RECONSTRUCTING
MACROECONOMICS

RECONSTRUCTING MACROECONOMICS

Structuralist Proposals and Critiques
of the Mainstream

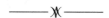

LANCE TAYLOR

HARVARD UNIVERSITY PRESS
Cambridge, Massachusetts
London, England
2004

Library of Congress Cataloging-in-Publication Data

Taylor, Lance
Reconstructing macroeconomics : structuralist proposals and
critiques of the mainstream / Lance Taylor.
p.   cm.
Includes bibliographical references and index.
ISBN 0-674-01073-6 (alk. paper)
1. Macroeconomics.   2. Macroeconomics—Mathematical models.   I. Title.

HB172.5.T393   2003   2003056775
339—dc22

Contents

Acknowledgments

I took over teaching first-term advanced macroeconomics at the New School from John Eatwell in 1995. The New School economics department tries to have its courses combine a critical review of mainstream analysis with a constructive presentation of more historically and institutionally founded ways of doing economics. The present volume builds upon Eatwell's course arrangement in doing just that.

So the main contributors to the material herein were the successive cohorts of New School students who had to suffer through my attempts to put a coherent presentation together. To all of them, my enormous gratitude, and thanks in particular to Thorsten Block, Christy Caridi, Ute Pieper, and Matias Vernengo. Many passages of this latest version could not have been written without critical inputs from Nelson Barbosa Filho, Per Gunnar Berglund, and Codrina Rada.

Also, thanks to Robert Blecker and Amitava Dutt, who read the whole manuscript and offered numerous, very helpful suggestions. Ideas built into several passages came from Jaime Ros, Duncan Foley, Ron Baiman, Yilmaz Akyuz, and Jan Kregel. Mike Aronson and Elizabeth Gilbert at Harvard University Press and Butch Montes at the Ford Foundation were quiet but substantial contributors.

My wife Yvonne, daughter and son Signe and Ian, son- and daughter-in-law Joel and Elisabeth, and grandkids Lyla and Imogen were enormous supportive, even if the last two didn't know it. The same goes for all the canine, caprine, feline, equine, porcine, gallinaceous, and (last but most obnoxious) anserine critters at Black Locust Farm.

RECONSTRUCTING
MACROECONOMICS

——————————————————)(——————————————————

Introduction

Macroeconomic frameworks that constrain social and economic actors and aggregates of their actions are the topic of this book. Diverse schools of economists have proposed such schemes. A "structuralist" approach, based on social relations among broad groups of actors, is emphasized here.

In the North Atlantic literature, structuralism's intellectual foundations lie within a complex described by labels such as [original, neo-, post-]–[Keynesian, Kaleckian, Ricardian, Marxian] which nonmainstream economists have adopted; numerous variants exist in developing countries as well. The fundamental assumption of all these schools is that an economy's institutions and distributional relationships across its productive sectors and social groups play essential roles in determining its macro behavior.

The approach adopted here also puts a great deal of emphasis on accounting relationships as built into national income and product accounts and flows of funds. These relationships constrain the numbers presented in the accounts, which are the fundamental data of macroeconomics. Almost needless to say, the conventions used in building macro-level accounts are anything but objectively given. They arose historically out of the debates over the Keynesian system, and serve social and political ends. The accounts are mostly estimated on the basis of data collected for other purposes, such as taxation, and are by no means a clear reflection of what is going on in the "real" economy, out there. But they still define the realm of macroeconomic discourse and have to be accepted and utilized as such.

More important, market-balance restrictions constrain the outcomes of decisions made by economic actors—not every actor can have a trade surplus with all the others, for example. In practice such statements can be rephrased in terms of macro-level "sectors" and "institutions" such as households, nonfinancial business, financial business, government, and the rest of the world (in one familiar scheme). A distinguishing feature of structuralist theories is that they are constructed directly in terms of aggregates such as household consumption, business investment, total exports, and so on. Few if any appeals are made to optimizing decisions allegedly made by individual "agents," in contrast to most mainstream (especially Anglo-American) macroeconomics.[1]

In practice, two sorts of accounting restrictions matter—those that concern flows (for example, GDP is the sum of payments to labor, payments for indirect taxes, and payments for "surplus" or profits) and those that cumulate flows into the corresponding stocks (such as the fact that a country's net foreign assets are the sum over time of its current account surpluses). "Stock-flow consistent" (SFC) macro modeling takes all such restrictions into account.[2] They remove many degrees of freedom from possible configurations of patterns of payments at the macro level, making tractable the task of constructing theories to "close" the accounts into complete models.

Two such tasks are attempted in this book. One is to present a critical review of mainstream macroeconomics from a structuralist perspective. The focus of the critique is on monetarist, new classical, new Keynesian, and recent growth theory models with an effort to study these contributions from a historical perspective. Various forms of monetarism are traced from the eighteenth century, and current monetarist and new classical models are compared (unfavorably) to those of the post-Wicksellian, pre-Keynesian generation of macroeconomists (Knut Wicksell himself, Dennis Robertson, Joseph Schumpeter, the young John Maynard Keynes). The new Keynesian vision is contrasted to Keynes's own in *The General Theory of Employment, Interest, and Money* from 1936, and contemporary growth theories are analyzed against a long backdrop of thought about questions of structural economic change and development.

The theories presented as alternatives to the mainstream draw upon work by Keynes's immediate disciples (mostly at Cambridge University, including Nicholas Kaldor and Joan Robinson) in the 1950s and 1960s, and contemporary and subsequent scholars including Michal Kalecki, John Hicks, Roy Harrod, Richard Goodwin, Amartya Sen, Stephen Marglin, Amitava Dutt, Robert Blecker, Bob Rowthorn, John Eatwell, the American "social structure of accumulation" school (Samuel Bowles, David Gordon), other Marxists (Duncan Foley, Anwar Shaikh), and Anglo-American post-Keynesians (Hyman Minsky, Jan Kregel, Wynne Godley, Thomas Palley). As already noted, their emphasis is on setting out models with clear and complete macro accounting and explicit statements of socioeconomic relationships among the main groups of actors.[3] In the chapters to follow, a fairly complete structuralist macroeconomics is presented, including output determination, distributive conflict and inflation, growth, cycles, relationships between the real and financial sectors, and open economy complications. Many conclusions run counter to standard results, and can be empirically supported.

The discussion draws upon both formal models and historical and institutional considerations. The models are pitched roughly at a first-year graduate student level, requiring calculus, matrix algebra, and the rudiments of optimal control theory. Keynes's strictures against applying formal probability theory to finance and economics are heeded, so there is scant use of that sort of mathematics. A brief chapter outline follows.

1. *Social Accounts and Social Relations.* Much of the formal argument is framed in terms of social accounting matrixes (SAMs) and their associated balance sheets, which are introduced in this chapter. They are used to illustrate questions of model causality or "closure" (selection among various behavioral restrictions to append to SAM accounting balances to give an algebraically complete model). For example, given hypotheses about how diverse groups of economic actors respond to one another (saving decisions by households with different sorts of income flows, distribution of profit flows and investment decisions by nonfinancial and financial business, demand choices by the government and rest of the world, and financial linkages among all these groups), is it more appropriate to postulate that output is determined by full employment of labor and capital (Say's Law in its modern guise) or the Keynes-Kalecki principle of effective demand? Besides addressing such analytical questions, the chapter uses SAM-based accounting to display and analyze recent U.S. macro data.

2. *Prices and Distribution.* This chapter begins with a review of cost-based theories of price determination—classical "prices of production" and neoclassical formulations under perfect and imperfect competition. The next topic is the neoclassical approach to measuring productivity change, which is shown basically to boil down to manipulation of accounting identities. Questions are raised for later discussion about the interactions between distribution (measured by the real wage and profit rates) and labor and capital productivity growth. On the basis of neoclassical production theory, the discussion returns to the issue raised above as to whether macro equilibrium is determined by effective demand or in labor markets according to new classical and/or new Keynesian formulations. A critique of the new Keynesian approach is formulated on Marxist and Austrian grounds. The chapter closes with a discussion of wage-wage and price-wage distributive conflict theories of inflation, and their contrasts with monetarist inflation theory.

3. *Money, Interest, and Inflation.* The discussion begins with a histori-

cal overview of different positions regarding the effects of money/credit on prices and quantities. It then turns to the diverse roles the interest rate is supposed to play: interest rate cost-push theories of inflation (the "Wright Patman effect"), loanable funds and real interest rate theories (Böhm-Bawerk, Fisher, Ramsey), the overlapping generations (OLG) model and the financing of pension plans, and a Wicksellian monetarist model of a "cumulative process" inflation when the market rate of interest differs from the "natural rate." The "inflation tax" central to the Wicksell model is at the heart of monetarist inflation models, and the chapter closes with a quick review of the related "Olivera-Tanzi effect" and "tight money paradox" (Sargent-Wallace).

4. *Effective Demand and Its Real and Financial Implications.* The principle of effective demand is presented in Kaleckian and Keynesian variants, with discussion of the irrelevance of neoclassical labor demand theory to Keynes's model and the theory's empirical lack of support. The role of income distribution in determining effective demand is analyzed—is demand "wage-led" (the likely developing-country case) or "profit-led" (industrialized countries)? Following a discussion of liquidity preference and diverse interpretations of the liquidity trap (Keynes versus Fisher and Krugman), Hicks's IS/LM model is set out in terms of SFC accounting. Next come discussions of own-rates of interest and theories of investment demand (Tobin's q versus post-Keynesian formulations), the consumption function and implications, and "disequilibrium" macroeconomics (Malinvaud). The chapter closes by asking: how well does Keynes's own model stand up after almost seventy years? The answer is generally positive.

5. *Short-Term Model Closure and Long-Term Growth.* This chapter marks a transition between older and more contemporary approaches to macroeconomics. It starts out with a review of the various closure assumptions and "effects" discussed in previous chapters. The next topic is how these assumptions and effects feed into supply-driven growth models, with investment and growth determined by available saving in Solow (with more discussion of growth accounting) and Marxist specifications, and by investment with an endogenous income distribution for Kaldor. Demand-driven models come next—Harrod, Robinson, and an initial presentation of a distribution/effective demand model used extensively in later chapters. An illustration contrasts the model's results regarding the financing of social security schemes with those from an OLG specification.

6. *Chicago Monetarism, New Classical Macroeconomics, and Mainstream Finance.* The discussion covers the emergence of post–World War II reactions against Keynes—critical reviews from SFC and effective de-

mand perspectives of Chicago monetarism (Friedman, Phelps), new classical macroeconomics (Lucas, Sargent), the role of government debt ("old fiscal conservatives" versus Barro's "Ricardian equivalence"), complete information finance theory, and the Modigliani-Miller theorem.

7. *Effective Demand and the Distributive Curve.* A complete real-side structuralist macro model is constructed in the capacity utilization versus wage-share plane. It is based on an effective demand curve that can be either wage- or profit-led and a "distributive curve" representing a steady-state (possibly locally stable or unstable) wage share that emerges from differential equations for money-wage inflation, money-price inflation, and labor productivity growth. Dynamics are shown to depend on interactions between income distribution and productivity growth. The real-side model is then extended to incorporate money and bonds. Finally, an open economy version is set out in which currency devaluation can be either expansionary or contractionary with respect to real output.

8. *Structuralist Finance and Money.* The story begins with a historical reconstruction of the evolution of Anglo-American monetary and financial systems—the roles of "endogenous" money and finance. A model of endogenous or passive money is presented within an SFC accounting framework (an approach not often taken by post-Keynesians). A post-Keynesian growth model is then constructed, based on an effective demand function that can be either "debt-led" or "debt-burdened" and a differential equation for the growth of business sector debt. The chapter closes with a quick review of a couple of "asymmetric information" (new Keynesian) approaches to money and finance.

9. *A Genus of Cycles.* Models of business cycles are presented in a two-dimensional-phase plane, in which one variable has positive feedback into itself, and is stabilized by damping from the other—hence the "genus." Models presented include Goodwin's predator-prey distributive cycle between labor and capital, an extension based on the Chapter 7 macro model with application to the U.S. economy, a cycle based on contractionary devaluation, destabilizing expectations in the Tobin monetary growth model, a financial cycle drawing upon the ideas of Minsky (explicitly rejecting the Modigliani-Miller theorem), and a cyclical version of the Chapter 8 model of borrowing by business that can generate "overinvestment" of the sort frequently discussed in connection with the 2001–2002 U.S. recession.

10. *Exchange Rate Complications.* Open economy macroeconomics is reviewed with an emphasis on the determination and economy-wide effects of the exchange rate. It is argued that existing models all fail to pro-

vide exchange rate "fundamentals." Purchasing power parity (PPP) and uncovered interest rate parity (UIP) exchange rate theories are sketched from this perspective. Next, the familiar portfolio balance model is shown to be treated incorrectly in the literature. When its full SFC accounting is respected, it has just two independent equations for asset market clearing and so can only determine home and foreign interest rates but not the exchange rate. If asset market equilibria vary smoothly over time, it follows that the balance of payments equation in the Mundell-Fleming model is not independent and cannot set the exchange rate either. The "correct" model is a two-country IS/LM specification coupled with exchange rate dynamics. Cyclical properties of a version incorporating dynamics based on UIP are briefly explored. It is contrasted with the well-known monetarist and Dornbusch models, which are also based on correct accounting but make use of PPP and classical as opposed to Keynesian behavioral relationships. Finally, a model of exchange rate and debt cycles in a developing country context is presented.

11. *Growth and Development Theories.* Growth and development theories from several different streams over the past two centuries are presented and contrasted with recently popular endogenous growth models and subsequent purported explanations for convergence—or lack of same—of per capita income levels internationally. Drawing on material from earlier chapters, seven lines of thought are explored: full employment, savings-driven mainstream growth models; models with full employment, endogenous distribution, and an independent investment function à la Kaldor; classical models with savings-driven dynamics and class-determined distribution; demand-driven growth models as described in Chapters 7 and 9; models built around a binding resource or sectoral output level; development accounting schemes; and specific effects such as economies of scale and externalities. Development policy recommendations derived from these families of models (including those presented in previous chapters and more mainstream formulations) are reviewed and criticized.

As should be clear from these summaries, some topics are covered in several different chapters, for example productivity growth in Chapters 2, 5, 7, 9, and 11. There is a lot of cross-referencing in the text so the cross-chapter connections should be fairly apparent.

Finally, quite a few distinct algebraic models are presented, each requiring its own set of symbols. As a consequence, some symbols change meaning between sections. Full definitions and redefinitions have (one can hope) all been provided, but the reader should be on the lookout for them.

CHAPTER ONE

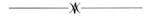

Social Accounts and
Social Relations

Another way of putting the points raised in the Introduction is to say that macroeconomics is framed by social accounting and social relations. The social accounts form a skeleton, and social relations change the skeleton's position over real, historical time. Specifying just which relations drive the motions is not a trivial task, as subsequent chapters attest. But the objects that move—the observable phenomena in macro—are mostly the numbers making up the national income and product accounts (NIPA), the flow of funds (FOF) accounts, and allied systems. We begin with those.[1]

1. A Simple Social Accounting Matrix

Table 1.1 presents a social accounting matrix (or SAM) of the sort promoted by two economists from the University of Cambridge—Richard Stone and Wynne Godley.[2] In all SAMs the two main accounting rules have been borrowed from the input-output system and can easily be implemented in computer spreadsheet programs: each entry along a row should be valued at the same price, and the sums of corresponding rows and columns should be equal. A good part of macroeconomics comprises theories about processes that drive these sums toward equality.

As its title suggests, column (1) of the SAM summarizes the costs of producing the value of output PX. The symbol X stands for "real" output, in practice some index of production gross of intermediate inputs with P as the corresponding price deflator (the more usual notation for output is Y, but in this book that symbol is reserved for real or nominal income flows as discussed in the next paragraph). The costs of producing PX include outlays for intermediate inputs aPX, wages wbX, and profits πPX. Intermediate uses are assumed to be proportional to gross output through the input-output coefficient a, and employment L is related to output X through a similar relationship, $L = bX$. "The" (average) money-wage rate is w, and π is the share of PX paid out as profits.

Table 1.1 A small SAM with production, income, expenditure, and flow of funds accounts.

	Current expenditures				
	Output costs (1)	Wages (2)	Profits (3)	Capital formation (4)	Totals (5)
(A) Output uses	aPX	PC		PI	PX
Incomes					
(B) Wages	wbX				Y_w
(C) Profits	πPX				Y_π
Flows of funds					
(D)			S_π	$-PI$	0
(E) Totals	PX	Y_w	Y_π	0	

Social relations enter the SAM's structure with the decomposition of gross output less intermediate costs or "value-added" $(1 - a)PX$ into wage payments and profits. From the "Output costs" column (1) and "Incomes" rows (B) and (C) we have $(1 - a)PX = wbX + \pi PX = Y_w + Y_\pi$, where Y_w and Y_π stand for wage and profit income flows in nominal terms. They are carried separately on the hypothesis that people who (mostly) get wages behave differently in economic terms from the corporations and real persons who (mostly) share flows of profits, rents, interest, dividends, and capital gains.

The extreme case is illustrated in the "Current expenditures" columns (2) and (3) of Table 1.1. All wage income Y_w goes to consumption PC (price P, "real" quantity C) and all profit income Y_π is saved as S_π. This sort of class distinction fits the facts. Of course, in practice some wage income is saved and some profits are consumed (corporate CEOs receive income for their labor services, and who besides CEOs, extremely successful entrepreneurs, or rentiers could support commerce in Beverly Hills or Manhattan's Upper East Side?), but different savings rates across incomes from different sources clearly exist. Besides being empirically relevant, the differential saving hypothesis is a key component of the heterodox models described in this book. For reasons to be discussed in this and following chapters, most orthodox or mainstream economists steer away from class-linked savings rates and even income flows.

So far, we have analyzed a cost-of-production decomposition and income-expenditure accounts for wages and profits. The expenditures include "current" outlays only, implying that capital accumulation has to be treated in another set of accounts. To lead into them, note that row (A) of the SAM sums up the uses of output: $PX = aPX + PC + PI$, where C and I respectively stand for "final demands" for consumption and investment (gross fixed capital formation plus increases in inventories) in real terms.[3] The value of investment, PI, is reflected via a minus sign in column (4) from row (A) into row (D) for flows of funds, or changes in assets and liabilities. Despite the fact that there are two groups of income recipients, only one flow-of-funds row is needed in the present setup. With no saving from wage income, its recipients cannot build up real or financial claims.

The sign convention is that "sources" of funds (saving plus increases in liabilities in SAMs which contain detail on financial transactions) are positive while "uses" (investment plus increases in financial assets) are negative. In Table 1.1, row (D) says just that. The "net lending" or "financial surplus" of profit recipients is nil ($S_\pi - PI = 0$) because they put all their newly saved resources into capital formation. It is easy to derive this saving-investment "identity" from the costs and uses of production statements and the income-expenditure balances, or vice versa. In other words, a balanced set of accounts already puts significant restrictions on the degrees of freedom of the variables it contains. This mundane observation will be of great concern in the chapters that follow.

2. Implications of the Accounts

Some implications of macroeconomic accounting balance are worth exploring in more detail.

First, the SAM in Table 1.1 embodies "circular flow" à la Joseph Schumpeter (1934), but with characteristic macroeconomic modifications:

The value of output decomposes into intermediate purchases, the wage bill, and profits, all of which are production costs.

Wage and profit payments generate incomes.

Wage incomes generate final consumer demands and intermediate purchases are also sales. Not all income flows are spent for current purposes, however, because profits are saved.

The level of investment is set by enterprises, more or less independently of current savings flows. Investment goes together with consumption and intermediate demands for goods to use up or "realize" total output.

The saving-investment identity, $S_\pi = PI$, follows from these flows as a theorem of accounting. Its ramifications are many, but the trunk of the tree is the fact that in capitalist economies the households or divisions of corporations which save are not the same as those which invest. In other words, there is a potential problem of coordination between different economic actors. It is made more acute by a second fact: savings and investment flows must be equilibrated through financial markets that have their own proper dynamics and are prone to instability.

These particular social relations are the gist of modern macroeconomics, as enunciated by John Maynard Keynes and Michal Kalecki in the 1930s.[4] The roles of different social actors are illustrated by the column structure of Table 1.1—firms' production operations and relations with their labor forces dominate column (1), workers' consumption summarizes (2), rentiers' and corporations' saving is in (3), and long-term planning by firms interacting with financial markets sets investment in column (4).

Investment behavior is crucial because from the SAM balances, it is clear that even if it is entirely consumed, the wage bill cannot exhaust total product—a corollary of the saving-investment accounting theorem recognized in 1935 by Kalecki in an article on "The Mechanism of the Business Upswing." The implication is that investment (or some other "injection") has to be present for demand to be realized. With imperfect coordination, it is not obvious that the macro system will arrive at a balance between saving and investment with socially desirable properties—for example, "full employment" of the potentially available labor force and capital stock is not guaranteed. These observations can be illustrated with a couple of examples.

In the first one, we can "close" the accounts of Table 1.1 with the Keynes-Kalecki principle of effective demand, which asserts that changes in the level of output X are the means by which saving and investment are brought into equality, with investment being determined independently of potential savings flows. The algebra is well known and simple. From row (B) and column (2) of the SAM, we have $PC = wbX$, or $C = \omega bX$ with $\omega = w/P$ as the real wage. Substituting into row (A) and manipulating gives

$$X = \frac{I}{1 - a - \omega b} = \frac{I}{\pi}$$

where the denominator in the expression after the second equality follows from the cost decomposition in column (1).

Through a multiplier process, output X and employment $L = bX$ are determined by investment I and the profit share π. The level of economic activity will be low, for a low injection I or a high saving "leakage" π. The model is simplistic, but it does illustrate the basic insight that output, employment, and saving can adjust to meet the level of effective demand as driven by the net effect of offsetting injections and leakages.

Much macroeconomic effort after Keynes has been devoted to refuting this causal scheme, as will be discussed in great detail in later chapters. Full employment can then be guaranteed on the basis of appropriate assumptions.

One variant of this alternative vision goes as follows. Let K stand for the aggregate capital stock, implicitly assumed to be made from the same "stuff" as output X.[5] Moreover, X is constructed from available labor L and capital K according to an aggregate production function $X = F(L, K)$, with properties to be described in detail in later chapters. Further assume that the real wage is set according to the marginal productivity rule $\omega = \partial F/\partial L$, and that the rate of profit $r = \pi PX/PK$ (total profits divided by the value of the capital stock at replacement cost) is determined by $r = \partial F/\partial K$.

With such input pricing rules, one can construct Walrasian macro models in which values of ω and r exist such that L and K take on predetermined, "full employment" levels. If L and/or K shift, moreover, ω and/or r will adjust so that markets for these production inputs continue to clear. Stated somewhat differently, we can put enough mathematical restrictions on the production function and other descriptors of the macro system to ensure that full employment of labor and capital comes about. When that happens, the total saving supply $S_\pi = \pi PX = rPK$ is also determined by the marginal productivity formulas and full employment (the level of the price level P comes from a cost function "dual" to the production function, as discussed in later chapters).

But if saving is fixed, then there is no room in this system for an independently determined level of investment I. The principle of effective demand and a full employment Walrasian description of the economy are incompatible. In a Keynes-Kalecki world, the way to stimulate output and economic growth is to raise investment; by reducing consumption demand, an increase in potential saving would have the opposite effect. If Walras rules, growth will be faster if there are increases in saving supply (due to, for example, reductions in government spending). The two models give dramatically different policy recommendations, because of the causal relationships that they have built in. The question of how best to "close" macro accounts such as those of Table 1.1 with an appropriate set of behavioral hypotheses is one that arises throughout this volume.

Three further observations are worth making, before going on to other sets of accounts. The first is that in principle a construct like a SAM summarizes all that can be observed about economic transactions at the macro level. It adds up all purchases and sales, incomes transferred and taxes paid, and so on in an economy at a "point in time" and aggregates them into certain categories. Economists, however, want to go beyond mere observation and ask counterfactual questions about how X might change in response to a shift in I, how P might react to w, and so on (with the influences possibly running in the opposite directions as well). We just went through two such exercises and will soon go through another.

Precisely because they are counterfactual, such thought experiments are irrefutable. Cohorts of econometricians to the contrary, the best that the numbers extracted from a quarterly or annual sequence of SAMs can do is give correlations—how else could so many mutually contradictory macro models have been "verified" on the basis of (say) American data over time? As it turns out, both pairs (I, X) and (w, P) tend to move together across SAMs. However, whether one variable causes the other in the algebraic sense of the models worked out above is a query the data themselves cannot answer. This is the major reason why macroeconomics is so theory driven, and why so many theories will have to be reviewed in this book. To cull the good ones from the bad, to a large extent one has to go outside SAM-type data and bring in opinions about how individuals and societies function as a whole, along with aesthetic criteria such as Occam's razor (bearing in mind that parsimony is in the eye of the beholder).

Second and related to the Occam question, the Keynes-Kalecki version of macroeconomics has a clear, almost linear causal structure, as will be seen in Chapter 4. Imposing such an order on the macro system makes it possible to tell clean theoretical narratives. But it violates ingrained Walrasian notions that the economy is a seamless web, everything depends on everything else in general equilibrium, and so on. In his *History of Economic Analysis,* Schumpeter (1954) reached back five generations before Keynes to label his style of theorizing the "Ricardian vice." The theories that David Ricardo and John Maynard Keynes constructed were in their details quite dissimilar, but they both had crisp causal structures. Whether vice or virtue was implicit is a question to be addressed in subsequent discussion.

Finally, in 1990s pop-culture imagery from the field of "chaoplexity" (a name blending chaos and complexity, coined by Horgan 1996), macroeconomics is an "emergent" phenomenon because its properties cannot be deduced solely from the individual economic actions of households, enterprises, and players in financial markets. With regard to the first model above, for example, in *The General Theory* Keynes observes that "the reconciliation of the identity between saving and investment with the apparent 'free-will' of the individual to save irrespective of what he or others may be investing, essentially depends on saving being . . . a two-sided affair. For . . . the reactions of the amount of his consumption on the incomes of others makes it impossible for all individuals simultaneously to save any given sums. Every . . . attempt to save more by reducing consumption will so affect incomes that the attempt necessarily defeats itself" (p. 84). This typically macroeconomic scenario "emerges" in the form of the quantity and price changes through which the "free wills" of individuals are forced to conform to the economy-wide accounting restrictions implicit in a SAM. This insight hovered at the edge of economic theory for many decades after Adam Smith; only in the 1930s did Keynes and Kalecki bring it into the full light of the principle of effective demand.

3. Disaggregating Effective Demand

As it turns out, the economy's overall behavior is influenced not just by the income distribution but also by differing forms of injections (investment, government spending, exports) and leakages (saving, taxes, imports). In this section, we pursue that logic as applied to the U.S. macro system. Along the lines of Table 1.1, in macroeconomic equilibrium totals of injections and leakages must be equal. Broadly following Godley (1999), we can use this fact to set up a useful decomposition methodology for effective demand.

At the one-sector level (ignoring intermediate outputs and sales along with the distinction between wage and profit income flows), the aggregate supply of goods and services available for domestic use (X) can be defined as the sum of total private income (Y_P), net taxes (T), and "imports" or (for present purposes) all outgoing payments on current account (M):

$$X = Y_P + T + M. \tag{1}$$

In NIPA categories, we have GDP $= Y_p + T = X - M$ so the accounting in (1) is nonstandard insofar as X exceeds GDP. As in row (A) of Table 1.1, the aggregate supply and demand balance can be written as:

$$X = C_P + I_P + G + E, \tag{2}$$

that is, the sum of private consumption, private investment, government spending (on both current and capital account), and "exports" or incoming foreign payments on current account. It is convenient to define leakage parameters relative to aggregate supply, yielding the private savings rate as $s_P = (Y_P - C_P)/X$, the import propensity as $m = M/X$, and the tax rate as $t = T/X$.

From all this one gets a typical Keynesian income multiplier function

$$X = (I_P + G + E)/(s_P + t + m), \tag{3}$$

which can also be written as

$$X = (s_P/\lambda)(I_P/s_P) + (t/\lambda)(G/t) + (m/\lambda)(E/m), \qquad (4)$$

in which $\lambda = s_P + t + m$ is the sum of the leakage parameters, and I_P/s_P, G/t, and E/m can be interpreted as the direct "own" multiplier effects on output of private investment, government spending, and export injections with their overall impact scaled by the corresponding leakage rates (respectively, savings, tax, and import propensities). That is, aggregate supply is equal to a weighted average of contributions to demand from the private sector, government, and the rest of the world. If two of these contributions were zero, then output would be equal to the third.

Another representation involves the levels of $I_P - s_P X$, $G - tX$, and $E - mX$, which from (4) must sum to zero. Moreover, the economy's real financial balance can be written as

$$\dot{D} + \dot{Z} + \dot{A} = (I_P - s_P X) + (G - tX) + (E - mX) = 0, \qquad (5)$$

where $\dot{D}$ ($= dD/dt$), $\dot{Z}$, and $\dot{A}$ stand respectively for the net change per unit time in financial claims against the private sector, in government debt, and in foreign assets.

Equation (5) shows how claims against an institutional entity (the private sector, government, or rest of the world) must be growing when its demand contribution to X exceeds X itself. So when $E < mX$, net foreign assets of the home economy are declining, while $G > tX$ means that its government is running up debt. A contractionary demand contribution from the rest of the world requires some other sector to be increasing liabilities or lowering assets, for example, the public sector when $G > tX$. Because from (5) it is true that $\dot{D} + \dot{Z} + \dot{A} = 0$, such offsetting effects are unavoidable.

The offsets, however, can cumulate over time. "Stock/flow" disequilibrium problems threaten when ratios such as D/X, Z/X, or $-A/X$ (or D/Y_P, Z/tX, or $-A/E$) become "too large." Then the component expressions in (4) and the accumulation flows in (5) have to shift to bring the system back toward financial "stock-flow" or "stock-stock" equilibrium. Such adjustments can be quite painful.

Without making predictions about whether the American economy will have recovered from its 2001–2003 slowdown (an outcome not known as of this writing), it is interesting to see how its macro data fit into equations (4) and (5) in the twentieth century. The lines in Figure 1.1 show the evolution of supply and private, government, and foreign contributions to effective demand since World War II, in nominal terms

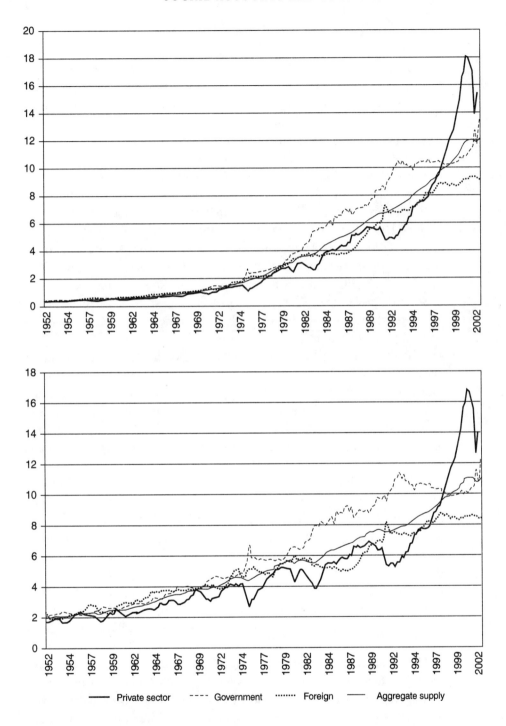

Figure 1.1
Multiplier effects on output from each sector—trillions of nominal dollars (upper) and real dollars
of 1996 (lower).

in the upper panel and in real terms below. Three observations can be made.

First, since 1982, the "foreign" curve has generally been below the supply line. This means that the external deficit (the excess of payments outgoing on current account over those coming in) has had a contractionary effect on economic activity, with current account leakages or imports outweighing injections or exports. This drag was briefly lifted in the early 1990s, as a consequence of dollar devaluation of about 30 percent between 1985 and 1990 (which stimulated exports and cut back the import share of supply), the (George H. W.) Bush recession (which also reduced import penetration), and transfers from the rest of the world of about $100 billion in connection with the Gulf War. All these favorable factors receded after 1992, and the gap between supply and foreign effective demand steadily widened, leading authors such as Godley (1999) and Blecker (1999a) to warn of impending stock/flow imbalances.

Second, governments at all levels—federal, state, and local—combined to stimulate demand through 1997. The federal deficit was responsible for this outcome, because state and local governments suffer from chronic budget balances or surpluses. As the "government" curve shows, the policy choice to run a federal surplus to "pay down the debt" along with the fact that fiscal stimulus tends to drop off as the economy expands (tax revenues rise and transfer payments such as unemployment compensation fall) led to a contractionary fiscal stance from 1995 through 2000. Thereafter, government began to support demand again.

Third, with demand from the rest of the world lagging and fiscal demand in retrenchment, in the late 1990s the private sector had to pick up the slack. Its effective demand grew rapidly after 1992, because of rising investment and a falling saving rate. Private demand peaked at the end of 1999, and with the onset of recession there was a very rapid decline. By the end of 2001 the private and public sectors were both offsetting the net export drag, but with strongly divergent trends. It will be interesting to see if the two sectors go back to (respectively) dampening and supporting aggregate demand as they did from the mid-1970s through the mid-1990s.

These demand shifts had financial consequences. As shown in (5), if a sector's effective demand lies above total supply, it has to borrow to finance the excess. Quarterly increases in net claims among the sectors are shown in Figure 1.2 (again, nominal data in the upper diagram and real below). Two private sector curves are included, for household and "other" flows of investment minus saving (with the latter basically coming from nonfinancial and financial business).[6] Except for the 1992 blip,

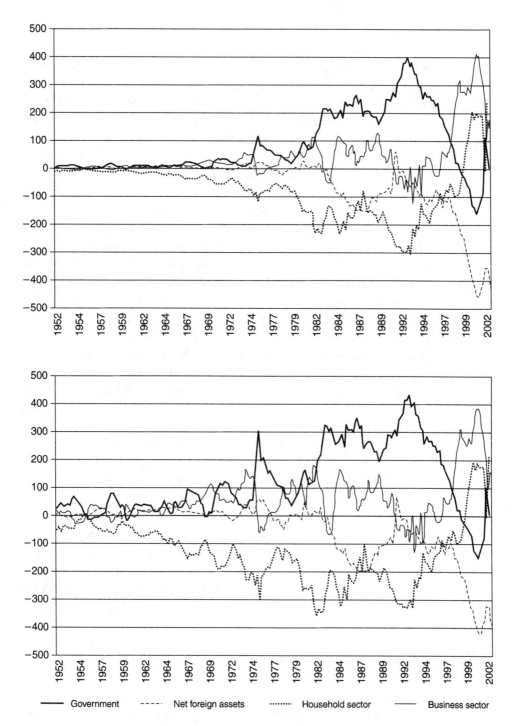

Figure 1.2
NIPA-based financial needs of the private, government, and foreign sectors—billions of nominal dollars (upper) and real dollars of 1996 (lower).

U.S. imports consistently exceeded exports, $E - mX < 0$, so the economy was decumulating net foreign assets.

Flow accumulation of government debt ($G - tX > 0$) reached its peak in mid-1992 and then declined; government began to build up positive net claims—or reduce its net liabilities—in 1997. There was another reversal in 1999–2000 and by 2001 the government sector once again was running up debt in the range of $100–$200 billion per year. With an external deficit on the order of $400 billion in nominal terms, the private sector had to run the offsetting internal deficits.

Both components of the private sector behaved in unhistorical fashion in the 1990s. Ever since the early 1950s, the household sector had run a consistently positive financial balance (or negative deficit in the figure) which beginning early in the 1970s tended to vary countercyclically between around $300 billion in real terms in recessions and $100 billion in booms. But beginning in 1992, the sector's level of gross saving fell from about $600 billion to $200 billion in 2000. Investment rose from a bit over $200 billion to $400 billion. The outcome was that households started to run a historically unprecedented deficit in 1997.

The business sector had tended to run deficits during upswings and then revert to approximate financial balance or a small surplus in recessions as in the early 1980s and early 1990s. But as with households, the business deficit took off later in the 1990s. In 1991–92, both saving and investment were about $700 billion. They climbed in tandem (with investment rising somewhat faster) to about $1.0 trillion in 1997–98. Thereafter, investment shot up to almost $1.3 trillion in 2000, with saving falling off to $850 million (with investment dropping significantly faster) in 2001. As Figure 1.2 shows, the swing of business into a consistent deficit position occurred in 1994–95; the household shift came a year or two later. Thereafter both sectors' deficits climbed hand in hand, amply collateralized by rising asset prices, into the bubble that began to deflate in the year 2000.

In other words, the Clinton boom was uniquely supported by net increases in private sector liabilities. The fiscal deficit played a negligible role in stimulating demand, in sharp contrast to previous upswings. In the first half of the 1990s, the public sector did issue liabilities to finance the foreign deficit. But in the second half of the decade private debtors took over that function.

As of early 2003, how the rapid reversal of trends in private and public sector deficits in 1999–2000 will play out remains to be seen. What can safely be said is that if the structural foreign deficit remains in the $400–$500 billion range and the household and business sectors continue to move toward the combined surplus they used to run in economic downswings, then there will have to be a large fiscal stimulus if effective demand is to be maintained. Otherwise the foreign deficit will have to be sharply reduced by recession and/or devaluation as in the early 1990s. Toward their right-hand sides, Figures 1.1 and 1.2 illustrate interesting times.

4. A More Realistic SAM

The next step is to introduce a more realistic set of accounts, bringing in elements missing from Table 1.1 with which macroeconomists have to deal on an ongoing basis. Table 1.2 illustrates some of the complications.[7]

An initial extension is a more ample collection of economic actors, with incomes flowing to wage earners, "rentiers" or households receiving dividends and interest, business enterprises, the banking system, the government, and the rest of the world in rows (B) through (G) respectively. These six groups undertake financial transactions summarized in the flows of funds rows (H) through (M). Underlying the accounts for sources and uses of incomes are the decompositions of production costs and demands for output in column (1) and row (A) respectively. These take the same general forms as their analogs in Table 1.1, with new wrinkles in column (1) related to taxes and foreign trade that are discussed presently.

Turning to the details of sources and uses of incomes in rows (B)–(G) and columns (2)–(7), first note that in addition to their labor earnings wbX (cell B1), wage recipients get (modest?) interest payments at rate i on the money (currency and deposits) M_w they hold as a claim on the banking system (cell B5). More significantly, as discussed later, they receive transfer payments Q_w from the government in cell B6. In column (2), they use their income Y_w for consumption PC_w, taxes T_w, and saving S_w. Rentiers make similar uses of their income Y_r in column (3). Their income sources are interest earnings iM_r in cell C5 and dividends on business equity that they hold in cell C4, where V is the amount of equity outstanding, P_v is its price, and δ is the dividend payout rate.

In row (D), business income Y_b is equal to gross profit flows πPX. In column (4), part of Y_b is used to pay interest on loans from abroad in cell G4 (i^* is the foreign interest rate, e is the exchange rate in units of local currency to foreign currency, and Z_b^* is the stock of foreign loans to domestic business). Other uses include dividend payments in cell C4, taxes T_b in cell F4, and local interest payments iL_b in cell E4, where L_b is the stock of loans to business from the banking system and (for simplicity) it is assumed that the interest rate on both bank loans and deposits is the

Table 1.2 An expanded SAM with production, income, expenditure, and flow of funds accounts.

	Output costs (1)	Wages (2)	Rentiers (3)	Business (4)	Banks (5)	Government (6)	Foreign (7)	Capital formation (8)
				Current expenditures				
(A) Output		PC_w	PC_r			PG	PE	PI
Incomes								
(B) Wages	wbX				iM_w	Q_w		
(C) Rentiers				$\delta P_v V$	iM_r			
(D) Business	πPX							
(E) Banks				iL_b		iL_g	$i^* eR^*$	
(F) Government	T_x	T_w	T_r	T_b				
(G) Foreign	eaX			$i^* eZ_b^*$		$i^* eZ_g^*$		
Flows of funds								
(H) Wages		S_w						
(I) Rentiers			S_r					
(J) Business				S_b				$-PI$
(K) Banks					S_l			
(L) Government						(S_g)		
(M) Foreign							S_f	
(N) Totals	PX	Y_w	Y_r	Y_b	Y_l	Y_g	Y_f	0

same.[8] In cell J4, business saving S_b appears as retained earnings after payments for interest, dividends, and taxes. Banks' income Y_l in row (E) comes from interest on loans to business and government (iL_b and iL_g in cells E4 and E6 respectively) and interest on foreign reserves ($i^* eR^*$ in cell E7). In column (5), Y_l is used to pay interest on deposits and for saving S_l.[9]

In row (F), government income Y_g comes from taxes on production (T_x in cell F1), and income taxes on wage, rentier, and business incomes. In column (6), Y_g is used for public consumption PG as well as for transfers to wage earners (Q_w) and interest payments at home (iL_g) and abroad ($i^* eZ_g^*$). Government wage payments that would appear in cell B6 are ignored, although as will be seen below they account for large shares of GDP in most industrialized economies. The parentheses around government saving (S_g) suggest that its value is often less than zero.[10]

Cell G1 shows one component of foreign income as imports scaled to the gross value of output—a is the relevant input-output coefficient and the "world price" P^* of imports is implicitly set equal to one.[11] Business and government pay foreign interest in cells G4 and G6 respectively. In column (7), foreign income is used to pay for "our" exports PE in cell A7, that is, national products are sold abroad at their local prices. As already noted, in cell E7, the rest of the world pays interest at rate i^* on the local currency value eR^* of foreign reserves held by the banking system.

Table 1.2 (continued)

Changes in national claims			Changes in foreign claims		
Business equity (9)	Bank assets (10)	Bank liab. (11)	National liab. (12)	National assets (13)	Totals (14)
					PX
					Y_w
					Y_r
					Y_b
					Y_l
					Y_g
					Y_f
		$-\dot{M}_w$			0
$-P_v\dot{V}$		$-\dot{M}_r$			0
$P_v\dot{V}$	$\dot{L}_b$		$e\dot{Z}_b^*$		0
	$-\dot{L}$	$\dot{M}$		$-e\dot{R}^*$	0
	$\dot{L}_g$		$e\dot{Z}_g^*$		0
			$-e\dot{Z}^*$	$e\dot{R}^*$	0
0	0	0	0	0	

Consolidating row (G) and column (7) shows that "foreign saving" S_f is equal to the external current account deficit—if we are sending more money abroad than we are taking in, then the rest of the world is saving for us.

The last use of output in row (A) is investment PI in column (8), which includes both gross fixed capital formation and the increase in business inventories. Along row (A), consumption of households and government, exports, and investment sum to the gross value of output PX. Down column (1), PX emerges as the sum of wages (wbX), profits (πPX), and indirect taxes less subsidies on production activity (T_x) plus the value of imports at domestic prices. The first three items make up total value-added "at market prices," or GDP (the sum of wbX and πPX is called value-added "at factor cost").

From the equality of row (A) and column (1) totals, the national accounts breakdown of aggregate demand and the aggregate cost of production becomes $P(C_w + C_r + G + E + I) - eaX = GDP = wbX + \pi PX + T_x$. As in last section's discussion of effective demand, it is often convenient to work with X as an output indicator even though it is bigger than GDP.

Next we turn to flows of funds. Wage earners in row (H) have the simplest financial account, with their saving S_w being directed solely toward an increment in money balances, $\dot{M}_w = dM_w/dt$ in cell H11. To keep the mathematics underlying Table 1.2 within the realm of simple calculus, we assume that stock variables such as M_w increase or decrease smoothly in continuous time. In row (I), rentiers use their saving to build up money holdings $\dot{M}_r$ in cell I11 and to acquire new equity $P_v\dot{V}$ at the going price P_v in cell I9.

Business firms in row (J) have other financial options. The balance between business saving and investment varies widely across capitalist economies. In Japan, firms before the slump of the 1990s typically invested more than they saved, with household saving making up the shortfall. In abnormal circumstances such as those of Russia and South Africa (for different reasons) in the 1990s, business saving substantially exceeded firms' capital formation. As can be seen in Figures 1.1–1.2, prior to the go-go late 1990s, private saving in the United States ($S_w + S_r + S_b$) tended to exceed private investment (PI) by a margin in the range of \$200 billion per year.[12] Nevertheless, American business engages in many financial transactions. In Table 1.2, for example, firms are assumed to have access to three sources of funds—new borrowing from banks $\dot{L}_b$ (J10), new borrowing from abroad $e\dot{Z}_b^*$ (J12), and new issues of equity $P_v\dot{V}$ (J9). In line with standard practice, incremental flows of foreign credits and equity are valued at their ruling prices, respectively e and P_v.

In row (K), sources of funds for banks are their saving S_l in cell K5 and new deposit liabilities $\dot{M}$ in K11. Uses of these funds are for new loans $\dot{L}$ in K9 and acquisition of international reserves, $e\dot{R}^*$ in K13.[13] In row (L), government's (negative) saving S_g is covered by new loans from banks, $\dot{L}_g$, and from abroad, $e\dot{Z}_g^*$.

In Chapter 10, it will be shown that a row like (M) for the rest of the world's flows of funds with the home economy or the "balance of payments" does not appear when a full SAM is set up for two countries. The balance of payments is no more than a derived set of flows that summarizes changes in the home country's net foreign assets. However, in accounts for a single country it is convenient to carry a line saying that S_f or the current account deficit must be offset by capital movements, that is, $S_f + e\dot{R}^* = e\dot{Z}^*$.

Finally, note in columns (9) through (13) that changes in claims add up across different groups—in column (10) total new bank loans ($\dot{L}$) go to business ($\dot{L}_b$) and government ($\dot{L}_g$), and so on. Summing the flows of funds rows (H) through (M) vertically gives the standard saving-investment "identity,"

$$S_w + S_r + S_b + S_l + S_g + S_f - PI = 0,$$

as a theorem following from Table 1.2's other accounting balances. As the quotation from Keynes at the end of section 2 underlines, just how this equation gets satisfied can be a complicated matter.

5. Stock-Flow Relationships

The financial flows in Table 1.2 naturally cumulate over time. Also, the increase in the capital stock K is the result of investment, $\dot{K} = dK/dt = I$ (ignoring depreciation). The stock variables that are the outcomes of these processes appear in the balance sheets in Table 1.3. For each broad group of actors, assets are on the left and liabilities and net worth on the right.

As usual, wage earners have the simplest balance—their money holdings M_w make up their total net worth or wealth Ω_r. Similarly, rentiers' money M_r plus the value of their equity holdings $P_v V$ add up to their wealth Ω_r. The government's "asset" is the "full faith and credit" Δ behind its debt obligations L_g and eZ_g^*—as will be seen in Chapter 6, some modern macroeconomists do not take this sovereign claim very seriously. If we impose the accounting convention that the banking sector does not save, it does not build up net worth. Foreign wealth Ω_f is $e(Z^* - R^*)$, or "our" external debt minus the banking system's foreign reserves.

Analysis of the balance sheet for businesses is slightly more complicated. Their capital stock can alternatively be valued at "replacement cost" PK, or else at an "asset value" qPK. The "q" term was brought to prominence by James Tobin (1969), and represents the valuation put on firms by financial markets.[14] Under various interpretations, q will figure in much discussion to follow. At present, if business net worth Ω_b in Table 1.3 is equal to zero, then "average" q is given by

$$q = (L_b + eZ_b^* + P_v V)/PK, \qquad (6)$$

or the ratio of enterprise total liabilities to the replacement cost of capital stock. As will be seen in Chapter 4, one can restate this definition (at

Table 1.3 Balance sheets corresponding to Table 1.2.

Wage Earners		Rentiers	
M_w	Ω_w	M_r	Ω_r
		$P_v V$	
Business		**Banks**	
qPK	L_b	L	M
	eZ_b^*	eR^*	
	$P_v V$		
	Ω_b		
Government		**Rest of the World**	
Δ	L_g	eZ_g^*	eR^*
	eZ_b^*		Ω_f

least formally) in terms of asset rates of return. Either way, q is often interpreted as a rough-and-ready indicator of the performance of firms and figures as an argument in investment demand functions. A firm is in a sort of financial equilibrium when its q equals one. A higher value suggests that it should be building up its capital stock, and a lower one signals that it may be ripe for an external takeover. The American merger and acquisition wave of the 1980s (discussed in note 12 and later chapters) took place during a period when corporate q-values tended to be well below unity.

A final point is worth noting before we take up how the flows of funds in Table 1.2 and the balance sheets in Table 1.3 interact. Summing across all the balance sheets and equating demands and supplies for claims (for example, $L_b + L_g = L$), gives the wealth "identity"

$$\Delta + qPK = \Omega_w + \Omega_r + \Omega_b + \Omega_f.$$

In words, "primary wealth" is made up of the government's debt (said to come from "outside" the financial system) plus the capital stock valued at its asset price. Through a web of financial claims, primary wealth constitutes the net worths of workers, rentiers, business, and the rest of the world.

To begin to see the linkages of balance sheets with flows of funds, observe that combining row (H) of Table 1.2 with the differentiated version of the wage earners' balance sheet gives the equalities

$$S_w = \dot{M}_w = \dot{\Omega}_w.$$

That is, the change in workers' net worth in the form of an increase in bank deposits is just equal to their saving.

For rentiers, similar maneuvers with their balance sheet and row (I) of Table 1.2 give the result

$$S_r + \dot{P}_v V = \dot{Q}_r, \tag{7}$$

or the capital gains on rentier's holdings of business equity must be added to their saving to arrive at their change in wealth. Note that levels of wealth like Ω_r only change over time and are constant in the "short run" unless an asset price like P_v discontinuously jumps. These accounting restrictions help determine macro behavior, as will be illustrated in several later chapters.

The dynamics get more complicated for business net worth, for which the relationship is

$$S_b + (q - 1)\dot{P}I + \dot{q}PK - \dot{P}_v V = \Omega_b. \tag{8}$$

To understand the implications of equation (8), one can work through three special cases.

First, suppose that q is identically equal to one (so that Ω_b is identically zero) and that $\dot{P} = \dot{e} = 0$. Then (8) reduces to $S_b = \dot{P}_v V$, or enterprise saving is automatically reflected into capital gains on equity. Under appropriate assumptions about capital accumulation and asset demands, this situation could correspond to the steady state of a neoclassical optimal growth model (see Chapters 3 and 4 for examples). In such a world, the financial structure of enterprises is a veil. They have no net worth and their saving automatically redounds to the wealth of their stockholders, that is, combining (7) and (8) gives $S_r + S_b = \dot{\Omega}_r$. Such assumptions underlie the mainstream's aversion to the class-differentiated saving behavior discussed above. If finance is a veil and identical, "representative" households receive both wage and profit income, then diverse savings rates applied to different income streams make no sense.

Second, we can let q take values different from one but still set enterprises' net worth Ω_b to zero. This is the financial world described by the celebrated Modigliani-Miller (1958) theorem, discussed in detail in Chapter 6. Still assuming $\dot{P} = \dot{e} = 0$, business saving in (8) now shows up in changes in both q and P_v: $S_b = \dot{P}_v V - \dot{q} PK$. The asset prices q and P_v will also be linked by q's defining equation (6). As shown in Chapter 4, plausible asset demand equations will determine both variables jointly. There is little substantive difference from the steady state case just discussed. For the financial side of the economy the Modigliani-Miller theorem closely resembles a full employment assumption on the real side. These hypotheses lead naturally to models in which prices of goods and services (on the real side) and rates of return to asset and liability claims (on the financial side) adjust smoothly to remove any incipient market disequilibria. Beginning with Keynes, structuralist economists have viewed such models critically; they want to see a world in which real and financial quantity adjustments play essential roles.

Third, financial side structuralism comes into its own when business net worth Ω_b is allowed to be nonzero, that is, asset markets do not instantaneously transform a firm's valuation qPK into equity prices (given the levels of its other liabilities). Nonzero, endogenous net worth creates room for independent dynamics (including possible jumps) for q and/or P_v due to Keynes's "animal spirits" or the forces producing "financial fragility" à la Hyman Minsky (1986). This world has a richer tapestry and is far less predictable than the two just discussed. It figures in some of *The General Theory*'s more dazzling insights but is alien to mainstream macroeconomics.

6. A SAM and Asset Accounts for the United States

To get a feel for the wealth of information that a social accounting matrix can convey, it makes sense to work through a numerical example. In this section we present a SAM—or rather a SAM plus supporting tables describing changes in asset/liability portfolios and the capital stock—for the United States. The setup is somewhat different from that in Tables 1.2 and 1.3 (and the SAMs in the rest of this book), which are basically designed to summarize macroeconomic models set up in continuous time. Rather, the emphasis in Tables 1.4–1.6 is on presenting the annual numbers as they appear in current prices in the U.S. NIPA and FOF accounts for 1999 (the latest year with a full set of data available as of this writing).

Rows and columns are given mnemonic labels based on terminology that national income accountants like to use, for example, I-O for "input-output" at the northwest corner of Table 1.4 or A for "Absorption of domestic final output" for the row immediately below. The matrix is organized with "headlines" for groups of rows—each number in a headline row is the sum of the entries immediately below. Thus 6,286.8 (billion dollars) in row H and column X is the sum of the "Household and institution" income entries down through row HINT. Five sectors are considered: households and institutions (including nonprofit entities such as foundations and churches), nonfinancial business, financial business, general government (combining federal, state, and local),[15] and the rest of the world.[16]

The general layout of Table 1.4 resembles that of Table 1.2, but with differences in the details. One showing up immediately in columns XH through XG is that all four domestic sectors engage in "production." The rationale is that sectors defined on an institutional basis both generate income flows (thereby "producing" output in columns of the SAM) and receive those and other incomes in rows. This worldview contrasts sharply with that of most formal macro models, which are set up in terms of opposing categories like producers versus consumers, and so on. In NIPA-land, there is no conceptual overlap between, say, "households" and "consumers."

The entries in columns XH through XG are summed in column X. As usual, the total of all entries or "gross value of output" in column X, 10,543.4, corresponds to the sum of final demand items in row A. Gross domestic product (GDP) can be defined as total absorption minus imports in cell (EIMP, X) or 10,543.4 − 1,244.2 = 9,299.2. A numerically less significant fact is that financial business provides "business services" as an intermediate input into nonfinancial business. This flow is reflected in the positive and negative entries of 204.8 appearing in the I-O row (the number was extracted from the U.S. input-output table and nets recorded payments flows going both ways).

Also in contrast to Table 1.2 (and the rest of the book), depreciation or "consumption of fixed capital" appears explicitly in Table 1.4. For the sectors, depreciation figures as a cost of production in rows HCFC, BCFC, and GCFC. Besides (mostly residential) depreciation of 163.2, the household production account (column XH) includes payments to labor (row HW&S), rental income (HRIP) and a fairly hefty intrasectoral interest flow of 340.4 (HINT) paid by households in their capacity as final owners and suppliers of factors of production to households in their capacity as producers and users of those factors. There is also a small net subsidy of −16.1 from government in row GTXI.[17]

Production accounts for nonfinancial business in column XN are more complicated. Under the "Households and institutions" headline are payments to labor in rows HW&S (wages and salaries) and HOLI (many "other" income flows). Incomes of proprietors of unincorporated firms appear in row HPI. The "Domestic business" headline covers payment flows that stay within the corporate sectors themselves. For nonfinancial business the major items are undistributed profits (170.9 in row BUDP), dividend and interest payments within the sector (250.9 and 260.1 in rows BDIV and BINT), and depreciation of 715.7. Even omitting business direct taxes in cell (GTXD, XN), the nonfinancial business "surplus" of 1,415.6 amounts to 0.1797 of the sector's output of 7,876.4 (the column XN and row AN sum). In other words, the after-tax gross "profit share" of nonfinancial business is around 18 percent (or 22 percent of nonfinancial business value-added = gross value of output − imports − intermediate inputs from financial business = 6,435.6).

Other headline payments include various forms of taxes of 1,118.7 to general government (row G) and imports of 1,236.0 from the rest of the world (rows E and EIMP). As in Table 1.2, the accounting convention is that imports of goods and services are undertaken by the business sectors for resale to the rest of the economy. Finally, in row Z there is a small discrepancy (−60.7) between the cost- and demand-side estimates of nonfinancial business activity. The accounting for financial business in column XF is broadly similar. Its after-tax gross profit share is 229.2/602.7 or a robust 38 percent. In relation to gross value added, the share is 229.2/799.3 = 28.7%.

Accounting for government in the SAM reflects the fact that separate cost- and demand-side estimates of its activities do not exist. "Production" of government services in column XG has two major components: depreciation of its capital in cell (GCFC, XG), and labor payments in cell

Table 1.4. Social accounting matrix for the U.S. economy: Generation, distribution, and uses of income, 1999 (billions of $).

		Current account						
			Generation of income				Uses of income	
		Total, resid. sectors	House-holds & institu-tions	Non-financial business	Financial business	General govern-ment	House-holds & institu-tions	Non-financial business
		X	XH	XN	XF	XG	DH	DN
CURRENT ACCOUNT								
Net purchases of intermediate inputs	I-O	0.0		204.8	−204.8			
Absorption of domestic final output	A						6,268.7	
From households and institutions	AH						1,039.3	
From nonfinancial business	AN						4,669.4	
From financial business	AF						560.0	
From general government	AG							
Households and institutions	H	6,286.8	1,055.5	3,962.1	440.5	828.8		13.3
Wage and salary disbursements	HW&S	4,475.3	408.5	3,068.4	346.2	652.2		
Other labor income	HOLI	501.0		297.1	27.3	176.6		
Proprietors' income with IVA and CCAdj	HPI	663.4		596.5	66.9			
Rental income of persons with CCAdj	HRIP	143.4	143.4					
Consumption of fixed capital	HCFC	163.2	163.2					
Dividends	HDIV							
Interest	HINT	340.4	340.4					
Current transfers	HTRC							13.3
Domestic business	B (F&N)	1,644.8		1,415.6	229.2		535.2	881.5
Nonfinancial	N	1,415.6		1,415.6				
Financial	F	229.2			229.2		535.2	881.5
Wage and salary accruals less disbursements	BUDW	5.2		4.7	0.5			
Undistributed profits with IVA and CCAdj	BUDP	159.7		170.9	−11.2			
Consumption of fixed capital	BCFC	827.5		715.7	111.8			
Dividends	BDIV	328.9		250.9	78.0			314.9
Interest	BINT	283.8		260.1	23.7		535.2	566.6
Current transfers	BTRC	39.7		13.3	26.4			
General government	G	1,439.5	−16.1	1,118.7	140.8	196.2	1,490.5	
Indirect taxes less subsidies	GTXI	689.7	−16.1	676.4	29.5			
Contributions for social insurance	GTXW	323.6		275.7	22.0	25.9	338.5	

Table 1.4 (continued)

	Current account		Capital account								
	Uses of income		Investment						Net capital trans-fers	NIPA & FOF residuals	Total
Financial business	General govern-ment	Rest of the world	House-holds & institu-tions	Non-financial business	Financial business	General govern-ment	Rest of the world				
DF	DG	DE	JH	JN	JF	JG	JE	TRK	ZNF	T
										0.0
	1,325.7	990.2	408.1	1,158.4	138.2	254.1				10,543.4
										1,039.3
	305.9	952.5	408.1	1,158.4	138.2	243.9				7,876.4
	5.0	37.7								602.7
	1,014.8					10.2				1,025.0
1,350.5	986.5	−5.4								8,631.7
		−5.4								4,469.9
										501.0
										663.4
										143.4
										163.2
370.3										370.3
963.8										1,304.2
16.4		986.5								1,016.2
370.5	357.0	280.3								4,069.2
370.5										1,786.1
	357.0	280.3								2,283.2
										5.2
		69.6								229.3
										827.5
64.0		76.3								784.1
306.5	357.0	134.4								2,183.4
										39.7
93.1										3,023.1
										689.7
										662.1

Table 1.4 (continued)

		Current account						
			Generation of income				Uses of income	
		Total, resid. sectors	House-holds & institu-tions	Non-financial business	Financial business	General govern-ment	House-holds & institu-tions	Non-financial business
		X	XH	XN	XF	XG	DH	DN
Direct taxes	GTXD	255.9		166.6	89.3		1,152.0	
Consumption of fixed capital	GCFC	170.3				170.3		
Dividends	GDIV							
Interest	GINT							
Rest of the world	E	1,244.2		1,236.0	8.2		26.6	
Imports of goods and services	EIMP	1,244.2		1,236.0	8.2			
Dividends	EDIV							
Interest	EINT							
Current transfers	ETRC						26.6	
CAPITAL ACCOUNT								
Gross saving and capital transfers	S						310.8	891.3
Households and institutions	SH						310.8	
Nonfinancial business	SN							891.3
Financial business	SF							
General government	SG							
Rest of the world	SE							
Net purchases of nonproduced assets	NPN							
NIPA-FOF reconciliation	Q							
Memo: Implied net lending NIPA	QLIN							
Itemized discrepancy NIPA-FOF	QZIT							
Memo: Conceptually adjusted net lending	QLCA							
Residual discrepancy NIPA-FOF	QZZ							
Net lending	L							
Households and institutions	LH							
Nonfinancial business	LN							
Financial business	LF							
General government	LG							
Rest of the world	LE							
Discrepancy	Z	−71.9	0.0	−60.7	−11.2	0.0	−0.1	0.0
Total	T	10,543.4	1,039.3	7,876.4	602.7	1,025.0	8,631.7	1,786.1

Table 1.4 (continued)

	Current account			Capital account							
	Uses of income			Investment							
	Financial business	General government	Rest of the world	Households & institutions	Non-financial business	Financial business	General government	Rest of the world	Net capital transfers	NIPA & FOF residuals	Total
	DF	DG	DE	JH	JN	JF	JG	JE	TRK	ZNF	T
											1,407.9
											170.3
	0.4										0.4
	92.7										92.7
	295.8	11.6									1,578.2
											1,244.2
	34.5										34.5
	251.4										251.4
	9.9	11.6									48.1
	173.2	342.2	313.2						0.0		2,030.7
									−36.2		274.6
											891.3
	173.2										173.2
		342.2							36.8		379.0
			313.2						−0.6		312.6
							7.2	−7.2		0.0	0.0
				−2.9	−94.4	−26.1	0.0	−0.1		123.5	0.0
				−133.5	−267.1	35.0	117.7	319.8		−71.9	0.0
				−3.8	1.7		2.1			0.0	0.0
				−129.7	−268.8	35.0	115.6	319.8		−71.9	0.0
				0.9	−96.1	−26.1	−2.1	−0.1		123.5	0.0
				−130.6	−172.7	61.1	117.7	319.9		−195.4	0.0
				−130.6							−130.6
					−172.7						−172.7
						61.1					61.1
							117.7				117.7
								319.9			319.9
	0.1	0.1	−0.1	0.0	0.0	0.0	0.0	0.0	0.0	71.9	0.0
	2,283.2	3,023.1	1,578.2	274.6	891.3	173.2	379.0	312.6	0.0	0.0	0.0

(H, XG) plus social insurance contributions in cell (GTXW, XG). How government's output of its own services filters over to the demand side of the economy is taken up below. For the moment, note that its labor-related payments of 854.7 amount to almost 8 percent of the economy's output of 10,543.4.[18]

We next take up income generation and then go on to patterns of demand and savings. Besides incomes originating from production, households and institutions receive relatively large inflows in the columns headed "Uses of income" (DH–DE). The biggest single item is 986.5 (9.3 percent of total output) of transfers from general government in cell (HTRC, DG)—even in resolutely free enterprise America, the government plays a major redistributive role. Next in size are interest receipts of 963.8 in cell (HINT, DF). This is *inter*sectoral interest income. The U.S. accounting convention is that all cross-sector interest and dividend payments are channeled through financial business, that is, that sector is supposed to take in all such flows and then pass them along to their ultimate recipients (the United States lags countries such as Sweden in not providing a full matrix of intersectoral movements of interest, dividends, and all other financial stocks and flows). Thus gross household interest receipts in row HINT are the sum of intra- and intersector payments, 340.4 + 963.8 = 1,304.2 (12.4 percent of total output and 15.1 percent of household income, largely to the benefit of institutions and persons in the upper reaches of the size distribution of income).

Turning to the two business sectors, we find several interest payments flows in row BINT. Under the accounting convention just described, households pay 535.2 to financial business in cell (BINT, DH). To save white space in the SAM, only *inter*sectoral interest payments figure in columns DN and DF—nonfinancial business pays 566.6 to financial business on its outstanding obligations, and 306.5 flows the other way. Similar observations apply to dividends in row BDIV. Finally there are net undistributed profit, dividend, and interest payments from the rest of the world in column DE. As usual, they are assumed to go to financial business for a total of 280.3 in cell (F, DE).

"General government" income largely comes from indirect taxes less subsidies (including a small subsidy to households, the total is 689.7, with the taxes paid by business), contributions to social insurance (662.1, from business, households, and the government itself), and direct taxes (1,407.9, with 82 percent coming from households). It also receives minor dividend and interest payments from financial business.

Finally, the rest of the world's income is from U.S. imports of goods and services, dividends and interest channeled through financial business, and transfers. The total of 1,578.2 is 15 percent of the gross value of output.

The columns headed "Uses of income" are broadly similar to those in Table 1.2, though affected by the maneuvers already discussed. In cell (AH, DH) households purchase 1039.3 "from themselves." This amount is the household services "produced" with the cost structure of column XH. They also buy goods and services from the two business sectors, pay intersectoral interest to financial business, render social insurance payments and direct taxes to government, and make transfers to the rest of the world. What's left over is gross saving of 310.8 in cell (SH, DH). This flow amounts to 3.6 percent of household income. "Personal saving" subtracts consumption of fixed capital (163.2 in row HCFC) from the gross figure, leaving 147.6 or 1.7 percent of income (subject to considerable media attention, this figure went negative for a time after 1999). Aside from a small transfer to households in cell (HTRC, DN),[19] nonfinancial business uses its income of 1,786.1 to pay interest and dividends to financial business in rows BDIV and BINT and to save 891.3 in row SN. Financial business uses its income of 2,283.2 to distribute dividend, interest, and transfer payments to the other sectors and to save 173.2 in row SF.

The government's income is 3,023.1, or 29 percent of the gross value of output. Its current demands for goods and services total 1,325.7 in cell (A, DG). Adding government investment of 243.9 in cell (AN, JG), total purchases from business come to 554.8. The rest of the government's spending takes the form of using its own-produced services of 1,025.0 with the cost structure described in column XG emphasizing labor payments and depreciation (giving a total outlay of 1,579.8). In the United States at least, the traditional Keynesian injunction to "increase G" 35 percent boils down to buying more goods and services from the business sectors and the rest to hiring more government employees and charging depreciation.

The rest of the world uses its income of 1,578.2 to purchase exports from the United States and make payments (described above) to financial business. Its "saving" or the U.S. current account deficit is 313.2 in row SE. As noted above, this flow is interpreted as foreign saving because the United States sends greater payments abroad than it takes in, covering the resulting deficit by emitting liabilities or running down external assets. Both maneuvers feed into increased holdings of wealth abroad. In fact, the U.S. external deficit of a billion dollars per day absorbs well over half of the rest of the world's surplus of saving over investment (Eatwell and Taylor 2000).

Sectoral investment demands—for gross fixed capital formation and changes in inventories—are presented in columns JH through JE. Note that household and nonfinancial business gross savings flows from rows SH and SN fall sort of the corresponding investment levels by $100 billion or so, and financial business and government savings exceed their investments by lesser amounts. Some other sector must make up the overall domestic savings shortfall—as noted just above and illustrated in Figures 1.1 and 1.2, this task gets passed to the rest of the world.

Table 1.4 does not follow Table 1.2 in using "flows of funds" rows to summarize the changes in asset and liability holdings of the different sectors that are the financial counterparts of their differences between saving and investment. This sort of information is presented in greater detail in Tables 1.5 and 1.6 below. To set up links with these stock-flow tables, we need to present net financial accumulation flows (or net increases in financial claims) for each of the sectors. The numbers appear in Table 1.4 under the headline "NIPA-FOF reconciliation."

The word "reconciliation" suggests that the NIPA and FOF numbers are not consistent, which in fact is the case. But before we get into that, we have to complete the NIPA accounts. Their full definition (rather more complicated than the simple saving-investment comparisons underlying Figure 1.2) of a sector's financial accumulation or net lending to other domestic sectors and the rest of the world is

Net lending = (Gross saving + Net capital transfers receivable)
− (Gross investment + Net purchases of non-produced assets).

Net capital transfers in column TRK are basically estate taxes; net purchases of nonproduced assets in row NPN refer to mineral deposits, uncultivated forests, and so on (the two entries for transactions between government and the rest of the world are the only ones present in the accounts). The NIPA numbers that come out of the net lending balance appear in row QLIN. The next row presents "itemized discrepancies" between the two sets of accounts, with results in row QLCA.

The bottom lines are the FOF net lending estimates in rows LH through LE (summarized in row L) and the sectoral "residual discrepancies" between the two sets of estimates in row QZZ. The net lending estimates feed into Table 1.5, subject to the caveat that some numbers in the QZZ row are pretty big, for example, the nonfinancial business discrepancy amounts to almost $100 billion, or about 1 percent of the gross value of output and 10.7 percent of the sector's gross saving. Such imprecision is unavoidable in the economic statistical game.

The next step is to consider changes in holdings of financial assets, launched from rows LH through LE of Table 1.4 and presented in detail in the three sections of Table 1.5. As can be seen, financial instruments in the table are classified under nine headings (consolidated from the thirty presented at the highest level of aggregation in the "Flow of Funds Ma-

Table 1.5a Net financial assets accounts for the U.S. economy, 1999 (billions of $).

	Net financial assets (1)	Money (2)	Other bank credit (3)	Government paper (4)	Business bonds (5)	Other bus. paper (6)	Mortgages (7)	Household invest. & borrowing (8)	Equity (9)	Other (10)	FOF sector discrep. (11)	Residual FOF discrep. (12)
Opening balances	1748.3	-508.6	-207.1	25.4	0.0	-31.9	0.0	0.0	0.0	2659.9	-189.3	126.4
Households and institutions	24376.8	4139.5	51.0	1058.6	584.7	0.0	-4075.4	11986.1	10715.9	105.7	-189.3	126.4
Nonfinancial business	-17706.0	783.3	-1072.6	-172.0	-1829.6	282.4	-1358.2	165.9	-15935.9	1430.6	0.0	0.0
Financial business	-1769.5	-5393.0	642.7	1962.7	944.1	163.5	5263.3	-11496.8	5409.7	734.3	0.0	0.0
General government	-4694.7	170.9	158.6	-4441.7	61.2	-525.3	170.3	-655.2	102.0	264.4	0.0	0.0
Rest of the world	1541.7	-209.3	13.1	1617.7	239.6	47.5	0.0	0.0	-291.8	124.8	0.0	0.0
Net lending	195.4	-60.1	-32.2	-3.1	-0.1	-49.9	0.1	0.2	0.0	340.3	0.2	0.0
Households and institutions	-130.6	208.2	-20.5	154.6	52.6	-1.8	-431.8	300.4	-387.1	-5.1	-0.1	-0.2
Nonfinancial business	-172.7	101.4	-89.1	-17.1	-229.9	-41.8	-161.2	3.6	172.7	88.6	0.1	0.0
Financial business	61.1	-416.7	58.1	-281.9	18.2	58.2	588.9	-265.6	227.2	74.5	0.2	0.4
General government	117.7	77.6	5.0	55.5	12.6	-22.9	4.2	-38.2	3.5	20.3	0.1	0.0
Rest of the world	319.9	-30.6	14.3	85.8	146.4	-41.6	0.0	0.0	-16.3	162.0	-0.1	-0.2
Holding gains	-11.9	-2.4	-29.9	-116.7	0.0	-60.0	-0.1	-0.2	0.2	7.6	189.5	-125.8
Households and institutions	4253.2	-116.3	0.0	113.0	73.8	-60.4	-5.4	1201.7	2857.3	0.0	189.6	-126.0
Nonfinancial business	-3748.0	0.0	0.1	0.0	0.0	0.0	-20.6	24.7	-3992.1	240.0	0.0	0.0
Financial business	13.7	113.1	-29.9	-171.6	-31.7	-2.6	-7.1	-1226.6	1320.9	49.7	-0.5	-0.4
General government	43.1	-1.0	-0.1	10.0	0.0	0.4	33.0	0.0	9.5	-8.5	0.0	0.0
Rest of the world	-573.9	1.9	0.0	-68.0	-42.1	2.6	0.0	0.0	-195.2	-273.5	0.5	0.6
Closing balances	1931.8	-571.1	-269.3	-94.4	-0.1	-141.9	0.0	0.0	0.2	3007.8	0.6	0.8
Households and institutions	28499.4	4231.4	30.5	1326.2	711.1	-62.2	-4512.6	13488.2	13186.0	100.6	0.2	0.2
Nonfinancial business	-21626.2	884.7	-1161.6	-189.1	-2059.5	240.6	-1540.0	194.2	-19755.3	1759.2	0.1	0.0
Financial business	-1694.7	-5696.6	670.9	1509.2	930.6	219.1	5845.1	-12989.0	6957.8	858.5	-0.3	0.0
General government	-4533.9	247.4	163.5	-4376.2	73.8	-547.9	207.5	-693.4	115.0	276.2	0.2	0.2
Rest of the world	1287.7	-238.0	27.4	1635.5	343.9	8.5	0.0	0.0	-503.3	13.3	0.4	0.4

Table 1.5b Gross financial assets accounts for the U.S. economy, 1999 (billions of $).

	All financial assets (1)	Money (2)	Other bank credit (3)	Government paper (4)	Business bonds (5)	Other bus. paper (6)	Mortgages (7)	Household invest. & borrowing (8)	Equity (9)	Other (10)	FOF sector discrep. (11)	Residual FOF discrep. (12)
Opening balances	76890.6	6508.2	2593.8	8558.0	4102.4	2985.7	5736.6	15759.1	19800.5	10783.0	−63.2	126.4
Households and institutions	30592.6	4139.5	276.7	1058.6	584.7		109.3	13317.8	10715.9	326.9	−63.2	126.4
Nonfinancial business	7250.7	783.3	3.3	79.4		1605.6	122.2	165.9		4491.0		0.0
Financial business	31811.5	896.4	2083.3	5302.1	2796.9	1089.2	5334.9	2254.1	7867.3	4187.4		0.0
General government	1617.5	198.3	158.6	500.3	61.2	124.3	170.3	21.3	102.0	281.2		0.0
Rest of the world	5618.4	490.7	72.0	1617.7	659.6	166.6			1115.4	1496.4		0.0
Net acquisition of financial assets	4665.3	606.8	302.1	601.3	465.8	362.2	613.6	556.2	−53.9	1211.2	0.0	0.0
Households and institutions	491.7	208.2	42.0	165.0	52.6	5.3	−0.6	394.8	−387.1	11.6	0.1	−0.2
Nonfinancial business	725.8	101.4	0.9	−3.2		125.2	16.0	3.6		481.9		0.0
Financial business	2569.0	175.4	239.4	316.7	240.0	246.2	594.0	153.5	231.6	372.0	−0.2	0.4
General government	164.8	74.6	5.0	37.0	12.6	6.5	4.2	4.3	3.5	17.1		0.0
Rest of the world	714.0	47.2	14.8	85.8	160.6	−21.0			98.1	328.6	0.1	−0.2
Holding gains	6161.3	−11.5	−30.2	10.4	42.5	65.3	25.9	1564.0	4473.2	84.7	62.9	−125.8
Households and institutions	4258.6	−116.3	−0.1	239.9	73.8	65.2	−0.1	1201.8	2857.3	0.4	63.0	−126.0
Nonfinancial business	65.6							24.7		40.9	0.0	0.0
Financial business	1779.3	105.7	−30.1	−171.6	−31.7	−2.6	−7.1	337.5	1296.6	282.7	0.2	−0.4
General government	45.6	−1.0	−0.1	10.0	0.4		33.0		9.5	−5.8		0.0
Rest of the world	11.9	0.1		−68.0	0.4	2.7			309.8	−233.4	−0.3	0.6
Closing balances	87717.2	7103.5	2865.7	9169.7	4610.7	3413.1	6376.1	17879.3	24219.8	12078.9	−0.4	0.8
Households and institutions	35343.1	4231.4	318.6	1463.5	711.1	70.5	108.6	14914.4	13186.0	338.9	−0.1	0.2
Nonfinancial business	8042.1	884.7	4.2	76.2		1730.8	138.2	194.2		5013.8	0.0	0.0
Financial business	36159.8	1177.5	2292.6	5447.2	3005.2	1332.8	5921.8	2745.1	9395.5	4842.1	0.0	0.0
General government	1827.9	271.9	163.5	547.3	73.8	130.7	207.5	25.6	115.0	292.5	−0.1	0.2
Rest of the world	6344.3	538	86.8	1635.5	820.6	148.3	0	0	1523.3	1591.6	−0.2	0.4

Table 1.5c Gross financial liabilities accounts for the U.S. economy, 1999 (billions of $).

	All financial liabilities (1)	Money (2)	Other bank credit (3)	Government paper (4)	Business bonds (5)	Other bus. paper (6)	Mortgages (7)	Household invest. & borrowing (8)	Equity (9)	Other (10)	FOF sector discrep. (11)
Opening balances	75142.4	7016.8	2800.9	8532.7	4102.4	3017.6	5736.7	15759.1	19800.6	8123.1	252.6
Households and institutions	6215.8		225.7				4184.6	1331.7		221.2	252.5
Nonfinancial business	24956.7	0.0	1075.9	251.4	1829.6	1323.2	1480.4	13750.9	15935.9	3060.4	0.0
Financial business	33581.0	6289.4	1440.6	3339.3	1852.8	925.7	71.6	676.5	2457.6	3453.1	0.0
General government	6312.3	27.5		4941.9	420.0	649.6				16.8	0.0
Rest of the world	4076.7	700.0	58.9			119.1			1407.1	1371.6	0.0
Net incurrence of financial liabilities	4469.7	666.9	334.3	604.4	465.9	412.1	613.5	556.0	-53.9	870.9	-0.4
Households and institutions	622.2		62.5	10.4		7.1	431.2	94.4	-172.7	16.7	-0.1
Nonfinancial business	898.5		90.0	13.9	229.9	167.0	177.2		4.4	393.3	-0.1
Financial business	2507.8	592.1	181.3	598.6	221.8	188.0	5.1	419.1		297.5	-0.1
General government	47.1	-3.0				29.4	0.0	42.5		-3.2	-0.1
Rest of the world	394.1	77.8	0.5	-18.5	14.2	20.6			114.4	166.6	0.0
Holding losses	6173.4	-9.2	-0.3	127.0	42.5	125.3	26.0	1564.2	4473.0	77.1	-252.2
Households and institutions	5.7		-0.1				5.4	0.1	0.4	0.4	-252.5
Nonfinancial business	3813.6		-0.1	126.9		125.6	20.6		3992.1	-199.1	0.0
Financial business	1765.8		-0.1					1564.1	-24.3	233.0	0.4
General government	2.5	-7.4		0.1		-0.4				2.7	0.1
Rest of the world	585.8	-1.8		0.1	42.5	0.1			505.1	40.1	-0.2
Closing balances	85785.4	7674.6	3135.0	9264.1	4610.8	3555.0	6376.1	17879.3	24219.6	9071.1	-0.2
Households and institutions	6843.7		288.1	137.3		132.7	4621.2	1426.2		238.3	-0.1
Nonfinancial business	29668.8		1165.8	265.3	2059.5	1490.2	1678.2		19755.3	3254.6	-0.1
Financial business	37854.5	6874.1	1621.7	3938.0	2074.6	1113.7	76.7	15734.1	2437.7	3983.6	0.3
General government	6361.8	24.5		4923.5		678.6		719.0		16.3	-0.1
Rest of the world	5056.6	776	59.4		476.7	139.8			2026.6	1578.3	-0.2

trix" tables of the FOF accounts): money, other bank credit, government paper including "agency securities,"[20] business bonds, other business paper, mortgages, household investment and borrowing, equity, and other. There are also columns for discrepancies.

Several accounting conventions differ between Tables 1.2 and 1.5. In the "Flows of funds" rows of Table 1.2, increases in liabilities are given a positive sign while increases in assets are negative. Tables 1.5a–c treat their flow entries as being (normally) positive.

Second, Table 1.2 does not incorporate capital (or "holding") gains and losses on claims. They are carried in Tables 1.5a–c, subject to the balance conditions:[21]

> Opening balances of financial liabilities + Net increases in financial liabilities + Holding losses on financial liabilities = Closing balances of financial liabilities

and

> Opening balances of financial assets + Net increases in financial assets + Holding gains on financial assets = Closing balances of financial assets.

Table 1.5a presents net financial accounts, consolidating asset and liability positions. The first panel shows levels of stocks coming into 1999. The second panel gives financial accumulation flows by sector, with the numbers coming from the "Net lending" panel of Table 1.4. The third panel summarizes holding gains during 1999, and the fourth gives current value net asset positions at yearend.

In the first panel, households and institutions can be seen to have relatively large net holdings of money (4,139.5), government paper (1,058.6), equity (10,715.9), and "household investment and borrowing" or HIB (11,986.1). This last item combines a number of household asset and liability categories, with details presented later. Other lines of the "Opening balances" panel show that equity is the biggest "liability" of nonfinancial business, while HIB is largely a net liability of financial business. Households' biggest net liability is mortgages (−4,075.4). Their net worth in early 1999 was 24,376.8, or 2.3 times that year's gross value of output.

Nonfinancial business has net worth of −17,706.0. The chief net liability item is equity (−15,935.9, reflecting the cumulative effect of the 1990s bull market in stocks), followed distantly by business bonds and bank credit. Its net position with banks is only slightly negative (−289.3) because of its holdings of money. As might be expected, financial business has a fairly complicated net portfolio position. Its liability categories are money and HIB. It has large net asset holdings of government paper, business bonds, mortgages, and equity.

General government has negative financial net worth, with the big net liability being its bonds. The major net asset of the rest of the world is government paper, including treasury and municipal bonds and agency securities.

The second panel shows net lending by the different sectors, coming from Table 1.4. Without going through all the numbers, the table's striking feature is that portfolio *re*allocations on the flow basis are as large as or larger than portfolio expansion due to net lending. Households, for example, increased their holdings of money, government paper, and HIB by amounts substantially exceeding the absolute value of their net lending flow of −130.6. They also increased their mortgage debt and ran down holdings of equity. Both business sectors likewise practiced portfolio churning. The government mostly used its net saving of 117.7 to build up deposits and holdings of its own securities. The rest of the world directed 162.0 of its saving of 319.9 to "Other" securities. The FOF guide needs 36 pages to describe its Other category completely. One important component is foreign direct investment or FDI,[22] in which the U.S. net position coming into 1999 was 119.2. At the end of the year, it was 34.6.

As befits a bull market, net holding gains and losses during 1999 are imposing. Households gain 4,253.2 and nonfinancial business loses −3748.0, with the big component being equity. Households also pick up 1201.7 in their investment and borrowing transactions with financial business, itself another major beneficiary of rising share prices. The rest of the world had net holding losses of −573.9, on equity and "other."

Asset and liability positions are presented in Tables 1.5b and 1.5c respectively. We just point to a few of the highlights. In Table 1.5c, it can be seen that households enter 1999 with a debt level of 6,215.8, made up of mortgages (4,184.6) and loans under the HIB heading (1,331.7), that is, consumer credit mostly coming from financial business. From Table 1.4, the interest payment flow is 340.4 in cell (HINT, XH) on mortgages, of which 324.3 truly comes from households and the rest from nonprofit institutions. The implied interest rate on the opening balance is 8.1 percent (or 7.4 percent on the closing balance and 7.7 percent on the geometric mean of the initial and final levels of debt). Interest on consumer debt is the difference between 535.2 from cell (BINT, DH) and 340.4 on mortgages, or 194.8. The implied rate on the initial balance is 14.6 percent (13.7 percent on the closing balance and 14.1 percent on the geometric mean).

Table 1.6 Produced assets and net worth accounts for the U.S. economy, 1999 (billions of $).

| | Net worth (1) | Net financial assets (2) | All produced assets (3) | Fixed assets | | | | Inventories (8) | Revision discrepancy prod. assets (9) | Pre-revision produced assets (10) |
| | | | | Structures | | Equipment and software | | | | |
				Residential (4)	Nonresidential (5)	Residential (6)	Nonresidential (7)			
Opening balances	26865.2	1748.3	25116.9	9337.5	9976.9	67.6	4409.2	1325.6		
Households and institutions	33279.1	24376.8	8902.3	8044.4	734.7	23.7	99.5			
Nonfinancial business	−6307.1	−17706.0	11398.9	1079.9	5724.7	43.9	3224.9	1325.6		
Financial business	−889.7	−1769.5	879.7	213.3	429.3		450.4			
General government	−758.8	−4694.7	3936.0		3088.3		634.4			
Rest of the world	1541.7	1541.7								
Net increase by transaction	953.6	195.4	758.2	252.7	205.2	3.0	238.8	58.6	−39.6	797.8
Households and institutions	128.4	−130.6	259.0	231.7	17.5	0.9	8.8		14.1	244.9
Nonfinancial business	187.1	−172.7	359.8	18.8	104.7	2.1	175.6	58.6	−82.9	442.7
Financial business	119.0	61.1	57.9		15.6		42.3		31.5	26.4
General government	199.2	117.7	81.5	2.2	67.3		12.0		−2.3	83.8
Rest of the world	319.9	319.9								
Increase by transaction	6574.9	4665.3	1909.6	400.0	452.1	8.8	990.1	58.6	−49.2	1958.8
Households and institutions	913.8	491.7	422.1	356.3	32.5	2.9	30.3		14.0	408.1
Nonfinancial business	1788.7	725.8	1062.9	38.4	263.7	5.9	696.3	58.6	−95.5	1158.4
Financial business	2743.3	2569.0	174.3		27.3		147.0		36.1	138.2
General government	415.2	164.8	250.4	5.3	128.6		116.6		−3.7	254.1
Rest of the world	714.0	714.0								

Less: Decrease by transaction	5621.1	4469.7	1151.4	147.3	247.0	5.8	751.3		−9.6	1161.0
Households and institutions	785.3	622.2	163.1	124.6	15.0	2.0	21.5		−0.1	163.2
Nonfinancial business	1601.5	898.5	703.0	19.6	159.0	3.8	520.7		−12.7	715.7
Financial business	2624.2	2507.8	116.4		11.8		104.6		4.6	111.8
General government	216.0	47.1	168.9	3.1	61.3		104.5		−1.4	170.3
Rest of the world	394.1	394.1								
Holding gains	732.5	−11.9	744.4	346.5	329.0	−0.7	31.4	38.2		
Households and institutions	4568.1	4253.2	314.9	287.9	27.7	−0.2	−0.5	38.2		
Nonfinancial business	−3488.2	−3748.0	259.8	48.0	153.3	−0.5	20.8			
Financial business	34.7	13.7	21.1		16.7		4.4			
General government	191.8	43.1	148.7	10.7	131.3		6.7			
Rest of the world	−573.9	−573.9								
Closing balances	28551.3	1931.8	26619.5	9936.7	10511.1	69.9	4679.4	1422.4		
Households and institutions	37975.5	28499.4	9476.1	8564.0	779.9	24.3	107.9	1422.4		
Nonfinancial business	−9608.2	−21626.7	12018.5	1146.6	5982.7	45.5	3421.3			
Financial business	−736.0	−1694.7	958.7		461.5		497.1			
General government	−367.7	−4533.9	4166.2	226.1	3287.0		653.1			
Rest of the world	1287.7	1287.7								

On the asset side in Table 1.5b, the household portfolio is quite diversified with big holdings of money, government paper, equity, and HIB. The large items in the latter basket are shares in mutual funds (2,501.0), bank personal trusts (1,001.0), life insurance reserves (718.3), and pension fund reserves (an impressive 9,097.6).

Nonfinancial business has 7,250.7 in financial assets, over half of them "Other." The dominant liability is equity. Financial business has claims of 31,811.5 on all other sectors and itself, under virtually all headings (including 997.3 of mutual fund shares in HIB). Its total liabilities or "supplies" of finance are even larger at 33,581.0, concentrated in money, government paper (agency securities again), bonds, equity, other, and especially HIB. General government holds some assets, and its liabilities are concentrated under the heading of government paper. The rest of the world's liabilities are equity and other; its assets are spread under several headings.

Substantial churning is revealed under the "Net acquisition of financial assets" and "Net incurrence of financial liabilities" headlines in Tables 1.5b and 1.5c respectively; holding gains and losses are also large. Presumably all this financial activity underpins accumulation of physical capital. A summary appears in Table 1.6.

The first three columns of the table present summary net worth accounts, breaking net asset holdings into "financial" and "produced" (with the categories excluding nonproduced nonfinancial assets and also consumer durables). The opening total of produced assets is 25,116.9, giving a capital/output ratio (with respect to the gross value of output) of about 2.4 in 1999. All four domestic sectors hold produced assets, with around 45 percent of the total in nonfinancial business and 35 percent held by households. Columns (4) through (7) give a breakdown of "fixed" assets by four categories. Most household fixed assets take the form of residential structures. Nonfinancial business holds all four types of fixed assets plus a stock of inventories of 1,325.6 or 12.6 percent of the gross value of output.

Changes in holdings of produced assets are shown in panels lower in the table. Households, for example, acquire 356.3 of residential structures and dispose of 124.6 for a net increase of 231.7. The observed 287.9 in holding gains on their houses (most of which are *not* "realized" for taxation purposes via actual sales of residences) gives an overall increase of 519.6 in the value of the housing stock.[23]

Similar decompositions apply to the other categories of produced assets. Though they are sizable (in the hundreds of billions of dollars), the increments and decrements are smaller for physical assets in Table 1.6 than for many financial categories in Table 1.5. Which broad asset category wags what dog is an enduring question in macroeconomics, to be addressed throughout the remainder of this book.

7. Further Thoughts

All the accounting discussed in this chapter reflects broad themes of this volume—there are many ways in which macroeconomic models can be "closed" mathematically, with different "closures" reflecting diverse perceptions of socioeconomic reality. Such diverse formulations impinge on all aspects of the macroeconomy. Consider the variables already introduced in Tables 1.1–1.3:

Nominal prices and values: w, P, e, i, P_v, qP, etc.
Real prices and distributional variables: ω, e/P, $j = i - \hat{P}$,[24] π, q, etc.
Quantity variables: X, L, K, C_w, C_r, G, E, etc.
Income flows: Y_w, Y_b, Y_r, etc.
Real and nominal accumulation variables: I, S_w, S_r, etc.
Financial stocks (and associated flows): L, M, Z^*, V, etc.

We obviously have a great deal to explain. The next chapter begins the task by describing theories proposed over many years about income distribution and price determination.

CHAPTER TWO

Prices and Distribution

Can macroeconomics truly be grounded on social relations among broad groups of economic actors? An affirmative answer would run directly counter to the reductionist program of mainstream economics over the past few decades. Orthodoxy seeks to derive aggregate behavior from micro-level decisions based on postulates of "methodological individualism" and "rational action" (or MIRA for short). MIRA-based analysis has spread throughout the social sciences,[1] but it finds its fullest representation in the theories of demand and supply of scarce resources built into Walrasian microeconomics.

In the Walrasian context, methodological individualism asserts that "agents" (households, firms, investors, and so on) act solely in their own interests, without direct, personal interactions of any sort. Each agent works only with its set of "endowments" and the market opportunities which permit it to alter that set's composition. It makes these choices "rationally," in light of built-in preferences among or technologies for transforming commodities which are assumed to be predetermined. These postulates find their fullest expression in neoclassical theories of price formation, the topic of much of this chapter.

In a way, the following discussion is a detour from our main concerns, but price theory is an unavoidable input into the efforts in later chapters to set out macrofoundations for microeconomic behavior. In particular, we will argue that through distributional channels, movements in "macro" prices like the interest rate, the exchange rate, and the wage can have profound effects on the economic possibilities of individuals and enterprises. As a prelude, it makes sense to examine conventional views about how they react to changing prices in their local economic environments.

1. Classical Macroeconomics

But before we get into MIRA price formation as such, both respect for history and ease of exposition point toward beginning with a review of a more macro theory of prices, that of the "classical" economists who flourished from the late eighteenth through the mid-nineteenth centuries. The names that figure in this and the next sections' discussion are those of the French physiocrats (especially François Quesnay), Jean-Baptiste Say, Thomas Malthus, David Ricardo, and Ricardo's divergent successors Karl Marx and John Stuart Mill.[2]

Quesnay's *Tableau Economique* has the distinction of being the first SAM in history, with a clear recognition of mutual transaction flows among landlords, manufacturers, and farmers.[3] It shows an economy firmly based on agriculture, with farmers producing food for everybody and raw materials for manufacture, and landlords appropriating "surplus" product in the form of land rents. Such a macro structure was postulated by all the early classical economists, and formed an essential part of their analyses.

One conclusion that the classicists drew from observing their relatively poor, largely agricultural countries was that most of what got produced found some economic use—in western Europe famines still occurred in the years around 1800 and were attributed to an overall scarcity of food. The largely empirical observation that creation of one product opens a "vent" for sales of others in exchange was enunciated by Say in 1803, and came to be known as "Say's Law."

There were also business cycles (including the big post–Napoleonic War downswing in England beginning in 1815) which were said to create "general gluts" of commodities not consumed. In the first edition of his *Principles* (1820) Malthus advanced arguments which (generously interpreted) asserted that insufficient consumption by landlords might hold down effective demand, leading to a general glut in the long run. Most classicists followed Say in asserting that gluts were transitory at worst. This analytical stance has implications that are worth pointing out.

First, there is no explicit theory of supply underlying Say's (own) Law. Flows of commodities are produced by habitual actions of farmers and manufacturers, and most are habitually used either as intermediates or to satisfy final demands. If Malthus's landlords, like the leading characters in *Tom Jones,* do their duty as enthusiastic spenders, there will be no glut.[4]

Second, there is no assertion that labor will be fully employed as in modern versions of Say's Law. How could there be full employment when the poorhouse reigned? As will be seen, the classicists thought that the real wage was determined by social processes, not labor market clearing.

Third, the macro balance implicit in the *Tableau Economique* implies that saving equals investment. Indeed, with full utilization of all commodities, the quantities not used as intermediates, exported, or consumed must be invested—there is no other vent. The institutional structure is such that capital formation is largely undertaken by the same actors who save via their "abstinence," so that the coordination problems emphasized in Chapter 1 do not arise. It was pointed out, notably by Mill, that the rate of interest could vary in the market for "loanable funds" to help equate investment demand with saving supply. This extension is best seen as a friendly amendment to Say's Law.

Against this macro background, then, how did the classicists determine income distribution and prices?

2. Classical Theories of Price and Distribution

There are two interpretations (at least). One, put forth by Alfred Marshall and developed more recently by Hollander (1979), is that in their basic instincts the classicists were neoclassical. They never quite figured out marginal utility and productivity theory but came close—Ricardo's treatment of land rent being the prime example. In this narrative, the theory of production that the classicists could not fully elaborate would presumably have been some sort of cross between Walras's and Marshall's.

The other interpretation considered here is associated with the University of Cambridge, post-Marshall. The simplest statement is that the classicists took the vector of commodity output flows as given by non-economic processes having to do with traditional agricultural practices, guild hall rules for craft production, and so on. However, they did set forth variants of a distribution-driven theory of price, later highly elaborated in Piero Sraffa's (1960) book on *Production of Commodities by Means of Commodities* and subsequent contributions. Essays in the collection edited by Eatwell and Milgate (1983) take the further step of combining Sraffian price theory with determination of output not by Say's Law but by effective demand. Whether prices and quantities can be so neatly separated is a complication to be discussed presently.

Two versions of classical price theory are presented here. The first sets out "prices of production" in two incarnations involving circulating and fixed capital respectively. The second embeds prices of production with fixed capital into a "natural" accounting system proposed by Pasinetti (1981).

In modern notation, the basic accounting scheme with circulating "capital" takes the form of intermediate goods in process in N sectors. (The sectors are indicated in the usual fashion by i and j subscripts, which should be fairly easy to distinguish from the i and j labels used throughout this book for nominal and real interest rates respectively.) Cost decompositions for the sectors take the form

$$P_j X_j = \sum_{i=1}^{N} P_i X_{ij} + W_j + \Pi_j, \qquad j = 1, \ldots, N \qquad (1)$$

where P_j and X_j are respectively the price and output of commodity j, X_{ij} is the intermediate use of commodity i in the production of commodity j, and W_j and Π_j are respectively wage and "surplus" (rent, profit, etc.) flows in sector j.

Prices of production models add two hypotheses to this accounting. First, input-output coefficients of the form $a_{ij} = X_{ij}/X_j$ are stable in the face of "reasonable" variations in prices and quantities. Second, wage and profit *rates* per unit of labor and capital respectively are equalized across sectors.

The accounting in equation (1) and first hypothesis are not strikingly counterfactual. The second hypothesis is, meaning that prices of production are often interpreted as "centers of gravitation" toward which processes of competition will make observed sectoral prices tend as capital and labor are reallocated across sectors as their respective returns in all productive activities tend toward equality. In a standard example, if wages are paid at the end of the period of production and surpluses are generated by a real interest rate j charged on the use of circulating capital, then "in the long run" in a two-sector model the price system will be given by the equations

$$\begin{aligned} P_1 &= (1 + j)(P_1 a_{11} + P_2 a_{21}) + w b_1 \\ P_2 &= (1 + j)(P_1 a_{12} + P_2 a_{22}) + w b_2, \end{aligned} \qquad (2)$$

where w is the wage. Both j and w are assumed to apply economy-wide. Wage bills are $W_j = w b_j$ and surplus flows are $\Pi_j = j(P_1 a_{1j} + P_2 a_{2j})X_j$ for $j = 1, 2$.

If one price (say, P_1) is taken as a numeraire, then (2) will solve for the relative price P_2/P_1 and *either* the real wage w/P_1 *or* the interest rate j. In other words, if in the long run competition equalizes rates of payments across sectors and social processes set one of the two distributional variables w/P_1 or j, then relative prices and the other distributional variable will follow. In Garegnani's (1984) description, the value and distribution "core" of the macroeconomic system is determined independently of output levels, so long as the a_{ij} coefficients are stable.

The story is broadly similar in models with fixed capital. Generalizing Table 1.1, an economy-wide two-sector SAM for this case appears in Table 2.1. For the moment, we concentrate on the cost decompositions in

Table 2.1 A SAM for Pasinetti's "Natural System."

	Sec. 1 (1)	Sec. 2 (2)	Wages (3)	Profits		Capital formation		Totals (8)
				(4)	(5)	(6)	(7)	
Output uses								
(A) Sec. 1			P_1C					P_1X_1
(B) Sec. 2						$P_2g\mu_1X_1$	$P_2g\mu_2X_2$	P_2X_2
Sources of incomes								
(C) Wages	wb_1X_1	wb_2X_2						Y_w
(D) Sec. 1 profits	$\pi_1P_1X_1$							$Y_{\pi1}$
(E) Sec. 2 profits		$\pi_2P_2X_2$						$Y_{\pi2}$
Flows of funds								
(F) Sec. 1				S_1		$-P_2g\mu_1X_1$		0
(G) Sec. 2					S_2		$-P_2g\mu_2X_2$	0
(H) Totals	P_1X_1	P_2X_2	Y_w	$Y_{\pi1}$	$Y_{\pi2}$	0	0	

columns (1) and (2), which give price equations of the form $P_i = wb_i + \pi_iP_i$, where w again is the economy-wide wage rate, b_i is the sector i labor-output ratio and π_i is its profit share.

Suppose that the first sector produces consumer goods and the second capital goods (leaving intermediates in accounting limbo, as is often the case in macro models). Also, let each sector's "technically determined" capital/output ratio be μ_i and r be the "pure" rate of profit on fixed capital, equalized across sectors.[5] The value rate of profit will be rP_2, because P_2 is the market price of capital goods. If nonwage income is entirely made up of profits, by definition we have $r = \pi_iP_iX_i/P_2K_i$, where K_i is sector i's capital stock. Because $\mu_i = K_i/X_i$, we get $\pi_iP_i = rP_2\mu_i$. Finally, letting $\omega = w/P_1$ be the real wage and $\rho = P_2/P_1$ be the relative price of capital goods, we can write the cost decompositions as

$$1 = \omega b_1 + r\rho\mu_1$$
$$\rho = \omega b_2 + r\rho\mu_2. \tag{3}$$

This system has three unknowns—ω, r, ρ. Again, given one of the distributional variables r and ω, we can solve for the other distributional indicator as well as relative prices. Classicists typically invoked costs of reproduction of human labor or a reserve army of the unemployed to peg a variable like ω. In Chapter 7, we will see how such ideas along with Garegnani's "core" carry through into recent structuralist models.

Distributional conflict can be underlined if we eliminate ρ from equations (3) to get a relationship known as the "wage-profit curve" or "factor-price frontier":

$$(1/\omega r)(1 - \omega b_1)(1 - r\mu_2) = b_2\mu_1. \tag{4}$$

It is easy to see that the partial derivatives of the left-hand side with respect to both ω and r are negative. The implication is that there is an inverse trade-off between the real wage and the profit rate, or if one broad class of income recipients gains the other inescapably loses. This sort of class conflict characterizes many classical and neoclassical macro models, and often hinges on Say's Law. If output levels were to rise in response to distributional changes, for example, then both workers and profit recipients could gain because of the resulting decreases in the μ_i ratios in (4).

Finally, note that if $b_1/\mu_1 = b_2/\mu_2$ then (4) simplifies to the linear form $\omega b_1 + r\mu_2 = 1$. This famous case of "equal organic compositions of capital" (or equal labor/capital ratios) across the two sectors is one in which distributional conflict is quite clear. If we scale coefficients so that $b_1 = b_2 = b$ and $\mu_1 = \mu_2 = \mu$, then $P_2 = \omega b/(1 - r\mu) = P_1$ so that a labor theory of value applies—prices in both sectors are formed with the *same* markup rate on labor costs. The markup factor $(1 - r\mu)^{-1}$ increases when the profit rate r goes up.

In practice, profit rates across different sectors (and firms) never equalize but on the other hand they rarely differ by more than a factor of two or so. In industrialized economies, wages make up the larger proportion of value-added and even variable costs. Hence a labor theory of value is not a bad empirical approximation—Ricardo's perception, as Stigler (1958) famously pointed out. Marx, however, turned the labor theory into a political question by tying it to surplus extraction or exploitation. Since then, generations of progressive economists have toiled to set out analytical conditions delineating circumstances in which prices will be formed as simple markups on labor costs. Three cases in which such a price theory is valid are of interest.

First, as just noted, there can be equal organic compositions of capital across sectors.

Second, Sraffa (1960) discovered in a circulating capital model that if a special set of weights is used to construct an economy-wide price index (based on the ruling set of prices), then a linear wage-profit curve falls out of the computation. The weights make up a "standard commodity" characterized in two sectors by equality of the ratios $X_i/(a_{i1}X_1 + a_{i2}X_2)$, $i = 1, 2$. The proportions of total output to intermediate sales are the same across sectors, and in fact equal $1 + j^*$, where j^* is the highest real interest rate the system will support when the wage w is set to zero in (2). In terms of the standard commodity, prices can all be reduced to their content of direct-and-indirect or "dated" labor. What Sraffa cleverly did was to choose his index weights to mimic the effects of a "technologically" determined equal organic composition.[6]

He also Delphically suggested that the real interest rate on circulating capital "is susceptible of being determined from outside the system of production, in particular by the level of the money rates of interest" (p. 33). How the structure of "own-rates of return" to physical and financial assets anchored by the short-term financial interest rate might serve to set all asset prices and corresponding profit rates was a theme developed by Sraffa, Keynes, and Kaldor. It is discussed in Chapter 4.

A third example of a labor theory of value is Pasinetti's "natural system" exemplified in Table 2.1. It configures saving and investment flows (instead of technical coefficients or a commodity bundle) to fix each sector's price as a markup on its output's labor content.[7] In the Table 2.1 SAM, it can be seen that as in Table 1.1, all wage income is consumed (cell A3). Pasinetti accepts Say's Law in its modern, full employment version, so that total employment $b_1 X_1 + b_2 X_2$ equals labor supply $\bar{L}$. Combining this assumption with row (C) and column (3) gives $C = \omega \bar{L}$—consumption equals the real wage times the labor supply.

Investment demand in Table 2.1 is based on the premise of steady-state growth. Output and the capital stock in each sector grow at the same rate g: $\dot{K}_i = \mu_i \dot{X}_i = \mu_i g X_i$, where in the absence of technical progress g is also the growth rate of the labor force. Cells B6 and B7 show the resulting purchases of commodity 2. The last key assumption is that investment in each sector is directly financed by its own profit flows—at the industry level there is no discoordination between abstinence and capital formation.

As noted in connection with Tables 1.2 and 1.4, this hypothesis is not strictly valid, because enterprises typically pay over some share of their profit flows to households and financial intermediaries as dividends, interest payments, and so on, and also tap the financial system for funds to pay for part of their investment demand. The relevant empirical question is whether or not fully self-financed investment is a plausible first approximation. As illustrated in Figure 1.2 and Table 1.4 for the United States, Pasinetti's assumption may not be completely misleading (if we ignore the bubble of the late 1990s). Retained earnings of the business sector more or less track its gross capital formation, and household saving somewhat exceeds investment in housing. The household net lending position is roughly equal to business borrowing.

If self-financing applies, equating profit and investment flows in each sector shows that $r_i = \pi_i P_i / P_2 \mu_i = g$. Profit rates across sectors equalize to the economy-wide rate of growth—a situation that modern neoclassical economists call the "golden rule" after Phelps (1961).[8] From columns (1) and (2) of Table 2.1 the price equations become $P_i = P_2 g \mu_i + w b_i$, with solutions

$$P_1 = [w/(1 - g\mu_2)][b_1 + g(\mu_1 b_2 - \mu_2 b_1)]$$
$$P_2 = wb_2/(1 - g\mu_2).$$

(5)

In sector 2, a simple markup applies. In sector 1, the price depends on labor content wb_1, but the relationship involves the expression $(\mu_1 b_2 - \mu_2 b_1)$, which measures the difference in organic compositions between the two sectors. As emphasized by Pasinetti, similar rules apply in the more complicated case in which growth (and profit) rates differ across industries.

A labor theory of value (though with sector-specific price/wage relationships except when there are equal organic compositions in both sectors) emerges from Pasinetti's system, essentially from his assumptions about how investment is financed. A result about income distribution which will figure in later chapters also follows. Suppose that the capacity growth rate g increases, requiring additional investment. An output adjustment of the Keynes-Kalecki sort cannot occur, because full employment is presupposed in the natural system. The saving counterpart can only come from increases in operating surpluses $\pi_i P_i$ or (as can be verified by manipulating equations (5)), a fall in the real wage ω and workers' consumption $\omega \bar{L}$.

This sort of crowding-out of consumption by a greater injection of investment demand is known as "forced saving," whereby the extra saving effort is extracted by income redistribution from (in the present case) low-saving workers to high-saving firms. After World War II, macroeconomic adjustment via forced saving was emphasized mainly by Nicholas Kaldor (1957). Three decades previously it had figured as the main equilibrating mechanism in Keynes's *Treatise on Money* (1930), Schumpeter's *Theory of Economic Development* (1934), and the macroeconomics of a whole generation that Amadeo (1989) calls the "post-Wicksellians."

The bottom line to the foregoing discussion of classical price theory (and even the labor theory of value) is that it is not likely to be far wrong as a "center of gravitation" in a circulating capital model or even a fixed capital model so long as output levels and thereby the capital-output ratios μ_i are fairly stable. But if Say's Law for commodities does not generally hold, then it is conceivable that effective demand at the sectoral level will be sensitive to income distribution. More precisely, demand-determined output levels X_i may respond to changes in the real wage and profit rates, which themselves depend on the X_i via the ratios $\mu_i = K_i/X_i$. Classical supply-side determination of output ceases to apply. Such potential linkages between distribution and effective demand did not figure in classical theory (save perhaps for the work of the perpetually muddled

Malthus), but are central to the structuralist models discussed in later chapters. They are not considered in the classically influenced papers collected in Eatwell and Milgate (1983), which, as already noted, suggest that a reasonable macro framework ought to combine Ricardian price theories with determination of output by effective demand. This program has problems if demand depends strongly on income distribution as captured in most macro models by the values of variables such as ω and r. As will be seen, there are reasons to believe that such linkages exist.

3. Neoclassical Cost-Based Prices

The emphasis switches wholly to the supply side in neoclassical price theory. The base case is pure competition in input markets, with the MIRA individuals being "small" firms hiring inputs according to their market prices. The model's emphasis is on adding substitution wrinkles to prices of production, turning a parameter like the labor-output ratio $b = L/X$ into a function of the real wage as well as of other real input prices. Such details appear clearly in a "dual" specification which uses cost instead of production functions to describe price formation and input demands. In this section we spin the basic story, and then go on to a couple of applications.

To begin with the traditional production function, assume that a firm can produce output X using inputs Z_1 and Z_2 according to a "technical" relationship such as $X = F(Z_1, Z_2)$. The usual hypothesis added for macroeconomics is that the "aggregate" production function $F(..)$ demonstrates constant returns to scale or CRS (in other words, $F(..)$ is homogenous of degree one so that for a positive constant κ, we have $F(\kappa Z_1, \kappa Z_2) = \kappa F(Z_1, Z_2)$). As is well known, if the firm pays its inputs their marginal products, then from Euler's Theorem under CRS the total value of payments will just exhaust the value of output. Moreover, average cost per unit output will be independent of the scale of production.

If the real market price of input i is c_i, then the firm is supposed to minimize the total cost $\Gamma = c_1 Z_1 + c_2 Z_2$ of producing a given level of output X. Let the function $C(c_1, c_2)$ be equal to the value of Γ when the firm has chosen its cost-minimizing input basket. "Duality" means that the following production and cost relationships apply:

Production	Cost
$X = F(Z_1, Z_2)$	$\Gamma = C(c_1, c_2)$
$\partial F/\partial Z_i = c_i, \quad i = 1, 2$	$\partial C/\partial c_i = Z_i, \quad i = 1, 2$

In the literature, the result that the partial derivative of the cost function with respect to an input's price gives the level of use of that input is known as Shephard's Lemma (1953). Setting the partial derivative of the production function with respect to an input (the "marginal product") equal to its cost is the standard rule for determining input demand.

It is easy to sketch a proof of Shephard's Lemma using the "envelope theorem" about the behavior of functions which have been optimized with respect to some of their arguments. For example, let $M(y)$ be the value that the function $f(x, y)$ takes when it is minimized with respect to x,

$$M(y) = \min_x f(x, y) = f[x(y), y], \tag{6}$$

where $x(y)$ is the x that solves the minimization problem for a given y.

The question is what happens to $M(y)$ in (6) when y changes. The answer is that dM/dy is equal to the partial derivative of f with respect to y, holding x to its optimized value. In Shephard's Lemma, for example, the derivative of the cost function $\Gamma = c_1 Z_1 + c_2 Z_2$ with respect to c_1 when the Z_i are at their optimal values is just Z_1. Because Z_1 and Z_2 have already been chosen to minimize cost, any "small" or "second-order" changes ($d^2 Z_1/dc_1^2$ and $d^2 Z_2/dc_1^2$) they make in response to shifts in c_1 will not reduce Γ any further.[9]

A first example illustrates further implications of duality. Switching to macroeconomic labels for inputs, suppose that X is produced by labor L and capital K. The output price level is P and the nominal wage is w. In the characteristic aggregate contortion mentioned in Chapter 1, capital goods are assumed to be made of the same "stuff" as X, meaning that their replacement cost is also P, as opposed to a specific capital cost index P_K (which, for example, in a small open economy depending on capital goods imports would surely depend on the exchange rate e). With a pure profit rate r, the nominal cost of using capital is rP.

A commonly used production function presupposes a constant elasticity of substitution (CES), with the elasticity σ being a measure of the curvature of an isoquant.[10] The explicit form of a CES production function is

$$X = [\beta_L L^{-\lambda} + \beta_K K^{-\lambda}]^{-1/\lambda}, \tag{7}$$

where $\lambda = (1 - \sigma)/\sigma$ and the β_i are scaling parameters which can be estimated using the payment shares of inputs in the value of output. Setting the partial derivatives with respect to L and K equal to the real wage ω ($= w/P$) and profit rate r give input demand functions as

$$L = X(\omega/\beta_L)^{-\sigma} \quad \text{and} \quad K = X(r/\beta_K)^{-\sigma}. \tag{8}$$

Input demands are proportional to the output level X, with the new twist being that the input coefficients or factors of proportionality between inputs and output (the terms in parentheses taken to the power $-\sigma$) now depend on real costs. The same is true of input shares $\psi = wL/PX$ and $1 - \psi = \pi = rK/X$.

A CES cost function has the same functional form as the corresponding production function, a convenience demonstrated by plugging the expressions in (8) into (7) and rearranging:

$$P = [\gamma_L w^{1-\sigma} + \gamma_K (rP)^{1-\sigma}]^{1/(1-\sigma)} \quad \text{or} \quad 1 = (\gamma_L \omega^{1-\sigma} + \gamma_K r^{1-\sigma})^{1/(1-\sigma)}, \tag{9}$$

where $\gamma_i = (\beta_i)^\sigma$, for $i = K, L$.

The second equation in (9) shows that the real wage ω and profit rate r vary inversely—if one falls the other must rise as along the classical wage-profit curve (4) discussed above. The first equation makes P into a linearly homogeneous function of nominal input costs w and rP, not different in spirit from the prices of production relationships (1) and (2). By permitting its input coefficients and cost relationships to depend on relative prices, neoclassical production theory generalizes classical theory to a degree, but the differences between the two approaches are not profound.

4. Hat Calculus, Measuring Productivity Growth, and Full Employment Equilibrium

In practice, much of the neoclassical story follows from accounting identities, as an extended example in this section illustrates. It relies on a useful bag of tricks known informally as "hat calculus," where a "hat," or circumflex accent, over a variable denotes its logarithmic differential (or log-change): "X-hat" $= \hat{X} = d(\log X) = dX/X$.[11] As already observed in Chapter 1 (note 24), one can also interpret $\hat{X}$ as a growth rate, that is, $\hat{X} = \dot{X}/X = (dX/dt)/X$.

We can begin with a version of the "Output cost" columns of the SAMs already presented:

$$PX = wL + rPK,$$

where we ignore interindustry transactions, taxes and transfers, and other complications. This equation is a cost function like the expressions in (9), but with less regalia. Log-differentiated and rearranged, it can be written in the form

$$\hat{P} + \hat{X} = \psi(\hat{w} + \hat{L}) + (1 - \psi)(\hat{r} + \hat{P} + \hat{K}),$$

where as before ψ is the share of labor payments wL in the value of output PX. For this formula to be able to track changing SAMs, ψ would have to shift over time (contrary to the Cobb-Douglas case, for example). The algebra can be rearranged to give a decomposition of quantity and price log-changes in "Divisia indexes" with time-varying weights ψ and $(1 - \psi)$:

$$0 = \psi[(\hat{w} - \hat{P}) - (\hat{X} - \hat{L})] + (1 - \psi)[\hat{r} - (\hat{X} - \hat{K})], \tag{10}$$

where the hats implicitly signify growth rates.

Several general points can be made regarding (10). The first is that the terms $(\hat{X} - \hat{L})$ and $(\hat{X} - \hat{K})$ respectively measure shifts in the output/labor and output/capital ratios, or average "productivity" levels of the two inputs. Long-run evidence reviewed by Foley and Michl (1999) suggests that observed technical change (as reflected in shifting productivity levels) in capitalist economies is sometimes but not always "Marx-biased" in the sense that labor productivity X/L tends to rise over time while capital productivity X/K falls.

Another "stylized fact" often but not always supported by the data and built into many growth models is that real wage growth $(\hat{w} - \hat{P})$ tends to run at about the same rate as labor productivity growth $(\hat{X} - \hat{L})$, when both variables are averaged over time. If this relationship is observed, then persistently negative trend growth $(\hat{X} - \hat{K})$ in capital productivity has to be associated with a falling rate of profit $(\hat{r} < 0)$ in (10), because the bracketed term multiplied by ψ will be close to zero. Marx-biased productivity changes go together with the traditional Marxist distributive theme that a falling rate of profit (FROP) is to be expected under modern capitalism.

Of course, observed country histories add complications. The plots in Figure 2.1 present growth rates for the real wage and (nonresidential) capital and labor productivity levels in the United States (lower diagram) and Japan (upper) after the Japanese "miracle" period ended in the mid-1960s. The data are presented year-on-year, to give some feeling for cyclical fluctuations.

Capital productivity in the United States has fluctuated strongly, basically in step with the business cycle. The growth rate's jumps up and down, however, are close to being centered around zero (the average growth rate is 0.0008). Early in the period, growth rates of labor pro-

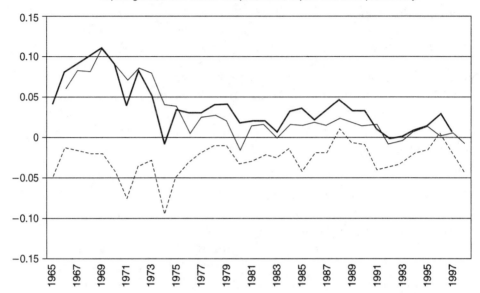

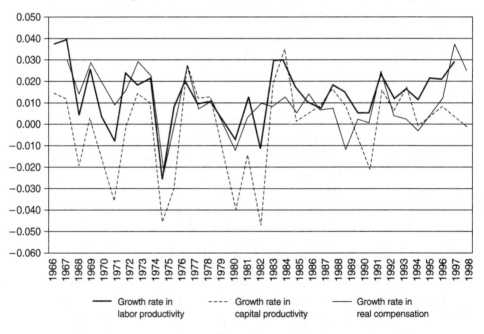

Figure 2.1
Comparative growth performance of the United States and Japan, 1965–1998.

ductivity and the real wage move roughly in step, with the latter tending to lag after the early 1980s (a Reagan effect?). By contrast, with just a couple of exceptions, yearly capital productivity growth in Japan was negative throughout the period—a rather standard observation for East Asia. The Japanese economy avoided a FROP only insofar as its real wage tended to grow less rapidly than labor productivity.

The neoclassical approach to measuring technological change takes the form of "sources of growth" accounting, which blends separate growth rates of labor and capital productivity together into one term, ϵ:

$$\epsilon = \psi(\hat{X} - \hat{L}) + (1 - \psi)(\hat{X} - \hat{K}) = \hat{X} - \psi\hat{L} - (1 - \psi)\hat{K}. \quad (11X)$$

The number ϵ emerging from these expressions is often called "total factor productivity growth" (TFPG) because it is supposed to represent how overall productivity of the input factors L and K jointly rises over time (Solow 1957). In other words, output growth $\hat{X}$ is decomposed into a weighted average of the growth rates of the inputs, $\psi\hat{L} + (1 - \psi)\hat{K}$, plus TFPG.

In much mainstream analysis ϵ, $\hat{L}$, and $\hat{K}$ are treated as predetermined variables so that the output growth rate $\hat{X}$ is set from the side of supply. However, the accounting would be the same if $\hat{X}$ were determined by effective demand and ϵ were a "residual" (another name it frequently goes by, perhaps more descriptive than TFPG). To repeat a point made previously, the causal scheme to be imposed on an accounting identity like (10) requires serious thought.

Substituting ϵ as defined in (11X) into (10) gives decompositions of price growth,

$$\epsilon = \psi\hat{w} + (1 - \psi)(\hat{r} + \hat{P}) - \hat{P} = \psi\hat{\omega} + (1 - \psi)\hat{r}. \quad (11P)$$

The expression after the first equality states that $\hat{P}$ will be lower, the greater the value of ϵ. This productivity rein on price increases is observed in the data. It has to be present in a consistent accounting scheme.

The second equality, $\epsilon = \psi\hat{\omega} + (1 - \psi)\hat{r}$, is more interesting. It supports a critique of the mainstream advanced by Shaikh (1974) among others, and elaborated by Felipe and McCombie (2002) in one of a series of papers. The starting point is that the value of ϵ coming from (11X) represents a "surplus" of output growth over a weighted average of the growth rates of input uses. Somehow it must be distributed to actors in the economy, and (11P) sets out the relevant accounting restriction. Trend versus cycle considerations become important in this regard.

As hinted above, the trend value of profit rate growth $\hat{r}$ may be zero or negative. However, over periods on the order of one to ten years $\hat{r}$ is more volatile than real wage growth $\hat{\omega}$ as it oscillates through the business cycle. For example, the (transient?) TFPG acceleration during the cyclical upswing in the United States in the late 1990s seemed to spill over into positive values of $\hat{r}$. In general, labor productivity growth itself appears to vary "pro" the output/distribution share cycle in the United States (see Chapter 9).

Over a longer term (decades, perhaps), if real wage growth runs at about the same rate as labor productivity growth and there is no strong trend in capital productivity, it will be true that $\epsilon \approx \psi\hat{\omega} \approx \psi(\hat{X} - \hat{L})$, or secular TFPG is roughly equal to the rates of real wage and productivity growth multiplied by the wage share.

The bottom line is that TFPG plays multiple roles. In the medium run, ϵ in (11P) feeds into distributive conflict over the cycle. Its long-run behavior will be driven by the technological and social forces that influence labor productivity growth and the adjustment of the real wage thereto. Sorting out how all these factors interact in historical time is a formidable task. Just summing them up into an index like ϵ and claiming it measures "technological change" is not terribly helpful, despite the enormous effort devoted to such exercises in the decades following Solow's 1957 paper. Looking at separate trends in $(\hat{X} - \hat{L})$ and $(\hat{X} - \hat{K})$ à la Foley and Michl while considering concurrent shifts in the real wage and profit rate makes more sense.

A modest step in this direction by the mainstream is to bring in "factor-augmenting" technical change in the context of a production function. To see how it works, we can begin with another identity,

$$\hat{X} = \psi[\hat{L} + (\hat{X} - \hat{L})] + (1 - \psi)[\hat{K} + (\hat{X} - \hat{K})]. \tag{12}$$

This equation basically says that $\hat{X} = \hat{X}$ and holds for any value of ψ. However, if ψ is set equal to the labor share and rates of productivity growth are defined as $\epsilon_L = \hat{X} - \hat{L}$ and $\epsilon_K = \hat{X} - \hat{K}$, it can be used for growth accounting in the form

$$\hat{X} = \psi(\hat{L} + \epsilon_L) + (1 - \psi)(\hat{K} + \epsilon_K) = \psi\hat{L} + (1 - \psi)\hat{K} + \epsilon. \tag{12ϵ}$$

After the first equality, output growth is decomposed into a weighted average of growth rates of the inputs plus their factor-augmenting rates of technological change. After the second equality, this construct is seen to boil down to TFPG. If ψ is assumed not to change over time, then (12ϵ) is a Cobb-Douglas production function in growth rate form— a fancy reinterpretation of the identity (12) and nothing more. As illustrated in a moment, other production functions differ from Cobb-Douglas only in imposing auxiliary "marginal productivity" equations to determine ψ as some function of ω and r. The bottom line is that the mainstream production function/TFPG story just adds bells and whistles to the task of tracing changes over time in the accounting identities (10) and (12). Isn't it more sensible to work with the identities themselves, instead? Attempts to do so are presented in several chapters to follow.

From the mainstream perspective, the answer to this question is "no." Production functions and marginal productivity conditions are the way to go. To illustrate a common neoclassical interpretation of factor augmentation, we can combine (12ε) with the (locally) constant elasticity of substitution σ. Technical change is supposed to make "effective" labor and capital inputs L^* and K^* grow over time according to rules such as $L^* = L \exp(\epsilon_L t)$ and $K^* = K \exp(\epsilon_K t)$. If producers still minimize costs with respect to "ordinary" input levels L and K, then it can be shown (Taylor 1979, app. D) that in log-change form demands for labor and capital can be written as

$$\hat{L} = -\sigma\hat{\omega} + \hat{X} - (1 - \sigma)\epsilon_L \quad \text{and} \quad \hat{K} = -\sigma\hat{r} + \hat{X} - (1 - \sigma)\epsilon_K. \quad (13)$$

The effects of factor-augmentation on input demands are ambiguous; only for values of $\sigma < 1$ will positive productivity growth reduce demand for the corresponding input. This curiosum is relevant to the discussion of "new" or "endogenous" growth theories in Chapter 11.

Setting $\epsilon = \psi\epsilon_L + (1 - \psi)\epsilon_K$ as above, a bit of substitution shows that equations (13) are consistent with (12) so long as one of two relationships (11X) and (11P) is independently valid. As already discussed in section 3, the usual neoclassical "dual" interpretation of these manipulations is that factor-demand equations like (13) combined with a cost equation generate a production function, and vice versa. But a clearer rationale is that if the decompositions in (10) or (12) fit the data (as they must, if the numbers are constructed properly), then equations for factor demands as in (13) are the only functional forms with a single substitution parameter σ that are compatible with SAM accounting. In econometric practice, such a one-parameter restriction is weak enough to be difficult to refute.

Finally (setting $\epsilon = 0$ to concentrate on comparative statics), the log-change version of the wage-profit curve from (11P) is

$$\psi\hat{\omega} + (1 - \psi)\hat{r} = 0. \quad (14)$$

If we define $u = X/K$ as a rough-and-ready measure of capacity utilization, then plugging (14) into the capital-demand equation in (13) and simplifying gives the expression

$$\hat{\omega} = -[(1 - \psi)/\sigma\psi]\hat{u}. \quad (15)$$

In words, the real wage is an inverse function of capacity utilization, or the level of economic activity. The "story" is that if firms are to produce more output, they have to be presented with a lower real wage to induce them to hire the necessary labor. Macroeconomically, this adjustment is a variation on the distributional scenario discussed in connection with Table 2.1, combining the real wage reduction of forced saving with a positive employment response.

On the other hand, labor supply may rise with the real wage, according to a (locally) constant elasticity ϕ: $\hat{L} = \phi\hat{\omega}$. Substituting into the production function in (11X) with $\epsilon = 0$ gives

$$\hat{u} = \psi\phi\hat{\omega} - \psi\hat{K}. \tag{16}$$

In words, a higher real wage will pull more workers into the labor market. If they get jobs, the level of economic activity will rise. In the present setup, the invisible hand will presumably make sure that the jobs are there, as the real wage varies to equilibrate labor supply and demand. More formally, for a given value of $\hat{K}$, (15) and (16) are a pair of simultaneous equations for $\hat{u}$ and $\hat{\omega}$ or for u and ω more generally. Their solution determines the activity level and real wage. All this is illustrated in Figure 2.2, a diagram with axes that will become achingly familiar in this volume. The curves crossing in the graphs, however, will have drastically

Figure 2.2
Determination of macroeconomic equilibrium from the labor market.

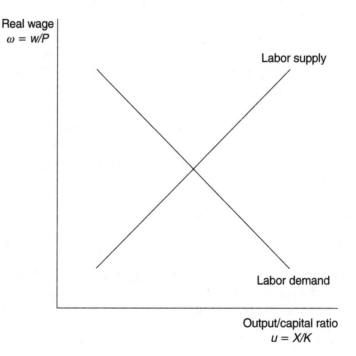

Real wage
$\omega = w/P$

Labor supply

Labor demand

Output/capital ratio
$u = X/K$

differing contents. Labor demand and supply are the key relationships in Figure 2.2, which embodies "full employment" along the supply curve. Such an updated version of Say's Law is congenial to many modern economists but alien to the visions of Kalecki and Keynes.

5. Markup Pricing in the Product Market

The major omission in Figure 2.2 is the principle of effective demand, as will be pointed out in later chapters. A more immediate, technical point, however, is the fact that the inverse relationship between the real wage and the level of economic activity built into (15) is difficult to establish empirically. In *The General Theory*, Keynes went to great (some say excessive) lengths to render his ideas acceptable to orthodoxy. One of his ploys was to accept the "first classical postulate" that to get higher employment, labor must accept a lower real wage.[12]

A few years after *The General Theory* was published, Dunlop (1938) and Tarshis (1939) challenged this postulate empirically—if anything, real wages appeared (and, depending on how they are measured, still do appear) to vary pro-cyclically.[13] In a response, Keynes (1939) had no problem accepting this amendment to his own theory, but it remains vexing to neoclassicists. Thereby hang many tales, some to be developed in this and the following sections. The theme they share is that it is possible to replace the "new classical" or Walrasian curves in Figure 2.2 with more plausible constructs, while still retaining the picture's message that the macroeconomy obeys rules closely akin to the modern, full employment version of Say's Law. This message is central, for example, to the mainstream "new Keynesian" research project that flourished in the 1980s (Mankiw and Romer 1991).[14] The following discussion gives a taste of new Keynesian analysis.

A basic idea is that market imperfections can generate macroeconomic relationships resembling those of Figure 2.2, with the curves crossing at a point that determines "natural rates" of capacity utilization and employment. The most obvious departure from pure competition in commodity markets is monopoly power used to drive wedges between prices and costs. In the simplest example, the MIRA individual is a single-market monopolist firm seeking to

Maximize $PX - wbX$
  subject to $X = X_0 P^{-\eta}$,

where the absolute value of the price elasticity of demand facing the firm is $\eta > 1$.

Solving this problem gives a pricing rule of the form

$$P = wb/[1 - (1/\eta)] = (1 + \tau)wb = wb/(1 - \pi). \tag{17}$$

The price P is set by a margin over variable cost wb, with the markup rate τ depending on the firm's market power as captured by the elasticity η. The cost decomposition is $P = wb + \pi P$, where π is the profit share, so that $1 + \tau = (1 - \pi)^{-1}$. If η tends toward infinity, price is just equal to variable cost ($P = wb$), while the markup rate tends toward infinity as η approaches one from above.

With a constant η, we get a constant markup rate—a good first approximation to what is observed. Besides monopoly power, moreover, there are numerous theoretical justifications for markup pricing. They include a desire on the part of firms to generate cash flow sufficient to finance capital formation along forced saving lines (Eichner 1980). Historically, stable markups provided a basis for intrafirm coordination in multidivisional enterprises like General Motors (Semmler 1984).

But why a constant markup rate? Is there a more accurate second approximation? Long ago, Pigou (1927) proposed that the markup may vary countercyclically, contrary to the first classical postulate and forced saving.[15] This possibility has been picked up by new Keynesians, with one suggestion being that when aggregate demand rises, novel products enter the market (Weitzman 1982). If they substitute closely with old ones, price elasticities may increase overall, reducing markup rates from the first equation in (17). Another idea is that price-setting collusion among firms may falter when demand surges (Rotemberg and Saloner 1986). Third, a firm is likely to find that the proportion of new to old customers in its clientele varies pro-cyclically, in a twist on the "kinked demand curve" explanation for markup pricing proposed by Sweezy (1939). In an attempt to lock in the loyalty of its new buyers, the firm may shave prices (Phelps and Winter 1970).

Finally, the presence of decreasing average costs may lead to lower real prices during a boom. The two obvious candidates for lower costs per unit output are the inputs of labor and capital. Although detailed discussion of the phenomenon is postponed for several later chapters, we have already noted that labor productivity does appear to respond positively to economic activity. In the short to medium run, Okun's Law (1962) states that the elasticity of the unemployment rate with respect to U.S. GDP is about one-half (in Okun's day, the value was more like one-third). An earlier, longer-term analog is Verdoorn's Law (1949) asserting a cross-cyclical or cross-country positive relationship between productivity growth and the level of output (especially in the manufacturing sector). Using appropriate econometric techniques, Vernengo and Berglund (2000) find support for both relationships in U.S. time-series data.

On the side of capital, costs can also shift counter-cyclically and feed into a similarly varying markup rate. Following Hazledine (1990), this scenario can be illustrated by a typical applied industrial organization model, where N oligopolistic firms of the same size are active in a sector.[16] The basic idea is that firms face a fixed cost of using capital ρK (with $\rho = rP_K$, where r is the sector's profit rate as "required" by its financiers and P_K is the cost of its capital input bundle). Redefining Γ as the average cost of production, we have

$$\Gamma = wb + \rho(K/X) = wb + [(K/N)/(X/N)] = wb + \rho\kappa/(X/N), \quad (18)$$

where $\kappa = K/N$ is the industry-wide average capital stock per firm. Average cost falls as output per firm X/N rises, that is, firms can "spread" their fixed capital charge $\rho\kappa$ over a greater volume of sales when demand swings up. In log-change form we have

$$\hat{\Gamma} = (1 - \lambda)\hat{w} + \lambda(\hat{\rho} + \hat{N} - \hat{X}), \quad (19)$$

where $\lambda = \rho\kappa(X/N)/\Gamma$. As in the SAM of Table 1.4, the share of enterprise "operating surpluses" in value-added (or, more appropriately, the share in the gross value of a sector's output, which includes intermediate input costs) will be on the order of 0.2 or less. Fixed capital costs of the sort considered here necessarily appear as part of operating surpluses in the data. Hence, the elasticity $-\lambda$ of Γ with respect to X in (19) will be negative but "small" in absolute value. Decreasing average cost should be visible but not strikingly so in the sector's time-series numbers.

The overall cost decomposition is $PX = \Gamma X + \pi PX$ so that the price level is $P = (1 + \tau)\Gamma$, where the markup rate τ satisfies the relationship $1 + \tau = (1 - \pi)^{-1}$ as in (17).[17] Let $\phi = 1 + \tau$ be the "force" of the markup, and assume that $\phi = \phi_0\Gamma^{-\gamma}$ so that $P = \phi\Gamma = \phi_0\Gamma^{1-\gamma}$. Here the assumption is that competition means that all cost increases cannot be passed along into higher prices. In an economy open to competitive imports of goods "similar" to those produced at home, for example, γ might approximate the import share in total demand of home and foreign goods. In an economy closed to trade, γ could be close to zero in a sector without much competition.

We can also assume that new firms enter the sector when its markup rises, $N = N_0\phi^{\mu}$. In a sector with relatively free entry, μ could be on the order of ten or higher. If there are strong barriers to entry, it could be one or less. Finally, because new firms require investment finance, ρ may rise with the number of firms, $\rho = \rho_0 N^\beta$ (presumably, β is "small").

Log-differentiating all these relationships and putting them together gives an expression for the log-change in the sector's price level:

$$\hat{P} = \frac{1-\gamma}{1 + \lambda(1+\beta)\mu\gamma}[(1-\lambda)\hat{w} - \lambda\hat{X}]. \tag{20}$$

A nominal wage increase is passed into a higher price, although with an elasticity likely to be less than one. Higher output makes the price level fall. The elasticity could be near zero for relatively large values of the price-cost retardation elasticity γ and the entry elasticity μ and approximately equal to $-\lambda$ for low values of these parameters—a countercyclical markup response is likely to be stronger in an economy closed to competitive imports and with high barriers to entry.

If such industry-level outcomes can be blown up to the economy as a whole, they suggest that the real wage $\omega = w/P$ would tend to rise in line with increases in the both the money wage w and the level of economic activity X. The relevant elasticities would have absolute magnitudes in the range of 0.1 or smaller.

6. Efficiency Wages for Labor

In new Keynesian theory, markup pricing for output is often combined with market power with respect to labor. In a variant perhaps more relevant to Europe than to the United States, monopoly unions may be able to drive up real wages when employment rises.[18] The American literature, by contrast, endows firms with monopsony power over their employees. This position enables them to "extract labor from labor power" in Marx's phrase, by combining wage carrots and coercion sticks to enhance workers' productivity and reduce shirking (Bowles and Gintis 1990).

Such a labor-extraction process is often modeled with the firm as a "principal" (or Stackelberg leader) which minimizes labor cost subject to the productivity response functions of its workers or "agents." In a typical example, the labor-output ratio might be adjusted by workers reacting to their perceived "cost of job loss" Z. A higher cost of being fired means that they would be willing to work harder. In the usual formulation the firm solves the following problem:

Minimize $\omega b(Z)$
    subject to $Z = \omega - \epsilon\omega_a - (1-\epsilon)\omega_b,$

where ω is the real wage, ϵ is the overall rate of employment ($\epsilon = L/\bar{L}$, where $\bar{L}$ is labor supply), ω_a is the wage paid by employers alternative to the worker's present firm, and ω_b is the level of benefits paid to the unemployed. Because people raise their productivity when their cost of job loss goes up, the labor-output ratio b is a decreasing function of Z.

The firm chooses ω—it is in a position to tell labor both how many jobs will be available (given the output level X) and the level of the wage. Its optimality condition can be written out as

$$-Zb'/b = Z/\omega = (1 - \epsilon)(\omega - \omega_b)/\omega, \tag{21}$$

where ω_a is set equal to ω in the substitution for Z after the second equality. Toward the other end of the expression, $b' = db/dZ$. Let θ stand for the elasticity of b with respect to Z at the extreme left. Then roughly speaking, (21) will be satisfied for numbers such as $\theta = 0.475$, $\epsilon = 0.05$, and $(\omega - \omega_b)/\omega = 0.5$. All these values are econometrically plausible. For θ (locally) constant, (21) shows that a higher unemployment benefit ω_b raises the real wage ω—firms have to pay more to extract labor from workers if their cost of job loss falls. Aggregate demand can also affect ω—there is no presumption of full employment in the efficiency wage model. By reducing Z at an initial level of ω, a higher employment rate ϵ forces firms to raise the real wage.[19]

7. New Keynesian Crosses and Methodological Reservations

This positive response of the real wage to the level of economic activity is central to the new Keynesian project. The narrative starts with an increase in capacity utilization $u = X/K$ and thereby the employment rate $\epsilon = bu(K/\bar{L})$, where conventionally both the capital stock K and the available labor force $\bar{L}$ are assumed to be fixed in the short run. As we have seen, the higher value of ϵ bids up the real wage; it also (slightly) reduces the labor/output ratio b, consistent with the Okun and Verdoorn laws. If such effects are important economy-wide, the upward-sloping "Efficiency wage" schedule in the (u, ω) plane emerges in Figure 2.3.

The "Markup" schedule in the diagram draws on the model of section 5, which generated a weak inverse relationship between the level of economic activity and the price/wage ratio. This linkage is captured by the shallow positive slope of the "Markup" curve. The crossing point of the curves defines "natural" capacity utilization and real wage rates $\bar{u}$ and $\bar{\omega}$, at which firms satisfy their goals with regard to both price formation and labor extraction. If in addition money wages and prices tend to rise rela-

Figure 2.3
Determination of
macroeconomic
equilibrium via mar-
ket imperfections.

tive to trend for values of u above $\bar{u}$ and fall under other circumstances, then (in one of the more gruesome acronyms coined by an illiterate profession) the natural rate becomes a NAIRU, or "non-accelerating inflation rate of unemployment."

In the American policy debate late in the 1990s and early in the decade of the "aughts," the NAIRU lost a lot of its earlier cachet because after 1995 the economy was growing rapidly and operating at high levels of capacity utilization with little visible inflation. How this "failure" of the concept will affect its future acceptance remains to be seen. But if we look backward, the NAIRU had a formidably successful history; whether it was deserved or not will be thoroughly discussed in subsequent chapters.

One reason why NAIRU-like ideas are likely to live on lies in the similarity between Figure 2.3 and the purely competitive, labor market-based analysis of Figure 2.2. A strength of the Figure 2.3 worldview is that it at least admits the possibility of unemployment, because the employment ratio ϵ can be less than one. Interventions to raise ϵ become possible in the form of "incomes" or incentive policies aimed at shifting the two schedules, as discussed by Layard, Nickell, and Jackman (1991) and Carlin and Soskice (1990). Concerted attempts to change the level of effective demand are bound to fail, however, because the rate of capacity utilization cannot lie above its "equilibrium" value $\bar{u}$ "in the long run" (except possibly in the "Goldilocks economy" of the United States in the late 1990s, when everything was "just right").

This basic message of Figure 2.3 has been transmitted in many ways. For example, Lindbeck (1993) crosses an upward-sloping "wage-setting" curve with a first classical postulate labor demand function; Phelps (1994) replaces the labor demand curve with a pricing relationship from a dynamic oligopoly model. Regardless of the rationales underlying the curves of Figure 2.3, its practical implications are hard to distinguish from Figure 2.2's version of Say's Law. Two curves originating on the supply side cross and determine ω and u, independent of aggregate demand.

A final decision about the mechanism behind the curves—pure or impure competition—does not have to be reached at this point. However, two reasons why models based on pure competition may merit deeper consideration are worth pointing out. One is rhetorical, the other ontological.

The rhetorical argument is that a fundamental critique of the capitalist system should be mounted on capitalism's strongest theoretical ground, that is, perfect competition. Although their final theories were far apart, this strategy was shared by Marx and Keynes. As will be seen in Chapter 4, Keynes took on the model underlying Figure 2.2 on its own terms. By replacing the second classical postulate with the principle of effective demand—reversing the Walrasian causal structure—he revoked the full employment statement of Say's Law. The most powerful new classical counterarguments also are founded on pure competition.

By comparison, new Keynesian imperfect competition looks a bit like window dressing. It does not rest on the deepest foundation of *The General Theory*, which as observed in Chapter 1 is a social structure involving distinct roles for workers, enterprises or "business," and rentiers. Political choice underlies the socioeconomic distinctions among these actors—under modern capitalism society cedes control over production and accumulation to corporate elites (Lindblom 1977). This decision is neither inevitable nor sacrosanct. Indeed, as Polanyi (1944) forcefully argued, societies at times take back powers granted to the market, when it creates such inequality or provokes such financial instability as to generate widespread unrest. Polanyi's view that societies move toward and away from full market liberalization in "double movements" is the best reason to take economic analysis embodying less than perfect competition seriously. But Polanyi and Lindblom stand well outside of economics as it is usually practiced—they are interested in society and the state, not the latest technical tricks in modeling imperfect competition.

The ontological argument for concentrating on pure competition is also sociopolitical, but relies on process as opposed to structure. Simply put, its conclusion is that imperfect competition in all its forms—oligopolies, efficiency wages, externalities, indivisibilities, and so on—is doomed to disappear in some not very lengthy run. It will be undone by entrepreneurial forces. Through entry of firms into oligopolized markets, markups will be driven toward zero. Unemployed workers will toil with high productivity at low pay to bid down efficiency wages until every willing hand finds a job. Economic externalities or production indivisibilities will be "internalized" through bargained market solutions until socially optimal marginal benefit = marginal cost equalities apply (Coase 1960).

This view of competition as a process that inevitably grinds away economic barriers because someone can make money by doing the grinding is characteristic of the Austrian school of economics, launched by Carl Menger in Vienna during the second half of the nineteenth century.[20] The best-known latter-day Austrian is undoubtedly Friedrich von Hayek. In Milton Friedman's heyday, the Chicago School offered a complementary synthesis of Austrian ideas with monetarism and the perfect competition economics of demand and supply.

In modern terminology, Menger and Hayek viewed the socioeconomic system as an evolutionary game in which the forces of entrepreneurship will finally prevail, leading to a socially optimal competitive resource allocation. Formally speaking, no proofs of convergence were provided. Rather, von Hayek (1988) argued that the existence and benefits of a trend toward capitalism worldwide are demonstrated by the rapid expansion of the human population observed over the last few hundred years.

There are immediate doubts. Whether modern capitalism arose spontaneously is one question (Polanyi said it did not, stressing the role of nineteenth-century European and American states in establishing market systems). Whether it is a sufficient cause of fast population growth is another. "Reasonable" answers tending toward the negative suggest that arguments for the existence and convergence of Austrian entrepreneurial processes boil down to assertion. As it turns out, economists around the North Atlantic are trained to take the Austrian assertion to heart.

8. First Looks at Inflation

We will revisit queries about the durability of noncompetitive structures, for example in the theory of economic growth. But to wind up this chapter, one topic remains: the origins of trends in nominal prices, or inflation.

The initial question is which part(s) of the price system serve(s) as "nominal anchor(s)," in a recent phrase (Bruno 1993). The parentheses suggest that the answer can be either singular or plural. There are two main candidates.

First, the overall level of prices can be determined from the side of costs, along the lines of equations (2), (5), (9), (17), and so on. In this case, the nominal wage (so many dollars per hour) is the likely anchor for the system—when it moves so will all other prices, more or less in proportion. In an economy open to trade (especially in the wake of very high or hyperinflations which have destroyed local price relations), another obvious candidate is the nominal exchange rate in units of local currency to foreign.

Second, the money supply (billions of dollars) can anchor prices through a relationship known as the "equation of exchange," $MV = PX$, where M is money, P is the aggregate price index, X is real output, and V is a parameter called "velocity." It is supposed to measure how rapidly the value of output PX "turns over" with respect to the money supply M. For a broad definition of "money," Tables 1.4 and 1.5 suggest that V for the U.S. economy is around 1.5. It would have to be approximately constant for M to be able to regulate P.

These anchors are not mutually exclusive. Both could hold the price level at the same time, or prices could be breaking away from both in an inflation hurricane—an event not infrequently observed. However, one or the other of the two price-level regulators often appears to dominate, giving rise to "structuralist" and "monetarist" inflation theories respectively. This distinction has been around for a long time. As discussed in Chapter 3, Kindleberger (1985) traces it to debates among eighteenth-century Swedes.

Inflation is unavoidably dynamic, a process of trending prices which has to be understood in terms of its own history, not to mention the institutions and conventions of the economy in which the process is taking place. How well do the two theories explain inflation in such terms?

The monetarist story is deceptively simple. The first approximation is that V is constant, and the second is that it is an increasing function of the inflation rate $\hat{P}$. The rationale is that as inflation runs faster, it erodes the real value of the money stock more rapidly so that MIRA agents flee to other assets; after all, the return to holding money is $-\hat{P}$. Differentiating the equation of exchange with respect to time and rearranging shows that

$$d\hat{P}/dt = (V/v)(\hat{P} + \hat{X} - \hat{M}),\qquad(22)$$

where $v = dV/d\hat{P} > 0$ and the hats signify growth rates.

Suppose that $\hat{X}$ is determined by forces of supply (there is little room for effective demand in monetarist analysis) and that money supply growth $\hat{M}$ is also predetermined (mechanisms are discussed in Chapter 3). Then (22) is a differential equation giving the change of the inflation rate $d\hat{P}/dt$ as a function of predetermined variables and the inflation rate itself. Dynamically, (22) is unstable because a higher value of $\hat{P}$ increases $d\hat{P}/dt$, which feeds back into a further increase in $\hat{P}$. This sort of instability is characteristic of many recent macro models. The mainstream eliminates it by fiat. Asset holders are supposed to have perfect foresight (up to a random error term) about present and future inflation. They will avoid the instability by jumping to a perfect foresight or "rational expectations" inflation path along which

$$\hat{P} = \hat{M} - \hat{X}, \tag{23}$$

with $d\hat{P}/dt = 0$ and V is constant by construction.

Equation (23) is *the* monetarist theory of inflation: price increases are driven by exogenous money creation. Stop "printing money," the story goes, and inflation will disappear. Whether such a simplistic statement can even be approximately true in practice is a hotly debated question.[21] At a more theoretical level, a couple of observations are worth making.

First, like the Austrians, monetarist analysts resolve causal questions by assertion—$\hat{M}$ and $\hat{X}$ are simply postulated to be exogenous variables in (22) and (23). In reality, money may be created in response to rising prices or output may rise in response to money creation. There is no obvious way to sort out such causal links from money and price data by themselves; outside information of an institutional or historical nature has to be brought to bear.

Second, regardless of price trends, cost breakdowns as discussed earlier in this chapter continue to apply. Concretely, if $\hat{P}$ is determined by $\hat{M}$, then nominal wage inflation $\hat{w}$ must follow through the cost function. But it is easy to observe social processes independently affecting $\hat{w}$. They are ignored by monetarism. It cannot be a complete theory of inflation.

So how do we bring in price-cost relationships from the supply side? Social conflict over real values of input prices such as the nominal wage can easily combine with price-propagation mechanisms such as contract indexation to create an inflation spiral. Conflict and propagation mechanisms are the essential elements of structuralist inflation theory. But the equation of exchange $MV = PX$ is valid as an identity, and velocity is not observed to tend to infinity (even in chronically inflationary Brazil, the ratio of GDP to money supply only reached a level of around 65 in the mid-1990s). Therefore, structuralists implicitly have to assume that causality runs from right to left in the formula: money is "passive" in Olivera's (1970) phrase. Central bankers of sufficiently inflationary mentality can easily arrange for passivity to be the rule (just as their colleagues of deflationary inclination can revoke it).

Conflict can arise for many reasons. In the famous German hyperinflation of the early 1920s there was tension between workers' income claims and the low real wage implicit in an exchange rate weak enough for the economy to be able to run a trade surplus big enough to pay the World War I reparations claims imposed by the Treaty of Versailles. Latin American theory after World War II emphasized low real wages due to high food prices. Besides "price-wage," there can also be "wage-wage" competition. In *The General Theory,* Keynes stressed that different groups of workers seek to maintain their relative income positions. He was thinking of resistance to piecemeal money-wage cuts, but similar logic applies to wage inflation. Each group will seek to have its money wage rise at least as fast as all others.

Keynes's insight was picked up after World War II in the United States by institutionalist labor economists such as Dunlop (1957). American labor unions still mattered at the time, negotiating contracts that lasted for more than one year. Each year's round of wage increases served as a target for the unions bargaining the following year, as the staggered contracts added a degree of permanence to the inflation process. Without Dunlop's institutionally rich description of "wage contours" across industries and other social relationships, the staggered contract idea was picked up by John Taylor (1980) in an influential new Keynesian model of wage-wage competition as a means of propagating inflation.[22] A sketch of his analysis follows, set up in discrete time to emphasize the periodic nature of wage adjustments.

At time t, wages for half the workers are set, for periods t and $t + 1$. At time $t + 1$, wages are set for the rest of the labor force, for periods $t + 1$ and $t + 2$, and so on. With labor productivity normalized to unity and no markup, algebraic simplicity dictates that the price level should be a geometric mean of wage costs,

$$P_t = w_{t-1}^{1/2} w_t^{1/2} \tag{24}$$

where subscripts are used to denote time periods.

Velocity is also conveniently equal to one, so that in a transformation of the equation of exchange from a description of asset preferences into an effective demand curve (a sleight of hand discussed at length in subsequent chapters), output X_t is given by

$$X_t = M_t/P_t, \tag{25}$$

where M_t is the money supply at time t.

In standard Cobb-Douglas or "log-linear" form, Taylor assumes that wages at time t are determined in response to last period's observed level w_{t-1} and the level expected next period, w_{t+1}, along with positive effects of current and future demand X_t and X_{t+1},[23]

$$w_t = [w_{t-1}X_t^\gamma]^\beta[w_{t+1}X_{t+1}^\gamma]^{1-\beta}. \tag{26}$$

The parameter β indicates whether wage adjustment looks backward ($\beta = 1$ in the extreme case) or forward ($\beta \to 0$). It is argued below on institutional grounds that $\beta = 1$ is more likely, but in much discussion β is set to 1/2. The elasticity γ measures the strength of the demand boost to wage claims.

Plugging (24) and (25) into (26) and going through some algebra give the relationship

$$1 = (M_t^\beta M_{t+1}^{1-\beta})^{\phi-1} w_{t-1}^\beta w_t^{-\phi} w_{t+1}^{1-\beta}, \tag{27}$$

where $\phi = [1 + (1/2)\gamma]/[1 - (1/2)\gamma] > 1$. This formula shows how wage levels have to adjust over time to satisfy the indexing rule (26). As it turns out, the equation is satisfied by a wage adjustment of the form $w_{t+1} = w_t^\alpha$, where $\alpha > 1$ signifies wage growth over time. To solve for α, one can take logs in (27) to get

$$0 = \{\beta + (\phi - 1)[\beta \log(M_t) + (1 - \beta)\log(M_{t+1})]/\log(w_{t-1})\}$$
$$- \phi\alpha + (1 - \beta)\alpha^2.$$

Since $\phi > 1$, the solution of this quadratic equation in α that can permit stable wages (or $\alpha = 1$) takes the form

$$\alpha = \frac{\phi - [\phi^2 - 4(1 - \beta)(\beta + \mu)]^{1/2}}{2(1 - \beta)} \tag{28}$$

in which $\mu = (\phi - 1)[\beta \log(M_t) + (1 - \beta)\log(M_{t+1})/\log(w_{t-1})]$.

The $\alpha = 1$ stability condition implies that $\mu = \phi - 1$ or $[M_t^\beta M_{t-1}^{1-\beta}]^\gamma/w_{t-1} = 1$. Suppose this equality is satisfied but that M_t unexpectedly jumps upward. In (28) μ will increase, driving up α and making w_t exceed the level w_{t-1} it would have had with M_t unchanged. From (24), the price level P_t will increase by less than the money supply, and from (25) aggregate demand will rise. Output, the price level, and wages will remain above their initial levels in subsequent periods, only converging back to where they began as higher wages gradually reduce μ over time. Persistent inflationary and expansionary effects of the monetary shock are built into the dynamics by staggered contract indexation. This linkage has emerged as a repeated theme in new Keynesian analyses of inflation.

Despite sporadic attempts at forward indexation ($\beta \to 0$ in Taylor's formulation), in practice wage adjustment schemes are almost always backward-looking, because contrary to much recent economic theorizing, union leaders and business people are not blessed with perfect foresight about future price and output changes. We can illustrate how indexation interacts with social conflict in a simple model incorporating adjustment periods that can change. Shortening or increasing the time span between price and wage revisions is a policy issue that has been important in many inflationary economies over the past few decades. The basis for the discussion is a corrected version of an early model for Italy, worked out by Modigliani and Padoa-Schioppa (1978).[24]

Prices in period t are assumed to be set according to the lagged markup rule

$$P_t = h(1 + \tau)w_t b + (1 - h)P_{t-1}, \tag{29}$$

where a fraction h of current wage cost $w_t b$ is passed into prices via the markup at rate τ. The lagged price P_{t-1} feeds into the current level with a coefficient $1 - h$.

Wages are fully indexed between periods according to the formula

$$w_t = \bar{\omega}P_{t-1}, \tag{30}$$

where $\bar{\omega}$ stands for a highest instantaneous real wage that workers get. At the beginning of period t, w_t is set according to (30), and then real labor income erodes as prices rise during the period (a year, a quarter, or perhaps even less). Avoiding wage erosion is the workers' game in this model—the details come shortly.

The price inflation rate $\hat{P}_t$ coming from (29) and (30) is

$$\hat{P}_t = [(P_t - P_{t-1})/P_{t-1}] = h[(1 + \tau)\bar{\omega}b - 1] = hF, \tag{31}$$

so that inflation runs at a steady rate when F > 0, that is, when desired markup and peak real wage claims conflict. On the demand side of the economy there must be some mechanism to ration output among the conflicting groups. Forced saving would serve, as would the "inflation tax" implicit in the flight from money discussed above in connection with the equation of exchange.

Equation (31) shows that $\hat{P}_t$ will be larger, the more rapidly wage costs are marked up according to the coefficient h. For the non-Pigovian (but conventional) case in which the markup rate increases with capacity utilization, the model is illustrated in Figure 2.4. There will be inflation at any utilization level u exceeding $\bar{u}$. Moreover, one can show that $w_t/P_t =$

Figure 2.4
Conflicting claims
with price and wage
indexation.

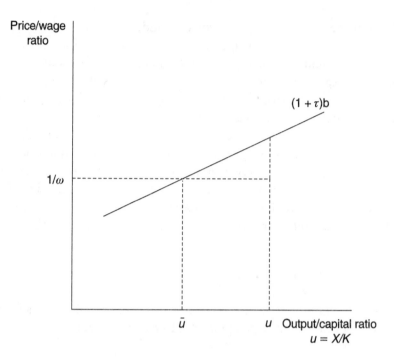

$\bar{\omega}/(1 + \hat{P}_t)$, so the real wage that workers actually get at the point of indexation is lower as inflation runs faster.

When trending prices settle in, history in Latin America and other inflationary corners of the world demonstrates that pressures to shorten indexation periods always develop. With an annual rate of up to 30 percent (say), workers may accept yearly readjustment, but if inflation is much more rapid, they are likely to press for semiannual or quarterly contracts. At 100 percent per year (just under 6 percent per month), monthly readjustments may come into play. The analytical question is: what is the impact of shortening indexation intervals on the inflation rate? Our first major conclusion is that more frequent indexation may well make inflation speed up.

Suppose that suddenly the rules are changed so that there are N indexation periods per year instead of just one (from now on we use t and $t - 1$ to stand for the end and beginning of a year respectively). A point of reference for the pricing behavior of firms is the new inflation pass-through coefficient h_N that would hold the annual inflation rate constant. With an indexation period of one year, (31) can be restated as $P_1/P_0 = hF + 1$. The analogous formula for N indexation periods per year is $P_N/P_0 = (h_N F + 1)^N$. Setting $P_N = P_1$ it is easy to solve for h_N in terms of h, that is,

$$h_N = (1/F)[(hF + 1)^\xi - 1], \tag{32}$$

Table 2.2 Responses of the inflation rate to more rapid wage indexations.

| Number of wage adjustments per year | Annual inflation rate for an initial value of h | | | |
| | $h = 0.5$ | | $h = 0.8$ | |
	h unchanged	$h \to h/N$	h unchanged	$h \to h/N$
1	0.15	0.15	0.24	0.24
2	0.32	0.155	0.54	0.254
4	0.75	0.159	1.36	0.262
12	4.35	0.162	12.21	0.269

where $\xi = 1/N$ is the length of the new period of indexation. Experimentation shows that the value of h_N from (31) is a little bit less than h/N.

If annual inflation stays constant when the pass-through coefficient shifts from h to h_N, what happens if it is set to h/N (an easier adjustment for firms) or simply doesn't move? Table 2.2 provides some illustrative answers with $F = 0.3$.

The moral of these numbers is that inflation rates can be highly unstable in an upward direction if firms do not modify their pricing behavior to conform to the new indexation rules. Even if they make the "obvious" $h \to h/N$ adjustment, inflation can inch up with indexation, and it can easily take off if h is not changed or only adjusted slightly downward,

To pursue the discussion further, we set aside markup dynamics for the moment to ask how the peak real wage $\bar{\omega}$ in (30) in fact gets set. To that end, let ω stand for the *average* real wage over the indexation period. Figure 2.5 is a diagram familiar in inflation-prone countries, showing how ω oscillates under an indexation scheme in which wages are readjusted every ξ units of time. If $\lambda = \xi/2$ and inflation is steady, then ω is given (approximately) by the formula

$$\omega = \bar{\omega}(P_{t-\lambda}/P_t) \tag{33}$$

while the annual inflation rate is

$$Z = (\bar{\omega}/\omega)^{1/\lambda} - 1. \tag{34}$$

Finally, suppressing institutional detail, historical discontinuity, and partial irreversibility in one blow, we can assume the indexation period is determined according to a simple rule of the form

$$\lambda = \lambda_0/(1 + Z). \tag{35}$$

Lying behind the real wage peak $\bar{\omega}$ is a *target* real wage ω^* that workers wish to receive. This target in fact will evolve over time in light of changing bargaining positions, the employment situation, government

Figure 2.5
Real wage fluctua-
tions under inflation.

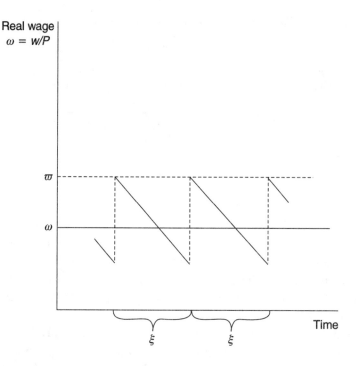

policy, and many other factors. But to illustrate what happens when ω^* is stable in the short to medium run, we can start from a nonconflict situation in which there is ongoing inflation but the wage target has in fact been attained between times $t - 2\xi$ and $t - \xi$, as illustrated in Figure 2.6.

Suppose that there is a crop failure, devaluation, or some other such shock at $t - \xi$. Inflation accelerates during the next period, and the average real wage falls below its previous (and target) level ω^*. Workers respond with increased money-wage claims, pressing for an increase in the peak from its old level $\bar{\omega}_{t-\xi}$ to a new level $\bar{\omega}_t$. Following Ros (1988), we can say that "inertial inflation" describes the situation in which they succeed. The peak wage moves upward to allow workers to recover the target in the period between t and $t + \xi$. They suffer only a one-period, transitional real income loss as inflation accelerates. There is inertia in the sense that when steady inflation returns, workers regain 100 percent indexation at their target real wage.

The problem with this scenario is that it ignores both markup dynamics and potential shortening of the indexing period coupled with incomplete adjustment of their inflation pass-through coefficient by firms. Both factors are likely to provoke a new jump in the inflation rate, with subsequent adjustment of the wage peak $\bar{\omega}$, another upward movement in the inflation rate, and so on. As stressed by Amadeo (1994) and many other authors, this situation is unstable in the sense that any adverse price development, originating for example in supply-limited "flex-price" sectors or foreign trade, can easily provoke price increases to speed up.

This general conclusion also applies to "heterodox shock" anti-inflation packages which attempt to stop the process by combining price freezes with contract de-indexation. Their goal is to eliminate the inflation spiral by freezing prices and wages and de-indexing contracts at a stroke. Unfortunately, there are likely to be unfavorable demand effects from the shock and balance-of-payments complications as well (Taylor 1994).[25] The policy conclusion is that even if inflation is inertial, it cannot be attacked solely from the side of costs. Contract de-indexation may be a necessary condition for stopping inflation, but other policies have to be applied as well. And beyond "policy" in the usual sense of the word, unless conflicting income claims are ameliorated inflation is likely to recur.

"Conflict inflation" can be said to occur when workers' aspirations in Figure 2.6 are not fulfilled. The wage peak is increased less than proportionately to the real wage loss between times $t - \xi$ and t; hence workers' real income losses persist. Suppose that they resort to pressing for a shorter indexation period along the lines of (35). One possible outcome is an indexation spiral as illustrated in Figure 2.7.

The "Wage inflation" schedule in the diagram represents (34), and the "Indexing rule" is (35); the curves can intersect twice. The lower equilibrium at point A is stable while B is unstable. At B, an inflationary shock

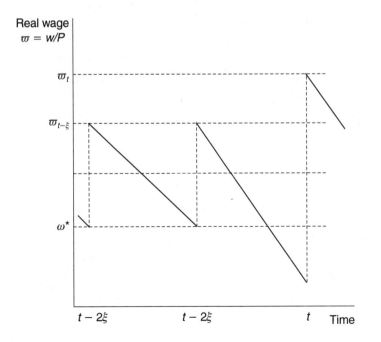

Figure 2.6
Adjustment of the peak real wage to acceleration in inflation.

Figure 2.7
Interaction between
conflict inflation and
the frequency of in-
dexation.

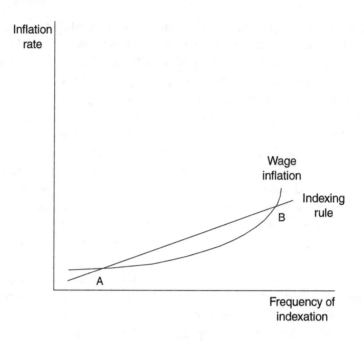

Figure 2.7
Interaction between conflict inflation and the frequency of indexation.

leads Z_t to rise, provoking a large increase in the indexation frequency *N*, another upward jump in inflation, and so on. Such a divergent process is often invoked in structuralist analyses of hyperinflations such as Germany's after World War I (Franco 1986). If, because of an upward jump in the peak wage or an increase in the overall frequency of indexation, the Wage inflation schedule lies completely above the Indexing rule, not even the unstable equilibrium at B can exist.

This interpretation of Figure 2.7 here is structuralist, but there are orthodox versions as well. The government may incur so much debt that it outstrips the market's willingness to lend in a "debt trap" (Chapter 6) or emit so much money that it overwhelms the resource-mobilizing capabilities of the inflation tax (Chapter 3). An alarmist diagram like Figure 2.7 has many incarnations; some, like hyperinflation, can even occur in practice.

CHAPTER THREE

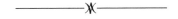

Money, Interest, and Inflation

This chapter continues our discussion of "macro" price theory. Following on from Chapter 2's sketch of the monetarist/structuralist inflation debate, it begins with a review of the different visions that economists have developed over a couple of centuries about the interactions of money, interest, and prices. The next topics are diverse theories of the interest rate: its role as a component of cost; its interpretation as a relative price between present utility and future production in Irving Fisher's "real" formulation (which influenced Keynes); and then fairly complete presentations of the Ramsey optimal saving and overlapping generations models, which are the frameworks for most current mainstream macroeconomics. The chapter continues with a formal statement of Wicksell's cumulative process inflation model based on a "natural" rate of interest. With its effective demand implications, Wicksell's model is a stepping stone to *The General Theory*. One of its major components is an "inflation tax" on money balances. We close with a quick look at some of the tax's applications, post-Wicksell.

1. Money and Credit

How does money affect macroeconomic equilibrium? This question has been hotly debated among economists and more sensible people since before 1750. It can be posed from at least three angles:

First, does money largely control, or just respond to, developments elsewhere in the economy? Is money "active" (exogenous and determined prior to other variables) or "passive" (endogenous) as in structuralist inflation theory?

Second, do changes in the money supply mostly affect the volume of activity, or the price level? What are the channels via which money has its impacts on quantities and prices?

Third, should we concentrate analysis on changes in "money" (banking system liabilities) or "credit" (banking system assets)?

Over the long sweep of economic analysis, one can find eminent partisans of all eight analytical positions implicit in this three-way classification. Table 3.1 presents an outline. We will go through the entries to sketch informally the theoretical views underlying each cell, roughly in chronological order.[1] Lessons for subsequent analysis will also be drawn.

Early participants in the matrix include two political parties—the "Hats" and the "Caps"—that appear in the active/quantities/credit and active/prices/credit slots. They flourished in a parliamentary democracy for a few decades between Divine Right despots in Sweden in the mid-eighteenth century. As their names suggest, the parties represented the big and small merchant bourgeoisie respectively. These rather obscure historical groupings are of interest because the Hats and Caps were the first proponents of distinctively "structuralist" and "monetarist" positions in macro theory (Kindleberger 1985).

The Hats were policy activists, urging credit creation to spur the Baltic trade. The Caps countered with arguments that excessive spending could lead to inflation, payments deficits, and related ills. The Hats took power after a period of slow Cap growth and (as often happens with expansionist parties) pushed too hard—they lost power in an inflation and foreign exchange crisis in 1765. Despite their respective policy failures, the intellectual points raised by the politically warring Swedes carry down through the years.

Table 3.1 Positions of different monetary analysts.

Causal status of money/credit	Main effects of money/credit			
	On prices		On quantities	
	Via money	Via credit	Via money	Via credit
Passive	Hume	Thornton Wicksell Schumpeter	Malthus Banking School	Marx Kaldor Minsky Real Business Cycle School
Active	Ricardo Currency School Mill Monetarists	"Caps"	Keynes	"Hats" Law

Both parties were fundamentally mercantilist. Had they stooped to algebra, they might have summarized their basic macro model as

$J = I + B = J$(interest rate, credit)
$S = S$(population, unemployment, real wage)
$J - S = 0$

where J stands for demand injections (investment I and the trade surplus B) and S represents saving leakages. Various policy instruments and social processes could regulate the variables in the equations, namely, Malthusian checks for population, the poorhouse for unemployment, forced saving for the real wage, and tariffs and export subsidies for trade balance.

Investment could be spurred by low interest rates ensured by usury laws or credit creation. The importance of credit was stressed by John Law, a Scotsman who sought to stimulate French growth early in the eighteenth century by setting up development banks. That his scheme led to the Mississippi Bubble—one of the earliest speculative booms—has echoes in the financial instability theories of Hyman Minsky (1975, 1986), a contemporary economist who also emphasizes that banks actively create credit which can have a strong influence on output via "Keynesian" channels. As will be seen in Chapter 8, moreover, financial innovations help make this credit expansion an endogenous variable in the overall macro system. Minskyan feedbacks between real output and expansionary finance can be so strong as to lead to macro instability. John Law's fortunes might have fared better had perfect foresight enabled him to grasp what his distant analytical descendent Minsky had to say.

Caps, Hats, and Law all argued as if money and credit could be controlled by the relevant authorities. Part of the intellectual reaction against mercantilism took the form of making money (or "specie") as well as the trade surplus endogenous in the short run. David Hume (1969), a world-class philosopher turning into a best-selling historian circa 1750, is usually credited with this advance in economic analysis. Its implications will figure in Chapter 10 on open economy macro.

Hume's location in the passive/prices/money slot follows from a model that might be written as

$D = D(M/P)$
$X = X$(employment)
$MV = PX$
$\dot{M} = X - D(X/V) = B(P^*/P)$

As in John Taylor's inflation model discussed in the last chapter, aggregate demand D depends on the real money stock M/P while (assuming full employment) output X is predetermined. The expansion in the money supply $\dot{M}$ ($= dM/dt$) is given by specie inflow resulting from the trade surplus $B = X - D$—in this sense money is passive or endogenous. Because money drives the price level P via the equation of exchange, money expansion $\dot{M}$ is an inverse function of P and thereby of M itself. The last expression for $\dot{M}$ normalizes this response around a "world" price P^*. The stable dynamics here contrasts sharply with the unstable monetarist inflation process discussed toward the end of both Chapter 2 and this chapter. Open-economy monetarism is a beast rather different from its closed-economy cousin.

The behavioral story is simple, and well known. A big money stock means that there is a high domestic price level and excess demand. The trade surplus becomes negative when D is high, forcing specie to flow out of the country and prices to fall. Aggregate demand ceases to draw in imports, and "our" exports sell better—the trade deficit declines toward equilibrium. Policymakers' attempts to stimulate output by monetary expansion (say, by raising the banking system's money/specie multiplier) will backfire in this model; their attempt will just drive up prices and worsen the trade deficit. Although they reasoned on different grounds and far less cogently, the Caps would have approved of this conclusion. The same is true of contemporary exponents of policy ineffectiveness discussed in several subsequent chapters.

The next major players in Table 3.1 are Malthus and Ricardo, who stand opposed in the northeast and southwest corners. We have already seen that the former argued along proto-Keynesian lines that food prices should be kept high by import restrictions, so that landlords (notoriously low savers) would spend on luxuries to support industrial demand. A precursor of the structuralist Banking School, Malthus thought that the money supply and/or velocity adjusted endogenously to meet demand, or the "needs of trade."

Ricardo, a superb monetary theorist, differed from Malthus in accepting supply-side determination of output, the nineteenth-century version of Say's Law. He naturally followed the monetarist trail, most notably in 1810 when he attacked "excessive" British note issue to finance the war against Napoleon. His evidence included a premium on gold in terms of notes within Britain, and a fall of the exchange value of sterling in Hamburg and Amsterdam. His logic was based on the quantity theory and purchasing power parity—standard components of all subsequent open-economy monetarist models.

Ricardo's main policy recommendation was a Friedmanite rule called the "currency principle," recommending that the outstanding money stock should be strictly tied to gold reserves. Money should not be created for frivolous pursuits such as combating tyranny, and its supply should only be allowed to fluctuate in response to movements of gold. In effect, Ricardo sought to steer monetary policy along the trail blazed by Hume.

The Currency School, which took the monetarist side in British financial debates well into the nineteenth century, was founded on Ricardo's principle. Its great victory was Peel's Charter Act of 1844 for the Bank of England, which put a limit on the issue of notes against securities. Above the limit, notes had to be backed by gold. This triumph of principle over practice was short-lived, since there was a run against English banks in 1847. The Bank of England acted (correctly) as what the many-sided Walter Bagehot ([1873] 1962)—the defining editor of the *Economist* magazine—in the 1870s christened a "lender of last resort." It pumped resources into commercial banks in danger of collapse. To this end, the Charter Act had to be suspended. As will be seen in Chapters 9 and 10, in its essentials this financial instability scenario remains unchanged today.

As the Currency School flourished, John Stuart Mill was putting together his own economic synthesis. Although he had some sympathy for the Banking School (see below), Mill is placed in the active/prices/money slot because he codified the doctrine of "loanable funds" which underlies much subsequent mainstream thought as discussed later in this chapter. Following Henry Thornton, a contemporary of Ricardo, Mill thought the interest rate would adjust to erase any difference between aggregate saving and investment, thereby clearing the market for loanable funds. As already observed in Chapter 2, this theory undergirds Say's Law by bringing in changes in the interest rate to ensure full employment investment-savings balance.

Loanable funds is a nonmonetary theory of the rate of interest, of the sort later criticized by Keynes (see Chapter 4). It incorporates Patinkin's (1966) "dichotomy" in that money can affect only the price (and presumably the wage) level, without any influence on the volume of production. This is the ultimate monetarist position, with echoes in both Irving Fisher's suggestion that monetary policy should be actively deployed to control prices and Milton Friedman's argument against active policy (because its effects on output only are visible with "long and variable lags" while money rules the price level best in the long run).

The final entries in the broadly monetarist left columns of Table 3.1 are Thornton, Knut Wicksell, and Schumpeter (with respect to the short-run macro adjustment scenario in his *Theory of Economic Develop-*

ment, at least) in the passive/prices/credit niche. Schumpeter's vision transcends mere monetary analysis; for purposes of later discussion, it makes sense to present an outline here.

Schumpeter took over much of Marx's emphasis on the importance of technical change in generating supply and combined it with a provocative analysis of how the economy responds to such innovation in forging his own defense of capitalism—he called his teacher Böhm-Bawerk (to be discussed presently) a "bourgeois Marx" but could have applied the label equally to himself. His theories are also very Keynesian (or Wicksellian) in building the growth process around the supply of credit and making macro adjustments to changes in investment demand.

The starting point is rather like the mainstream's Walrasian models of steady growth, which Schumpeter calls "circular flow." An economy in circular flow may be expanding, but it is not "developing" in his terminology. Development occurs only when an entrepreneur makes an innovation—a new technique, product, or way of organizing things—and shifts production coefficients or the rules of the game. He gains a monopoly profit until other people catch on and imitate, and the economy moves to a new configuration of circular flow.

The invention or insight underlying the innovation need not be the entrepreneur's—Schumpeter's "new man" simply seizes it, puts it in action, makes his money, and (more likely than not) passes into the aristocracy as he retires. Ultimately, his innovation and fortune will be supplanted by others in the process of "creative destruction" that makes capitalist economies progress.

The key analytical question about this process refers to both the financial and the real sides of the economy—how does the entrepreneur obtain resources to innovate? An endogenous money supply and redistribution of real income flows are required to support his efforts.

To get his project going, the entrepreneur must invest—an extra demand imposed upon an economy already using its resources fully in circular flow. To finance investment, he obtains loans from the banks; new credit and thereby money are created in the process. The bank loans are used to purchase goods in momentarily fixed supply. Their prices are driven up, so that real incomes of other economic actors decline. The most common examples are workers receiving temporarily fixed nominal wages or the cash flows of noninnovating firms. There is forced saving along the lines discussed in Chapter 2 as workers' lower real incomes force them to consume less; groups which receive windfall income gains are implicitly assumed to have higher saving propensities so that overall aggregate demand declines. Meanwhile, routine investment projects may be cut back.

The transition between states of circular flow is demand driven from

the investment side (though, of course, the innovation may involve production of new goods or increases in productivity) and short-run macro
adjustment takes place through income redistribution via forced saving
with an endogenously varying money supply. The Walrasian "marginal
this equals marginal that" resource allocation rules that reign in circular
flow are necessarily ruptured by the price changes underlying redistribution (a point that Kaldor (1956) later emphasized in his discussion of distribution). In a longer run, there can be a cyclical depression due to
"autodeflation" as bank loans are repaid; workers can regain real income via falling costs. In later versions of the model, Schumpeter emphasized that bankruptcy of outdated firms can also release resources for in-
novators, but the essentials are the same.

A very similar macro adjustment story appears in Wicksell (1935), although much of his analysis was anticipated by Thornton almost one
hundred years before. We have already noted that the Keynes of the
Treatise on Money (1930) was a stalwart post-Wicksellian along with
Schumpeter. Only his revised views in *The General Theory* (1936) place
him in the active/quantities/money cell.

Wicksell extended loanable funds theory by proposing that inflation is
a "cumulative process" based on the discrepancy between new credit demanded by investors and new deposit supply from desired saving (corresponding to a zero rate of inflation) at a rate of interest fixed by the
banks. Anticipating the formal model of section 8, it is worthwhile now
to talk through the cumulative process, by way of introduction.

Suppose that the banks set the interest rate too low. Then an excess
of new credits over new deposits leads to money creation; via the equation of exchange at presumed full employment, the consequence is rising prices. Inflation is the outcome of endogenous monetary emission,
driven by credit creation.

The key analytical question is how saving and investment are brought
together to secure macroeconomic equilibrium ex post. Forced saving
can provide part of the adjustment, if wages are incompletely indexed to
price increases. The rest comes from the "inflation tax," a dynamic version of the well-known "real balance effect," which states that people increase their saving to restore the real value of their money stock M/P
which is squeezed when P rises. To keep to essentials, let output X and
(temporarily) velocity V be constant in the equation of exchange $MV = PX$. The inflation tax interpretation rests on the equations

$$\dot{M}/PX = \dot{P}(M/P)/PX = \hat{P}/V,$$

which follow from the growth rate version of the equation of exchange,
$\hat{M} = \hat{P}$. After the first equality, $\dot{P}(M/P)$ is the instantaneous loss in real

balances from price increases $\dot{P}$, which wealth-holders are supposed to make good by extra saving so that the "tax" effectively cuts aggregate demand. The expression after the second equality shows that the tax base erodes if V rises when inflation speeds up (the monetarists' favorite stylized fact).

Wicksell thought that after a time, bankers would raise the interest rate to its "natural" level to bring the cumulative inflation to a halt, but for present purposes this ending is not essential to his story. The key point is that through both the inflation tax and forced saving, a rising price level liquidates ex ante excess aggregate demand. This model is the clearest monetarist alternative to the structuralist inflation theories already discussed.

Returning attention to Table 3.1, the next point of interest is the passive/quantities/money Banking School, the main rival of the Currency School in last century's British debate. The group is famous (or notorious, depending on one's perspective) for espousing the doctrine of "real bills." In the early nineteenth century, the banking system devoted most of its efforts to accepting (at a discount) paper issued by merchants in pursuit of trade. The Banking School's doctrine stated that the banks should discount all solid, nonspeculative commercial paper, that is, true or real debts. How in practice a banker should identify paper tied firmly to the needs of trade was not spelled out; indeed Adam Smith (an early proponent of the doctrine) advised that banks should concentrate on real trade to avoid ratifying currency speculation.

Extreme members of the Banking School finessed Smithian fears with a "law of reflux" through which excessive lending would drive up activity and/or prices and lead the private sector to pay off loans and buy gold: there would be an automatic contraction of the money supply in response to too aggressive attempts to expand it. Hume's policy irrelevance reappears in structuralist guise, albeit without his specie flow considerations.

Real bills ideas have downside implications as well. If credit needs are not satisfied by banks, then new, nonbank financial instruments are likely to be invented to meet the needs of trade (Minsky puts a lot of emphasis on this sort of financial innovation). Such a Coase (1960)-style outcome sometimes happens, sometimes not, but it is implicit in Banking School views. Among structuralists, reflux notions show up in the 1959 report on the British monetary system by the Radcliffe Committee and in Kaldor (1982). The latter is worth quoting: "If . . . more money comes into existence than the public, at the given or expected level of incomes or expenditures, wishes to hold, the excess will be automatically extinguished—either through debt repayment or its conversion into interest-bearing assets." One notes a certain affinity in structuralist positions across 150 years.

The final entries in the matrix are the Real Business Cycle School and Marx, perhaps demonstrating that economic perceptions can unite strange political bedfellows. The former group is a recent offshoot of new classical economics, at the mainstream's Walrasian verge extreme as discussed in Chapter 6. Its members argue that business cycles in advanced economies are due to strong substitution responses (labor versus leisure choices, and so on) to supply-side shocks to the macro system. They deem money unimportant and subject to "reverse causality." They are joined by Kaldor and the post-Keynesians Davidson and Weintraub (1973) in their view that typical Central Bank responsiveness to trade plus the presence of inside money render monetary aggregates endogenous: their leads and lags with output depend on institutions and contingencies beyond the analytical reach of Granger-Sims causality tests and similar econometric probes.

Marx, as always, is more complex. The existence of money was central to his view of capitalism, incarnated in the famous $M - C - M'$ sequence, in which exploitation arises as money M is thrown into circulation of commodities C (incorporating labor power and the means of production), which yields a money return M': surplus value is $M' - M$. Access to M gives capitalists a leg up in the economy, making their extraction of surplus possible. At a more applied level of abstraction, Marx roughly adhered to Banking School ideas, at times arguing that velocity varies to satisfy the equation of exchange. This view is consistent with the endogeneity of inside money, for example, financial obligations created and destroyed by transactions among firms. Building on the reproduction schemes in Volume II of *Capital*, Foley (1986) extended this approach to set up real/financial "circuit of capital" models in which endogenous fluctuations can occur.

2. Diverse Interest Theories

If we turn to the interest rate per se, an initial observation is that it very well may be a price, but the price of what? The answer has changed over time. Classical economists through Marx largely treated interest as a category within the general flow of surplus (along the lines of Chapter 2, the portion of the gross value of production not devoted to purchases of labor services or intermediate inputs). Interest payments were just another transaction among capitalists. There are vestiges of this perspective in growth models such as the famous one by Pasinetti (1962). He postulates two classes of income recipients—rentiers and workers. The latter receive a share of total profits (perhaps proportional to the profit rate), which authors following Laing (1969) call "interest." To a certain extent, this line of thought is pursued in later chapters with models in which different economic classes hold diverse portfolios of financial assets with differential rates of return.

The interest rate could also be the price of holding nonfinancial assets such as the vehicles lined up neatly in a car dealer's lot. Business people think so, and in the following section we trace through the implications of treating interest payments as a component of cost.[2] Most economists, however, prefer to think of interest as a payment for deferred gratification and/or the possibility of making higher profits in years to come. This interpretation of the interest rate as a relative price mediating transactions between the present and future is built into "real" theories such as those constructed early in the past century by Irving Fisher and Frank Ramsey, among many others.

As already noted, Fisher influenced Keynes, while Ramsey's optimal saving model (along with its "overlapping generations" analog) dominates contemporary mainstream thought. Applied in practice, real theories tend to treat the interest rate as the variable which adjusts to clear the market for loanable funds, as in the teachings of J. S. Mill. Loanable funds interest rate models contrast with the "liquidity preference" theory developed by the Keynes of *The General Theory* (to be reviewed in the following chapter). Keynes's "monetary" analysis dominated the mainstream for a few decades. But it has been eclipsed by the real and loanable funds models presently in vogue.

3. Interest Rate Cost-Push

Regardless of how the interest rate is determined, a model developed by Anyadike-Danes, Coutts, and Godley (1988) provides a framework for treating it as a cost that enterprises have to pay to hold inventories—a useful point with which to begin our discussion. To see the details, we can write out a modified version of the cost and sales decompositions appearing in column (1) and row (A) of Table 1.2's SAM:[3]

$$wbX + \pi PX + iL = P(C + I + G) + P\dot{Z} + \dot{P}Z. \tag{1}$$

The notation is familiar, except that Z stands for the stock of inventories held by firms and the value of investment PI does not include changes in inventories, which are represented by the term $P\dot{Z}$. The profit share π should be figured net of interest payments and i is a nominal or money rate of interest as determined in the market.

There are two nonstandard features in the income-expenditure statement (1). First, the interest bill on a volume of loans L at rate i that enterprises pay is treated as a component of cost and not as a transfer. Second, the capital gain (or loss) $\dot{P}Z$ on inventories appears on the right-hand side. The rationale is that stocks turn over "within" the accounting period, so that firms have to adjust outlays to compensate for price changes.

Suppose that firms take loans to finance inventory: $L = PZ$. Let X stand for output, as usual: $X = C + I + G + \dot{Z}$. Finally, assume that inventory is held in proportion to output: $Z = \xi X$ (Tables 1.4 and 1.6 suggest that the ratio of the stock of inventories to GDP is about 0.15). Plugging these hypotheses into (1) and simplifying gives the pricing rule

$$P = \frac{wb}{1 - \pi - (i - \hat{P})\xi}. \tag{2}$$

In words, the price level is formed as a markup on wage cost, with the markup rate increasing as a function of the profit share π *and* the real interest cost $(i - \hat{P})\xi$ of financing inventory. The partial derivative of P with respect to $i - \hat{P}$ is equal to $P\xi/\psi$, where ψ is the labor share. With P normalized to one initially, the implication is that an increase in the interest rate of 1 percent might raise the price level by, say, $[0.15/0.75]\% = 0.2\%$—a nontrivial impact.

The notion that the price level (and, by extension, the inflation rate) depends positively on the interest rate has a checkered history. It flies in the face of conventional wisdom. Suppose that a NAIRU exists, and that as the activity level strays above it inflation speeds up. A central bank intervention to raise the interest rate and cut aggregate demand is always proposed as the remedy of choice. The higher cost of borrowing is supposed to brake rising prices. But the remedy can fail when an equation like (2) applies, especially with a high value of ξ and a low wage share (more characteristic of developing than industrialized economies).

An early opponent of tight money was Thomas Tooke, a founding member of the Banking School who wrote an influential *History of Prices*. A century later in his *Treatise*, Keynes (1930) labeled the positive interest rate/price level correlation that Tooke emphasized (and which many others have observed) the "Gibson paradox." He and Wicksell explained it away on the grounds that the money rate of interest lags the business cycle.

Despite this impressive weight of authority against it, interest rate cost-push continues to appeal to both business people and expansionist economists. In the United States it is sometimes called the "Wright

Patman effect" in honor of an easy-money Texas congressman who jousted with the Federal Reserve in the 1950s. The current Latin American label is the "Cavallo effect" (1977) after the Argentine minister of economy of the 1990s who found empirical support for the phenomenon in his Harvard Ph.D. thesis. He later found it politic to repudiate the doctrine. Perhaps surprisingly, at about the same time the arch–new classical economists Sargent and Wallace (1981) came up with another argument tying tighter money (though not higher interest rates) to faster inflation. Details in section 9 below.

4. Real Interest Rate Theory

The role of the real interest rate as a relative price between present and future economic choices was stressed by many of the founders of neoclassical economics, especially the Austrian School; members of the school placed great weight on the roundabout nature of production. Their definitive statement came in the late 1800s from Eugen von Böhm-Bawerk, who also made a name for himself as finance minister, for criticizing Marx, and for being Schumpeter's thesis advisor. He proposed three reasons for the existence of a nonzero real rate of interest.

The first was "different circumstances of want and provision" in present and future, with one example being different income levels that affect the marginal utility of consumption (in more modern jargon). Second came "underestimation of the future," or pure time preference. Finally, we get technical differences between the present and future, for example, more or less roundaboutness. These three reasons all fit into contemporary optimal savings models, as discussed in the following section.

Before getting into that, however, it makes sense to sketch the fullest elaboration of Böhm-Bawerk's own ideas, in models presented in final form by the Yale economist Irving Fisher (1930) after a maturation period of several decades. One took the form of a familiar diagram presented in Figure 3.1. Another was his well-known "arbitrage" relationship between a "real" asset return (an interest rate j or a profit rate r) and a nominal return i as mediated by the inflation rate $\hat{P}$,

$$j = i - \hat{P}.$$

Ex ante, $\hat{P}$ has to be interpreted as an expected inflation; ex post, the observed rate is often plugged into the equation.

Fisher's argument in support of this proposition does indeed rest on arbitrage, in a form that will become familiar in later chapters. In discrete time, assume that the price of some asset with a real return j is expected to increase at the rate $\hat{P} = (P_{t+1} - P_t)/P_t$. If (short-term) bonds are to be held as an alternative to the asset in question, their nominal return i has to satisfy the condition

$$1 + i = (1 + j)(1 + \hat{P}).$$

Expanding the right-hand side gives the Fisher relationship when the product $j\hat{P}$ is "small."

Fisher arbitrage is not supported by the data (Summers 1983; Henwood 1998). As argued in Chapter 4, it is dynamically inconsistent with Keynesian liquidity preference theories of the rate of interest. Nonetheless, the real rate/nominal rate distinction is central to much economic discourse. Good analytical (as opposed to weak empirical) support is why it holds its own as an intellectual center of gravity.

Turning to Fisher's real interest rate theory (a theory of j), Figure 3.1 is the basic diagram for an isolated individual ("Robinson Crusoe," in the economists' drastic misreading of that personage's vivid social interactions with his capitalist cronies, enemies, and slaves). It illustrates the trade-offs between income flows "today" and "tomorrow."

The "Opportunity" curve concave to the origin is a production-possibility relationship, showing how much of today's income has to be sacrificed to generate more tomorrow. Convex to the origin is a "Willingness" curve. Its absolute slope is assumed be less than -1 when it crosses

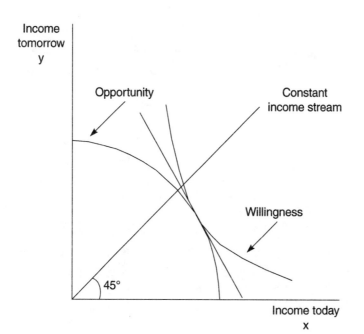

Figure 3.1
The Fisher diagram.

the "constant income stream" line with a slope of 45 degrees (or +1). This condition ensures "positive time preference" from Böhm-Bawerk's first two reasons. The implication is that the point of tangency between the willingness and opportunity lines lies below the 45-degree line. The (absolute) slope of the line through the tangency is $1 + j$, where $j > 0$ is the equilibrium real interest rate.[4]

The next step is to allow market transactions. The key observation is that an economic actor will take advantages of opportunities with returns exceeding the current interest rate j. In Figure 3.2, for example, someone beginning at point A can "invest" α with a "return" β to get to point B. She or he can then borrow the sum $\alpha + \gamma$ to arrive at an equilibrium C (with the slope of the "interest rate" schedule determining the relative positions of B and C).

An analogous picture can be drawn for someone who lends. Presumably, there are people elsewhere in the system who are in fact willing to lend to offset our individual's net borrowing γ—there is a market for loanable funds. Also, it is usually inadmissible to borrow more than one saves indefinitely. As will be seen, this "no Ponzi game" condition comes into its own in models in which time lasts longer than just tomorrow.[5]

To summarize, the real interest rate in Fisher's world equilibrates the market for loanable funds. The nominal rate adjusts to the real rate when there is inflation. As Keynes later emphasized, how markets for *stocks* of financial assets are to be cleared is left unexplained; this weak-

Figure 3.2
Transactions in the
Fisher diagram.

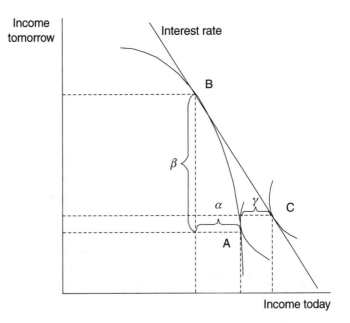

ness led him to develop his own monetary theory of the rate of interest. Like Keynes's approach, a strength of Fisher's model is that it can handle financial transactions among a multiplicity of agents—as discussed in Chapter 6, it underlies the Modigliani-Miller theorem in a world populated by well-informed, optimizing financial actors. Such diversity is lacking in other contemporary formulations based on "representative" firms and households. Frank Ramsey's (1928) optimal saving model is the prototypical example.[6] The standard update of Ramsey, usually attributed to Cass (1965) and Koopmans (1965), is the topic of the following two sections.

5. The Ramsey Model

Following Abel and Blanchard (1983), we can start by working separately with resource allocation decisions over time by firms and households, although the institutional distinction between these two sorts of "agents" will prove to be slight. Subsequently, their optimal time paths will be combined to solve the "social" dynamic allocation problem. We measure all variables relative to the supply of labor L, which for the moment is assumed not to grow (that steady-state growth is a minor extension of the stationary state is illustrated in the following section). The capital/labor ratio is $k = K/L$, consumption per household is $c = C/L$, ω is the real wage, and $g = I/K$ is the growth rate of capital (ignoring depreciation as usual). To finance investment, firms issue bonds Z with a short-term real interest rate j, and $z = Z/K$.

Both firms and households are assumed to share perfect foresight about an infinite future—the incredibility of this hypothesis will be lamented from time to time. If they can foretell all that lies ahead, firms might plausibly be supposed to maximize the present discounted value V of their real cash flow (output less investment and wages) per capita,

$$V = \int_0^\infty \rho[f(k) - gk - \omega]dt = \int_0^\infty \rho J dt, \tag{3}$$

subject to the restriction

$$\dot{k} = gk. \tag{4}$$

In (3), $f(k)$ is a neoclassical production function in which output per capita is determined by the capital stock per capita, presupposing Say's modern law. The "extensive" form of the production function, $X = F(K, L)$, is assumed to have constant returns to scale so that $X/L = F(K/L, 1) = f(k)$. The discount factor ρ is based on the changing bond interest rate over future time, $\rho(t) = \exp[-_0\int^t j(t)dt]$, where exp(..) is the exponential function. Since firms issue bonds to pay for investment, we have $\dot{Z}/L = gk$. Bond purchases and interest payments show up below in the household budget constraint (11).

The contemporary standard version of the calculus of variations techniques that Ramsey imported into economics from mathematical physics is known as optimal control theory. The solution procedure starts out by introducing a "costate variable" or undetermined function of time μ to adjoin the differential equation constraint (4) to the performance function being integrated in (3) to get a "Hamiltonian" expression $H = \rho J + \mu \dot{k}$. When there is a discount factor like ρ in the maximand, it is convenient to work with a costate written as $\mu = \rho q$ to generate a "present-value" Hamiltonian of the form

$$H = \rho(J + q\dot{k}) = \rho[f(k) + (q - 1)gk - \omega].$$

The Hamiltonian is a function of time, in the present problem running from $t = 0$ to $t = \infty$. In line with the discussion in Chapter 1, $q(t)$ as it emerges from H will turn out to be the asset price of capital at time t.

The partial derivatives of H with respect to the "state" (or stock) variable k and "control" (or flow) variable g can be used to set up "Euler equations" defining the firm's optimal investment path. Dynamics of the costate variable follow from the partial of H with respect to k:

$$d(\rho q)/dt = -\partial H/\partial k = -\rho[f'(k) + (q - 1)g], \tag{5}$$

where $f'(k)$ is the marginal product of capital, df/dk. If this equation is interpreted as running forward in time (perhaps not the most sensible procedure, as discussed later), then the discounted capital asset price ρq declines more rapidly as the marginal product is higher.

The accumulation equation "dual" to (5) is just (4) once again:

$$dk/dt = \partial H/\partial(\rho q) = gk.$$

In principle, (4) and (5) solve the firm's dynamic planning problem. Both formulas depend on the capital stock growth rate g, which according to the optimal control recipe *should* be determined by one last Euler condition: $\partial H/\partial g = 0$. But here a small mathematical spanner falls into the works: the Hamiltonian H is *linear* in g. There is no simple way to solve this marginal condition.

More sophisticated evasions exist, but mainstream aggregate growth theory gets around this difficulty in straightforward fashion. It introduces "installation" or "shut-down" costs $\dot{k}h(g) = gkh(g)$ associated with capital formation or decumulation. So long as $h(g)$ is conveniently nonlinear,[7] its presence in the Hamiltonian permits an interior solution for g. This revision of Ramsey's original model, first popularized by Eisner and Strotz (1963), may make empirical sense, but it should be recognized for what it is: a mathematical trick designed to ensure smooth accumulation dynamics over time.

Cash flow including investment costs is $J = f(k) - gk(1 + hg) - \omega$. From an appropriately modified Hamiltonian, the condition $\partial H/\partial g = 0$ becomes

$$q = 1 + h(g) + gh'(g). \tag{6}$$

With the properties of the function $h(g)$ listed in note 7, (6) makes $q = 1$ when $g = 0$. By an arbitrary choice of functional form, the capital asset price is set to its benchmark value of unity when the economy is in a steady state with $\dot{k} = 0$.

The evolution of q itself is determined by plugging (6) into (5) as rewritten to take into account the presence of $h(g)$. Making use of the fact that $\hat{p} = -j$, the differential equation for q becomes

$$\dot{q} = jq - [f'(k) + g^2h'(g)]. \tag{7}$$

Equations (4), (6), and (7) describe the behavior of the optimizing firm, based on joint determination of k and q over time.

Postponing consideration of the dynamics of this system until Chapter 4, assume for the moment that the economy always has been and ever will be at a stationary state with $\dot{k} = \dot{q} = 0$. Combining (6) and (7) then gives

$$q = f'(k)/j = 1. \tag{8}$$

The capital asset price is the marginal product of capital $f'(k)$ capitalized over an infinite horizon at the (constant) market interest rate j. In long-run equilibrium the marginal product equals the interest rate, $f'(k) = j$, so that $q = 1$.

This condition is an application of the q-theory of investment demand proposed by Tobin (1969). To explore the causal structure of the Ramsey model, it is helpful to consider a linearized version of (8), setting $r = f'$ so that the profit rate is equal to the marginal product of capital. Noting that (6) makes g an increasing function of q, we get an investment demand function of the form

$$g^j = g_0 + \alpha r - \theta j, \tag{9}$$

where perturbation terms from linearization of $q = r/j$ fit into g_0.

Investment rises with the profit rate and falls with the bond interest rate. Keynes would not be greatly surprised. Where he and Minsky would differ from the modern interpretations of Ramsey (as discussed in Chapters 4 and 8) is with regard to the simple-mindedness of believing that firms can even pretend to solve an infinite horizon optimizing problem of the sort we are discussing here.

Next we turn to the immortal, identical households making up the citizenry. They choose consumption paths by maximizing lifetime utility,

$$U = \int_0^\infty \exp(-\epsilon t)u(c)dt, \tag{10}$$

subject to the intertemporal budget relationship

$$\dot{z} = (\omega - c)/k + z(j - g), \tag{11}$$

where $u(c)$ is a "felicity" (or instantaneous utility) function, ϵ is a subjective discount factor, and the term $z(j - g)$ takes into account interest payments to households from firms on their outstanding debt and the "scaling" effect of capital stock growth g on the ratio variable $z = Z/K$.

Details about the Hamiltonian dynamics of a problem similar to (10) and (11) are presented in the following section, as well as in Abel and Blanchard (1983), Blanchard and Fischer (1989), Romer (2001), and many other sources. If the household felicity takes the frequently postulated form $u(c) = c^{1-\eta}/(1 - \eta)$ (discussed in more detail below) then integration over time of a household behavioral equation of the form (19) or (20) derived below followed by substitution of the integral of the household income-expenditure balance gives a per capita consumption function

$$c = C/L = \beta(j)[qk + (\omega/j)] = [\beta(j)/j](X/L) \tag{12}$$

with C as total consumption. After the second equals sign, c is proportional to total wealth comprising the value of capital per head qk and capitalized wage income ω/j. The proportionality factor $\beta/(j)$ depends on the interest rate. The last expression follows when one notes that $q = r/j$ at the steady state. For (12) to make sense economically, the condition $\beta(j)/j < 1$ is required. From equation (8) for q, c will depend positively on the marginal product of capital or profit rate. Depending on the balance of income, substitution, and wealth effects, dc/dj can take either sign but it is conventionally assumed to be negative.

Dividing k through (12) gives expressions for the capital stock growth rate permitted by available saving,

$$g^s = u - (C/K) = \{1 - [\beta(j)/j]\}u = s(j)u \tag{13}$$

with $s(j) < 1$ and $\partial s/\partial j > 0$.

The full employment assumption that we have been making all along sets $u = \bar{u}$, where $\bar{u}$ is constant. Marginal productivity conditions fix the profit rate r and profit share $\pi = r/u$. From (9) and (13) the standard macroeconomic balance condition $g^i - g^s = 0$ for the Ramsey model linearized around its stationary state comes out as

$$g_0 + \alpha\pi\bar{u} - \theta j - s(j)\bar{u} = 0, \tag{14}$$

with the real interest rate j as the implicit adjusting variable.

As will be seen in the following section, the full solution to the Ramsey model is dynamically unstable, because its asset price equations (7) or (18) below incorporate positive feedback. If we ignore this aspect for the moment, then (14) boils down to a relationship in which the real interest rate could vary to bring saving and investment into equality with full employment. The market involved is the one for bonds issued by firms, or loanable funds. A few pages of clunky mathematics and we are steering right back toward John Stuart Mill.

6. Dynamics on a Flying Trapeze

Now we take up the unstable dynamics, which call for a few special assumptions to make the loanable funds story go through. Along with many other authors, Abel and Blanchard (1983) show that the separate optimizations of firms and households are equivalent to a single planner's problem of maximizing household utility

$$U = \int_0^\infty \exp(-\epsilon t)u(c)dt$$

subject to two restrictions,

$$c + gk[1 + h(g)] - f(k) = 0$$

and

$$\dot{k} = gk.$$

As usual in neoclassical CRS models, this "command economy" optimizing problem can be implemented by decentralized "agents," provided that they keep their accounting straight and faithfully carry out their assigned maximization tasks. This equivalence between planning and the market is often credited to the cleverness of the invisible hand in guiding optimal growth. In the present context, competitive forces are supposed to lead the interest rate (or the structure of present and future short-term rates, if the economy is out of the stationary state) to adjust in the market for loanable funds to ensure that saving is equal to investment at full employment. Investing firms are differentiated from saving households only by capital stock installation or shut-down costs, a pale reflection of the institutional structure of capitalism that Keynes and Kalecki emphasized.

For looking at dynamics, an immediate simplification is to suppress the minor distinction between households and enterprises altogether (also getting rid of capital stock installation and shut-down costs), so that household saving is directly channeled into capital formation without intermediation through enterprises obtaining loanable funds. On the other hand, to explicate technical debates in the mainstream it is convenient to introduce labor force growth at a constant rate n: $L(t) = \exp(nt)$ with $L(0)$ normalized to one. It is also customary to weight felicity in the utility integral by the population in existence at any point in time, that is, the payoff function takes the "Benthamite" form $\exp(-\epsilon t)L(t)u[c(t)]$. After substitution for $L(t)$, "society's" planning problem boils down to

$$\max U = \int_0^\infty \exp[-(\epsilon - n)t]u(c)dt \tag{15}$$

subject to

$$\dot{k} = f(k) - c - nk, \tag{16}$$

where the final term in (16) reflects the fact that ongoing population growth cuts into the existing level of capital per head. As before, it is convenient to assume that felicity $u(c)$ takes the constant elasticity form, $c^{1-\eta}/(1 - \eta)$, with $u(c) = \log c$ for $\eta = 1$.[8] The elasticity of substitution between values of c at two points in time can be shown to be $1/\eta$. The lower the value of η, the more slowly marginal utility falls as consumption rises. That is, a household with a low η is willing to let its consumption levels swing substantially over time.

The maximand in (15) now incorporates a constant (net) discount rate $\lambda = \epsilon - n$, which will have to be positive for a solution to (15) and (16) to exist (without the condition $\lambda > 0$, the utility integral (15) will be unbounded). An equivalent statement based on results to be developed immediately below is that a long-run real interest rate ϵ smaller than the steady-state output growth rate n is not consistent with a dynamic equilibrium. As discussed in Chapter 6, the $\epsilon > n$ condition doesn't make a lot of sense outside a dynamic optimization framework, because it is hard for a borrower to make ends meet in the long run when the ruling interest rate exceeds the growth rate of real income. But for now we leave that complication aside.

Proceeding as with the firm's investment problem discussed above, we can work with a costate variable written as $\exp(-\lambda t)\xi$, with ξ as society's capital asset price analogous to the firm's q. The present value Hamiltonian becomes

$$H = \exp(-\lambda t)\{u(c) + \xi[f(k) - c - nk]\}.$$

The Euler conditions for a locally optimal growth path are

$$u' = du/dc = \xi, \tag{17}$$

and

$$-\hat{\xi} = f' - \epsilon. \tag{18}$$

Hat calculus shows that the growth rate of u' is $\hat{u}' = -\eta\hat{c}$, in turn equal to ξ from (17). Substituting into (18) gives a condition known as the "Ramsey-Keynes rule,"[9]

$$\eta\hat{c} + \epsilon = f'. \tag{19}$$

This equation could just as well be called the Böhm-Bawerk rule, because it combines his three reasons for a positive interest rate. The $\eta\hat{c}$ term reflects how changing "circumstances of want and provision" as captured by $\hat{c}$ affect saving choices, while ϵ captures "underestimation of the future." The profit rate f' summarizes investment possibilities, for the third reason. The rule basically says that an interest rate (or "social rate of discount") on the left of the equals sign has to be set equal to a profit rate on the right to arrive at an accumulation optimum. At steady state with $\hat{c} = 0$ and $\hat{K} = n$, the rule boils down to $f' = \epsilon$ or rate of profit = rate of time preference = steady-state rate of interest.

As is often the case with neoclassical macroeconomics, these results look very neat; only their underlying hypotheses and verisimilitude are open to question. In particular, the intertemporal behavior of dynamic models like the present one can seem implausible. The details are what we take up next.

Equation (16) restated for convenience and a rearranged version of (19) form a coupled dynamic system:

$$\dot{k} = f(k) - c - nk \tag{16}$$

and

$$\dot{c} = (c/\eta)(f' - \epsilon). \tag{20}$$

The two equations clearly allow for a steady state at which $\dot{c} = \dot{k} = 0$. To investigate the dynamic behavior of c and k in the vicinity of this point, we can form the 2×2 Jacobian matrix of first partial derivatives of the right-hand side of the equations, and plug in steady-state values of k and c. The matrix takes the form

$$M = \begin{bmatrix} f' - n & -1 \\ (c/\eta)f'' & 0 \end{bmatrix} \tag{21}$$

in which $f'' = d^2f/dk^2 < 0$.

The necessary condition for local stability of the system (16)–(20) is that both eigenvalues of M should be negative at the steady state. Because the trace of a matrix is the sum of its eigenvalues and the determinant is their product, we need Tr $M < 0$ and Det $M > 0$ for stability.[10] The determinant condition is violated in (21). With regard to the trace, we have already observed that $f' = \epsilon$ at the steady state. Because the condition $\epsilon > n$ is required for a solution of (15) and (16) to exist, Tr M is positive. The steady-state solution is dynamically unstable. There is one positive and one negative eigenvalue (Det $M < 0$), and the positive root has greater absolute magnitude (Tr $M > 0$).

Figure 3.3 is a "phase diagram" which attempts to illustrate what is going on. Let k^* be the solution of the equation $f'(k) = \epsilon$. Then from (20), $\dot{c} = 0$ when $k = k^*$, as illustrated by the vertical line. For values of k less than k^*, $\dot{c} > 0$ and the reverse is true for $k > k^*$ (as indicated by the small arrows). The locus of points along which k is stationary or $\dot{k} =$

Figure 3.3
Saddlepath dynamics in the Ramsey model.

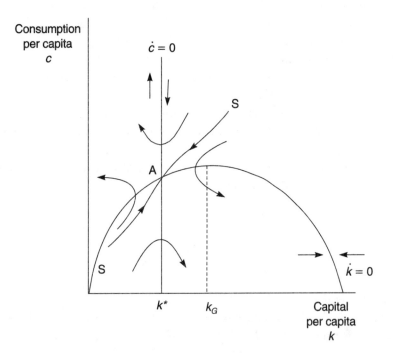

0 is hump-shaped, taking on a negative slope for high values of k as capital's "marginal product" drops off due to decreasing returns to a single factor.[11] From (16), the capital/labor ratio rises for points below the hump and falls for those above it.

The steady state with $\dot{c} = \dot{k} = 0$ is at point A. However, as the curved arrows illustrate, the equilibrium is a saddlepoint. Only trajectories beginning along the "saddlepath" SS will reach the steady state.[12] All others bend toward and then away from SS in the fashion of the "turnpike" dynamics beloved by mainstream theorists in the 1960s. An immediate conclusion might be that describing macroeconomic dynamics with an equation pair like (16) and (20) is not a reasonable strategy to pursue.

The current generation of mainstream economists, however, prefer to treat (16) and (20) as an accurate description of how agents behave. Not being satisfied with the saddlepath as a referential turnpike, they want the economy always to be on it (or even better, always at steady state). If such a short-run equilibrium is perturbed, the "jump" or control variable c will immediately adjust to put the system back on the straight and narrow.

An example appears in Figure 3.4, in which the $\dot{k} = 0$ locus moves upward because of a technical advance, so that point B is the new steady state and the old steady state, point A, becomes an initial position. An "ordinary" trajectory beginning at A would head southeast toward the horizontal axis and zero consumption, like many an old sailing ship with luckless navigation in the "roaring forties" south of Cape Horn. An instant jump of consumption from point A to point B can prevent this catastrophe. Under full rationality, the argument goes, this unique event will occur.

Put a bit more formally, fully competent agents would avoid the Ponzi-like strategy of running down the capital stock to support rising consumption, as finally happens along trajectories to the left of SS in Figure 3.3. Such behavior will not be observed. Trajectories to the right of SS all lead the ratio of households' discounted consumption to discounted income to go to zero as they engage in overinvestment (Romer 2001). They can surely do better by sticking to the saddlepath. For the immortal, omniscient Beings solving (15) and (16), adding such a "transversality condition" to their local optimizing rule (20) may not be too much to ask; all they have to do in a multisectoral version of the model is steer the economy within a set of measure zero in a high-dimensional phase space.

Four final points. The first is that a planning problem with dynamics like (16) and (20) but with a finite horizon T instead of ∞ in the integral in (15) sidesteps some of the metaphysical trappings of the standard

Figure 3.4
Effects of a produc-
tivity increase in the
Ramsey model.

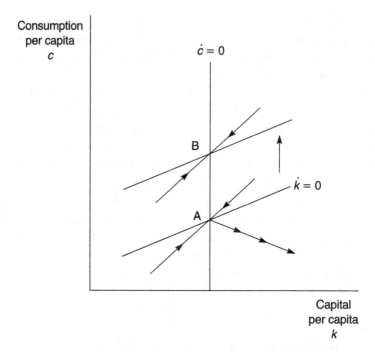

Figure 3.4 Effects of a productivity increase in the Ramsey model.

Ramsey model, and moreover is easy to solve. It is a "two-point bound-ary value" problem with an initial value $k(0)$ of the state variable and "reasonable" final values for $c(T)$ and $k(T)$, which emerge from solving (16) and (20) with $\dot{c} = \dot{k} = 0$.

Substituting $c(T)$ into (17) gives a final value $\xi(T)$ for the costate vari-able. A revised version of (18),

$$\dot{\xi} = -\xi(f' - \epsilon), \tag{18'}$$

can be solved *backward* in time from the terminal value $\xi(T)$. Backward integration of this differential equation for ξ is stable, and from (17) gives values of c over time as well. Plugging these into (16) integrated *forward* in time from $k(0)$ amounts to a feedback decision rule for the state variable. Iterating on (16) and (18') in this fashion easily solves the planning problem from a "plausible" initial reference path (Bryson and Ho 1969; Kendrick and Taylor 1970), and for $T = 100$ or 10,000 years the results will not differ noticeably from the infinite horizon problem.

The question that arises is why such a planner's problem (which might be an interesting reference path for policy discussion) is taken by the mainstream as an *exact* description of how decentralized agents behave as T goes to infinity. For the reasons discussed above, many people find such a notion strange. Moreover, as discussed in Chapter 6, even the planner's problem becomes computationally infeasible once uncertainty is brought into the equations. That is perhaps the fundamental difficulty for economists willing to take the Ramsey model as descriptive of individual behavior on its own terms. Even armed with supercomputers, "agents" could not comply with their assigned behavioral model.

The second observation is that in Figure 3.3 the equilibrium capital/labor ratio k^* is less than the "golden rule" ratio k_G at which steady-state consumption per head is maximized (by setting $f' = n$ in (16) with $\dot{k} = 0$). In contrast to Pasinetti's model discussed in Chapter 2, the profit rate exceeds the growth rate because $k^* < k_G$. A Ramsey steady-state equilibrium is not a "natural system."[13]

Third, full employment dynamic adjustment in Ramsey models basically relies on supportive changes in the whole structure of interest rates over time. An example in the present case is given by a reduction in the discount rate ϵ. In Figure 3.3, k^* would shift to the right, dragging the saddlepath with it. Consumption c would jump down from point A to the dislocated SS schedule, and then increase back along it to the new equilibrium on the "$\dot{k} = 0$" locus. Because $-\eta\hat{c} = \hat{\xi} = \epsilon - f'$, asset prices and thereby interest rates would adjust to accommodate this movement over infinite time (for more details about the asset price/interest rate linkage, see Chapter 4).

What happens if the term structure of interest rates is not fully flexible, because of slowly changing expectations and large bond reserves held by speculators? Then the Say's Law assumption underlying the Ramsey model becomes difficult to sustain. Excess aggregate demand is more likely to be driven toward zero by changes in the level of economic activity than by price-driven movements in investment and savings schedules. This argument, made in a classic paper by Kaldor (1960a), goes unanswered in optimal savings exercises, in which perfect foresight supersedes the workings of real world financial markets.

Finally, introducing artifacts like money (typically entering into the utility function) and slow price adjustment to a discrepancy between aggregate demand and aggregate supply can permit transient unemployment in Ramsey-style models—Ono (1994) neatly works through one such exercise. Hahn and Solow (1995) engage in similar maneuvers for the overlapping generations model we take up next. These more "Keynesian" approaches, however, do not alter the basic causal structure of the models—they just resemble a shift from a system like the one in Figure 2.2 of last chapter to Figure 2.3.

7. The Overlapping Generations Growth Model

As the foregoing discussion suggests, over the last decades of the twentieth century mainstream macroeconomists devoted a good deal of effort to generating MIRA foundations for capital accumulation. Besides Ramsey and Tobin q exercises, the other major thrust went toward construction of overlapping generations (OLG) models in which "young" and "old" agents cohabit the same economy.

Because we have just worked through a Ramsey formulation, it makes sense at this point to set up a simple discrete-time OLG model to draw contrasts and also point out instability and inefficiency problems. With aging populations in industrial economies, the OLG story has influenced the pension policy debate. The section closes with an OLG-based analysis of social security systems, to be compared with a more Keynesian discussion developed in Chapter 5.

The story in the canonical Diamond (1965) version of the model is that each "agent" lives two periods, working in period t and subsisting on accumulated saving before s/he (it?) dies at the end of period $t + 1$. Faced with such a life history, an agent optimizes two-period consumption. A common statement of the choice problem is to maximize a non-Benthamite (felicity *un*weighted by population size), discrete-time version of the utility integral (15) of the Ramsey model,

$$U = [(c_t)^{1-\eta}/(1 - \eta)] + [(c_{t+1})^{1-\eta}/(1 - \eta)]/(1 + \epsilon)$$

subject to the intertemporal budget constraint

$$c_t + c_{t+1}/(1 + r_{t+1}) = \omega_t, \tag{22}$$

where the subscripts denote time periods. Future consumption is discounted at "next" period's profit rate r_{t+1}, so that agents require perfect foresight only over their own lifetimes. Their saving automatically takes the form of physical capital accumulation because of Say's Law. The income available for saving and first-period consumption comes from the real wage ω_t; second-period consumption is paid for by first-period saving and accumulated profit income.

After routine grinding,[14] saving per person at time t (that is, $\omega_t - c_t$) is given by the expression

$$\left[\frac{(1 + r_{t+1})^{(1-\eta)/\eta}}{(1 + r_{t+1})^{(1-\eta)/\eta} + (1 + \epsilon)^{1/\eta}} \right] \omega_t = s(r_{t+1})\omega_t.$$

The algebra is intimidating, but simplifies nicely. When $\eta = 1$ (the Cobb-Douglas case of logarithmic utilities),

$$s(r_{t+1}) = 1/(2 + \epsilon). \tag{23}$$

For values of η "close" to one, changes in the $s(r_{t+1})$ term in response to movements in the profit rate will not be important and in the following discussion are ignored. We assume $s(r_{t+1}) = s$, a constant.

The parameter s stands for saving per person, so that total saving is $s\omega_t L_t = s\omega_t b_t X_t$ (with b_t being the labor/output ratio and X_t output). The capital stock growth equation is

$$K_{t+1} = K_t + s\omega_t b_t X_t$$

or

$$(K_{t+1} - K_t)/K_t = g_t = s(u_t - r_t) \tag{24}$$

(with $u_t = X_t/K_t$), after substitution from the accounting identity $u_t = \omega_t b_t u_t + r_t$. The direct effect of a higher profit rate r_t is to *reduce* g_t in (24). From Chapter 2's wage-profit frontier ω_t and r_t vary inversely, while saving and growth rise with wage income. The resulting "perverse" response of accumulation to profitability can produce dynamic instability, as we now demonstrate.[15]

The state variable of interest is $k_t = K_t/L_t$, with assumed full employment of labor and population growth at rate n: $L_{t+1} = (1 + n)L_t$. Dropping subscripts for the moment, one can use hat calculus tricks to get the following differential change relationships from neoclassical production theory:

$$du = -(1 - \pi)(u/k)dk \quad \text{and} \quad dr = (r/\sigma u)du,$$

where π is the share of profits in output and σ is the elasticity of substitution between capital and labor. Plugging these results into (24) minus subscripts and using the identity $r = \pi u$ shows that

$$dg = -\frac{su}{k}(\frac{\sigma - \pi}{\sigma})(1 - \pi)dk. \tag{25}$$

The sign of dg/dk depends on the term $\sigma - \pi$, with implications to be discussed presently.

The next step is to set up a growth equation for k_t. Using the relationships $K_{t+1} = (1 + g_t)K_t$ and $L_{t+1} = (1 + n)L_t$, it comes out as

$$k_{t+1} = \frac{1 + g_t}{1 + n}k_t = \frac{1 + s(u_t - r_t)}{1 + n}k_t. \tag{26}$$

In discrete time, the local stability condition for this nonlinear difference equation is that the absolute value of dk_{t+1}/dk_t has to be less than one. With its dynamic responses thus limited, an equation like (26) becomes a "contraction mapping" converging to a stationary solution k_{t+1} = k_t = k^*. Stable dynamics are shown in the upper diagram of Figure 3.5, with the "accumulation" line showing k_{t+1} as a function of k_t. There is convergence from an initial capital/labor ratio k_0 to k^*. The lower picture illustrates the unstable case.

Figure 3.5
Stable and unstable dynamics in a saving-driven OLG model.

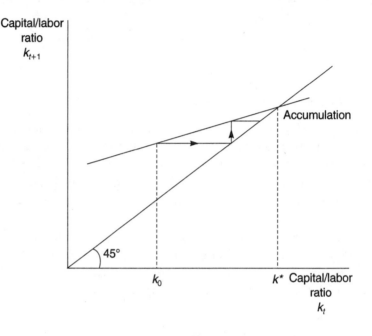

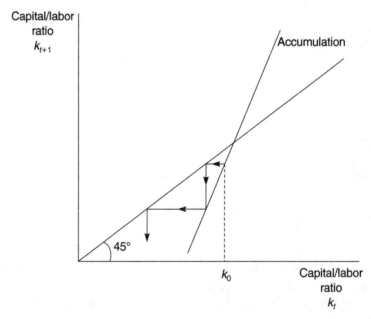

Combining (25) with subscripts restored and (26) shows that the relevant differential expression is

$$dk_{t+1} = \frac{1}{1+n}[(1+g_t) - su_t(\frac{\sigma - \pi_t}{\sigma})(1-\pi_t)]dk_t. \tag{27}$$

At an initial steady state, $g_t = n$. Then dk_{t+1}/dk_t will be less than one and the OLG growth process will be stable so long as the term after the minus sign in the brackets in (27) is positive, that is, $\sigma > \pi_t$.

The narrative is that the profit rate responds more strongly to changes in u_t when σ is small. There is a constant profit share when σ equals one in the Cobb-Douglas (production function) special case. For values of σ near zero, on the other hand, redistribution toward the elderly becomes important in the macro adjustment process. When k_t decreases or the labor/capital ratio increases, the increased labor input makes the output/capital ratio u_t go up as well. The higher u_t leads to a big increase in r_t when σ is small. But the elderly agents who receive profit income just spend it to consume. As a consequence, overall saving and the growth rate g_t decline, k_{t+1} falls further, and the economy diverges from steady state. With savings-driven accumulation, macro adjustment via income redistribution breaks down, if the beneficiary group has a high propensity to consume. In American terms, let Generation X beware![16]

Rather than potential instability in OLG models, the mainstream has focused on another problem—their potential inefficiency because the equilibrium capital/labor ratio k^* can exceed the golden rule value k_G. If that is the case, the profit rate (or marginal product of capital) r will be below the population growth rate n because capital is very plentiful. From the hump-shaped relationship in Figure 3.3 (which broadly applies in an OLG world as well), consumption per head is maximized when $k = k_G$. Hence for $k > k_G$, consumption could be increased by cutting back on the capital stock. This is the inefficiency.

This problem does not arise in Ramsey models because growth trajectories to the right of the separatrix SS in Figure 3.3 are ruled out by a transversality condition. Immortal, omniscient actors won't get themselves on such a path. However, coordination problems across generations could push an OLG economy into Pareto inefficiency.[17] Because saving comes from real wages, which are high when the profit rate is low, one signal could be a small saving rate. Look at equations (26). At a steady state, $k_t = k_{t+1}$ and $g_t = n$. If we drop subscripts, the relationship reduces to $n = s(u - r)$, or

$$r = u - (n/s). \tag{28}$$

It is easy to see from (28) that $r < n$ when $u < n(s + 1)/s$. For $u = 0.3$ (observed values for the GDP/capital ratio rarely go outside the range 0.2–0.4) and $n = 0.01$, $s < 0.035$ would give inefficiency. It doesn't have to happen, but s in such a range is possible—consider American household or even private saving rates as discussed in Chapter 1.[18]

An alternative is to test directly whether the profit rate lies below the growth rate. More generally, under "risk" in the sense that complete probability distributions can be put on future events (an epistemological position which Keynes deemed absurd, as we will see), Abel, Mankiw, Summers, and Zeckhauser (1989) show that the appropriate test for efficiency is that the profit share of GDP should exceed the investment share—capital income contributes to consumption when it exceeds social accumulation needs. Seven industrialized economies turn out to pass this test. For economists intrigued by academic debates, such results may be comforting. Much more fundamental is the fact that while overall profit income may exceed investment, it is also true that in industrialized capitalist economies corporations distribute a substantial portion of their profits to households. In turn, households' acquisition of new business liabilities may represent an important supplement to retained earnings in funding capital formation. All the financial churning that stands out in Tables 1.4 and 1.5 is simply ignored in the OLG (in)efficiency discussion. Are those big financial flows completely a veil?

For future reference, both Marxist and "Austrian" business cycle models (the latter originating from the London School of Economics in the 1930s) invoke "excessive" investment in the recent past as a fundamental cause of cyclical downswings. There is certainly a family resemblance to inefficiency in the OLG framework. For more details, see Chapter 9.

Despite its peculiar assumptions about saving, the OLG model has emerged as the principal theoretical vehicle for the analysis of pension and social security systems. The standard approach is based on modifications to the household budget restriction (22). The general idea is that households are taxed (in lump-sum fashion) an amount q in the first half of their lives and receive a lump-sum transfer z in their second period. Under such a scheme (22) has to be rewritten as

$$c_t + c_{t+1}/(1 + r_{t+1}) = \omega_t - \{q - [z/(1+r_{t+1})]\}. \tag{22SS}$$

Most existing pension schemes can be modeled as a blend of two extreme forms:

"Fully funded" plans simply take the payroll deduction q and invest it at the going return r_{t+1} so that $z = (1 + r_{t+1})q$. The budget constraint under social security, (22SS), reduces to (22) and the foregoing analysis is unchanged.

"Pay-as-you-go" (or "pay-go") schemes sum up all young households' payments of q and transfer them to the less numerous older cohort. Each such household thereby receives $z = (1 + n)q$. In (22SS) the last term to the right doesn't vanish, and there will be effects on the accumulation equation (26). It is easy to see that if $r_{t+1} > n$, the term in brackets in (22SS) will be positive, reducing wealth and presumably inducing households to save less. Even in the opposite "inefficient" case, one can show (Blanchard and Fischer 1989 for the details in the Cobb-Douglas utility case) that the increase in saving from greater wealth due to the pension scheme will be less than the saving loss due to the tax q. Hence overall saving will decline in general.

In the upper diagram of Figure 3.5, the effect will be to shift the Accumulation locus downward. The economy will converge to a steady state with a lower capital/labor ratio k^*, implying lower wealth per capita, a lower steady-state real wage, and a higher rate of profit. The U.S. social security program is close to being pay-go. Results of the sort just described are prominent in the propaganda of people who want to change the system. In their view, Roosevelt's creation creates an unconscionable reduction in social saving.

8. Wicksell's Cumulative Process Inflation Model

A soupçon of Irving Fisher aside, the foregoing real interest rate models do not figure in *The General Theory*. The circle of economists in which Keynes moved was much more focused on the distinction between natural and market rates of interest. The macroeconomic background in the decades on both sides of the year 1900 involved business cycles in which price fluctuations up and down were relatively more significant than output changes, with the shift toward production adjustments only coming with the 1920s and 1930s (Nell 1992; Sylos-Labini 1993).[19] Price adjustments due to the market and natural rates getting out of gear were a natural analytical construct. The market rate(s) could be observed, while the unobservable natural rate was believed to emerge from marginal conditions of the sort developed in the Ramsey model or, better, from a Fisherian market in which all participants are solving their own private utility maximization programs while engaging in financial transactions with one another.

Macroeconomic debate centered around this perspective. As Amadeo (1989) argues, a post-Wicksellian macroeconomic model certainly did exist. It was a blend of credit-driven endogenous money creation as described by Wicksell (1935) and Schumpeter (1934), and the inflation tax and forced saving as macro adjustment mechanisms analyzed by Schumpeter, Robertson (1933),[20] and Keynes (1930). Effective demand was implicit, despite a general acceptance of Say's Law (perhaps an adequate rough-and-ready description of the relatively minor output fluctuations over the cycle). The full employment, zero inflation natural rate was a "center of gravitation" for the system, but played little role in its day-to-day operation.

What did matter in Wicksell's own cumulative process model—the intellectual prelude to *The General Theory*—were interactions between the inflation tax and the interest rate charged by banks, as mediated by a saving-investment process. The accounting appears in the SAM of Table 3.2. (Until the following section, ignore the entries in column 7 and cell B4.)

The financial side of the economy is treated as a pure credit banking system—the only financial claims are those associated with banks. Their consolidated balance sheet is $A_f + A_g = D + M$, where A_f and A_g stand for advances (credits, loans) from the banks to firms and the government respectively. "Desired" deposits from households are D, and M is an endogenously adjusting money (or currency) supply. Column (6) in the SAM restates the banks' balance sheet in flow terms (where a "dot" above a variable as usual denotes its time derivative).

The driving force in this system is the evolution of total bank credit $A = A_f + A_g$, which rises with capital formation and government spending.

Table 3.2 A SAM incorporating the inflation tax (all variables scaled by the value of capital stock).

	Current expenditures					Change in banks' claims (6)	Change in government bonds (7)	Totals (8)
	Output costs (1)	House-holds (2)	Firms (3)	Government (4)	Investment (5)			
(A) Output uses		γ_h		γ_g	g			u
Incomes								
(B) Households	$(1-\pi)u$			jB/K				ξ_h
(C) Firms	πu							ξ_f
(D) Government								0
Flows of funds								
(E) Household "noninflationary"		σ_h				$-\dot{D}/PK$	$-\dot{B}/K$	0
(F) Seigniorage		$(\hat{P}+g)/V$				$-\dot{M}/PK$		0
(G) Firms			σ_f		$-g$	$\dot{A}_f/PK$		0
(H) Government				(σ_g)		$\dot{A}_g/PK$	$\dot{B}/K$	0
(I) Totals	u	ξ_h	ξ_f	0	0	0	0	

The key variable driven is household saving or (in Robertson's terminology) "lacking" induced by faster price increases. The mechanism appears in the "seigniorage" (another term for the inflation tax) row (F). Before exploring the model's causal structure, we should look at the rest of the SAM.

All variables are normalized by the value of the capital stock PK (the only nonfinancial asset in the system), and $u = X/K$ as usual. Say's Law is presumed, so that u is predetermined. Column (1) shows how output is split between household and enterprise income flows, where π is the profit share. Because forced saving will not be brought into the present discussion, π will also be predetermined (by marginal productivity conditions, for example, if one is so inclined).

Row (A) shows that on the demand side, u is appropriated by household consumption γ_h, government consumption γ_g, and investment spending $g = I/K$ (all three components of final demand are scaled to the capital stock). We will shortly specify an investment function, while γ_g is presumably set as a policy variable. How, then, is γ_h going to adjust endogenously to satisfy the row (A) accounting balance $\gamma_h + \gamma_g + g = u$?

To begin to answer from the blueprints, observe that in the flows of funds row (G) firms fill their financial deficit $g - \xi_f = g - \pi u$ by taking new net credits from the banking system in the amount $\dot{A}_f/PK$.[21] Government is assumed to have no income in row (D), but it spends γ_g in column (4). In row (H), its negative saving (σ_g) is financed by banks' advances $\dot{A}_g/PK$. In the absence of inflation, households in row (E) desire to save σ_h, which (because they have no other option) they hold as new bank deposits $\dot{D}/PK$.

What happens if $(\dot{A}_f + \dot{A}_g)/PK > \dot{D}/PK$, that is, new loans from the banking system exceed new deposits? To balance their books, banks will issue currency M in the quantity $\dot{M}/PK = (\dot{A}_f + \dot{A}_g)/PK - \dot{D}/PK$. In addition to all the foregoing accounting, we assume that the equation of exchange, $MV = PK$, applies with a constant value of V (a restriction to be relaxed soon). With Say's Law in force, it is a matter of convenience to use PK instead of PX on the equation's right-hand side. Hat calculus shows that $\hat{M} = \hat{P} + g$, or $\dot{M}/PK = (\hat{P} + g)/V$.

The last equation is row (F) of the SAM. The interpretation is that households are hit by the inflation generated by credits created to "finance" demand for commodities by government and firms. These actors have a prior claim on output, ratified by money creation. Households are crowded out of the market, and have to cut back their consumption as a consequence. To make the accounts work out so that macro balance $\gamma_h + \gamma_g + g = u$ will hold, the required reduction is $(\hat{P} + g)/V$.

How can this particular amount be rationalized? The usual story is that the loss in real balances M/P induced by a price increase $\dot{P}$ is $-(M/P)\dot{P}$. The public is supposed to raise its saving by this amount to reconstitute its wealth when the price level rises—a rational act. Alternatively, faster inflation means that people need to hold more money for transactions purposes; operating with the impoverished asset and liability structure of column (6) of the SAM, the only way that they can build up currency holdings is to save more. Similar reasoning applies to the higher transactions balances needed to deal with growth of the real capital stock at rate g.

The next steps are to consolidate the accounts to get an aggregate demand or investment-saving balance, and then to postulate an investment function. Presumably, the latter should depend on the real interest rate j $= i - \hat{P}$, where the nominal rate i is set by the banking authorities. Indeed, Wicksell's central argument is that inflation is provoked when the interest rate in his pure credit banking system is pegged below its "natural" level. To see how, we can consolidate rows and columns in Table 3.2 to get the following equation for aggregate demand:

$$\gamma_g + [1 - (1/V)]g(i - \hat{P}) - s(i - \hat{P})u - (1/V)(\hat{P}) = 0, \qquad (29)$$

where $su = \sigma_h + \sigma_f$. We assume (with scant empirical justification) that household saving apart from the inflation tax responds positively to the real interest rate as in the models of previous sections, and that investment demand g is an inverse function of the same variable. Equation (29) says that if the nominal rate i is pegged so that there is incipient excess aggregate demand,

$$Q(i, \hat{P}) = \gamma_g + [1 - (1/V)]g - su > 0, \qquad (30)$$

then $\hat{P}$ will immediately jump up to squeeze real household expenditure via the inflation tax to restore macroeconomic balance.[22]

Is this adjustment stable? To address this question, we must look at the partial derivatives of $Q(i, \hat{P})$ in (30). Because g falls and s rises with a higher interest rate, it is clear that $\partial Q/\partial i < 0$. On the other hand, $\partial g/\partial\hat{P}$ is positive, because a faster inflation rate reduces the real interest rate, thereby cutting saving and stimulating investment demand.[23] Although it is built into most models, there is no reason to take the investment linkage seriously, especially in high-inflation economies. The reason is that a faster price spiral adds so much uncertainty to the system that investment plans are almost always cut back. More formally, $\hat{P}$ itself should enter as a separate argument in the investment function, with a negative impact. Similarly, the partial derivative $\partial s/\partial\hat{P} < 0$ can be taken with a grain of salt, especially after an inflation process has settled in and non-

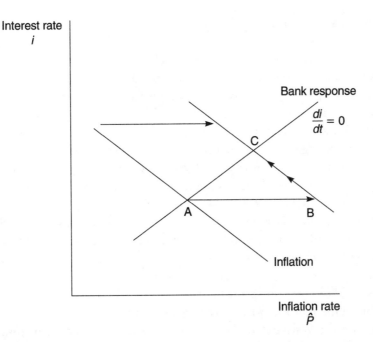

Figure 3.6
Dynamics of a
Wicksellian cumula-
tive process.

affluent people find that their real spending power has been eroded accordingly.

The upshot is that the effects of $\hat{P}$ in the function $Q(i, \hat{P})$ in (30) are of uncertain magnitude and sign. From (29), overall aggregate demand $Q(i, \hat{P}) - (1/V)\hat{P}$ almost certainly depends negatively on the rate of inflation via the inflation tax. Because demand also responds inversely to the interest rate i, the "Inflation" locus along which (29) is satisfied in Figure 3.6 has a negative slope.

To play against this schedule, Wicksell argued that after inflation persists for a time, banks (or the Central Banker) will voluntarily raise the interest rate to limit loan demand and cut down on losses of reserves, say, according to a rule such as

$$di/dt = \theta\hat{P} + \phi(i - i^*), \tag{31}$$

where i^* is the target or natural nominal interest rate. Usages of the word trace far back in time, but the proximate sources for modern "natural" employment rates or NAIRUs are the Wicksellians. The diagrams sketched in Chapter 2 and developed at great length later basically substitute the real wage ω or the labor share ψ for the nominal interest rate i on the vertical axis of Figure 3.6.

Coming back to equation (31), another possibility is that the banking authorities might seek to stabilize the real interest rate $j = i - \hat{P}$,

$$di/dt = \theta'\hat{P} + \phi[j^* - (i - \hat{P})].$$

This equation reduces to (31) with $i^* = j^*$ and $\theta = \theta' + \phi$, so we can consider either case. If the real rate is targeted, then $\theta > \phi$ in (31), a condition that turns out to be of interest below.

The "Bank response" curve in Figure 3.6 represents the condition $di/dt = 0$ giving a positively sloped relationship between i and $\hat{P}$. An autonomous increase in aggregate demand (say, from higher public spending γ_g) immediately makes the inflation rate jump upward from A to B. Banks then begin to raise interest rates until a new steady state is reached at C. Inflation will be forced back closer to its initial level insofar as the Bank response schedule is steep, that is, $\theta >> \phi$ in (31), but for finite parameters $\hat{P}$ will increase at least somewhat.

The diagram also shows that the nominal interest rate will be higher in the new steady state, while a bit of manipulation indicates that the real rate will increase when $\theta > \phi$. But then investment g will decline, and so will the steady-state rate of growth. In other words, if banks respond aggressively to inflation by raising interest rates (in particular, if they try to stabilize the real rate j by substantially raising the nominal rate i), they may force investment to be reduced enough to make fiscal dissaving crowd out growth in the medium run. In Wicksell's canonical monetarist inflation model, there is no automatic transition from inflation stabilization to renewed capital formation, a lesson that is too familiar in developing economies afflicted with the medications of the International Monetary Fund.

Moreover, persistent inflation means that the desired level i^* of the interest rate in (31) is not attained. Despite its marginalist anchors, the nominal "natural" rate becomes a moving target, depending on the underlying inflationary trend (a result of the interactions of aggregate demand with wage indexation and bank responsiveness, in a minimally realistic model)—a point perhaps first raised by Myrdal (1939).

As a final exercise, we can elaborate on analysis already sketched in Chapter 2 by introducing the monetarists' preferred stylized fact that velocity tends to increase with the inflation rate, say,

$$V = V_0 + v\hat{P}. \tag{32}$$

That is, people "flee money" by reducing their currency and deposit balances as inflation speeds up. Econometric estimates of the parameters V_0 and v usually take values between one and ten.

Assume, realistically, that the current inflation rate $\hat{P}$ is accurately observed but that there is uncertainty about its rate of change. If the expected value of $d\hat{P}/dt$ is $E(d\hat{P}/dt)$ and households adjust their money balances according to this expectation,[24] then (32) suggests that the change in velocity over time should be written as $\dot{V} = dV/dt = vE(d\hat{P}/dt)$. Substituting this expression into the growth rate version of the equation of exchange (interpreted as a dynamic money demand function), $\hat{M} + \hat{V} = \hat{P} + g$ and rearranging gives an expression for $E(\hat{P})$,

$$E(d\hat{P}/dt) = (V/v)(\hat{P} + g - \hat{M}).$$

The natural next step for a modern economist of monetarist or new classical inclination is to assume rational expectations or (more precisely in the present context in which we are ignoring random prediction errors) myopic perfect foresight with regard to the change in the inflation rate, $E(d\hat{P}/dt) = d\hat{P}/dt$. Households correctly estimate $d\hat{P}/dt$, so that the formula above can be restated as a differential equation

$$d\hat{P}/dt = (V/v)(\hat{P} + g - \hat{M}). \tag{33}$$

Evidently, there is a positive feedback of $\hat{P}$ into $d\hat{P}/dt$. What are the implications of such a possibly destabilizing linkage? After substitution of various relationships from Table 3.2, (33) can be rewritten in the form

$$d\hat{P}/dt = (V/v)[\hat{P} - VQ(i, \hat{P})], \tag{34}$$

where $Q(i, \hat{P})$ is defined in (30). This differential equation replaces the static relationship (29), which can be restated as

$$VQ(i, \hat{P}) - \hat{P} = 0. \tag{35}$$

The steady-state solution of (34) at $d\hat{P}/dt = 0$ satisfies (35), but superficially the dynamics are richer because (34) is coupled with (31) in a two-dimensional system. The most realistic case is probably the one in which the inflation tax dominates other responses to $\hat{P}$ in the bracketed term on the right-hand side of (34) so that $d(d\hat{P}/dt)/d\hat{P} > 0$.[25]

We are following the recipe spelled out in connection with the Ramsey model, and to check on stability we have to investigate the properties of the two equations' Jacobian matrix. The sign pattern of the partial derivatives turns out to be

$$
\begin{array}{ccc}
 & \hat{P} & i \\
d\hat{P}/dt & + & + \\
di/dt & + & -
\end{array}
$$

The negative determinant signals a saddlepoint, with the two eigenvalues having opposite signs. The phase diagram is in Figure 3.7.

From an initial equilibrium at A, the figure shows the adjustment path when the curve along which $d\hat{P}/dt = 0$ shifts rightward to give a new steady state at C. Inflation jumps from A to B, and then both $\hat{P}$ and i in-

Figure 3.7
The cumulative pro-
cess with rational
expectations.

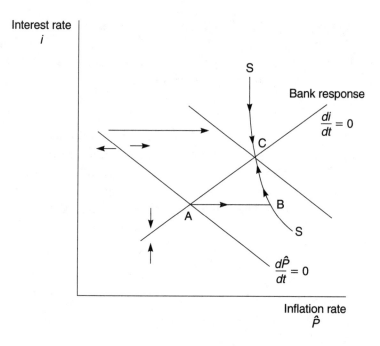

crease along the saddlepath SS until they get to the new equilibrium. This scenario closely resembles the one in Figure 3.6, with the main difference being that the initial jump in inflation is a bit smaller in Figure 3.7.

To summarize, the Wicksellian model presented here presupposes Say's Law and involves macroeconomic adjustment via interest rate changes and (more spectacularly) the inflation tax. The inflation rate is the "jump" variable that permits rapid equilibration of the equation of exchange in growth rate form. At least short-run perfect foresight about $d\hat{P}/dt$ or the change in the inflation rate has to be invoked if the economy is to leap to a saddlepath as in Figure 3.7. Such hypotheses always beg questions about the sources of the precise economic knowledge that they entail, but perhaps the interrogation can be less severe for the Wicksell model than for an infinite horizon Ramsey machine.

More important from the perspective of *The General Theory* is the foundation of Wicksellian models on injections and leakages as sources and sinks of effective demand, along with their recognition of the fact that some variable has to adjust in the short run to ensure macro-economic equilibrium. Compared with Wicksell, one contribution of Keynes and Kalecki was to recognize that prices are more credibly deter-mined by "slow" dynamics (of the sort already sketched in the struc-turalist inflation models of Chapter 2) than by saddlepath trapeze leaps. Their more important innovation was to drop Say's Law. In line with the nature of the twentieth-century business cycle, capacity utilization becomes the jump variable par excellence.

The final point worth noting and to be developed at length later in this volume is that overthrowing Say's Law turned out to be no trivial task. Both the new classical and new Keynesian models currently at the profession's center stage bear a much closer relationship to the formulations of Wicksell and his successors than they do to those of Kalecki and Keynes.[26] The main difference is that the stable inflation rest point is now called a NAIRU instead of a natural rate of interest.

9. More on Inflation Taxes

Inflation taxes are hardy perennials in monetarist and new classical gardens. Before turning to the Keynesian interpretation of effective demand, it makes sense to peek briefly at three species that have flourished in recent years—the inflation tax in public finance, its stability or instability in non-Wicksellian contexts, and an exotic new classical orchid called the "tight money paradox."[27] The thrust of the argument is that these recent models work with an even more limited set of assets than the one used by Wicksell, and are correspondingly less relevant to realistic policy choice.

In most monetarist discourse, the fact that firms can finance the gap between their investment and saving by borrowing from banks is ignored—the government gets all the blame for the inflation tax. In most models, the tax is analyzed in terms of monetary "real balances" $m = M/P$ held by households. They evolve over time according to the relationships

$$\dot{M}/P = \hat{M}m = \dot{m} + m\hat{P}. \tag{36}$$

In a stationary state, $g = \dot{m} = 0$. Under such circumstances, inflation tax or seigniorage revenue $\dot{M}/P$ is equal to $m\hat{P}$. It is used to finance the real fiscal deficit Δ.

Under inflationary conditions, the standard mainstream money demand function was introduced by Cagan (1956):

$$m = m_0 \exp(-\alpha\hat{P}). \tag{37}$$

Setting $m_0 = 1$ gives the following expression for seigniorage:

$$\dot{M}/P = \hat{P} \exp(-\alpha\hat{P}). \tag{38}$$

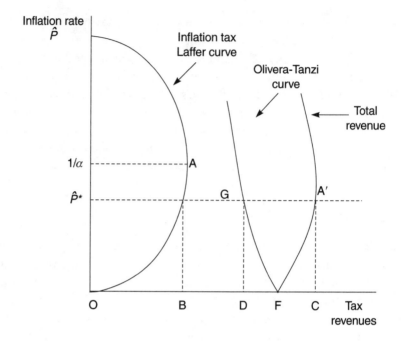

Figure 3.8
Inflation and other
tax revenues.

This formula generates the "Laffer curve" for the real proceeds of the inflation tax sketched in Figure 3.8. It is easy to show that revenue is maximized when $\hat{P} = 1/\alpha$ at point A.

The next step is to consider the effects of inflation on "ordinary" tax revenue. If the tax system is not indexed to the inflation rate—an institutional shortcoming that is remedied sooner or later in most inflation-prone economies—so that there are lags in the collection process, real tax returns will decline as $\hat{P}$ goes up.[28] This "effect" was emphasized in a Latin American context by Olivera (1967) and Tanzi (1978). Using tricks like those deployed to analyze conflicting claims inflations in Chapter 2, the latter considers a collection lag of n months. If $T(\hat{P})$ stands for real tax revenue when the annual inflation rate is $\hat{P}$ (in discrete time), he shows that

$$T(\hat{P}) = T(0)/(1 + \hat{P})^{n/12}. \tag{39}$$

The declining revenue is illustrated by the "Olivera-Tanzi curve" in Figure 3.8. The inflation rate $\hat{P}^*$ that generates maximum fiscal revenue is less than $1/\alpha$ because of the Olivera-Tanzi tax drag. At $\hat{P}^*$, revenue from the inflation tax is OB, from other taxes it is OD, and the total is OC.

Although it is unlikely that real-world finance ministers ever seriously ponder a diagram like Figure 3.8, they are certainly aware of the considerations it includes. When the annual rate gets well into the double digits, the effects of inflation on a government's ability to finance itself become a matter of serious policy concern.

So how do the economic authorities handle the inflation tax? Can it be destabilizing? Many mainstream economists have addressed such questions over the years—Bruno and Fischer (1990) summarize and extend their arguments. An alternative interpretation is offered here, ignoring Olivera-Tanzi effects and based on the analysis around Figure 3.7 above.

We stick with the Cagan money demand function (37) with $m_0 = 1$ in a zero growth/zero interest rate economy, and assume that the government finances its nominal deficit $P\Delta$ only with monetary emission $\dot{M}$,

$$\Delta = \dot{M}/P = \hat{M}m = \hat{M}\exp(-\alpha\hat{P}), \tag{40}$$

using (36) and (37) to set up the various equalities. The final expression for Δ is plotted as the "Inflation tax" schedule in Figure 3.9. Since $\Delta = \hat{M}$ when the inflation rate is zero, Δ itself pins the intercept of the curve along the horizontal axis. The economy is assumed to satisfy (40) at all times so that for a given Δ, $\hat{M}$ depends on $\hat{P}$ or vice versa.

The "Steady-state" schedule (the 45° line along which $\hat{M} = \hat{P}$) can intersect the Inflation tax curve at two, one, or zero points. The last case is analogous to a nonintersection of the "Wage inflation" and "Indexing rule" curves in Figure 2.7; in the present context it represents a deficit

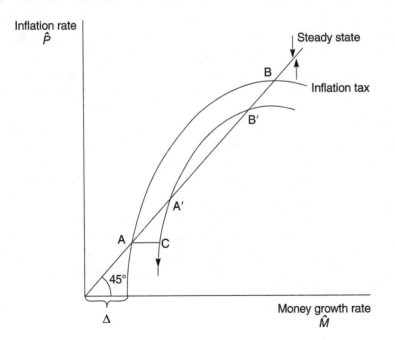

Figure 3.9
The inflation tax and
stationary equilibria.

Inflation rate $\hat{P}$

Steady state

Inflation tax

Money growth rate $\hat{M}$

too big to be covered by the expedient of printing money. If the curves intersect twice, there are potential steady states with low and high inflation rates at points A and B on the "right" and "wrong" sides of the Laffer curve respectively.

What happens if the fiscal deficit suddenly increases at the low inflation steady state? To trace through the dynamic response we can maintain the assumptions leading to equation (33) above to show that households adjust their real balances according to the rule

$$\dot{m} = -\alpha[\exp(-\alpha\hat{P})]E(d\hat{P}/dt) = -\alpha m E(d\hat{P}/dt), \tag{41}$$

where as before $E(d\hat{P}/dt)$ is the expected change in the inflation rate. Since $\dot{m} = \hat{M} - \hat{P}$, we find that

$$E(d\hat{P}/dt) = (1/\alpha)(\hat{P} - \hat{M}). \tag{42}$$

With myopic perfect foresight or $E(d\hat{P}/dt) = d\hat{P}/dt$, (42) amounts to a restatement of (33). The principal difference between the present model and Wicksell's is that the latter contains an explicit macro framework for the real side of the economy with the interest rate as a medium-run adjusting variable according to the theory of loanable funds. Such an adjustment scenario is conspicuously absent in Cagan-style models.

The effects of this limited specification show up clearly in Figure 3.9. If the deficit Δ shifts up, the Inflation tax curve (40) moves rightward and $\hat{M}$ has to jump from point A to point C as monetary emission runs faster. But under myopic perfect foresight the Steady-State locus now represents (42), building in unstable dynamics for $\hat{P}$. Since C lies below the new steady state at A′, both $\hat{M}$ and $\hat{P}$ will decline after $\hat{M}$ jumps while real balances m steadily *rise*. Falling inflation and increased money demand are not supposed to happen when the government prints more money.

In Cagan's day, monetarists got around this embarrassing outcome by postulating "adaptive expectations" for the inflation rate. Later, when rational expectations came in, this recourse fell out of fashion and the model itself became less popular. Nevertheless, it still serves as the mainstay for the mainstream's empirical analyses of inflation, for example, the World Bank studies presented in Easterly and Rodriguez (1995). To illustrate how the model can be made to work with adaptive expectations for changes in inflation, let a (for "acceleration") stand for $d\hat{P}/dt$ and $a^e = E(d\hat{P}/dt)$. The key hypothesis is that a^e changes over time according to an error-correction mechanism,

$$\dot{a}^e = \rho(a - a^e). \tag{43}$$

In rather plausible fashion households adjust their ideas about how inflation is likely to change on the basis of the error in their present perceptions (ρ is a constant describing their speed of adjustment).

Stability analysis for (43) is tedious but straightforward. Using (43), (42) can be restated as

$$\hat{P} = \alpha a^e + \hat{M}.$$

Differentiating with respect to time gives

$$a = \alpha \dot{a}^e + d\hat{M}/dt.$$

Substituting this expression back into (43) and simplifying gives

$$\dot{a}^e = [1/(1 - \rho\alpha)][d\hat{M}/dt - a^e]. \tag{44}$$

The next step is to express $d\hat{M}/dt$ in terms of growth of the fiscal deficit $d\Delta/dt$. Since $\hat{M} = \Delta/m$ from (40), we have

$$d\hat{M}/dt = (1/m)(d\Delta/dt - \Delta\hat{m}) = (1/m)(d\Delta/dt + \Delta\alpha a^e),$$

where the expression after the second equality follows from (41). Substitution into (44) and simplification using (40) give a final equation

$$\dot{a}^e = [1/m(1 - \rho\alpha)][d\Delta/dt + m(\hat{M}\alpha - 1)a^e]. \tag{45}$$

If the fiscal deficit starts to increase when the economy is at point A in Figure 3.9, then $\hat{M} < 1/\alpha$ since seigniorage is not being maximized. The coefficient on a^e on the right-hand side of (45) will be negative. Then so long as money demand is not overly responsive to the inflation rate (small α) and/or expectations are sluggish (small ρ) the condition $\rho\alpha < 1$ will hold and (45) will be a stable differential equation for a^e. A growing deficit $d\Delta/dt$ drives up a^e in (45). As the system arrives at a new steady state with $a = a^e = 0$ when $d\Delta/dt$ returns to zero,[29] from (42) the inflation rate itself converges to the new, higher level of $\hat{M}$. Monetarist sanity returns, at the cost of a few tranquilizing assumptions to hold down the volatility built into rational expectations.

Although it is not usually described in such terms, the last model to be considered can be viewed as an attempt to retool Cagan-type equations into a full macro system à la Wicksell. It gives rise to a "tight money paradox" resembling the peculiar dynamics in Figure 3.9. The original version was developed by Sargent and Wallace (1981) in an opaque overlapping generations setup; a simpler version provided by Liviatan (1984, 1986) is adopted here.

The basic accounting appears in Table 3.2, including column (7) and cell B4. It is simplest to drop deposits D from the model and assume that the accounts of firms and households are consolidated into the hands of the latter. There is no growth, so investment g is zero. The government's deficit (scaled to the capital stock) is $\Delta/K = \gamma_g + jB/K$, with B as the outstanding stock of inflation-indexed bonds that the authorities have placed on the market. Including bond finance is the step that Sargent and Wallace take beyond Cagan. The bonds carry a predetermined real interest rate j, perhaps set on the basis of time preference. The fiscal deficit is financed by bond sales and money emission,

$$\Delta/K = \dot{B}/K + \dot{M}/PK.$$

Liviatan solves an optimization problem to scale consumption and money demand to household real wealth $\Omega = M/P + B + K$, consistent with the full use of capacity presupposed in row (A) of the SAM with u predetermined. Without much violence to the data, it is simpler to use the capital stock as the scaling variable for the demand functions,[30]

$$C = \gamma_b K \quad \text{and} \quad M/P = m = [(j - \gamma_b)/(j + \hat{P})]K. \tag{46}$$

Assuming that the inflation rate is correctly observed, one can combine the money demand function in (46) with the relationships in (36) to get a differential equation for real balances,

$$\dot{m} = (j + \hat{M})m - (j - \gamma_b)K. \tag{47}$$

The government's consolidated accounts give an equation for emission of bonds,

$$\dot{B} = -\hat{M}m + jB + \gamma_g K. \tag{48}$$

The Jacobian of (47) and (48) is

$$\begin{bmatrix} j + \hat{M} & 0 \\ -\hat{M} & j \end{bmatrix}$$

It has two positive eigenvalues, so expect some fireworks.

Assume that the economy is in an initial steady state, with $\dot{m} = \dot{B} = 0$ and $\hat{M} = \hat{P}$. What happens if the government tries to switch from monetary to credit financing by reducing the rate of growth of the money supply? The answer is pretty clear. From (47), the reduction in $\hat{M}$ makes $\dot{m} < 0$. Because of the positive feedback in the equation, m falls over time at an increasing rate. From the money demand function in (46) with the interest rate j constant, the only way m can decline is through an increase in the rate of inflation, which induces people to hold lower real balances. So $\hat{P}$ rises, at an increasing rate. This burst of inflation in response to tighter money is the first part of the "paradox." It amounts to the Figure 3.9 story with lower as opposed to higher levels of Δ and $\hat{M}$.

A second stage follows from the bond market. In equation (48), the jump downward in $\hat{M}$ makes $\dot{B}$ positive; the subsequent reduction in m and positive feedback accelerates the growth of B. Ultimately bond demand is supposed to saturate so that suddenly $\dot{B} = 0$.[31] Rewriting (48) gives $\hat{M} = (1/m)[jb - \dot{B} + \gamma_g K]$. The only potentially free variable in this equation is $\hat{M}$, so the jump down in $\dot{B}$ forces money supply growth to jump up. Somehow m stays constant during and forever after this earthquake so a new steady state sets in with $\dot{m} = \dot{B} = 0$. To complete the paradox, the inflation rate $\hat{P}$ has to jump to meet the higher $\hat{M}$.

In sum, monetary contraction leads first to a steadily rising inflation rate and then a leap in $\hat{P}$ to a new steady state that somehow maintains itself despite the manifest instability built into (47)–(48). Rising interest rates, falling output, and even interest rate cost push into faster inflation are potentially important responses to tight money which the Sargent-Wallace paradox leaves out. Wicksell thought seriously about all three.

Some part of economic reality is conspicuously missing from the new classical vision. It is time to turn to Keynes.

CHAPTER FOUR

Effective Demand and Its Real and Financial Implications

Subject to strong caveats set out below about how volatile, subjective expectations can destabilize all the behavioral relationships it includes (especially liquidity preference and the marginal efficiency of capital), *The General Theory*'s basic model has a clear and simple causal structure.[1] It can be illustrated as follows:

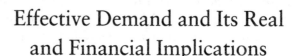

$$
\begin{array}{c}
w \Rightarrow P \\
M
\end{array} \Rightarrow i \Rightarrow I \Rightarrow \begin{array}{c} C \\ Y \\ X \end{array} \quad \textit{from} \quad \begin{array}{l} X = C + I \\ Y = X \\ C = f(Y) \end{array} \tag{1}
$$

The linkages are easy to describe from left to right. The nominal wage w is the principal determinant of the price level P, through a price-cost relationship of the sort discussed in Chapter 2. With the money supply M predetermined, real balances M/P (in non–*General Theory* terminology) set the interest rate i according to Keynes's liquidity preference theory. Investment I follows as enterprises compare the interest rate with the marginal efficiency of capital that they see emerging from their portfolios of potential projects. Consumption C, real output X, and real income Y emerge from the material balance relationship $X = C + I$, the output-income mapping $Y = X$, and the consumption function $C = f(Y)$.

After an initial review of Kaleckian macroeconomics, this chapter presents the relationships underlying (1) in detail, concentrating on a question central to *The General Theory*: will wage reduction stimulate employment? We then discuss some of the many reactions that Keynes's generally negative answer provoked. These basically took two forms. One was a move to revise the causal structure (1) toward the "modern" version, in which real macroeconomic equilibrium is determined in the labor market as in Figure 2.2 or Figure 4.4, rather than in the commodity market that Keynes and Kalecki emphasized. At the same time, Keynes's insights into financial markets were systematically repressed. The beginnings of these decades-long processes are examined here, and subsequent high points are presented in Chapter 6.

The second set of revisions aimed at putting macroeconomics on a more MIRA or Walrasian basis by emphasizing "micro foundations" of macro behavior and respecifying *The General Theory*'s consumption and investment functions. As the new Keynesian movement demonstrates, this effort is still in full swing. The story here begins with the ideas behind *The General Theory* and goes on to currently popular formulations.

1. The Commodity Market

It is convenient to discuss Kalecki's and Keynes's approaches to the determination of commodity market equilibrium in sequence, beginning with an updated version of the former because it is a bit simpler and leads naturally into the structuralist models discussed in Chapters 5 and 7–10. Two basic questions are addressed: First, in an economy closed to foreign trade, do real wage increases cause effective demand to fall or rise? Second, if we take such linkages into account, do nominal wage cuts stimulate employment? Keynes's answer to the second query was a resounding no, but the matter is still subject to intense debate.

The mode of argument is to impose different causal schemes on simple models, to ask which ones fit macroeconomic stylized facts and institutions the best. The starting point is Kalecki's (1971) analysis of output adjustment, with extensions independently due to Rowthorn (1982) and Dutt (1984) regarding how changes in the real wage affect output, the profit rate, and growth. A substantial literature has emerged in the wake of their papers—see Blecker (2002a) for a survey.

As we observed in Chapter 1, Kalecki believed that commodity output is not limited by available capital stock or capacity, and that final goods prices are determined from variable costs (for labor only in the simplest model) by a markup rule:

$$P = (1 + \tau)wb, \tag{2}$$

where the notation is the same as in previous chapters: P is the price level, w the nominal wage rate, b the labor-output ratio, and τ the markup rate. We assume that w is fixed at any point in time, from institutions and a history of bargaining or class struggle (Keynes's ideas about these matters were introduced in Chapter 2 and are extended below). For the moment, the coefficient b is assumed to be determined by technology and custom.

For a given money wage w, we concentrate on the macroeconomic effects of changes in the real wage $\omega = w/P$ or the profit share π. Like w, both variables are determined by historical forces and policy interven-

Table 4.1   Closed economy macroeconomic relationships

$P = wb/(1 - \pi)$	(3)
$\omega = (1 - \pi)/b$	(4)
$u = X/K$	(5)
$r = \pi u$	(6)
$g^i = g_0 + \alpha r + \beta u = g_0 + (\alpha\pi + \beta)u = g^i(\pi, u)$	(7)
$g^s = [s_\pi\pi + s_w(1 - \pi)]u = s(\pi)u$	(8)
$g^i - g^s = 0$	(9)
$MV = PX$ or $\omega = wKu/MV$	(10)
$u = \bar{u}$	(11)
$s_\pi = s_\pi(M/P);$ $s_w = s_w(M/P)$	(12)
$P = f(w, rP);$ $b = L/X = f_\omega(\omega, r)$;	(13)
$\quad 1/u = K/X = f_r(\omega, r)$	

tions. The latter can range from tax/transfer policies through actions such as price and import controls to labor market regulation and nationalization of firms. Shifts in distribution can be specified by changes in π, τ, or ω.

Any one of these parameters identifies the others. For example, $1 + \tau = 1/(1 - \pi)$. We use this formula to restate the markup rule (2) as equation (3) in Table 4.1, which is a compact rendition of Kaleckian macroeconomics in an economy closed to foreign trade. Equation (4) expresses the real wage in terms of the profit share. The output-capital ratio u (which as usual we take as a measure of economic activity) is defined by (5). The profit rate r is identically equal to the product of the profit share and the output-capital ratio, equation (6).

Let g^i stand for investment demand, expressed as the growth rate of the capital stock (ignoring depreciation, g^i is the ratio of real investment to capital). Kalecki assumed that g^i depends on the profit rate r as an index of expected future earnings. Kaldor (1940) and Kalecki's colleague Steindl (1952) introduced the output-capital ratio u as another variable affecting g^i. Its influence can be rationalized by the observation that when the economy normally operates below full capacity, then a higher level of capacity utilization is likely to stimulate faster accumulation. Dutt and Rowthorn picked up on the Kaldor-Steindl formulation, writing investment functions in forms similar to the one appearing after the first equals sign in (7). The expression after the second equality follows from (6), and the function $g^i = g^i(\pi, u)$ with both partial derivatives positive can be postulated as a general description of investment demand.

Let g^s stand for the capital growth rate permitted by saving supply, that is, national saving divided by the value of the capital stock PK. In

(8), saving comes from markup and wage income at rates s_π and s_w respectively. If workers don't save ($s_w = 0$), (8) reduces to the "Cambridge equation" embedded (with $s_\pi = 1$) in Table 1.1: $g^s = s_\pi \pi u = s_\pi r$. More generally, we have $g^s = s(\pi)u$, with $s(\pi)$ an increasing function of π when $s_\pi > s_w$.[2]

Macro equilibrium based upon (3)–(8) occurs when excess commodity demand is zero, or (9) is satisfied. Before we use this equation to figure out the effect on output of changes in the income distribution, a word should be added about the formulas in (10). They complete the model with the simplest possible money market specification, omitting interest rate effects to force a sharp contrast between structuralist and monetarist views.

The main point is that the system (3)–(9) solves for all variables appearing in (10) except M and V. The simplest Kalecki model presupposes endogenous money in the Banking School tradition discussed in Chapter 3. Relative *and* absolute prices are being determined in the nonmonetary part of the economy by institutional forces; therefore, M and/or V must be endogenous. It is easy to verify that proportional changes in absolute prices leave the real equilibrium unchanged, so that the model "dichotomizes" in the sense of Patinkin (1966).

An alternative approach is to assume that M is predetermined and V an institutional constant. Then for a predetermined real wage or income distribution, the money wage w has to be endogenous. This reading is crucial to orthodox recommendations to cut money wages to raise output, and to impose tight money to slow inflation. In practice, proactive monetary policy is usually only attempted in connection with aggressive stabilization packages, as in the United States under the lash of Paul Volcker's interest rate hikes in 1979. Predictably, instead of rapidly slowing inflation, very tight money forced the economy into a prolonged recession. As is usually the case, the output and employment slump did finally wring out inflation, but at substantial social cost.

For now, we take macro equilibrium to follow from (3)–(9) with w predetermined and M and/or V tagging along from (10). The real wage is also predetermined, and output (or the output/capital ratio u) adjusts to ensure demand-supply balance. Standard arguments show that this system will be stable when investment responds less strongly than saving to an increase in output. Formally, the stability condition is[3]

$$\Delta = s_\pi \pi + s_w(1 - \pi) - g^i_u > 0, \tag{14}$$

where g^i_u is the partial derivative of the investment function with respect to u. If this inequality is violated, short-run equilibrium will be unstable.

For future reference, note that Harrod's (1939) growth model can be interpreted as a dynamic extension of the unstable case. As discussed in Chapter 5, his "knife-edge" of instability was sharp because of an accelerator-based investment function with dg^i/dt instead of g^i as the left-hand-side variable.

To show the effect of a change in the profit share on output, we can differentiate the macro-balance condition (9) to get

$$\frac{du}{d\pi} = \frac{g_\pi^i - (s_\pi - s_w)u}{\Delta}. \tag{15}$$

From (14), the denominator on the right-hand side is positive. Equation (15) shows that income redistribution in favor of profits will stimulate economic activity if workers have a relatively high saving share and/or the effect of the profit share on investment is strong. From the linearized investment function in (7), the latter condition applies when the profit rate coefficient α is big. Real wage cuts boost aggregate demand when saving propensities from different income flows are similar and/or investors react with agility to profit signals.

With regard to other key variables, one can show that the profit rate r rises with a higher real wage if β in (7) exceeds s_w. Redistribution toward labor stimulates consumer demand. A strong investment response to higher consumption offsets the lower value of π in (6) with a higher u. This "win-win" distributional scenario runs directly counter to the inverse wage/profit trade-off built into the prices of production and neoclassical cost function models of Chapter 2, and is an intriguing aspect of Kaleckian macroeconomics.

Similar reasoning applies to the capital stock growth rate. The sign of $dg/d\pi$ is positive if $\alpha s_w - \beta(s_\pi - s_w) > 0$. A lower real wage speeds growth in the absence of the accelerator. It slows the economy if the accelerator is strong ($\beta >> 0$) and saving from wage income is lower than saving from profits. As discussed in later chapters, an extended version of the present model arrives at steady-state growth upon convergence of dynamic processes affecting the income distribution; the condition just stated signifies that the growth rate is "endogenous" in the sense that it differs across steady states.

As noted above, the ambiguous effects of real wage changes on output, the profit rate, and growth have been the subject of much recent debate in the structuralist literature. Following Bhaduri and Marglin (1990), an output increase in response to redistribution toward labor may be called "stagnationist" or "wage-led"—redistribution favoring workers activates an otherwise stagnant system (in an example of the "paradox of costs," to apply another label). The opposite case in which output is "profit-led" also becomes "exhilarationist" as a natural piece of jargon.

As we will see shortly, there is no certainty with regard to the shape or slope of the income distribution versus aggregate demand relationship, but one might "naturally" suppose that a higher profit share will stimulate capital formation more strongly when the share itself is low, that is, α in (7) is an inverse function of π or a direct function of ω. If so, the "Output response" relationship between the real wage ω and the output/capital ratio u is illustrated by Figure 4.1, which reintroduces the capacity utilization/real wage plane already used in Chapter 2. Macro equilibrium always lies somewhere along the curve—the activity level is picked out by the profit share or real wage. As the schedule is drawn, the economy is wage-led for low values of ω and profit-led for high ones because of stronger profit effects on investment as the real wage rises. Of course there are other possibilities, such as wage-led growth at low levels of capacity utilization (the 1930s?) and profit-led otherwise. This scenario would make the Output response curve look like an inverted U instead of the backwards C in Figure 4.1.

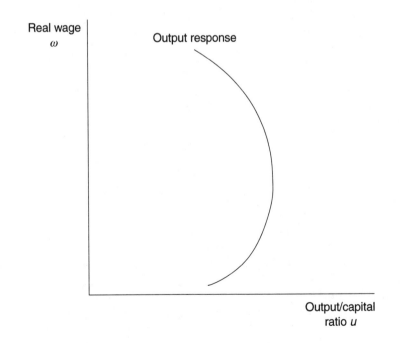

Figure 4.1
Relationship between the real wage and output with no capacity constraint.

2. Macro Adjustment via Forced Saving and Real Balance Effects

Mainstream authors often want to make production subject to an upper bound. In the basic version of Say's Law for industrialized economies, the limiting factor is the supply of labor $\bar{L}$, so that in equation (11) $\bar{u} = b\bar{L}$. This restriction appears as the vertical line for a "Capacity limit" in Figure 4.2. What are the implications in a Kaleckian model?

In the diagram, macro equilibrium lies on the thickened segments of the curves. The economy may operate below capacity either along the wage-led segment AB or in the profit-led range CD of the Output response curve. Along the segment BC, production constraints bind. Below full capacity, adjustment of output toward the relevant curve is usually assumed to be rapid, as shown by the small arrows.

The interesting question is how demand is limited to supply when capacity constraints start to bind, due for example to progressive income redistribution in a wage-led economy, expansionary policy which shifts the entire Output response curve to the right, or an adverse supply shock that makes $\bar{u}$ drop. Three mechanisms are likely to be important in practice—forced saving, real balance effects, or the inflation tax. In an open economy, changes in net imports can play a major role.

In the model of Table 4.1, forced saving kicks in when the capacity

Figure 4.2
Modes of adjustment with and without a binding capacity constraint.

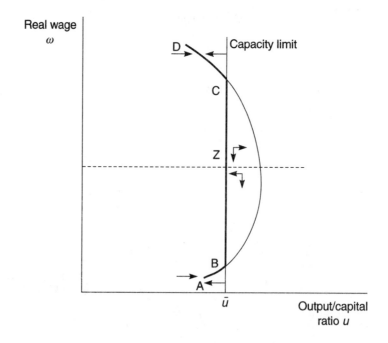

constraint (11) is added to the preceding equations. There is a standard overdetermination problem with one more equation than there are variables. This problem resolves itself, however, insofar as an incipient excess of aggregate demand over capacity makes prices rise. If the money wage is not fully indexed to inflation, the markup τ and profit share π increase, becoming endogenous, equilibrating macroeconomic variables. The real wage falls, reducing demand, output, and very possibly the rate of capital stock growth in a wage-led system.

This form of short-run inflationary adjustment via workers' forced saving toward limited capacity is stable in the wage-led case—the segment BZ in Figure 4.2.[4] If the economy is profit-led—segment ZC—price increases raise profits, stimulate investment, and lead toward hyperinflation in response to an initial increment in demand. Harrodian instability shows up in divergent prices instead of output levels.

Although it still hovers in the background, forced saving lost its star role in mainstream macroeconomics between 1930 and 1936, the respective publication years of Keynes's *Treatise on Money* and *General Theory* (perhaps in line with the shift in the business cycle from price toward quantity variations, as discussed in Chapter 3). Much macroeconomic discourse, however, centers around an inverse relationship between the price level and real effective demand (the "aggregate demand curve") of the sort that forced saving provides. When such a linkage was again needed after the Great Depression, it found its mainstream rationale not in real wage reduction, but in lower real wealth.

The real balance or quantity theory explanation for the inverse price-demand relationship is an essential component of the orthodox argument for cutting money wages to stimulate employment, as we will see in section 3. Its prominence helps explain the disinterest in differential saving propensities across income classes that most post–World War II economists have displayed (recent exceptions are mentioned in section 12).

The adjustment scenario resembles the inflation tax, but with a jump in P instead of $\hat{P}$. An initial price increase when capacity limits are reached will reduce real balances or the money stock divided by the price level. With the real value of their assets cut back by this change, wealth-holders save more to compensate, cutting consumption. From an investment function like (7), capital formation follows in train.

The real balance process runs parallel to forced saving. In practice, the two modes of adjustment are hard to tell apart. In the model world, however, the real balance effect is easy to incorporate by adding (12) to the full capacity specification. The saving rates s_π and s_w become inverse functions of M/P, the real value of the nominal money stock M. But

P is directly related to τ and π (a higher markup goes together with higher prices and lower real balances), so the saving rates rise with π. Another negative term $-u[\pi(ds_\pi/d\pi) + (1 - \pi)(ds_w/d\pi)]$ shows up in the numerator of (15). Profit-led adjustment to distributional changes becomes more likely, since markup increases cut demand by reducing both real wages and wealth.

Another way to evade capacity limitations is to bring in imports freely—such a move could be treated formally in the model structure here by including imports relative to capital stock as one more negative term in (9). Macro adjustment via wholesale importation has been important in practice (recall France under early Mitterrand where household durable goods highly prized by wage earners led the import surge after progressive redistribution, the United States under Reagan's expansionary fiscal policy and Clinton's household consumption boom, and countless external crises in the Third World) and no doubt will remain so in the future.

3. Real Balances, Input Substitution, and Money-Wage Cuts

So far, wage cutting is no panacea. If capacity limits don't bind, policies aimed at shifting the income distribution in favor of profits may well reduce output and employment. When the economy tends toward demand levels exceeding capacity, real wage reductions induced by inflation may help restore equilibrium, but will be less necessary when real balance effects are strong.

In view of these observations, why does wage restraint remain a central orthodox theme? At least as far as output responses are concerned, the answer hinges on positing the real balance effect as the unique or at least dominant macro adjustment mechanism, in conjunction with neoclassical input substitution. Building on Pigou (1943), Patinkin (1966) is the central text in this regard. The work it summarizes established the "neoclassical synthesis" (or "bastard Keynesianism" in Joan Robinson's phrase) that flourished through the early 1960s and pointed the way toward the monetarist and new classical revolutions that followed. New Keynesianism can be viewed as a high-tech attempt to steer the profession back toward an imperfectly competitive version of Patinkin.

To see the logic, we proceed by stages, first recalling that Keynes in *The General Theory* was adamant in insisting that cutting money wages would not effectively raise employment. He presented arguments along two lines.

We have already encountered the first in connection with Dunlop's wage contours and the Taylor inflation model in Chapter 2. It was essentially practical ("not theoretically fundamental" in Keynes's words). Wage reductions have to be made in piecemeal fashion, but each such attempt would be resisted by the affected group because not only its real but its relative income position would be eroded. Even if, as Keynes accepted in *The General Theory*, a lower economy-wide real wage is essential to stimulate employment, "wage-wage" conflicts will make this goal very difficult to achieve by negotiated contract revisions.

The second argument is that at least insofar as its first-order effects are concerned, cutting the money wage cannot result in real wage reduction. This result is easy to see in a Kaleckian model. In light of the markup equation (1), such a change does not affect the output level. Prices just fall in proportion to wages, the profit share and real wage are unchanged, and macro equilibrium remains wherever it was along the output response schedule in Figure 4.1.

The General Theory differs from Kalecki by building in the "first classical postulate" that the real wage equals the marginal product of labor under a regime of decreasing returns to additional employment. Following the analysis in Chapter 2, a contemporary way to fit this view into our equations is to drop the markup rule (3) of Table 4.1, and use the neoclassical supply specification appearing in (13) instead. This move amounts to replacing imperfect competition in the product market and a constant marginal (= average) product of labor with perfect competition and a marginal product that falls when output rises. In (13), $P = f(w, rP)$ is a linearly homogeneous cost function consistent with an aggregate production function having constant returns to scale in capital and labor. As we have seen, it can be restated as a wage-profit frontier in the form $f(\omega, r) = 1$. Input demands follow from Shephard's Lemma, where f_ω and f_r stand for partial derivatives.

To see how the argument works, assume for a moment that the real balance effect is inoperative. In terms of the real wage ω, the macro balance equation (9) can be written as

$$g^i(\omega, u) - [s_\pi - (s_\pi - s_w)\omega b]u = 0, \tag{16}$$

where the profit share π can be replaced by the real wage in the investment function since one depends monotonically on the other along the wage-price frontier. Equation (16) is a restatement of the Output response curve, redrawn in Figure 4.3.

As observed in Chapter 2, this model also implies an inverse relationship between the output-capital ratio and the real wage. Lower labor cost means that more workers can be profitably employed, leading u to rise. This linkage underlies *The General Theory*'s real-side macro clo-

Figure 4.3
Keynesian determi-
nation of output and
the real wage.

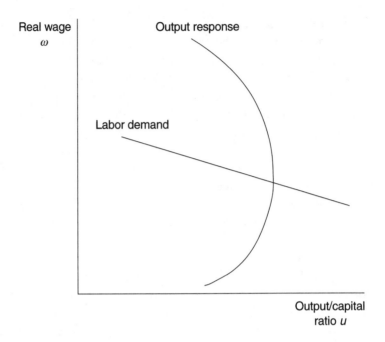

sure. It combines (13) with (4)–(10) in Table 4.1. For the moment, we retain the hypothesis of passive money.

The graphical solution is instructive. The negatively sloped "Labor demand" curve representing (13) in Figure 4.3 uniquely picks out macro
equilibrium, determining output and the real wage. Shifts in the Output
response schedule (from changing investment demand or fiscal moves)
modify the equilibrium position. Higher effective demand moves the
schedule to the right, causing employment to rise and the real wage
to fall. Reducing the money wage has no effect in this formulation precisely because the *real* wage is determined in Figure 4.3. A lower w
makes P drop in proportion, given effective demand. In a nutshell, this is
Keynes's "theoretically fundamental" argument against the power of
money-wage cuts.[5]

The conclusion does not depend on the slope of the Labor demand
schedule, as Keynes (1939) admitted after Dunlop and Tarshis showed
that the real wage rose with output over the business cycle. As discussed
in Chapters 7 and 9, extrapolating such a cyclical result to a steady-state
relationship of the sort depicted in Figure 4.3 is not a foolproof maneuver. But subject to this reservation, Keynes was willing to scrap the first
classical postulate and accept a positive association between the real
wage and output as an empirical likelihood, so long as his reasoning
about money wage changes went through.

Now we can reintroduce the real balance effect, which makes the saving rates s_π and s_w functions of real balances M/P, *not* the real wage w/P. Cutting the money wage reduces P through the cost function, raises M/P, and stimulates demand since wealth-holders feel richer. If the linkage is strong, Keynes's effective demand argument is undone (leaving out interest rate effects, which are brought in below).

Strong assumptions about model causality and empirical legitimacy are built into the real balance story. The causal question is whether money supply M is determined prior to the price level P. As noted in Chapter 3, there is no historical dearth of eminent economists willing to argue that endogenous rather than active money may usually be the rule. The empirical doubt is whether the postulated positive effect of price changes on saving rates in (16) overrides the other linkages in that equation.

The standard mainstream model answers both queries in the affirmative, dropping effective demand. In a popular stripped-down version, the quantity theory of money is transferred from the asset market to the real side of the system, and pressed into action as a shorthand representation of dominant real balance effects in demand. The model comprises equations (4)–(6), the second version of the quantity equation in (10) with predetermined M and V, and (13). Effective demand equations such as (7)–(9) don't get around much any more.[6]

In this setup, it is easy to verify from (10) that for a given money wage, the real wage increases along with capacity utilization. Higher output means that the price level must fall (and real wage rise) from the equation of exchange. The direction of macro causality is the reverse of the one pursued heretofore. It supports a "monetarist wage-led" theory of aggregate demand.

Equation (10) appears as the "Velocity" schedule in Figure 4.4. Its cross with the Labor demand curve (the same as in Figure 4.3) determines macro equilibrium. The new twist is the dependence of the Velocity relationship in (10) on the money wage w. Cutting w shifts the curve downward to the dashed position, reducing the real wage and raising output. A bigger money supply also leads u to rise and ω to fall because of a higher price level. With their relative importance depending on how easily new workers can be utilized (that is, on the value of a parameter like the elasticity of substitution), both employment gains and forced saving play roles in adjustment to the bigger money supply. As already observed in Chapter 3, over a period of fifty years, mainstream macroeconomics returned very close to post-Wicksell/pre-*General Theory* views about how equilibrium is attained.

In a preview of the mainstream models developed in Chapter 6, we can also sketch how the return extends to the long run, with a "natural"

Figure 4.4
The effect of a money-wage cut when aggregate demand is determined by the equation of exchange.

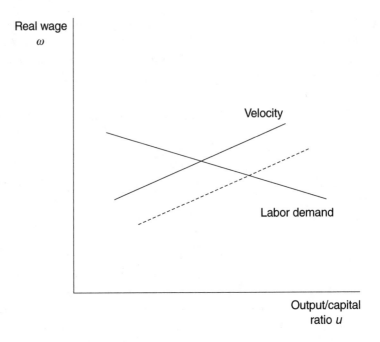

Figure 4.4
The effect of a money-wage cut when aggregate demand is determined by the equation of exchange.

rate of employment replacing Wicksell's rate of interest. It is easy to turn Figure 4.4's short-run adjustment into a process leading to the natural rate in steady state, following Friedman (1968) and later Fischer (1977) and John Taylor (1980). Suppose that for reasons of "expectational errors" (Friedman) or "staggered contracts" (Fischer and Taylor), the money wage responds to labor market disequilibrium according to a Phillips curve differential equation such as

$$\dot{w} = h(bu - \bar{\lambda}), \tag{17}$$

in which bu is the current labor/capital ratio, and $\bar{\lambda}$ is the ratio corresponding to zero wage pressure or the natural rate.

For a given capital stock, employment is an inverse function of w from Figure 4.4. The implication is that if bu drops below $\bar{\lambda}$, then w begins to fall, leading to real wage reduction, new hiring, and restoration of equilibrium at $bu = \bar{\lambda}$. At this long-run stable position, u is at its natural rate level and ω comes from (13). Hence from (10) the money wage is also determined. All nominal prices follow from $MV = PX$; there is no room in a monetarist steady state for institutional influences on either the real or the money wage. Macroeconomic adjustment relying on real balance effects is institutionally overdetermined.

This observation harks back to the discussion of "nominal anchors" for the price system in Chapter 2. In the monetarist long run of Figure 4.4, the money supply is the anchor; through the cost function the money wage must adjust to ratify the price level emerging from the equation of exchange. In his preferred short run, Keynes reasoned in exactly the opposite direction. Institutional forces in the labor market don't necessarily hold the money wage constant, but do dictate how it varies over time. The price level follows from the cost function, and the role of the policy-determined money supply is to regulate the interest rate and thereby effective demand. Just how this is supposed to happen is the topic we take up next.

4. Liquidity Preference and Marginal Efficiency of Capital

Go back to scheme (1). Keynes's treatment of the interest rate and investment demand determines its linear causal chain. He forged it in the early 1930s after breaking away from the natural rate theory of Wicksell and the *Treatise on Money*.

Reading left to right in (1), a key link ties investment I to the interest rate i. In fact, there are at least two distinct investment models in the book: the "marginal efficiency of capital" (MEC) story in Chapter 12 and a much more interesting discussion of asset pricing in Chapter 17, sketched in section 8 below.

MEC analysis is pretty standard. It follows from Keynes's mentor Marshall and the profitability calculations characteristic of Irving Fisher. Each firm is supposed to have a schedule (probably a step function) with a generally negative slope relating the expected return on investment on the vertical axis to the volume undertaken on the horizontal. The firm invests until the rate of return on its "last" project falls to the market rate of interest. Aggregating across firms gives the economy-wide MEC schedule.[7] If rate of return and interest rate do not get fully equalized (for a variety of "frictional" reasons), then the investment demand function (7) in Table 4.1 extends naturally to the form

$$g^i = g_0 + \alpha r + \beta u - \theta i, \tag{18}$$

which we have already met (without the accelerator term βu) in connection with the Ramsey model in Chapter 3.

Like all algebra, (18) elides a major theme in Keynes's thought—the existence of fundamental uncertainty. Its essence is best seen using the distinction drawn by the early Chicago economist Frank Knight (1921) between "risk" and "uncertainty." Probability distributions can be assigned for risk; human knowledge is insufficient to apply probability calculus to much of our future prospect, which is truly "uncertain."[8]

The General Theory and follow-up contributions such as Keynes (1937a) are replete with eloquence (some reproduced below) about how the "dark forces of time and ignorance" require that investment decisions be undertaken in conditions of fundamental uncertainty in Knight's sense. Therefore, the "expectational" element in investment looms large. In algebraic terms, r in (18) should be replaced by an expected profit rate r^e with properties that cannot be formalized, the intercept term g_0 can jump up or down unpredictably as "animal sprits" change, and so on. For computation of economic prospects even in the near future, there is no reason to expect the parameters in an investment function like (18) to be stable or even well defined.

The same observations apply to the "liquidity preference" relationship which determines the interest rate from the real money supply M/P. The formal part of the story is that demand for real money has two components. The first is for "transactions," proportional to the level of output X or capacity utilization u along the lines of the equation of exchange (another hand-me-down to Keynes from Marshall). "Speculative" demand, on the other hand, depends inversely on the rate of interest i. Keynes rationalized its existence by invoking the market for bonds (an institutional feature that may or may not be present in any given economy).

The simplest version of the argument rests on the well-known inverse relationship between the price of a bond and its current interest rate (discussed in detail in the following section). Suppose that somebody expects the interest rate next "period" to be higher than it is now, so that the bond price is necessarily expected to be lower at that time. Then if the player buys a bond today, she or he will anticipate a capital loss that may be big enough to offset the bond's coupon payment. Given the low current interest rate, it may be wiser not to buy at all, and stay "liquid" by holding money instead. After all, the bond is expected to cost less in the future.

At worst, this narrative suggests that the interest rate is at the level it is because it isn't at another. A more generous interpretation is that liquidity preference involves "bootstrap" dynamics whereby the "tone and feel" of the financial market evolve over time, with changing perceptions about future interest rates affecting current preferences for liquidity. There may or may not be a steady-state "natural" interest rate as a center of gravitation for this process. Keynes's pronouncements on this point were Delphic, for reasons to be discussed in the following sections.

But he was clear that like investment demand (18), the money demand function

$$M/P = \mu(X, i) \tag{19}$$

is not going to be notably stable over time.

A final comment is that a specification like (19) marks a significant break from previous analysis by relating the interest rate and rates of return more generally to *stocks* of real and financial claims rather than *flows* of the sort built into real and loanable funds theories. Beyond liquidity preference, moving from a flow to stock formulation for financial analysis ranks with the principle of effective demand as one of Keynes's greatest contributions in *The General Theory*. Tables 1.4 and 1.5 show that outstanding liabilities of the business sector and government are about two times GDP. Many of these securities turn over every day, and derivative contracts effectively make the turnover of outstanding paper many times larger. Bringing these transactions in stocks into the purview of macroeconomics was a major accomplishment.

5. Liquidity Preference, Fisher Arbitrage, and the Liquidity Trap

Thinking about financial markets in terms of stocks, in particular stocks of bonds subject to capital gains and losses, raises many analytical questions. One set came to the fore in the 1990s in policy debates about the relevance of Keynes's "liquidity trap" to issues such as the effects on interest rates of changing inflation rates, for example, in Japan's "post-bubble" economy. A flash forward makes sense before we summarize *The General Theory*'s central messages in section 6, and go on to mainstream reactions thereto.

Kregel (2000) points out that there are at least three theories of the liquidity trap in the literature—Keynes's own analysis in Chapter 15 of *The General Theory*, Hicks's glosses in his 1936 and 1937 reviews of the book, and a view that can be attributed to Irving Fisher in the 1930s and Paul Krugman (1998) in latter days. We will take these alternatives in order, devoting the most space to Keynes. His central question was about how prices of long bonds react to changes in their interest rates. As pointed out above, an investor is likely to opt for "liquidity" or holding (something like) money as opposed to a long bond if she or he expects the relevant interest rate to rise, causing a capital loss on the bond that may exceed the interest or "running yield" it will provide.

To make this insight more precise, we can work through the details for two sorts of bonds—"consols" (a nickname for British government securities resulting from a loan consolidation in 1751) which promise to pay a coupon value of one dollar in perpetuity and "zeros" with no coupon but which will be redeemed at face value upon maturity. Zeros thereby sell at a discount until they can be cashed out. The relevant interest rates are i_c and i_z respectively. For reference, the short-term nominal and real rates are i and j respectively. For Fisher and Krugman, in particular, j amounts to a natural rate emerging from the market for loanable funds.

In continuous time, the value C of a consol is

$$C = \int_0^\infty \exp(-i_c t)dt = 1/i_c.$$

The question at hand is how C changes in response to a shift in i_c. The log-derivative (called "modified duration" in finance jargon, as an indicator of the "length" of the bond's payment stream) is

$$dC/C = (-1/i_c)di_c.$$

Keynes was interested in how a change in i_c would affect the return R_c to holding a consol for a short time δ. From the equation just above, the answer turns out to be

$$R_c\delta = \frac{(i_c C + dC)\delta}{C} = (i_c + \frac{dC}{C})\delta = i_c(1 - \frac{di_c}{i_c^2})\delta. \qquad (20C)$$

Formulas like the one to the right are sometimes called "Keynes's square rule" after a notably obscure numerical example on p. 202 of *The General Theory*. Obscurity notwithstanding, its conclusion is worth quoting: "If, however, the rate of interest is already as low as 2 per cent, the running yield will only offset a rise in it of as little as 0.04 per cent per annum. This, indeed, is perhaps the chief obstacle to a fall in the rate of interest to a very low level. . . . [A] long-term rate of interest of (say) 2 per cent leaves more to fear than to hope, and offers, at the same time, a running yield which is only sufficient to offset a very small measure of fear." At $i_c = 0.02$ (or something similar), the risk of capital loss due to being illiquid is very high if the rate is one day expected to rise to a "normal" level, while the return itself is very low. Hence most investors will already be liquid and the rate is unlikely to fall much further.

The story is broadly similar for a "zero" held at time zero and maturing at time T. Its value is

$$Z = \exp(-i_z T).$$

The analog to (20C) is

$$R_z\delta = i_z(1 - \frac{T}{i_z}di_z)\delta. \tag{20Z}$$

Note that the coefficient on $-di_z/i_z$ is T which will be "large," in many cases more than 10. By the square rule, the same observation applies to the coefficient $1/i_c$ on $-di_c/i_c$ in (20C).

On the basis of these examples, let i_l stand for a generic long rate and $E(di_l)$ be its expected change. If the ongoing inflation rate is $\hat{P}$, Fisher-style arguments about time preference combined with liquidity preference suggest that under near-perfect arbitrage i_l should satisfy a relationship such as

$$i_l[1 - (\phi/i_l)E(di_l)] = \rho + i = \rho + j + \hat{P}, \tag{21}$$

in which ρ is a "risk premium" on long bonds that would equal zero under long-range completely perfect foresight. As in (20C) and (20Z) the coefficient ϕ/i_l multiplying the expected change in the long rate is "large."

Three conclusions follow.

First, for a given inflation rate, $E(di_l) > 0$ means that asset-holders will think twice about investing long. The equality in (21) could easily be violated, with the left-hand side being less than $\rho + i$ or $\rho + j + \hat{P}$ and very possibly negative. This is the essence of liquidity preference, at least with regard to holding bonds.

Second, if arbitrage rules and equality holds in (21), a jump in the inflation rate will *not* be met by a proportional increase in i_l if $E(di_l) \neq 0$. As stressed by Kregel (2000), Fisher arbitrage does not apply in general to long rates and one has to tell a more complicated story. An example is presented momentarily.

Finally, a "normal" yield curve is characterized by the inequality $i_l > i$—long rates are generally higher than short. The main observed exception for the U.S. economy is a flat or inverted yield curve in advance of the onset of recession (Estrella and Mishkin 1996), due mainly to upward movements in short rates. A typical regression equation takes the form $i_l = \alpha + \beta i$, with α having a value of a few hundred basis points (a few percentage points) and β a bit less than one. From (21), the risk premium ρ is small and the implicit expectation underlying a rising curve must be $E(di_l) > 0$. However, given the likely magnitude of the coefficient ϕ/i_l and the fact that β is close to one, the anticipated upward drift in i_l need not be brisk.

From a contemporary perspective, it is tempting to use (21) in a dynamic context to analyze the interactions of the interest and inflation rates. Naturally, this is done assuming myopic perfect foresight or $E(di_l)$ = di_l.[9] Setting $\rho = 0$ for simplicity, we get a differential equation for i_l,

$$di_l/dt = (1/\phi)(i_l - \hat{P} - j). \tag{22}$$

Unsurprisingly, the positive effect of i_l on its time-derivative makes (21) unstable. However, the interest rate response to a shock to the right-hand side will be sluggish since the coefficient $1/\phi$ will be "small." In practice, long rates tend to be substantially less volatile than shorts.

In a stripped-down model, it is simplest to assume that the time-derivative of the inflation is observed perfectly, and satisfies

$$d\hat{P}/dt = -\eta i_l - v\hat{P} + \Gamma. \tag{23}$$

The coefficient η would normally be assumed to be positive but small— an increase in the long rate would slow inflation by reducing aggregate (especially investment) demand but the effect might not be very strong. If $v > 0$ inflation tends to be self-stabilizing, and Γ represents an inflationary shock. It is easy to verify that the Jacobian of the system (22)–(23) has a negative determinant and an ambiguously signed trace—we are back in saddlepoint country with i_l as the jumping variable. The phase diagram appears in Figure 4.5.

Figure 4.5
Dynamics of long-term interest and inflation rates.

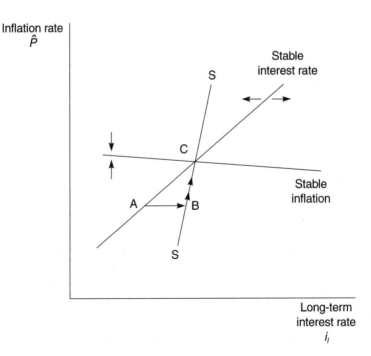

Suppose the system is initially at point A, but then Γ increases so that the Stable inflation locus along which $d\hat{P}/dt = 0$ shifts upward. The new equilibrium is at C, where the inflation curve intersects with the Stable interest rate curve along which $i_l = j + \hat{P}$ and $di_l/dt = 0$. As illustrated, the dynamics involve an upward jump of i_l from A to B, and then a steady increase in both variables to the new steady state (at which, a bit unrealistically, there is a flat yield curve with $i_l = i$).[10] Reading the diagram in reverse, a deflationary shock would cause i_l to jump downward, and then both variables would decline. Either way, although in a standard rational expectations (and bond market?) narrative the interest rate jumps in anticipation of an oncoming inflation or deflation, it undershoots in the sense that it does not immediately arrive at its new equilibrium level.

We will return to the policy implications of Figure 4.5, but first a few words about the two other interpretations of the liquidity trap mentioned above. In his first review of *The General Theory*, Hicks (1936) saw a stable value of the interest rate as requiring an elastic supply of consumption goods (in other words, output is the macroeconomic adjusting variable) and an elastic supply of money at some (low) level of i. In the IS/LM diagram that Hicks (1937) introduced in his second review, the LM curve will have a horizontal section that may coexist with low levels of u and i "on the left side" of the picture. For an example, see Figure 4.7 below. With low effective demand and the flat LM schedule, monetary policy becomes ineffective—the traditional metaphor is "pushing on a string."

In postulating an elastic money supply (at least at a low rate), Hicks joined hands with the Banking School and the post-Keynesians but was not wholly consistent with Keynes, as the latter pointed out in correspondence. On the other hand, the horizontal LM segment *is* a visually striking way of representing the flight to liquidity that can ensue when i_l is low, $E(di_l)$ is positive, and the expression on the left-hand side of (21) has a value close to or less than zero.

The Fisher-Krugman theory can be illustrated with the standard loanable funds diagram in Figure 4.6. Saving and investment are supposed to depend on the real return to capital j, which by Fisher arbitrage in turn should be equal to $i - \hat{P}$. For historical reasons investment demand may have declined (shifted left) and saving supply increased (shifted right) to such an extent that they only intersect at a negative real rate j_{trap}. The nominal rate i, however, can only fall to zero. To get a negative real rate and raise investment, the only recourse is to increase the rate of inflation with the nominal rate somehow held constant to make $i - \hat{P} < 0$. Such was Fisher's advice to President Franklin D. Roosevelt in the 1930s and

Figure 4.6
A Fisher-Krugman
liquidity trap.

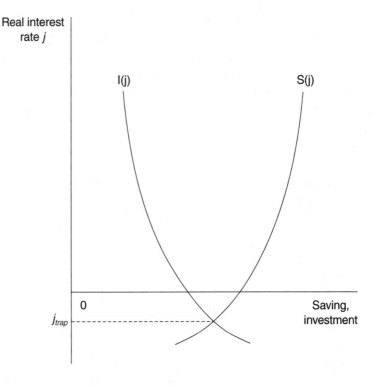

Krugman's to the Japanese central bank sixty-odd years later. Moreover, according to Krugman the bank has a credibility problem in that it truly has to make an effort to emit money in increasing volume over time to set off a Cagan-style inflationary process. A simple once-off increase will just make P jump from the equation of exchange and not force $\hat{P}$ to become convincingly positive.

With regard to practical matters, Keynes himself saw the appearance of a true liquidity trap as hypothetical: "whilst this limiting case might become practically important in the future, I know of no example of it heretofore" (p. 207). Suppose we take Japan as the "future example." What can be said with regard to policy?

The traditional "Keynesian" recommendation is to take advantage of the horizontal LM segment by boosting aggregate demand. In Japan beginning in the 1990s, after a period of highly contractionary monetary policy aimed at deflating the 1980s asset price bubble once and for all, such efforts took the form of fiscal expansion in an economy in which demand had historically been export-led. One important outcome was a big increase in the fiscal debt/GDP ratio—a potential stock/flow disequilibrium of a sort not addressed by Keynes but of great concern to successors such as Wynne Godley (see Chapters 1 and 8 herein). If the government has become debt-constrained and export growth prospects are limited, then boosting consumption demand is the only remaining option. It may or may not be possible to convince Japanese households to save less and thereby boost demand (a linkage sometimes called the "paradox of thrift"), but in analytical terms their spending behavior has no direct connection with a liquidity trap. Keynes, to be sure, did see a high national saving rate and a yearning for liquidity as a combined recipe for stagnation. More on that in Chapter 8.

Inducing inflation also has its complications, on rational choice grounds. If Fisher arbitrage happens and the right-most equality holds in (21) with the real rate j taking a value somewhere between Figure 4.6's j_{trap} and zero, then any successful attempt to raise $\hat{P}$ will simply increase i as well, leaving the real return to investment unchanged. This is, after all, the traditional quantity theory story about how the nominal interest rate gets determined. Furthermore, the rational expectations extension of (21) to the dynamic system (22)–(23) suggests that the nominal long rate i_l will jump in anticipation of any future inflationary process, inflicting capital losses on long bonds and raising the short-term cost of financing investment projects, thereby making the current effective demand shortfall worse. For an economy successfully to inflate its way out of a liquidity trap, the monetary authorities would have to be able to control both the short and the long segments of the nominal yield curve (as well as, one might add, the volume of capital movements across their borders). It is not obvious that the Bank of Japan could or ever would choose to wield such extensive powers.

6. The System as a Whole

Perhaps it is a relief to turn from the late-twentieth-century problems of Japan—with clear Keynesian characteristics but no obvious solutions—to ask how *The General Theory*'s model hangs together. Using equations written out above, a revised version of the causal chain in (1) takes the form:

$$\begin{matrix} w \Rightarrow P \\ M \end{matrix} \Rightarrow \begin{matrix} i \text{ from (19)} \Rightarrow g^i \text{ from (18)} \\ s_\pi, s_w \text{ from (12)} \Rightarrow g^s \text{ from (8)} \end{matrix} \Rightarrow u \text{ from (9).} \qquad (24)$$

Besides feedback effects of X or u (and $r = \pi u$) in (18) and (19) which are taken up in section 7, (24) incorporates two major changes in comparison with (1). First, a lower nominal wage causes the price level to fall, the real money stock M/P to rise, and thereby savings rates s_π and s_w to decline—this is the real balance effect. Second, via the liquidity preference relationship (19), a higher level of M/P will drive the interest rate down, stimulating investment demand through the "Keynes effect." Nominal wage reductions stimulate effective demand and employment in two ways, contrary to a central tenet of *The General Theory*. What has gone wrong?

"Very little," the Master might reply. Keynes did not mention the real balance effect in *The General Theory*. If he had, he almost certainly would have dismissed it as a theoretical curiosum with scant empirical relevance. As discussed in section 10, the significance of wealth changes for saving and consumption decisions remains controversial to this day, especially in the Keynesian short run. The American stock market plunges of 1987 and 2000–2001 did not reduce aggregate consumption visibly, although they did cut back on sales of yuppie artifacts like $30,000 imported cars.

Keynes's counterargument to his own "effect" is that cutting money wages to reduce prices to reduce interest rates to stimulate investment demand is a tricky maneuver. The first lesson that every applied economist learns is not to give a lot of credence to long causal chains. Why not just increase the money supply directly? This is in fact his recommendation in Chapter 19 of *The General Theory*.

In sum, based on thoroughly neoclassical production theory and the principle of effective demand, the first-order argument in *The General Theory* is that reducing nominal wages will not successfully stimulate employment. Two distinctly second-order arguments (one introduced by Keynes himself) go the other way. Insofar as any debate in economics can be settled a priori, one might think that Keynes had won.

Posterity, however, judged differently, reversing the priority of the arguments just mentioned. Less than a decade after *The General Theory* was published, we find Modigliani (1944) observing that "it is the fact that money wages are *too high* relative to the quantity of money that explains why it is unprofitable to expand employment to the 'full-employment' level" (emphasis added).

Why are wages "too high" instead of the money supply "too low"? One answer is that an economic expansion induced by increasing M might well be more inflationary than one resulting from a lower w. With rising prices, debtors would benefit and the real wealth of creditors would go down. Regardless of the motives behind the young Franco Modigliani's choice of wording six decades ago, it is pretty clear on which side of the debtor/creditor divide the majority of the economics profession would like to (and probably does) reside. Their preference for deflation over (moderate) inflation is in part class-determined, a thought developed further in Chapter 7.

7. The IS/LM Model

The missing elements in the discussion just concluded are the effects of changes in the output/capital ratio u and profit rate r on money demand in (19) and macroeconomic balance in (9). Such linkages were first brought into an explicit model with the celebrated "IS/LM" formulation of Hicks (1937), who also threw in a positive effect of the interest rate on saving for good measure.

IS/LM can be interpreted in many ways. One (voiced at times by Keynes) is that it is not a bad representation of at least the formal side of *The General Theory*. Another, expressed for example by Pasinetti (1974) and the papers in Eatwell and Milgate (1983), is that Hicks's machine perverts Keynes's vision by turning its clear causal structure into a mushy set of simultaneous equations while ignoring the social structures, incomplete information, and potential financial instability that are at its roots (perceptions that, in writing much later, Hicks (1980–81) seemed to share). In this reading, the underlying thrust of IS/LM effort was to turn *The General Theory* into an empirically dubious Special Case.

Be that as it may, it is still important to get Hicks on record. On the LM side of the economy, the presentation here is based on Tobin's (1969) approach to financial modeling. Tobin is faithful to Keynes in determining rates of return in markets for stocks of assets and liabilities. However, Tobin-style models like the one to follow usually take a Special Case or Walrasian tangent by adopting the "full employment" Modigliani-Miller (1958) financial market specification discussed in Chapter 1. Financial markets are cleared solely by adjustments in asset prices and rates of return (for alternative perspectives, see the following section and Chapter 8). By way of compensation for a super-orthodox LM as well as to avoid the complications introduced by the "first classical postulate," we then set up the price/quantity or IS side of the system along Kaleckian lines.

Table 4.2 presents balance sheets for the main financial actors. The wage earners and rentiers of Table 1.3 are consolidated into "households." Their portfolios contain money M, bonds or "T-bills" T_h emitted by the government, and the value of business equity $P_v V$. Following contemporary convention, bonds are treated as very short term ("overnight," say), so they pay only a running yield and we do not need to carry their price in the accounting. The benefit is convenience, at the cost of leaving out Keynes's liquidity preference rationale for holding money in the first place. Households' wealth Ω is the sum of their asset holdings: $\Omega = M + T_h + P_v V$ (note that V now stands for equity and not ve-

Table 4.2 Balance sheets for an IS/LM model.

Households		Business	
M	Ω	qPK	L
T_h			P_vV
P_vV			

Commercial Banks		Central Bank		Government
H	M	T_c	H	T
L				

locity). Households, business, banks, and so on are assumed to satisfy such restrictions at all times—there are no "black holes" in their balance sheets.

The asset value of business capital stock is qPK, with PK as replacement cost. Securities issued by business comprise equity and loans from banks L, and the sector's net worth is set to zero. The valuation ratio is "average q": $q = (L + P_vV)/PK$. Commercial banks lend to firms and issue money. Their reserve against deposits or "high-powered money," $H = M - L$, takes the form of claims on the central bank. The offsetting central bank asset is held as T-bills T_c, where T is the government's outstanding liability with a market-clearing condition

$$T_h + T_c = T.$$

The central bank can expand the stock of high-powered money by buying T-bills from households. The purchase drives up notional bond prices in the very short run, and thereby reduces the T-bill interest rate i.

Even highly aggregated financial systems like the one in Table 4.2 need a wagonload of symbols and equations to analyze. To begin with accounting, first note that consolidating entries across balance sheets and imposing the market-clearing condition for bonds shows that "primary wealth" in the system is

$$\Omega = qPK + T, \tag{25}$$

all ultimately held by households. As rationalized in Chapter 6, the Modigliani-Miller theorem says that businesses have zero net worth,

$$qPK = L + P_vV, \tag{26}$$

and that the sum of returns on business liabilities uses up the return to capital,

$$i_lL + i_vP_vV = \rho qPK = rPK.$$

The symbols are i_l as the rate of interest on loans from banks (not the long-term interest rate, as in section 5), i_v as the rate of return to holding equity, and ρ as the profit rate on the asset value of the capital stock (r is the profit rate figured with respect to replacement value). The total return to equity $i_v P_v V$ follows as the return to capital minus interest costs on loans.

If we let

$$\lambda = L/qPK, \tag{27}$$

then combining the equations above gives an expression for q:

$$q = r/[\lambda i_l + (1 - \lambda)i_v]. \tag{28}$$

That is, q is the ratio of the profit rate to a weighted average cost of financing a unit of capital (a result less compelling than appears at first glance since the weights themselves depend on q). Because $\rho q = r$, it follows that

$$\rho = \lambda i_l + (1 - \lambda)i_v.$$

The behavioral action subject to these accounting restrictions comes from the households' asset demand balances. They are

$$v(i_v, i, u)\Omega - P_v V = 0 \tag{29}$$

$$\tau(i_v, i, u)\Omega - T_h = 0 \tag{30}$$

$$\mu(i_v, i, u)\Omega - M = 0. \tag{31}$$

Equations (29)–(31) say that households spread their wealth over their three assets in the proportions v, τ, and μ subject to the constraint $v + \tau + \mu = 1$.[11] The demand proportions for shares, government bonds, and money are assumed principally to depend on the equity return i_v, the T-bill interest rate i, and the output/capital ratio u respectively.

As already noted, these equations work in the same way as do excess factor and commodity demand functions in a Walrasian system. In (29)–(31), rates of return and the price of equity adjust so that households absorb predetermined stocks of assets. Specifically, for given u and Ω, i_v and i in (30) and (31) follow from the supplies of money M and T-bills T_h. The equity price P_v is given by the demand function $v(i_v, i, u)\Omega$ and the supply of securities V in (29).

The last equations describe behavior of the banking system along highly traditional lines (analysis of asset and liability management on the part of banks is deferred to Chapter 8). Money supply is determined as a multiple of commercial bank reserves:

$$M = \zeta H = \zeta T_c. \tag{32}$$

The corresponding supply of bank loans is

$$L = (\zeta - 1)H. \tag{33}$$

The multiplier ζ will typically be the inverse of a required reserve ratio imposed by the banking authorities. Loan supply follows in (33) from the commercial banks' balance sheet identity.

The nine equations (25)–(33) determine nine variables: Ω, q, P_v, i_v, i_l, i, λ, M, and L. Variables coming from outside this system include r, u, and P from the IS part of the economy; V, T, and K from historical accumulation processes; and T_c and T_b from open market policy decisions.[12]

The implicit message of all this algebra is that the financial system works in myriad ways to balance claims among "agents" via movements in appropriate rates of return. Modifying the model to avoid this manifestly unreliable conclusion is a task left for later completion. For the moment, as far as money demand and supply are concerned, we can combine (31) and (32) to get the relationship

$$\mu(i_v, i, u)[(qPK/T) + 1] - \zeta(T_c/T) = 0. \tag{34}$$

The Hicksian interpretation is that the money demand proportion μ is an inverse function of the bond interest rate i and (perhaps) the return to equity i_v, and an increasing function of economic activity u. Demand for M is scaled by the expression $(qPK/T) + 1$, where the ratio qPK/T reflects the breakdown of primary wealth between physical capital and government liabilities. A higher value of capital relative to claims on the government means that money demand rises, bidding up interest rates. On the other hand, an increase in the outstanding stock of government debt T would reduce i, *if* the share T_c/T that is "monetized" is held constant.[13]

The overall money supply $\zeta(T_c/T)$ can be boosted by open market purchases to increase T_c or by an increase in the money/reserve ratio ζ. When $\zeta(T_c/T)$ goes up, the interest rate i has to fall to restore equilibrium. If (34) is interpreted as an excess money demand equation with i as the accommodating variable, then this adjustment is locally stable because $\partial\mu/\partial i < 0$.

Figure 4.7 gives the standard picture, with (34) represented by the upward-sloping LM curve. As discussed in Chapter 8, the Pasinetti/post-Keynesian position is that the interest rate is determined prior to the real

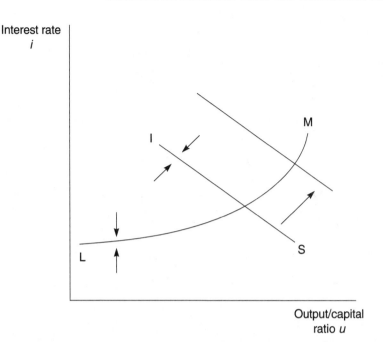

Figure 4.7
An IS/LM diagram with a Hicksian liquidity trap.

side of the system, so that LM has a shallow or horizontal slope.[14] The monetarist/Say's Law story is a near-vertical LM. Hicks deserves credit for coming up with a model which can capture such diametrically opposed ways of looking at the world.

An IS curve to cross with the LM is already implicit in equation (9) in Table 4.1. We can leave out the distributional issues discussed at length in sections 1–3 by holding the profit share π constant. To look at fiscal effects, it is convenient to bring in government spending (scaled by the capital stock) γ_g as a demand injection. Putting equations in the table together with the investment function (18) gives the condition that excess aggregate demand should be equal to zero:

$$\gamma_g + g_0 + (\alpha\pi + \beta)u - \theta i - [s_\pi\pi + s_w(1 - \pi)]u = 0. \tag{35}$$

If the output/capital ratio rises when the left-hand side of this equation is positive, short-term adjustment dynamics will be stable when the higher u stimulates investment less than saving, as already observed in connection with equation (14). If stability is assumed, excess aggregate demand is an inverse function of both u and i, meaning that the two variables trade off inversely to hold it equal to zero. The implication is that the IS curve slopes downward in Figure 4.7.

The standard thought experiment is to raise γ_g. IS shifts to the right, and both u and i increase. As the small arrows indicate, short-run adjustment dynamics to such a shock in (34)–(35) are stable. Because the interest rate goes up (at least outside the liquidity trap/post-Keynesian/Minskyan flat LM curve case), capital formation may be partially crowded out.

These results are not dissimilar to those of the Wicksellian model of Chapter 3, except that u replaces $\hat{P}$ as the jump variable and Figure 4.7 presupposes "fast" dynamics for i instead of its "slow" evolution in Figure 3.5. The first change is by far the more important. It explains why between the *Treatise* and *The General Theory* Keynes became the most important economist of the twentieth century instead of remaining merely a brilliant post-Wicksellian.

8. Maynard and Friends on Financial Markets

One of the joys of reading (and re-reading) *The General Theory* is to learn from Keynes how "really existing" capital markets really function. They are a far cry from the smoothly adjusting rates of return in equations (29)–(31), as illustrated with a couple of examples in this section. One shows how financial markets can help ratify macroeconomic equilibria in which Say's Law does not apply—they are a significant reason why capitalist economies may *not* be optimally self-adjusting.[15] The other demonstrates that insofar as capital markets generate sensible investment decisions, they do so only because social arrangements provide relatively stable background structures of expectations, prices, and costs. The contrast with the perfect market-clearing, rational expectations models set out in Chapter 6 is striking.

One source of instability and/or the persistence of socially undesirable macroeconomic situations lies with the behavior of individual market participants.[16] Speaking from his own time and place, in Chapter 12 on "The State of Long-Term Expectation" Keynes described financial markets as "beauty contests." He was thinking not of Miss Great Britain but rather of 1930s competitions in English tabloid newspapers in which readers were asked to rank photos of young women in the order of beauty that they thought would be given by the average preferences of all other competing readers. The winning player would express not his or her own preferences, nor a guess at genuinely average preferences, but rather would reach "the third degree where we devote our intelligences to anticipating what average opinion expects the average opinion to be." In financial markets, professionals dig even deeper; "there are some, I believe, who practice the fourth, fifth, and higher degrees" (p. 156).

There is no reason to expect a market—a financial market in particular—operating on such principles either to make correct assessments about the "beauty" or somewhat more tangible attributes of corporations such as their potential profitability, or to be stable against shocks: "A conventional valuation which is established as the outcome of the mass psychology of a large number of ignorant individuals is liable to change violently as a result of a sudden fluctuation of opinion due to factors which do not really make much difference to the prospective yield, since there will be no strong roots of conviction to hold it steady. In abnormal times, . . . the market will be subject to waves of optimistic and pessimistic sentiment, which are unreasoning and yet in a sense legitimate where no solid basis exists for a reasonable calculation" (p. 154).

Markets driven by average opinion about what average opinion will be demonstrate two special behavioral patterns. As the quotation states, in "abnormal times" they can be volatile and prone to severe loss of liquidity when all opinion shifts the same way. The liquidity squeeze can drive up the cost of capital, reduce investment, and slow growth in the medium run.

On the other hand, the prophecies of the market can be self-fulfilling: "We should not conclude from this that everything depends on waves of irrational psychology. On the contrary, the state of long-term expectations is often steady" (p. 162). Even so, such "equilibria" need not be socially desirable. Because it is shared by "a large number of ignorant individuals" (be they highly paid Wall Street professionals or otherwise), market opinion crystallizes around Keynes's "conventions," often in the form of simple slogans.

Eatwell (1996) argues that beginning in the 1970s, for example, market opinion insisted on government "credibility" in terms of tight monetary policy and a "prudent" contractionary fiscal stance. If the authorities did not comply by raising interest rates and cutting taxes and (especially) spending, the government's bonds would be sold off, cutting their prices and driving up interest rates anyway. In developed countries, at least, governments may have become prudent enough to accommodate to pressures from volatile bond and foreign exchange markets, and by the late 1980s volatility had declined. But at the same time real interest rates trended upward (on the whole, real rates in the 1990s were at historical highs with levels exceeding even those of the gold standard era one hundred years earlier), growth outside the United States was not outstanding, private firms cut back investment to levels consistent with slower output growth, and with reduced tax takes governments became even more fiscally constrained. And in developing economies after 1995, even extreme fiscal prudence could not ward off periodic financial crises spurred by capital flight—abnormal times were not few and far between.

The notable exception to this interpretation was the very Keynesian

"Goldilocks economy" in the United States in the late 1990s, when both liquidity preference and private savings rates were very low and the output surge plus rising tax revenue (in part made up of healthy capital gains taxes during the stock market boom) pushed the government into surplus. How the rapid reversal of these tendencies at the end of the decade (illustrated in Figures 1.1 and 1.2) will play out will only be known in years to come.

Chapter 17 on "The Essential Properties of Interest and Money" in *The General Theory* turns financial market stability on its head in an illuminating way. A major implication is that price inertia in real and financial markets is essential to a capitalist system. Following Galbraith and Darity (1994) and Panico (1988), the basic ideas are the following.

One can imagine a durable asset—a house, say—which can be purchased for a price P_t^a this period or else at a price P_{t+1}^a (paid now) for delivery next period. Typically $P_{t+1}^a > P_{t+1}^a$ so that there is a "spot premium" $(P_t^a/P_{t+1}^a > 1)$ or "forward discount" $(P_{t+1}^a/P_t^a < 1)$ on the asset. Both and P_t^a and P_{t+1}^a are observed in the market, but the same is not true of an expected price P_{t+1}^e for spot sales next period. This price can be used to define an "own-rate of return" ρ for the asset as[17]

$$\rho = [P_{t+1}^e - P_t^a]/P_t^a . \tag{36}$$

Besides a return, an asset is also likely to have a carrying cost between periods for storage, insurance, etc. On the other hand, if it can be sold rapidly for cash, it might also carry a liquidity premium (which would be low or negative for assets such as half-constructed houses). Let c and l stand for carrying cost and liquidity premium respectively. Then the overall return to owning the asset is $\rho - c + l$.

Fisher had already worked through the analytics of own-rates late in the nineteenth century (Schefold 1997). Sraffa (1932a,b) picked them up in a polemic with von Hayek (1931). From a contemporary perspective, Hayek resembles an OLG theorist contemplating an economy on the "wrong" side of the golden rule. Along Austrian lines, he argued that business cycles result from excessive capital deepening and production round-aboutness that occur because banks tend to hold the market interest rate below its "natural" level (for a formal example of such a cycle, see Chapter 9). Only a slump can undo the excessive capital formation. Moreover, attempts at expansionary policy during the downturn will just make the underlying situation worse.

In opposition, Sraffa said that the short-term interest rate i is at best a center of gravitation for the diverse own-rates of other assets. That is, for each commodity's and capital good's variables ρ, c, and l on the right-hand side, the relationship

$$i = \rho - c + l \tag{37}$$

will only hold approximately. Out of full equilibrium there are myriad observed own-rates. Even in equilibrium they will differ because they represent diverse trends in relative prices, as Fisher realized and as Pasinetti (1981) discusses at length. It is not possible to ascertain what the "natural" rate might be. No observable natural rate, no theory of the trade cycle, and no justification for Hayek's preferred contractionary monetary stance (especially because he himself did not think it makes a lot of sense to compute averages of rates of return across different sectors).

Ironically, Keynes to an extent argued along Hayek's lines. He observed that if an investor is building up holdings of an asset, his or her cost of funds is i. With a stable or sluggish expected price P_{t+1}^e, more purchases will tend to drive up the current asset price P_t^a until ρ from (36) falls far enough to satisfy (37). At that point, the investor will stop buying. In other words, there *are* market forces driving $\rho - c + l$ toward the value i, although they may not complete the task in any short period of time.

Now suppose that i declines. A buying process will begin, driving up P_t^a. As the expected return to acquiring the asset today begins to drop off from (36), it becomes more appealing to buy forward. But then P_{t+1}^a will also increase, because spot and forward prices of producible assets tend to move together. This co-movement is in fact what triggers capital formation. To see why, we have to bring in another price P_t^c, or the "cost price" of manufacturing the asset. When P_{t+1}^a / P_t^c, entering into production for forward sale becomes an appealing option.

This Sraffa/Keynes theory of investment demand is deeper than the standard MEC chronicle. Several observations are worth making. The first is that the decision-making process just described relies on stability of the expected price P_{t+1}^e and the cost price P_t^c. Suppose that P_{t+1}^a moves in proportion to P_t^a (the spot premium is stable) *and* that P_{t+1}^e moves in proportion to P_{t+1}^a. Then the investment increase just described can never happen. An initial rise in P_t^a will be matched proportionately by a higher P_{t+1}^e and from (36) a reduction in ρ cannot occur (ultimately the interest rate would have to rise back up to meet ρ, as in the steady state of Ramsey growth models). Similarly, if the cost price P_t^c jumps up when P_{t+1}^a does, no one can make a profit by producing more of the asset.

This latter observation shows that nominal cost anchors are an essential attribute of capitalist accumulation. Investment can not take place unless costs (and in particular wage costs) are relatively stable. Similarly, the current economic situation cannot move unless changes in expectations are sluggish. Stated differently, we have just proved a "policy ineffectiveness" proposition: even if investment is very low, reducing the interest rate will not stimulate more capital formation when P_{t+1}^e and P_t^c rapidly adjust to the lower level of i. In the context we are considering, postulating such speedy price adjustment looks a little bit crazy; after all, the economy does accumulate as it moves from one configuration to another in historical time.

Contrariwise, if one believes that the current configuration is "optimal" in some sense, then rapidly adjusting or "rational" expectations become a powerful rhetorical weapon—we're in the best of all possible worlds and speedy adjustment of expectations will keep us there. Subsequent chapters describe how aggressively new classical economists have sold this line.

Finally, the more relatively stable are prices such as P_{t+1}^e and P_t^c, the more important are likely to be quantity shifts in mediating macroeconomic adjustments (a point already raised in the context of the Ramsey model in Chapter 3). But what stabilizes asset prices and rates of return? In an unjustly neglected pair of papers written in the late 1930s, Kaldor (1960a,b) built on Keynes by demonstrating that speculators in the bond market can do the job of stabilizing the own-rate structure with the short-term interest rate set by the central bank as the anchor, unless expected asset and commodity prices are highly elastic to changes in current conditions. Among the own-rates will be profit rates in production. Closing a great circle, Kaldor's work supports Sraffa's (1960) suggestion (mentioned in Chapter 2) that the money rate of interest regulates the income distribution along the wage-profit frontier.

If expected prices *are* sensitive to changes in the current situation, then speculation can be destabilizing, with the losses of many unsuccessful speculators keeping the profits of a successful few quite healthy. Kaldor did not presume the existence of super-rational representative agents, and failed to see the possibility of a perfect foresight interest rate and asset price saddlepaths as discussed in sections 5 and 9. Perhaps that was because he thought he was theorizing about the real world.[18]

9. Financial Markets and Investment

The foregoing discussion leads naturally to consideration of other factors that may influence the investment decision. In this section, we take up two approaches—the first post-Keynesian[19] as propounded by people like Minsky (1986) and the second based on Tobin's q.

It is clear from the own-rate models just discussed that the investment decision hinges on comparing the asset price P^a with the cost price P^c of the bundle of capital goods under consideration. An immediate complication is that the enterprise making the comparison can draw on three disparate sources of finance: liquid assets on hand; the enterprise's current flow of gross profits after payment of existing debt service and interest obligations, dividends on equity, taxes, and expenditures for "business style"; and finally external funds to be obtained by issuing new liabilities. These sources of funding carry different costs and obligations which fundamentally influence investment decisions. Enterprises operate in highly imperfect capital markets; they do not live in a Modigliani-Miller world.

For firms apart from Microsoft in its glory days, liquid assets are not going to be substantial.[20] Moreover, as already noted in Chapter 1, their desired investment may well exceed retained gross earnings on a continuing basis so that external funds are required. In American practice, firms will often initially finance a project by borrowing from banks or the money market, and then refinance with longer-term obligations.[21] Figure 4.8 illustrates the complications.

The schedule for the "Internal funds limit" on investment is a rectangular hyperbola: $P^c I = F$, where I is the volume of investment, P^c is its cost price, and F is the available flow of internal funds. The cost price

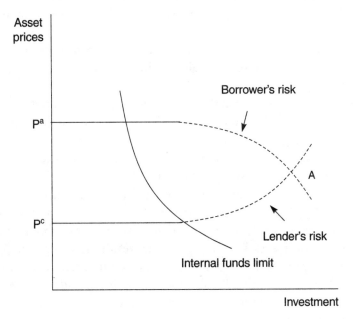

Figure 4.8
Post-Keynesian investment theory.

begins to rise for levels of investment lying to the right of this curve. There are several reasons why. Supply costs may begin to go up as capital goods producers begin to hit capacity limits. Meanwhile, "lender's risk" becomes increasingly important.[22] As a firm borrows more from its banks, they are likely to raise interest rates, shorten loan maturities, and attach "covenants and codicils" to loan agreements to force the borrower to restrict current dividends, restrain further borrowing, not sell assets, and even keep a floor under business net worth. Higher interest rates do not give a full picture of rising financial costs, which is why the "Lender's risk" curve is drawn with dashes.

"Borrower's risk" also goes up with the volume of investment. To quote Minsky (1986) directly, the investing firm either has "to run down holdings of financial assets that are superfluous to operations, or to engage in external finance. If financial assets are run down, then margins of safety in the asset structure are reduced. If new issues of common shares are undertaken, the issue price will have to be attractive, which may mean the present stock owners will feel their equity interest is being diluted. If debts, bonds, or borrowing from banks or short-term markets are used, then future cash-flow commitments rise, which diminishes the margin of safety of management and of equity owners. . . . [B]orrower's risk will increase as the weight of external or liquidity diminishing financing increases. This borrower's risk is not reflected in any objective cost, but it reduces the demand price of capital assets" (pp. 191–192).

In diagrammatic form, P^a drops off for high levels of investment, as shown by the dashed "Borrower's risk" schedule. There is a notional "equilibrium" at point A, which determines the level of investment actually undertaken. Typically, A will lie to the left of a neoclassical investment equilibrium just because lender's and borrower's risk restrain capital formation. These schedules as drawn may also shift for several reasons.

First, a less severe internal funds restriction (represented by a rightward shift of that schedule) would push both the dashed schedules to the right, stimulating capital formation.

Second, by pulling down own-rates of return as discussed above, lower short-term interest rates will push the asset price P^a upward. Because as discussed in Chapter 3 interest rates enter into production costs (especially for investment projects with long periods to maturity), their reduction will move the cost price P^c downward. Both shifts will move the intersection point A to the right. The resulting inverse relationship between the interest rate and new capital formation reflects not just "decreasing returns to capital," but rather the financial and institutional adjustments that permit more rapid accumulation to take place.

Third, when this environment changes, so will investment behavior. A boom will increase corporate profits and shift the Internal funds limit curve to the right, reducing the rate of increase of lender's risk. It is also likely to shift P^a up. We get an "accelerator" investment response, but again one dependent on institutions.

Finally, if we return to Keynes's beauty contest, attitudes of financial market actors affect the slopes of the Lender's and Borrower's risk schedules. They may change configurations suddenly, or stay locked in place for extended periods of time. If the dashed curves in Figure 4.8 are steep and at the same time internal funding possibilities are low, there is scant reason to expect high investment and a socially desirable rate of economic growth.

These downside "uncertainties" (in Frank Knight's terminology) are blissfully ignored in recent mainstream investment theories. Their focus is on the dynamics of capital formation resulting from postulated optimizing behavior of firms facing perfect capital markets. The paradigmatic q-model was presented in section 5 of Chapter 3, and we explore its dynamic properties here.

Restating the relevant Euler equations for convenience, we have an accumulation rule for the growth of a firm's capital-labor ratio k,

$$\dot{k} = gk, \tag{38}$$

where g is the growth rate. There is an asset price q corresponding to k, and g is optimally determined by the formula

$$q = 1 + h(g) + gh'(g), \tag{39}$$

where $gkh(g)$ is an "installation" or "shut-down" cost associated with the change $\dot{k}$ of the capital/labor ratio caused by a nonzero value of the control variable g (which can be either positive or negative). Inverting the expression on the right in (39) makes g an increasing function of q, and the properties of the cost factor h can be cunningly chosen to make the value $q = 1$ correspond to a steady-state growth path along which $g = \dot{k}/k = 0$.

Finally, there is an optimizing rule for the growth of q. It can be stated in two ways,

$$i = [f'(k) + g^2 h'(g)]/q + \dot{q}/q \tag{40a}$$

or

$$\dot{q} = iq - [f'(k) + g^2 h'(g)]. \tag{40b}$$

At an initial steady state with $\dot{q} = g = 0$, (40a) reduces to $i = f'(k)/q$. Taking into account the transition from discrete to continuous time, this formula amounts to a combination of Keynes's equations (36) and (37) tying an asset's own rate of return ρ to the interest rate i (ignoring the liquidity premium l and carrying cost c), with the own-rate in the present case being $\rho = f'(k)/q$.

Now let the interest rate shift downward. As discussed above, the own-rate must also jump down via an increase in the asset price q. Because g is an increasing function of q from (39)—this *is* the "q" theory of investment demand—$\dot{k}$ will be positive from (34). The positive value of g will also make $\dot{q} < 0$ in (40b), even though $iq - f'(k) = 0$ in the "instant" that the interest rate moves. To summarize, the asset price jumps upward when the interest rate is cut, inducing investment demand and a gradual reduction of the price itself.

This process looks vaguely under control, *except* for the iq term on the right of equation (40b). As in the previous perfect foresight models that we have encountered, this term sets up a positive feedback loop in which a reduction in q makes $\dot{q} < 0$ and reduces q further still. What factors can make this cascade of capital losses (negative own-rates of money return in Keynesian jargon) come to a halt? There are two possibilities. One is to postulate that expectational dynamics for asset prices are a lot more sluggish than those built into (40b) for q. To a degree, this solution was adopted by Kaldor (1960a).

The other ploy is to stick with (40b) because it has MIRA foundations, and push rationality to the hilt. As illustrated in Figure 4.9, the system (38)–(40) has saddlepoint dynamics. A lower interest rate shifts the locus

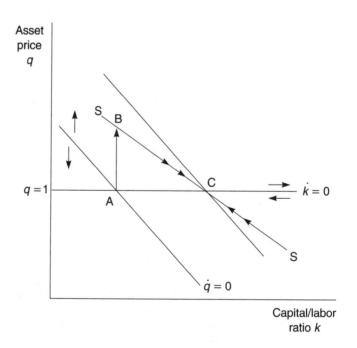

Figure 4.9
Saddlepoint dynamics for capital accumulation when the interest rate is reduced.

along which $\dot{q} = 0$ upward, setting up a saddlepath SS. The asset price jumps from its initial steady-state level of unity at A to a higher value at B on the new saddlepath, and begins a gradual decline to a new steady state at C. Capital accumulation k also initially jumps up and then gradually slows back to zero.

Appropriate transversality conditions on q and k can make this process work out, avoiding dynamic trajectories along which q goes to infinity or zero (Blanchard and Fischer 1989; Romer 2001).[23] One question is whether the capitalist enterprises one reads about in the *Wall Street Journal* and *Financial Times* have the market agility required to leap to and remain in balance along the saddlepath. One can perhaps be permitted a modicum of doubt.

Second, even if the Figure 4.9 capital formation path were to work out, it lacks verisimilitude. As any reader of Keynes and Minsky is well aware, investment dynamics in any observable market economy are far richer than the story just recounted. Interest rate reductions do not just cause investment immediately to jump up and then gradually die off— repercussions within the firm and on both the real and the financial sides of the economy bring much more oscillatory accumulation processes into action. Some are discussed in Chapter 9.

10. Consumption and Saving

If investment is at the heart of the injection side of the Keynesian calculus, then saving has equivalent importance as a leakage. In Anglo-American financial structures, at least, the biggest shares of gross national saving are provided by businesses and by households in the top few percent of the size distribution of income. One might expect that the bulk of research would be on the generation and allocation of corporate and high personal income flows. Most professional attention, however, has concentrated on average saving rates. In part this emphasis follows *The General Theory* itself, but it also reflects mainstream perceptions. If the Modigliani-Miller theorem means that finance is a veil, then it makes sense to concentrate on households as the ultimate savers. And the representative agent hypothesis makes all households look the same.

In the beginning, Keynes himself thought that the overall marginal propensity to consume dC/dY (where in *The General Theory* Y stands for an income concept resembling real GDP) would be less than the average propensity C/Y. Keynes did not write out an explicit equation for his consumption function $C(Y)$, but the literature soon came to accept a linear version

$$C = a + mY \tag{41}$$

(with a and m both positive and $m < 1$). Keynes went so far as to term the $m < 1$ condition a "fundamental psychological law" (p. 96). Pop psychology from a genius, alas, turned out to be no more reliable than similar pronouncements from less august sources.

Problems showed up within a decade of *The General Theory*. One was that even though real disposable income in the United States fell between 1945 and 1947, there was no postwar consumption slump (as had been generally predicted). Spending from wealth in forms such as savings bonds built up during the war and a general recuperation from the national vicissitudes beginning in 1929 provided ad hoc explanations, but left the "psychological law" suspect.

Analysis of time-series data by Kuznets (1946) and others also posed problems. The marginal propensity to consume appeared to vary countercyclically, falling in booms and rising in slumps (a possibility already recognized by Keynes, who had access to Kuznets's preliminary empirical results). Over longer time spans, a companion finding was that the intercept term a in (41) tended toward zero. The reason is easy to see if we consolidate household accounts for income and expenditure, flows of funds, and change in wealth:

$$Y - C = S = \dot{\Omega},$$

where Y now represents real household income, S is household saving and $\dot{\Omega}$ is the increment in household wealth (all variables are figured per capita). In a steady state or over a long period of averaged data, let the growth rate of Ω be g. Then manipulation of the accounting statement above gives

$$C/Y = 1 - (\Omega/Y)g. \tag{42}$$

For g amounting to a few percentage points and Ω/Y in the range of one to three, C will be around 90–95 percent of Y. This theorem of accounting underlies a diagram like Figure 4.10, where the "Keynes" consumption function crosses a long-run relationship like (42). Over periods of quarters or a few years, data points may (or may not) cluster along the Keynes relationship, but the schedule itself cannot be stable. In an economy with real per capita income growth it has to shift upward over time to permit the average ratio C/Y to satisfy (42).

Beginning in the 1940s, an active cottage industry grew up attempting to explain these findings. Here we sketch three early approaches in increasing order of influence on the mainstream (and decreasing order of institutional interest). The first was advanced by Duesenberry (1949). One basic idea was that each household's consumption behavior is the

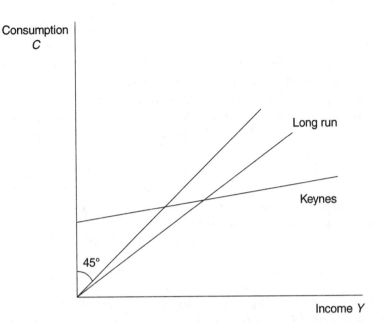

Figure 4.10
Alternative consumption functions.

result of learning, custom, and habit (points already made in *The General Theory*). People do watch each other as well as the movies and TV, and shape the level and composition of their spending accordingly.

Second, consumption is somewhat inertial. When *Y* swings up, *C* rises but with a lower rate of growth. When *Y* declines, households try to retain existing real standards of living, so that *C* drops off with a lag. In formal terms, Duesenberry argued that *C* is likely to depend on past peak real income as well as current *Y*, giving rise to a "ratchet effect." In an upswing, *C* moves along a "Keynes" curve in Figure 4.10, but it doesn't fall very much when *Y* declines. Thus in the next upswing the intercept of the "Keynes" schedule has risen, providing a mechanism for its drift upward over time.

Duesenberry's model explained the stylized facts of its time (the high consumption level after World War II, the countercyclical marginal propensity to consume, and equation (42)) parsimoniously and with a bit of flair. It would be interesting to see how well it would apply to the period of stagnant household income (but rising income inequality) between around 1970 and the late 1990s. But such studies have not been made. Although it sounds sensible, the ratchet effect lacks MIRA foundations, and consequently vanished from professional view.

The "life cycle" consumption model of Modigliani and Brumberg (1954) and Ando and Modigliani (1963) took a step from Duesenberry toward MIRA fundamentals, but at least tried to describe the ways in which people plan their economic lives. The households considered, however, are of a certain age and kind. As Marglin (1984) observes, "People whose employment prospects are reasonably certain, who follow a reasonably predictable career path, and whose lives are otherwise sufficiently ordered that long-term planning makes intellectual and emotional sense might . . . make decisions according to the life-cycle hypothesis . . . (A colleague of mine once remarked that the life-cycle hypothesis is just what one would expect of a tenured college professor!)" (p. 431).[24]

Such a well-ordered person might be T years old, expecting to live to age L and to work to age N. Let ω be expected yearly average wage income for the rest of his or her working life. Then his or her consumption function at age T could take the form

$$C_T = \frac{\Omega + \omega(N - T)}{L - T},$$
(43)

where it is understood that the term $\omega(N - T)$ drops out when the person retires (that is, $\omega = 0$ when $T > N$). Somebody aged forty-five who expects to work to sixty-five and die at seventy-five will thus consume 3.33 percent of his or her wealth per year and 66.67 percent of expected average wage income. Evidently these coefficients will change over a person's life cycle, but the population-wide numbers add up to something like the Keynesian consumption function (41).

Except for those who are about to die, the consumption coefficient on wealth in this setup is pretty small—a few percent per year for the middle-aged and near zero for the young. Such models correctly predicted that the paper losses of one or two trillion dollars in the stock market crash of October 19, 1987, would not be large enough to cause a recession in 1988. (As of this writing, what will happen as a result of dropping asset prices in 2001–2003 remains to be seen.) Life-cycle considerations also suggest that the real balance effect is of extremely limited significance for consumption behavior, because in the United States total "liquid assets" (currency and deposits, money market funds, and cash surrender value of insurance and pension accounts) amount to less than 20 percent of household wealth (Wolff 1995). This observation is ignored by the mainstream.

There are other problems with the life-cycle model. The version in (43) includes no "bequest" motive for a person to die with $\Omega > 0$ so as to ensure the livelihoods of her or his heirs, although that could easily be added. More fundamentally, to quote from Marglin (1984) again, the group to whom the Modigliani et al. hypothesis applies

is hardly representative of the population as a whole—neither of the top 1 or 2 percent of the income distribution who account for a disproportionate amount of total saving and for whom other motives than provision for retirement appear to be significant, nor of the bottom 80 to 90 percent of the distribution who account for most savers, if not for most saving. . . . [Their prospects] are so uncertain that deliberate choice and planning are beside the point. . . . The life-cycle hypothesis may adequately account for the . . . professionals and executives whose futures are sufficiently secure to make deliberate provision for the future a reasonable notion and whose relative means make the pressure to spend less imperative. . . . This leaves us with the upper end of the income distribution, not just the super-rich but the top 1 to 2 percent . . . candor compels the admission that we know very little about the saving behavior of the people who do most of the saving. (p. 432)

With regard to the super-rich, moreover, standard theory fails to explain why anyone would want to build up a huge fortune in the first place—after the first few hundred million dollars, providing consumption possibilities for oneself and one's heirs must cease to be a concern. Desires for power and prestige along with the thrill of playing the money-making game are obvious motivations, but they don't fit well into most economists' models.

More on Marglin's ideas about saving behavior below, but next we have to discuss the most influential mainstream theory—Milton Friedman's (1957) permanent income hypothesis (PIH). The simplest rationale is provided by someone with a known, finite lifespan and an income stream that fluctuates over time. This person is assumed to have access to a perfect capital market, and can borrow or lend at a zero interest rate. What plan will maximize the integral of his or her consumption "felicity" (or utility from consumption at each point in time)?

The answer is that consumption per unit time will be a constant equal to the sum of the person's expected lifelong income flows divided by the length of his or her life. The reason for this is that any blip upward from a level consumption path would have to be matched by an equal blip downward at some other time to satisfy the lifetime budget constraint. But with diminishing marginal utility of consumption, the "utils" gained in the upward blip are less than those lost from the one going down. The implication is that all blips (let alone trends or more complicated fluctuations) will be avoided.

Such a person's consumption would be unaffected by "transitory" income fluctuations above or below his or her lifelong average (or "permanent") level and would satisfy (42) with saving varying procyclically. We have another explanation for the post–World War II stylized facts—one that makes the marginal propensity to consume out of current income vanishingly small.

This last observation explains why the PIH was an important early salvo in the orthodox attack on the Keynesian edifice. If the marginal propensity to consume out of current income is near zero (or the marginal propensity to save is near one) then injection/leakage and multiplier calculations fall apart. A "temporary" tax change such as Lyndon Johnson's surcharge of 1968 will not reduce consumer spending, as in fact it did not appear to do. A "permanent" change such Ronald Reagan's tax reduction of 1982 might be expected to have more bite, as "verified" by the boom that followed.

Such macroeconomic correlations can be explained in a thousand ways, of course, which is why one has to ask about the nature of the theories underlying the explanations. The PIH is attractive to the mainstream because of its optimizing foundations. The maximizing problem stated above is a special case of the Ramsey optimal saving model, in which both the return to alternative uses of funds (or the profit rate) r and the person's pure rate of time preference j are set equal to zero. Recall from equation (20) of Chapter 3 that consumption behavior in the general case is described by the Ramsey-Keynes rule

$$\dot{C} = (C/\eta)(r - j), \tag{44}$$

where η is the elasticity of the marginal utility of consumption (and $1/\eta$ is the intertemporal elasticity of substitution in consumption). We have $\dot{C} = 0$ when $r \to 0$ and $j \to 0$, or Friedman's result.

Relationships like (44) have generated enormous academic churning, due in part to the post-PIH mainstream fashion of basing consumption theory on Ramsey-type models solved under the assumption that complete probability distributions can be put on future household income flows, including returns to assets. For the reasons mentioned above in connection with the liquidity preference and investment functions, this approach is strikingly anti-Keynesian.

With regard to asset valuations in particular, Keynes thought that "the existing market valuation [of an asset] . . . cannot be uniquely correct, since our existing knowledge cannot provide a sufficient basis for a calculated mathematical expectation" (p. 152). He continued: "Human decisions affecting the future, whether personal, political, or economic, cannot depend on strict mathematical expectation, since the basis for making such calculations does not exist; and it is our innate urge to activity which makes the wheels go round, our rational selves choosing between the alternatives as best we are able, calculating where we can, but often falling back for our motive on whim or sentiment or chance" (pp. 162–163).

Details about how to ignore Keynes and solve Ramsey models under quantifiable risk using stochastic dynamic programming are postponed until Chapter 6. For the moment, we can briefly mention three topics that have been hotly debated in the literature before going on to more interesting material—the random walk hypothesis, interest rate effects on saving, and the puzzle of the equity premium.

The random walk model shows up if we set $r = j = 0$ in (44) but compensate by throwing in a random error term ϵ on the right-hand side,

$$\dot{C} = \epsilon. \tag{45}$$

It is straightforward to show that (45) will be an optimal decision rule for the Friedman problem described above when felicity takes the form of a quadratic function and income per unit of time is subject to a random shock (again assumed to be described by a calculable and complete probability distribution as opposed to being "uncertain" à la Keynes and Knight).[25]

The significance of equations like (45) as "tests" of the PIH and similar optimizing formulations was pointed out by Hall (1978), who provided econometric support for the hypothesis that period-on-period changes in consumption are an uncorrelated random process, that is, a random walk. Countless econometric exercises later, the mainstream consensus seems to be that despite the attractiveness of (45), both the level and the change in C are affected by permanent and transitory factors, in Friedman's terminology (Romer 2001). We come down not too far from Keynes's model of consumption.

The potential effects of interest rate changes on consumption are most easily contemplated in a Fisher diagram like the one in Figure 3.1. A higher interest rate rotates the corresponding schedule clockwise, giving a real income loss "today" (presumably reducing saving) and inducing a shift along an indifference curve toward more consumption "tomorrow" (and thereby saving "today"). If real wealth goes up because of a lower interest rate, saving will presumably fall. Which effect will dominate is not immediately clear. The ambiguous diagram aside, casual observation suggests that people don't adjust their saving much in response to interest rate changes. In a Ramsey model framework, however, Summers (1981) tried very hard to argue the opposite case. In the notation of (44), he thought about a long-lived individual for whom r is slightly bigger than j and $1/\eta$ is small. The growth rate of consumption is thus slightly positive, meaning that the level of C at a long life's end will be noticeably bigger than at its beginning.

To satisfy this plan, the individual will have to save a lot in his or her early years, put the money into assets with a return r, and then dis-save massively toward the end along the lines of the life-cycle equation (43). This particular pattern of behavior will be quite sensitive to changes in r. Summers makes a good lunge at forcing saving at the aggregate level to be interest rate–sensitive, but in light of Marglin's observations above, he doesn't get the ring. To repeat, just how many people in the population are in a position to make such precise calculations, and what proportion of total saving do they provide?

Finally, the "puzzle of the equity premium" refers to Mehra and Prescott's (1985) observation that the average long-term return to holding stocks in the U.S. economy is about 7–8 percent while the "riskless" real return on Treasury bills is about 1–2 percent. The "puzzle" emerges from the following line of reasoning in a standard finance theory model in which asset-holders maximize expected consumption under calculable risk (Kocherlakota 1996)—the capital-asset pricing model (CAPM) is the standard story.

If the covariance of an asset's return with its holder's consumption growth is high, then it makes sense for the holder to sell that asset and buy another one with a low (or, better, negative) covariance—in that way overall variance of consumption is reduced. To induce the holder to keep the high covariance asset in his or her portfolio, then, those holdings have to pay a high return. The puzzle is that in the United States the covariance of equity returns and consumption growth is well less than 0.005 while the differential in rates of return between T-bills and equity is 0.06. If holding equity poses such a tiny covariance risk, why is its return so much higher than that on bonds?

Mainstream economists have no clear explanation for the difference in returns. They mumble about transactions costs in the stock market, but sound unconvinced. Readers of Keynes could respond that these observers' perception of how the market functions is not correct. Its driving participants are not households interested in maximizing expected utility from consumption, but rather professionals competing against one another in search of high short-term returns, probing market opinion to "the fourth, fifth, and higher degrees."

In such a game among insiders, the carrying and illiquidity costs of taking positions are important matters; in terms of equation (37) the own-rate of return to holding shares must be correspondingly high. Nifty little formalizations may now (and forever) be lacking, but it is hard to see how this Keynesian institutional explanation of the elevated return to equity as a compensation for speculation's Knightian "uncertainty" could be badly wrong. Its active players segment the stock market away from the rest of the economy in which passive investors are happy to get a good rate of return; within the market's own precincts, the stakes are very high.

11. "Disequilibrium" Macroeconomics

To end a survey of Keynesian economics, one last debate about short-term adjustment is of interest. The key issue can be illustrated by the sharp distinction between two theories of consumption demand discussed in the last section. One is Keynes's "fundamental psychological law" stating that current real consumption is mainly a function of current real income. In other words, consuming households are constrained in their decision making by whatever money happens to be coming in. On the basis of rules of thumb, slow adjustment to income fluctuations, and maybe a little bit of saving for a rainy day, at time t they basically scale $C(t)$ to the amount of income $Y(t)$ that is available.

Friedman's permanent income hypothesis, on the other hand, says that households have a present and future "endowment" of income flows that they can foresee pretty accurately. With access to a (nearly) perfect capital market they can borrow and lend to smooth away income fluctuations and keep a stable consumption path. The only income (or wealth) constraints they face are their fixed lifetime endowments. This view is Walrasian in that it presumes that prices will adjust smoothly to generate full employment income flows over time. Households plug this information into their dynamic optimizing programs, and buy accordingly.

Three decades after *The General Theory*, Clower (1965) stirred up waves by pointing out that Keynes did not think like Friedman or Walras. Clower propounded a "dual decision hypothesis." In one choice, households base consumption expenditure on the current income they receive, which depends on the overall level of employment. In the other decision, firms choose employment levels based on their current volume of sales. Such decision procedures boil down to an injections/leakages calculus, not a Walrasian scenario in which prices rapidly adjust to ratify full employment levels of incomes and sales.

Building on Clower, Leijonhufvud (1968) soon added that expected prices and wages are likely to respond sluggishly to changing events and that "perverse" responses to macroeconomic dislocations can be expected.[26] All this could not have been surprising to anyone who had taken *The General Theory* (as opposed to Patinkin-based and IS/LM glosses) to heart. The Clower-Leijonhufvud tempest blew itself up because by the mid-1960s in (especially) the United States and the United Kingdom authentic Keynesians were a rare breed; neoclassical synthesizers were in full cry.

In Europe, on the other hand, Malinvaud (1977) took the dual decision line a step or two further, drawing on his experience working with the French "indicative" planning bureaucracy in the 1950s and 1960s. A frequent argument between the labor unions and the bureaucrats concerned the effects of an increase in the real wage—would it add to employment by raising aggregate demand, or reduce it by driving up labor costs? Malinvaud's answer took the form of a variation on Figures 4.2 and 4.3.

The gist is illustrated by the "arrowhead diagram" of Figure 4.11, in which aggregate demand is assumed to be wage-led along the positively sloped schedule. Firms will only employ more workers, on the other hand, when the real wage falls along the "Labor demand" curve. Malinvaud's innovation was to assume that employment is determined by a "short-side rule" operating across the commodity and labor markets. For example, if the real wage is low, then aggregate demand along its schedule will be less than the output firms would be willing to produce with cheap labor. Output and employment will be limited by demand on the "short" side of the market, in a situation of "Keynesian unemployment."

Alternatively, for a high real wage, desired commodity demand will

Figure 4.11
Malinvaud's arrow-head.

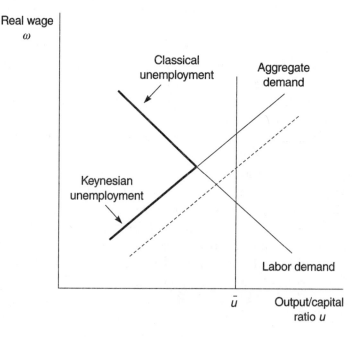

exceed the quantity firms are willing to provide. "Classical unemployment" along the labor demand curve will be in force. Given the level of the real wage, the economy will find itself somewhere on the darkened segments of the curves. The model generalizes *The General Theory* insofar as Keynes operated at the point of the arrowhead where both schedules are in force.[27]

As discussed above, Keynes thought that higher aggregate demand (dashed line) would be associated with higher output and a lower real wage. With the model closure of Figure 4.11, this conclusion is modified depending on the level of the real wage ω. If ω is low, higher demand will raise output at a constant wage. If ω is high, expansionary policy simply will not work. In both cases, if at a given ω the aggregate demand locus crosses the "full employment" activity level $\bar{u}$, then an intuitively obscure "repressed inflation" equilibrium will kick in.

Just listing all these cases suggests why disequilibrium macroeconomics did not take hold. Malinvaud and colleagues such as Benassy (1986) took the nonlinear MIRA mathematics (not to mention econometrics) underlying Figure 4.11 quite seriously. By the time they had written down all the switching rules among regimes in formal terms, the equations were intractable and ugly. A more flexible, institutionally based analysis of the adjustment possibilities implicit in the diagram might have proved enlightening. But because they were locked into their "non-Walrasian" MIRA way of thinking, qualitative, history-based analysis was not within the reach of the best Continental economists of the 1970s.

12. A Structuralist Synopsis

The foregoing arguments have been lengthy and convoluted. It makes sense to step back and review the major macroeconomic points. Following Gordon's (1997) econometric summary, they include the following.

Investment demand does appear to respond positively to the profit rate r and capacity utilization u, and negatively to the interest rate i. The standard econometric tests suggest that savings flows do not "cause" investment either by being important right-hand-side variables in regression equations or by chronologically "leading" capital formation.

Aggregate consumption responds positively to u and negatively to profit income flows, consistent with different propensities to consume from wage and nonwage income. Consumption and saving react weakly, if at all, to changes in the interest rate, but do appear to have a strong inertial component à la Duesenberry. Marglin's (1984) "disequilibrium hypothesis" via which household "saving occurs when income rises faster than households can adopt their spending habits; dissaving occurs when income falls faster than households can rein in their spending" (p. 145) appears to fit the data reasonably well.

The essentials of the principle of effective demand thus appear to have survived sixty years of intense scrutiny. Moreover, strong attacks to a greater or lesser extent have misfired.

First, even impeccably mainstream economists such as Carroll and Summers (1991) reject the permanent income hypothesis by admitting that consumption growth tracks income growth, and that savings rates differ across income classes. One reason is that households with scant wealth are recognized to be subject to "liquidity constraints," and consume according to "rules of thumb" as opposed to optimizing scenarios (Shefrin and Thaler 1988).

Second, anomalies such as the "equity premium puzzle" suggest that all is not well with the axiom that financial markets perform perfectly. The views of Keynes and colleagues on the significance of essential uncertainty, financial "beauty contests," and institutional structures have not been overturned. The implication is that idealized models of investment and saving along Ramsey's lines are far removed from macroeconomic reality.

Third, as argued more fully in following chapters, Say's Law is not true—saving does not drive investment and full utilization of labor and installed capacity are not observed.

Effective demand remains *the* valid approach to macroeconomics. The question is how to use it to understand and improve the social impacts of the existing macroeconomic system.

———————— ✕ ————————

Short-Term Model Closure
and Long-Term Growth

Effective demand may be alive and kicking, but it is under intense competition from macroeconomic theories with opposing ethical and epistemological foundations. The alternatives are considered together in this chapter, in a journey over once-trod ground with some new attractions thrown in. The goals are to take a breather after racing through a lot of different models, and to set the stage for further analysis.

We begin by summarizing how the models we have discussed behave in the short run (concentrating on the real as opposed to the financial side of the economy), and go on to consider their extension into theories of growth rooted at least partly on the supply side—Solow, Kaldor, and Marxist formulations. The next section focuses on the demand side, covering stability or lack of same in Harrod-style growth models. We close with an introduction to a demand-driven model used extensively in later chapters. It is used to analyze pension programs as was done with the OLG model in Chapter 3. The supply- and demand-driven formulations come to virtually opposite conclusions about the macro effects of pay-go and fully funded social security programs.

1. Model "Closures" in the Short Run

Two fundamental points are that the accounts in the SAM underlying a one-sector macro model plus a small number of additional "behavioral" assumptions serve completely to determine the model's properties, and that these properties can differ strikingly depending on just which behavioral relationships are imposed.

Although they are implicit in Keynes's transition from his forced-saving *Treatise* to the output-adjusting *General Theory*, explicit statements of these ideas emerged only after his death from his immediate disciples in Cambridge, for example, Robinson (1956) with her various "ages" of growth and Kaldor (1956) on alternative theories of distribution. They were picked up by Sen (1963), Harris (1978), Taylor and Lysy (1979),

Marglin (1984), and Dutt (1990). Taylor and Lysy (1979) popularized the not overly felicitous word "closure" as a shorthand description of a model's causal structure.

Table 5.1 sets the stage for closure analysis in an economy without foreign trade and in which monetary linkages are ignored (for the moment). It follows along the lines of Table 4.1 in presenting two similar but not identical macro models—the one to the right with neoclassical assumptions about uses of inputs and income distribution is more internally constrained or closed than the one to the left with markup pricing. The causal structure of both versions rests on determination of price and input-output relationships from equations (1)–(4), and the level of demand from (4)–(7). How the two sets of equations interact is determined by a handful of additional restrictions. We can quickly run through cases that appear in the literature—models characterized by output adjustment, forced saving, loanable funds, IS/LM, real balance effects, inflation effects, determination of investment by saving supply, and closure by adding extra variables.

Output Adjustment

In the markup model, assume that the nominal wage w is fixed by historical wage bargains and custom, the capital stock K by previous in-

---

Table 5.1 Basic macro relationships for a one-sector model

Markup Pricing		**Neoclassical Cost Function**	
$P = (1\ t)wb = wb/(1 - \pi)$		$P = f(w, rP)$	(1)
$L/X = b$		$L/X = f_\omega(\omega, r)$	(2)
$u = X/K$		$u = X/K$	(3)
$r = [\tau/(1 + \tau)]u = \pi u$		$K/X = f_r(\omega, r)$	(4)

Macroeconomic Balance	
$g^s = [s_\pi \pi + s_w(1 - \pi)]u = s(\pi)u$	(5)
$g^i = g^i(r, u) = g^i(\pi, u)$	(6)
$\quad = g_0 + \alpha r + \beta u = g_0 + (\alpha\pi + \beta)u$	
$\gamma_g + g^i - g^s = 0$	(7)

Definitions

$\pi = rPK/PX = \tau/(1 + \tau)$
$\omega = w/P = (1 - \pi)/b$
$\gamma_g = PG/PK$

vestment, and government spending G and (for the given K) the spending ratio $\gamma_g = G/K$ by policy. Then with a fixed markup rate τ, the price level P and the income distribution follow from (1). The demand equations (5)–(7) and the distributional identity (4) jointly determine r and u. Output X follows from (3) and employment L from (2). We have a macro system in which causality runs toward employment and output from the side of demand; output is implicitly assumed to lie below the full capacity level κK determined by the available capital stock, where κ is a "technically determined" capacity/capital ratio.

The neoclassical story is similar, but more tightly constrained. Only γ_g, w, and K can be predetermined—distributional variables such as τ, the profit share π, and the real wage ω are endogenous to the system. This complication is reflected in the fact that (1) must be combined with (4)–(7) to solve jointly for u, r, and ω. Output and employment follow from (3) and (2) as before, while (1) gives the price level. As we have seen, one interpretation (essentially Keynes's interpretation) is that the real side of the model underlying *The General Theory* comprises the neoclassical equations (1)–(7) closed from the side of demand. Graphical illustrations appear below and in Chapter 4.

Comparative statics of the two versions can be illustrated with three experiments: changing government dis-saving γ_g, the money wage w, and the real wage ω. In both versions, a higher value of γ_g raises u and X through a multiplier process that converges so long as saving supply increases more strongly than investment demand as a function of u—the Harrodian stability condition already explored in Chapter 4.

In the neoclassical model, (1) can be inserted into (4) to eliminate ω. The upshot is a positive relationship between r and u. But then from (1) stated as a wage-profit curve

$$1 = f(\omega, r), \tag{8}$$

ω must fall as u goes up. As observed in Chapters 2 and 4, this "first classical postulate" implies that an increased demand injection is associated with greater output and a lower real wage, with decreasing returns setting in as more labor is combined with the available capital stock. Since the nominal wage is fixed, P must rise to reduce ω—the demand injection drives up the price level as well as the output.

Neither the real wage decrease nor the price increase occurs in the markup model, since τ is set from the outside and diminishing returns do not set in so long as capacity exceeds output. A demand injection could even cause real wage increases and price deflation (at least with respect to money wages) if the markup rate is an inverse function of u, as discussed in Chapter 2. Empirically, this sort of response to rising output is not unknown.

A change in the money wage w has no real effects in the markup system. From (1), P just adjusts in proportion, and the real side is unchanged. The neoclassical equations can easily be seen to depend only on ω or w/P; therefore the same conclusion applies. For a given demand injection γ_g, the real wage is an outcome of the neoclassical model. Hence money wage changes will affect only the price level and not employment. This is basically Keynes's argument about the uselessness of money wage reduction in Chapter 19 of *The General Theory*, presented in detail in Chapter 4 above.

Because the real wage is endogenous in the neoclassical system, it cannot be shifted exogenously in a thought experiment. In the markup model, if the markup rate τ is changed by macroeconomic shocks or policy (price controls, revised public enterprise charges, trade policy, and so on), the real wage will also move. As noted in Chapter 4, a real wage increase may make effective demand go either up or down. The latter, "profit-led" case arises when there is a small differential between rentiers' and workers' saving shares and/or the responsiveness of investment demand to the profit share is strong. Such conditions are important to determining stability of the adjustment mechanism we are about to discuss.

Forced Saving

Forced saving occurs when u and X cannot vary, for example, because the economy is using all its available capacity (u is at its "technical" maximum κ) or employment L is predetermined at a "full" level from the second classical postulate. In what follows, we concentrate on closure by a fixed L along the lines of Kaldor (1956), but the analysis extends to a supply-side restriction on output due to available capital or a labor supply function such as $L = L(\omega, X, K)$. A "surplus labor" specification, for example, would make L highly elastic to the real wage, effectively fixing ω. Such an assumption underlies a family of neo-Marxian growth models as illustrated graphically below.

In the markup model, setting employment adds a restriction to (1)–(7). In algebraic terms, the system becomes overdetermined, and some variable must become endogenous to meet the new constraint. If incipient excess demand with fixed output leads to upward pressure on prices, the obvious candidate for endogeneity is the markup rate τ or profit share π, and thereby the price level P from (1). The causal structure is that L determines X in (2), and then (3) sets u. The demand equations (5)–(7) give the profit rate r that balances saving and investment at the supply-determined level of u. The markup rate then comes from (4) and P from (1). Through price movements relative to the fixed money wage (presupposing a greater saving propensity from profits than wages), the income distribution adjusts endogenously to force the creation of enough saving to meet the new injection of demand.

In the neoclassical version, (1) and (4)–(7) determine u, r, and ω as in the output adjustment closure. But then the model falls apart. Equations (2) and (3) give inconsistent values for X—the only recourse is that one equation be dropped. Two excisions generally appear in the literature. The first is to leave out the investment demand function, with implications to be taken up below. The other is to omit (2) and replace (4) by the identity $r = \pi u$. These moves are tantamount to abandoning marginal productivity input demand functions and returning to the markup system.

This forced retreat underscores Kaldor's (1956) doubts about the usefulness of macroeconomic distribution theory based on marginal productivity; it also illustrates why implementation of a Schumpeterian innovation via credit creation and forced saving is a disequilibrium process from the neoclassical point of view. Alternatively, forced saving can be seen as a macro adjustment scenario in which the neoclassical combination of output and price increases in response to higher demand degenerates into a pure price (and distribution) change when output is determined from the side of supply.

This last observation leads into comparative statics in the markup model. With u fixed, if the demand injection γ_g increases, then in (5)–(7) the profit rate is the free variable that goes up to provide the corresponding saving supply. From (4) and (1), the markup and price level rise and the real wage goes down. Reduced real spending on the part of wage earners caused by higher prices is the adjustment vehicle.

An obvious question is whether this adjustment process is stable. Figure 4.2 already shows that it converges only when demand is wage-led, but it is worthwhile to demonstrate this result formally. With u predetermined, we can solve the model of Table 5.1 for π as

$$\pi = \frac{\gamma_g + g_0 + (\beta - s_w)u}{[s_\pi - (s_w + \alpha)]u}. \tag{9}$$

The macroeconomic stability condition with π as the adjusting variable in the short run is $\partial(g^i - g^s)/\partial\pi < 0$. Mindless differentiation based on the linearized investment function in the second lines of (6) shows that this inequality is equivalent to

$$s_\pi - (s_w + \alpha) > 0, \tag{10}$$

or that the denominator in (9) is positive. Consulting the discussion of equation (15) in Chapter 4 shows that condition (10) describes an economy in which effective demand is wage-led if output is the adjusting variable. In the present context, the message is that instability occurs when an increase in π sets off demand pressures which make it increase further still, as in the "Harrodian hyperinflation" section ZC of Figure 4.2.[1] If adjustment is stable, then contemplation of (9) shows that $\partial\pi/\partial s_\pi < 0$. This is the standard "widow's cruse" result of forced-saving macro models—a reduction in the saving rate from profits makes the profit share go up.[2]

Because π follows from effective demand, a money wage increase would just drive up the price level proportionally under forced saving. A similar outcome could befall an attempt at redistribution. Suppose in a simple case that $s_w = 0$, investment is stable at the level $\bar{g}$, and that a tax $trPK$ is levied on profit income and transferred to wage earners. Saving-investment balance becomes $r = \bar{g}/s_r(1 - t)$. The profit rate rises along with the tax rate increase, and the real wage correspondingly falls.

Real income per worker after the transfer is $Y_w = \bar{\omega} + trK/L$. Substituting from the expression for r above and drawing on Table 5.1, one can show that $Y_w = (1/b)[1 - (\bar{g}/su)]$, *independent of* the tax-*cum*-transfer rate t. The transfer does not go through, in a reverse example of the widow's cruse. The cruse bedevils any transfer attempt when output is at an upper bound.

In closing, note that although forced saving has been described here in terms of wages and profits, similar redistributive effects can occur among any savings flows. Applied models will include saving from the business sector, one or more household income classes, the rest of the world, and the government. Movements in financial surpluses (saving less investment) as prices shift will differ across these classes and institutions, allowing forced saving to occur. The presence of flows fixed in nominal terms—transfers and state spending are common examples— makes redistribution induced by changing prices even more important.

Loanable Funds

Changes in "the" interest rate (say i, ignoring the real/nominal distinction for the moment) mediate the adjustment mechanism already discussed at length in connection with the Ramsey/Tobin-q optimal accumulation and Wicksell cumulative process inflation models. If saving increases as a function of i,[3] while investment demand g^i declines, then even with u and/or X predetermined, all seven equations of Table 5.1 compose a well-behaved system. An exogenous increase in γ_g will make the left-hand side of (7) positive, and i will increase to restore equilibrium by cutting investment and inducing extra saving.

This loanable funds story sounds sensible, but is subject to at least two objections (both emphasized by Keynes). The first, already discussed in Chapter 4, is structural. Rates of return to assets in principle are determined in markets for stocks, not by savings and investment flows. The second question is about the strength of interest rate effects. As we have seen, there is not much evidence anywhere that overall saving responds to interest rate movements (although portfolio compositions certainly do). With much investment controlled by the state and large enterprises with good access to finance, interest rate effects on aggregate demand may be limited to only part of gross capital formation (housing construction?) and perhaps consumer purchases of durable goods. Empirical questions arise, but low elasticities can cripple adjustment based on interest rate movements in and of themselves. They may have more widespread effects by inducing changes in asset prices, but the underlying processes of arbitrage among own-rates of return only sometimes appear to be important in macroeconomic terms. Japan after its bubble burst is an obvious case in which they were. Will the United States in the decade of the aughts be another?

IS/LM

These empirical worries are to an extent dispelled if the interest rate is not forced to be the only variable equilibrating injections and leakages in (7). Rather, i itself can emerge from some behavioral equation and then help determine the levels of g^s and (especially) g^i, with output changes bearing the major burden of macroeconomic adjustment. As discussed in Chapter 4, this sort of causal scheme appears to be what Keynes principally had in mind when he wrote *The General Theory*. Although Keynes did mention them in his narrative, the subsequent mainstream emphasis on feedback effects involving u via a money demand equation

$$\mu(i, u)[qPK/T) + 1] - \zeta(T_c/T) = 0$$

as well as making saving a function of the interest rate are the handiwork of Hicks. In a streamlined setup where bonds issued by firms and the government (both paying an interest rate i) are the only nonmonetary financial claims, the asset price q is given by $q = r/i = \pi u/i$ so that money demand can be restated as

$$\mu(i, u)[(\pi uZ/i) + 1] - \zeta(T_c/T) = 0, \tag{11}$$

where the state variable $Z = PK/T$ is fixed at any point in time.

Equation (11) is a simplified version of (34) in Chapter 4, dropping the return to holding equity i_v as an argument of μ.[4] How it interacts with an IS curve to generate macro equilibrium has already been discussed. The novelty in (11) is that by bidding up q, a higher profit share will increase money demand and thereby the interest rate—financial responses can push the economy in the direction of being wage-led. For growth theory, a key question is how the stock ratio or state variable PK/T evolves over time. The analysis is presented in Chapter 7.

The Real Balance Effect

If output is predetermined and there is an independent investment function, consumption is the main demand component that must vary to permit macro equilibrium. If consumer demand is an inverse function of the price level so that the aggregate demand curve slopes downward in the (X, P) or (u, P) plane, the outcomes are straightforward: increased investment crowds out consumption by driving prices up. As noted in Chapter 4, forced saving provides such a linkage, but it lost theoretical favor (apart from Kaldor and colleagues) fifty or sixty years ago. In contemporary macroeconomics, its place is taken by the real balance effect. The story is familiar, although as we have seen it leads toward an over-determined model in a neoclassical specification. Adjustment pivots on an exogenous money supply, M. A price increase will reduce national wealth by eroding real balances M/P. Wealth-holders might be expected to try to restore their position by saving more; hence the overall saving rate becomes $s = s(M/P)$. A higher P cuts consumption by increasing s. Crowding out by rising prices becomes feasible again.

Comparative statics of the real balance effect were worked out in Chapter 4. The key result in a markup model is that money-wage cuts can raise output from the demand side by reducing P—this is the reason why the real balance story is congenial to the mainstream. With neoclassical price formation, an even stronger result emerges. Marginal productivity rules plus full employment determine the real wage w/P. But if P varies to bring aggregate demand into line with predetermined supply by altering real balances, then there is no room in the neoclassical specification for independent determination of the money wage w. How wage changes are neutralized by neoclassicists in the long run is a major theme of Chapter 6.

The Inflation Tax

The inflation tax is a dynamic version of the real balance effect, analyzed in Chapter 3. Its demand-reducing effect at times is practically relevant, for example in the consumption surges that have followed attempts to stabilize inflations by banning indexed contracts and imposing price controls in heterodox shock anti-inflation programs in Israel, eastern Europe, and Latin America. For that reason, it makes sense to merge an inflation tax with structuralist inflation theories emphasizing distributive conflict and propagation mechanisms in applied models (Taylor 1991, 1994).

Other Effects of Inflation on Demand

Inflation may affect other demand injections or leakages. Suppose that i, the nominal loan rate of interest, is pegged or comes from the financial side of the economy. Then faster inflation reduces the real rate $i - \hat{P}$, perhaps stimulating capital formation via the Mundell-Tobin effect mentioned in Chapter 3. Contrariwise, by adding to fundamental economic uncertainty, inflation may reduce capital formation. If either possibility is deemed relevant, it is easily built into an investment function. The same observation applies to effects of inflation on competitive imports, demand for consumer durables, the efficiency of tax collection,[5] or other variables.

Determination of Investment by Saving

Forced saving, loanable funds, and real balance effects provide means for accommodating a labor supply function into the macro system. Dropping the independent investment demand function (6) is another, as pointed out in Chapter 1. This artifice is widely used. For example, it is at the heart of Solow's (1956) neoclassical growth model analyzed in the following section.

Causal links are straightforward. In the markup model, K, L, w, and τ are predetermined. In Table 5.1, P comes from (1), X from (2), u from (3), r from (4), and g^s from (5). In a savings-driven economy there is no room for (6), so that capital stock growth g^i comes from (7). The solution of the neoclassical version is similar, except that as usual there is no room for a predetermined distributive index such as τ. With w fixed, equations (1)–(4) solve jointly for P, X, r, and u, and the story thereafter goes as in the markup model.

Output, income distribution, and saving all come from the supply side in the neoclassical version of this closure, which emphasizes productivity and thrift. A higher value of γ_g reduces g^i from (7). In the key rationale for President Clinton's fiscal policy of the 1990s, government spending "crowds out" investment demand. The real wage can't be altered, and a money-wage increase reflects itself solely in higher prices.

The markup model also demonstrates a pure price increase from a higher money wage and investment crowding-out by γ_g. A real wage increase is represented by a lower τ. From (4) and (5), the profit rate and saving supply fall. Hence, (7) shows that the growth rate must decline. Such outcomes are opposite those in the output adjustment closure discussed above. To reiterate, with potential results so different, empirical awareness and institutional understanding of the economy are required to judge how an apposite macro model should be closed.

Adding Endogenous Variables to the System

Finally, suppose that the investment demand function (6) in Table 5.1 is reinstated along with predetermined employment, but that γ_g is endogenous. Then all equations can be retained, with γ_g coming from (7). The interpretation is that the government regulates its spending to ensure full employment. Another possibility would be for the government to adjust some tax variable (though not the ineffective rate t of the tax-cum-transfer program discussed above) to the same end. The spending scenario is spelled out in Meade (1961), while Johansen (1960), when he set up the first-ever computable general equilibrium model, used an endogenous income tax to accommodate both an independent investment function and full employment.

2. Graphical Representations and Supply-Driven Growth

The foregoing arguments are easy to summarize in diagrams. The pictures used here are complementary to those in Chapter Four. We first describe equilibrium in the short run, and then show how growth models converging (at times) to steady-state solutions emerge from the various closures.

Figure 5.1 illustrates macro equilibrium under a markup pricing specification, using the linearized version of the investment function in the second line of (6).

The topmost quadrant to the right plots capital stock growth as a function of the profit rate. Equilibrium is defined by the intersection of the schedules for saving leakages g^s and demand injections $g^i + \gamma_g$ (two levels of investment demand, labeled by subscripts, are shown). In the quadrant just below, capacity use is related to the profit rate by the rule $r = \pi u$ until a capacity limit $\bar{u}$ is reached at a profit rate $\bar{r}$. To the left of the kink at $\bar{u}$, r and π vary independently of u. To the right, $u = \bar{u}$ and the investment functions become sensitive to variations in π only in the profit rate identity $r = \pi u$. Hence they are less steep as functions of r.

The lowest quadrant shows that the real wage ω (and therefore the

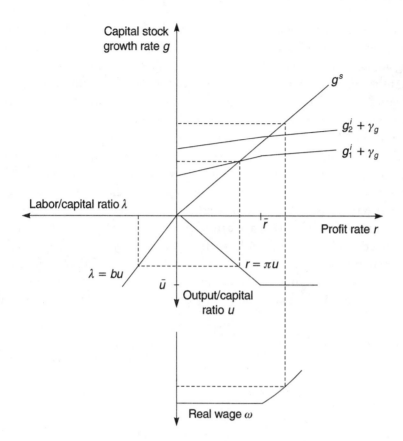

Figure 5.1
Markup macroeconomic equilibrium.

markup rate τ and profit share π) is constant for $u \leq \bar{u}$ and $r \leq \bar{r}$. To the right of the kink, ω becomes a decreasing function of r as forced saving applies with a binding output constraint. Finally, in the quadrant to the left, the labor/capital ratio $L/K = bu$ increases with u until $u = \bar{u}$. For later use, let λ stand for L/K.

The intersection of $g_1^i + \gamma_g$ with g^s depicts a closure in which output adjustment reigns. A small increase in γ_g will shift the injection schedule up, leading g, u, and λ to rise with a constant real wage. With a predetermined π, the macro equilibrium will be stable when condition (14) in Chapter 4 applies. An overly strong investment response to an increase in u can create short-run instability. Figure 5.1 shows the stable case; instability would require $g_1^i + \gamma_g$ to have a steeper slope than g^s.

The intersection of $g_2^i + \gamma_g$ with g^s corresponds to a forced saving model with $r > \bar{r}$. A higher γ_g initially shifts the injection schedule upward, leading g and r to rise while ω declines. Final equilibrium is reached after a further readjustment of $g_2^i + \gamma_g$ induced by the rise in π corresponding to the lower real wage. The new solution will be stable in the short run when condition (10) is satisfied.

The model with neoclassical price formation is illustrated in the right-hand quadrants in Figure 5.2; the story combines output and forced saving adjustments as discussed above. The main contrast with Figure 5.1 is that the kinks at $u = \bar{u}$ and $r = \bar{r}$ have been replaced by smooth curves indicating that the profit rate is an increasing function of capacity utilization, while r and ω trade off inversely along the factor price frontier. An increase in γ_g now leads g, r, and u to rise and ω to decline.

The quadrant to the left shows that u $(= X/K)$ rises smoothly with the labor/capital ratio λ along a neoclassical production function. This observation becomes of interest when we switch closures in the model. Suppose that instead of reading Figure 5.2 clockwise in an investment-determined scenario, we trace causality counterclockwise from a predetermined level of λ. Now u follows from the identity $\lambda = bu$, determining r which in turn sets ω and g^s. As we have already noted, there is no room in this reading for an independent investment function: g^i must adjust to satisfy the macro balance condition $g^i + \gamma_g - g^s = 0$. The injection sched-

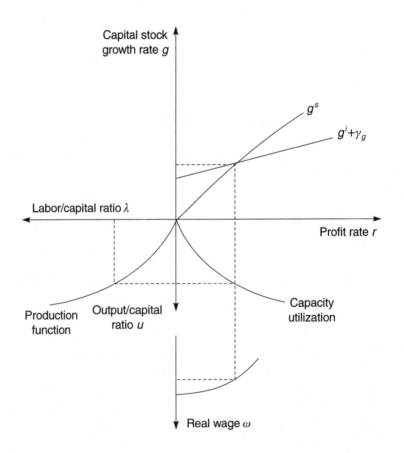

Figure 5.2
Neoclassical macro-economic equilibrium.

ule $g^i + \gamma_g$ can be viewed as sliding up and down until it meets g^s at the supply-determined profit rate r. As we will see, the resulting capital stock growth rate g varies to ensure steady-state stability in Solow's (1956) mainstream standard model.

Stories about Steady States

Contemporary economists use one or the other of two approaches to formal stability analysis in macro growth models. The one adopted heretofore in this book (except for the OLG model in Chapter 3) involves perfect foresight leaps between saddlepaths on the part of some flow or control variable(s) while the state variable(s) stay constant in an "instant" of time. This way of doing dynamics became popular in the 1970s, when saddlepoint "instability" in dynamic optimizing models was miraculously transformed into "stability" via jumps in control variables at initial time points induced via "backward" differential equations for costate variables subject to transversality conditions at final times. How long the jumps stay fashionable remains to be seen. The scenarios we have looked at so far suggest that intelligent leapers may plausibly land on their feet in the short run, but almost certainly not over endless stretches of time.

The more traditional approach followed by Solow, Kaldor, and many others is to assume that short-run variables such as the ones pictured in Figures 5.1 and 5.2 converge "rapidly" to equilibrium. The behavioral relationships satisfied by the "fast" variables shift in response to changes in "slow" or "state" variables set up as ratios of two growing quantities. The time derivative of each state variable comes from short run equilibrium, and when it is equal to zero, both the numerator and the denominator will be growing at the same rate—this is a steady state which can be used to characterize the economy "in the long run." Two exercises in stability analysis are built into this procedure—for the short-run adjustment and the steady state. The implicit time frame for the former might be months or quarters, and years or decades for the steady state. Presumably a steady state is not worth investigating if the economy is not stable in the short run.[6]

The Solow Growth Model

One interpretation of Solow and Kaldor is that they proposed their growth models as a means to bring a growth rate g^w "warranted" by short-term macro balance into equality line with a "natural" growth rate n via shifts in the capital/labor ratio and the overall saving rate respectively. These maneuvers were supposed to let the economy avoid

Harrod's "knife-edge" discussed below. This interpretation works better for Solow, although it is easy to argue that he did not so much avoid as ignore Harrod's investment-driven causal scheme. Be that as it may, his model has been put to many uses and merits examination on its own terms.

For the Solow model, K/L is usually used as the state variable. That procedure is adopted here in Chapter 9 when the model is reintroduced to lead into Tobin's monetary growth and cycle theory. But since it already appears in Figures 5.1 and 5.2, we can just as well work with the inverse $\lambda = L/K$. The relevant differential equation is

$$\dot{\lambda} = \lambda[\hat{L} - g(\lambda)] = \lambda[n - g(\lambda)], \tag{12}$$

where the employment (= population) growth rate $n = \hat{L}$ is taken as predetermined.

Suppose that $g < n$. Then $\dot{\lambda} > 0$, and the consequent increase in λ will lead in Figure 5.2 to higher values of u, r, *and* g in the counterclockwise reading. The upshot of this short-run adjustment is that g is an increasing function of λ, so that in equation (12) $d\dot{\lambda}/d\lambda < 0$ around the long-run rest point where $g = n$. The implications are that λ is locally stable, and that marginal productivity rules and the cost function determine the long-run income distribution from the level of λ at steady state.

Solow emphasized the role of real wage (and more generally, price) adjustment in leading to full employment in the short run. However, Figure 5.2 suggests that wage changes are a sideshow in the southeast corner. In the constant markup area of Figure 5.1 (with causality running counterclockwise and the independent investment function suppressed), it can be seen that a reduction in λ will lead u, r, and g to decline in the short run. Steady-state growth equilibrium is stable in a price-*in*sensitive saving-driven model. Short- and long-run distribution both follow from the predetermined markup rate τ.

The moral is that the key to stability in saving-driven models is the determination of accumulation by saving supply as an increasing function of capacity utilization or the profit rate, not flexible prices. If the saving rate is a *decreasing* function of the profit rate, the growth process can be unstable as we saw in the OLG model in Chapter 3.

Along with the Ramsey model, Solow's story is the workhorse of mainstream growth theory. It has figured recently in the debate over endogenous growth that is touched upon in Chapter 11. A few points are worth introducing here.

Away from the steady state at which $\dot{\lambda} = 0$ and $\lambda = \lambda^*$, the model says that the labor/capital ratio will be falling more rapidly, the higher the level of λ. That is, growth of capital and output per worker will be faster, the poorer the economy. This prediction is counterfactual in that countries which do manage to enter into sustained economic growth usually do so at a faster rate at middle income levels of a few thousand dollars per capita. Japan's extremely rapid labor productivity growth during its catch-up phase toward the left side of Figure 2.1 is the classic example.

More generally, growth accounting in the Solow framework boils down to applications of equations (10) and (12) in Chapter 2 across time. In purchasing power parity terms, real income levels per capita in rich countries are on the order of ten times as high as they are in poor ones. To examine potential sources of this discrepancy, we can restate equation (12ε) from Chapter 2 as

$$\hat{X} - \hat{L} = (1 - \psi)(\hat{K} - \hat{L}) + \psi\epsilon_L + (1 - \psi)\epsilon_K, \tag{13}$$

where ψ is the labor share and ϵ_L and ϵ_K are the growth rates of labor and capital productivity respectively. If we let ξ_L and ξ_K stand for productivity *levels* and hold ψ constant (implicitly slipping in a Cobb-Douglas approximation), then integrating this differential expression gives

$$X/L = (K/L)^{1-\psi}(\xi_L)^{\psi}(\xi_K)^{1-\psi} \tag{14}$$

as an equation for per capita output.

It is not easy to measure ψ in poor countries, because much economic activity is undertaken by independent proprietors (peasants, petty traders, and so on) who receive diverse blends of "wage" and "profit" incomes. However, a consensus view is that ψ is well less than 0.5 in a very poor economy and perhaps 0.8 in a rich one (recall Table 1.4). If ψ were, say, 2/3, then if a tenfold difference in income per capita were to be explained only by variation in the capital/labor ratio, K/L would have to be $10^3 = 1,000$ times as high in the rich country as in the poor one. Such a differential (and on neoclassical grounds a correspondingly enormous profit rate spread) is not observed. A labor productivity differential of $10^{3/2} = 31.6$ would suffice, as would combined capital/labor ratio and labor productivity differentials of ten each (all assuming no capital productivity differential or Marx bias). A principal concern of contemporary mainstream growth theorists is to "explain" how cross-country labor productivity differentials on the order of ten can possibly arise. Their most recent ploys are to enhance the importance of saving and thrift by invoking accumulation of "human," "intangible," "organizational" or other forms of capital which are supposed to raise ξ_L, to redefine the accounting to raise the capital contribution $1 - \psi$, or both. See Chapter 11 for some details.

A Kaldor Growth Model

Decades in advance of the contemporary mainstream, Kaldor (1957) was concerned with the role of endogenous technical change in growth. He also wanted an independent investment function and full employment of labor. As discussed above, in the short run forced saving permits the investment function and full employment to coexist. Kaldor's model is a dynamic extension of this closure, coupled with his "technical progress function."

The short-run story can be read from Figure 5.1. Capacity utilization u follows from the full employment level of λ in a counterclockwise reading of the southwest quadrant based on the relationships $u = \lambda/b = \xi_L\lambda$. The capital stock growth rate and the profit rate and share are determined by the intersection of $g_2^i + \gamma_g$ with g^s, as outlined above. For use below, the explicit solution for the growth rate is

$$g = \frac{(s_\pi - s_w)(g_0 + \beta u) + \alpha(\gamma_g - s_w u)}{s_\pi - (s_w + \alpha)} \tag{15}$$

Kaldor's (1961) stylized facts about advanced economies included a stable output/capital ratio and profit rate combined with steady increases in labor productivity and the capital/labor ratio over time. Along the lines of the Verdoorn (1949) and Okun (1962) "Laws" mentioned in Chapter 2, he bundled the latter two observations into a "technical progress function" for labor productivity, $\xi_L = f(K/L)$. In growth rate form,

$$\hat{\xi}_L = \epsilon_L = \phi_0 + \phi_1(g - n). \tag{16}$$

The natural state variable for the Kaldor model is the output/capital ratio u. If its differential equation is stable, u presumably will not be observed differing greatly from its value at steady state, fitting the stylized fact. Since $u = \xi_L\lambda$, using (16) the time derivative $\dot{u}$ is given by

$$\dot{u} = u[(1 - \phi_1)(n - g) + \phi_0]. \tag{17}$$

Old-fashioned stability analysis is based on the hypothesis that $0 < \phi_1 < 1$, so that labor productivity growth in (16) does not generate its own knife-edge. We then have $d\dot{u}/du < 0$ when $dg/du > 0$ from (15). With a positive denominator in this formula (the short-run forced saving adjustment process is stable from (10) because aggregate demand is wage-led), $dg/du > 0$ when $(s_\pi - s_w)\beta - \alpha s_w > 0$, or there is a big difference in saving propensities and the accelerator coefficient β is large. From Chapter 4, these are just the conditions required for growth to be wage-led in an economy where output is the adjusting variable. Forced saving supports steady-state stability when *both* the output/capital ratio and the capital stock growth rate are wage-led.

From (17), the long-run, natural rate of growth when $\dot{u} = 0$ is

$$g = n + \phi_0/(1 - \phi_1),$$

which depends only on population expansion and the parameters of the technical progress function. The steady-state output/capital ratio and profit share follow from the conditions for short-term equilibrium. In a widely discussed special case, if there is no government dis-saving ($\gamma_g = 0$) and $s_w = 0$, then the "Cambridge equation" (simplified from (5) in Table 5.1)

$$g = s_\pi \pi u = s_\pi r \tag{18}$$

determines long-run income distribution from the steady-state values of r, π, and u. Moreover, because $\pi = 1 - \omega b = 1 - \omega/\xi_L$ and is constant, we have $\hat{\omega} = \epsilon_L$, or the real wage increases at the rate of labor productivity growth. This 100 percent pass-through of productivity gains into real wage increases is characteristic of growth model steady states which hold factor shares constant. It shows up in the Solow and Ramsey formulations as well.[7]

In the spirit of his times, Kaldor concentrated on such steady-state outcomes, rather than on the possibilities of "endogenous" growth or contraction occurring in the dynamically unstable case when $\phi_1 > 1$. Such possibilities are examined in Chapter 11.

Marxist Models

For reasons sketched in Chapter 11, it is extremely difficult to shoehorn Marx into simple formal models. Regardless, people continue to try. One example is another counterclockwise reading of Figure 5.2 which fixes the real wage in the southeast quadrant, say from "class struggle"—see Sen (1963), Marglin (1984), and Dutt (1990). Again, there is no room for an independent investment function, as u, λ, r, and g all follow from ω. Capital stock growth g will in general not be the same as the natural growth rate n, which eventually may lead the model to break down.[8]

One problem with this formulation is that Marx was well aware of the role played by technological change in generating crises and growth. If there is labor productivity growth and a fixed real wage, equation (10) in Chapter 2 already shows that the profit rate would have to trend steadily upward—a tendency that is never observed. From a Marxist perspective, a model with a predetermined wage share as opposed to Sen's fixed real wage is a more appropriate vehicle for the analysis of productivity growth. Foley and Michl (1999) develop such a specification and work through several applications. Their setup is consistent with the cyclical growth models analyzed in Chapter 9.

3. Harrod, Robinson, and Related Stories

Growth models driven from the side of demand are much less common than their supply-side cousins in the literature. Nevertheless, they have considerable intrinsic interest, and also serve as the framework for much of the analysis in Chapters 7–11. We present an introduction here, beginning with the controversy over Harrod's instability problem and then going on to the more stable formulation used in the rest of the book.

As noted above, Solow seems in part to have seen his dynamics as a means of getting around the "knife-edge" that Harrod (1939) emphasized in his pioneering growth model. That is, for Solow λ adjusts smoothly to let the capital stock growth rate $g(\lambda)$ converge to labor force growth n. As we have seen, the basic mechanism is a counterclockwise reading of Figures 5.1 and 5.2.

Harrod, as it turns out, was a clockwise economist. His knife-edge exists not because saving drives investment but because causality runs the other way and the investment function is rambunctious enough to cause long-term instability. We can fill in some details and also discuss another potentially unstable investment-driven model proposed by Robinson (1956).

Harrod's paper is not easy to read, and contains no explicit model. For that reason, three proposed formalizations are quickly presented here. In the first, due to Barbosa-Filho (2001a), output is the short-run adjusting variable (which can jump), and the capital stock grows steadily over time. For reasons to be made clear soon, it is interesting to carry "autonomous" real expenditures A as a component of demand, $X = C + I + A$. The variable A could comprise the intercept term in a Keynesian consumption function, government spending, net exports, and so on. With $a = A/K$, $g = I/K = \hat{K}$, and s as the overall saving rate, macro balance takes the form $su = g + a$ in a slight extension of the familiar "Harrod-Domar" equation. By simple differentiation, it is also true that

$$dg/dt = g(\hat{I} - g) \tag{19}$$

and

$$da/dt = a(\hat{A} - g). \tag{20}$$

This system of equations has a nontrivial solution only when $\hat{I} = \hat{A} = g$, that is, the growth rates of investment, autonomous spending, and capital are all equal. In the discussion to follow, $\hat{A}$ is treated as a predetermined "forcing" variable in (19)–(20).

A standard interpretation of Harrod is that his model is based on strong accelerator dynamics, say

$$\hat{I} = f(u) = f[(g + a)/s] \tag{21}$$

with f as an increasing function.[9] On this hypothesis, the Jacobian of (19) and (20) evaluated at a stationary point becomes

$$J = \begin{bmatrix} g[(f'/s) - 1] & gf'/s \\ -a & 0 \end{bmatrix},$$

in which $f' = df/du$.

The system will be stable when $f' < s$, in a dynamic analog to the usual Keynesian stability condition discussed in Chapter 4. If this inequality is violated, the variables will follow a diverging counterclockwise spiral in the (g, a) plane, along lines discussed in Chapter 9. The formulation captures at least part of what Harrod had in mind with his knife-edge. An overly strong investment response can easily push the growth rate away from its steady state value $\hat{A}$.

If the model is stable, the autonomous spending term can be used to address concerns raised during the 1930s by "secular stagnationist" Keynesians like Hansen (1938). They thought that active fiscal policy would be needed to offset what they saw as a long-term collapse in investment demand. It is easy to see that an increase in the growth rate of autonomous spending $\hat{A}$ will increase the long-term economy-wide rate of growth in (19) and (20). Hansen did not foresee how "military Keynesianism" during and after World War II would make his fiscal worries disappear.

Besides thinking about accelerators, Harrod also contrasted the natural growth rate n with a "warranted" capital stock growth rate g^w. To see what he may have had in mind, it is simplest to drop autonomous spending and to define variables relative to the labor force (and population). The output/labor ratio (or average labor productivity) is $\xi_L = X/L$, investment per worker is $\iota = I/L$, and $k = K/L$ is the capital stock per capita. The per capita macro demand balance is $\xi_L = (1 - s)\xi_L + \iota$, where again s is the saving rate from output. Clearly, $\xi_L = \iota/s$, and can jump in response to shifts in investment and saving rates. It is easy to see that

$$\dot{k} = k(g - n) = \iota - nk = s\xi_L - nk. \tag{22}$$

A steady state exists when $\dot{k} = 0$. Implications are that $\iota = s\xi_L = nk$ and $g = \iota/k = s\xi_L/k = s/\mu$, where $\mu = K/X$ is the capital/output ratio.[10] The "warranted rate" is $g^w = su = s/\mu$. If savings equals investment thanks to short-run market clearing (which may or may not have been assumed by Harrod), the warranted rate will be the observed growth rate as well. In steady state, the warranted and natural rates are equal. Harrod's question was, is such a steady state stable?

Once again, the answer could be no. As we have seen in (21), in which $\hat{I} = (dI/dt)/I$ responds to $g = I/K$, one way to build instability into the model is by positive feedback of investment demand into itself. For example, we can replace (6) with a function determining the *change* in investment instead of its *level*. Suppose that firms have a target level of output per capita given by the expression $\bar{\xi}_L = k\bar{u}$ with $\bar{u}$ as a "normal" level of the output/capital ratio (not necessarily equal to the steady state value n/s). Then the investment function might be

$$d\iota/dt = \phi(\xi_L - \bar{\xi}_L) = \phi[(\iota/s) - k\bar{u}] \tag{23}$$

with ϕ as a response coefficient.

The Jacobian of (22) and (23) is

$$J = \begin{bmatrix} -n & 1 \\ -\phi\bar{u} & \phi/s \end{bmatrix}$$

with $\text{Tr } J = (\phi/s) - n$ and $\text{Det } J = \phi[(\bar{u} - (n/s)]$. Instability can show up in a couple of ways. First, if firms set their target output/capital ratio too low, $\bar{u} < n/s$, then $\text{Det } J < 0$ and there will be saddlepoint dynamics. If the target output level is higher, $\bar{u} > n/s$, then a moderately strong accelerator coefficient, $\phi > sn$, could destabilize the system. If $\bar{u} = ns$ exactly, (23) reduces to

$$i = (\phi/s)(\iota - nk) \tag{23a}$$

so that $\text{Det } J = 0$ and the system is indeterminate. Since it incorporates changes in investment rather than the capital stock, (23a) has "faster" dynamics than (22) and would presumably lead to instability if some shock perturbs the steady-state equality $\iota = nk$.

This scenario seems to catch more of the essence of Harrod, although it suffers from relying on the specific investment function (23) and having an output/capital ratio that is endogenous as opposed to being "technically determined" in the short run. A basically similar story is proposed by Sen (1970), with less emphasis on the natural rate and more on an investment function based on a Marx/Keynes dialectic between expectations and realizations.

Translating Sen's analysis from discrete to continuous time, let X stand for current output, $X^r = X + \dot{X}^r\delta$ for output to be "realized" a short time δ from now, and $X^e = X + \dot{X}^e\delta$ for expected future output. The warranted rate is $\dot{X}^r/X = s/\mu$ with μ (or u) treated as a parameter instead of a variable as in the previous example. The warranted and natural rates are implicitly assumed to be equal in an initial steady state.

More precisely, μ can be interpreted as a "marginal" capital/output ratio. Then investment demand is determined by an accelerator relationship $I = \mu\dot{X}^e\delta$ so that $X = I/s = (\mu/s)\dot{X}^e\delta$. If $\dot{X}^e = \dot{X}^r$, the economy stays on the warranted growth path. Instability arises when it is somehow pushed away from this perfect foresight trajectory. To see the details, let $g^i = \dot{X}^i/X$ for $i = r$ and e. A bit of algebra shows that

$$g^r - g^e = (\mu/s)[(X^r - X^e)/X]g^e.$$

If expected growth is stimulated when realizations outrun expectations,

$$dg^e/dt = \phi(g^r - g^e) = \phi(\mu/s)[(X^r - X^e)/X]g^e \tag{24}$$

then we have positive feedback of g^e into itself and a knife-edge. Any small blip of X^r over X^e will make the right-hand side of (24) positive and set off explosive growth. The investment equations (21), (23), and (24) all share a family relationship and give rise to similar dynamic outcomes.

Harrod-style assumptions can be used in the analysis of cycles (Shaikh 1989) and also underlie much of "new" or "endogenous" growth theory (Chapter 11). However, they are counterfactual insofar as capitalist economies (not even Japan in the 1990s) are not observed to have rapidly accelerating or decelerating rates of growth. A growth model with an accelerator investment function that *can* maintain a steady state was proposed by Robinson (1956).

If all wage income is consumed, equation (5) in Table 5.1 shows that from the side of saving the growth rate must satisfy the "Cambridge equation" (18) introduced above. Suppose that the investment function takes the form

$$\dot{g} = \phi[f(r) - r], \tag{25}$$

in which $f(r)$ gauges the extent to which entrepreneurs are stimulated to greater capital formation. When expected profits $f(r)$ exceed the cost of capital r, they bid up the capital stock growth rate. Presumably, the incentive diminishes as r goes up.

Appropriately drawn, (18) and (25) create "Joan Robinson's banana"

Figure 5.3
Joan Robinson's
banana.

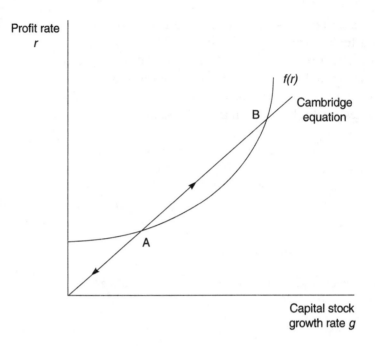

in Figure 5.3. The lower equilibrium at A is a knife-edge à la Harrod. At point B, $f(r) = r$ and $f'(r) < 1$, producing a stable steady state. We will see in Chapter 9 how dynamic expectations about expected profits in the model can generate cyclical growth.

4. More Stable Demand-Determined Growth

Sticking with an investment function of the form of (6), is it possible to construct growth models based on clockwise readings of Figures 5.1 and 5.2? The answer is certainly in the affirmative—it makes perfect sense to consider capital stock growth trajectories when there is an independent investment function and unemployment is possible in the long run (a "bastard golden age" in Joan Robinson's (1956) terminology). At present, the existence of readily employable labor is not a bad assumption in most economies of western Europe and is certainly a good one in the developing world (especially for those countries afflicted with IMF-style austerity programs in recent years). Over extended periods of time, output adjusting in Keynes/Kalecki fashion becomes an obvious closure to consider.

Moreover, it is possible to bring in IS/LM by assuming that the investment function takes the form

$$g^i = g_0 + \alpha r + \beta u - \theta i = g_0 + (\alpha \pi + \beta)u - \theta i$$

as in previous chapters. Then in short-run equilibrium with an institutionally determined profit share π or wage share $\psi = 1 - \pi$, the reduced-form equations for capacity utilization and the capital stock growth rate are

$$u = \frac{g_0 + \gamma_g - \theta i}{s(\pi) - (\alpha\pi + \beta)} \tag{26}$$

and

$$g = \frac{(\alpha\pi + \beta)\gamma_g + s(\pi)(g_0 - \theta i)}{s(\pi) - (\alpha\pi + \beta)} \tag{27}$$

where $s(\pi) = s_\pi\pi + s_w(1 - \pi)$ from (5).

There are several paths to be explored with (26) and (27). One involves distribution as it emerges from productivity- and cost-based inflation dynamics. With the profit or wage share given at a point in time, g is a function of the interest rate i emerging from a short-run IS/LM system comprising (11) and (26). As we will see in the following chapters, there are reasons to believe that distributive indicators change in response to several forces. As they move, then so will the growth rate. For example, in (27) g is both a direct and an indirect (through IS/LM) function of π or ψ, which in turn evolves according to its own proper dynamics.

A steady state is reached in such a model when the dynamic process for the wage share reaches a point at which $\hat{\psi} = 0$. As already noted in Chapter 4, g can vary across such steady states, which is not the case with employment-constrained growth. Demand-driven growth models are useful for asking how certain policies affect prospects for sustained economic expansion. A question relevant in developing countries, for example, is whether there is a natural way for recently popular external liberalization policy packages to lead an economy to socially acceptable rates of employment and growth. The observed answer to this particular query very often seems to be no (Pieper and Taylor 1998; Taylor 2000).

Second, one can ask similar questions about monetary policy, using equation (11), which includes the state variable $Z = PK/T$. The task is to consider its evolution over time coupled with ψ in a two-dimensional system, after solving for i, u, and g in (11), (26), and (27). Intriguing dynamic scenarios can emerge from such systems, as we will see in Chapters 7 and 8.

Third, it is of interest to analyze pension schemes from a Keynesian perspective as opposed to the supply-determined OLG model of Chapter 3 with its odd assumptions about saving. To keep the algebra within bounds, we can assume a zero saving rate from wage income and ignore

LM linkages. As in the OLG model, we work with cohorts of employable households H_t which work in period t and live off pension income in period $t + 1$. At time t, overall macro balance can be written as

$$X_t = (1 - s_\pi)\pi X_t + (1 - \pi)X_t - qH_t + Z_t + I_t.$$

Household numbers grow between periods at the rate n so that $H_{t+1} = (1 + n)H_t$. In the period when they can work, all households (whether employed or not) are assessed an amount q which is used to finance pensions.[11] Total social security disbursements to the retired population are Z_t. Both the households in the labor force and the retirees have zero savings rates, so the pension program basically shifts resources from one high-consuming group to another.

A "pay-go" scheme in this model just uses contributions directly to pay retirees, $Z_t = qH_t$, with no impact on effective demand. The number of retirees is $H_t/(1 + n)$ so their benefit per household is $(1 + n)q$, just as in the OLG model. The difference is that in an OLG world a pay-go scheme has visible effects on macro performance, whereas in a Keynesian world it doesn't.

A fully funded scheme, in contrast, has effects on output and growth in the Keynesian model but not in the OLG. The total pension outlay in period t is $Z_t = q[H_t/(1 + n)](1 + r_t)$, which need not be equal to qH_t. That is, each of the $H_t/(1 + n)$ employable households in period $t - 1$ paid a contribution q which was invested to give them a return at the interest (= profit) rate r_t. Let $\eta_t = H_t/K_t$. Then taking into account the effects of the pension program, one can write out an expression analogous to (26) as follows:

$$\{s_\pi\pi - (\alpha\pi + \beta) - [\pi q\eta_t/(1 + n)]\}u_t = g_0 - [nq\eta_t/(1 + n)].$$

Letting $B > 0$ stand for the bracketed expression multiplying u_t, one finds that

$$du_t = B^{-1}[(r_t - n)q/(1 + n)]d\eta_t,$$

so a higher population/capital ratio η_t will raise capacity utilization u_t and growth $g_t = s_\pi\pi u_t$ when the profit rate exceeds the rate of population growth (the empirically relevant case). The intuition is that the demand injection from the pension investment "last period" is outrunning the increased leakage due to population growth. A similar condition will come into play when we consider debt dynamics in Chapter 6.

It will also be true that

$$\eta_{t+1} = \eta_t\{1 + (1 + g_t)(n - g_t)\}. \tag{28}$$

At an initial steady state with $\eta_{t+1} = \eta_t = \eta^*$, the warranted and natural growth rates will have to be equal, $g_t = n$. Differentiating (28) with respect to η_t and using this condition gives the result

$$d\eta_{t+1}/d\eta_t = 1 - \eta_t(1 + g_t)(dg_t/d\eta_t).$$

For dynamic stability we need $d\eta_{t+1}/d\eta_t < 1$. This condition can apply if $dg_t/d\eta_t > 0$, which from the discussion above appears to be the case. The dynamic analysis will be the same as in the upper diagram of Figure 3.5. One can ask, for example, what will happen if the scale of the pension scheme is expanded via an increase in q. With $r_t > n$, it is easy to see that there will be an increase in effective demand and output growth in the short run. The accumulation locus will shift downward, leading to a new, lower value of η^*. The shift signals a *higher* level of capital per household, or a richer population. In Keynesian models, long-run outcomes of pension schemes and all other fiscal innovations are driven by the paradox of thrift. The effects of the policy change are 180 degrees removed from those emerging from the OLG model in Chapter 3.

This sort of outcome leads to one last question about demand-determined models. It implies that there are no "normal" long-term levels of capacity utilization u, the capital stock growth rate g, and the steady-state household/capital ratio η^*. Such results seem to bother a lot of people, and set off a debate summarized by Lavoie (1995). The central questions appear to be (1) whether it makes sense to postulate that a "natural rate" of capacity utilization u^* exists, and (2) if it does exist what forces will make u converge to u^* in the long run?

With regard to the second question at least two answers show up in recent literature. One involves modifying the investment function (6) in Table 5.1 to make g^i depend on a term such as $(u - u_n)$, where u_n stands for normal capacity use. Following Lavoie, if one further postulates adaptive evolution for u_n,

$$\dot{u}_n = \rho(u - u_n),$$

as well as for the animal spirits term g_0 in the investment function,

$$\dot{g}_0 = \mu(g - g_0)$$

then Dutt (1997) shows that this two-dimensional system will end up at a point where $u = u_n$. The equilibrium values of g_0 and u_n will depend on initial conditions, moreover, so that "history matters" in the determination of economic performance.

Although no one seems to have done it, the Lavoie-Dutt specification could be combined with another approach suggested by Barbosa-Filho

CHAPTER FIVE

198

(2000). The central point is that u in (26) depends on various parameters *and* the profit share π. One could then set up dynamics on π to steer u toward a predetermined u^* or an evolving u_n. Once again, capacity utilization would tend toward a "natural" or "normal" level.

Referring to the first question above, however, one can ask whether such a procedure makes modeling sense. As discussed in Chapters 7 and 9, profit and wage shares have their own proper dynamics in terms of wage and price inflation rates and the growth rate of productivity. It may be more appropriate to work directly with such variables to determine a long-run distributive equilibrium which can shift in response to economic forces. At the end of the day, structuralist models don't blend happily with natural rates.

CHAPTER SIX

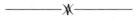

Chicago Monetarism, New Classical Macroeconomics, and Mainstream Finance

In the mainstream's eyes, ruling macroeconomic doctrines from the 1960s through century's end were built on the rubble from the neoclassical demolition of the castle of Keynes. Before returning to structuralist analysis, it makes sense to undertake a critical review of the new theories that were constructed.

By around 1960, the main building blocks of *The General Theory*—the principle of effective demand and determination of output through the income-expenditure linkage (Clower's "dual decision hypothesis" mentioned in Chapter 4)—had been effectively supplanted by the real balance effect and determination of the value of output *PX* by the talismanic letters *MV*.[1] The counterrevolutionary task remaining was to restore the second classical postulate and determine *X* by labor supply.

This operation took two stages. The first was the "natural rate" or "accelerationist" model advanced by Milton Friedman (1968) and Edmund Phelps (1968), and the second was the rational expectations/perfect market clearing hypothesis put forth by new classicists such as Robert Lucas (1972), Thomas Sargent (1973), and Robert Barro (1976). The difference between the two approaches is a matter of timing. Both assert that macroeconomic equilibrium is determined by the first and second classical postulates, or the intersection of schedules for labor demand and supply derived from MIRA foundations. The natural rate model just makes convergence to this position run a little slower.

As previewed in Chapter 4, strong "policy ineffectiveness" propositions emerge from both versions, basically because the economy can't be budged from its postulated "natural" stationary or steady state. A widely debated extension of this fundamental new classical message is the argument that bond and tax financing on the part of the government are equivalent—a translation of the Modigliani-Miller theorem to the public domain under the rubric of "Ricardian equivalence."

The most recent thrust from the Right has been an effort (anticipated many decades previously by Marx, Schumpeter, Wicksell, and Hayek) to explain economic fluctuations from the supply side using "real business cycle" models. Their formal foundation is stochastic dynamic optimization, which also underlies the mainstream finance results quoted in previous chapters. The story here continues with reviews of these "pseudo-mathematical" reifications of the institutional complexities emphasized throughout this book.[2] They lead naturally to a couple of proofs of the Modigliani-Miller theorem, with which the chapter closes.

1. Methodological Caveats

Before we get into the algebra, a few general observations are in order. The first is that all new classical analysis is devoid of social content—the richly detailed capitalist world described by Keynes and Kalecki stands out by its absence.

The monetarist and rational expectations/perfect market clearing models' only difference from a purely atomistic Walrasian scenario is that information about prices and the money supply may take a while to get transmitted. In an "islands" parable advanced by Phelps (1969), for example, corporations, financial houses, and organized labor don't exist, because all production is in the hands of independent contractors (one for each commodity) who live on semi-isolated islands. Each such agent is on its labor supply curve (the second classical postulate) and knows the price of the product it sells. However, knowledge of the general price level travels at finite speed and picks up random "noise" while diffusing across islands. This "information asymmetry" is the sole source of macroeconomic dis-coordination. Other economic and social relations within and between islands don't exist.

Second, the epistemology underlying the models oddly combines an Austrian insistence on the powers of entrepreneurship to cut through market imperfections with a rigidly positivistic approach to the acquisition of knowledge—this is the (post–Frank Knight) Chicago angle. The central message of traditional Austrian economics that an unfettered market is the best guarantor of human well-being is given a philosophical twist more characteristic of the Vienna of Rudolf Carnap than of Carl Menger—fundamental uncertainty about future events yields to stochastic perfect foresight.

As noted in Chapter 4, Knight, Keynes, and Hayek all thought that human decisions are made under conditions of unavoidable ignorance—there is no means by which complete probability distributions can be imposed on the future. Indeed, the presence of uncertainty opens room for the entrepreneur to maneuver. When people have different ideas about the future, entrepreneurs can back their own judgments against those of others and succeed. They wouldn't have the chance if we all held common expectations and acted according to them in the same "rational" way (as the representative agent hypothesis suggests).

Keynes talked about "expectations" on almost every page of *The General Theory,* but (in roughly increasing order of precision) his use of word meant something like "adivinations," "anticipations," or "views" about events to come. We have seen how he thought that attempts to calculate expected values of future happenings in a probabilistic sense were worse than useless.

Knight's and Hayek's doubts and Keynes's objections were overthrown in the 1960s, when for most economists the meanings of "expectation" and "expected value" in the sense of probability theory became identical.[3] Moreover, the ideas took hold that an "objective" model of the economy exists and that its structure is shared knowledge among all agents—concepts unthinkable to Knight, Hayek, and Keynes. In contemporary usage, "rational" really means "model-consistent" expectations under quantifiable risk—nonsense from anything but a particular epistemological point of view. For the new Austrians, incomplete knowledge à la Hayek is replaced by (nearly) perfect prescience in support of a welfare-optimizing economic system which seeks its ends independent of policy moves.[4]

Third, as Mirowski (2002) argues, after World War II there was a concerted effort, with the Cowles Commission, MIT, and (to a degree) Chicago in the vanguard, to mathematize microeconomics in support of Walrasian models and subsequently Nash equilibrium game theory (in Mirowski's view the Mephisto who provoked this campaign was none other than the "Hungarian wizard" or mathematical "demigod" John von Neumann). On this account, related developments in macroeconomics such as the neoclassical synthesis and new classical and new Keynesian modeling were automatic by-products because they could sell themselves as being analytically high tech.

The new tricks included Lucas's importation of the rational expectations idea from the microeconomics of commodity markets, and extensive new classical use of the deterministic and stochastic optimal control methodologies being perfected by applied mathematicians in the 1960s. The notion that there is a "true" model of the economy may have come from this source.

After all, if optimal control models building on Newton's (true) laws enable NASA to guide a rocket to the moon under statistically noisy conditions, why can't stochastic optimization analysis also be applied to an "islands" economy for which we are assured a unique model exists? The difference is that when in 1684 Edmund Halley (of later comet fame)

went up from London to Cambridge to ask the celebrated but somewhat strange mathematician Isaac Newton to clarify the rumors that
were running around about inverse square gravity laws, he got the definitive answer in the form of *Principia Mathematica* within three years;
Walrasian economists have not produced anything remotely comparable
in over one hundred. The economy rests on changing social relations—
all attempts to describe it in terms of timeless constructs like Newton's
laws, Einstein's field equations, or Feynman's diagrams are bound to fail.
Stochastic but rational expectations built upon a nonexistent "true"
model correspondingly have no content.

Finally, the alleged intellectual power of the new techniques was but-
tressed by the convenient "collapse" of the empirical Phillips curve in the
late 1960s. The story is that Phillips (1958) found a century-long association in the United Kingdom between changes in unemployment and
wage inflation. Samuelson and Solow (1960) observed a seemingly similar inverse correlation between price inflation and the unemployment
rate in post-Depression U.S. data. This relationship continued to fit the
numbers well until around 1970, when inflation accelerated while unemployment rose in a burst of "stagflation." This breakdown of the Phillips
relationship left the gates of macroeconomics wide open for anti-
Keynesian theories to charge in.

With hindsight and in terms of structuralist inflation theory, the events
of the 1970s are not so startling. We now know that the institutional consensus which supported the historically unprecedented output
growth rates of the Golden Age between the late 1940s and the late
1960s had fallen apart, with worldwide reductions in productivity
growth and capital accumulation (Glyn et al. 1990). Conflict was on the
rise, spilling over into faster inflation and social unrest. As will be shown
in Chapters 7 and 9, wage and price inflation and their expectations interact in complicated fashion. An upward shift in pressure for wage increases together with downward movements of productivity growth and
the investment demand function provide the basis for a coherent, socially based theory about events in the 1970s that is verified herein and
elsewhere (see Bowles, Gordon, and Weisskopf, 1990, for example).

Even with the Samuelson-Solow period included, longer-term data for
industrialized economies on inflation versus the rate of employment or
capacity utilization such as those presented by Galbraith and Darity
(1994) and Romer (2001) typically show up as a cloud of points in the
$(u, \hat{P})$ plane, perhaps with a gentle inclination from southwest to northeast. One interpretation is that $\hat{P}$ on the vertical axis is the "dependent"
variable driven in the long term by u and its determining factors on the
horizontal. The most obvious statistical association is a line with a slight
positive slope ("the" Phillips curve) or maybe a curve that undulates as

in Figure 7.1 below in Eisner's (1996) tentative interpretation. One implication is that the unemployment cost of policies aimed at substantially reducing inflation is likely to be high.

Were u the "dependent" variable, the regression line through the data cloud would be near-vertical (instead of near-horizontal) with an intercept not far to the left of u's sample mean. This is the "vertical Phillips curve" at the heart of monetarist and new classical models. The data themselves no more point toward a vertical curve than a flat one; the causal structure to be imposed on the numbers has to come from outside the $(u, \hat{P})$ plane. Monetarists and new classicists happen to prefer a Walrasian interpretation in which u responds to price changes (plus random error terms) but is basically fixed;[5] structuralists see $\hat{P}$ as responding to u in a fairly complicated system which may include feedbacks such as the inflation tax and forced saving.

Friedman, Lucas, and friends would have painted their preferred model on the data regardless of whether the American Phillips curve had "collapsed" or not, but there is no denying that the break in Samuelson and Solow's phenomenological relationship came at just the right time to give anti-Keynesian arguments tremendous polemical force.

2. A Chicago Monetarist Model

In stripped-down form, both monetarist and new classical models can be described in three equations. In the (u, ω) plane used throughout this book, there is a reduced form aggregate demand relationship which can be written as

$$u^a = f^a(\gamma_g, M/P), \tag{1}$$

where γ_g is the fiscal deficit (scaled by the capital stock) and M/P stands for real money balances.

In Friedman's version of the model, labor is demanded by firms which can perfectly observe the product wage $\omega = w/P$. By Keynes's first classical postulate, the number of people they employ and therefore the level of economic activity u^d will be an inverse function of ω along an f^d schedule which combines a "production function" relationship between u^d and the labor/capital ratio λ, and a "labor demand" relationship between λ and ω (recall the hat calculus discussion in Chapter 2):

$$u^d = f^d(\omega). \tag{2}$$

Finally, workers rely on out-of-date price information, because either there are lags in contracts, it is not easy to gather information on a big set of prices to recalculate the consumption wage continuously, or it takes time for price data to diffuse across Phelps's islands. The labor supply decision is thereby based on an expected price P^e. If we let $\xi^p = P/P^e$, labor supply will depend on $w/P^e = \omega\xi^p$. Running this response through the production function gives

$$u^s = f^s(\omega\xi^p). \tag{3}$$

In many presentations of the accelerationist model, (3) is treated as a "notional" relationship with macro equilibrium being determined by (1) and (2). An upward shift in aggregate demand (from a higher money supply M, say) would shift the u^a schedule to the right from an initial point A, as in Figure 6.1. The new short-run equilibrium would be at B, ratified by a lower real wage ω. Presumably the reduction in ω is achieved by a jump in the price level P, which also would shift the u^a schedule back toward the left. Workers aren't quite with it because they think the real wage is still $\omega\xi^p$ at the "old" level of ω. But with a lag they revise expectations according to an error-correction rule such as

$$\dot{\xi}^p = \rho^p(1 - \xi^p), \tag{4}$$

and the u^s schedule begins to shift downward.

The story doesn't end there, however. Workers are getting paid a real wage lower than they want so long as the value of ω along the u^s curve lies above its value at the intersection of u^a and u^d; they may start pushing for higher money wages as a consequence. The price level will re-

Figure 6.1
Standard diagram for the Friedman-Phelps model.

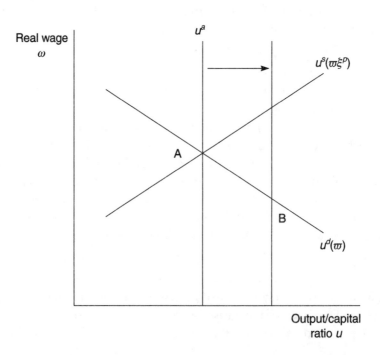

Real wage ω

u^a

$u^s(\varpi\xi^p)$

A

B

$u^d(\varpi)$

Output/capital ratio u

spond through producers' cost functions, pushing the u^a curve further back to the left via the real balance effect. After some sort of dynamic process, the economy will end up again at point A, with the demand jump eroded by higher prices and Say's Law in force. This "policy neutrality" result is the central thrust of both monetarist and new classical analysis; it just takes a while to work itself through in the Chicago version.

3. A Cleaner Version of Monetarism

The foregoing narrative is all right as far as it goes, but it leaves the details of dynamic adjustment a bit fuzzy. The plot can be clarified if we stick with Say's Law, but assume fast adjustment of *both* nominal variables P and w. Such a use of separate market-clearing equations for prices and wages is characteristic of recent structuralist models such as those in Flaschel, Franke, and Semmler (1997).

The price level naturally varies to clear the commodity market,

$$f^a(\gamma_g, M/P) - f^d(w/P) = 0. \tag{5}$$

That is, an increase in P reduces aggregate demand via the real balance effect and raises output because firms hire more workers.

A higher money wage w clears the labor market,

$$f^d(w/P) - f^s(w/P^e) = 0, \tag{6}$$

by reducing labor demand and increasing supply.

Workers' adaptive expectations in (3) can be rewritten as

$$\hat{P}^e = \hat{P} + \rho^p[(P - P^e)/P], \tag{7}$$

where ρ^p again is a response coefficient. Equations (5)–(7) make up a complete dynamic model.

The first two relationships can be analyzed using comparative statics. Their behavior in the short run can be illustrated if we use hat calculus to rewrite them in log-linear form,

$$a\hat{\gamma}_g + b(\hat{M} - \hat{P}) + c(\hat{w} - \hat{P}) = 0 \tag{5'}$$

and

$$-c(\hat{w} - \hat{P}) - d(\hat{w} - \hat{P}^e) = 0, \tag{6'}$$

where a, b, c, and d are all elasticities. Restating these equations in matrix notation gives

$$\begin{bmatrix} -(b+c) & c \\ c & -(c+d) \end{bmatrix} \begin{bmatrix} \hat{P} \\ \hat{w} \end{bmatrix} \begin{bmatrix} -(a\hat{\gamma}_g + b\hat{M}) \\ -d\hat{P}^e \end{bmatrix} \tag{8}$$

Because $(b + c)/c > 1 > c/(c + d)$, the slope $d(\log w)/d(\log P)$ of the Commodity market schedule is greater than one, and the slope of the Labor market curve is less than one, as shown in Figure 6.2. A shift to the right of the commodity schedule induced by $\hat{\gamma}_g > 0$ or $\hat{M} > 0$ increases the P/w ratio, or the real wage falls. An upward shift in the labor market locus when $\hat{P}^e > 0$ increases w/P.

With this information at hand, we can quickly run through a couple of adjustment scenarios, beginning at an initial equilibrium where $P^e = P$. As just noted, a higher γ_g makes P jump up more than w, leading firms to hire more workers and output to increase. From (7), P^e begins to rise, pushing up w and P with less than unit elasticities (as is easily verified from the algebra in (8)) but raising w/P. Aggregate demand u^d declines with the continuing increase in P, supply u^s falls back as w rises less than P, and the output level u^d corresponding to labor demand drops off with a higher w/P.

These three shifts together drive the system back to its initial output level, but with higher nominal values of w, P, and P^e. Consumption demand is 100 percent crowded out by higher fiscal spending through a reduction in real balances M/P. There is a similar long-run response to a jump in the money supply, except that after the adjustment is complete levels of government and private consumption remain the same. In the short run, monetary stimulus may be effective through the Pigou/Patinkin and Keynes effects, but its long-term potency is nil. Be-

Figure 6.2
Nominal price and wage adjustment in the Friedman-Phelps model.

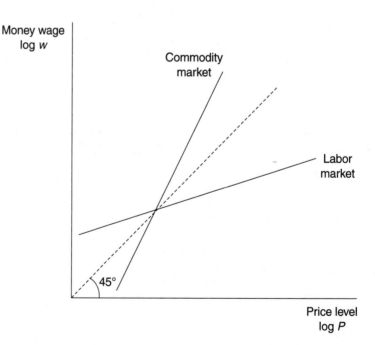

cause in Friedman's world the permanent income hypothesis makes demand multipliers vanish, fiscal policy is weak in both the short and the long runs.

To summarize, we have a story in which the real balance effect makes sure that Say's Law holds in a static model. Price and wage increases fully offset efforts at inducing higher employment by expansionary policy. Contractionary policies would be symmetrically frustrated by price and wage reductions. These exercises all take the form of comparative statics, with no dynamic processes except changes over time of P^e. After all the uproar about overthrowing the Phillips curve, whatever has happened to inflation?

The only way that ongoing price increases can be kindled in the present model is by persistent growth of the money supply, perhaps supporting Friedman's slogan that "inflation is always and everywhere a monetary phenomenon." But with a lag of decades, his dynamics (implicitly based on "helicopter drops" of currency) lack the institutional richness of Wicksell's. The liveliest story involves conscious acceleration of inflation by the authorities. With luck, they might keep employment above its Say's Law level for a time, thereby giving the model its "accelerationist" nickname. For all its enormous impact on politics and policy, the intellectual content of the monetarist counterrevolution is remarkably thin.[6]

4. New Classical Spins

The main difference between new classical macroeconomics and its monetarist progenitor is that it makes policy ineffectiveness propositions come true instantaneously. The Lucas et al. model can be viewed as a special case of Friedman's machine in which the adjustment coefficient ρ^p in (7) goes to zero so that $\hat{P}^e$ becomes very nearly equal to $\hat{P}$. Equation (8) can be restated as

$$\begin{bmatrix} -(b+c) & c \\ (c+d) & -(c+d) \end{bmatrix} \begin{bmatrix} \hat{P} \\ \hat{W} \end{bmatrix} = \begin{bmatrix} -(\alpha\hat{\gamma}_g + b\hat{M}) \\ 0 \end{bmatrix} \tag{9}$$

As shown in Figure 6.3, the Labor market schedule now coincides with the 45° line. Expansionary policy in the form of a positive value of $\hat{\gamma}_g$ or $\hat{M}$ will shift the Commodity market schedule rightward and immediately increase w and P in equal proportion, so that real output stays constant. Attempts at government intervention rapidly dissipate into nominal price jumps up or down; in the jargon, policy "super-neutrality" reigns.

As noted in previous chapters, the assumption that $\hat{P}^e = \hat{P}$ is not obvi-

Figure 6.3
Nominal price and
wage adjustment in
the new classical
model.

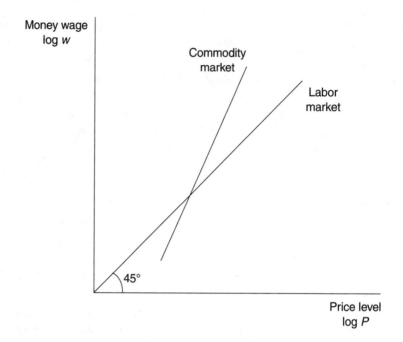

ously crazy. After all, people do learn rapidly about the state of play on the inflation front. The more relevant questions are whether it makes sense to use the real balance effect to suppress effective demand and replace it with the second classical postulate, and whether it is more appropriate to pass a flat or steep summary line through the inflation rate versus activity level data cloud. People can have honest disagreements about the answers, no doubt linked to their political positions and social predilections. Only extremely careful scrutiny of the data combined with institutional and historical knowledge coming from beyond technical economics per se can help to resolve them.

Such circumspection was not for the new classicists. Rather, on the basis of their radical Austrian positivism they spelled out additional propositions in support of Say's Law. The best known is the Lucas (1972) "supply function," which justifies dependence of u on $\hat{P}$ (broadly interpreted) rather than the reverse structuralist causality. In detail, the analysis involves symmetrical producers on Phelpsian islands, each specialized in selling a single product with price P_i and all consuming the same basket of goods made up of products from the whole archipelago.

Demand for each good is subject to a random shock z_i so that its sales volume is $X_i = X(P_i/P)^{-\eta}z_i$, where η is the price elasticity of demand (the same for all goods),[7] P is a consumption price deflator, and X is total real demand obeying the quantity theory rule $X = M/P$. When equilibrium is attained and error terms average out, normalization "per island" will make $P_i = P$ and $X_i = X$. The money supply M is also subject to random shocks. Together with the z_i, the shock to M makes observation of the price index P subject to probabilistic errors or noise.

Up to its stochastic specification, this model has the same structure as the ones discussed previously in this chapter. The first and second classical postulates apply because each producer maximizes a function based on utility from consumption and disutility from work, giving rise to curves similar to the u^s and u^d schedules, which shift with the z_i. The $X = M/P$ rule with M subject to random shocks has the same content as a schedule for u^a. The error terms are the new elements.

Rational or model-consistent expectations enter when we assume that all agents have complete knowledge of the technical details of production and consumption (the new classical "laws" of economics), and that they estimate P subject to known probability distributions for the z_i and the shock to M. Under strong behavioral assumptions—the main ones being that the island agents all share the same quadratic utility function in logs of employment and consumption, and that there are Gaussian probability distributions for $\log z_i$ and the log of the shock to M—a log-linear supply rule emerges from this formulation (Romer (2001) gives a clear presentation of the manipulative details). Each agent will end up supplying its product in accordance with an economy-wide equation that can be written as

$$\log X - \log \bar{X} = b[\log P - E(\log P)]. \tag{10}$$

Quadratic utility and Gaussian shocks together guarantee that $\log X$ depends in *linear* fashion *only* on $E(\log P)$ or the mathematical expectation of the log of the overall price level and not on this random variable's higher moments. According to Keynes, of course, even the expected value has no meaning.

Equation (10) is the famous "surprise" supply function. Output will differ from its Walrasian level $\bar{X}$ when $\log P$ randomly departs from its expected value. "Unexpected" price excursions or "inflation" explains any observed deviation of output and employment from the "natural" levels which fix the position of the vertical Phillips curve.

This formulation is a methodological refinement of the "expectations-augmented Phillips curve" which emerged in the wake of Friedman and Phelps,

$$\hat{P} = \hat{P}^e + a(\log X - \log \bar{X}) + \zeta, \tag{11}$$

where $\bar{X}$ is the NAIRU output level at which $\hat{P}^e = \hat{P}$ and ζ stands for supply shocks. When estimated subject to a rule like (7) for formation of expectations (not probabilistically expected values, necessarily) with $\hat{P}$ as the endogenous variable, equation (11) yields a small positive regression coefficient a, that is, a "horizontal" short-run Phillips curve. Because $\hat{P}^e$ is a linear combination of lagged values $f(\hat{P}_{lag})$ of $\hat{P}$, the change in inflation as measured by $\hat{P} - f(\hat{P}_{lag})$ will be positive when X exceeds $\bar{X}$.

This "accelerationist" interpretation is neat, but depends on econometric sleight-of-hand which gives the intercept of the regression equation (11) the particular label $-a(\log X)$. Without this trick, (11) becomes

$$\hat{P} = A + \hat{P}^e + a(\log X) + \zeta, \tag{12}$$

where $A < 0$ is an intercept term estimated in the usual way (scaling $\log X$ around its sample mean will make A negative when $a > 0$).

As noted above, if a convergent process is postulated for $\hat{P}^e$, then the Phillips curve (12) turns out to be nearly flat, or possibly configured like a snake crawling gradually northeast in the $(\log X, \hat{P})$ plane. In steady state, the effects of changes in $\log X$ on the inflation rate are small and may be of uncertain sign. A vertical long-run Phillips relationship emerges from (11) only when the intercept term A in (12) is said to define a NAIRU output point at which $\hat{P}^e = \hat{P}$ and $\zeta = 0$.

For new classicists, the Lucas model (10) rules out such undesirable outcomes by reversing causality to make X a function of random shocks to $\log P$, rather than having $\hat{P}$ depend on X. If a in (11) or (12) is small and positive, then its inverse b in (10) will be satisfyingly large. Log X will respond strongly to a shift in the variable $[\log P - E(\log P)] \approx \hat{P}$ and the Phillips curve will be nearly vertical. Such a robust short-run response of output and labor supply to price changes underlies the real business cycle models discussed later in this chapter. Unfortunately for its proponents, a large b coefficient is not easily inferred from industrialized economy employment data.

Utilizing his supply function, Lucas (1976) launched a well-known critique of phenomenological constructs like the Samuelson-Solow Phillips curve. The basic story is that if the authorities speed up money-supply growth to raise employment, this trick will work only so long as it drives a "surprise" increase of $\log P$ in (10). More likely sooner than later, people will catch on and raise $E(\log P)$, driving X back to its natural level where it belongs. Econometric estimates of the Phillips curve during this transition process may look good, but really don't mean anything.

The idea that the statistical relationship between X and $\hat{P}$ may change if policymakers attempt to take advantage of it became *the* mainstream rationale for the acceleration in inflation observed in industrialized economies in the 1970s. In the United States in particular, poor Lyndon Johnson and his neoclassically synthesizing economic advisors just didn't realize that the public would smoke out their efforts to drive the unemployment rate down and keep it there by pursuing monetary and fiscal expansion (the Vietnam-related contribution to these policies was not anticipated by the advisors, but that's another story).

As already discussed, from a structuralist perspective shifts in the functions underlying the model presented in Chapters 7 and 9 in association with observed social and political changes seem a less-contrived explanation for faster inflation in the 1970s. As a structuralist model would further predict, inflation then slowed after interest rates were raised dramatically in 1979 and Ronald Reagan moved to break labor militancy by firing the air traffic controllers in 1981 and to cut production costs by appreciating the real exchange rate. No endogenous shifts in mathematically expected inflation rates need be postulated to explain observed events. But to repeat a thought from Chapter 1, parsimony in explanation in the sense of William of Occam rests in the eye of the beholder.

5. Dynamics of Government Debt

Barro (1974) stars in the next episode in the new classical chronicle. He kicked off an enormous debate about the "Ricardian equivalence" of tax and debt financing of government spending. The basic idea is that only government purchases and not the means by which they are financed affect the real side of the economy.[8] The SAM in Table 6.1 leads into the argument. Its setup is similar to the one in Table 3.2, which we used to analyze the Wicksell and (much more akin to Barro) Sargent-Wallace inflation models.

To begin with the accounting, households receiving wage income hold the debts D_g and D_f of government and firms. The corresponding interest payments (at the real rate j) show up as income flows in cells B3 and B4 of the matrix, where $\delta = D/PK$, $\beta = D_f/D$, $1 - \beta = D_g/D$, and $D_f + D_g = D$. Other items of note include the entry τ_h in cell D2, representing lump-sum taxes on households (like all other variables in the matrix, τ_h is scaled by the value of the capital stock PK).

Household income is $\xi_h = (1 - \pi)u + j\delta$. The corresponding saving flow, $\sigma_h = \xi_h - \gamma_h - \tau_h$, is used to acquire more debt $\delta\hat{D} = \dot{D}/PK$ in the flow of funds row (E). In rows (F) and (G) firms and government issue new debt to cover their deficits $g - \sigma_f = g + j\beta\delta - \pi u$ and $-\sigma_g = \gamma_g + j(1 - \beta)\delta - \tau_h$ respectively (profit flows remaining after interest payments by firms are assumed to be saved). As usual, $g = I/K$ is the growth rate of the capital stock.

Table 6.1 A SAM incorporating government debt and taxes (all variables scaled by the value of capital stock).

| | Current expenditures | | | | Loans to firms | |
	Output costs (1)	Households (2)	Firms (3)	Government (4)	Investment (5)	& government (6)	Totals (7)
(A) Output uses		γ_h		γ_g	g		u
Incomes							
(B) Households	$(1-\pi)u$		$j\beta\delta$	$j(1-\beta)\delta$			ξ_h
(C) Firms	πu						ξ_f
(D) Government		τ_h					ξ_g
Flows of funds							
(E) Household		σ_h				$-\delta\hat{D}$	0
(F) Firms			σ_f		$-g$	$\beta\delta\hat{D}_f$	0
(G) Government				σ_g		$(1-\beta)\delta\hat{D}_g$	0
(H) Totals	u	ξ_h	ξ_f	ξ_g	0	0	

Definitions

$\delta = D/PK$

$\beta = D_f/D$

$1-\beta = D_g/D$

From row (A) of the SAM, we have

$$\gamma_h = u - \gamma_g - g. \tag{13}$$

In the steady state of a neoclassical growth model of the Ramsey or Solow type g is predetermined by labor force growth (assuming that productivity growth is zero). The output/capital ratio u and profit share π will be set by marginal productivity rules. For given values of u and g, equation (13) shows that if government spending γ_g goes up, then household consumption γ_h has to be crowded out 100 percent, regardless of whether the extra public spending is paid for by higher taxes or issuing more debt. Moreover, with γ_h as an endogenous variable in cell A2 and the tax burden τ_h determined by policy in cell D2, household saving σ_h must be endogenous in cell E2. The relationship

$$\sigma_h = (g - \pi u) + (\gamma_g - \tau_h) + j\delta \tag{14}$$

can be derived from the SAM accounting. The saving/capital ratio σ_h has to move to cover financial deficits arising in other sectors as well as total interest payments $j\delta$.

These tautologies of accountancy are the basic Ricardian equivalence results, with the key element being the endogenous adjustment of σ_h in (14) to offset changes in the tax and debt variables τ_h and $j\delta$ for a given γ_g. If taxes go down, then σ_h goes up in equal measure, "in anticipation" of the inevitably increased fiscal debt burden to come. Barro offers a rationale for the endogeneity of σ_h in a Ramsey model, but before we get into that it makes sense to explore debt dynamics without household optimization.[9]

The key equation for the increase of $\delta = D/PK$ follows from substitutions within the SAM. It is

$$\dot{\delta} = (g - \pi u) + (\gamma_g - \tau_h) - (g - j)\delta. \tag{15}$$

The state (or ratio) variable δ goes up with the "primary" deficits $g - \pi u$ and $\gamma_g - \tau_h$ of firms and the government respectively. It is self-stabilizing with $d\dot{\delta}/d\delta < 0$ when $g > j$, or the rate of growth of output exceeds the real rate of interest.[10] The economy can "grow out" of the burden of debt if the $g > j$ condition is satisfied. Note the similarity to the profit rate > population growth rate condition for stability of the Keynesian fully funded pension model toward the end of Chapter 5. In both cases, a "growth factor" has to exceed a "leakage factor" for the dynamics to be stable.

When the $g > j$ condition holds, setting $\dot{\delta} = 0$ in (15) shows that the steady-state ratio of debt to capital is[11]

$$\delta = [(g - \pi u) + (\gamma_g - \tau_h)]/(g - j). \tag{16}$$

In words, the debt ratio settles down to the sum of business and government primary deficits as scaled to the value of capital stock, capitalized by the difference between the growth and real interest rates. In real world markets, national "solvency" can become worrisome when the debt/GDP ratio exceeds, say, 100 percent. A critical value for δ thereby might be in the vicinity of one-third.

Even with the steady-state hypothesis $\hat{D} = g$ (or a constant δ along with a constant P) imposed on the accounting in Table 8.1, the real interest rate j remains undetermined. A traditional fiscal economist might use this degree of freedom to introduce a saving function of the form

$$\sigma_h(j) = \delta\hat{D}, \tag{17}$$

adding behavioral content to SAM row (E).

In the standard scenario, the total primary deficit Q of firms and government is positive: $Q = (g - \pi u) + (\gamma_g - \tau_h) > 0$. The steady-state equation (16) can be rewritten as

$$j = g - (Q/\delta), \tag{16'}$$

which becomes the Debt schedule in Figure 6.4. Along this curve, the interest rate is zero when $\delta = Q/g$, and rises asymptotically to the level g as δ goes to infinity.

The Saving schedule represents (17) in steady state. As drawn, it cuts the debt locus twice, with a stable equilibrium at A and an unstable one

Figure 6.4
Debt dynamics in a
traditional model.

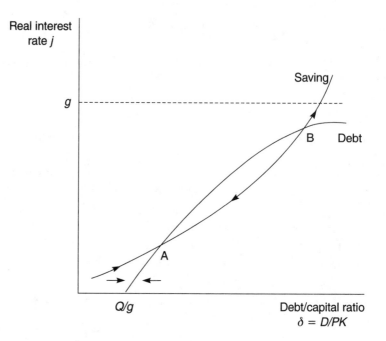

at B. Suppose that the economy is initially at A, but that the government chooses "permanently" to increase its primary deficit $\gamma_g - \tau_b$. This policy change will make Q go up, shifting the intercept of the Debt curve on the horizontal axis to the right and raising the steady-state values of δ and j. From (17), the increase in j will call forth more household saving to finance the government's bigger deficit and cut household consumption to satisfy the accounting restrictions (13) and (14). In a Keynesian formulation as in Chapter 4, a higher interest rate would also reduce investment demand and the growth rate g^j. The intercept Q/g^j of the debt schedule would shift further to the right, in a potentially destabilizing feedback.

If the government further pursues its profligate ways, the Debt schedule may shift far enough to the right not to intersect with the saving curve. Then the economy will fall into a true debt trap, with j and δ both diverging toward infinity until someone on horseback canters in and straightens out the fiscal mess.

6. Ricardian Equivalence

This last scenario is the stock-in-trade of old-fashioned fiscal conservatives, who exist all across the political spectrum. In India, for example, the Left traditionally raises the specter of an imminent debt trap. In the

United States, the main official rationale for the tight fiscal policy of the Clinton administration was its alleged effectiveness in holding interest rates down (even though in the late 1990s real long rates were at all-time highs). Sometimes such notions are not off the mark, as is their labor market analog illustrated in Figure 2.7 and even the inflation tax Laffer curve in Figure 3.8. But Barro is after bigger game. He wants to show not that the government is capable of fiscal (ir)responsibility, but that how it finances its excesses really doesn't matter, a cheering thought for American conservatives like the writers for the editorial page of the *Wall Street Journal* during the times of Ronald Reagan's (and more recently George W. Bush's) exploding public deficits. Regardless of how it is paid for, all that government expenditure can do along an optimal growth model is crowd out (worthy?) private consumption.

Barro consolidates the households and firms of Table 6.1 into a private sector, and normalizes variables by the fully employed labor force L as opposed to the capital stock PK. The corresponding SAM appears in Table 6.2, with $x = X/L$, $k = K/L$, $gk = (I/K)(K/L) = I/L$, $\Delta = D/L$, and so on. Row (A) can be rewritten as

$$c_p = x - c_g - gk, \tag{18}$$

where c_p and c_g are private and government consumption per capita. As in (13), there is 100 percent crowding-out of private by higher public consumption, because x and gk are fixed by Say's Law and steady-state assumptions.

Table 6.2 Another SAM incorporating government debt and taxes (all variables scaled by labor supply).

| | Current expenditures | | | Loans to | |
	Output costs (1)	Private sector (2)	Government (3)	Investment (4)	government (5)	Totals (6)
(A) Output uses		c_p	c_g	gk		x
Incomes						
(B) Private sector	x		$j\Delta$			y_p
(C) Government		t				y_g
Flows of funds						
(D) Private sector		s_p		$-gk$	$-\Delta\hat{D}$	0
(E) Government			s_g		$\Delta\hat{D}$	0
(F) Totals	x	y_p	y_g	0	0	

Definitions
$\Delta = D/L$
$x = X/L$
$k = K/L$

To reach full Ricardian equivalence whereby the government's shifts between tax and debt financing are offset by shifts in private saving, two steps are required. The first is to cut links between debt dynamics and changes in the interest rate such as those discussed in section 5. The second is to avoid debt traps. In a mode of argument dear to all economists, new classicists take both strides by making the appropriate assumptions.

They begin by postulating that household saving decisions follow from a Ramsey model like the one discussed in Chapter 3, with Euler equations of the form

$$\dot{k} = f(k) - c_p - c_g - nk \tag{19}$$

and

$$\dot{c}_p = (c_p/\eta)(f' - \epsilon), \tag{20}$$

where n is the rate of population growth (in steady state, $g = I/K = n$), η is the elasticity of the marginal "felicity" of consumption, and ϵ is a pure rate of private time preference.

Recall from Chapter 3 that for a solution to the Ramsey problem to exist, the condition $\epsilon > n$ is required, that is, the discount rate has to exceed the rate of population growth. At a steady state with $\dot{c}_p = 0$, (20) shows that $f' = \epsilon$, or the marginal product of capital equals the discount rate. Competition in the financial market will further ensure that the real interest rate j equals f'. In line with most of the literature, we focus on these steady-state results.

The equality between j and ϵ is tricky, because manipulation of accounting balances in the Table 6.2 SAM shows that the debt/labor ratio evolves according to the rule

$$\dot{\Delta} = (c_g - t) - (n - j)\Delta, \tag{21}$$

where t stands for lump-sum taxes per capita. With $j = f' = \epsilon > n$ this equation is unstable with $d\dot{\Delta}/d\Delta > 0$. How can the economy avoid a debt trap?

To lead up to an answer, we have to examine the stability of the whole system (19)–(21). Linearized around a steady state, its partial derivative matrix has the form

	k	c_p	Δ
$\dot{k}$	$\epsilon - n$	-1	0
$\dot{c}_p$	$(c_p/\eta)f''$	0	0
$\dot{\Delta}$	0	0	$\epsilon - n$

The zero entries in the last row and column show that debt dynamics are delinked from k and c_p—this is the first step toward Ricardian equivalence. As we have seen in Chapter 3, subject to enough transversality conditions the differential equations for $\dot{k}$ and $\dot{c}_p$ will "converge" to a saddlepoint steady state. The presence of c_g in (19) makes sure that the accounting balance (18) is satisfied. An argument like the one made in connection with Figure 3.4 shows that if c_g changes in (19), then c_p will "jump" to bring the economy to a new steady state. Otherwise, k and c_p would go off on a divergent path.

For a dedicated new classicist, adding one more potentially unstable process to the already divergent Ramsey model (19) and (20) is not to worry: "[I]ndividuals who optimize over an infinite horizon would not hold public debt that grows asymptotically at a rate as high as the interest rate. . . . This condition rules out Ponzi games or chain letters where the government issues debt and finances the payments of interest and principal by perpetual issues of new debt" (Barro 1989, pp. 203–204). The omniscient market will force the government to keep its finances from blowing up. Ponzi games will be avoided if the state runs a primary surplus $t - c_g > 0$ to pay the interest required to keep the debt stock per capita at the level

$$\Delta = (t - c_g)/(\epsilon - n) \tag{22}$$

that holds $\dot{\Delta} = 0$ at the (unstable) steady state.

Analogously to (14), the accounting relationships in Table 6.2 can be used to show that private saving per capita s_p at steady state will satisfy the equations

$$s_p = (c_g - t) + j\Delta + nk = n(k + \Delta), \tag{23}$$

where it is assumed that $j = \epsilon$ and the expression after the second equality follows by substitution from (22). Saving adjusts to cover the expansion of capital and debt required to keep up with population growth, and the debt/labor ratio Δ itself varies to offset tax and spending changes. If c_g or t shifts in (23), then s_p will jump to preserve the first equality.

The biggest worry with all this, of course, is that infinite perfect foresight may falter. What if it fails to guide the economy to comply with all the transversality conditions required at the end of time to offset dynamic instability arising from the two positive eigenvalues of the system (19)–(21)? One might feel safer with an old-fashioned stability condition such as a higher growth rate than interest rate. Barro, however, argues that such caution is misplaced. In an overlapping generations framework, "optimal" bequests will chain the decisions of mortals together over time to ensure that the steady-state conditions sketched here will be satisfied.

Before such a grand vision, objections such as the facts that pure lump-sum taxes don't exist and that most households face liquidity constraints and do not optimize their saving decisions pale to insignificance. However, it *is* fair to say that Barro did not make the mainstream *really* believe that the Reagan fiscal deficits were beside the point. In the Clinton years, enough deficit hawks thinking along the lines of Figure 6.4 survived to convince politicians that public spending should be cut and taxes (slightly) raised. Whether they or Barro along with newly resurgent supply-siders and a few remaining pro-deficit Keynesians will carry the day during the decade of the aughts is a question yet to be decided.

7. The Business Cycle Conundrum

Seemingly cyclical fluctuations of output and almost all other macro variables are an enduring feature of advanced capitalist economies. Two different ways of thinking about these movements coexist uneasily in the current literature. One traces back to the late 1800s and found its most influential form in the United States in the work of the National Bureau of Economic Research (NBER), in particular Burns and Mitchell (1946) and Zarnowitz (1992). Thoroughly empirical, the NBER methodology concentrates on interconnections between phases within one cycle and across cycles; the severity (amplitude) of cycles; and the co-movements of a wide range of economic indicators and activities.

New classical economics is the foundation of more recent "real business cycle" (RBC) models, which in contrast to the NBER approach emphasize random as opposed to systematic behavior, ahistorical analysis in place of history-based discussion, and statistically independent sequencing of phases and cycles instead of their interconnections. As discussed in the following section, RBC models generate fluctuations with random shocks to an otherwise stable system; opposing scholars such as Goldstein (1996) see cycles as endogenous to capitalism.

A fundamental stylized fact for real business cycle models is that in the United States, for example, "detrended" real output demonstrates significant positive autocorrelations over short periods and weak negative autocorrelations over longer ones. With trends removed by a moving average, the quarterly time series for log GDP is tolerably well modeled by a two-period autoregression,

$$\log GDP_t = \alpha(\log GDP_{t-1}) - \beta(\log GDP_{t-2}) + \epsilon, \qquad (24)$$

where $\alpha > \beta > 0$ and ϵ is the usual error term. The negative coefficient on the second lag generates the "hump-shaped" response to disturbances which is typically observed (Blanchard and Quah 1989). Of course, if log GDP_t is highly correlated with log GDP_{t-1} (a truism), then with the double lag the computer is almost certain to come smiling back with two oppositely signed "highly significant" coefficients which sum to a value close to the coefficient in the single-lag regression. How seriously one should take the hump emerging from this construction is an open question.

Although we won't go into the details until Chapter 9, models in which output is driven by effective demand can track the business cycle reasonably well. Variants include multiplier-accelerator formulations stemming from Samuelson (1939) through distributional shifts in Goodwin (1951, 1967) and onto financial cycles as in Minsky (1975). Recent mainstream discussion has focused on how central bank interventions to stem U.S. inflation tend to throw the economy into recession (a finding belied by Fed tightening in 1999–2000 unless what is termed "inflation" is extended from goods prices as discussed by Romer and Romer (1989) to asset prices as well). The cycle models presented in Chapter 9 incorporate many of these themes.

8. Cycles from the Supply Side

Demand-driven cycles, however, do not completely dominate the discussion. In terms of the diagrams in Chapter 5, "counterclockwise" readings of macro causality from the supply side also have a long tradition in the literature on price, employment, and output fluctuations.

On the left, the adverse cyclical effects of rising capital per worker—an increasing organic composition of capital—have long figured in Marxist discourse. On the Right, Wicksell and Austrian economists such as von Hayek (1931) saw depressions as an essential antidote to an overhang of excess investment resulting from banks' holding the market interest rate below its "natural" level (the same "inefficiency" that can crop up in the OLG models sketched in Chapter 3). This view underlay Schumpeter's contemporary description to credulous Harvard undergraduates of the Great Depression as an unavoidable capitalist "cold douche" (Heilbroner 1999). In a clear extension of the entrepreneur-driven technical change in his *Theory of Economic Development,* Schumpeter grounded his own massive work on cycles on "waves" of innovation, which could underlie output fluctuations ranging from periods of a few years to grand fifty-year Kondratiev cycles.

Minus the marvelous political economy of his *Capitalism, Socialism, and Democracy,* Schumpeter's (1947) temporally fluctuating technical progress has been picked up by the recent mainstream RBC school as the key factor underlying output fluctuations. The formal models assume that the level of output is determined by a neoclassical production function with a multiplicative term for shifts in total factor productivity as discussed in Chapter 2, for example in period t, $X_t = z_t F(K_t, L_t)$, with z_t as the time-varying productivity term.

The basic RBC trick is to assume that z_t "this period" depends strongly on its level z_{t-1} "last period" plus a current random error. The stochastic term transforms the standard Ramsey model into a problem of dynamic optimization under risk—a nontrivial extension as discussed in section 9. With enough ad hoc assumptions imposed to give it a closed-form solution, the stochastic Ramsey model cranks out a set of standard RBC results.

The first is that if there is a one-period lag between investment and completed capital formation, then the accounting is in place to make output in period t depend on its levels in periods $t - 1$ and $t - 2$.[12] Cunning choice of parameters enables such a model to replicate the hump-shaped two-period auto-regression of log output displayed in equation (24) above. Stadler (1994) reviews the best-known variants, beginning with the original by Kydland and Prescott (1982). Most of the cyclical action comes from the productivity growth–forcing function. Just why z_t should fluctuate so vigorously (with a quarterly standard deviation of its random shock term of about 1 percent in most applications) is never fully explained.[13]

What about real wages and employment? As in the Ramsey and Kaldor models discussed previously, under a full employment assumption, higher productivity automatically raises output per worker and the real wage. Although the results are built in by the closure assumptions of RBC models, their ability to generate pro-cyclical productivity and real wage movements is usually taken as a major point in their favor. Less enthusiastically received has been their presumption that employment fluctuations over the cycle are due to labor/leisure substitution in response to wage and interest (= profit) rate changes.

In detail, the "island" households making up the population are supposed to maximize a universally shared utility function with consumption and "leisure" as its arguments. A two-period optimization exercise like the one discussed in connection with the overlapping generations model in Chapter 3 makes labor supply in period t depend positively on the real wage ω_t and the expected interest rate r_{t+1} as in equation (33) below. The gist of the interest rate story is that with a high value of r_{t+1}, working and saving the proceeds in period t becomes attractive in comparison to working in period $t + 1$.

As discussed in section 4, strong employment responsiveness along these lines underlies the Lucas supply function. Facile labor/leisure trade-offs also have to be built into RBC models if they are to replicate the stylized fact that employment correlates positively with output in the United States over the cycle (remember Okun's Law). Unfortunately for the theory, microeconomic evidence like that presented by Ball (1990) suggests that changes in labor supply are quite insensitive to fluctuations in real wages and interest rates.

The last criticism usually voiced by new Keynesian critics such as Summers (1986) and Mankiw (1989) is that RBC models ignore monetary disturbances as a major perturbation of aggregate demand. In making this assertion, RBC people are true to their conservative mentors Friedman and Lucas in treating output as being determined from the supply side. However, they go one step further in assuming "reverse causality" in the equation of exchange: PX/V drives the "inside" (or commercial bank–generated component of) M in RBC models, as credits and deposits rise to meet a higher transactions volume required by an increase in X. This tendency toward heterodoxy goes only so far, however. RBC modelers ultimately need a nominal anchor to fix the price level. They are much happier to find it in a predetermined level of outside money than in a social process determining the money wage.

Finally, beyond new Keynesianism there is a question about informational and computational requirements implicit in models of how economic decisions get made. As noted above, RBC formulations boil down to a Ramsey model with a technological error term thrown in. Such exercises in dynamic optimization under quantifiable risk are extremely difficult to solve if they do not incorporate special assumptions such as the quadratic preference functions and linear constraints which produce the simple closed-form results discussed in connection with Lucas's supply function (10) and Hall's "random walk" consumption model discussed in Chapter 4. Besides Lucas and Hall, they underlie the equity premium puzzle and the Modigliani-Miller theorem. Because such formulations are pervasive, it makes sense to present a sketch of how they can be analyzed and (possibly) solved.

9. Optimal Behavior under Risk

Early RBC models were set up in discrete time, and we continue with that convention here. In intuitive terms, continuous-time stochastic optimization is not difficult to follow, but the formal mathematics (Itô's lemma, Kolmogorov's backward equation, Feynman-Kac integrals, and all the rest) can be a bit daunting.[14] Thus the discrete-time RBC Ramsey problem at hand is

$$\max V_t(t = 0) = E[\sum_{t=0}^{T} \beta^t U(C_t, 1 - L_t)] \tag{25}$$

subject to

$$K_{t+1} = (1 - \delta)K_t + z_t F(K_t, L_t) - C_t \tag{26}$$

and

$$E[K(T)] = K^*. \tag{27}$$

The notation $E(\ )$ stands for the probabilistic expectation operator over the "known" distribution of the z_t. The maximand V_t in general varies as a function of time, with its value depending on the date t at which optimization begins to take place. The parameter $\beta < 1$ is a discount factor, U is the maximizing agent's "felicity" function based on consumption C_t and "leisure" $1 - L_t$ (where the agent can provide one unit of labor at most), and δ is a "radioactive" depreciation coefficient via which a proportion δK_t of the entering capital stock disappears in each time period. This formulation mainly differs from (15) and (16) in Chapter 3 by including the random error terms z_t in (26), which force the agent to maximize expected utility in (25). The way the model works is most easily illustrated if the planning problem is assumed to end at some "distant" future time T, when the expected capital stock should arrive at its balanced growth level K^* (the presence of the stochastic terms means that the target cannot be hit exactly).

Recall from Chapter 3 how the nonstochastic Ramsey model can be solved numerically using a feedback control rule based on backward integration of the differential equation for its costate variable (say, ξ) from a terminal condition $\xi(T)$ coupled with forward integration of the state variable K from an initial condition $K(0)$, with optimal choice of the control variable(s) at each point in time. This procedure is "local" or "open loop" in the jargon of control engineers (Bryson and Ho 1969). From a given initial value $K(0)$, it can find an optimal path to K^* at time T. Several such "extremal" trajectories are illustrated in Figure 6.5, starting

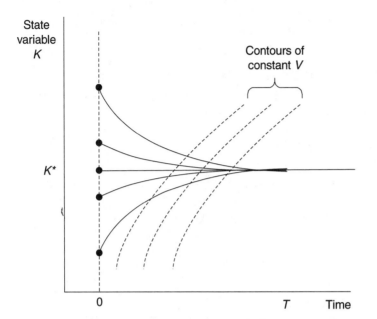

State variable K

Contours of constant V

K^*

0   T Time

Figure 6.5
Optimal dynamic paths and contours of the return function in a stochastic Ramsey problem.

out from different levels of $K(0)$. Each one is fully optimal because it satisfies the initial and terminal conditions of the Ramsey model's two-point boundary value problem as well as the relevant Euler equations.

Along each extremal (in discrete time), the value of the maximand $V_t(K_t)$ in (25) will vary, in general depending on the time t and value of the state variable K_t at which it is evaluated. The dashed curves are contours of constant V, which need not be orthogonal to the capital stock trajectories. In the diagram, one can imagine "sweeping" V backward from contour to contour over time, picking out optimal values of K (and associated control variables) along extremals, in a global "feedback" or "closed-loop" control environment. This procedure is the essence of "dynamic programming." The contemporary version is due to the mathematician Richard Bellman (1957), who built on the Hamilton-Jacobi partial differential equation of classical physics.

Bellman was the first to admit that dynamic programming is bedeviled by a "curse of dimensionality." To solve a general problem, one has to compute and store values of V and K over the entire state space. With personal computers of the early twenty-first century, such a calculation is feasible for a few state variables. Supercomputers can do far more, of course, but can we safely assume that island-bound optimizing households are equipped with such machines?[15]

Supercomputing power is needed, unfortunately, to do dynamic optimization under quantifiable risk. In terms of Figure 6.5, the presence of stochastic shocks means that the state variable randomly jumps from one extremal path to another. To compute expected values over all these paths as required by (25), the full backward sweep of the dynamic programming solution has to be worked out. Applied RBC modelers can and do throw in enough special assumptions to make their models soluble analytically or with simple computer routines. Problem solvers in the real economic world are not likely to be so lucky.

It is still of interest to go through the formal details of what they are supposed to do. Bellman's "principle of optimality" states that the backward sweep of the return function V_t can be taken in steps, with optimal decisions about the control variables (C_t and L_t, in the present case) made during each one. This "recursive" principle boils down to finding V_t (for successively lower values of t) according to the rule

$$V_t(K_t) = \max_{C_t, L_t} \{U(C_t, 1 - L_t) + \beta E[V_{t+1}(K_{t+1})]\}, \tag{28}$$

subject to the stochastic difference equation (26) tying K_{t+1} to C_t and L_t. The backward sweep begins at time T with V_T computed on the basis of terminal or transversality conditions as sketched in Chapter 3.

Let $U_{C,t}$ and $U_{L,t}$ stand for the (positive) partial derivatives of the felicity function with respect to C_t and $(1 - L_t)$ at time t, and let $F_{K,t}$ and $F_{L,t}$ be the partials of the production function. Also, let V_t' be the derivative of V_t with respect to K_t. Plugging (26) into (28) and maximizing with respect to C_t and L_t gives the rules

$$U_{C,t} - \beta E(V_{t+1}') = 0 \tag{29}$$

and

$$-U_{L,t} + \beta E[V_{t+1}'(z_t F_{L,t})] = 0. \tag{30}$$

Also, in light of the envelope theorem, differentiating both sides of (28) with (26) substituted in (after C_t and L_t are optimized) with respect to K_t gives

$$V_t' = \beta E\{V_{t+1}'[z_t F_{K,t} + (1 - \delta)]\}. \tag{31}$$

This formula is a discrete-time, stochastic analog of the "backward" equation for the costate variable of the nonstochastic Ramsey model discussed above, with V' taking the role of ξ.[16] In light of (29), one can replace $\beta E(V_{t+1}')$ by the nonstochastic variable $U_{C,t}$ in (31) to get

$$V_t' = U_{C,t} E[z_t F_{K,t} + (1 - \delta)].$$

Changing the time subscript from t to $t + 1$ and substituting back into (29) gives the expression

$$U_{C,t} = \beta E\{[U_{C,t+1}][z_{t+1}F_{K,t+1} + (1 - \delta)]\} \tag{32}$$

to determine consumption at time t.

Equation (32) is a Ramsey-type optimal consumption rule (its continuous-time, nonstochastic analog is equation (20) above). To see how it works, suppose that the agent slightly reduces C_t, leading to capital accumulation and a higher expected value of output in period $t + 1$. The left side of (32) gives the utility loss from this maneuver; the right side gives the expected discounted utility gain from more consumption next period. At the margin, these expected costs and benefits should be equal.

The expectation in (31) is taken over the product of the stochastic variables $U_{C,t+1}$ and $z_{t+1}F_{K,t+1} + (1 - \delta)$. By definition, for random variables X and Y, $E(XY) = E(X)E(Y) + \text{cov}(X, Y)$, where $\text{cov}(X, Y)$ is the covariance of the two. Suppose, for example, that consumption is high when the marginal product of capital is high. Then the covariance of $U_{C,t+1}$ and $z_{t+1}F_{K,t+1} + (1 - \delta)$ will be *negative,* because marginal utility is an inverse function of C_t. The resulting low value of the right side of (32) means that $U_{C,t}$ will also be low. In other words, C_t will be optimized at a *higher* value than would be the case if the covariance were zero. Pro-cyclical variation of consumption and the rate of profit should be associated with lower saving overall (a proposition difficult to test in practice, insofar as most saving is done by enterprises and their profit share moves pro-cyclically).

One can go through similar manipulations to show that the agent's labor supply rule takes the form

$$U_{L,t} = U_{C,t}E(z_tF_{L,t}). \tag{33}$$

Marginal utility of leisure $U_{L,t}$ is a decreasing function of $(1 - L_t)$. Hence a higher expected marginal product of labor (or real wage) $E(z_tF_{L,t})$ calls forth a higher level of work L_t. Similarly, from (32) a higher expected future marginal product of capital (or profit rate) makes $U_{C,t}$ and thereby L_t rise in (33). These are the elastic labor supply responses of RBC models discussed in section 8.

In practice, model builders in the RBC world usually impose enough assumptions to make their dynamic programming problems soluble in closed form. For example, McCallum (1989) shows that in the model discussed here, Cobb-Douglas production and utility functions, purely circulating capital (or $\delta = 1$), and a log-normal productivity error term will do the trick. How well such a "tractable" specialization of the model reflects its general pattern of results is not made clear.

10. Random Walk, Equity Premium, and the Modigliani-Miller Theorem

As pointed out at the end of section 8, stochastic dynamic programming also provides derivations of the random walk consumption model, the equity premium puzzle, and the Modigliani-Miller Theorem. We can quickly run through the mechanics here.

The random walk follows directly from (32) when accumulation for period $t + 1$ is not considered ($F_{K,t+1} = \delta = 0$), and there is no discounting of the future ($\beta = 1$). The equation reduces to

$$U_{C,t} = E(U_{C,t+1}),$$

or

$$U_{C,t} = U_{C,t+1} + \epsilon'_{t+1},$$

where ϵ'_{t+1} is a "white noise" error term. Further, if the felicity function U is quadratic in the variable C_t, we get $U_{C,t} = aC_t$, where a is a coefficient. The equation for optimal consumption choice becomes

$$aC_t = aC_{t+1} + e'_{t+1},$$

which can be rewritten as

$$C_{t+1} - C_t = \epsilon_t,$$

where ϵ_t is also white noise. This equation describes the optimizing consumer's drunkard's walk.

The equity premium puzzle can be illustrated if we rewrite (32) as

$$U_{C,t} = \beta E[U_{C,t+1}(1 + r_{t+1})], \tag{34}$$

where r_{t+1} is the stochastic return (net of depreciation) from engaging in production activity in period $t + 1$. Now contrast two firms, which have returns positively and negatively correlated with $U_{C,t+1}$ respectively. The first firm is worth *more* because owning it allows the investor to hedge against *low* values of C_{t+1}, which are associated with *high* values of $U_{C,t+1}$. The implication is that the first firm can pay a *lower* return than the second one to its owners. This logic underlies the popular capital asset pricing model (or CAPM), which states that the higher the correlation of a firm's returns with overall returns on the market, then the higher the equilibrium yield on its stock has to be.[17]

The equity premium puzzle follows from (34), when one observes that equity yields have a small positive correlation with C, or a small negative correlation with U_C. Equity should therefore have to pay only a small premium over the return to riskless assets, nothing like the 5–6 percent historically observed in the U.S. market.

Equation (34) can be further tied into individual optimizing behavior, if the "investor" behind it is deciding whether to take over ownership of a firm with value Z_t and cash flow π_t (where π_t is profits net of investment expenditure).[18] The return to ownership becomes $1 + r_t = (Z_{t+1} + \pi_{+1t})/Z_t$. Substituting into (34) gives

$$U_{C,t} = \beta E\{U_{C,t+1}[(Z_{t+1} + \pi_{t+1})/Z_t]\}. \tag{35}$$

The Modigliani-Miller theorem is implicit in this formula, which in effect generalizes Irving Fisher's theory of real returns to asset ownership over wide domains of securities, agents, spaces of probabilistically expected events, and time. To extract the theorem, we can follow Lucas (1978) and multiply both sides of (35) by the nonstochastic variable $(Z_t/U_{C,t})$ to get the difference equation

$$Z_t = \beta E[(U_{c,t+1}/U_{C,t})(Z_{t+1} + \pi_{t+1})] \tag{36}$$

in Z_t and its expected future values. Because she has already worked through the relevant backward dynamic programming sweep (calculating optimal expected consumption levels along the way), it is no great task for the investor to solve (36) forward in time along the relevant extremals and let T go to infinity to get the expression,[19]

$$Z_t = E[\sum_{s=1}^{\infty} (\beta^s U_{C,t+s}/U_{C,t})\pi_{t+s}], \tag{37}$$

where expectations are taken sequentially over information available at time s. The worth of the firm is a fancy discounted present value of its expected returns, with a time-varying discount rate depending on the investor's expected future levels of marginal utility.

To get rid of the marginal utility terms, it is conventionally assumed that the existing set of securities "spans" all "states of nature" (indexed by n).[20] Then all investors will equate their discounted marginal utilities in (37) to asset prices $p_{n,t+s}$ which give the values of "goods and securities" in state of nature n at time $t + s$, relative to their prices in period t. That is,

$$p_{n,t+s} = q_{n,t+s}\beta^s U_{C,t+s}/U_{C,t},$$

where $q_{n,t+s}$ is the probability that state n will occur at time $t + s$. In Lucas's well-informed world, the $q_{n,t+s}$ must be interpreted as objective probabilities, known to all agents.

Substituting the state-contingent prices $p_{n,t+s}$ into (37) gives

$$Z_t = \sum_{s=1}^{\infty}\sum_{n=1}^{N} p_{n,t+s}\pi_{n,t+s}, \tag{38}$$

where the (finite?, countable?) number of states of nature is N.

The Modigliani-Miller theorem basically says that given all the optimizations and contingency-spanning securities we have postulated, it doesn't really matter how a firm chooses to package its ownership claims. In other words, the structure of its offering of securities is irrelevant.[21] In line with the arbitrage arguments underlying the theorem (sketched in the following section), suppose that a firm arbitrarily divides its cash flows into stream E ("equity") and stream B ("bonds") with $\pi_{n,t} = \pi_{E,n,t} + \pi_{B,n,t}$. If we expand upon (38), the value of each stream is

$$Z_{i,t} = \sum_{s=1}^{\infty}\sum_{n=1}^{N} p_{n,t+s}\pi_{i,n,t+s}, \qquad i = E, B, \tag{39}$$

with $Z_{E,t} + Z_{B,t} = Z_t$. The algebraic linearity of all these manipulations means that the firm's value Z_t does not depend on the labels it attaches to its securities. If, for example, it substitutes cheaper debt for equity, then as in Figure 6.6 below it has to pay a higher return on equity because its leverage has gone up.

The key assumptions are that the firm has zero net worth and that its total cash flows π are independent of their allocation into the boxes π_E and π_B. Modifications to the latter assumption such as the fact that only dividends and not interest payments are taxed at the corporate level (more bond finance increases π) and that greater leverage may drive up bankruptcy risk (reducing π) do not alter the argument's basic thrust.

11. More on Modigliani-Miller

Because the foregoing discussion is rather abstract, it makes sense to try to add some intuitive flesh to the algebraic bones. One way to do this is via Modigliani and Miller's original approach to their famous results.[22]

Another gloss on the theorem is that if all of a firm's publicly traded securities exhaust the value of its assets, then the returns imputed to these obligations exhaust all profits. The proof relies on arguments about gains from arbitrage that characterize much neoclassical thought and are implicit in the discussion of last section. Modigliani and Miller (1958) worked with firms 1 and 2, which both have an expected annual future profit flow Π. Their market valuations Z_1 and Z_2 should then satisfy the relationships $Z_1 = Z_2 = Z = \Pi/\rho$, where Π/ρ is their capitalized return at the rate ρ appropriate to their "risk class" (loosely defined as a group of firms with highly correlated returns).

The argument proceeds by contradiction, on the maintained hypothesis that both enterprises have zero net worth. Suppose that firm 1 issues only equity ($Z_1 = E_1$, where E_1 is the value of its shares outstanding) and that firm 2 is "leveraged" or "geared" because it issues both equity and bonds ($Z_2 = E_2 + B_2$). What happens if $Z_2 > Z_1$?

The holder of a portion α of firm 2's outstanding equity E_2 gets a total return $Y_2 = \alpha(\Pi - j_b B_2)$, where j_b is the ruling real interest rate on bonds. If there is a perfect capital market, he can sell his shares and also borrow the amount αB_2 to buy a fraction $\alpha(E_2 + B_2)/E_1$ of firm 1's equity, using his new share holdings as collateral for the loan. The return Y_1 to this new portfolio turns out to be

$$Y_1 = \alpha[(E_2 + B_2)/E_1]\Pi - \alpha j_b B_2 = \alpha(Z_2/Z_1)\Pi - \alpha j_b B_2.$$

That is, $Z_2 > Z_1$ means that $Y_1 > Y_2$. It makes sense to sell off E_2 so that Z_2 declines and buy E_1 so that Z_1 rises, until $Z_1 = Z_2$.

Similarly, if $Z_1 > Z_2$, an owner of a portion α of firm one (with total return $\alpha\Pi$) can sell off her shares E_1 and buy a new portfolio made up of firm 2's securities in the proportions E_2/Z_2 for shares and B_2/Z_2 for bonds. It is easy to show that the return to this portfolio is $\alpha(Z_1/Z_2)\Pi$, which is higher than the original return $\alpha\Pi$ when $Z_1 > Z_2$. The investor "undoes" firm 2's gearing, to get access to its underlying valuation Π/ρ.

These arguments imply that the value of a firm is independent of its financial structure. A similar statement applies to returns. If j_e is the real rate of return to holding equity, then "return exhaustion" implies that $\Pi = j_e E + j_b B$. Because $\Pi = \rho Z$ and $Z = B + E$, this equation can be restated as

$$j_e = \rho + (\rho - j_b)(B/E), \tag{40}$$

which is illustrated in Figure 6.6. The "required" return to equity increases linearly with the firm's debt/equity ratio B/E, perhaps tailing off a bit (dashed line) if the cost of borrowing goes up with increasing lender's

Figure 6.6
The return to equity
as a function of
debt/equity ratio.

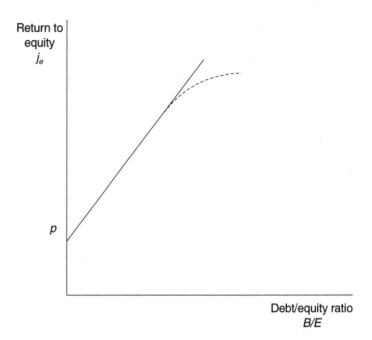

risk when B/E is high. A relationship like (40) does not fit the observed data badly.

Now the caveats. As noted above, the standard literature points out that if debt and equity claims are taxed differently and/or if there is risk of bankruptcy, asset-holders may not be indifferent to a firm's financial structure. To these factors, one can add all the forces underlying differentiated borrowers' and lenders' risks as discussed in Chapter 4.

Finally, problems can arise in general equilibrium. Intuitively, the theorem says that if a firm reduces its B/E ratio, then from (40) new equity owners will experience a reduction in their return stream. If asset-holders can borrow and lend on the same terms as firms, they can buy or sell financial assets to offset the change. But for the arguments above to go through in general equilibrium, all owners of securities have to adjust their portfolios. If, for whatever reason, some do not do so, then the bond market will fail to clear and asset prices will have to change. Simultaneous actions by all market participants are required to give the result that the financial structure of the firm is irrelevant.

12. The Calculation Debate and Super-Rational Economics

Maybe the best way to round out this chapter is to recall the outcome of the "calculation debate" of the 1920s and 1930s about the feasibility of socialist planning. The Left was represented by, among others, Lange

(1936–37) and Lerner (1936), who argued that if the economy behaves in proper Walrasian fashion, then by controlling relative prices intelligently, a planner can guide the system to an efficient allocation of resources. In other words, central planning can work.

Scholars on the right such as von Mises (1935) asserted that planning was bound to fail. "As if" socialist planners would merely "play" a market game, because they would not be disciplined by bankruptcy for making mistakes. Moreover, even if not misguided by such "agency" problems, planners could not possibly get all their calculations right. If they bungled even a few key price relationships, especially those feeding into the profitability calculus underlying investment decisions, they could badly upset production.

In retrospect, the Right appears to have won the debate—at least the Soviet version of socialism did not work out. The irony is that their intellectual heirs discussed in this chapter basically accept the Lange-Lerner argument that "really existing" capitalism is based on the actions of perfect optimizers. Hence there is no need for the state to intervene to guide the market's behavior, and indeed any attempts at intervention will be counterproductive.

But what if merely mortal and fallible financiers and businessmen make mistakes? Traditionalist Austrian economists believe that entrepreneurship in the market can overcome such "random shocks" while new classicists say they fit painlessly into agents' exercises in dynamic stochastic optimization. If both are wrong—if history, institutions, and socioeconomic structures matter in determining market outcomes—then the new Right's vision of capitalism in the social order will turn out to be as misleading as was the Left's optimism about the possibilities for socialism in the market.

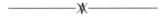

CHAPTER SEVEN

Effective Demand and the Distributive Curve

Chapters 7–10 cover recent ideas in structuralist macroeconomics—output determination, inflation, and distribution in this chapter, then money and finance (mainly from a post-Keynesian perspective), cycles, and open economy issues with an emphasis on the exchange rate. In a bit more detail, this chapter describes how determination of output and growth by effective demand interacts with the dynamics of distribution, inflation, and labor productivity growth emerging from market, institutional, and social forces. Attention is paid to the effects of expansionary policies, and how they may affect distribution by changing income shares and shifting real returns to financial assets. We begin with distribution, productivity growth, and inflation. Relationships between such "supply" factors and demand are then illustrated with examples: the differential effects of faster productivity growth in profit- and wage-led economies; possibilities for implementing expansionary policy in profit-led economies (without and then with financial repercussions); and three-way distributive conflicts in an economy open to foreign trade.

1. Initial Observations

Four introductory points are worth making. One is that social forces set the rules via which nominal prices evolve. Money-wage dynamics emerge from labor relations; commodity price and labor productivity growth depend on market power. In steady state, the rate of price inflation will equal the rate of wage inflation minus the rate of labor productivity growth so that the real wage and productivity grow at the same rate and the labor share of output is constant.

Second, in confronting such a model with the data on any industrialized capitalist economy, some means has to be found to deal with the presence of business cycles. An immediate question is: How does one compare outcomes over cycles to steady states emerging from a growth/distribution model? For example, if real wages vary pro-cyclically, does that mean that the long-term average wage would be higher if the economy could be managed in such a way as to maintain a higher average level of capacity utilization? There is no way to answer such a question apart from running the relevant experiment, but in historical time that rarely happens. One common practice is to ground growth models on stylized facts extracted from cyclical behavior, and trust that their "trend" implications are valid. As will be seen, such an exercise can call for fairly subtle interpretation of cyclical regularities. An alternative is to modify steady-state models so that they can generate cyclical growth. The first approach is adopted in this and the next chapters, with models of cyclical growth following in Chapters 9 and 10.

The third observation is about the mechanisms via which the labor share

$$\psi = wb/PX = \omega/(X/L) \tag{1}$$

and the level of economic activity $u = X/K$ can combine to permit a steady state with a constant inflation rate and a stable income distribution to exist. Under plausible assumptions, there is a curve in the (u, ψ) plane along which $\dot{\psi} = d\psi/dt = 0$ in steady state. A curve has a lot more points in it than the single $(\bar{u}, \bar{\psi})$ combination that defines a NAIRU as described in Chapter 2; working in one dimension rather than zero vastly extends the range of macro policy combinations to be considered. Some possibilities are discussed in following sections, after we think through the details of a bare-bones structuralist analysis of distribution, productivity growth, and inflation.[1]

Finally, both the real wage and the productivity growth vary cyclically in the U.S. economy, meaning that dynamics of the wage share are driven by changes in both ω and labor productivity $\xi_L = 1/b = X/L$. We discuss signs of wage, price, and productivity responses to shifts in ψ and u by drawing upon cycle-based econometric results presented in Chapter 9, thereby illustrating the particular American case.

2. Inflation, Productivity Growth, and Distribution

Beginning with the social relationships built into the model, a first question is how to define an object of interaction between labor and capital. Because workers are concerned with their standard of living and enterprises set prices as margins over costs, a complete formulation would work with separate "consumption" and "product" wages (the money wage deflated by the cost-of-living index and a relevant producer price index respectively), and also take into account nonwage production costs. To keep the algebra within bounds, these important details are omitted here (although section 8 does take up the implications of costs of imported intermediate inputs). In the labor and commodity markets respectively, wage and price dynamics are assumed to be keyed just to the labor share ψ, which does double duty as an indicator of worker/management conflict and a measure of per unit labor costs.[2] In keeping with the literature, the analysis is phrased in terms of expectations about ψ, although this approach is more a convention than a contribution to intellectual clarity.

In the labor market, the models in previous chapters suggest that workers key their bargaining about the nominal wage to their expected real income share wb/P^e because they can observe the money wage they receive and how hard they are working, but (especially when computing the cost-of-living index that determines their consumption wage) they cannot perfectly observe prices. If a higher wage share signals the presence of enhanced worker bargaining power, one might expect wage inflation to respond positively to an increase in wb/P^e. Greater resistance to wage demands on the part of firms as the profit share erodes and unit labor costs rise could give a negative response. From the econometrics in Chapter 9, more rapid wage increases when ψ is high appear to be the rule for the United States. There is also a weakly positive wage response to u. The typical business cycle pattern is a falling (rising) wage share as capacity utilization rises (falls) so that the two positive signs are consistent with a pro-cyclical nominal wage.[3]

Firms presumably make their pricing decisions in light of labor costs $w^e b/P$, where w^e is their expected money wage. This "expectational" (or inertial) element may enter because they do not fully pass through cost changes into price increases in the short run, as in the indexation scenarios in Chapter 2. A positive pass-through of labor costs into prices shows up in the Chapter 9 econometrics. The price level (and implicitly the markup rate) appears to respond negatively to u, consistent with not strongly cyclical price behavior.

Let $\chi^p = P/P^e$ and $\chi^w = w/w^e$; these variables will equal one in a steady state in which observations and expectations coincide for prices and wages. Easy substitution gives $wb/P^e = \psi\chi^p$ and $w^e b/P = \psi/\chi^w$ for the target variables in the labor and commodity markets respectively. For a model in the (u, ψ) plane, fairly general expressions for nominal wage and price inflation can be written as

$$\hat{w} = f^w(u, \psi\chi^p) + (1 - \sigma)\epsilon \tag{2}$$

and

$$\hat{P} = f^p(u, \psi/\chi^w). \tag{3}$$

In (2), $\epsilon = \hat{\xi}_L = \hat{X} - \hat{L}$ is the rate of labor productivity growth; a fraction $1 - \sigma$ of any productivity increase is immediately passed through into a higher money wage. Wages increasing in line with productivity are a common union bargaining claim. The case of full pass-through ($\sigma = 0$) is sometimes but far from universally observed.

Along the lines of Kaldor's technical progress function, we can write

$$\epsilon = f^{\epsilon}(u, \psi/\chi^{w}). \tag{4}$$

The general view is that productivity varies pro-cyclically. However, this observation has to be interpreted in terms of the typical pattern of the capacity utilization/distributive cycle described above. Along with a downswing in capacity utilization, the wage share rises. A *lagged* positive response of ξ_L to ψ would be associated with an upswing in productivity as the cycle bottoms out, the pattern typically observed. A positive response to u is then consistent with continued productivity growth during the first part of the upswing. In other words, positive values for both partial derivatives of f^{ϵ} in (4) are consistent with observed behavior of ξ_L, u, and ψ.

Equations (2)–(4) are "fairly general," because they say that the inflation rates observed in the labor and commodity markets both depend continuously on two variables—an expectation about ψ and an observation of u. A steady state in this model is defined by $\chi^{p} = \chi^{w} = 1$ and a constant value of ψ. To analyze stability, the first step is to substitute (2)–(4) into the definitional equation $\hat{\psi} = \hat{w} + \hat{b} - \hat{P}$ to derive

$$\begin{aligned}
\dot{\psi} &= \psi[f^{w}(u, \psi\chi^{p}) - f^{p}(u, \psi/\chi^{w}) - \sigma f^{\epsilon}(u, \psi/\chi^{w}] \\
&= \psi[f^{\omega}(u, \psi\chi^{p}, \psi/\chi^{w}) - \sigma f^{\epsilon}(u, \psi/\chi^{w})]
\end{aligned} \tag{5}$$

in which $f^{\omega} = f^{w} - f^{p}$. The natural equations for changes in χ^{w} and χ^{p} are a version of adaptive expectations,

$$\dot{\chi}^{w}\rho^{w}(1 - \chi^{w}) \tag{6}$$

and

$$\dot{\chi}^{p} = \rho^{p}(1 - \chi^{p}), \tag{7}$$

where ρ^{w} and ρ^{p} are positive response coefficients.[4] Equations (5)–(7) are a 3 × 3 dynamic system for $\dot{\psi}$, $\dot{\chi}^{w}$, and $\dot{\chi}^{p}$. Around a steady state, the sign of $\partial\dot{\psi}/\partial\psi$ is determined by $f_{\psi}^{\omega} - \sigma f_{\psi}^{\epsilon}$, where the subscripts stand for partial derivatives. The sign of this expression is ambiguous. It can be negative if real wage growth has a less strong positive response than productivity growth to a higher value of ψ, as appears to be in case in the long term for the United States. Another possibility is a negative productivity response to ψ, or a positive response to the profit share.[5] With $f_{\psi}^{\epsilon} < 0$ one could have $\partial\dot\psi/\partial\psi > 0$ or the wage share will be locally unstable. Even in this case, the adaptive expectations in (6) and (7) could stabilize the 3 × 3 system, and as will be seen there can be stabilizing feedbacks via effective demand as well.

The analysis so far refers to the distribution/inflation "core" of the economy in Garegnani's (1984) usage as discussed in Chapter 2. The immediate questions are about relationships between the level of economic activity and distribution. As pointed out above, the locus along which $\dot\psi$ = 0 traces a curve—a "Distributive" curve in the (u, ψ) plane—not a NAIRU-style point with fixed u and ψ and a stable "nonaccelerating" inflation rate. (How the curve can be forced to collapse to a point is taken up below.) Its slope is

$$\frac{du}{d\psi} = -\frac{f_\psi^\omega - \sigma f_\psi^\epsilon}{f_u^\omega - \sigma f_u^\epsilon}. \tag{8}$$

The sign of the numerator is ambiguous, as just discussed (with locally stable dynamics of ψ calling for a negative value). For the United States, $0 < f_u^\epsilon < f_u^\omega$, suggesting a positive denominator. With a negative numerator, the resulting positive slope $du/d\psi$ is a phenomenon given different names by different authors. The new Keynesian labor economists Blanchflower and Oswald (1994) call the distributive schedule a "wage curve," while for the Kaleckian radicals Boddy and Crotty (1975) its slope encapsulates a "cyclical profit squeeze." This usage carries over into the applied "social structure of accumulation" macro models of Bowles, Gordon, and Weisskopf (1990) and Gordon (1995).

More generally, the slope of the distributive schedule reflects several historical positions in the macroeconomic debate. Suppose for the moment that the numerator of (8) is negative, or $\partial\dot\psi/\partial\psi < 0$. Then for low values of u and ψ, a shallow positive or negative slope may occur because labor's bargaining power is weak. This situation approximates the elastic labor supply curve of the neo-Marxist growth model discussed in Chapter 5.

A rising section of the curve could underlie Marxist cyclical growth, in which an increasing real wage induces capitalists to increase investment levels and search for new labor-saving technologies as well as to reduce employment via input substitution. For various reasons, including a profit squeeze on investment at high levels of economic activity, excessive funds tied up in machinery, and sectoral imbalances, such a boom will finally collapse (Sylos-Labini 1984). The productivity advances during its course, however, can support a higher production level during the next upswing. If the economy cycles around a high activity level, will the full employment profit squeeze transform itself into a long-term FROP of the sort possible in the Japanese case discussed in Chapter 2?

Finally, the Distributive curve might display a consistently negative slope, for two reasons. As already discussed, one involves positive values of both the numerator and the denominator in (8)—this situation might be labeled an "unstable profit squeeze." The other cause for a negative slope is a combination of a negative denominator in (9) with a positive numerator (so that $\partial\dot{\psi}/\partial\psi < 0$). The negative sign of $f_\psi^\omega - \sigma f_\psi^\epsilon$ signals forced saving macroeconomic adjustment, perhaps more likely as the economy nears full capacity use (as discussed in Chapter 5). For high values of u, price inflation would accelerate more rapidly than wage inflation, strengthening downward pressure on the labor share.

A steep positive or negative slope for the Distributive schedule is a special case in the present model. Yet some such configuration is essential for picking out a NAIRU level of capacity utilization, which would correspond to a vertical curve, originating at some "full employment" output/capital ratio $\bar{u}$. In the most orthodox interpretation, marginal productivity conditions such as those in force along the "Labor demand" curve in the Figure 2.2 version of NAIRU theory would also fix the wage share $\bar{\psi}$. The solution set to our "fairly general" differential equation system (5)–(7) would reduce to a single point in the (u, ψ) plane.

The same result emerges under the new Keynesian variant in Figure 2.3. Ignoring productivity growth for simplicity, let $\hat{w}^n = \hat{P}^n = n$ be a NAIRU rate of inflation. Then one could rewrite equations (2) and (3) in the form

$$d\hat{w}/dt = \alpha^w[f^w(u, \psi\chi^p) - n] \tag{2n}$$

and

$$d\hat{P}/dt = \alpha^p[f^p(u, \psi/\chi^w) - n]. \tag{3n}$$

The functions f^w and f^p now stand for NAIRU-consistent configurations of (say) an efficiency wage and a markup schedule. If the curves somehow shift away from their "equilibrium" positions, then price and wage inflation will accelerate or decelerate accordingly. In equilibrium, the intersection of the curves defines the $(\bar{u}, \bar{\psi})$ point.

Another observation about price inflation is worth adding. Along a Distributive locus with $\dot{\psi} = 0$, ψ is implicitly a function of u at steady state. Plugging this relationship into (3) with $\chi^w = 1$ gives a reduced form for the steady-state price inflation rate, $\hat{P} = \hat{P}(u)$. NAIRU models shrink this function to a point, $\hat{P} = \hat{P}(\bar{u})$. One ought to be able to do better than that.

Figure 7.1
A possible relationship between price inflation and the output/capital ratio.

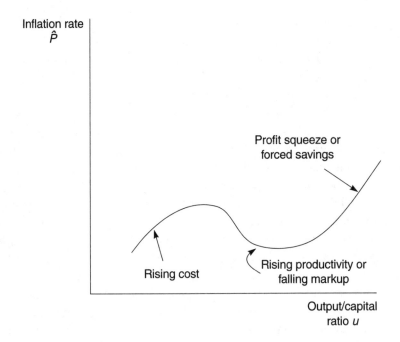

Figure 7.1 illustrates a not implausible relationship: for relatively low levels of u, $d\hat{P}/du > 0$ as costs increase. For intermediate levels of u, a countercyclical markup and/or pro-cyclical productivity growth can make $d\hat{P}/du$ negative. Finally at very high levels of capacity utilization and/or employment, inflation speeds up as either wage inflation (the profit squeeze) or price inflation (forced saving) takes off.

Free-form fitting of a cubic equation suggests that the diagram might not be a bad description of inflation in the U.S. economy.[6] However, insofar as it reflects more than just the multicollinearity of its explanatory variables, the snake depicted in Figure 7.1 represents a *long-run* relationship, like the one Phillips (1958) discussed in the original paper on his famous curve. In the context of the model just presented, there is no reason to expect price or wage changes year-on-year to demonstrate any simple pattern. The celebrated "failure" in the 1970s of short-run Phillips curves à la Samuelson and Solow (1960) was a case of monetarist and rational expectationalist hunters and hounds pursuing a fox that did not exist. Where the phantom chase led has already been explored in Chapter 6. After going down those trails it makes sense to work through how demand and distribution interact in a Keynesian/Kaleckian model.

3. Absorbing Productivity Growth

One question of interest is whether faster productivity growth raises real wage and output levels. In steady state the labor share will satisfy the relationships $\hat{\psi} = \hat{w} + \hat{b} - \hat{P} = \hat{\omega} - \epsilon = 0$ so that the real wage increases at the same rate as productivity growth—a standard result already pointed out in connection with the Ramsey and Kaldor growth models. Without their presumption of full employment, however, other consequences of faster productivity growth can be less beneficent. To see why, we have to set out a full macro model.

Complementing the inflation/distribution "core" (5)–(7), the price/quantity side of the economy is presented in Table 7.1, copied over from the "markup" specification in Table 5.1 with saving and investment in (13) and (14) tied to $1 - \psi$ instead of π as a representation of the profit share. As discussed at length in previous chapters, both effective demand and (through the investment function) capital stock growth can be either wage- or profit-led. The detailed conditions for $du/d\psi$ and $dg/d\psi$ to have the same sign are not identical, but quite similar. To avoid endless taxonomies, we simply assume forthwith that the signs of both growth and output responses to changes in ψ are the same.

Adding effective demand makes distributional dynamics more complicated. In (5), one has to consider not only direct effects of the labor share ψ on its time-derivative $\dot{\psi}$ via the functions f^w, f^p, and f^ϵ, but also indirect effects involving $du/d\psi$ through the equations of Table 7.1. In the locally stable distributive case with $\partial\dot{\psi}/\partial\psi < 0$ (assumed throughout this section), these linkages will not destabilize the entire system if the slope of the Distributive locus from (8) is "large" in absolute terms, that is, the curve has a visually *shallow* negative or positive slope in the (u, ψ) plane.

Figure 7.2 illustrates the argument. In the upper diagram for a profit-led economy, an outward shift in the effective demand curve makes out-

Table 7.1 Basic demand side and price relationships for a one-sector model.

$P = (1 + \tau)wb = wb/(1 - \pi) = wb/\psi$	(9)
$L/X = b$	(10)
$u = X/K$	(11)
$r = [\tau/(1 + \tau)]u = \pi u = (1 - \psi)u$	(12)
$g^s = [s_\pi(1 - \psi) + s_w\psi]u = s(\psi)u$	(13)
$g^i = g^i(u,r) = g^i(u, \psi) = g_0 + \alpha r + \beta u = g_0 + [\alpha(1 - \psi) + \beta]u$	(14)
$\gamma_g + g^i - g^s = 0$	(15)

Definitions

$\pi = rPK/PX = \tau/(1 + \tau)$
$\omega = w/P = (1 - \pi)/b = \psi/b$
$\psi = 1 - \pi$
$\gamma_g = PG/PK$

put jump from A to B. With a negatively sloped Distributive curve due to forced saving, the labor share will begin to fall, leading to a new steady state at C. In this case, forced saving and profit-led demand go together to create a strong long-term impact of expansionary policy. It is easy to imagine that if the Distributive curve were to cut the Effective demand

Figure 7.2
Stable expansionary adjustment in profit-led (upper) and wage-led (lower) economies.

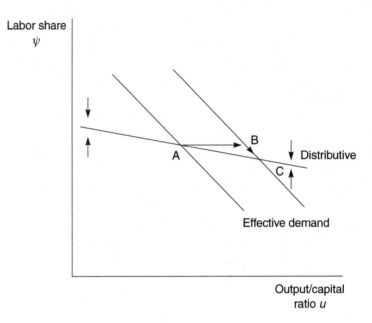

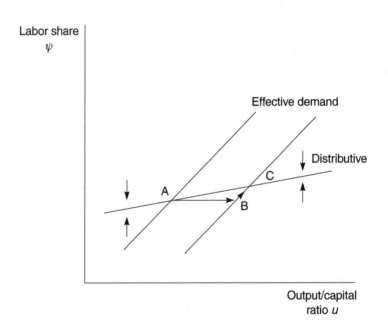

schedule from above instead of below, the labor share would diverge toward zero. If the Distributive curve has a positive slope, on the other hand, medium-term stability in a profit-led economy is assured (see the upper diagram in Figure 7.4 below).

Similarly, in the wage-led lower diagram, a Distributive schedule with a shallow positive slope $d\psi/du$ will amplify the effects of expansionary policy over the long term. If the schedule were steep enough to intersect the Effective demand curve from below, then an expansion would make the labor share rise, generating more demand and output, increasing the labor share further, and so on. Ultimately the economy would hit some form of output barrier, possibly forcing a shift over to forced saving adjustment modes as discussed in connection with Figure 4.2.

Such a scenario can be the Achilles' heal of expansionary, redistributive policies in wage-led systems. An example is a heterodox shock antiinflation package, where getting rid of rapid inflation by fiat boosts aggregate demand by eliminating forced saving and the inflation tax. A strong push for real wage increases after the shock could set off diverging wage-led output growth; well before forced saving kicks in, the stabilization program will probably have fallen apart.

Assuming such catastrophes away as in Figure 7.2, we can turn to the question of productivity growth. With a positively sloped Distributive schedule, Figure 7.3 illustrates the implications of an upward shift in the function f^ϵ. By cutting costs, this jump moves a stable Distributive locus downward. In the profit-led case in the upper diagram, the outcomes of the move from point A to a new steady state at B include a lower wage share due to reduced labor input with faster real wage growth, a higher level of economic activity, and faster capital stock growth—more rapid technical change is absorbed easily. In the open economy context, this could be the story of a successful exporter of manufactured goods. Lower unit labor costs stimulate the export component of aggregate demand, and the economy grows rapidly.

The scenario in the wage-led economy at the bottom is less pleasant. In the short run, if $\sigma > 0$ in (2), a lower labor/output ratio is not immediately followed by a proportionately higher real wage. At the initial level of output at point A, total wage payments fall as jobs are eliminated, reducing consumer demand. Because they stop being stimulated by demand pressure, investment and new capacity formation drop off.

These results persist in the new steady state at B, where along with the labor share, the output/capital ratio and (by our "same signs" assumption) the capital stock growth rate are lower. The real wage will rise faster if ϵ retains a higher value at B after both u and ψ go down, but it does so in the face of less employment expansion (output growth is

Figure 7.3
Effect of more rapid
labor productivity
growth in profit-led
(upper) and wage-led
(lower) economies.

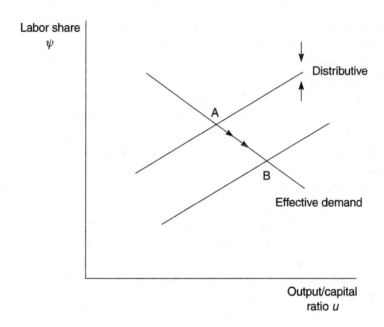

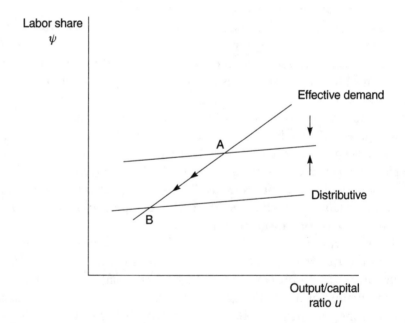

down and productivity growth may be up) and slower growth of consumer demand.

This scenario seems to run counter to capitalism's classic mechanism for real per capita income to rise, that is, sustained growth of real wages in line with productivity increases. What the bottom diagram of Figure

7.3 shows is that even if wages do go up to offset lower labor/output ratios, faster productivity growth does not necessarily lead to higher output and employment. This possibility dawned on the Luddites and economists such as David Ricardo two centuries ago.[7] If a tendency toward lagging consumer sales is not offset by other shifts such as falling savings rates, productivity growth not "realized" by effective demand could be a problem in wage-led developing economies today.

4. Effects of Expansionary Policy

As argued by Bowles and Boyer (1995) and substantiated for the United States in Chapter 9, demand in modern industrial economies appears to be profit-led. Even if they so avoid Luddite problems of absorbing productivity growth, profit-led systems are still affected by the shape and position of the Distributive schedule. The upper diagram of Figure 7.2 already illustrates a strong response to expansionary policy under a forced saving distributive adjustment. Figure 7.4 shows two additional possibilities when there is a profit squeeze.

In the upper diagram, a "permanent" outward shift in the Effective demand schedule because of expansionary policy will *not* have strong effects on employment and can even reduce medium-term growth. In the short run, economic stimulus looks good, as output jumps from point A to point B and investment rises (assuming that higher capacity utilization has some positive impact on investment demand). Over a longer stretch of time, however, unit labor costs ψ increase toward point C. Private investment could well decline in reaction to the high employment profit squeeze. The dynamic adjustment through points A, B, and toward C may lead toward slower growth in the medium run.

In the lower diagram, adjustment around the $\dot{\psi} = 0$ locus is not stable. As discussed in connection with equation (8), this "unstable profit squeeze" is associated with a negatively sloped Distributive schedule. The overall system can be stable, however, if the Distributive curve cuts the (profit-led) Effective demand curve from above. At least in terms of stimulating output and growth, expansionary policy is now clearly counterproductive since it drives the economy to a new equilibrium C lying to the left of the initial point A. The wage share does increase, but output and productivity growth could be substantially reduced.

There are potential feedback effects that could worsen these problems.

First, a positively sloped Distributive schedule may shift further upward or become steeper, as higher observed wages lead to labor militancy and still higher wage targets in contract negotiations. The importance of such processes depends on the social context. They were far less

Figure 7.4
Expansionary policy
in a profit-led econ-
omy when distribu-
tive dynamics are
stable (upper) and
unstable (lower).

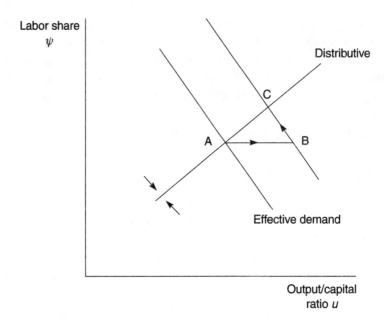

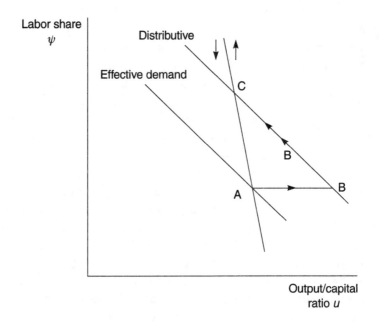

forceful in the United States of the 1990s than they were when the
Golden Age of postwar economic growth (Glyn et al. 1990) ended more
than a quarter-century ago. As discussed in Chapter 9, the economy may
have shifted from a borderline unstable to a stable profit squeeze configuration at the end of the Golden Age.

Second, the Effective demand schedule and capital formation may shift downward. Reduced investment demand in the short run may dampen "animal spirits" at home and lead to diversion of capital spending to projects abroad over the medium term. This observation is pertinent to industrialized economies today because of the opening of international capital markets over the 1970s and 1980s. Profitability comparisons between potential domestic and foreign projects play a much bigger role in enterprise decision making than they did even in the 1980s.

Third, such responses may be exacerbated if higher real wages and/or capacity utilization are associated with faster inflation toward the far right end of the curve in Figure 7.1. Combined with exogenous upward shifts in the cost schedule induced by the oil price shocks, such structuralist price and wage pressures triggered the staggering "anti-inflationary" American interest rate hikes just before and after 1980. Tight money was anti-employment, and curtailed investment spending. To explore such eventualities further, we have to bring in the financial side of the economy, as in following sections of this chapter. However, it should also be added that the experience of the late 1990s belied any strong tendency for inflation to speed up at relatively high levels of aggregate demand.

Fourth, widening trade deficits can be caused by higher wages and employment, meaning that interest rates may have to be increased to staunch the external gap. In the United States, such a scenario has become increasingly relevant as the economy has opened to foreign trade (the marginal import coefficient with respect to GDP in the 1990s is on the order of one-third). Alternatively, devaluation provokes further inflation. Because international capital movements have become highly responsive to interest rate differentials and expected exchange rate adjustments, there may be a contractionary bias to the world financial system (Eatwell and Taylor 2000).

Finally, on the brighter side, there *are* policies that can be used to offset many of these unfavorable effects. With regard to effective demand, intelligently directed public investment (in both physical and "human" capital) can help sustain overall accumulation, especially if it "crowds in" private capital via complementarities. Insofar as the fiscal deficit and associated interest obligations on outstanding debt (see Chapter 6) are considered "excessive," such spending initiatives in the United States could be financed by taxes on financial transactions (the volume of which has skyrocketed over the recent period) and/or wealth (Pollin 1998b; Wolff 1995).

On the "supply" or distribution/inflation side of the economy, steps to encourage greater worker "voice" in enterprise management can lead to less labor militancy and even higher investable profits by flattening or shifting the Distributive schedule downward (Freeman and Medoff 1984). Asset redistribution may enhance economic productivity over-all (Bowles and Gintis 1995). Controls and/or taxes on external cap-ital movements can make internal investment less sensitive to changes in interest and profit rates. Some of these proposals transcend mere macroeconomics, but illustrate how intimately it depends on the social fabric.

5. Financial Extensions

The next task is to bring in the dynamics of fiscal and monetary interven-tions as they cumulate through the private sector's, government's, and the banking system's flows of funds. Alongside the income level and share changes illustrated in Figures 7.2 and 7.4, the real interest rate $i - \hat{P}$ enters as an indicator of distributive strife. As in Chapters 4 and 5, the IS/LM analysis to follow is fairly conventional. The emphasis in the presentation is on how a generalized model of the real and financial economy hangs together. With more specific assumptions, detailed re-sults from post-Keynesian and Minskyan specifications are presented in Chapters 8 and 9.

The LM curve introduced as equation (11) in Chapter Five can be re-stated as

$$\mu(i - \hat{P}, u)[(qPK/T) + 1] - \zeta(T_c/T) = 0, \qquad (16)$$

where i is "the" nominal interest rate, qP is the asset price of capital, T is the outstanding stock of fiscal debt ("T-bills"), T_c is the part of T held by the central bank, and ζ is the credit multiplier blowing up high-powered money T_c to the outstanding money stock.

The balance sheets underlying (16) appear in Table 7.2. The main con-trast with Table 4.2 is that households now lend L_h to business, instead of holding equity $P_v V$. The nominal interest rate on bank and household

Table 7.2 Balance sheets for an IS/LM model.

Households		Business		
M	Ω	qPK	L_b	
T_h			L_h	
L_h				
Commercial Banks		**Central Bank**		**Government**
H	M	T_c	H	T
L_b				

loans and T-bills is assumed to be the same, with q as the accommodating variable.

The other new wrinkle in (16) is inclusion of the real interest rate as an argument in the money demand function μ. If households don't suffer money illusion, the real rate should also figure in the definition of q as

$$q = r/(i - \hat{P}). \tag{17}$$

This formula looks suspiciously close to Irving Fisher's arbitrage equality $r = i - \hat{P}$ between the profit rate and the real interest rate (derived in Chapter 3).[8]

In the financial world of Table 7.2, Fisher's formula would apply in asset market "equilibrium" when $q = 1$. In the more general setup of Table 4.2, however, the equation for q is longer,

$$q = r/[\lambda(i - \hat{P}) + (1 - \lambda)i_v], \tag{18}$$

where λ is the share of loans in qPK and i_v is the return to equity. From (18), one gets the Fisher relationship only when $q = 1$ and $i - \hat{P} = i_v$. The equity premium puzzle discussed in Chapter 4 makes sure that the latter condition does not apply. Moreover, the $r = 1 - \hat{P}$ equation does not fit the data from the U.S. economy. Faster inflation does not boost nominal interest rates automatically, a point relevant to the discussion to follow.

In any case, plugging (17) into (16) while observing that $r = (1 - \psi)u$ as an accounting identity produces a final form for an LM equation,

$$\mu(i - \hat{P}, u, \hat{P})\{[(1 - \psi)uZ/(i - \hat{P})] + 1\} - \zeta(T_c/T) = 0, \tag{19}$$

where $Z = PK/T$. In this formula, money demand *increases* as a function of $\hat{P}$ through the terms in $i - \hat{P}$. This is a nonstandard result, although it is consistent with Keynes's emphasis on the likelihood of asset holders' "fleeing to liquidity" when anything untoward happens. A less restricted financial model than the one in Table 7.2 would include "hedge assets" such as equity, land, collectibles, and so on, which could be used as inflation shields.

A full short-run macro model emerges if we adjoin (19) to the equations of Table 7.1. A couple of revisions, however, are useful. First, bringing in effects of inflation, the investment function (14) can be modified to the form

$$g^i = g_0 + [\alpha(1 - \psi) + \beta]u - \theta(i - \hat{P}) - \phi\hat{P}, \tag{14'}$$

where the net impact of a higher value of $\hat{P}$ on investment will be negative when $\phi > \theta > 0$. Throwing an extra $\hat{P}$ argument into the money demand function μ (with a negative partial derivative) similarly offsets the odd effects of inflation mentioned above.

A second change is to carry interest payments in the accounting, at least for T-bills, so that as in Chapter 6 we can study the macroeconomic role of government debt. If only rentiers hold T-bills, then the saving function (13) should be revised to read

$$g^s = [s_\pi(1 - \psi) + s_w\psi]u + s_\pi(i/Z), \tag{13'}$$

where it is tacitly assumed that all T-bill interest ultimately gets passed along to wealthy households and that we can continue to ignore interest payments on loans to business.[9]

6. Dynamics of the System

To get to full dynamic speed, we have to investigate how the ratio or state variable $Z = PK/T$ evolves over time. After substitution among the entries in Table 7.2, total household wealth can be written as $\Omega = qPK + T$, or the sum of the economy's "primary assets" comprising physical capital and "outside" debt. The ratio Z basically measures Ω's composition.

As discussed in Chapter 10, in an open economy national wealth is given by $\Omega = qPK + T + N$, with N standing for net foreign assets. Tables 1.5 and 1.6 show that (in trillions of dollars) the U.S. numbers at the end of 1999 were $qPK = 26.6$, $T = 4.9$, $N = -1.3$, and $\Omega = 30.2$ so that $(qPK - N)/T \approx 5.1$. In practical terms, a value of Z in the range of ten or above would suggest a very thin national bond market; a value below three might be taken as an indicator that government debt is "too high," as it allegedly is in Japan.

Along lines already developed in section 5 of Chapter 6, a differential equation for Z can be written as

$$\dot{Z} = Z[g - (i - \hat{P}) - \gamma_g Z], \tag{20}$$

with $\gamma_g PK$ as the primary fiscal deficit. To explore stability, we have to consider the effects of Z and ψ on i, $\hat{P}$, and g. In the LM equation (19), a higher value of Z increases money demand by raising the $(1 - \psi)uZ/(i - \hat{P})$ term, leading to a higher interest rate. Investment demand g^i will fall, reducing u as well. The impact effect of a lower u on markup inflation $\hat{P}$ can take either sign in (2), but is likely to be weak. Absent strong interest rate cost-push as discussed in section 3 of Chapter 3, we have $d\hat{P}/dZ$ small and of uncertain sign, $dg/dZ < 0$, $di/dZ > 0$, and $d\hat{T}/dz > 0$ for $\gamma_g > 0$. Plugging all this information into (20) gives $d\dot{Z}/dZ < 0$. This self-stabilizing response could vanish if interest rate cost-push were strong, an idea lurking at the fringes of macroeconomics since the times of Thomas Tooke.

The stability of (20) has interesting implications. The ratio variable $Z = PK/T$ can be interpreted as the "velocity" of fiscal debt with respect to the capital stock, in the sense that if it takes a high value then there is weak financial backup for tangible assets (just as a high ratio of GDP to the money supply signals that money is "scarce"). As long as the output/capital ratio u and the policy variables ζ and T_s/T do not vary over wide ranges, then if Z does not change very much, neither will other velocity ratios such as PX/H, PX/M, and so on. From the perspective of a demand-driven growth model, the widely heralded stability of money velocity, to the extent that it exists, is simply a consequence of the fact that the differential equation determining the evolution of its underlying determinant Z is stable and relatively unaffected by changes in income distribution and output.

Turning to the effects of changes in ψ on Z, $dg/d\psi$ can take either sign, depending on whether the economy is wage- or profit-led. By increasing unit labor costs, a higher ψ makes $\hat{P}$ increase in (2). In (19), it reduces money demand and thereby i. These interest rate and inflation effects may be weak, so that if investment demand is strongly profit-led the net outcome can be a negative value of $d\dot{Z}/d\psi$ in (20). In the interest of brevity, we consider only the locally stable case in which $d\dot{\psi}/d\psi < 0$ in (5). An increase in Z affects $\dot{\psi}$ by driving up the interest rate and reducing u. With a stronger output effect on wage than markup inflation, we get $d\dot{\psi}/dZ < 0$.

The sign pattern of the Jacobian matrix of (5) and (20) around a steady state becomes

$$
\begin{array}{c c c}
 & \psi & Z \\
\dot{\psi} & - & - \\
\dot{Z} & -(?) & - \\
\end{array}
$$

where the potential destabilizing effect of interest rate cost-push is ignored. The question mark in the row for $\dot{Z}$ refers to possible effects of a lower real interest rate combined with weakly profit-led investment on $d\dot{Z}/d\psi$.

7. Comparative Dynamics

A whole macro model is bundled into equations (5) and (20); working through the implications of all the own- and cross-effects is not easy. At most, the exercises to follow may help clarify whether expansionary and/or progressively redistributive policies have a chance to succeed in an economy in which effective demand is profit-led and the wage share and capacity utilization have a positive relationship along the distributive curve. The outcomes are not completely unfavorable, but may well have politically hard-to-handle adverse effects on the real return to financial assets.[10]

We first have to trace effects through the IS/LM system. In a standard diagram like Figure 4.7 for a profit-led economy, the IS curve will shift rightward (increasing both u and i) when the labor share ψ and inflation rate $\hat{P}$ decrease and/or government outlays γ_g go up. The LM curve will shift downward (reducing i and increasing u) when the capital/T-bill ratio Z declines, $\hat{P}$ decreases, ψ increases (reducing q), and the credit multiplier ζ or the part of T-bills used as high-powered money T_c/T goes up.

Taking into account shifts in both curves, the overall effects are likely to go as follows:

	ψ	Z	$\hat{P}$	γ_g	ζ	T_c/T
u	−	−	−	+	+	+
i	?	+	?	+	−	−
g	−	−	−	+	+	+

It is assumed that the outward shift in the IS curve makes $du/d\psi < 0$, and the ambiguous effects of both curves shifting make it hard to determine how i responds to ψ and $\hat{P}$. Effects of changes in the policy and state variables on the growth rate g are assumed to parallel those on u. From (3) we further have a positive effect of ψ and an ambiguous effect of u on the price inflation rate; these feedbacks are assumed not to override the signs just indicated.

Figure 7.5 shows how the schedules for $\dot{\psi} = 0$ ("Distributive") and $\dot{Z} = 0$ ("Velocity" of the fiscal debt) adjust in response to policy changes. From the signs and likely magnitudes of the derivatives discussed at the end of section 6, the Velocity schedule is not strongly affected by changes in the labor share in the (Z, ψ) plane. Its slope is negative and steep (or positive and steep) insofar as $d\dot{Z}/d\psi$ is small and negative (or small and positive if investment demand is only weakly profit-led). Because both $d\dot{\psi}/dZ$ and $d\dot{\psi}/d\psi$ are negative, the Distributive schedule slopes downward. With ψ and u varying together, the output increase associated with lower interest rates from a lower value of Z may make the Distributive schedule nonlinear.

A "permanent" increase in public spending γ_g pushes the Velocity schedule to the left by making public debt build up faster (reducing Z),

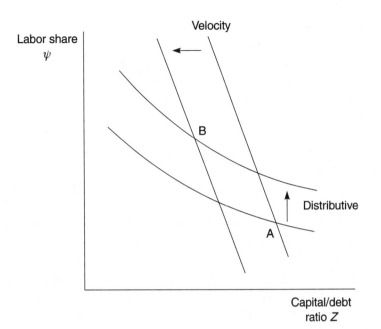

Figure 7.5
Effects of a higher
value of public
spending γ_g across
steady states.

and moves the Distribution schedule up by raising aggregate demand. Both shifts raise the labor share in the transition from point A to point B, partly offsetting the output and growth stimulus from the higher value of γ_g (as in Figure 7.4). The capital/debt ratio unambiguously decreases. Along with a higher ψ, the lower value of Z will bid down the nominal interest rate as long as T_c/T or the share of the fiscal debt that is "monetized" is not reduced. Inflation, on the other hand, could well speed up because of cost pressures. The real interest rate $i - \hat{P}$ could decline, displeasing bondholders. This last change could be the main political obstacle to a policy shift which otherwise has generally favorable effects (insofar as they are not partly or wholly reversed by the rising labor share, as in Figure 7.4).

Does expansionary monetary policy fare any better than its fiscal counterpart? By shifting the LM curve downward, the impact effects of a higher ζ or T_c/T include a lower interest rate, higher rates of economic activity and capital stock growth, and an ambiguous change in the rate of inflation. In equation (20) the balance of forces is unclear, but relatively strong growth and inflation effects might require a shift of Z to the right to hold $\dot{Z} = 0$, as shown in Figure 7.6. As in Figure 7.5, the expansionary policy makes the Distributive schedule shift up.

The new equilibrium at point B has a higher level of Z (if the shift in the Velocity schedule dominates) and a higher ψ (with the increase attenuated by the negative slope of the Distributive curve). Increased fiscal debt velocity bids up the interest rate, partly offsetting the initial monetary expansion. If the real interest rate is stable or rises (due to the increase in Z and weak effects of expansion on inflation), monetary expansion may prove politically feasible. A high interest rate is more likely if the Velocity schedule has a positive slope due to a weak effect of the higher labor share on investment demand.

Finally, Figure 7.7 shows what happens if labor costs fall, because of faster productivity growth, wage restraint, or institutional changes such as those discussed at the end of section 4. The Distributive schedule shifts downward, stimulating growth and reducing inflation as in the upper diagram of Figure 7.3. The higher capital/debt ratio bids up the interest rate. Bondholders might be happy, especially because people in their class position would also gain from a higher profit share in current income. Combined with neutral monetary and mildly restrictive fiscal policies, this scenario is not far from the U.S. experience in the late 1990s.

As mentioned above, the impacts of the policy changes illustrated in Figures 7.5–7.7 are a mixed bag. In a profit-led economy in which strong financial interests push for relatively high real interest rates and low inflation, expansionary policies may well have to be combined with institutional changes to hold down production costs. One way to shift down the Distributive schedule is through money-wage cuts along the lines hinted at by Modigliani (1944) in the quotation presented in Chapter 4.[11] The Modigliani (or Patinkin) line is that the nominal wage is "too high" with respect to the money supply; in terms of Figure 7.7, ψ should

Figure 7.6
Possible effects of expansionary monetary policy across steady states.

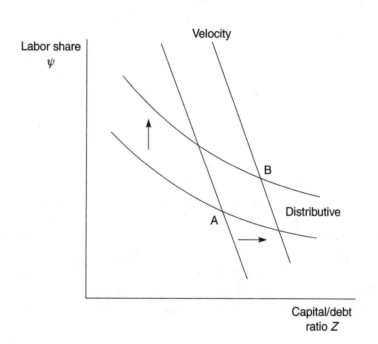

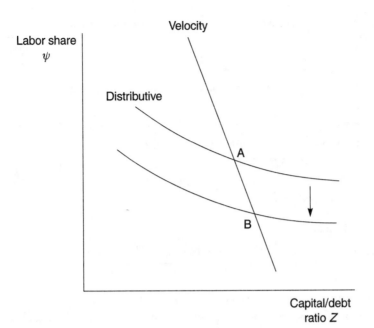

Figure 7.7
Steady-state effects of a reduction in labor costs.

decline for a given level of Z. Alternatively, NAIRU-style arguments assert that the real wage can be "too high" to clear the labor market; as we have seen in Chapter 6, a temporary price inflation may then be "needed" to erode it away.

The reasoning at the end of section 4 suggests that there are institutionally less painful ways than cutting money wages or running price inflations to shift the Distributive schedule downward to sustain investment demand. If powerful social actors favoring a low labor share and a high real interest rate can be kept in check, then both distributionally progressive and expansionary policies have a role to play, especially if they can be designed to stimulate productivity growth and accumulation.

8. Open Economy Complications

Financial considerations carry over full force to the open macro-economy, as described in Chapter 10. Here, we deal only with the demand side in the short run, to give a foretaste of things to come and to round out consideration of potential linkages between income distribution and the level of economic activity.[12]

The economy is assumed to export its product in volume E, with $\epsilon = E/K$ (note the redefinition of ϵ) depending positively on the real exchange rate $\rho = e/P$ where e is the nominal dollar/yen exchange rate.[13] The elasticity of ϵ with respect to ρ is η. If excess capacity is low, exports may de-

Table 7.3 Macro relationships for a one-sector, open economy model.

$P = (wb + ea)/(1 - \pi)$	(21)
$\phi = ea/(ea + wb)$	(22)
$\rho = e/P = \phi(1 - \pi)/a;\quad \omega = w/P = (1 - \phi)(1 - \pi)/b$	(23)
$u = X/K$	(24)
$r = \pi u$	(25)
$g^s = \{s_\pi \pi + [s_w(1 - \phi) + \phi](1 - \pi)\}u$	(26)
$g^i = g^i(r, u) = g^i(\pi, u)$	(27)
$\epsilon = E/K = \epsilon(\rho)$	(28)
$\epsilon + g^i - g^s = 0$	(29)

Definition

$\pi = rPK/PX = \tau/(1 + \tau)$, where $P = (1 + \tau)(wb + ea)$

cline when domestic activity picks up as producers more aggressively pursue internal sales, but this extension of the basic model is omitted for simplicity.

On the import side, as usual we assume a "workshop" economy which processes intermediate and raw material imports into final products for domestic use or export, or else a developing country that has pursued import-substituting industrialization far enough to be dependent on imported intermediate inputs. Import volume is the quantity aX, where a is an input-output coefficient which again for simplicity is assumed to be fixed. Total cost of output decomposes as $PX = wbX + \pi PX + eaX$, so we implicitly assume that the value of output PX is bigger than GDP because it includes the cost eaX of imports.

Table 7.3 sets out equations for the model. We return to using the profit share π as the key internal distributive variable, because in (21) the price level is determined as a markup on the sum of labor (wb) and import (ea) costs per unit of output. The definitions in (22) and (23) show that with a constant π, the real wage ω is an inverse function of the real exchange rate ρ. There is now a three-way distributional conflict among profit recipients, wage earners, and the rest of the world.

Scaled to the capital stock K, total real injections minus leakages Δ are equal to $\epsilon + g^i - g^s$; for macro equilibrium, (29) shows that Δ must equal zero. Total differentiation gives $d\Delta = 0 = (d\Delta/du)du + (d\Delta/d\rho)d\rho$, or $du/d\rho = -(d\Delta/d\rho)/(d\Delta/du)$. Standard Keynes/Harrod stability arguments require that $d\Delta/du < 0$, so that the sign of $du/d\rho$ is the same as that of

$$d\Delta/d\rho = (\epsilon/\rho)\{\eta - [\rho au(1 - s_w)/\epsilon]\}. \tag{30}$$

Effects of the change in ρ on investment demand are left out in this expression to keep the algebra within bounds (shifts in g^i are implicit in the diagrammatic analysis coming later).

Equation (30) shows how Δ and thereby u respond to currency devaluation in the form of an increase in the real exchange rate ρ. If a country devalues from an initial trade deficit (so that $eaX > PE$ in current prices) and its workers' saving rate s_w is small, then the term $\rho au(1 - s_w)/\epsilon = (1 - s_w)eaX/PE$ could easily exceed one. Certainly in the short run, the export elasticity η need not have so high a value. In other words, devaluation could be contractionary, improving the trade deficit not so much by increasing exports and encouraging substitution of domestic products for imports as by making the level of economic activity go down.

To shed further light on this possibility of "contractionary devaluation," we can consider the country's trade deficit in real terms (again scaled by the capital stock), $D = \rho au - \epsilon$. One can easily show that

$$dD/d\rho = (\epsilon/\rho)[(\rho au/\epsilon) - \eta] + \rho a(du/d\rho). \tag{31}$$

In the literature on open economy macroeconomics, "Marshall-Lerner" (or ML) conditions in various forms are often invoked to ensure that $dD/d\rho < 0$ so that devaluation reduces the trade deficit. Invariably, such conditions resemble the first term to the left of the equals sign in (31) and do not include a term in $du/d\rho$. Two points are worth making.

The first is that if we ignore $du/d\rho$ in (31), then a negative value of $dD/d\rho$ requires that $(\rho au/\epsilon) - \eta < 0$. This inequality is the standard issue ML condition for the present model. Leaving aside the term in s_w in (30), one can see that when the inequality holds, devaluation cannot be contractionary. A "perverse" macroeconomic result seems to be avoided because the trade deficit is empirically observed to decrease (usually) in response to devaluation.

The interesting thing about this argument is its unconscious acceptance of Say's Law. If the level of economic activity u is assumed to be constant, then it makes no sense to ask how its changes might influence the trade balance. Of course if u *can* change, then the bracketed term in (31) can be positive, combining contractionary devaluation and $dD/d\rho < 0$ just because $du/d\rho \neq 0$. In practice, this sort of scenario happens fairly often in developing economies where export elasticities can be low.

The other point is that from (31) the trade deficit may respond weakly to devaluation when $du/d\rho > 0$, or a devalued exchange rate stimulates effective demand. For a given profit share π, a "weaker" (or higher) ρ goes hand in hand with a lower real wage ω, so one might expect $du/d\rho > 0$ in a profit-led system. To see how this works out in detail, we can

Figure 7.8
Effects of devaluation
when demand is
profit-led (upper) and
wage-led (lower).

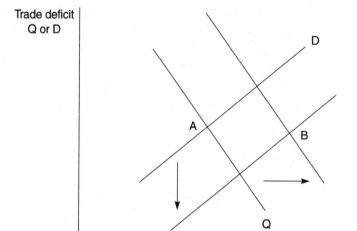

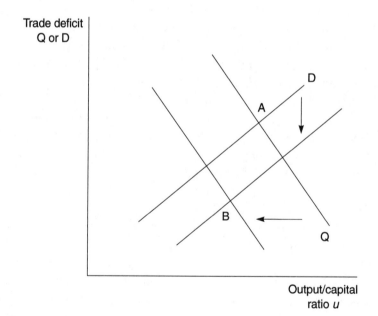

use the definitions in (22) and (23) to rewrite the macro balance condition (29) in the form

$$g^j - [s_\pi\pi + s_w\omega b]u = Q = D = \rho a u - \epsilon, \tag{32}$$

where Q stands for the domestic component of effective demand (investment minus saving) and D is again the trade deficit.

We know that $dQ/du < 0$ from a Keynesian stability condition, while for a constant profit share, $dQ/d\rho$ will be positive (negative) when demand is profit-led (wage-led) because of the negative effect of ρ on ω. If a Say's Law ML condition applies we have $dD/d\rho < 0$, but the opposite sign is also a possibility. Finally, $dD/du > 0$ because imports go up (and exports may go down) in response to higher economic activity.

Figure 7.8 shows the effects of devaluation in the two cases, with macroeconomic equilibrium observed at the points where the Q- and D-schedules cross. In a wage-led economy at the bottom, devaluation can be contractionary when the leftward shift in the Q-schedule is big (a lower real wage strongly reduces domestic demand) and the downward shift in the D-schedule is small (a relatively low export elasticity η). Both shifts lead the trade deficit to improve, in the sort of "overkill" of which the IMF is occasionally accused (Taylor 1991). Even if the Say's Law Marshall-Lerner condition is violated and the D-schedule shifts up, the trade deficit can still decline because of lower effective demand.

By contrast, in the profit-led economy at the top, the rightward shift in the Q-schedule counters the downward shift in the D-schedule, and the trade balance improvement may be slight. Following Blecker (1991) one might argue that the Reagan tax cuts of the 1980s pushed the U.S. economy in the direction of being more profit-led by reducing tax-induced income leakages from high, profit-based incomes and reducing differentials in "leakage" rates across different sources of income.[14] One consequence in line with the upper diagram was the small reduction in the trade deficit observed after the dollar depreciated in the mid-1980s. This result was only made worse by deteriorating American "competitiveness" or an upward drift in the D-schedule for a given level of u.

Once again, structural changes and distributional shifts interact in complicated fashion to generate observed macroeconomic events.[15]

CHAPTER EIGHT

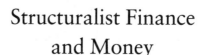

Structuralist Finance
and Money

The trouble with most macroeconomic models of finance is that they don't let anything interesting happen. In the standard LM apparatus (and even more so in new classical models), the only action involves rates of return adjusting to clear securities markets—there are no financial innovations such as money market funds and derivatives, no strong feedbacks between the real and financial sectors, no speculative booms and crashes. A few economists, mostly post-Keynesians, have built endogenous or passive money into their model frameworks; fewer still have dealt with endogenous changes in finance. Modest steps in these directions are taken in this chapter, on the basis of historical experience and stylized facts. We begin by reviewing the latter, in a logical reconstruction of financial (mainly banking) history, if not quite the history itself.[1] A short-run model of "endogenous money" in a complete macro accounting framework is then set out. It is followed by a post-Keynesian growth model focused on business borrowing under strong but not unrealistic simplifying assumptions about the financial accounts. The discussion closes with a quick review of new Keynesian models aimed at capturing the institutional (or, better, social) aspects of finance. Both post- and new Keynesian formulations foreshadow a model in Chapter 9 of Minsky's cyclical macro story as based on some of the micro detail presented here.

1. Banking History and Institutions

Over a long historical span, Chick (1986) traces the linkages among changes in bank liabilities ($\Delta M = \Delta C + \Delta D$, where C stands for "notes" or currency, and D for deposits), reserves (ΔH), and loans (ΔL) in "Anglo-American" commercial banks.[2] In the eighteenth century, finance houses across the United Kingdom gradually shifted from being "goldsmith-bankers" to "country banks," mostly sponsored by local merchants. These banks issued notes which circulated alongside merchants' bills of exchange as the main means for commercial payments (workers, insofar as they engaged in monetized transactions at all, continued to use the coin of the realm). The notes were short-term and, like deposits in gold, were used to support short-term lending as well as a precautionary level of reserves:

$$\Delta M \Rightarrow \Delta L \quad \text{and} \quad \Delta H. \tag{1}$$

In both countries, battles ensued over the right to issue notes. The Bank of England (still a private entity) spent much of the eighteenth century trying to revise the Bank Act to get a monopoly on issue. Deposit banking and a clearing system in London arose as responses to the progressive strengthening of the Bank of England's monopoly position. In the United States, a National Bank Act limited the right of issue to National Banks holding government debt—after all, the Union had to finance the Civil War. Systems of "correspondent banking" emerged in which U.S. money center banks (mostly in New York and Chicago) and the Bank of England held surplus funds of the country banks. Their "reserves" thereby shifted from being mainly specie to deposits in the money centers or notes of the Bank of England.

The presence of fractional reserves (legislated in the United States and subject to prudential good practice in the United Kingdom) permitted overall credit expansion. In the United States, the Federal Reserve System was originally set up with a dozen virtually independent regional Feds in charge of rediscounting operations with local banks on bills originating in each one's domain. Federal bonds issued to finance World War I soon pushed the system as a whole toward open market operations—an institutional change unanticipated by the original architects. A new, truly "central" bank run by the Board of Governors emerged in Washington, D.C., in the 1930s.

The implications of all these developments for the regulation of the money supply began to be recognized at the same time. The left Keynesian Lauchlin Currie (1934) and others deciphered the standard textbook causal chain

$$\Delta H \Rightarrow \Delta L \Rightarrow \Delta M = \zeta \Delta H, \tag{2}$$

where ζ is a deposit multiplier of the sort introduced in previous chapters. "Monetary policy" became possible insofar as the monetary authorities (the central bank) could influence the value of ζ or ΔH. In this system, a sharp exogenous reduction in reserves, say from a run against the local currency, forces loans and deposits to contract. As discussed in Chapter 3, central bankers eventually invented "lender of last resort," or LLR, interventions (necessity is the mother of . . .) to create compensating reserves and stave off systemic collapse.

These changes, however, took time. Around the turn of the nineteenth century, well before Currie arrived at his insights into the control of the money supply, the Banking School got the upper hand in the long debate with its Currency School antagonists. If banks prudently lend short term (that is, they accept only "real bills"), then it is not so much their reserves as the collateral on their loans that guarantees the security of their deposits. From this stance, it is a short step to consider a pure credit banking system like the one built into the Wicksellian inflation model in Chapter 3. If ΔL^d is the increase in loan demand, we have

$$\Delta L^d = \Delta L \Rightarrow \Delta M \Rightarrow \Delta H, \tag{3}$$

or "loans create money." In conformity with the local rules of the game, the "required" increase in reserves is determined by institutional arrangements within the banking system. Loan demand itself could be regulated by changes in the interest rate, again partially subject to control by the authorities.

As detailed for the United States in the following section, a more accurate story for the most recent turn of the century involves "liability management," whereby banks choose a level of new loan supply ΔL^s and then find reserves to cover:

$$\Delta L^s = \Delta L \Rightarrow \Delta M \Rightarrow \Delta H. \tag{4}$$

In the words of a former senior vice president of the New York Federal Reserve, "in the real world banks extend credit, creating deposits in the process, and look for reserves later" (Holmes 1969). The monetary authorities can abet this search by creating unborrowed reserves through open market operations. Alternatively, they can impose a "frown cost" on commercial banks while letting them obtain borrowed reserves at the discount window. Liability management (or the "doctrine of shiftability" in older literature) refers to any means by which commercial banks shift their reserve constraints onto the nonbank public. To build up ΔH, they may search more aggressively for loans from discounts or from the federal funds, Eurocurrency, and certificate of deposit (CD) markets.

Financial innovations underlay all the changes summarized in (1) through (4). One essential difference between the real and the financial sides of the economy is that "new technologies" in the latter are easily

copied—there are no long-lasting Schumpeterian returns to financial entrepreneurship. This is one key reason why a changing structure of financial claims (as just outlined) is endogenous to capitalism. This doctrine
found its prophet in Hyman Minsky (1975, 1986). Our next task is to
delve more deeply into what Minsky and his followers have to say about
the modern causal structures (3) and (4). In Pollin's (1991) usage, we
will also have to investigate the differences between Minsky's "structuralist" approach to monetary/financial innovation and Kaldor's (1982)
and Moore's (1988) "accommodationist" (or more strictly Banking
School) narrative in which the central bank usually acts to ratify the ongoing pace of credit creation at some fixed interest rate.[3]

It is also fair to add that in practice as opposed to in theory, the working monetary model of the macro economy espoused by central banks is
for practical purposes post-Keynesian, at least according to Fair's (2000,
pp. 2–3) description. The current standard model is based on three basic
equations, which are: (1) an "interest rate rule: The Fed adjusts the real
interest rate in response to inflation and the output gap (deviation of output from potential). The real interest rate depends positively on inflation
and the output gap. Put another way, the nominal interest rate depends
positively on inflation and the output gap, where the coefficient on inflation is greater than one" (harking back to Wicksell's endogenous money
model as described in Chapter 3); (2) a "price equation: Inflation depends on the output gap, cost shocks, and expected future inflation";
and (3) an "aggregate demand equation: aggregate demand (real) depends on the real interest rate, expected future demand, and exogenous
shocks. The real interest rate effect is negative. In empirical work the
lagged interest rate is often included as an explanatory variable in the interest rate rule. This picks up possible interest rate smoothing behavior
of the Fed."

2. Endogenous Finance

Two questions naturally arise: What have been the implications of twentieth-century financial innovations for the inflation and interest rate performance of the economy? How does endogenous finance enter the business cycle?

If we broadly follow Minsky (1986), Dymski and Pollin (1992), and
a more analytical treatment by Schroeder (2002), the key idea is that
economic actors are constrained by their inherited financial positions,
which Minsky describes as "hedge," "speculative," or "Ponzi." A unit is
practicing hedge finance when a "reasonable" lower bound on its anticipated cash flows from operations exceeds anticipated commitments at

all future times ("anticipated" is used in a Keynesian sense—expected values over well-defined probability distributions on all future events are alien to Minsky's world).

Speculative units anticipate that cash commitments will exceed cash flows at some points in the future, for example, when principal repayments on short-term debt fall due. They can run into trouble if the money market does not function normally at critical times, such as when debt has to be refinanced. If speculative positions are common, then upward pressure on interest rates can drive the whole system toward "financial fragility."

Fragility is much more likely if many firms are engaging in Ponzi finance, with anticipated cash inflows falling short of obligations at most or all future times. Like their namesake, Ponzi units have to borrow to pay interest as well as principal on their debts. Were they wise, they would carry big stocks of liquid assets, but they often do not. An enterprise with highly seasonal sales, for example, may hope that some year's bonanza will carry it through the next few. The Enron Corporation, to note the most notorious example of 2001, apparently "marked to market" anticipated energy-trading revenues far in the future, thereby providing nonexistent collateral for its Ponzi mountain of debt.

With these descriptions at the back of the mind, we can assess the evolution of the American financial system, beginning before the Great Depression. As already observed in Chapter 3, business cycles at that time involved significant price decreases (and, implicitly, rising real interest rates) in the downswing.[4] During a recession, debtors found their obligations mounting in real terms and were pushed toward speculative and Ponzi positions. Waves of debt repudiation followed. An increasing proportion of capital assets was controlled by individuals, directly or through corporate equity. Along with a collapse in effective demand on the part of the debtors, the entire financial system could be drastically simplified, requiring years to rebuild. Irving Fisher's (1933) "debt-deflation" chronicle is the classic description of such a process.

In the United States, debt-deflation became less important after the 1930s, as the Federal Reserve and Treasury began to engage in counter-cyclical policy aimed at moderating real/financial cycles of the sort discussed in Chapter 9. At the same time, "automatic stabilizers" such as unemployment insurance were created as part of the welfare state. Interacting with the responses of the financial system itself, these bits of economic engineering had unexpected consequences. One was that an inflationary bias was added to the system by the presence of demand supports. In terms of Figure 7.2, the level of economic activity was pushed toward the right, leading to increased inflation in either the upper (due to forced saving, Minsky's interpretation) or lower (profit squeeze) diagram.

A second unanticipated outcome was a move of corporations toward speculative and Ponzi positions, leading them to seek higher short-term profitability to try to keep their financial houses "in order." Absent fears of price and sales downswings, high risk/high return projects became more attractive. Such a shift was notable in the increased "short-termism" of investment activities and the push toward merger and acquisition (M&A) activity in the 1970s and 1980s when corporate q was less than one.

Third, the intermediaries financing such initiatives gained more explicit protection against risky actions by their borrowers through LLR interventions on the part of the Fed and (especially) savings and loan regulators. The resulting "moral hazard" induced both banks and firms to seek more risky placements of resources.[5] Financial institutions, in particular, pursued innovation.

Just after World War II, they started out with a big load of government bonds in their portfolios and strict upper bounds on interest payments on deposits (via the Fed's "regulation Q"). By the 1970s, however, liability management rapidly emerged, for at least two important reasons. One stemmed from the credit crunch of 1965–66. In the years immediately before, money center banks had started offering negotiable certificates of deposit to their corporate clients. They thus preserved their deposit base, but only as long as the regulation Q limit on CD interest rates was above the ninety-day T-bill rate. When the gap vanished, the commercial banks rapidly lost funding and had to start calling loans to the securities industry—some observers see the episode as a close encounter with a 1929-level crash.

The second reason is that at roughly the same time, unregulated Eurodollar and then Eurocurrency markets started to thrive. A Eurodollar deposit is just a deposit denominated in dollars in a bank outside the political jurisdiction of the United States. British and American authorities winked and nodded at such placements at the outset, because they seemed like a sensible way for commercial banks to make use of their excess reserves. A major contributing factor to growth in Eurocurrency markets was the American "interest equalization tax" of 1964–1973, enacted in an attempt to defend the capital controls in force at the time. Basically, the tax raised costs for banks to lend offshore from their domestic branches. The resulting higher external rates led dollar depositors such as foreign corporations to switch their funds from onshore U.S. institutions to Eurobanks.

Eurocurrency transactions rapidly taught market players that they could shift their deposits, loans, and investments from one currency to another in response to actual or anticipated changes in interest and exchange rates. These moves were early warnings of a pervasive regulatory problem that dominates the world economy today: any nation's financial controls appear to be made for the sole purpose of being evaded. Even the ability of central banks to regulate the supply of money and credit was undermined by commercial banks' borrowing and lending offshore. All national authorities were forced to scrap long-established interest rate ceilings such as regulation Q, lending limits, portfolio restrictions, reserve and liquidity requirements, and other regulatory paraphernalia.

In the United States, innovations proliferated rapidly in response to these challenges. Money market funds appeared, investing in government and high-grade commercial paper and using the proceeds to pay rates of return on "near-money" accounts which were high enough to draw deposits from banks. There was an upward shift in the whole structure of interest rates. Another outcome was the saving and loan (S&L) crisis. With higher-deposit interest rates, the fixed-rate mortgage-based asset portfolio of the S&L system became unviable. With LLR support in the background, these institutions turned to heavy investment in speculative assets like junk bonds and shopping malls, leading to an inevitable collapse.[6]

A further step was the formation of investment funds, in the first instance for "asset securitization," expanding upon the activities of Freddie Mac and Fannie Mae. Banks sold packages of assets to trusts which in turn issued shares, with dividend payments passing through the interest receipts to their equity-holders. In many cases the primary assets were high risk (credit cards, car loans), but packaging them permitted reduction of perceived risk through diversification. In effect, a new investment vehicle was created, paying high returns.

Finally, novel high risk/high return packages were put together for investors who inhabit that segment of the market. Innovations took the form of "derivatives" or complex contingent contracts based on underlying securities. "Hedge funds" appeared to trade in derivatives, typically financing their operations with heavy borrowing on the margin (with liabilities reaching ten times the value of their equity and more). Again, the outcome was more upward pressure on interest rates and increased financial instability worldwide (Eatwell and Taylor 2000).

As observed in Chapter 1 (note 12), these developments were associated with a substantial increase in the ratio of borrowed funds to gross capital formation for the U.S. nonfinancial corporate sector. As it turned out, however, most of the extra resources were used to finance M&A activity (Pollin 1997). For the reasons just discussed, increased credit availability was not associated with any downward trend in real borrowing costs (insofar as such movements can be isolated from the actions of the central bank).

All this history is consistent with a Minskyan or structuralist interpretation of the financial system. Perhaps it fits less well with the more hydraulic vision of the "accommodationist" Kaldor-Moore school, which postulates short-term endogeneity of the money supply via central bank or financial market ratification of commercial banks' lending behavior.

3. Endogenous Money via Bank Lending

This section is devoted to a simple model of an endogenous money supply, along accommodationist lines. It basically reworks the analysis in Palley (1996, chap. 7) in focusing on how money can be created in response to changes in the volume of loans in a fully specified Tobin-style financial market model.

The intellectual background is Nicholas Kaldor's crusade against Chicago monetarist analysis of the sort described in Chapter 6. Beginning in the late 1950s with testimony to the (British) Radcliffe Committee on the Working of the Monetary System and continuing until he died in 1986, Kaldor argued that under modern capitalism the central bank has little choice but to accommodate the lending activity of commercial banks, presumably at some stable rate of interest. A predetermined or exogenous money supply is the central dogma of monetarism; Kaldor hoped that if it were shown to be unrealistic, the rest of that particular form of anti-Keynesianism would disappear. Maybe so, but it is also fair to add that Kaldor underestimated the desire of economists to adhere to Say's Law. If they can't do it with exogenous money and the real balance effect, there is always some other channel.[7]

Moreover, just saying that the central bank has the option to peg the interest rate doesn't alter the supply-driven causality of the monetarist model. In a standard money supply framework like the one sketched in equation (2) and fully developed in Chapter 4, the central bank can always fix the nominal rate i by adjusting its holdings of T-bills T_c (thus changing the level of nonborrowed reserves of commercial banks) or by altering reserve requirements to shift the money multiplier ζ (essentially the inverse of the required reserve/deposit ratio). Despite the pegged rate, what the central bank chooses to do with high-powered money drives the system. Kaldor and successors such as Moore and other American post-Keynesians want the driving force for money creation to be

Table 8.1 Balance sheets for an "accommodationist" money supply.

Households		Firms		Commercial Banks	
M_b	Ω_h	qPK	L_f	H	M_b
M_a	L_h	M_f	Ω_f	L	M_f
T_h					D
Central Bank		**Money Market**		**Government**	
T_c	H	T_a	M_a		T
D					

lending activity by commercial banks. The balance sheets in Table 8.1 set up a framework in which bank credit creation has some traction. To keep the analysis simple, a stable money multiplier is anachronistically assumed to exist.

Table 8.1 differs from the more conventional Table 4.2 in four important ways. First, equity with a value P_vV is omitted from the accounting, because it is tangential to the present discussion. Absent asset prices such as P_v that can jump discontinuously, net worth Ω_h of business firms can only change gradually over time as retained earnings accumulate. It is constant in the short run.[8] Net worth Ω_h of households is similarly determined by the accumulation of savings flows.

The second difference is that the business sector holds deposits M_f such as CDs with commercial banks. The subscript reflects a "finance demand" for balances introduced by Keynes (1937b) in one of his many follow-up papers to *The General Theory*. He wrote that such balances "may be regarded as lying half-way so to speak, between active and inactive balances" (with active balances being used to satisfy transactions demands and inactive balances, liquidity and/or speculative demands for money). The interpretation here is that M_f is held by productive firms as a revolving fund to support capital formation. When firms borrow more from banks to support higher investment, their loans L_f and deposits M_f go up together, because Ω_f cannot vary in the short run. The importance of such transactions can be judged from Table 1.5. At the end of 1999, U.S. nonfinancial business had about $1.2 trillion in loans outstanding in the form of bank credit and held $900 billion of broad money, with both numbers on the order of 10 percent of GDP. Households are also assumed to take loans L_h (think of credit cards) from the banks.

Third, loans "create money" along the lines of the causal chain in (4). Commercial banks have numerous options to obtain the corresponding required reserves. For simplicity, only one is built into Table 8.1. The banks can draw advances D from the central bank discount window at a specified interest rate i_d. Such borrowed reserves along with non-borrowed reserves T_c sum to H, the supply of high-powered (or base) money. Discount borrowing allows the banking system to expand its loan supply while still respecting the reserve requirements that underlie the credit multiplier relationship $M_b + M_f = \zeta H = \zeta(T_c + D)$ with $\zeta > 1$.[9] Causality now runs from loans L to the money supply $M_b + M_f = [\zeta/(\zeta - 1)]L$, and back to base money $H = L/(\zeta - 1)$ and discount borrowing $D = H - T_c$.

Fourth, "money market funds" are assumed to exist, holding T-bills T_a as an asset and offering near-money deposits M_a to households as the corresponding liability. How this new sort of financial intermediary influences the structure of interest rates is discussed in the following section. For the moment, we set $T_a = M_a = 0$.

Before we jump into the algebra, one last observation is that asset and liability choices are assumed to depend only on the directly relevant interest rates. In principle, all portfolio decisions should depend on all the rates in the model (five in total), but in practice carrying a host of partial derivatives explicitly in the algebra just creates notational chaos in exchange for negligible economic insight. So in what follows, demand and supply functions for financial instruments are kept as simple as possible.

Two questions immediately arise: How does L get determined? Why do households agree to hold the quantity of money M_b that banks choose to provide them?

To answer the first query, let i_l be the interest rate on bank loans. It is natural to assume that firms have a loan demand function such as

$$L_f = \lambda_f^d(i_l, g^i)qPK, \tag{5f}$$

in which g^i stands for investment demand (scaled to the capital stock, as usual). The conventions are that $\partial\lambda_f^d/\partial g^i > 0$ and $\partial\lambda_f^d/\partial i_l < 0$, that is, demand for loans (and finance balances M_f) rises with the level of investment and falls when the loan interest rate rises. Total borrowing is scaled to the asset value of the capital stock.

Households' borrowing is naturally scaled to their net worth,

$$L_b = \lambda_b^d(i_l)\Omega_b, \tag{5h}$$

with a derivative $d\lambda_b^d/di_l < 0$.

If the level of bank credit is proportional to their base of unborrowed reserves, then the loan supply function can be written as

$$L^s = \lambda^s(i_l, i_d)T_c, \tag{6}$$

with the first and second partial derivatives of λ^s being positive and negative respectively.

Equilibrium in the loan market is determined by the condition that excess demand equals zero,

$$L_b + L_f - L^s = 0, \tag{7}$$

as illustrated in the upper quadrant of Figure 8.1. By the assumed signs of the partial derivatives of λ_b^d, λ_f^d, and λ^s with respect to i_l, this equilibrium will be stable when the loan rate adjusts to clear the market.

Households hold T-bills $T_h = T - T_c$ in an amount set by central bank open market policy. Their holdings of money M_b and firms' finance balances M_f enter into an excess demand function for money of the form

$$M_b + M_f - [\zeta/(\zeta - 1)]L = 0, \tag{8m}$$

while bond market equilibrium can be expressed as an excess supply relationship,

$$T - T_c - T_h = 0. \tag{8t}$$

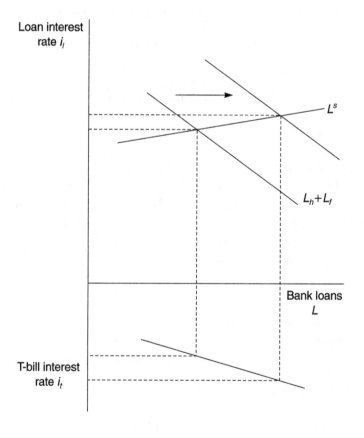

Figure 8.1
Determination of volume of bank lending and interest rates in an accommodationist model of the banking system.

Households can be assumed to allocate their total financial resources—net worth plus loans—to money and bonds according to relationships such as

$$M_b - \mu(i_b, i_t)(\Omega_b + L_b) = 0 \tag{9}$$

and

$$T_b - \tau(i_b, i_t)(\Omega_b + L_b) = 0, \tag{10}$$

where i_b and i_t are interest rates on bank deposits and T-bills respectively. Presumably, $\partial\mu/\partial i_b > 0$ and $\partial\mu/\partial i_t < 0$ with the partials of τ having the opposite signs. Because households satisfy their balance sheet restriction $M_b + T_b = \Omega_b + L_b$, the demand shares must sum to unity, $\mu + \tau = 1$. That is, only one of equations (9) and (10) is independent.

The model boils down to two equations. Plugging (5f), (5h), and (6) into (7) gives a loan supply-demand balance

$$\lambda_b^d(i_l)\Omega_b + \lambda_f^d(i_l, g^i)qPK - \lambda^s(i_l, i_d)T_c = 0, \tag{11}$$

which solves for i_l as a function of g^i. As already noted, the relevant schedules are in the upper quadrant of Figure 8.1. If the loan supply function λ^s is elastic with respect to i_l (as shown), then higher investment demand will lead to only a small increase in the loan rate.

Substituting through the portfolio choice relationships and the balance sheets in Table 8.1 reveals that just one of the two asset equilibrium conditions (8m) and (8t) is independent—if one of them clears then so will the other. It is simpler to work with the one for T-bills, assumed to equilibrate via changes in i_t with i_b held constant. The relevant equation is

$$T - T_c - \tau(i_b, i_t)[1 + \lambda_b^d(i_l)]\Omega_b = 0. \tag{12}$$

How (12) works is illustrated in the lower quadrant of Figure 8.1. Higher investment g^i bids up credit supply and the loan rate i_l. At the same time, the money supply increases through the credit multiplier. More expensive loans mean that households cut back their borrowing and reduce demand for bonds from (10). To ensure that they choose to hold the quantity of bonds supplied to them, $T_b = T - T_c$, i_t must rise, with i_l adjusting to clear the credit market.[10] Unsurprisingly, an increase in T_c via an open market bond purchase forces i_t to decline.

If, as shown, most of this financial adjustment takes place via quantity changes, then we have a fair representation of the Banking School/Robertson/Radcliffe Report/Kaldor vision of the monetary system in a model with a complete set of financial accounts. The keys to the results are the elastic loan supply from the banking system and the willingness of the central bank to provide borrowed reserves without stint.

4. Money Market Funds and the Level of Interest Rates

The next step is to bring in money market accounts, as a financial innovation of a sort which along Schumpeterian lines cannot happen if "full employment" of financial claims is imposed at all times. In the small, formalized world of Table 8.1, money market funds are the new idea. They are assumed to hold T-bills as assets, consolidating their running yield to offer liquid near-money deposits at a rate i_a close to that on government securities, say,

$$i_a = i_t(1 - \delta), \tag{13}$$

with a "mark-down" rate δ not far from zero. With their good liquidity characteristics, the new deposits M_a can be assumed to be close substitutes with ordinary bank deposits M_b. Hence, if banks are to stay in business they will have to offer deposit interest at a rate i_b not far from i_a. Regulation Q has to go by the boards.

Moreover, banks will have negative cash flow unless it is true that

$$i_l L > i_d D + i_b M_b, \tag{14}$$

so that the loan interest rate i_l will be subject to upward pressure as i_b rises.[11] As a major component of bank costs, the deposit rate i_b will enter as an argument in the loan supply function λ^s in (6), with a negative partial derivative.

To work through detailed implications of the innovation, first note that households now hold three assets—M_a, M_b, and T_b—in their portfolios. The interest rate i_a on money market deposits is linked to the T-bill rate by (13). So there are two freely varying interest rates, i_b and i_t, which adjust to clear the markets for deposits and T-bills.

After substituting from the firms' and households' balance sheets, the money market balance (8m) can be stated as

$$\Omega_f + [\lambda_f^d(i_l, g^i) - 1]qPK + \mu(i_b, i_t)[1 + \lambda_h^d(i_l)]\Omega_h$$
$$- [\zeta/(\zeta - 1)]\lambda^s(i_l, i_b)T_c = 0. \tag{15}$$

Using the household balance sheet, the bond market equilibrium condition is

$$T - T_c - [1 - \mu(i_b, i_t)][1 + \lambda_h^d(i_l)]\Omega_h = 0. \tag{16}$$

With positive own-responses and negative cross-responses of household asset demands to rates of return, equations (15) and (16) underlie Figure 8.2, in which a higher deposit rate bids up the T-bill rate in the market for government paper, and a higher i_t bids up i_b in the market for deposits. (The dependence of the loan supply function λ^s on i_b in (15) makes sure that the slopes of the two curves in the (i_t, i_b) plane differ.) Such mutually positive feedbacks are characteristic of financial rates of return. They will not destabilize the system so long as the effect of i_t on i_b is relatively weak and vice versa (the situation shown in the diagram).

From (15), if loan supply λ^s shifts upward, then μ or the portfolio share of deposits has to rise. The obvious mechanism is a higher deposit rate, so the "Deposit equilibrium" schedule in Figure 8.2 moves upward. Bank credit creation is thereby associated with increases in both i_b and i_t.

The system-wide analysis of Figure 8.1 has to be extended when the money market enters the scene. In Figure 8.3, the loan rate i_l and stock of bank credit L are determined in the northeast quadrant as before, except that the intercept of the loan supply function L^s is assumed to shift upward with an increase in the deposit rate i_b, as discussed above. This linkage creates a negative feedback from an increase in loan demand $L^d = L_h + L_f$ onto supply L^s. The impact effect of higher demand is to increase the deposit rate i_b (southeast quadrant) via the mechanisms outlined in Figure 8.2. But a higher i_b in turn shifts up the loan supply sched-

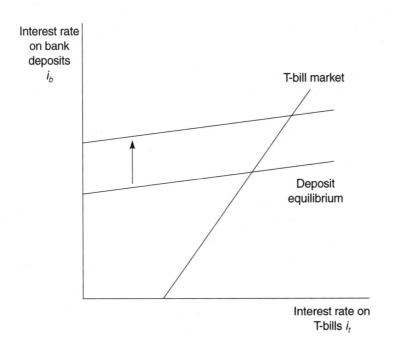

Figure 8.2
Effects of an increase in bank loans on the deposits and T-bill interest rates.

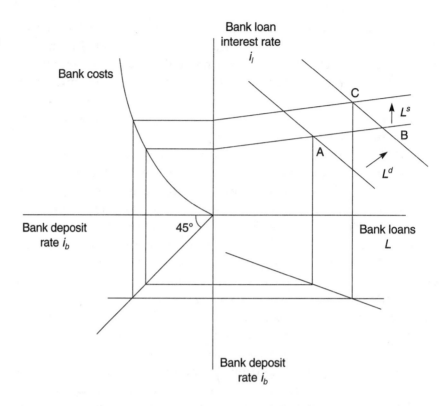

Figure 8.3
Effects of an increase in loan demand on financial equilibrium.

ule via the "Bank costs" curve in the northwest quadrant, choking off part of the initial credit increase and bidding up i_l. Instead of shifting from point A to B, the economy ends up in an inferior situation at C.

One implication is that the monetary system will be less accommodative than in the post-Keynesian Figure 8.1. The invention of money market funds "closes the loop" in the left-hand quadrants of Figure 8.3, and helps shift the whole interest rate structure upward. Asset owners no doubt benefit, and in a Walrasian world there would be an overall gain in welfare from filling in a "missing market" for near-money deposits. But the real world is Keynesian, not Walrasian. It is not clear that there are any gains in terms of progressive income redistribution and output growth from creating a financial instrument that as its major impact bids up the cost of finance for capital accumulation. As argued historically in Eatwell and Taylor (2000), more arcane financial entities emerging in the wake of money market funds only strengthened these unhappy results.

5. Business Debt and Growth in a Post-Keynesian World

The foregoing is not the end of the story, of course. Endogenous money in the short run should lead along the lines of Chapter 7 into a theory of long-term growth. The literature in the area is scarce, but Lavoie and Godley (2000) set up a parsimonious model to address interesting questions. A SAM and balance sheets appear in Tables 8.2 and 8.3.[12]

Table 8.3's menu of financial claims is substantially reduced from the one in Table 8.1. There is a pure credit Wicksellian banking system with money held by households (M) as its liability and loans to firms (L) as its asset. Wicksellian finance is a pretty good approximation of the freely lending and happily discounting commercial and central banks discussed above. The predetermined real interest rate on both money and loans is j. Firms have zero net worth, and the asset value of their capital stock, qPK, is exhausted by their outstanding loans and the value of their equity P_vV. Capital is the only primary asset and households are the only actors with net worth Ω, so $\Omega = qPK$. As will be seen, the natural state variable for dynamic analysis is the debt/capital ratio $\lambda = L/PK$.

As usual the flow variables in Table 8.2 are also scaled to PK. To study processes of accumulation, a good place to begin is with the flows of funds rows (E)–(G). Firms save a proportion s_f of their income net of interest payments $r - j\lambda$ (and transfer the rest to households as dividends $\delta = (1 - s_f)(r - j\lambda)$ in cell B3). Their other sources of funds are new borrowing $\lambda\hat{L}$ and issuance of equity. A working hypothesis is that they finance a share χ of their capital formation with new shares, so that $P_v\dot{V}/PK = \chi g$.[13] With $\sigma_f = s_f(r - j\lambda)$, row (F) in the SAM can be restated as

$$s_f(r - j\lambda) + \lambda\hat{L} - (1 - \chi)g = 0. \tag{17}$$

The post-Keynesian twist in this equation is the term for the growth of bank credit, $\lambda\hat{L}$. The profit rate r and growth rate g are determined on the real side of the model, so the supply of bank loans has to be endogenous to allow firms to carry through their investment plans.

Household consumption is assumed to depend on income and wealth,

$$\gamma_h = (1 - s_h)\xi_h + \phi q,$$

using the fact that $\Omega = qPK$. After substitutions from the row and column balances in the SAM and the flow of funds for the banking system, the household flow of funds row (E) can be restated as

$$\{s_h[(u - r) + (1 - s_f)r + s_f j\lambda] - \phi q\} - \chi g - \lambda\hat{M} = 0, \tag{18}$$

with the terms in brackets summing to σ_h. Because $L = M$ and $\hat{L} = \hat{M}$ from the banking system's balance sheet, accounting consistency ensures that households obligingly pick up the deposits that bank lending creates.

Table 8.2　A SAM for a post-Keynesian growth model (all variables scaled by the value of capital stock).

	Current expenditures					Changes in claims			
	Output costs (1)	Households (2)	Firms (3)	Banks (4)	Investment (5)	Bank assets (6)	Bank liabs. (7)	Firms' equity (8)	Totals (9)
(A) Output uses		γ_h			g				u
Incomes									
(B) Households	$(1-\pi)u$		δ	$j\lambda$					ξ_h
(C) Firms	πu								ξ_f
(D) Banks			$j\lambda$						ξ_b
Flows of funds									
(E) Household		σ_h					$-\lambda\hat{M}$	$-P_v\dot{V}/PK$	0
(F) Firms			σ_f		$-g$	$\lambda\hat{L}$		$P_v\dot{V}/PK$	0
(G) Banks						$-\lambda\hat{L}$	$\lambda\hat{M}$	0	0
(H) Totals	u	ξ_h	ξ_f	ξ_b	0	0	0	0	

Definitions

$\lambda = L/PK = M/PK$

$\delta = (1-s_f)(r-j\lambda)$

Table 8.3 Balance sheets for a post-Keynesian growth model.

Households		Firms		Banks	
M	Ω	qPK	L	L	M
P_vV			P_vV		

The growth rate of the capital stock permitted by the available saving, g^s, is the sum of (17) and (18),

$$g^s = [s_f(1 - s_h)\pi + s_h]u - s_f(1 - s_h)j\lambda - \phi q. \tag{19}$$

Post-Keynesian investment functions of the sort estimated by Fazzari and Mott (1986–87) and Ndikumana (1999) emphasize cash-flow considerations. If the interest burden $j\lambda$ increases, firms are likely to cut back on capital formation g^i. For symmetry with the saving function (19) it is convenient to make g^i depend on q (as opposed to the profit rate r and interest rate j separately), and we also carry a term in capacity utilization:

$$g^i = g_0 + \beta u + \eta q - \psi j\lambda. \tag{20}$$

The short-term macro equilibrium condition is $g^i - g^s = 0$, or

$$\begin{aligned} g_0 + (\eta + \phi)q + [s_f(1 - s_h) - \psi]j\lambda \\ - [s_f(1 - s_h)\pi + s_h - \beta]u = 0. \end{aligned} \tag{21}$$

The usual stability condition is a positive value for the term in brackets multiplying u in (21), $s_f(1 - s_h)\pi + s_h - \beta > 0$. Assuming that it is satisfied, note the ambiguous effect of $j\lambda$ on u. A bigger debt burden reduces investment demand through the coefficient $-\psi$ but also cuts into firms' saving. Filtered through profits distributed to households, lower retained earnings create a net leakage reduction of $s_f(1 - s_h)j\lambda$. If this term exceeds ψ, effective demand can be said to be "debt-led." Otherwise, it is "debt-burdened." The remaining term in (21) involves q. Through both investment and saving effects, a higher q increases the level of economic activity. How q itself gets determined is taken up below.

These distinctions become of interest in discussing the evolution of the debt ratio λ. From the business sector's flow of funds (17), its differential equation can be written as

$$\dot{\lambda} = (s_f j - g)\lambda + (1 - \psi)g - s_f\pi u. \tag{22}$$

Because firms typically don't save 100 percent of their net profits $\pi u - j\lambda$, the growth rate versus interest rate criterion for the stability of λ discussed in Chapter 6 is somewhat relaxed in (22). With $s_f < 1$, j can exceed g but the (partial) stability condition $s_f j - g < 0$ can still be satisfied. There are also effects of λ on u and g to be considered. From the discussion above and the reduced form direct dependence of g on u, they can take either sign. To keep discussion of possible outcomes of the model within limits, we assume overall stability, $d\dot{\lambda}/d\lambda < 0$.

By analogy to the stability analysis for ω in the (u, ω) plane presented in Chapter 7, it is tempting to apply the same treatment to λ in the (u, λ) plane. Lavoie and Godley (2000) use the terminology "normal" for the case in which $d\dot{\lambda}/du < 0$ via the coefficient $-s_f\pi$ in (22). An increase in profits $r = \pi u$ reduces the need of firms to borrow. The steady-state locus along which $\dot{\lambda} = 0$ thereby has a *negative* slope. An alternative, "Minskyan" case arises through the terms in g in (22). If $1 - \lambda - \psi > 0$ (as is likely), then a strong effect of u on g through the investment function could make $d\dot{\lambda}/du > 0$. The $\dot{\lambda} = 0$ locus would have a positive slope, with debt varying pro-cyclically as many of Minsky's writings seem to imply.

The four stable configurations of the "Effective demand" and "Stable debt" (or $\dot{\lambda} = 0$) schedules are shown in Figure 8.4.[14] The upper two diagrams depict the Lavoie-Godley normal case, and the lower two are Minskyan. Effective demand is debt-led in the northwest and southeast, and debt-burdened in the southwest and northeast. An immediate question is whether an expansionary shock (say, a reduction in the household saving rate) has effects that persist in the long run. The answer is that "it

Figure 8.4
Long-run adjustment in a post-Keynesian (Lavoie-Godley) growth model. Normal and Minskyan diagrams (upper and lower); effective demand is debt-led in NW and SE; debt-burdened in SW and NE.

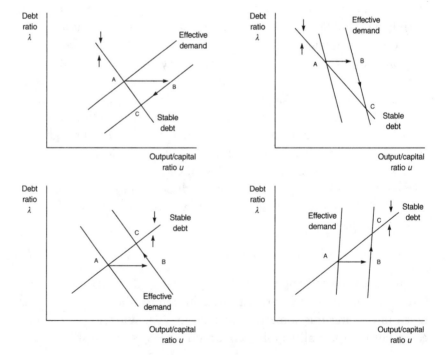

depends." For example, if the steady-state debt ratio rises with u (the Minsky case) and effective demand is debt-led, then as in the southeast diagram, debt will grow faster than the capital stock after the initial shock, further increasing capacity utilization (and almost certainly the growth rate) as the economy moves from point A through B to C. A similar scenario unfolds in the northeast if the steady-state debt ratio falls with u and demand is debt-burdened.

The two diagrams to the left show more conventional cases (like the Chapter 7 scenarios involving a profit squeeze in a profit-led economy) in which an initial positive demand shock generates responses tending to push u back down. The model behaves in Keynesian fashion in the short run, but is more classically inclined in the steady state (Duménil and Lévy 1999).

Turning to the financial side of the model, households' demands for the two assets can be written as

$$\mu qPK - M = 0 \tag{23}$$

and

$$vqPK - P_vV = 0. \tag{24}$$

Only one equation is independent, since $\mu + v = 1$ to make sure that the household balance sheet really balances. The adjusting variable is the equity price P_v, since $M (= L)$ and V are given by history and the real interest rate is fixed. One can solve for P_v and q as

$$P_v = (v/\mu)(L/V) \tag{25}$$

and

$$q = \lambda/\mu. \tag{26}$$

Suppose that liquidity preference declines, so that μ falls and v rises. Then P_v and q necessarily go up. There is a positive demand shock in (21) from the higher valuation ratio, and u and λ set forth on one of the trajectories in Figure 8.4. This demand expansion is consistent with Keynes's hints throughout *The General Theory* that high savers and bear speculators with high liquidity preference (with members of both groups coming from the same social class?) are the chief culprits behind lagging effective demand.

In the present setup, the positive effect of falling liquidity preference on asset prices and q follows directly from the rudimentary financial specification. However, similar results can be derived in the more complete market structure used in the previous sections, if it is extended to include equity. Instead of an exogenously fixed interest rate, the key assumptions would be that commercial banks have elastic loan supply functions and that the central bank stands ready to back up their lending decisions by creating reserves. These hypotheses may be appropriate for most advanced capital economies most of the time. But there *are* periods—say in the United States after the interest rate hikes in 1979—when they clearly do not apply.

Finally, it would not be terribly difficult to extend the model to take into account households' borrowing collateralized by their equity holdings. A reduction in the saving rate s_h to make room for loans as a household source of funds in (18) would give a demand kick, and also push the model toward a debt-led configuration. If the southeast diagram in Figure 8.4 applies, a substantial boom could result—the American case in the 1990s? Of course a subsequent downswing accompanied by rising saving rates and the threat of debt-deflation could be severe. A cyclical extension of the present model is set out in Chapter 9 to analyze some of these issues.

6. New Keynesian Approaches to Financial Markets

New Keynesians have also taken an interest in financial fragility, in part because it provides a means to amplify productivity shocks into big economic fluctuations in extensions of the real business cycle models discussed in Chapter 6. The same mechanisms can apply in the structuralist cycle models discussed in Chapter 9. The new Keynesian leitmotif is that higher net worth of enterprises is associated with more abundant credit, lower risk of bankruptcy, and higher investment and growth. Since net worth increases in a cyclical upswing, a positive financial feedback or accelerator mechanism is built into the system, analogous to debt-led growth in the southeast corner of Figure 8.4.

The popular models put great effort into providing formalized MIRA micro foundations for their results, and it would take us too far afield to crank up the machinery here. So a verbal sketch of two of the more important research programs is all that follows. In terminology introduced in Chapter 4 and here, they respectively conflate lender's risk and moral hazard, and borrower's risk and adverse selection. The world of these models is far from Modigliani and Miller's because "asymmetric information" held by different participants in financial markets rules their behavior, although the historical origins and sociological underpinnings of the asymmetries are things new Keynesians rarely discuss. And of course the models are all anti-Keynesian in that relevant probability distributions and the capacity of "agents" to calculate around them are automatically assumed to exist.

In one of series of papers, Bernanke and Gertler (1990) consider a case of moral hazard in which lenders and borrowers have the same knowledge about the probability of success of investment projects *before* they are undertaken, but only the borrowers/investors know ex post how they have worked out. This difference in knowledge creates a principal/agent relationship between lenders and borrowers, in which the former can set up some sort of monitoring apparatus to reduce their uncertainties about how well projects have succeeded. There is an "agency cost" associated with monitoring.

Bernanke and Gertler assume that agency costs decrease with firms' net worth. The cost of lender's risk being lower, the supply of credit goes up, providing the positive feedback mentioned above. There are a couple of significant macroeconomic implications. One is that the business cycle is not symmetric. Because net worth varies pro-cyclically, contractions are sharper and shorter than expansions.

Second, there is redistribution of wealth between creditors and debtors over the cycle. Output contraction and (perhaps) price deflation shift net worth from borrowers to lenders, forcing the former to cut back on capital formation. Bernanke and Gertler interpret this result as a formalization of Fisher's (1933) views about debt deflation.

In a specimen from another series of papers, Greenwald and Stiglitz (1993) analyze a case of ex ante asymmetric information in which firms issuing new equities know more than potential buyers about how their investment projects will work out *before* they are undertaken. Firms rely on selling stock to finance their projects, but run the risk of bankruptcy with associated costs if they don't succeed. If they have higher net worth, their bankruptcy costs are lower and their investment demand will be more buoyant. We have much the same macro story as in Bernanke-Gertler, but the micro foundations are different.

Greenwald and Stiglitz present a cyclical story not dissimilar to that of the model of last section or scenarios of the sort presented in Chapter Nine. In an upswing, an initial positive productivity shock leads both profits and real wages to rise. However, the labor market tightens and growth of net worth lags behind growth of the wage bill. Balance sheets become weaker. A profit squeeze and increased bankruptcy risk cause a downturn, during which demand for labor weakens, setting up conditions for a recovery.

To quote Mishkin (1990), "A financial crisis is a disruption to financial markets in which adverse selection and moral hazard problems become much worse, so that financial markets are unable to efficiently channel funds to those who have the most productive investment opportunities. As a result, a financial crisis can drive the economy away from an equilibrium with high output in which financial markets perform well to one in which output declines sharply."

Although new Keynesians perhaps overestimate the verisimilitude of their informationally asymmetric hobbyhorses as sources of cyclical oscillations, Mishkin's summary of historical financial disruptions is not far off the mark.

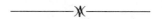

CHAPTER NINE

A Genus of Cycles

Although business cycles are always with us, constructing theories about them has been an off-and-on avocation among economists. Samuelson's (1939) multiplier-accelerator scenario was a landmark of early Keynesianism. But among his intellectual grandchildren, accelerators have disappeared from new Keynesian discourse, despite their apparent empirical superiority to formulations based on Tobin's q. Entrepreneur-driven cycles—whether linked to Schumpeter's (1947) waves of creative destruction and technical advance or to von Hayek's (1931) overinvestment due to banks' holding the interest rate below its natural level—have been supplanted on the Right by the real business cycle computable black boxes discussed in Chapter 6. As also observed in that chapter, some Marxists have seen cycles as the result of "excessive" levels of investment or capital per worker. Others emphasize distributive conflict, which was the basis for Goodwin's (1967) predator-prey model of cyclical growth. Goodwin serves as a natural jumping-off point for extending the structuralist models of Chapters 7 and 8 to deal with cycles.

This chapter is devoted to a half-dozen simple cycle models that attempt to capture the essentials of several ideas about economic fluctuations. The formal specifications all boil down to sets of two differential equations with a similar mathematical form—a genus of cycles. Consider the Jacobian J of the two equations evaluated at a stationary point:

$$J = \begin{bmatrix} j_{11} & j_{12} \\ j_{21} & j_{22} \end{bmatrix}, \tag{1}$$

with $\operatorname{Tr} J = j_{11} + j_{22}$ and $\operatorname{Det} J = j_{11}j_{22} - j_{12}j_{21}$. We will be considering systems in which the first variable has stable own dynamics, $j_{11} < 0$, while the second feeds back positively into itself, $j_{22} > 0$, creating a potential instability. If the system is to avoid a saddlepoint with $\operatorname{Det} J < 0$ and instead generate cycles, it has to be damped by oppositely signed off-diagonal entries, that is, $j_{12}j_{21} < 0$. An increase in the second variable sets off a response in the first that drives the second back down.

If the damping is strong enough, the differential equations will generate a convergent spiral around the stationary point in a two-dimensional phase diagram. Continuing exogenous "shocks" would be required to keep the damped cycle going over time. The spiral may also tend toward a "limit cycle" around a "closed orbit," or else it may diverge. In the following discussion, we will not be greatly concerned with which possible outcome occurs. To find out, one has to resort to relatively sophisticated mathematics which would take too much time to develop here.[1] Rather, the emphasis will be on describing economic mechanisms that can make the potentially destabilizing positive value of j_{22} and damping through j_{21} and j_{12} show up in the first place.

In the models presented in this chapter, instabilities arise in three ways—from distributional conflicts, destabilizing expectations, and a "confidence variable" that feeds back positively into itself. The Goodwin model is first presented, in original and structuralist variants, followed by a model in which the real exchange rate is at the root of distributive conflict. A monetary growth model initially set out by Tobin illustrates destabilizing expectations, and a multiplier-accelerator model, a Minsky-style model of cyclical finance, and a model of potential over-investment all are driven by confidence in one form or another. Two more models are sketched in Chapter 10—a fiscal debt cycle involving expectations-driven exchange rate dynamics in advanced economies, and confidence-based fluctuations in capital inflows that can provoke financial crises in capital-importing developing countries.

1. Goodwin's Model

Richard Goodwin (1967) rather neatly arbitraged mathematical models of species competition worked out in the 1920s (Lotka 1925; Volterra 1931) into economics, to set up a "predator-prey" scenario involving distributive conflict between capitalists and workers. The workers, as it turns out, are the predators with economic activity and employment as the prey. A whole econometric literature on a cyclical profit squeeze followed in Goodwin's wake. Representative papers include Desai (1973), Goldstein (1996), and Gordon (1997). A general finding is that profit squeeze cycles exist for the U.S. economy. They are only slightly damped and therefore are repetitive. Further supporting evidence is provided in sections 2 and 3.

Goodwin assumed full utilization of capital and savings-determined investment. Let $K = \kappa X$, with κ as a "technologically determined" capital/output ratio. The employed labor force is $L = bX$. If N is the total population, then the employment ratio λ is given by $\lambda = L/N = b(K/\kappa)/N$. The growth rate of N is n. The wage share is ψ, and if all profits are saved the growth rate g of the capital stock becomes $g = (1 - \psi)X/K = (1 - \psi)/\kappa$.

Over time, the evolution of the employment ratio is determined by growth in output and population,

$$\dot{\lambda} = \lambda(g - n) = \lambda\{[(1 - \psi)/\kappa] - n\}. \tag{2}$$

Along Phillips curve lines, the wage share is assumed to rise in response to the employment ratio,

$$\dot{\psi} = \psi(-A + B\lambda). \tag{3}$$

At a stationary point where $\dot{\lambda} = \dot{\psi} = 0$, the Jacobian of (2)–(3) takes the rather extreme form

$$J = \begin{bmatrix} 0 & -\lambda/\kappa \\ \beta\psi & 0 \end{bmatrix}.$$

The two variables basically damp fluctuations in one another, with no intrinsic dynamics of their own. Hirsch and Smale (1974, p. 262) show that with zeros along the diagonal of the Jacobian, λ and ψ chase each other endlessly around a closed orbit in the (λ, ψ) plane which encircles the stationary point (λ^*, ψ^*). See Figure 9.1, in which the particular orbit that the variables trace is set by initial conditions. The labor share is the predator since it rises with λ. The employment ratio, in turn, is the prey since a higher value of ψ squeezes profits and cuts back accumulation and growth.

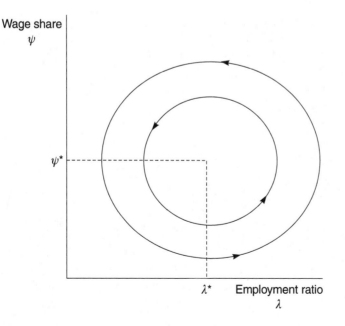

Wage share
ψ

ψ^*

λ^* Employment ratio
λ

Figure 9.1
Closed orbits in the Goodwin model.

2. A Structuralist Goodwin Model

In slightly modified form, the structuralist macro model presented in Chapter 7 generates Goodwin-style cycles.[2] In the discussion to follow, we first concentrate on real wage and productivity dynamics on the side of distribution and overall capacity utilization as an indicator of effective demand. Subsequently we take up behavior of the nominal wage and price levels, and the components of demand.

To model the output cycle, we can treat capacity utilization u as a continuously differentiable function of time. That is, instead of letting $u = X/K$ jump discontinuously as in Figures 7.2, 7.4, 8.4, and so on, we now assume that it varies according to the relationship

$$\hat{u} = \hat{X} - \hat{K}. \tag{4}$$

As will be seen, this "smoother" specification readily generates cycles, and is consistent with the relatively small changes quarter-by-quarter typically observed (for developed countries, at least) in macro time series for aggregate demand and distribution.

Similarly, we have $\psi = \omega/\xi$ as the labor share, where $\omega = w/P$ is the real wage and $\xi = X/L$ is labor productivity. The analog to (4) is

$$\hat{\psi} = \hat{\omega} - \hat{\xi}. \tag{5}$$

As in Chapter 7, we examine dynamics in the (u, ψ) plane. In growth rate form, the model can be restated in four equations:

$$\hat{X} = \alpha_0 + \alpha_u u + \alpha_\psi \psi, \tag{6}$$

$$\hat{K} = \beta_0 + \beta_u u + \beta_\psi \psi, \tag{7}$$

$$\hat{\omega} = \gamma_0 + \gamma_u u + \gamma_\psi \psi, \tag{8}$$

and

$$\hat{\xi} = \delta_0 + \delta_u u + \delta_\psi \psi. \tag{9}$$

If we set $\phi_i = \alpha_i - \beta_i$ and $\theta_i = \gamma_i - \delta_i$, then substituting (6)–(7) into (4) and (8)–(9) into (5) gives reduced-form equations for u and ψ:

$$\dot{u} = u(\phi_0 + \phi_u u + \phi_\psi \psi) \tag{10}$$

and

$$\dot{\psi} = \psi(\theta_0 + \theta_u u + \theta_\psi \psi). \tag{11}$$

What can we say about the signs of the coefficients in (10) and (11)? Beginning with equation (6), evidence presented in section 3 and elsewhere suggests that effective demand in the United States and other advanced countries is profit-led, so that $\alpha_\psi < 0$. There is a general consensus that the basic Keynesian stability condition $\partial \dot{X}/\partial X < 0$ is satisfied, or $\alpha_u < 0$. In (7), capital formation usually responds positively to both the level of economic activity and profitability, so that $\beta_u > 0$ and $\beta_\psi < 0$. It follows immediately that $\phi_u < 0$ so the differential equation (10) is locally stable in u. Via the multiplier, the overall negative demand effect of a higher value of ψ should outweigh its specific effect on investment, $|\alpha_\psi| > |\beta_\psi|$, so that $\phi_\psi < 0$. In both diagrams in Figure 9.2, the "Effective demand" schedule along which $\dot{u} = 0$ has a negative slope $d\psi/du = -\phi_u/\phi_\psi$ in the (u, ψ) plane.

The story about the "Distributive" curve along which $\dot{\psi} = 0$ is tangled. In the United States the real wage rises across cycles. During the course of one cycle, ω appears to respond more strongly than ξ to changes in capacity utilization and the wage share, which itself varies counter to the capacity utilization cycle (see Figures 9.3–9.5 below). The resulting pro-cyclical profit share is more likely to be observed if productivity also moves pro-cyclically. Does this pattern hold?

In the relevant equation (9), δ_u will be positive if higher output induces faster productivity growth. The effect of ψ on ξ has to be interpreted along cyclical lines. During a downswing in u, ψ tends to rise. A positive *lagged* response of ξ to ψ is then consistent with a rise in productivity during and after the cyclical trough—the observed pattern. In summary, U.S. data suggests that both δ_u and δ_ψ will be positive.

In equation (8) applied to the United States, the response coefficients γ_u and γ_ψ usually satisfy the relationships $\gamma_u > \delta_u > 0$ and $\gamma_\psi > \delta_\psi > 0$. A higher wage share appears to enhance labor's bargaining power, as does a higher level of capacity utilization. From the latter, we have $\theta_u = \gamma_u - \delta_u > 0$. One would also expect that $\theta_\psi = \gamma_\psi - \delta_\psi < 0$. For the most part with American data, this expectation is confirmed. However, during the period 1955–1970 the regression results reported below suggest that $\delta_\psi << 0$, with productivity growth responding strongly to increases in the profit share and making $\theta_\psi > 0$ so that $d\dot{\psi}/d\psi > 0$ as well.

This damped instability case is illustrated in the lower diagram of Figure 9.2. For the determinant of the Jacobian to be positive, the Distributive curve has to cross the Effective demand curve from above. As shown, starting from a low point for u along the Effective demand schedule, the two variables follow a counterclockwise spiral around the equilibrium point—predator-prey dynamics again. The upper diagram corresponds to $\theta_\psi < 0$, and represents a stable profit-squeeze of the sort emphasized by Boddy and Crotty (1975), Bowles, Gordon, and Weisskopf (1990), and the authors cited above.[3] Both diagrams, of course,

Figure 9.2
A structuralist
Goodwin model, with
stable (upper) and
unstable (lower)
wage share
dynamics.

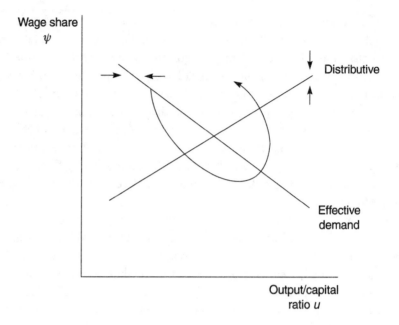

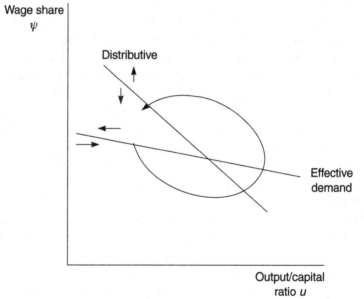

bear a close family resemblance to the ones in Figure 7.4. Their jumps in *u* have just been smoothed into cycles.

3. Evidence for the United States

Recall from the social accounting matrixes of Chapter 1 that there are numerous payments flowing toward households in the U.S. economy.

Just which should be called "wages" is by no means clear. A broad definition of labor payments incorporates wages and salaries paid separately by the private sector and the government, along with supplemental labor income (social security, health insurance, and other benefits) paid by both. Government wages tend to vary against the capacity utilization cycle, have an upward oscillating trend between 1950 and 1970, and a downward trend thereafter. Supplemental labor income trends upward from 4 percent of the total in the 1950s to around 14 percent in the mid-1990s with most of the growth prior to the mid-1980s. Wages paid by business vary pro-cyclically and the share has a slight downward trend through the early 1980s. On this definition, the real wage is weakly pro-cyclical in the sense that it picks up a positive response to u in regression equations like those discussed below.

Figure 9.3 shows smoothed annual observations of the broadly defined labor share and capacity utilization in the U.S. economy from 1950 through 2001. To scale u around a value of one, capacity utilization is measured relative to potential output calculated using Congressional Budget Office (CBO) methodology as opposed to the capital stock.[4] The trajectories in the figure broadly follow negatively inclined counterclockwise spirals, with capacity utilization fluctuating by five to seven per-

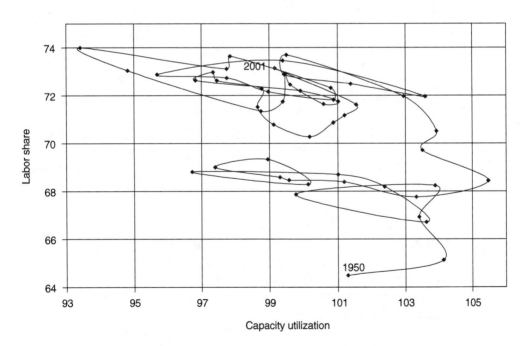

Figure 9.3
Capacity utilization and the broadly defined wage share in the U.S. economy, 1950–2001.

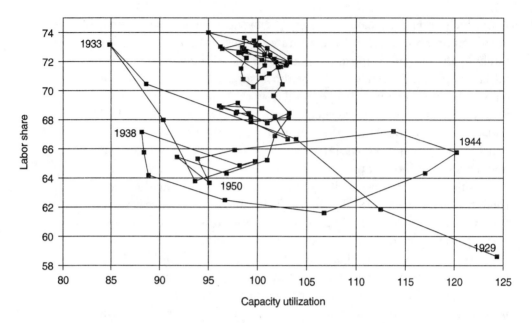

Figure 9.4
Capacity utilization and the broadly defined wage share in the United States, 1929–2001.

centage points over a cycle, and the labor share by two or three points. There is an upward shift in the spirals in the late 1960s, due to the trends in government wages and supplemental labor payments. Figure 9.4 presents the longer history beginning in 1929. With much wider fluctuations, the same general pattern shows up in the earlier period as well. The significant exception is the decline in the labor share between 1944 and 1950 as both capacity utilization and wages fell off from their wartime peaks.

The cycles for the United States bear more than a passing resemblance to the ones in Figure 9.2, which angle toward the southeast because the level of activity swings around the negatively sloped Effective demand curve. It makes sense to explore econometrically how well an extended version of last section's model applies to U.S. data.

For purposes of estimation, it is preferable to work with the labor share of the business sector only, for at least two reasons. The series is reliably stationary, because it does not incorporate the trending elements of supplemental income and government wages. Second, price/quantity data are not readily available for the nonbusiness sector. The labor share is measured as an index number (1992 = 100), constructed from Bureau of Labor Statistics series on the business sector implicit price deflator, hourly wages, and product per hour. To impose a linear decomposition of ψ into its components, regression equations were run for $\ln \psi$. More precisely, define $f(\psi_t) = \ln \psi_t - \ln \bar{\psi}$, where ψ_t is the wage share at time t and $\bar{\psi}$ is its sample mean. For sample values close to the mean, we have

$$\ln \psi_t - \ln \bar{\psi} \approx f(\bar{\psi}) + (1/\bar{\psi})(\psi_t - \bar{\psi}) = (\psi_t/\bar{\psi}) - 1.$$

There is an approximate linear relationship between ψ and $\ln \psi$, which in turn decomposes as $\ln \psi = \ln w - \ln P - \ln \xi$, parallel to the additive breakdown of aggregate demand into its components presented below.

Capacity utilization is measured as the ratio of observed to potential business sector product in percentage points. Potential output is calculated using the standard Hodrick-Prescott filter; results are much the same on the CBO definition. For decomposition analysis, we can write $u_t = c_t + i_t + n_t + g_t$ at time t, with the four demand components being consumption c_t, investment i_t, net exports n_t, and government spending g_t measured relative to potential GDP. Implicitly, potential GDP and potential business sector GDP are assumed to correlate closely, which they do.

Figure 9.5 presents annual data for capacity utilization and the labor share as just defined. A counterclockwise cycle persists in the (u, ψ) plane, beginning in 1947. Applying the Hodrick-Prescott filter to both variables suggests that movements in capacity utilization lead those of the labor share throughout most of the post–World War II period—predator is led by prey. Measured in index number form, variations in ψ slightly exceed those of u over cycles. Both series are stationary at the 1 percent level of significance on Augmented Dickey-Fuller tests.

Dynamics of u and $\ln \psi$ were studied using an off-the-shelf vector autoregressive (VAR) model of the form

$$y_t = \phi + \sum_{j=1}^{2} \Phi_j y_{t-j} + \epsilon_\tau,$$

where $y_t = [\ln\psi_t \, u_t]$ is a 2-by-1 vector containing the values of $\ln \psi$ and u at time t, ϕ and Φ_j, $j = 1, 2$ are coefficient matrices of appropriate dimensions and, by construction, ϵ_t is a vector of white-noise disturbances. To define the lag structure of the model, we set eight as the maximum length and computed Akaike information criteria for all specifications. The results indicated that two is the best lag length.

Table 9.1 summarizes results of the VAR model for the period 1948–2001. The wage, price, and productivity variables (especially) increase over time so all equations were estimated including trends. All coefficients were significant according to the standard tests, and the capacity utilization and labor share equations had adjusted R-squares of 0.75 and 0.83 respectively. Through the lags, capacity utilization responds posi-

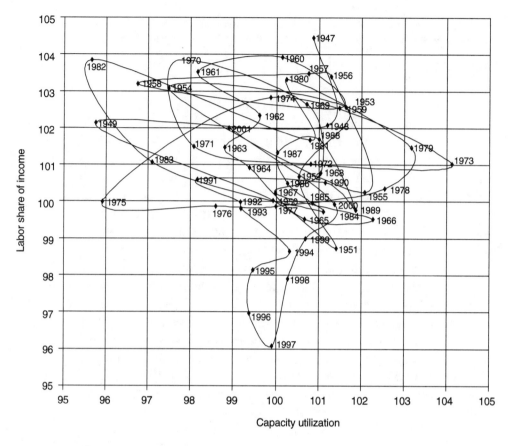

Figure 9.5
Scatter diagram of the labor share of income and capacity utilization in the U.S. business sector, 1947–2001.

tively to its own past values and negatively to the wage share. The equation for u can be rewritten as

$$u - u(-1) = 36.01 + (1.24 - 1)u(-1) - 0.51u(-2)$$
$$+ 0.28\psi(-1) - 0.36\psi(-2)$$

so that $\Delta u = u - u(-1)$ has an overall negative response to the two lagged values of u.

In formal terms, the main stability criterion for an autoregressive (AR) model is that the sum of coefficients on "own" AR terms must be less than one. From Table 9.1, this requirement is satisfied for the u process: $1.24 - 0.51 = 0.73 < 1$. Perhaps more intuitively, at a steady state it will be true that $u = u(-1) = u(-2)$, implying that $u - u(-1) = 0$, and $\psi = \psi(-1) = \psi(-2)$. The implied slope of the steady-state effective demand

Table 9.1 Estimated coefficients for capacity utilization and the labor share, 1948–2001.

	const	trend	$u(-1)$	$u(-2)$	$\psi(-1)$	$\psi(-2)$	Steady state $d\psi/du$
u	36.01	−0.00	1.24	−0.51	0.28	−0.36	−3.46
c	53.06	0.02	0.39	−0.15	−0.09	−0.05	
l	−13.62	0.00	0.86	−0.45	0.18	−0.30	
n	14.45	−0.01	−0.24	0.17	−0.18	0.12	
g	−17.88	−0.01	0.22	−0.08	0.36	−0.12	

	const	trend	$\ln u(-1)$	$\ln u(-2)$	$\ln\psi(-1)$	$\ln\psi(-2)$	Steady state $d(\ln\psi)/d(\ln u)$
$\ln\psi$	−1.34	0.00	0.04	0.16	0.70	0.20	2.02
$\ln w$	8.99	0.02	0.72	−0.60	1.15	0.53	
$\ln P$	4.23	0.01	−0.49	0.26	−0.51	0.59	
$\ln\xi$	6.10	0.01	1.17	−1.02	0.96	−0.27	
$\ln w/P$	4.76	0.01	1.21	−0.86	1.66	−0.06	

Table 9.2 Slopes of effective demand and distributive curves for subperiods, 1948–2001.

	Effective demand $d\psi/du$	Distributive $d(\ln\psi)/d(\ln u)$
1948–2001	−3.46	2.02
1954–2001	−3.24	2.11
1948–1970	−2.16	3.68
1954–1970	−1.58	−7.01
1971–2001	−8.01	1.23

curve is $d\psi/du = -(0.24 - 0.51)/(0.28 - 0.36) = -3.38$ (or, as shown in the table, -3.46 when more significant digits are carried in the calculation). Over the sample period, effective demand is profit-led, with a unit decrease in the index for the wage share resulting in a rise of about one-third of a point of capacity utilization.

The wage share responds positively to past values of capacity utilization and itself. The overall response of $[\ln\psi - \ln\psi(-1)]$ to $\ln\psi(-1)$ and $\ln\psi(-2)$ is $(-1 + 0.7 + 0.2) = -0.9$, so the difference equation for $\ln\psi$ is locally stable. The steady-state slope of the distributive curve $d(\ln\psi)/d(\ln u)$ is 2.02, signaling a profit squeeze.

Table 9.2 presents the slopes of the effective demand and distributive curves for the Golden Age period and thereafter. A convenient breakpoint is the year 1970, which contained the trough of an NBER business cycle. The initial year is alternatively 1948 or 1954 (the latter a trough year which omits the immediate post–World War II and Korean War periods).

Over both 1948–2001 and 1954–2001, demand is profit-led and there is a profit squeeze. Pre-1970, the demand effect is stronger (steady state $du/d\psi$ is bigger in absolute value), and weakens during 1971–2001. Further sample splits suggest that demand may have shifted to being wage-led during the 1970s but was profit-led in the preceding and following decades.[5] However, the number of observations per decade is too low to make a solid case.

During 1954–1970, the distributive curve takes a negative slope and the difference equation for ln ψ is locally unstable, as in the lower diagram of Figure 9.2. Along lines to be discussed below, the instability can be traced to a vigorous productivity response to the profit share.

In sum, the qualitative characteristics of the economy are described by the upper diagram in Figure 9.2. It follows that "permanent" distributive shocks favorable to labor (upward shifts of the distributive curve) lead to an increase in the labor share at the expense of a reduction in capacity utilization; and that positive demand shocks (upward shifts of the demand curve) lead to increases in capacity utilization and the labor share. Convergence around a "new" long-run intersection of the Effective demand and Distributive curve will of course be cyclical.

Although the technicalities can safely be left to Barbosa-Filho and Taylor (2003), it is possible to use VAR estimation subject to adding-up restrictions to express the demand components of u and the price/productivity components of ln ψ as functions of lagged values of these two variables. The results of these reduced-form estimates are also shown in Table 9.1.

The estimated coefficients suggest that c, or the ratio of private consumption to potential GDP, has a positive trend and is pro-cyclical (or as we have seen in Chapter 1, the household financial surplus varies countercyclically). Investment i also varies pro-cyclically. Net exports n have a downward trend and respond negatively to both capacity utilization and the wage share (interpreted as an index of labor costs). Government spending also has a negative trend, and responds positively to u and ψ. In the aggregate, the profit-led components predominate and there is no overall trend in u.

Trends are stronger in the logs of w, P, and ξ. The coefficients are consistent with the descriptions above for the long period 1948–2001. During 1954–1970, the sum of the coefficients on ln ψ in the productivity equation is -1.18, giving rise to the form of cyclical dynamics illustrated in the lower diagram of Figure 9.2.

4. A Contractionary Devaluation Cycle

The real wage or wage share is by no means the only object of distributional conflict. In part because it affects the real wage, the real exchange rate $\rho = e/P$ as analyzed in connection with Table 7.3 is often a bone of contention. (Recall that e is the nominal spot exchange rate and P is a national price level.) Its movements can set off cycles, especially when real devaluation has contractionary effects on output, apparently the case historically in many developing countries. With a lag, devaluation may lead to an export push, followed by wage increases that cut back on exports and ultimately demand and real wages themselves. Following Larrain and Sachs (1986) it is easy to model such interactions over time.

As in Table 7.3, let $\epsilon = E/K$ be the export/capital ratio. In equation (28) in the table, ϵ is assumed to respond immediately to a real devaluation, or an increase in ρ. A lagged response is more realistic, for example,

$$\dot{\epsilon} = \alpha[\epsilon^*(\rho) - \epsilon], \tag{12}$$

in which $\epsilon^*(\rho)$ is the "long-run" export level corresponding to a given value of ρ. Because of preexisting contracts, the need to search for new foreign outlets, and so on, exports do not immediately respond to price signals. Rather, their foreign currency value ϵ/e is likely to follow a "J-curve" (as a function of time) after a nominal devaluation, first dropping as e jumps up, and then gradually rising according to (12).

To keep the analysis conventional, suppose that there is a "natural" level $\bar{u}$ of the output/capital ratio at which wage inflation is zero. Money wages may then change according to a simple Phillips curve,

$$\dot{w} = \beta bw(u - \bar{u}),$$

in which β is a response coefficient and b the labor/output ratio. From this equation, a higher level of capacity utilization will make money wages begin to rise, reducing the import cost ratio ϕ in equation (22) in Table 7.3. The real exchange rate also appreciates (moves downward), leading export expansion to slow.

Real exchange rate dynamics are given by

$$\dot{\rho} = \rho(1 - \phi)[\hat{e} - \beta b(u - \bar{u})], \tag{13}$$

in which $\hat{e}$ is an exogenous growth rate of the spot exchange rate. If devaluation is contractionary, an increase in ρ pushes u down, making $\partial\dot{\rho}/\partial\rho > 0$ and creating a potential instability.

Around a steady state with $\dot{\epsilon} = \dot{\rho} = 0$ with positive ϵ and ρ, the signs of the entries in the Jacobian of (12) and (13) are as follows:

$$\begin{array}{ccc} & \epsilon & \rho \\ \dot{\epsilon} & - & + \\ \dot{\rho} & - & + \end{array}$$

Figure 9.6
Contractionary
devaluation
cycles.

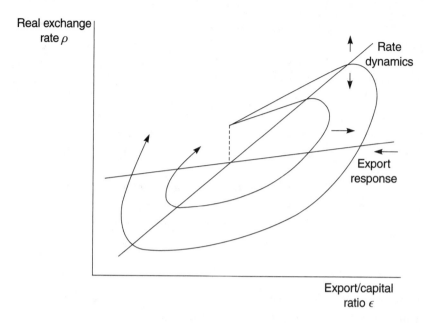

The off-diagonal terms have offsetting signs and can stabilize the system. In contrast to the Goodwin models, now the "prey" variable has unstable own-dynamics—instead of rapidly reproducing wage-share foxes, think of exchange rate rabbits.

Figure 9.6 illustrates the resulting cycles. The "Export response" curve corresponds to $\dot{\epsilon} = 0$ and the "Rate dynamics" to $\dot{\rho} = 0$. Starting from an initial equilibrium, a maxi-devaluation followed by an exchange rate freeze displaces the real rate upwards. There is further depreciation until a trajectory crosses the Rate dynamics schedule. Because of the lag in the export response, ϵ keeps growing until the spiral crosses that curve. A downswing follows, setting off a clockwise spiral with oscillating exports and real exchange rate (not to mention output and inflation), or else cyclical divergence. A closed orbit would be an intermediate case.

An alternative policy could involve a steady depreciation at a rate $\hat{e}$. Via (13), this would shift the Rate dynamics schedule to the right, leading to a long-term export gain but a lower real wage. If higher profits and more exports stimulated technical advance, the economy could jump to a higher growth path. Amsden (1989) suggests that elements of such a strategy contributed to the South Korean export miracle around the three-quarter mark of the twentieth century.

5. An Inflation Expectations Cycle

Talking about a Phillips curve already brings expectations into the picture. Inflationary expectations, in particular, have been extensively analyzed in a monetary growth model due to Tobin (1965). If adaptive expectations about the change in the inflation are strong enough, they can create cyclical instability, with the expected inflation rate as the predator and the real money stock per capita as the prey.[6] The predator is the one with unstable own-dynamics.

Tobin added simple fiscal and monetary accounts to Solow's (1956) Say's Law growth model (set up here in terms of the capital/labor ratio as opposed to its inverse as in Chapter 5). The government collects taxes T from and makes transfers Z to the private sector, comprising N individuals. If P is the price level, the real government deficit per capita is $\gamma_g = [(Z - T)/P]/N$. New money $\dot{M}$ is created to finance the deficit, so that $-\gamma_g + (\dot{M}/P)/N = 0$ is the government's flow of funds (government negative real saving per capita is $-\gamma_g$). The per capita real money supply is $m = (M/P)/N$. If $\mu = \hat{M}$ is determined by fiscal policy, it will be true that $(\dot{M}/P)/N = \mu m$.

Output per capita is $f(k)$, with k as the capital/labor ratio and $f(k)$ a neoclassical aggregate production function in intensive form. Taking into account transfers net of taxes that the private sector gets from the government, its real disposable income per capita y^{RD} is $y^{RD} = f(k) + \gamma_g$. There is an ongoing inflation at an expected rate π. The private sector knows how the (expected) inflation tax πm takes away real purchasing power, and so has a *perceived* real disposable income per capita of $y^{PD} = f(k) + \gamma_g - \pi m = y^{RD} - \pi m$.

Real consumption per head, c, is set by the rule $c = (1 - s)y^{PD}$. Per capita real saving σ thus becomes $\sigma = y^{RD} - c = s[f(k) + \gamma_g] + (1 - s)\pi m$. If the population is growing at a rate n, total real investment per capita is $\dot{k} + nk$ in standard fashion. Besides paying for investment, private sector saving is used to acquire the new money that the government deficit creates, so the sector's flow of funds is $\sigma - \dot{k} - nk - \mu m = 0$. Combining these two expressions for σ and substituting for γ_g from the government's flow of funds gives an expanded version of Solow's growth equation $\dot{k} = sf(k) - nk$,

$$\dot{k} = sf(k) - nk + (1 - s)m(\pi - \mu). \tag{14}$$

The Mundell-Tobin assertion that faster expected inflation speeds up capital formation is an immediate corollary. A higher value of π makes money a less desirable asset, so the private sector's portfolio shifts in flow terms toward real accumulation.

As with the structuralist Goodwin model's output/capital ratio in equation (4), it is convenient to assume that real money balances per capita change smoothly over time (that is, neither the money supply nor the price level jumps),

$$\dot{m} = m(\mu - \hat{P} - n). \tag{15}$$

A last step is to add a theory of inflation. In the literature around the Tobin model, it has become conventional to postulate that the inflation rate responds to "excess money supply." If for simplicity we stick to the quantity theory, then money demand M^D is given by $M^D V = PK$ (where the Say's Law assumption underlying the growth model means that demand can be scaled to the capital stock just as well as to output). Velocity V is presumably an increasing function of the expected inflation rate π: $V' = dV/d\pi > 0$. Real money demand per capita becomes $m^D = (M^D/P)/N = k/V$.

Fischer (1972) proposes that inflation dynamics be written down as

$$\hat{P} = \beta_p(m - m^D) + \pi. \tag{16}$$

That is, current inflation responds with a lag to money market disequilibrium and is also (somehow) influenced by the expected rate π.

Using (16) permits equation (15) for the change in real money balances to be restated as

$$\dot{m} = m\{\mu - \beta_p[m - (k/V)] + \pi - n\}. \tag{17}$$

If expectations about the inflation rate are formed adaptively, $\dot{\pi} = \beta_\pi(\hat{P} - \pi)$, then using (16) gives the differential equation

$$\dot{\pi} = \beta_\pi \beta_P \{m - [k/V(\pi)]\}. \tag{18}$$

Equations (14), (17), and (18) form a three-dimensional dynamic system with somewhat peculiar properties. Capital accumulation in (14) presumably unfolds over years and decades. On the other hand, (17) says that the money supply expands smoothly, and in (18) it is hard to believe that expected inflation differs from the actual rate for any extended period of time.

In an extreme case, therefore, one could solve $\dot{\pi} = 0$ in (18) for π, *given* values of k and m. This solution, together with the given k, could be used to solve for m with $\dot{m} = 0$ in (17). These solutions would involve the conditions $\pi = \hat{P} = \mu$ so that in the medium term (14) would revert to its basic Solow form. Sooner or later k would get close to an equilibrium value k^* with $\dot{k} = 0$.

This sort of solution procedure is known as an "adiabatic approximation" (Lorenz 1989). It basically says that the dynamics of a "slow" variable like k dominate the steady state of the system and that "fast" variables like m and π are "slaved" to k. Such an approximation will not work if the fast variables can act together in such a way as to destabilize the system.

In the present example, such an outcome depends on whether or not π and m can jointly generate an unstable predator-prey spiral. To try to find out if they can, we can examine the Jacobian of the subsystem (17)–(18) at its equilibrium point, for some given value of k:

$$J = \begin{bmatrix} -m\beta_p & -m[\beta_p m^D(V'/V) - 1] \\ \beta_p\beta_\pi & \beta_p\beta_\pi m^D(V'/V) \end{bmatrix}.$$

Brute-force calculation shows that $\text{Det } J = m$ and $\text{Tr } J = \beta_p[\beta_\pi m^D(V'/V) - m]$. At an equilibrium point, it will be true that $m^D = m$, so the condition for instability boils down to $\beta_\pi(V'/V) > 1$ or $\beta_\pi(\pi V'/V) > \pi$. The elasticity $\pi V'/V$ is likely to lie between zero and one, so an inflation adjustment parameter β_π exceeding the rate of inflation could set off a destabilizing spiral. An uptick in $\dot{m}$ would lead to higher real balances and a positive $\dot{\pi}$ in (18), amplified by the positive feedback in the southeast corner. A weak negative feedback in the northeast entry would let $\dot{m}$ continue to be positive, and a destabilizing spiral would be under way. According to (14), faster inflation would speed up growth. It is difficult to believe that this happy situation would continue for very long.[7]

6. Confidence and Multiplier

Expectations are of course unobservable. That fact of life can make empirical applications of models like the foregoing unconvincing. The same criticism applies to investment functions of the sort proposed by Keynes, which explicitly incorporated shifting expectations over the cycle. Despite this problem, it makes sense to try to think through how Keynesian investment (and saving) dynamics could work themselves out—the task of this and the following two sections.

We begin with a simple exercise in which investment demand shifts over time in response to a "confidence" variable ρ (redefined from being the real exchange rate) which feeds back positively into itself.[8] Much the same story underlies the many accelerator models proposed since the days of Samuelson (1939).

The setup here replaces the static expectation function $f(r)$ used in the model underlying Joan Robinson's banana in Figure 5.3 with the dynamics of ρ. The level of investment (per unit of capital) is g^i, and the macro balance condition is $u = (1 - s)u + g^i$, so that from the usual multiplier algebra we get $u = g^i/s$.

A typical accelerator story has investment responding to the change in output (and thereby to the change in itself). To get to such a model via a confidence variable, we can assume in line with the specification of the banana that the growth of investment depends on the difference between its expected return ρ and the profit rate $r = \pi u$ (with π now standing for the profit share instead of expected inflation) as an indicator of the cost of capital,

$$\dot{g}^i = g_0 + \alpha(\rho - \pi u) = g_0 + \alpha[\rho - (\pi g^i/s)]. \tag{19}$$

Positive feedback is added if confidence responds positively to itself. There is damping if ρ declines when the investment level is "too high,"

$$\dot{\rho} = \beta(\rho - g^i). \tag{20}$$

The Jacobian for the system (19)–(20) takes the form,

$$J = \begin{bmatrix} -\alpha\pi/s & \alpha \\ -\beta & \beta \end{bmatrix},$$

with Tr $J = \beta - (\alpha\pi/s)$ and Det $J = \alpha\beta[1 - (\pi/s)]$. For a positive determinant, the profit share has to be less than the aggregate saving rate. In other words, households and/or the government as well as firms must have visibly positive saving—the model might apply better to Japan than to the United States!

In a phase diagram in the (g^i, ρ) plane, the schedule corresponding to the $\dot{\rho} = 0$ condition would be the 45-degree line, and the $\dot{g}^i = 0$ locus would have a shallower slope (meaning that the base level of investment demand g_0 must be positive). The configuration of the curves would be the same as in Figure 9.6. An upward jump in confidence would kick off a clockwise spiral, unstable for a big β (highly responsive confidence) and/or a small α (unresponsive investment demand).

7. Minsky on Financial Cycles

This five-finger exercise becomes far more interesting when we bring in the financial side of the economy. It turns out that changes in investors' confidence can lead to potentially destabilizing macroeconomic cycles even when "the" interest rate is relatively stable in the face of aggregate demand shocks. The text is Minsky's (1975) book on Keynes, as partly put into algebra by Taylor and O'Connell (1985). For simplicity, inflation as well as debt accumulation complications of the sort discussed toward the end of Chapter 8 (and in the following section) are ignored.

To focus attention on the stock market and Minsky's interpretation of the valuation ratio q, we revert to supply-side determination of money and credit, as in the IS/LM model of Chapter 4. Balance sheets appear in

Table 9.3 Balance sheets for a Minsky-style financial instability model.

Households		Firms		Banking System	
M	Ω_h	qPK	L_h	T	M
L_h			L_b	L_b	
P_vV			P_vV		
			Ω_f		
		Government			
		T			

Table 9.3, with both households and banks lending to business. Corporate net worth Ω_f is not restricted to zero and is treated as an endogenous variable. The resulting degree of freedom will be filled by bringing investor confidence into the picture as a factor determining q.

With government debt T held only by the banking system, the money supply rule is $M = \zeta T$, so that the supply of bank loans to firms is $L_b = (\zeta - 1)T$. The economy-wide wealth balance is $\Omega_h + \Omega_f = qPK + T$. Given the shares v and λ_h^s of their wealth Ω_h that households direct toward equity and loans to firms respectively, we can use their balance sheet identity to scale their net worth to the money supply,

$$\Omega_h = M/(1 - v - \lambda_h^s) = M/\mu,$$

where μ (now) is the share of Ω_h held as money. The loan market equilibrium condition becomes

$$\lambda^d qZ - [(\lambda_h^s/\mu)\zeta + (\zeta - 1)] = 0, \qquad (21)$$

where $Z = PK/T$ is the capital/debt ratio to be used as a state variable for model dynamics.

Minsky can be read as saying that the arguments of the loan demand function λ^d are the interest rate i and an *expected* profit rate $r^e = r + \rho$, where r is the observed rate of profit and ρ is an indicator of business confidence with a dimension consistent with that of r. The shares of money and loans in household wealth (μ and λ_h^s, respectively) can be assumed to depend on i, r^e, and the output/capital ratio u as an indicator of the level of economic activity.

The expected profit rate $r^e = r + \rho$ also determines the capital asset valuation ratio q. Instead of emerging from the accounting as in Walras-Tobin models, q can reasonably be set equal to r^e capitalized by borrowing costs, that is $q = (r + \rho)/i$. When ρ is high and confidence is solid, the investing community ratifies its views by increasing its estimates of corporate wealth. From their balance sheet, the net worth of firms $\Omega_f = qPK - L_h - L_b - P_vV$ follows endogenously from the level of q and clearing of loan and equity markets. Evidently, with Ω_f not restricted to zero, Minsky and Modigliani-Miller don't mix.

For given levels of ζ and Z, excess demand for loans in (21) will be a decreasing function of the interest rate (when i goes up, λ^d will fall and λ^s_h will rise). An increase in the capital/debt ratio Z steps up demand for loans, thereby driving up i. Conversely, by raising loan supply, a higher ζ makes the interest rate go down.

Potential effects of changes in ρ (or r) on excess loan demand are more interesting. Minsky's (1975) discussion rests squarely on Keynes's idea that liquidity preference is high when times are uncertain or simply bad. It follows that "during a boom the speculative demand for money *decreases*" (p. 123, emphasis added). Further, on p. 76 if higher income from a boom "is interpreted as increasing the surety of income from capital-asset ownership, then the liquidity preference function will shift, so that for a given quantity of money, the higher income, the higher the interest rate, and the higher the price of capital assets" (or the higher the value of q, in the notation utilized here).

The natural interpretation is that as economic activity and business profits rise, speculative demand for money goes down more than transactions demand goes up. This portfolio switch helps bid up equity prices P_v in that market's equilibrium relationship,

$$(v/\mu)\zeta T - P_v V = 0,$$

and increases the relative supply of loans. Excess loan demand in (21) becomes *less* sensitive to changes in actual and anticipated profit rates r and ρ so that the slope of the LM or "Loan market" curve in the (r, i) plane becomes more shallow at high levels of r. See Figure 9.7 for an illustration.[9]

If investment demand depends on $q = (r + \rho)/i$, then the IS or "Commodity market" schedule determines macroeconomic equilibrium in Figure 9.7. A higher confidence level shifts the loan market schedule upward and the commodity market curve to the right, leading to a new equilibrium with higher values of r and i. The shift in liquidity preference, however, means that the increase in i *relative* to r will be greater at a low initial profit rate (point A) than at a high one (point C). These contrasting responses underlie Minsky's cyclical dynamics.

To trace an oscillatory trajectory, we can begin by observing that the state variable Z will evolve over time according to the rule[10]

$$\dot{Z} = Z(g - \gamma_g Z), \tag{22}$$

where g is the rate of capital stock growth from the IS/LM system and γ_g is the share of the fiscal deficit in the value of the capital stock. Because a

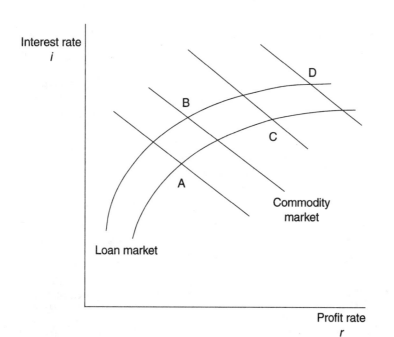

Figure 9.7
Effects of an increase
in investor con-
fidence ρ on macro-
economic equilib-
rium at relatively low
(A to B) and high (C
to D) levels of eco-
nomic activity in the
Minsky model.

higher value of Z raises the interest rate, $\partial g/\partial Z$ is likely to be negative; through both terms in parentheses we have $\partial \dot{Z}/\partial Z < 0$.

The other dynamic variable is of course the state of confidence ρ, which through positive feedback can generate cycles. A higher value steps up investment and the growth rate, so that $\partial \dot{Z}/\partial \rho > 0$. Changes in ρ itself presumably depend on the general state of the economy. Confidence might increase, for example, when the actual profit rate r is high or the interest rate i is low. The analysis underlying Figure 9.7 suggests that changes in confidence should depend on the ratio of r to i (or on q as "normally" measured without the confidence term included in the numerator):

$$\dot{\rho} = f(r/i), \tag{23}$$

where f is an increasing function.

Equations (22) and (23) can generate a clockwise cycle along the lines discussed in sections 4 and 6. The system is potentially unstable, because from Figure 9.7 a higher value of ρ can make the r/i ratio go up, that is, $\partial \dot{\rho}/\partial \rho > 0$. A higher Z raises the interest rate and reduces the level of economic activity and enterprise profits, so that $\partial \dot{\rho}/\partial Z < 0$. The dynamics are shown in Figure 9.8, for the possibly stable case in which the determinant of the Jacobian of (22)–(23) is positive. The "Confidence" schedule along which $\dot{\rho} = 0$ must be steeper than the "Velocity" schedule for which $\dot{Z} = 0$. The slope of the confidence curve is $-f_Z/f_\rho$ where

Figure 9.8
Dynamics of invest-
ment confidence and
the capital/debt ratio
in the Minsky model.

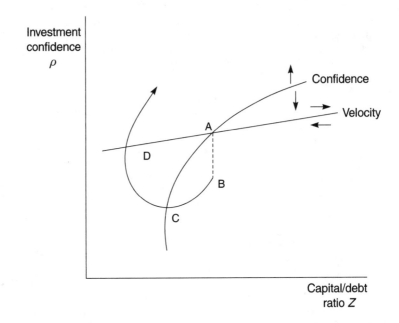

the subscripts stand for partial derivatives. The curve becomes flatter at high values of ρ because of the stronger effect of ρ on r/i shown in Figure 9.7.

A sudden loss of confidence at an initial steady state at A means that ρ jumps downward to B. It then continues to fall, with Z also declining because the interest rate is relatively high and investment drops off. After some time, Z may fall enough to reduce pressure on loan markets and allow the r/i ratio to start to rise (this transition will be quicker, insofar as the strong effect of ρ on r/i weakens as confidence declines).

After the trajectory crosses the Confidence curve at C, ρ will begin to rise, ultimately (at D) stimulating growth enough to permit $\dot{Z}$ to become positive. This upswing phase may last a considerable time, until the solution trajectory crosses the flattened Confidence schedule at high values of Z and ρ. Depending on the strength of the positive feedback to confidence, the system may then oscillate back to A, orbit the steady state forever, or diverge on a spiral path. The underlying real/financial interactions add a considerable degree of endogeneity to the cyclical process.

The swings in confidence underlying these events could be dampened by central bank interventions. In the present model they would affect ρ by shifting the interest rate through changes in the credit multiplier ζ. But if the authorities intervene to support confidence (which is by no means guaranteed), ρ itself may move upward over time, leading to increased moral hazard, more fragile financial positions, and the sorts of changes in financial structures discussed in Chapter 8.

8. Excess Capacity, Corporate Debt Burden, and a Cold Douche

Sticking to the post-Keynesian theme of a stable interest rate, it is interesting to ask how animal spirits and corporate (as opposed to fiscal) debt interact over the cycle. The Lavoie-Godley growth model presented in Chapter 8 provides an arena for several questions:

Is there a tendency for industrialized economies to generate excess capacity and/or a rising organic composition of capital, to prime the plumbing for a Schumpeterian "cold douche"?

If investment continues to rise while capacity utilization is falling, how does the implied "realization crisis" work itself out?

In particular, how long can investors' optimism persist when overcapacity begins to raise its head?

Such questions have been hotly debated in Left U.S. policy circles in recent years, for example, in Greider (1997) and many subsequent pieces. They obviously cannot be fully answered by contemplating a clockwise spiral in a two-dimensional phase plane, but perhaps the construct to follow can shed some light.

Recall that the key state variable for Lavoie and Godley is λ, the ratio of corporate debt to the capital stock. One distinction implicit in their model concerns the effect of λ on the output/capital ratio u. Is effective demand debt-burdened ($\partial u/\partial \lambda < 0$) or debt-led ($\partial u/\partial \lambda > 0$)? Second, if the debt ratio behaves in self-stabilizing fashion ($d\dot{\lambda}/d\lambda < 0$ in a total derivative through the dynamic system), then what about the sign of $d\dot{\lambda}/du$? Lavoie and Godley's label for a negative value is "normal" as opposed to a positive "Minskyan" response of debt growth to economic activity.

To set up a cycle model around λ, we can bring in confidence. The straightforward approach is to make the intercept term g_0 in the investment function[11] a dynamic variable,

$$\dot{g}_0 = f_g(\lambda, g_0). \tag{24}$$

Positive feedback can be introduced by making the second partial derivative of the function f_g positive; a degree of caution on the part of investing firms (borrower's and lender's risks, and so on) suggests that the first partial should be negative.

It is simplest to treat u as a fast variable, slaved to g_0 and λ. An increase in g_0 raises effective demand, so the interactions have already been sketched in Figure 8.4. Given the signs of the partial derivatives of f_g just postulated, the existence of a cyclical solution to (24) and the differential equation for λ,

$$\dot{\lambda} = f_\lambda(\lambda, g_0), \tag{25}$$

requires that $d\dot{\lambda}/dg_0 > 0$, that is, a Minskyan debt growth response to rising animal spirits.

Figure 9.9 shows the dynamics of (24) and (25), with the "Growth" schedule corresponding to $\dot{g}_0 = 0$ and the "Debt" curve to $\dot{\lambda} = 0$. The familiar clockwise spiral shows up.

An initial low-level temporary equilibrium at A will be associated with a falling debt burden and improving animal spirits until the (g_0, λ) trajectory crosses the Debt schedule at B. Then λ begins to rise while g_0 still increases until the Growth schedule is crossed (point D). Autonomous investment begins to fall, and the cycle bottoms out as the debt ratio declines after the trajectory crosses the corresponding schedule again at E. Around that point, presumably, the cold shower kicks in.

What happens to capacity utilization while this spiral uncoils? Almost certainly, u responds positively to g_0. It is also likely that effective demand is debt-burdened. On these assumptions ($\partial u/\partial g_0 > 0$ and $\partial u/\partial \lambda < 0$), we can sketch the positively sloped "Capacity utilization" contours in Figure 9.9. Each curve shows combinations of g_0 and λ that hold u

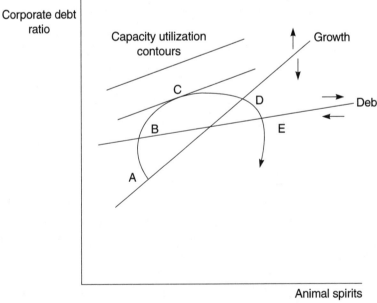

Figure 9.9
An animal spirits cycle in the Lavoie-Godley model.

constant, with its level increasing across contours toward the southeast. On this accounting, a realization crisis occurs at point C, where the trajectory is tangent to a contour line. Thereafter, u falls while animal spirits continue increasing until point D—growing overcapacity precedes a fall in optimism in this scenario. Together with a rising debt burden, a lower level of u slows investment demand; ultimately output $X = uK$ will begin to fall as well.

One argument in the late 1990s was that a cycle of the sort sketched in the diagram was especially threatening because industrial capacity had been growing worldwide since the mid-1980s under the stimulus of globalization. Instead of just one country's macro system, the whole world's was supposed to be going through a confidence squeeze. Apparent overinvestment in capital goods supporting information technology (excess capacity for computer components) and infrastructure for the Internet (thousands of miles of unused fiber optic cable) only made the situation worse.

Second, inflation had slowed almost everywhere, so that falling markup rates due to rising interest costs and decreasing capacity utilization were beginning to cause price levels to decline. Following Palley (1996) and the analysis in Chapter 8 it would be straightforward to add a more complete treatment of the financial system to the present setup to show how debt-deflation could further cut into economic activity.

Third, wage increases as advocated by people on the Left cannot restore aggregate demand if it in fact is profit-led. What is probably true is that demand is not stimulated by higher interest rates. So attempts to push rates down make sense in terms of the present model. Whether such a move would forestall massive worldwide output contraction combined with severe price deflation may still be an open question. As of mid-2003, hopes were still resting on a *non*-cyclical response of U.S. household savings rates to the downswing, so that aggregate consumption could continue to hold effective demand high.

9. Final Thoughts

There are numerous oscillatory processes at work in the real economy. Moreover, their import changes over time—recall the discussion in Chapter 3 of the differences between nineteenth- and twentieth-century business cycles. Simple little two-dimensional models cannot begin to cope with all the fluctuations (and fluctuations of fluctuations) that exist.

Nevertheless, they can focus attention on key oscillations. Devaluation and (in Chapter 10) external debt cycles in developing economies surely happen. In the United States, distributive and some sort of

Lavoie/Godley/Minsky financial cycles are visibly present. (Inflation expectation cycles probably are not that significant, despite their proliferation in the mainstream literature.) Trying to put the whole set of motions into a plausible package is the challenge, which neither econometrics nor computer simulation is likely to meet fully. But at least the toy models and their fancier cousins give a modicum of insight into some of the mechanisms underlying the intrinsic fluctuations of capitalism. In the future, of course, new models will have to be developed to track novel forms of cycles when they inevitably begin to spiral.

CHAPTER TEN

————————— ✕ —————————

Exchange Rate Complications

Macroeconomics in a world in which two or more countries are open to trade, factor payments, and capital flows raises issues well beyond those we have discussed. A full structuralist treatment would require another whole text. All we can do here is consider salient issues, mostly involving determination of the exchange rate as the key "macro price" in an open economy. Some results to follow are controversial; they will be flagged as we go along.[1]

As usual, we begin with accounting, and then go on to a series of exchange rate models. In sequence, they attempt to determine the rate as an asset price, or as a consequence of commodity price arbitrage, or as an endogenous variable in a portfolio balance, flow-based Keynesian, extended IS/LM, and a couple of monetarist macro models, or from other sorts of considerations (a more detailed preview of all these models appears in section 2). After a quick detour to consider exchange rate-based debt dynamics in a developing-country context, the chapter closes with the thought that although each model has serious problems on its own terms, perhaps the set may serve to surround the beast. How well the fencing may work is the final topic.

A warning: the discussion jumps between levels of abstraction, in keeping with the ways in which the different theories have been worked out. They all try to specify the "fundamentals" of exchange rate determination. Another summary of the chapter is that for all practical purposes fundamentals do not exist—except when market participants convince themselves that one or another of the many candidates truly matters. Once again, the beauty contest rules.

1. Accounting Conundrums

A central theme of this book is that often the best way to attack a problem in economics is to make sure your accounting is right. Tables 10.1 and 10.2 attempt this task for international trade and financial relations.

Table 10.1 A Two-country SAM with trade and interest flows and international capital movements.

	Output costs	Current home expenditures				Home ext. receipts		Changes in home claims				Exchange conversions	
		Private	Gov't.	Banks	Cap. form.	Exports	Foreign interest	Money	Home bonds	For. bonds	Totals	For. to Home	Home to For.
	(1)	(2)	(3)	(4)	(5)	(6)	(7)	(8)	(9)	(10)	(11)		
Output (A)		PC	PG		PI	Pa^*X^*					PX		
Incomes													
Private (B)	V		iT_h	Π_b			$ei^*T_h^*$				Y_h		
Gov't. (C)		τY_h									Y_g		
Banks (D)			iT_b				ei^*R^*				Y_b		
Flows of funds													
Private (E)		S_h			$-PI$			$-\dot{M}$	$-\dot{T}_h$	$-e\dot{T}_h^*$	0		
Gov't. (F)			S_g						$\dot{T}$		0		
Banks (G)				0				$\dot{M}$	$-\dot{T}_b$	$-e\dot{R}^*$	0		
External													
Imports (H)	eP^*aX											e	
Exports (I)						$-Pa^*X^*$							$1/e$
Int. in (J)							$-ei^*T_{ext}^*$					e	
Int. out (K)		iT_{ext}											$1/e$
Change (L) in ext. liab.									$-\dot{T}_{ext}$				$1/e$
Change (M) in ext. ass.										$e\dot{T}_{ext}^*$		e	
Totals (N)	PX	Y_h	Y_g	Y_b	0	0	0	0	0	0			

Unfortunately, full accounting in models containing real and financial sectors for the "home" and "foreign" countries requires a wagonload of symbols. The details in both tables are needed to demonstrate the results that follow. They follow broadly from a scheme proposed by Godley (1996).

Table 10.1 sets out flow accounts in the form of a SAM. Table 10.2 presents the corresponding balance sheets. Since the emphasis is on external transactions, economic actors in each country are aggregated into just three groups—a private sector comprising households and nonfinancial business, government, and the banking system, which consolidates commercial and central banks. Variables referring to the home and foreign private sectors are labeled with subscripts h and f respectively. The foreign country's stocks and flows are denoted by asterisks in both tables.

As shown in Table 10.2, primary assets include capital stocks valued at their asset prices (qPK and $q^*P^*K^*$) and outstanding short-term bonds or T-bills issued by the two governments (T and T^*, with interest rates i and i^* respectively). Both banking systems carry a subscript b, but they are distinguished by their asset portfolios. The home system's assets are home bonds T_b and foreign bonds as reserves with a value eR^*; the

Table 10.1 (continued)

Output Costs	Current foreign expenditures				Foreign ext. receipts		Changes in foreign claims				
	Private	Gov't.	Banks	Cap. form.	Exports	Home interest	Money	For. bonds	Home bonds	Totals	
(1*)	(2*)	(3*)	(4*)	(5*)	(6*)	(7*)	(8*)	(9*)	(10*)	(11*)	
	P^*C^*	P^*G^*		P^*I^*	P^*aX					P^*X^*	(A*) Output
											Incomes
V^*		$i^*T_f^*$	Π_g^*			iT_f/e				Y_f^*	(B*) Private
	$\tau^*Y_f^*$									Y_g^*	(C*) Gov't.
		$i^*T_b^*$				iR/e				Y_b^*	(D*) Banks
											Flows of funds
	S_f^*			$-P^*I^*$			$-\dot{M}^*$	$-\dot{T}_f^*$	$-\dot{T}_f/e$	0	(E*) Private
		S_g^*						$\dot{T}^*$		0	(F*) Gov't
			0				$\dot{M}^*$	$\dot{T}_b^*$	$-\dot{R}/e$	0	(G*) Banks
											External
					$-P^*aX$						(H*) Exports
Pa^*X^*/e											(I*) Imports
		$i^*T_{ext}^*$									(J*) Interest out
						$-iT_{ext}/e$					(K*) Interest in
									$\dot{T}_{ext}/e$		(L*) Change in ext. ass.
								$-\dot{T}_{ext}^*$			(M*) Change in ext. liab.
P^*X^*	Y_f^*	Y_g^*	Y_b^*	0	0	0	0	0	0		(N*) Totals

foreign system holds foreign bonds T_b^* and home bonds as reserves with a local value R/e. The banks have zero net worth and their liabilities are the money supplies M and M^* respectively. In their portfolios, the private sectors hold the relevant capital stock qPK or $q^*P^*K^*$, both flavors of bonds, and money M or M^*. Unrealistically, the private sector in each country is assumed to hold only the local currency. It is straightforward to deal with the general case by using more symbols, but the SAM already has too many.

Accounts for the home country appear to the left of the SAM, and for the foreign country to the right. Cross-border flows are mediated by "Exchange conversions" between the two sides (the conversions also involve a sign change because an inflow to one country is an outflow from the other). The spot exchange rate, e, is the home currency price of foreign currency.

Output and income generation relationships appear toward the northwest of each country's part of the SAM. Real output levels are X and X^* respectively, with prices P and P^*. The corresponding costs of production are broken down in columns (1) and (1*). Total values of output PX and P^*X^* include payments for nominal value-added (V and V^*) and imports (eP^*aX and Pa^*X^*/e). As in other chapters, imports are treated

Table 10.2 Balance sheets for two countries.

	Home Country	
Private Sector	**Banking System**	**Government**
M Ω	T_b M	T
T_h	eR^*	
eT_h^*		
qPK		

	Foreign Country	
Private Sector	**Banking System**	**Government**
M^* Ω^*	T_b^* M^*	T^*
T_f^*	R/e	
T_f/e		
$q^* P^* K^*$		

as components of cost.[2] Real imports are scaled to outputs by coefficients a and a^*, which could depend on relative prices such as the real exchange rate eP^*/P in models of the neoclassical persuasion.

Rows (A) and (A*) show that outputs are used for the usual purposes—private consumption, government spending, investment, and exports. For future reference, note how exports in cells (A6) and (A*6*) are valued at local prices. Rows (B)–(D) and (B*)–(D*) show how incomes of the private sectors, governments, and banks are generated; their outlays and levels of saving appear in columns (2)–(4) and (2*)–(4*). In rows (B) and (B*), the private sectors receive incomes from value-added and interest payments on their holdings of local and external bonds (for the home private sector, the receipts are iT_h and $ei^*T_h^*$ respectively). The simplest way to deal with interest incomes on bank assets is to assume that they are passed along to the private sectors. In row (D), for example, the home banking system has interest income $Y_b = iT_b + ei^*R^*$. It transfers these returns Π_b to the private sector in column (4): $\Pi_b = Y_b$. As a result of such maneuvers, savings of the banking systems are equal to zero in cells (G4) and (G*4*). The governments get their revenues from taxes on private incomes (τY_b and $\tau^* Y_f^*$) in rows (C) and (C*).

Rows (E)–(G) and (E*)–(G*) show the different sectors' flows of funds. As usual, "sources" of funds (saving and increases in liabilities) are positive and "uses" (increases in assets) are negative. The equation for the home private sector in row (E),

$$S_h - PI - \dot{M} - \dot{T}_h - e\dot{T}_h^* = 0,$$

shows that it uses its saving S_h for capital formation PI and increased holdings of home money $\dot{M}$, home bonds $\dot{T}_h$, and foreign bonds valued by the exchange rate $e\dot{T}_b^*$. Combined with differentiation of the home household balance sheet in Table 10.2, this flow of funds equation gives the change in nominal home private sector wealth as

$$\dot{\Omega} = S_h + e\dot{T}_b^* + (\dot{q}P + q\dot{P})K,$$

so that $\dot{\Omega}$ is the sum of saving and capital gains (or losses) from changing asset prices.

Row (F) shows that home government saving S_g must be negative if it is issuing a positive flow of new bonds ($S_g = -\dot{T} < 0$ when $\dot{T} > 0$). In row (G), the fact that the banking system's saving has been set to zero means that the growth of the money supply responds solely to changes in bank assets, $\dot{M} = \dot{T}_b + e\dot{R}^*$.

Three international payment flows go in each direction, for a total of six. See rows (H)–(M) and (H*)–(M*). In terms of their national prices, exports of the home and foreign countries (that is, foreign and home imports) take the values Pa^*X^* and P^*aX in cells (A6) and (A*6*). Between rows (I)–(I*) and (H*)–(H), home and foreign exports are converted to the other country's prices by the inverse of the exchange rate ($1/e$) and its level (e) respectively (together with the sign switches mentioned above) and then become imports in columns (1*) and (1).

Second, in column (7) the home private sector and banks hold foreign bonds in quantities T_b^* and R^*. The values of their interest receipts in home prices are ei^*T_b and ei^*R^*. With $T_{ext}^* = T_b^* + R^*$ as home's gross foreign assets, its total interest income is $ei^*T_{ext}^*$ in cell (J7). After an exchange conversion between rows (J) and (J*), the foreign government's interest payments in local prices on its bonds held abroad count as a fiscal outlay $i^*T_{ext}^*$ in cell (J*3*). The home government's interest payments on its gross external liabilities $T_{ext} = T_f + R$ are treated analogously in column (7*), rows (K*)–(K), and column (3).

Finally, foreign asset holdings change over time, for example, $\dot{T}_{ext} = \dot{T}_f + \dot{R}$ is the equation for foreign accumulation of the home government's bonds at home prices. The exchange conversion is between rows (L) and (L*), and column (10*) gives bond accumulation in foreign prices.

The transactions appearing in the SAM correspond to the usual categories in balance of payments accounts: trade in goods and services, factor payments, and movements of capital. In a formal model, the trade flows would be driven by activity levels and relative prices, and interest rates would adjust to make sure that asset markets (incorporating both foreign and home flows) clear. Interest rates on asset stocks would set the levels of factor payments.

As Godley (1996) emphasizes, an apparent puzzle in the SAM is the fact that while it includes numerous international transactions, there is no "balance of payments" per se. It is not obvious why all the cross-border flows with their exchange conversions should add up to some overriding "balance," especially since all have their own separate determinants.

But the standard accounting does make sense. To see why, it is helpful to think in terms of net foreign assets (NFA) N of the home country, which can be defined as

$$N = e(T_b^* + R^*) - (T_f + R) = e\dot{T}_{ext}^* - T_{ext}, \qquad (1)$$

or (in the present example) home's holdings of foreign bonds valued at the spot exchange rate minus the value of its own bonds held abroad. In (1) it is clear that N follows from historically given gross asset and liability positions in that its level is set by the home economy's history of current account deficits and surpluses and the ways in which they were financed. It is shown below that net foreign assets cannot "jump" in unconstrained fashion in temporary equilibrium—any change in the level of gross assets has to be met by an equal change in gross liabilities to hold N unchanged. In this way, (1) becomes a binding constraint on macroeconomic adjustment.

Net foreign assets can take either sign (including holdings of equity, they were about $-\$2$ trillion for the United States as of 2002). As nominal magnitudes, N and its foreign counterpart $-N/e$ are subject to capital gains and losses due to movements in the exchange rate. These are discussed below, so for the moment we concentrate on quantity changes in N. Summing and substitutions among the rows and columns of the SAM give the following chain of equalities:

$$S_b + S_g - PI = e(\dot{T}_b^* + \dot{R}^*) - (\dot{T}_f + \dot{R}) = \dot{N}$$
$$= [Pa^*X^* + ei^*(T_b^* + R^*)] - [eP^*aX + i(T_f + R)] = -S_f \quad (2)$$

where S_f stands for the home country's "foreign saving" or current account deficit (if the home country is saving less than it invests, then the rest of the world must be providing saving to make up the shortfall).

In the first line of (2) the sum of domestic sources of saving minus investment is equal to the increase in net foreign assets. In turn, in the second line $\dot{N}$ is equal to the surplus on current account (trade plus factor payments) or $-S_f$. All presentations of an economy's "balance of payments" are rearrangements of equations like those in (2). What they are basically saying is that (apart from capital gains and losses), net foreign assets evolve over time in response to the current account. Decisions about how net assets are "stored" in terms of national portfolio allocations (including amounts held in the form of international reserves) are discussed below.

2. Determining Exchange Rates

Exchange rate regimes come in two basic varieties—fixed and floating.

A "fixed" exchange rate sets a value for the local currency in terms of the currency of some other country (or a weighted average of other countries, if a "basket peg" is adopted). As a variation on the fixed theme, the rate may be allowed to fluctuate within a band, or be revised from time to time to guide its "real" value eP^*/P in a certain direction. One such scheme is a "crawling peg" in which small, frequent exchange rate changes are used to offset a differential between inflation rates in the home country and the rest of the world. Such a policy was examined in terms of the contractionary devaluation cycle discussed in Chapter 9.

Since the market in which currencies are bought and sold never closes, a fixed value of the exchange rate must be maintained by interventions in the market, typically undertaken by the home country central bank. Examples include spot and forward sales or purchases of reserves, or interest rate adjustments, which attempt to change the dynamics of exchange rate movements over time. Market players may support or attack a fixed rate by buying or selling spot or forward assets denominated in the home currency, but that does not mean that the rate will change. Rather, for reasons discussed below, the country concerned will accumulate or lose reserves. This will have further implications down the line.

Many developing countries pursue fixed-rate schemes of one form or another. The sustainability of the rate today or tomorrow depends, as we shall see, on players' perceptions of the economy's "fundamentals." In the wake of massive reserve losses in their crises of the late 1990s, Mexico, some East Asian countries, Russia, and Brazil adopted floating rates. How closely they will be managed or removed from immediate market pressure by capital controls remains to be seen.

Since the early 1970s the developed countries have floated their exchange rates, managed with greater or lesser concern by the authorities. At the end of the century, the major floating currencies were the dollar, the yen, the euro, and the pound sterling. Since the mid-1970s the United States has not been greatly concerned with the real value of its exchange rate and so comes closest to having a "pure" floating regime. But other rich countries, including "Euroland" or the eleven nations initially adhering to the euro, are not far behind.

One standard line of argument about the determination of floating rates is based on arbitrage in financial and/or commodity markets. A second focuses on stock and flow relationships involving asset portfolios and macro balances as in Tables 10.1 and 10.2. Finally, more institutionally oriented approaches attempt to pinpoint fundamentals that allegedly determine where the exchange market is likely to go.

Intertemporal forex arbitrage was analyzed in the 1920s by Keynes (1923), among others. It gives a rule known as "uncovered interest rate parity" (or UIP) by which the exchange rate can be calculated as an asset price from expected changes in its value over time. UIP is intrinsically dynamic, because it is based on arbitrage of own rates of return over time.

Also in the 1920s, the Swedish economist Gustav Cassell (1922) repopularized an old exchange rate rule known as "purchasing power parity" (or PPP) based upon current arbitrage in commodity markets. Exchange rates should be such that tradable commodities command the same prices in any country. Neither parity condition is observed in practice, rendering their underlying assumptions somewhat dubious. But both are commonly used to calculate exchange rate fundamentals. If one or the other of the hypotheses is badly violated, the market may conclude that the current exchange rate is at an inappropriate level.

Macro-level theories concentrate on the exchange rate's linkages with aggregates such as the trade balance, the composition of asset portfolios, or the overall balance of payments. If the rate is allowed to "float" or change freely, it is supposed to arrive at a level that "clears" macro balances. With the rate fixed, the balances may not achieve equilibrium in well-determined ways.

The macro relationships that must be considered in the contemporary world relate to both the current and the capital accounts. Before and in the first decades after World War II, it made sense to concentrate only on the trade account. A model proposed forty-odd years ago by Salter (1959) and Swan (1960) does contain a plausible exchange rate fundamental—the traded/nontraded goods price ratio. At least as far as trade is concerned, the exchange rate can be interpreted as becoming increasingly overvalued when this internal price ratio falls. But for the industrialized countries at least, payments related to trade are now such a tiny share of total external transactions that the model is obsolete (Eatwell and Taylor 2000).[3]

The two widely accepted Keynesian models incorporating the financial side of the balance of payments date from the 1960s and 1970s.[4] The younger concentrates on "portfolio balances," and claims that the exchange rate along with the two bond interest rates is determined by equilibrium conditions in three of four relevant financial markets—for home and foreign moneys M and M^* and bonds T and T^* (the fourth market is supposed to clear by Walras's Law). It is shown below that this claim is incorrect because there is just one independently clearing asset market in each country.

The other model is usually attributed to Mundell (1963b) and Fleming (1962). In an open economy described by a 3 × 3 system of equations, adjustment dynamics are based on the ideas that the output level responds to excess commodity demand from an IS relationship and the interest rate shifts in response to asset market imbalances in an LM. The floating rate is supposed to adjust when the balance of payments (or BP) does not clear. On the other hand, if the exchange rate is pegged then international reserves have to be the adjusting variable, making monetary policy endogenous. Solving all three equations simultaneously under the fixed or floating rate assumption gives the usual stability and comparative static results.

The Mundell-Fleming "duality" between reserves and the exchange rate evidently presupposes that a balance of payments exists, with a potential disequilibrium that has to be cleared. But as we have already seen in connection with Tables 10.1 and 10.2, the balance of payments is at most an accumulation rule for net foreign assets and has no independent status as an equilibrium condition—an argument spelled out in detail below. The Mundell-Fleming duality is irrelevant, and in temporary equilibrium the exchange rate does not depend on how a country operates its monetary (especially international reserve) policy.

The bottom line assessment of the portfolio balance and Mundell-Fleming models is that they are not satisfactory approaches to exchange rate determination. In contemporary markets it appears that the rate is extrinsic to macro equilibrium as it emerges from adjustments in variables such as interest rates or the general level of economic activity. A floating exchange rate is not a "price" that equilibrates markets—apart, perhaps, from the markets in which its own future values are set via UIP or other intertemporal behavioral practices.

Evidently dynamic considerations have to brought in. Although it does not fit the data (Blecker 2002b), UIP is the obvious intertemporal model to consider. A formulation incorporating IS, LM, and UIP is presented in section 8. It generates cyclical dynamics, as opposed to the saddlepath jumps characteristic of more recently popular dynamic optimization models discussed in earlier chapters.

A further strand of the exchange rate story is a monetary approach to the balance of payments worked out in the 1950s and 1960s (the reaction raging against Keynesianism at the time extended itself vigorously in the open economy direction). A sketch is given in section 9. There is also a discussion of econometric attempts to specify fundamental causes of exchange rate changes, largely along monetarist lines. They all failed dismally. Finally the monetarist approach led into a well-known model of exchange rate dynamics by Dornbusch (1976). It is outlined in section 10.

Two other analyses of the behavior of exchange rates are worth mentioning. First, "twin deficit" models assume that the balance on external accounts is determined by the fiscal balance, which immediately emerges as another fundamental. In particular, deterioration in the external position is attributed to growing fiscal deficit. Second, the so-called trilemma suggests that its three component policies—liberal capital markets, a fixed exchange rate, and an independent monetary (or indeed, fiscal) policy—may be mutually incompatible. Because the Mundell-Fleming duality principle is invalid, it is argued below that the trilemma per se makes no sense. But it still is of some use in underlining the fact that the state of expectations in the market is the exchange rate's ultimate arbiter.

3. Asset Prices, Expectations, and Exchange Rates

Recall from Chapter 4 the definition of an own-rate of return to an asset as $i = (R^{exp}/V) - c$, that is, the net expected income flow (R^{exp}) per unit value of the asset (V) minus the carrying cost (c). Keynes thought that asset prices like V "should" adjust to bring revenue streams net of carrying costs into broad alignment with one another and with "the" interest rate as well. The quotation marks are meant to call attention to the fact that arbitrage very often fails (in part for reasons he advanced in his beauty contest). Fully arbitraged asset prices represent a center of gravitation in the market that is often honored in the breach.

The exchange rate becomes an asset price when it responds to potential capital gains or losses in forward markets. Consider a Japanese investor who wants dollars in one month's time. He or she has two basic options. The first is to buy dollars now at the spot exchange rate e and hold them at the American (monthly) interest rate i. The total dollars available at the end of the month will be $e(1 + i)$. The alternative is to hold resources in yen at an interest rate i^* and then buy dollars at the expected forward rate $f = e + \epsilon$ where ϵ is the expected change in the dollar/yen exchange rate. The total at hand after a month would be $f(1 + i^*)$.

Arbitrage in forward markets should ensure that returns to both strategies are equalized, or $e(1 + i) = f(1 + i^*)$. Under normal conditions, the expected exchange rate change and the monthly interest rate will be around a percentage point or less. The product ϵi^* of these two valuation changes per month will be "small" (well less than 0.01 percent) and can be ignored. If this is true, then a bit of algebra applied to the arbitrage condition shows that

$$e = \epsilon/(i - i^*). \tag{3}$$

The current exchange rate should be equal to its expected change, capitalized by the difference between the two interest rates, $i - i^*$.

There are two interpretations of the ϵ term. The first applies to exchange markets among industrialized countries. They are usually "thick" in the sense of having a large volume of daily transactions and a wide spectrum of forward contracts. There is free capital mobility, and an absence of political or country risk (of the imposition of capital controls, for example). Future values of the exchange rate can be readily hedged by setting up forward contracts so a relationship like (3) can safely be assumed to apply. In markets with myopic perfect foresight, (3) can be restated as a differential equation for the exchange rate, with properties to be explored in section 8 below.

On the other hand, pure exchange risk may remain, for a variety of reasons, in what is known as the *uncovered* interest rate parity or UIP case. For any individual investor, the expected change in the exchange rate ϵ cannot be readily hedged by available contracts (with minimal transaction costs). It thereby unavoidably depends on the outcome of all investors' expectations about the future (the sum of average opinion). In own-rate form,

$$i = i^* + \epsilon/e, \tag{4}$$

Keynes's relationship says that the home interest rate will exceed the foreign rate whenever the home currency is generally *expected* to depreciate or weaken, that is, $\epsilon > 0$. A Japanese investor who goes into dollars subjectively anticipates a capital loss and has to be compensated by an American rate i that exceeds i^*. The "spread" between the interest rates will become greater as ϵ/e, the expected relative change in the exchange rate, rises.

"Testing" the validity of interest rate parity models has been a playground for econometricians for the past few decades. They have enormous fun trying to formulate and quantify expectations. Covered parity in "thick" markets for the currencies of developed economies does indeed appear to be widely observed. At least this is true when markets are behaving in tranquil fashion. Then covered interest rate differentials have become negligible in countries with unrestricted capital flows. On the other hand, when stable market expectations break down (as in the

1992 European crisis and in many developing country cases), the evidence indicates that UIP does not hold—expected exchange rate changes (however measured) do not reliably correlate with interest rate differentials.

4. Commodity Arbitrage and Purchasing Power Parity

Arbitrage in commodity as opposed to asset markets underlies a long-run theory of exchange rate determination that can be traced back to the sixteenth century. The basic idea is that the dollar should buy as much of a traded good in a foreign country as at home. Let P_t be a price index for traded goods in the home country and P_t^* a similar index abroad. Then the spot exchange rate should satisfy the PPP relationship $eP_t^* = P_t$.

If P_t exceeds eP_t^*, then the home country should be inundated with goods from its foreign providers until P_t is forced down or e up to restore market balance. If the latter adjustment occurs in an inflationary context, the exchange rate should rise along with the domestic price level (perhaps with fluctuations around the trend, or "overshooting" when e jumps to satisfy UIP in response to shifts in the expected rate of inflation). In the "overvalued" $P_t > eP_t^*$ case, violation of PPP should be associated with a widening trade deficit, so that two well-known fundamental indicators reinforce each other.

Despite its long pedigree, and the fact that it is widely believed to hold, PPP does not apply in practice. Consider two examples.

The introduction of the euro prompted a flurry of international price comparisons. They showed that prices for the "same" consumer good across the eleven nations of Euroland spanned a range of 50 percent up or down from the one in the middle. The range for producers' goods was almost as wide.

In a longer run, the association of PPP "overvaluation" with a wide trade deficit is not always observed. By most price comparisons the United States is "undervalued." In one frequently noted example, price quotations in the local currency for many consumer goods in the United Kingdom and United States are just about the same, although in exchange markets it usually costs somewhere around $1.50 to buy one pound. At the same time the chronic U.S. trade deficit signals that the dollar is too strong (probably even after visible depreciation in early 2003).

A plethora of similar observations may be found throughout the literature. The market's enforcement of the "law of one price" across borders, or even within one country, is notably lax. Even so, a persistently higher rate of inflation at home than abroad is usually interpreted as an unfavorable fundamental, and accordingly the market requires that the exchange rate adjust. As already noted, many developing countries have countered such a tendency with crawling peg regimes in which the exchange rate is adjusted frequently to keep eP_t^* approximately equal to P_t and maintain PPP.

5. Portfolio Balance

The portfolio balance model was introduced as a natural extension of Tobin's (1969) financial market analysis from closed to open economy macroeconomics. The basic idea was that a floating exchange rate should be determined by some contemporary market-clearing mechanism—the message of subsequent surveys such as those by Branson and Henderson (1985) and Isard (1995). In this section, we will see how this rather plausible notion fails. In other words, if it is not fixed by the authorities, the exchange rate is determined by forces beyond those contained in a temporary equilibrium asset allocation model.

The basic assumptions in this section are as follows.

Private sectors and banking systems at home and abroad are the only actors holding financial assets. They take the form of national money supplies and short-term government bonds or T-bills that pay home and foreign interest rates i and i^* respectively. The money supplies are backed by home and foreign bonds held by the two banking systems.[5]

Both private sectors and banks satisfy their balance sheet restrictions, that is, the total values of their assets are always equal to the total values of their liabilities plus net worth.

Apart from capital gains and losses induced by jumps in the exchange rate, total net foreign assets N (or $-N/e$) held by banks and the private sector in each country are constant in the short run. The reason is already clear from equation (2) above, which shows that N can only change over time in response to a surplus or deficit on current account.

A portfolio balance model is assumed to re-equilibrate in the short run to shocks such as operations of the monetary authorities and exogenous shifts in asset preferences. In the new temporary equilibrium, portfolio compositions may shift. In line with their key role in clearing asset markets, home and foreign interest rates are taken as the main endogenous variables.

Under these hypotheses, it will be shown that if the two markets for bonds clear, then so will the two markets for national moneys and vice versa. There are just two independent asset market equilibrium conditions in the system.

Traditionally, portfolio balance models are set up to deal with only the financial side of an open economy. Following this practice, capital stocks are ignored in the rest of this section. In the home banking system, the stock of M changes with open market operations in home T-bills (purchases and sales of bonds by the banking authorities) and shifts in the level of reserves. That is, M responds to its asset base as manipulated by banks. Notation to represent such interventions is introduced below. Many presentations treat banking system *liabilities* as predetermined. But since T_b and R^* can jump in the short run, just setting M instead of considering shifts in its underlying *assets* mis-specifies the analysis.

For algebraic convenience, asset holdings are set up as shares of private sector wealth levels Ω and Ω^*. The shares can depend on interest rates, wealth levels themselves, the level of economic activity, the exchange rate, its expected change, and other variables. The home excess demand and supply functions can be written as

$$\mu\Omega - M = 0, \tag{5}$$

$$T_b - \eta\Omega = 0, \tag{6}$$

and

$$eT_b^* - \phi\Omega = 0. \tag{7}$$

Similarly, asset balance equations for the foreign private sector are

$$\mu^*\Omega^* - M^* = 0, \tag{5*}$$

$$T_f/e - \eta^*\Omega^* = 0, \tag{6*}$$

and

$$T_f^* - \phi^*\Omega^* = 0. \tag{7*}$$

If the private sectors respect their balance sheets, the demand proportions must satisfy the restrictions $\mu + \eta + \phi = 1$ and $\mu^* + \eta^* + \phi^* = 1$.

There are four asset market equilibrium conditions. Two state that excess demands for money vanish in (5) and (5*). The others set excess supplies for the two flavors of T-bills equal to zero,

$$T - T_h - T_f - T_b - R = T - \eta\Omega - e\eta^*\Omega^* - T_b - R = 0 \tag{8}$$

and

$$T^* - T_h^* - T_f^* - T_b^* - R^* = T^* - \phi\Omega/e - \phi^*\Omega^*$$
$$- T_b^* - R^* = 0. \tag{8*}$$

Finally, as noted above, the home economy's net foreign assets N are defined by equation (1). To explore the implications, we can use home's gross external assets and liabilities as already defined in connection with Tables 10.1 and 10.2, $T_{ext}^* = T_h^* + R^*$ and $T_{ext} = T_f + R$. Then N is set in the "point-slope" representation of (1) in Figure 10.1. Its controlling variables are the exchange rate and historically given levels $\bar{T}_{ext}^*$ and $\bar{T}_{ext}$ of external claims. Exchange rate changes generate capital gains or losses in N. Devaluation or a higher value of e rotates the "External assets" line representing (1) counterclockwise around the $(\bar{T}_{ext}^*, \bar{T}_{ext})$ point, bidding up home's net foreign assets in home (N) and foreign (N/e) currency terms.[6] The line also constrains external asset positions when they jump away from their initial values if the model's temporary equilibrium is perturbed. The totals T_{ext}^* and T_{ext} have to rise or fall together to hold N constant. This simultaneous increase in home's foreign assets and liabilities is directly analogous to a firm running up deposits at a bank from which it takes a loan, as in the Lavoie-Godley model discussed in Chapters 8 and 9. Because N is *defined* by e, $\bar{T}_{ext}^*$, and $\bar{T}_{ext}$ in (1), it is argued below that the equation cannot sensibly be "solved" for the exchange rate.

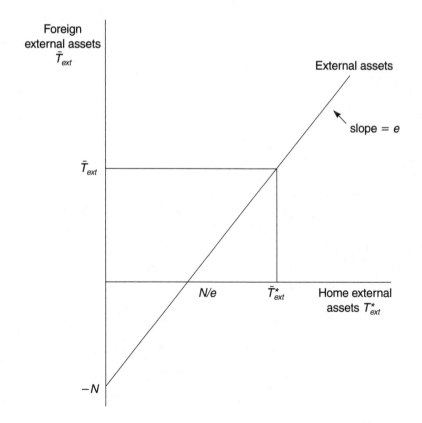

Figure 10.1
Determination of net foreign assets from initial external holdings.

Uniformly in the literature, the portfolio balance model has been set up with the balance sheet identities $\Omega = M + T_b + eT_b^*$ and $\Omega^* = M^* + T_f/e + T_f^*$ used to define levels of wealth. Then Ω and Ω^* are plugged into asset market balances, which are solved for the interest and exchange rates. This algorithm makes sense insofar as private wealth is predetermined at any time by a history of capital gains and saving flows (instantaneous capital gains due to a contemporary exchange rate movement can also be taken into account). But the standard formulation leaves out the fact that asset holdings of the private sectors are not fully free to vary. Besides Walras's Law, they are constrained by the balance sheets of the banking systems and (especially) the NFA constraint. These restrictions make dependent not just one but two of the market equilibrium conditions (5), (5*), (8), and (8*), reducing from three to two the number of independent relationships involving the underlying triplet of variables i, i^*, and e.

One way to incorporate balance sheet restrictions into Tobin-style models is to express the wealth levels Ω and Ω^* in the market balance equations in terms of national primary assets.[7] Walras's Law takes a step in that direction. It can be written as

$$(M - \mu\Omega) + e(M^* - \mu^*\Omega^*) + (T - \eta\Omega - e\eta^*\Omega^* - T_b - R)$$
$$+ e[T^* - (\phi\Omega/e) - \phi^*\Omega^* - T_b^* - R^*] = 0.$$

If the banking systems satisfy their balance sheets and the "adding up" restrictions $\mu + \eta + \phi = 1$ and $\mu^* + \eta^* + \phi^* = 1$ on portfolio allocations apply, this equation reduces to

$$\Omega + e\Omega^* = T + eT^*, \tag{9}$$

or worldwide wealth is equal to the value of outstanding government debt.

Equation (9) is familiar but not immediately helpful since it does not pin levels of national wealth. To determine Ω and Ω^* explicitly it suffices to assume that either (8) or (8*) holds, or that at least one bond market clears. Along with the maintained assumption that there are "no black holes" in balance sheets, if (8) holds then we can write the balance sheet for the home private sector in the forms

$$\Omega = M + T_b + eT_b^* = (T_b + eR^*) + (T - T_f - T_b - R)$$
$$+ eT_b^* = T + e(R^* + T_b^*) - (T_f + R)$$

or from (1),

$$\Omega = T + N. \tag{10}$$

Substitution into Walras's Law (9) then gives

$$\Omega^* = T^* - N/e. \tag{10*}$$

Each nation's wealth is made up of its outstanding government debt plus its net foreign assets. By shifting the values of N and N/e (as discussed above), changes in the exchange rate affect Ω and Ω^*. Home devaluation raises home and reduces foreign wealth.

Now we can use (10) and (10*) to show that equations (5) and (8) for money and T-bill market balance in the home country are equivalent (similar manipulations work for the foreign country as well). With (10) setting Ω, equation (5) for money demand-supply balance becomes

$$\mu(T + N) = M = T_b + eR^*. \tag{11}$$

Using (10) and (10*), equation (8) for the bond market can be written as

$$\eta(T + N) + e\eta^*(T^* - N/e) = T - T_b - R. \tag{12}$$

Formulas (11) and (12) superficially look different, but a few quick substitutions show that they are the same. To get (11) from (12), for example, one can substitute for R from (1), rearrange the resulting expression, and impose the condition $\eta + \phi + \mu = 1$. This result parallels the standard finding that in a closed economy, if the bond market clears then so does the money market. The net foreign asset constraint is the bridge that allows this reasoning to be extended to a two-country capital market.

As already noted, equation (1) enters the system as a binding restriction on spot transactions in external securities. Consider a shift in foreign preferences toward home bonds, so that T_f and T_{ext} jump up. If the foreign country's reserves R stay constant, then some element in the term $e(T_b^* + R^*) = eT_{ext}^*$ has to jump up as well. The obvious candidate is R^*. To acquire more home bonds, the foreign private sector must transfer foreign bonds that it holds across the frontier, valued at the spot rate e. They will immediately show up in home's international reserves, as eT_{ext}^* and T_{ext} slide up from their initial values $\bar{T}_{ext}^*$ and $\bar{T}_{ext}$ along the External assets line in Figure 10.1. More reserves feed immediately into an increase in home's money supply. Empirically, reserve upswings after capital inflows that lead to growth of the money supply are frequently observed. Since the Southern Cone crises around 1980, they have been a familiar precursor to emerging market debt cycles touched off by surging capital inflows. See section 12 below for more of this story.

Although recent experience underlines the practical difficulties, in principle such a monetary expansion can be controlled. This observation leads to a comment made by readers of previous versions of this analysis. They accepted the equivalence of each country's two asset market balances, but sought to preserve the traditional portfolio balance model by banning reserve changes. For example, one reader wrote that "the exchange rate could float and each country's central bank could control both components of its monetary base. *The exchange rate would adjust so as to keep net foreign assets N constant.* This is the outcome under flexible rates. Note that it determines perfectly the current exchange rate" (emphasis added).

There are at least two fatal errors in this argument. One is that the banking system *does* have tools at its disposal to control both components T_b and eR^* of the money supply with N constant and no need for a floating rate. The other problem is that if one simply follows the reader and postulates constant reserves without specifying what the banking system does to hold them steady, then an exchange rate that varies to satisfy the NFA constraint generates implausible results.

To see how the home banking system can control its asset position, suppose that the interest rates i and i^* adjust to clear the excess supply functions for home and foreign bonds. These relationships shift in response to changes in the spot exchange rate (through substitution effects and its wealth effects on N, $-N/e$, Ω, and Ω^*), the expected change in the exchange rate (via substitution effects), levels of wealth and output, and so on. Continuing with the example above, assume that the foreign demand functions for foreign and home bonds shift from $\phi^*\Omega^*$ and $\eta^*\Omega^*$ to $\phi^*\Omega^* - \Delta^*$ and $\eta^*\Omega^* + \Delta^*$ respectively. Home's immediate capital inflow makes its reserves and money supply increase by $e\Delta^*$. It is well known (Isard 1995) that home's central bank can counter such a shock to portfolio holdings in at least two ways. It can offset the reserve increase by selling a quantity $e\Gamma^*$ of foreign bonds and using the proceeds to buy home bonds (perhaps with the help of the foreign central bank), and reverse the monetary expansion by selling a quantity Λ of home bonds in a domestic open market operation.

After these portfolio adjustments, the home bond market balance can be written as

$$T - [\bar{T}_b + e\Gamma^* - \Lambda] - R - \eta\Omega - e(\eta^*\Omega^* + \Delta^*) = 0, \qquad (8a)$$

where $\bar{T}_b$ stands for the *initial* level of banking system holdings of home bonds and $[\bar{T}_b + e\Gamma^* - \Lambda]$ is the level after the interventions, and the foreign balance as

$$e(T^* - T_b^* - R^*) - \phi\Omega - e(\phi^*\Omega^* - \Delta^*) = 0. \qquad (8a^*)$$

From (1) extended to include Δ^* and Γ^*, the *new* level of reserves is

$$eR^* = N - \phi\Omega + R + e(\eta^*\Omega^* + \Delta^*) - e\Gamma^*. \qquad (1a)$$

To hold home banks' bond stock at $\bar{T}_b$, the authorities can de-monetize (or "sterilize") the effects of their foreign bond sale by setting $\Lambda = e\Gamma^*$ in the bracketed term on the left-hand side of (8a). Then after a substitution from (1a) into (8a*) to remove terms in eR^*, we get the simultaneous equations

$$T - \bar{T}_b - R - e\Delta^* - \eta\Omega - e\eta^*\Omega^* = 0 \qquad (13)$$

and

$$e(T^* - T_b^*) - N - R + e\Gamma^* - e(\phi^* + \eta^*)\Omega^* = 0. \qquad (13^*)$$

Assuming existence conditions are satisfied, for any value of e (13) and (13*) will solve for i and i^* as functions of Δ^* and Γ^*. Plugging the interest rate solutions into ϕ and η^* in (1a) gives

$$eR^* = N + R + f(\Delta^*, \Gamma^*) + e(\Delta^* - \Gamma^*) \qquad (1b)$$

as a reduced form. The function $f(\Delta^*, \Gamma^*)$ gauges the amount by which Γ^* would have to differ from Δ^* to hold R^* to its initial value. Although practical applications could prove difficult, (1b) shows that for a given Δ^* the central bank can use Γ^* to steer R^* to the level it desires. Net foreign assets stay constant and bond markets clear via changing interest rates, with no need for e to be an endogenous variable "dual" to the policy-determined stock of reserves.[8]

Of course, following the reader's suggestion above one might simply postulate that reserves do not change, without taking into consideration tools such as Λ and Γ^* that the banking authorities can use to make this situation come about (this was the theoretical stance taken by Mundell and Fleming in setting up their model, which the reader carried over to portfolio balance). It might then look reasonable to assume that e adjusts to hold N constant in (1) if the system is perturbed. But there are difficulties.

One is that in the real world (as opposed to optimal growth models in which asset prices can jump to hold net worth constant), it is hard to find cases in which wealth determines the values of its components, especially in the short run. The nominal net worth of a household, firm, nation, or the world is *determined* by its real asset positions and the relevant asset prices. For players individually and in the aggregate, their net worth does *not* determine asset valuations—causality runs the other way.

Further, in empirical practice, (1) or (1a) would not be a good "third equation" for the exchange rate, because the impact of a jump in T_f (with the other variables in the equation held constant) would be to *increase* the value of e. This depreciation could reverse if portfolio compositions shift strongly with e, or when feedback through the bond markets is taken into account. However, it is disturbing. Capital inflows are supposed to strengthen, not weaken, the local currency. The portfolio balance model, traditionally interpreted, gives the expected appreciation. If the two interest rates varied to clear each country's money market (with reserve levels and money supplies held constant by assumption), then the third equation could be the home country bond balance (8) or (8a). Under standard assumptions discussed below, one would have $\partial\eta/\partial e > 0$ and $\partial(e\eta^*)/\partial e > 0$ so (absent a strong wealth effect via Ω^*) e would decline in response to an exogenous portfolio shift of the sort discussed above. Trying to save the model by replacing dependent equation (8) with independent (1) subverts its original intent.

To close, it makes sense to work through the short-run comparative static implications of the equilibrium conditions (13) and (13*), with home and foreign interest rates as the endogenous variables. In home's financial markets, changes in i and i^* are usually assumed to have effects with opposite signs. A higher level of i will reduce excess demand for home money and excess supply of home bonds, with a higher i^* working the other way. If home and foreign bonds are close substitutes in (8a) or (13), then the Home bond market schedule in Figure 10.2 will have a slope of a bit more than 45 degrees.

With the effects of the net foreign asset constraint in the foreign bond market taken into account in (13*), interest rate effects are likely to have the *same*, negative sign. In (13*), $(\phi^* + \eta^*)\Omega^* = (1 - \mu^*)\Omega^*$ and presumably foreign money demand $\mu^*\Omega^*$ declines with increases in both i and i^*. For a "small" home country, the Foreign schedule representing (13*) will have a slightly negative slope if changes in i have minor effects on i^*.

Obvious comparative static shifts to consider are an expansionary open market operation (with home's central bank buying local T-bills), a capital inflow and an exchange of foreign for home bonds as discussed above, and movements in the expected and current exchange rates.

In (8a), an open market bond purchase (a negative Λ) reduces the left-hand side, forcing i to decline. The Home schedule shifts left, reducing the home and (marginally) raising the foreign rate. The bond swap (a positive Γ^*) shifts the Home schedule rightward and the Foreign schedule up. The home rate rises. The shift in the foreign rate is ambiguous, but if $e\Gamma^*$ is offset by an equal Λ in (8a), i^* will rise because the Home schedule does not shift. A capital inflow Δ^* compensated by these ma-

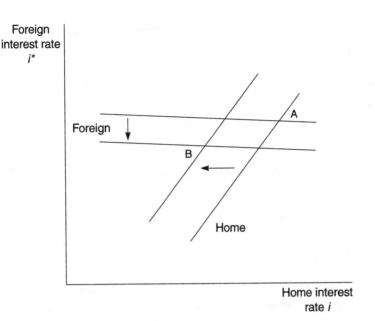

Figure 10.2
Effects of devaluation of the Home currency. Home monetary expansion is similar, except that only the Home schedule shifts.

neuvers shifts the Home schedule left. Higher external demand for home bonds strengthens their price, forcing a lower asset return i and a higher i^*. To offset the lower rate, the home central bank would have to use Λ and Γ^* to shrink the money base. Without such an intervention, if UIP rules the capital inflow will make the exchange rate appreciate over time (see note 8 and section 8).

Faster expected devaluation ϵ will presumably reduce the desired share of home bonds in the foreign portfolio, η^*. From (13), the home interest rate will have to rise (the Home schedule moves to the right) to restore market balance. In (13*), if foreign wealth-holders switch even partially from home's bonds into foreign money, the $(\phi^* + \eta^*)$ term will become negative, shifting the Foreign schedule upward. In the new equilibrium, i will rise and there will be an ambiguous (probably small) shift in i^*.

In both (13) and (13*), dimensionally alert asset-holders will deflate expected depreciation by the current exchange rate e to create a rate of return ϵ/e comparable to the others in the model. For a given ϵ, a discrete (jump) devaluation of the spot rate e will increase η^*, forcing i to decline and i^* to shift either way. These responses could be reversed by devaluation's effects on various terms in the market balance and net foreign asset equations, but in keeping with most of the literature we ignore such wealth effects.

Finally, stocks of bonds and the real side of the economy with its transactions demands notwithstanding, in an extreme case the *only* relevant arguments in the home asset equation (13) could be i, i^*, e, and ϵ. Although uncovered interest rate parity applies to expectations about future values of the spot rate, the literature often postulates that contemporaneous partial derivatives force these four variables to be related in a UIP form such as $-i + (i^* + \epsilon/e) = 0$. Because foreigners know as much about arbitrage as do home-dwellers, this formula would be their asset market equation too. The whole world would have just one asset relationship. Nonmarket or institutional forces would have to set most asset prices and rates of return. This situation is far from the original goal of the portfolio balance model to determine all financial variables by contemporary market clearing only.

6. Mundell-Fleming

Compared with portfolio balance, the Mundell-Fleming model is an accounting mare's nest. It puts a *flow* commodity market balance (the IS curve) together with a *stock* asset market equilibrium (the LM curve), and throws in part of (2) above as a BP relationship. Will this last equation be satisfied when commodity and asset markets are in balance?

In this section, the answer is shown to be "Yes," regardless of central bank interventions. The BP equation is *not* independent, that is, there cannot be an external imbalance for an exchange rate adjustment to remove.

To demonstrate this result, the key assumption is that asset market balances are satisfied continuously over time, that is, the existence of stock equilibria implies that flow equilibria exist as well. The relevant specification is in terms of flow-of-funds relationships from Table 10.1, which when supplemented by terms for capital gains and losses are time derivatives of balance sheets in Table 10.2.[9] The equilibrium condition needed from the real side is savings-investment balance. We will assume that adjustment mechanisms exist to generate the relevant equality in IS equation (16) below.

To be consistent with the presence of investment in cells (A5) and (A*5*) of the SAM in Table 10.1, private sectors must now be allowed to hold capital stocks. In the home economy the three asset demand functions (5)–(7) continue to apply, along with a stock demand for capital

$$\kappa\Omega - qPK = 0,$$

with $\mu + \eta + \phi + \kappa = 1$. The valuation ratio q adjusts to clear this equation, and may also enter as an argument in the investment demand function. This brusque treatment of capital finance could be considerably expanded as in Franke and Semmler (1999), but it suffices in terms of our present preoccupations with the exchange rate and balance of payments.

The immediate task is to show how Mundell-Fleming flow equations relate to portfolio balance. The following discussion focuses on relationships among the flows in Table 10.1 and the definitions of the change in home's net foreign assets in (2). It is consistent with any equilibrium theory of asset accumulation and portfolio choice—Keynesian, intertemporal optimization, or otherwise.

The first point to recall is that from (2), foreign savings S_f is equal to the current account deficit,

$$S_f = [eP^*aX + i(T_f + R)] - [Pa^*X^* + ei^*(T_b^* + R^*)], \tag{14}$$

and the flows of funds of the rest of the world with the home economy become

$$S_f + [e(\dot{T}_b^* + \dot{R}^*) - (\dot{T}_f + \dot{R})] = 0. \tag{15}$$

Foreign savings and flow capital inflows to home's private sector and central bank are the foreign country's sources of funds. Flow acquisitions of home's securities by its private sector and banks are its uses.

In other words, S_f equals the increase in home's foreign debt $(\dot{T}_f + \dot{R})$ less the increase in its foreign holdings $e(\dot{T}_b^* + \dot{R}^*)$. For this Mundell-Fleming BP relationship to be independent, it must be possible for the home economy's increase in net foreign assets (the bracketed term in (15)) to *differ* from its current account surplus $-S_f$ when home and foreign IS and LM relationships are satisfied. Only in such circumstances will the exchange rate or some other variable have play to restore the balance of payments to temporary equilibrium.

It is easy to see that this situation normally does not arise. First note that the sum of the flow of funds in rows (E)–(G) in Table 10.1 and (15) gives

$$S_h + S_g + S_f - PI = 0, \tag{16}$$

or macroeconomic saving-investment balance applies. Because equality in (16) is assumed to be assured by real side IS equilibrium, only three of the four flows of funds (including (15)) can be independent relationships. They are further constrained by flow clearing of asset markets. The relevant equations appear in columns (8)–(10) and (9*)–(10*) in the SAM, together with associated exchange conversions.

All asset markets can be assumed to clear in flow terms if the interest rates i and i^* are free to adjust, the banks satisfy their flows of funds restrictions, and the results of last section apply. Then the proof that the balance of payments must clear is trivial. Substitutions through the flows of funds under the assumption that commodity markets are in equilibrium (that is, (16) is valid) immediately produce equation (15).

There is no need for the exchange rate or anything else to vary to ensure that this equality will hold. In the textbook diagram, BP always passes through the IS/LM intersection, regardless of the value of e. As in the portfolio balance model, the triple intersection will occur whether or not central banks use flow transactions such as $\dot{\Gamma}^*$ and $\dot{\Lambda}$ (which could be incorporated in the foregoing accounting in straightforward fashion) to regulate changes in their holdings of home and foreign bonds.

It may be helpful to explore the implications of this result in more intuitive terms. If equality did not hold in (15), then in the double-entry bookkeeping of the flows of funds and flow asset balances some other equality would have to be violated. For example, suppose that the home country is running up external arrears by not meeting contracted payment obligations on outstanding debt, so that the current account surplus $-S_f$ falls short of the bracketed term in (15). There are two possible forms of repercussion on home's flow asset market balances and flows of funds. One is that some other flow-of-funds relationship is not satisfied. The other is that if home's domestic flows of funds equalities hold, then some flow asset market balance must fail to clear.

Consider the second case. The obvious counterpart to a nonclearing balance of payments is the domestic bond market in columns (9) and (10*) and rows (L) and (L*) of the SAM. The run-up in external arrears would be reflected into a flow excess supply of home bonds—foreigners are not picking up enough domestic securities to provide home the wherewithal to meet its external obligations. Under such circumstances (as discussed above), a spot devaluation of appropriate magnitude could be expected to erase the excess supply through a substitution effect and remove the disequilibrium.

The rub is that if home's other financial markets are in equilibrium, then this sort of adjustment is unnecessary—we know from the analysis of the portfolio balance model that if the home money market clears then so will the market for bonds. And with both money and bond markets in balance, there is no room in the accounting for an open balance of payments gap.

The other possibility is that the nonclearing balance of payments is reflected into another flow of funds relationship subject to the equilibrium condition (16). For example, one can imagine and even observe—as in recent Asian, Latin American, and Russian experiences—situations in which the home country is running up external arrears at the same time as the domestic private sector is undertaking investment projects that aren't working out (the sum of the terms in row (E) exceeds zero). An exchange rate realignment might even reverse such simultaneous buildups of external and internal bad debt. But at the macroeconomic level such situations are unusual. A normal, well-regulated banking sector at home is not in the business of providing nonperforming loans to corporations. In harmonious times, the balance of payments emerges automatically from output and asset market equilibria.

Finally, taking exchange rate movements into account, net foreign assets evolve according to the relationship

$$\dot{N} = e(\dot{T}_b^* + \dot{R}^*) - (\dot{T}_f + \dot{R}) + \dot{e}(T_b^* + R^*). \qquad (17)$$

If $\dot{N}$ were predetermined, then (17) could be treated as an "extra" equation to be solved for $\dot{e}$ in a "floating rate" case in which central banks use flow interventions like $\dot{\Gamma}^*$ and $\dot{\Lambda}$ to control $\dot{R}^*$ and $\dot{R}$. But in line with the discussion of (1) above, there are no obvious economic forces that would make $\dot{N}$ anything but the passive sum of the variables on the right-hand side. Even if $\dot{N}$ were predetermined, faster capital inflows $\dot{T}_f$ in (17) would in counterintuitive fashion speed up exchange rate depreciation $\dot{e}$. The usual Mundell-Fleming floating-rate story does not emerge naturally from consistent stock-flow accounting.

7. IS/LM Comparative Statics

The model thus reduces to linked IS/LM systems for the two countries. Financial markets are described by equations (8a) and (13*), which clear (after home central bank interventions and other shocks) via adjustments in i and i^*. Commodity markets are described by (16) and its analog in the foreign country. Saving and investment functions can be assumed to respond to the usual variables—interest rates, activity levels, profit rates emerging from the technology and institutions underlying V and V^*, perhaps q and q^*, and so on.

For present purposes, it makes sense to see how a Keynesian version behaves, with activity levels in both countries determined by effective demand. Because BP equations are not independent, the spot exchange rate has to be taken as a predetermined variable in the short run. We also assume that the home country is "small" in commodity markets, in that the foreign country's reserves stay constant, and in the sense of Figure 10.2.

Table 10.3 Signs of market responses in a linked IS/LM model.

	X	i	X^*	i^*	e	ϵ
IS	−	−	+	0	±	0
LM	+	−	+	+	−	+
IS*	0	0	−	−	±	0
LM*	0	0	+	−	+	−

Table 10.3 gives signs of responses of commodity excess demand and bond excess supply functions to the endogenous variables—output levels X and X^* and interest rates i and i^* in the two-country model—as well as to e and ϵ. The IS row shows that as usual, home excess demand is reduced by increases in both X and i. Higher foreign output X^* stimulates home demand via exports while changes in the foreign interest rate i^* are assumed to have no direct effects. In line with the possibility of contractionary devaluation as discussed in Chapter 7, a higher value of e may either reduce or increase home's aggregate demand. Faster expected depreciation ϵ has no direct effect.

In the LM row, by increasing transactions demand for money, a higher X raises the excess supply of home T-bills, while a higher i cuts it back. Increases in X^* and i^* also raise excess supply, while e and ϵ have the effects discussed in connection with Figure 10.2. Foreign IS* and LM* schedules are not affected by output and interest rate changes in a small home country, and the remaining signs in the last two rows are analogous to those already discussed.

Given the assumptions of Table 10.3, it is easy to work out how X and i respond to the other variables. (For simplicity, we consider only direct effects of e and ϵ in the IS and LM rows, without solving through IS* and LM*.) Increases in both i^* and ϵ reduce X and raise i. Even if home and foreign bonds are close substitutes in home portfolios as in Figure 10.2, it will be true that $\partial i/\partial i^* < 1$ because the fall in X reduces excess supply of T-bills. A higher X^* puts pressure on home financial markets and bids up i. The effect on X is ambiguous—increased export sales versus domestic demand contraction due to a higher interest rate.

If devaluation is expansionary, a higher e raises X but has an ambiguous impact on i. The interest rate will rise if the output increase is strong and/or the wealth and substitution effects of devaluation on home asset equilibrium are weak. A weaker currency is supposed to take pressure off interest rates, but that outcome does not have to happen.

If devaluation is contractionary, it unambiguously reduces i. The feedback effect on effective demand leaves the final response of X unclear.

Exchange appreciation in this case will be associated with a higher interest rate and possibly a reduction in output. Strong exchange rates, high interest rates, and slow growth have been characteristic of many semi-industrialized economies in the 1990s. If the fall in e is the driving force (perhaps because exchange appreciation is pursued as an anti-inflationary tool), the output and interest rate responses may reflect a situation in which effective demand is reduced or not strongly stimulated by devaluation.

So what happens to the balance of payments while these changes are going on? As in the portfolio balance model, reserve changes (as manipulated by central banks) will be the accommodating variables in both countries when their current accounts (driven largely by IS adjustments and interest rate changes) and holdings of external T-bills (driven by portfolio choices) shift over time. In the medium run, the current account will be the "autonomous" component of the balance of payments, as long as asset markets clear smoothly. Unless foreign portfolio preferences shift away from home's T-bills as its current account deficits or debt-service obligations become "too large," there is nothing in the model to prevent a country from running an external deficit indefinitely. Perhaps the United States since the 1980s is a case in point.

8. UIP and Dynamics

To summarize the last three sections, the exchange rate is not set by temporary macro equilibrium conditions. It must evolve over time subject to rules based on expectations about its values in the future. In a world of shifting and perhaps unstable expectations, no simple dynamic theory is likely to emerge. The best candidate is UIP and it does not reliably fit the data. However, because UIP relies on arbitrage arguments which "should be true" and has interesting dynamic properties, a scenario based upon it is worth sketching as an illustration of the sorts of results that a standard hypothesis can generate in conjunction with a demand-driven IS/LM-based growth model operating along Keynesian lines. Of course, other model "closures" or causal structures are possible. The Dornbusch model discussed in section 10 is one of many possibilities.

Under myopic perfect foresight (or MPF) about changes in the exchange rate with $\epsilon = \dot{e} = de/dt$, the UIP formula (3) or (4) can be restated as a differential equation

$$\dot{e} = e(i - i^*). \tag{18}$$

In the two-country IS/LM system the interest rates i and i^* are functions of the exchange rate and other variables. A long-run "equilibrium" rate $\bar{e}$, which may or may not easily be attained, is defined by the condition $i = i^*$.

Together with the IS/LM model, (18) makes up a well-defined dynamic system. On the right-hand side, i and i^* are functions of e, $\dot{e}$, and other variables Q, so (18) becomes $\dot{e} = f(e, \dot{e}, Q)$. This equation can be converted to the standard form $\dot{e} = g(e, Q)$. Assuming MPF, if the portfolio balance model really did have three independent equations among i, i^*, e, $\dot{e}$, and other variables, it would itself be a dynamic system for the exchange rate, inconsistent in general with UIP (not to mention full intertemporal arbitrage and optimization).[10]

Differential equations incorporating MPF in growth and financial models are usually unstable. An asset price feeds back positively into its own rate of growth, giving rise to saddlepath dynamics (under appropriate transversality conditions) or a bubble. However, at an initial equilibrium at which $i = i^*$ and $e = \bar{e}$, $d\dot{e}/de < 0$ in (18) if devaluation reduces the home interest rate as discussed above. This local stability opens up possibilities for cyclical exchange rate dynamics not present in most MPF formulations.[11]

Before turning to that, however, it is worth noting how UIP supports standard Mundell-Fleming conclusions. From the comparative statics discussed above, a capital inflow with the money supply held constant is likely to make i fall and i^* rise. If the differential equation (18) is stable, the exchange rate will decline over time, driving the interest rates back together. The "floating rate" scenario of a capital inflow leading to appreciation applies dynamically, except that e is not floating in the traditional sense, but is being determined in forward markets via UIP.

As an illustration of a full dynamic system, we can trace how the exchange rate interacts with home country government debt. The relevant state variable from the IS/LM system is $D = T/PK$, in which T is the outstanding stock of T-bills, P is the home price level, and K is the home capital stock. Ignoring depreciation, K increases over time according to the rule $\dot{K} = I = gK$, where I is the level of investment undertaken by business and g is the growth rate of K. Indeed, g can be treated as the model's investment function. As noted above, it can be assumed to depend on the interest rate i, the output/capital ratio $u = X/K$ as a measure of "capacity utilization," and the profit rate $r = \pi u$, where π is the share of profits in total income. Alternatively, the valuation ratio q can be taken as the principal argument of the function g.

The time derivative of T is $\dot{T} = \gamma PK + iT$, where γ is the government's "primary deficit" (outlays apart from interest payments less revenue) as scaled to the value of the capital stock. Using the foregoing information, a differential equation for D becomes

$$\dot{D} = \gamma + [(i - \hat{P}) - g]D, \tag{19}$$

where $\hat{P} = \dot{P}/P$ is the inflation rate. The steady-state value of the debt/capital ratio is $\bar{D} = \gamma/[g - (i - \hat{P})]$. As discussed in Chapter 6, an economy with $\gamma > 0$ can only sustain a stable debt/capital ratio when its capital stock growth rate exceeds the real rate of interest. This condition has tended to fail recently in industrialized economies (and fail strongly in developing debtor countries such as Argentina). We will assume, however, that at least some of the time g can exceed $(i - \hat{P})$.

Another complication is that the components of the bracketed term on the right-hand side of (19) depend on D. A higher value is analogous to an increase in T in (8). The excess supply of T-bills goes up, forcing their interest rate i to rise. In most IS/LM models with an inflation equation adjoined, the inflation rate $\hat{P}$ and growth rate g would go down. The derivative of the bracketed term in (19) with respect to D would be positive, which could make the total derivative $d\dot{D}/dD$ positive around a steady state with $\bar{D} > 0$. This potentially unstable case is the topic of the following discussion.

Effects of the exchange rate e on $\dot{D}$ in (19) go through the interest rate directly, as well as through shifts in g and $\hat{P}$ induced by interest and output changes. If $\partial i/\partial e < 0$ in the IS/LM system, we get a direct negative impact of e on $\dot{D}$. If the inflation and growth rates rise with a lower i, it is clear that $d\dot{D}/de < 0$. Finally, because a higher D increases i, $d\dot{e}/dD > 0$ in (18).

Figure 10.3 is a phase diagram for the system (18)–(19) in which there is a chance for cyclical stability. The initial equilibrium at which $\dot{D} = \dot{e} = 0$ resides at point A. Suppose that there is a permanent monetary expansion, driving down i. To bid up the interest rate again, D would have to rise and e to fall. The curves shift as illustrated.

Along the dynamic trajectory, the lower interest rate initially sets off exchange appreciation and a declining debt/capital ratio. The falling exchange rate begins to push up the interest rate, increasing the bracketed term in (19) until D starts to rise at point B. Both variables are now putting upward pressure on the interest rate. When i rises above i^* in (18), the exchange rate begins to depreciate. The trajectory may or may not converge to the new equilibrium at E.[12] Even if it does, the economy is likely to go through cycles. An initial monetary contraction would create a depreciation-then-appreciation exchange rate history. Since the late 1970s, the secular U.S. external deficit has been accompanied by (so

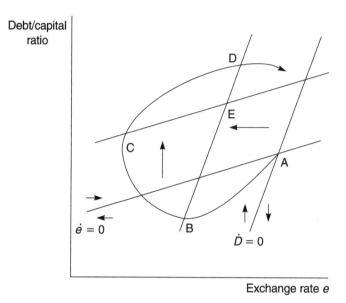

Figure 10.3
Adjustment dynamics for exchange rate and debt/capital ratio after a "permanent" monetary expansion.

far) two such cycles with periods exceeding ten years. As of mid-2003, maybe a third one is getting under way.

One should not take results from a two-dimensional dynamic system too seriously, but the foregoing narrative illustrates that a properly specified open economy macro model does contain interesting possibilities. Moreover, they would carry over to intertemporal models which incorporate UIP, but replace effective demand with Say's Law and derive a private savings (= investment) rate from a Ramsey-style dynamic optimization. Even with these changes, intertemporal models have to satisfy accounting relationships like those in Tables 10.1 and 10.2. Their dynamics cannot be less complicated than the trajectory of Figure 10.3, and as sketched in note 11, outright instabilities are also possible. There is no reason to expect monotonic or saddlepoint "stability."

This observation differs strikingly from early predictions based on the portfolio balance and Mundell-Fleming models. In one familiar example based on the former, suppose that the home country runs a current account deficit. Its reserves will fall, leading to monetary contraction and a higher interest rate. If UIP applies, the exchange rate will depreciate over time, presumably leading to a better trade performance and a new long-run equilibrium in which the current account is balanced and exchange and interest rates are stable. In the traditional model "stock-flow adjustments in the presence of capital mobility will generally move the exchange rate in the right direction to eliminate a current account deficit in the long run" (Blecker 1999b, p. 57).

This comforting story follows the pattern of Hume's price/specie flow chronicle in asserting that the existence of a current account deficit stimulates price adjustments such as depreciation that will make the deficit disappear. But in fact there is *no* reason for such adjustments to happen. In (18), a floating exchange rate has no fundamentals such as a real rate of return or a trade deficit that can make it self-stabilizing.

9. Open Economy Monetarism

Fundamentals, of course, are a Holy Grail with no dearth of errant seekers. At about the time the Keynesian models we have been discussing were invented, many other economists sought monetarist vessels for the balance of payments, the exchange rate, and macroeconomic performance more generally. Arguably, monetarism was the most influential approach to open economy questions in the latter part of the last century. It makes sense to devote a couple of sections to trying to understand why.

A starting point is the money-supply portion of (11), which can be restated as

$$M = T_b + eR^*. \tag{20}$$

We can combine this equation with a Cagan-style money demand function of the sort introduced in Chapter 3 (with the nominal interest rate i instead of the inflation rate $\hat{P}$ affecting money demand),

$$M/P = X^\phi \exp(-\lambda i). \tag{21}$$

Transactions demands depend on real output X with an elasticity ϕ (presumably with a value close to one for quantity theory reasons). If money demand equals supply, we get

$$T_b + eR^* = PX^\phi \exp(-\lambda i). \tag{22}$$

This equation can be used to tell several stories. For one, suppose for simplicity that the home private sector holds no foreign assets and that the foreign country does not bother to hold home's securities as reserves. Home's net foreign assets thus become

$$N = eR^* - T_f. \tag{23}$$

Additionally, if the exchange rate is fixed and is not expected to change, then UIP implies $i = i^*$. If Say's Law holds we have $X = \bar{X}$ at full employment. With PPP we also get $P = eP^*$. These assumptions, labeled "global monetarism" in the literature, pretty much tie up all the terms in (22).

The policy change of interest is an increase in central bank holdings of home bonds, T_b. If the bank attempts this sort of monetary expansion in the form of an upward jump in T_b, then from (22) international reserves eR^* will immediately drop because all the assumptions hold the right-hand side of the equation constant. From the NFA restriction (23), the reserve loss will take the form of a downward jump in foreign holdings of home bonds, or an immediate capital outflow.

If the attempted monetary expansion is undertaken in flow terms with $\dot{T}_b > 0$ and $e\dot{R}^* = -\dot{T}_b$ from (22), then a simplified version of (15) applies,

$$S_f = \dot{T}_b + \dot{T}_f. \tag{24}$$

The attempted monetary expansion leads either to a higher current account deficit S_f or a flow capital outflow, $\dot{T}_f < 0$.

Whether monetary expansion is attempted as a jump or a flow, it is bad medicine. Balance of payments problems are caused by "excessive" money creation, and the solution lies in tighter monetary policy. Moreover, along the lines of Hume's model sketched in Chapter 2, expansionary policy is self-defeating on the domestic front, since it just worsens the economy's external position without affecting output.

The International Monetary Fund adds a fiscal corollary. More government bonds to be purchased by the central bank are created in flow terms by the fiscal deficit or "quasi-fiscal" deficits originating in public enterprises, transactions between national and provincial governments, and so on, so the way to improve the balance of payments is to cut public spending (assuming that higher taxes invariably have distorting effects on incentives). Countless Third World recessions have found their origins in this particular recipe.

The other standard application of monetarist models has been in econometric efforts to find "fundamentals-based" models of the exchange rate, which have resoundingly failed empirically. The evidence is well summarized by Frankel and Rose (1995). The monetarist exercises usually start out correctly by postulating just two equations linking money demand to the interest rate and price level in the home and foreign countries (the exchange rate and its expected change are not included as arguments in these functions, though from the analysis herein they should be). The models add the assumption that money markets clear via price adjustments with supplies predetermined; in other words, price levels are set by the equation of exchange modified for interest rate effects. Purchasing power parity is then used as an "extra equation" to determine the exchange rate from the two national price levels. Because neither a tight link between an economy's money supply and its price level nor

PPP is ever strongly supported by the data (except possibly in the very long run), it is scarcely surprising that these formulations failed. Similar observations apply to extensions based on UIP, rational expectations, gradual price adjustment, and so on.

10. Dornbusch

The most influential model based on monetarist foundations was the one by Dornbusch (1976). It satisfies the accounting and closure restrictions set up in sections 5 and 6 and, despite many peculiarities, is cunningly designed to maximize the long-run role of fundamentals.

Dornbusch's economy reliably arrives via stabilizing expectations at a steady state defined by PPP. The closure assumptions feature determination of output by Say's Law (an assumption that could be relaxed by using new Keynesian tricks to permit unemployment in the short run). The money market balance, correctly utilized as the sole independent asset market relationship in the home economy, is combined with UIP and regressive exchange rate expectations around PPP (an "extra equation") to make the *nominal* exchange rate e depend on the *real* money supply M/P. Changes in P over time are caused by "excess demand" or the difference between aggregate demand and output. Because this difference is non-zero away from the steady state, the short-run current account is endogenous and implicitly offset by capital flows or reserve movements. They are (again implicitly) sterilized along the lines discussed above to let the central bank control M.

The principal—and famous—result is that the exchange rate "overshoots" en route to a new steady state when an initial one is perturbed. One basic assumption is that the Cagan money demand function (21) applies. UIP is assumed to apply in the form $\epsilon = e(i - i^*)$. The expected change in the exchange rate, in turn, is determined by "regressive" expectations around a long-term "equilibrium" rate $\bar{e}$ which is ultimately set (as will be seen) by PPP,

$$\epsilon = \theta(\bar{e} - e). \tag{25}$$

Plugging UIP and (25) into (21) gives

$$M/P = X^\phi \exp\{-\lambda i^* - \lambda\theta[\bar{e}/e) - 1]\}. \tag{26}$$

As noted, (26) ties the nominal exchange rate to the real money supply, which is mildly mysterious. The reasoning begins with the observation that more real money M/P should lead to a lower home interest rate i. Given UIP and regressive expectations one has $i = i^* + \theta[\bar{e}/e) - 1]$,

Figure 10.4
Dynamics in the
Dornbusch model.

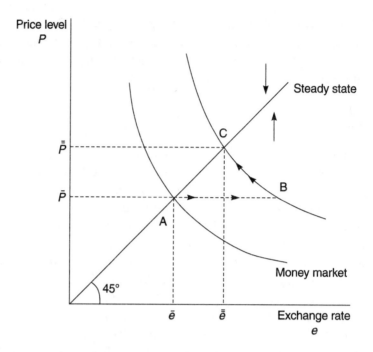

and (26) follows directly. It implies that e has to rise (depreciate) when M/P goes up. *Lower* domestic prices force a *weaker* exchange rate by reducing the interest rate, along the "Money market" curve in Figure 10.4. For future reference, a long-run price level $\bar{P}$ appears when $e = \bar{e}$,

$$\bar{P} = \frac{M}{X^\phi \exp(-\lambda i^*)}. \tag{27}$$

Dornbusch follows a strategy (used extensively in this book) of setting up a differential equation for P over time, to explore dynamics by crossing the steady state $\hat{P} = 0$ condition with the short-term relationship (26) and using e as a jump variable. He begins with a function for aggregate demand D,

$$D = (e/P)^\delta X^\gamma i^{-\sigma}, \tag{28}$$

in which δ, γ, and σ are all assumed to be positive ($\delta > 0$ means that real devaluation is expansionary, or inflationary in the present context).

The inflation rate follows from "excess demand," $\exp(\hat{P}) = (D/X)^\pi$, or

$$\hat{P} = \pi(\log D - \log X). \tag{29}$$

As noted above, besides causing inflation, a level of D exceeding X means that there will be a trade deficit, with potential draw-downs of international reserves which somehow have to be offset to let the money supply be predetermined.

When $\hat{P} = 0$, the exchange rate is assumed to be at its long-run level $\bar{e}$ with $i = i^*$ and $D = X$, so (28) becomes

$$\bar{e}/\bar{P} = [X^{1-\gamma}(i^*)^\sigma]^{1/\delta}. \tag{30}$$

Because X and i^* are assumed to be predetermined, the exchange rate and price level vary in proportion across steady states. If PPP or $P = eP^*$ holds at an initial steady state, it will continue to do so when the economy arrives at a new one. The level of $\bar{P}$ itself is determined by the money supply in (27).

The dynamics in Figure 10.4 are straightforward, with the "Steady state" schedule corresponding to $\hat{P} = 0$. Its slope of 45° is the result of the proportionality between $\bar{e}$ and $\bar{P}$ in (30). From an initial equilibrium at A, monetary expansion will lead to an immediate devaluation (just the opposite story from Figure 10.3), with e jumping to B. The exchange rate will then steadily appreciate while (contrary to the usual expectation) the price level rises until a new steady state is attained at C with price and exchange rate levels $\bar{\bar{P}}$ and $\bar{\bar{e}}$. The trade deficit immediately jumps up after the monetary shock and then narrows while the real exchange rate e/P is appreciating during the transition from B to C.

The Dornbusch model was a big hit, because it combined a stable (almost quantity theory) money demand story with Say's Law, long-run PPP, and overshooting dynamics (or "regression to mean" in financial market jargon) for the exchange rate. Like most formal exchange rate models, however, its empirical performance has been indifferent at best. In Figure 10.4, a change in monetary policy is supposed to lead to a one-time jump in the exchange rate in one direction, followed by steady movement the other way toward the new steady state. In practice exchange rate responses to monetary policy seem more gradual than the model suggests, and a long-run equilibrium may not be attained (Engel and Hamilton 1990). Maybe the real world looks more like the cycles in Figures 10.3 above and 10.5 below.

11. Other Theories of the Exchange Rate

The main, frequently repeated, theme of this chapter is that the exchange rate is not determined in asset or commodity markets apart from those involving its own forward values. On the other hand, current market relationships do suggest the existence of "fundamentals" that may well influence how a floating rate is affected by forward transactions. The price-based fundamentals mentioned so far include PPP, UIP, and the ratio of nontraded to traded goods price indexes. On the quantity side, we have the current account deficit and changes in international reserves. In present-day discussion, the fiscal deficit is often treated as another fundamental factor influencing expectations about the exchange rate.

A couple of channels are usually mentioned. One presupposes along monetarist/IMF lines that the government mainly borrows from the banking system to finance a revenue shortfall. The resulting expansion in bank loans or assets has to be accompanied by greater liabilities, usually money. If "printing money" drives up the domestic price level (which may or may not happen) and the nominal exchange rate does not increase at the same rate, then PPP violation, an increasing ratio of nontraded to traded goods prices, and a widening trade deficit are supposed to loom.

The other view is based upon the saving-investment balance (16). Suppose that the value of investment PI is stable. Then a reduction in government saving S_g due to a bigger fiscal deficit must be met by higher saving from other sources. Greater economic activity spurred by the fiscal stimulus might be expected to raise saving from households, business, and the rest of the world all together. In Reagan-era discussion, however, the focus was on foreign saving—a lower level of S_g was supposed to be matched by a "twin" increase in the current account deficit S_f. In practice, a close linkage was not observed, but that did not prevent twinned deficits from becoming part of the conventional wisdom.

Related to the twin deficits is a policy "trilemma" among (1) full capital mobility, (2) a fixed exchange rate, and (3) independent monetary and fiscal policy. In line with the (supposed) Mundell-Fleming duality—a fixed money supply and a floating exchange rate versus endogenous money and a fixed rate—the conclusion is that only two of these policies can be maintained. If the authorities try to pursue all three, the story is that they will sooner or later be punished by destabilizing capital flows. The run-up to the Great Depression around 1930 and Britain and Italy's difficulties during the 1992 European financial crisis more than sixty years later are standard examples.

But as we have seen, the exchange rate is determined by forces *not* contained in the Mundell-Fleming/portfolio balance apparatus. The exchange rate regime—fixed, floating in forward markets, or something in between—has no impact in principle on the ability of the monetary authorities to control central bank assets, even with capital mobility. The practice, however, may prove more difficult. A capital outflow, for example, could be remedied by reversing the transactions described in section 5. The negative effects on reserves and the money supply of the outflow

$-e\Delta^*$ could be roughly offset by a purchase $-e\Gamma^*$ of foreign bonds in exchange for home bonds in the central bank's portfolio, with the home bond stock being reconstituted by open market purchases. The question is how long the central bank could continue to sell home bonds into an adverse foreign market. Depending on the momentary elasticity of demand, bond prices could collapse overnight and interest rates soar. The United States has successfully carried out such sales for three decades; other countries have far less room to maneuver.

In other words, trilemmas exist in the eyes of "the market." The constant fear is that the home country's monetary and fiscal policy may not be in accord with what players "believe" to be reasonable and consistent objectives. The usual watchword is that policy must not be "excessively expansionary." Monetary stimulus may be associated with low home interest rates, which could lead to problems with UIP. Fiscal expansion might lead to the problems noted above. Macro stability is threatened when players with significant market power begin to sense that however the exchange rate is being determined, the home current account deficit (or, perhaps, the fiscal deficit or "reasonable" growth of reserves) cannot be financed by plausible levels of new foreign borrowing.

The destabilizing capital movements that may result originate in a beauty contest. Players "at higher degrees" of market perception begin to divest or sell short assets denominated in the home currency in anticipation of the capital losses they will suffer if the exchange rate significantly rises. A crisis can hit when reserve losses accelerate, the market raises its estimate of expected depreciation ϵ in the UIP calculus, and more players start stripping assets. The exchange and interest rates soar, and the early attackers sit back to count their profits.

How does the market decide when a trilemma is ripe to be pricked? The fact that no single form of transaction or arbitrage operation determines the exchange rate means that governments have some leeway in setting both the scaling factor between their country's price system and the rest of the world's and the rules by which it changes. However, their sailing room is not unlimited. Almost any rate (and the rule by which it is determined) is always in some danger of violating what average market opinion regards as a fundamental. Even a floating rate amply supported by forward markets can be an invitation to extreme volatility. Volatility can lead to disaster if asset preferences shift markedly away from the home country's liabilities in response to shifting fundamentals or adverse "news."

The fact the conventions can change unexpectedly and rapidly in beauty contests in exchange markets is the key to the trilemma. The crises of the late 1990s were caused in part by questions about the *perceived* policy stances of the governments concerned—why did the "Asian miracle" turn virtually overnight into "crony capitalism"? Underlying trends in the region were not fully favorable during the 1990s, but they did not affect the "miracle" of the conventional wisdom until mid-1997. In Keynes's phrase, "the mass psychology of a large number of ignorant individuals" was difficult to budge, until, that is, it reversed itself completely.

12. A Developing Country Debt Cycle

As a final topic, it is of interest to ask how exchange rates expectations in connection with other forces may influence potentially unstable foreign debt dynamics. The instability in (19) underlying Figure 10.3 is due to the cumulating burden of interest on debt. Coupled with destabilizing dynamics of confidence of the sort discussed in Chapter 9, similar effects have been important in the debt cycles observed in many developing countries in the 1990s. A simple formal model emphasizing short- to medium-term dynamics follows, drawing heavily on ideas proposed by Frenkel (1983) and Neftci (2001). The model also provides an opportunity to impose an alternative, basically post-Keynesian monetary closure on the IS/LM model used before we went off on the monetarist excursions in sections 9 and 10.

We can begin by rewriting the UIP equation in the form

$$i = i^* + (\epsilon/e) + \sigma. \tag{31}$$

It is assumed that there is a "credible" forecast ϵ of expected depreciation, perhaps based on a crawling peg being pursued by the central bank. But even taking that into account, there is an observed "spread" between the home and foreign interest rates, with the former being substantially (as much as 1,000 or 1,500 basis points) higher. In effect, at least some market participants believe that there is a possibility of a large devaluation at some future time, and thereby insist on a return far exceeding $i^* + (\epsilon/e)$ if they are to hold home's securities. The magnitude of the spread is measured by σ, and its dynamics have been crucial in observed crises. Falling well short of the drama of the real world, a simple example is presented below.

The post-Keynesian wrinkle is that (31) can be interpreted as fixing (at least a floor under) the home interest rate on loans. That is, on the right-hand side of (31) the total cost of funds for a firm borrowing abroad to finance a project at home will be foreign rate + expected cost from depreciation + spread. Lending rates at home are unlikely to fall below this sum. But with i being set this way, the home supplies of credit and money will have to be endogenous, as in Chapter 8. We forgo the analytical details here.

Adopting the simplified NFA restriction (23), foreign demand for home bonds can be written as

$$T_f = e\eta^*\Omega^* = e\eta^*(q^*P^*K^* + T^* - N/e) \tag{32}$$

in an immediate extension of (6*).

Since i as determined by (31) will far exceed any plausible rate of capital stock growth, it is simplest to save a symbol by setting $g = I/K = 0$ and concentrating on the dynamics of home's external debt T_f and reserves eR^* (as opposed to their ratios to PK). The coefficient η^* in (32) will be determined in temporary equilibrium by the interest rates, expected rate of depreciation, and the spread, so to see what happens to T_f over time, we can just examine the behavior of the equation $\dot{T}_f = e\eta^*\dot{\Omega}^*$. Substituting through flows-of-funds relationships gives

$$\dot{T}_f = \eta^*[eA^* + (eP^*auK - Pa^*u^*K^*) + iT_f] \tag{33}$$

with

$$A^* = (q^*g^* + \gamma^*)P^*K^*.$$

The term eA^* represents the increase in demand for home's T-bills induced by growth in foreign wealth (with q^* as the foreign country's asset valuation ratio, g^* its capital stock growth rate, and γ^* its primary fiscal deficit as a share of the value of the capital stock P^*K^*). The term $(eP^*auK - Pa^*u^*K^*)$ in (33) is the home trade deficit which must be financed by external borrowing, and the last term iT_f shows that the home country is pursuing Ponzi finance in the sense that it is running up more external debt to meet existing interest obligations.

The change in home's foreign reserves (ignoring its interest receipts ei^*R^* as being trivial) is

$$e\dot{R}^* = \dot{T}_f - (eP^*auK - Pa^*u^*K^*) - iT_f,$$

or flow capital inflows minus the trade deficit and interest payments abroad. Substituting (33) into this expression shows that

$$e\dot{R}^* = e\eta^*A^* - (1 - \eta^*)[(eP^*auK - Pa^*u^*K^*) + iT_f]. \tag{34}$$

So reserves grow faster with "autonomous" capital inflows $e\eta^*A^*$, and otherwise are eroded by the trade deficit and interest payments (with the term $1 - \eta^*$ taking spillovers into growth of foreign wealth into consideration).

Figure 10.5
Cyclical adjustment
of reserves and the
return spread after a
shift in foreign port-
folio preferences
toward Home
bonds.

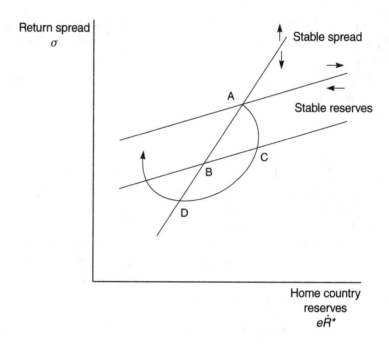

Figure 10.5
Cyclical adjustment of reserves and the return spread after a shift in foreign portfolio preferences toward Home bonds.

As discussed in section 5, reserve increases are likely to lead to expansion of money and credit. Both economic activity u and the trade deficit $(eP^*auK - Pa^*u^*K^*)$ should rise, reducing the growth of reserves: $\partial(e\dot{R}^*)/\partial(eR^*) < 0$. A higher rate spread σ will push up the interest rate i from (31). The cost of external debt service iT_f will increase, but the trade deficit is likely to fall. We assume the latter effect dominates, so $\partial(e\dot{R}^*)/\partial\sigma > 0$. The "Stable reserves" schedule in Figure 10.5 corresponds to the condition $e\dot{R}^* = 0$. Suppose that η^* increases in a foreign portfolio shift toward home bonds. Since in (34) we have $\partial(e\dot{R}^*)/\partial(eR^*) < 0$, eR^* would have to rise to hold $e\dot{R}^* = 0$, that is, the Stable reserves schedule shifts outward.

Turning to the evolution of the spread over time, it is likely that higher reserves reduce anxiety in forward markets, so that $\partial\dot{\sigma}/\partial(eR^*) < 0$. Following the cycle models in Chapter 9, there may be positive feedback of expectational changes into themselves, $\partial\dot{\sigma}/\partial\sigma > 0$, as a fall in the spread induces less perceived risk to holding home securities (and a rise creates greater preoccupations). We get the differential equation

$$\dot{\sigma} = f(eR^*, \sigma), \tag{35}$$

with the partial derivatives just indicated. The "Stable spread" schedule in Figure 10.5 represents the condition $\dot{\sigma} = 0$.

Figure 10.5 shows local dynamics for the system (34)–(35). As in several models in Chapter 9, the dynamic system generates clockwise spirals. By shifting the Stable reserves schedule outward, an increase in η^* moves the steady-state equilibrium from A to B. With the capital inflow, reserves start to increase, in turn making $\dot{\sigma} < 0$. These trends continue until the economy reaches point C, where an increasing trade deficit makes $e\dot{R}^* < 0$. At point D, reserve losses become severe enough to force the return spread to start to rise, pushing up the interest rate as well. In the diagram, a stable or unstable cycle may ensue. In practice in the 1990s, rising rates and currency imbalances in developing country balance sheets (with assets mostly denominated in local currencies and liabilities in foreign) forced σ to jump upward and crises followed. But the cyclical dynamic path that led into the collapses was exactly the one illustrated in the transition from points A through D in Figure 10.5.

13. Fencing in the Beast

Exchange rates are central to the understanding of the international financial system. The problem is that no one can say with certainty how they get determined, or even point out the main channels through which they are affecting the macroeconomy at any time.

This chapter has explored two issues: why exchange rates between different countries' currencies are at the levels at which they are, and how and why the levels are changing. Four central conclusions emerge.

First, exchange rates are determined not by so-called market fundamentals, but rather by investors' expectations and conventions as they interact in cross-border forward markets for exchange rates and other asset prices.

Second, as key components in a financial beauty contest, conventions can change (sometimes very rapidly) in response to shifts in fundamentals, but such changes are historically contingent and impossible to foretell in detail by the vast majority of market players. Indeed, the distinction between conventions and fundamentals is blurred because they play off against each other in the beauty contest.

Third, when conventions do shift, they can feed back on market performance and the fundamentals themselves in highly destabilizing fashion.

Fourth, subject to this essential uncertainty, models of the exchange rate do exist, and suggest certain variables that may play important roles in setting its level under specific circumstances. Unfortunately, often one cannot easily say when a particular model (or a closure thereof) reliably applies.

On the principle that a little knowledge is better than none, it makes sense to carry the analytics in the back of one's head when attempting applied policy analysis. But the models only put broad conceptual bounds on the forces setting the exchange rate and the forces it in turn is exerting on the real and financial sides of the economy. Within the bounds, especially with liberalized capital markets, the details of what is really going on with the exchange rate always have been, and no doubt will continue to be, remarkably unclear.

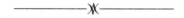

CHAPTER ELEVEN

Growth and Development Theories

Most chapters in this book say something about economic growth, from various angles. The purpose of this one is to pull the threads together against the backdrop of the many theories of growth and economic development that have been proposed over the past couple of hundred years. Somewhat arbitrarily, six theoretical traditions are categorized in summary fashion in sections A–F of Figure 11.1, with additional effects cataloged in section G. "Filiation" (a phrase coined by Schumpeter (1954)) runs roughly horizontally in the different sections, with cross-category linkages pointed out by solid lines. Dashed lines show oppositional reactions of importance. As it turns out, some rows have been described more fully in previous chapters than others, but it is useful to have all of them together in one diagram for purposes of comparison.

The schematic is the background for the three main themes of the chapter. The first is that past thinking about growth and development does encompass diverse lines of thought; many are relevant to the current policy debate. "New" growth theories draw upon just a few of these ideas, and are correspondingly deficient. Second, "new" or "market friendly" development strategies which became popular in the 1980s suffer from the same problem. Their orthodox advocates have an extremely limited perspective. How both mainstream discourses might be widened is the final topic. It can be clarified in part by considering specific issues with regard to the generation and absorption of technical progress, which are mentioned at various points.

1. New Growth Theories and Say's Law

Interest in economic growth on the part of the mainstream renewed itself in the mid-1980s, if only because by that time people were sick and tired of trench warfare between the new classical and new Keynesian camps. The two important early papers on "new" growth theory were by Romer (1986) and Lucas (1988).

Their concerns appeared to be twofold. One was to break away from

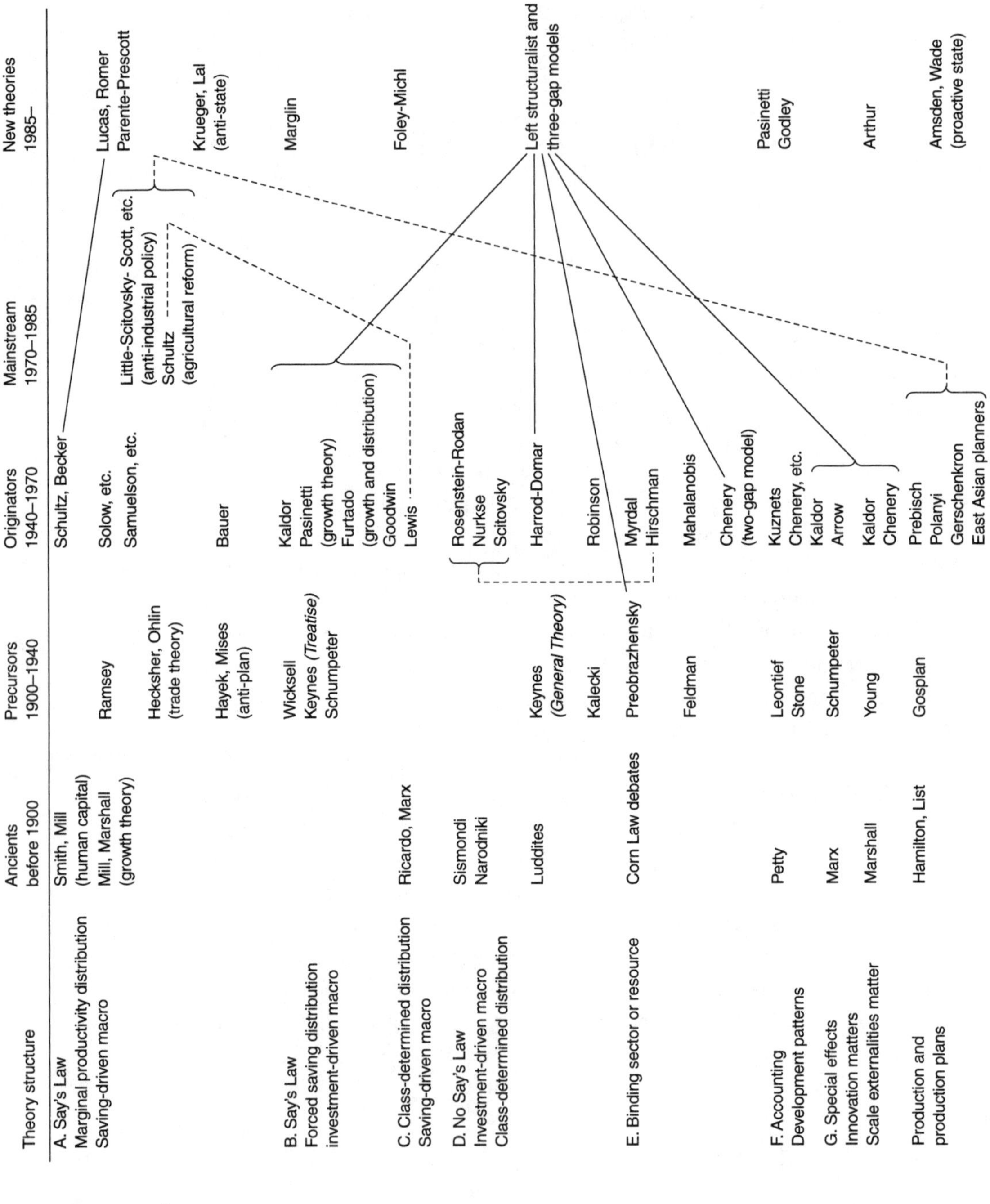

Figure 11.1
Filiations and oppositions in growth and development theory. Solid lines denote filiations, and dashed lines denote oppositions.

Theory structure	Ancients before 1900	Precursors 1900–1940	Originators 1940–1970	Mainstream 1970–1985	New theories 1985–
A. Say's Law / Marginal productivity distribution / Saving-driven macro	Smith, Mill (human capital) / Mill, Marshall (growth theory)	Ramsey / Heckscher, Ohlin (trade theory)	Schultz, Becker / Solow, etc. / Samuelson, etc.	Little-Scitovsky- Scott, etc. (anti-industrial policy) / Schultz (agricultural reform)	Lucas, Romer Parente-Prescott / Krueger, Lal (anti-state)
B. Say's Law / Forced saving distribution / investment-driven macro		Hayek, Mises (anti-plan) / Wicksell, Keynes (*Treatise*), Schumpeter	Bauer		Marglin
C. Class-determined distribution / Saving-driven macro	Ricardo, Marx		Kaldor, Pasinetti (growth theory), Furtado (growth and distribution), Goodwin, Lewis		Foley-Michl
D. No Say's Law / Investment-driven macro / Class-determined distribution	Sismondi, Narodniki / Luddites	Keynes (*General Theory*) / Kalecki / Preobrazhensky	Rosenstein-Rodan, Nurkse, Scitovsky / Harrod-Domar / Robinson / Myrdal, Hirschman		Left structuralist and three-gap models
E. Binding sector or resource	Corn Law debates	Feldman	Mahalanobis / Chenery (two-gap model)		
F. Accounting / Development patterns	Petty	Leontief, Stone	Kuznets, Chenery, etc. / Kaldor, Arrow		Pasinetti, Godley
G. Special effects / Innovation matters / Scale externalities matter	Marx / Marshall	Schumpeter / Young	Kaldor, Chenery		Arthur
Production and production plans	Hamilton, List	Gosplan	Prebisch, Polanyi, Gerschenkron, East Asian planners		Amsden, Wade (proactive state)

Solow's (1956) regime in which output and employment (plus exogenous labor productivity) growth rates are forced to be equal in steady state. Mathematical tricks were used to widen the spectrum of possible output growth rates.

The second goal was to "endogenize" productivity growth by tying it to other variables in the system, ideally through the use of rational actor "microfoundations." One approach was to relate the level of productivity to a stock variable such as physical capital or the human capital built into the (fully employed) labor force. Some sort of externality could be postulated to this end. The other way to endogenize productivity has been to tie its observed increases to realized economies of scale. To carry out this task, tractable formal models of imperfect competition are required. Most were borrowed from the new industrial organization literature, with their verisimilitude subject to doubt.

More recently, there has been a shift in focus toward levels of income as opposed to rates of growth, leading authors such as Parente and Prescott (2000) to invent "intangible capital" as the factor behind the divergence in per capita income between rich and poor countries that was noted in Chapter 5. Perhaps characteristically, Lucas (2000) wants it both ways. Diffusion of knowledge should allow the income distribution across the nations of the world to narrow substantially—by the year 2100 we should all be "equally rich and growing."

All the new theories inhabit Tory Row in section A of Figure 11.1. They postulate Say's Law that all scarce production inputs are fully utilized, and claim that flexible prices in markets dominated by MIRA "agents" vary to permit the economy to arrive at such a state. As charted by Chakravarty (1980), from Mill through Marshall to Solow and beyond, this vision of the economic system has animated orthodox thought. Its way of analyzing productivity growth has already been discussed in Chapters 2 and 5. Despite the fact that TFPG and similar constructs basically boil down to manipulation of accounting identities, they are viewed as engines of great analytical power by the mainstream.

Let n be the rate of population (= labor force) growth and ϵ_L the rate of labor productivity growth. One of the new theory's advertised advances was to get away from Solow's (1956) boring steady state with its exogenous growth rate $n + \epsilon_L$. For example, the output/capital ratio $u = X/K$ was simply set constant in Rebelo's (1991) "AK" model. If I is investment and s the average saving rate, the implication is that

$$\hat{X} = \hat{K} = I/K = su = n + \epsilon_L \tag{1}$$

automatically in a restatement of the "Harrod-Domar equation" used to crank out growth rates in numerous development planning exercises since the 1950s (the quotation marks signal the fact that the equation does not reflect the stability questions raised by both Harrod and Domar).

To satisfy (1), the productivity growth rate ϵ_L becomes an endogenous variable in an AK world, adjusting as a true "residual" (in the traditional growth theory usage of that word) to satisfy the growth accounting balances. The fact that Solow's introduction of capital-labor substitution was originally billed as an improvement over Harrod's and Domar's formulations is usually not mentioned in descriptions of AK models. Affinities between AK machines with several capital goods and von Neumann's (1938) and Sraffa's (1960) formulations are not pointed out either.

A more dramatic break with Solow was to render his growth equation unstable so that output per capita diverges from a steady growth path toward either infinity or zero—a knife-edge with policy implications to be developed later. As in Chapter 2, let ξ_L stand for the level of labor productivity and let $L^* = \xi_L L$ be the "effective" labor force. An effective labor/capital ratio can be defined as $\theta = L^*/K = \xi_L L/K$, and the Solow growth equation (12) from Chapter 5 can be restated as

$$\dot{\theta} = \dot{\theta}[n + \epsilon_L - sf(\theta)] = \theta[n + \epsilon_L - g(\theta)]. \tag{2}$$

The usual hypothesis is that the production function $f(\theta)$ is increasing in θ so that for a given capital stock, output and the capital stock growth rate $g(\theta)$ rise when there is a bigger labor input. Subject to "Inada conditions" on the shape of $f(\theta)$, (2) will be a stable differential equation with a steady state at which the equalities in (1) hold and $\dot{\theta} = 0$. The main requirement is that $f(\theta)$ be concave from below, so that there are decreasing returns to the use of additional labor in an environment of overall constant returns to scale for labor and capital.

In effect, Romer (1986) asserts that externalities generated by investments in R&D can be a source of aggregate *increasing* returns so that the Inada conditions fail to hold. In a typical formal representation, this hypothesis is observationally equivalent to Kaldor's (1957) "technical progress function" $\xi_L = f(K/L)$, introduced in Chapter 5. In growth rate form,

$$\hat{\xi}_L = \epsilon_L = \phi_0 + \phi_1(g - n), \tag{3}$$

so that faster capital stock growth relative to labor speeds the growth of labor productivity.

Equations (2) and (3) can be combined to give

$$\dot{\theta} = \theta[(1 - \phi_1)(n - g) + \phi_0)], \tag{4}$$

so that stability is going to depend on the sign of $1 - \phi_1$. On neoclassical assumptions about model closure (counterclockwise economics, in terms of Figure 5.1), an increase in θ or the effective labor/capital ratio means that total savings su and the growth rate g rise. The $\dot{\theta} = 0$ steady state is stable when $\phi_1 < 1$ in (4), with a capital stock growth rate $g = n + \phi_0/(1 - \phi_1)$ just as in the Kaldorian model presented in Chapter 5.

The Romer case is $\phi_1 > 1$. Now a higher θ still increases g. But from (3), it increases labor productivity growth ϵ_L even more. The outcome is that $d\dot{\theta}/d\theta > 0$—an instability similar to those in the Harrodian models of Chapter 5 and the structuralist Goodwin growth cycle model in Chapter 9. A similar form of "endogenous" growth can be extracted from Kaldor's model. Forty-odd years ago, he just didn't think of a catchy label for the divergent case of his growth equation.

Most new growth theorists, of course, go beyond Solow and Kaldor in treating savings rates not just as fixed coefficients. Rather, they want to follow the Ramsey route mapped in Chapters 3 and 4 by assuming that savings decisions come from infinite horizon exercises in dynamic optimization. New fonts of endogeneity are thereby brought into play.

As in Chapter 3, let $k = K/L$ and assume that there is an aggregate production function $X = F(K, \xi_L L)$. If the technical progress function can be written as $\xi_L = k^\phi$, then with the usual assumption that F is homogeneous of degree one, we have $X/L = f(k, k^\phi)$ in intensive form.

The world is supposed to be populated by small, identical firms that do not perceive the externality implicit in the k^ϕ argument of f. As far as its own plans are concerned, each firm believes that the marginal product of capital is just f_1, the first partial derivative of $f(k, k^\phi)$. On this hypothesis, the Euler equations emerging from a Ramsey model take the form

$$\dot{k} = f(k, k^\phi) - c - nk \tag{5a}$$

and

$$\dot{c} = (c/\eta)(f_1(k, k^\phi) - j), \tag{5b}$$

where c is consumption per capita, $-\eta$ is the elasticity of the marginal utility of consumption (with respect to c), and j is an exogenously given rate of time preference that households are supposed to apply to their choices regarding consumption now and later. Equation (5a) is another version of the growth equation (4), while the optimization exercise replaces a fixed national saving rate with the Ramsey-Keynes dynamic consumption equation (5b).

The Jacobian of this system is

$$
\begin{bmatrix}
f_1 + f_2 \phi k^{\phi-1} & -1 \\
(c/\eta)[f_{11} + f_{12} \phi k^{\phi-1}] & 0
\end{bmatrix}.
$$

Without the externality terms (those with "2" in their subscripts), this matrix would have a positive trace ($f_1 > 0$, capital has a positive marginal product) and a negative determinant ($f_{11} < 0$, capital has decreasing returns). In other words, it would have one positive and one negative eigenvalue and demonstrate "saddlepoint stability" as illustrated in Chapter 3.

Bringing in the externality takes a step further the mainstream's optimal growth gambit of specifying a locally unstable dynamic system and then driving it to a desirable solution via transversality conditions. Typically f_{12} will be positive (a stronger externality raises the marginal product of capital). With a big enough ϕ, therefore, the southwest entry in the Jacobian can become positive and the determinant becomes positive as well. The Jacobian has two positive eigenvalues and the dynamic system (5a, 5b) has an unstable node about the steady growth path $\dot{k} = \dot{c} = 0$.

Barro and Sala-i-Martin (1995), among others, inscribe the incantations about transversality conditions that will bring this locally completely unstable dynamic system to a steady growth path with $\hat{c} = \hat{k}$ so that consumption and capital per head grow at the same rate (determined by the larger of the two positive eigenvalues). Output and consumption per unit of capital stay constant, on the assumption that f_1 tends toward a constant level as k goes to infinity. Restating (5a) and (5b) in growth rate form and equating $\hat{c}$ and $\hat{k}$ shows that saving per unit of capital becomes $su = u - (c/k) = n + (1/\eta)(f_1 - j)$. From (5b), for positive growth of c we need $f_1 > j$, or the marginal product of capital as perceived by firms must exceed the private rate of discount.[1] In terms of the traditional accounting of equation (1), the rate of labor productivity growth ϵ_L will equal $(1/\eta)(f_1 - j)$—perhaps a lucid explanation for a variable which has always proved difficult to understand.

How can these convenient outcomes be arranged? One device is the AK model already mentioned. So long as the average (= marginal) product of capital A exceeds j, endogenous growth is assured. Slightly more generally, Jones and Manuelli (1990) in effect postulate that the production function $f(k)$ has a range strictly bounded from below. A constant elasticity of substitution (CES) production function will do the trick as long as the elasticity exceeds one. Econometric estimates of CES functions usually reject this hypothesis (even though it is also a convenient neoclassical explanation for a positive relationship between productivity growth and the profit share, a possibility noted in Chapter 9).

Whether these endogenous growth formulations—with either fixed savings rates or dynamically optimizing consumers—are credible empirically is a relevant question. For example, equation (5b) of the optimal growth variant suggests that consumption and saving decisions will be sensitive to differences between the private return (f_1) and cost (j) of capital. Strong sensitivity of this sort has been hard to demonstrate in practice for both saving and investment choices. Moreover, in the data profit rates and/or marginal products of capital (insofar as they can be measured) and interest rates do not vary over wide ranges. It is not obvious that basing big national differences in estimated rates of productivity growth (ϵ_L) on such foundations is a fruitful endeavor.

These observations can be sharpened. For one, both optimizing and fixed saving coefficient endogenous growth models demonstrate knife-edge dynamics—$\hat{c}$ can equal $\hat{k}$ for both positive and negative rates of growth as both variables diverge from the zero (per capita) growth path. In the optimizing models, does it make sense to say that knife-edges result from observed cross-country differences in savings parameters and rates of return? In fixed-rate formulations, can they come from small deviations above and below unity on the part of a parameter like ϕ_1 in equation (4)? Asserting that large differences across national economies in growth performance depend on such factors sidesteps a mass of historical experience, some of it discussed below.

Second, as illustrated in Chapter 5, knife-edges have long been postulated in growth theory from the side of investment demand, which cannot figure in neoclassical models based on Say's Law. And third, unstable growth dynamics can arise from many other sources. Some fifty years ago, Leibenstein (1954) and Nelson (1956) pointed out that high labor/capital ratios accompanied by Malthusian population dynamics and an absence of externalities can lead to poverty traps. Following many Latin American authors, Taylor and Bacha (1976) argued in an investment-driven model that the growth rate may rest on a knife-edge determined by distributive conflicts and tastes for different sorts of commodities by different social classes—a poverty trap or unequalizing growth led by luxurious consumption can result.

If we turn to microfoundations, we find that two sorts of behavioral rationales have been proposed for endogenous productivity growth. One is externalities, via which a productivity level like ξ_L can be tied to a stock or state variable in a growth model. As already observed, such specifications long predate Romer (1986). Besides Kaldor (1957), a widely cited precursor is Arrow (1962), who tied ξ_L to "learning by doing," as proxied by accumulated output over the years.[2] To fit such phenomena into optimal growth models, however, a dilemma that plagued Marshall has to be resolved.

One horn is the desire of neoclassical economists to retain marginal productivity distribution theory under conditions of perfect competition. To carry out that project, they have to assume that economic agents behave as if there are nonincreasing (preferably constant) returns to the scale for all inputs. Otherwise, second-order conditions for dynamic optimization cannot be satisfied and marginal productivity distribution rules make no sense. As Schumpeter (1947) pointed out long ago, such niceties are irrelevant to real capitalist practice in which firms are disciplined not by anonymous prices but rather by "creative destruction" caused by the "unending gale" of technical change. For better or worse, this disequilibrium, dialectical process is alien to the concerns of mainstream economics.

The dilemma's other horn is that positive externalities give rise to increasing returns. For example, in his well-known new growth model,[3] Lucas (1988) postulates an aggregate production function of the form

$$X = K^{\beta}[(1 - \tau)H]^{1-\beta}(H^*)^{\gamma}, \tag{6}$$

where H is the total stock of human capital and τ is the share of their time that agents devote to acquiring new H (ambitious beings, they are fully employed in commodity production the rest of the time). "Normal" production takes place according to constant returns of scale for work effort $(1 - \tau)H$ and physical capital K, but via the externality factor (H^*), more human capital raises the overall productivity level. The asterisk in the H^* term is a reminder that human capital is subject to personal decisions but also boosts overall productivity.

The agents make their saving and time allocations by maximizing the discounted utility of consumption subject to (6) and accumulation equations over infinite time. Like Romer's small, identical firms discussed previously, they cannot recognize the externality due to H^*, else their calculations fall apart for the reasons just noted.

Solving infinite horizon optimal growth problems with unrecognized externalities has been billed as a mathematical step forward, a claim which would make a real applied mathematician smile. More disconcerting should be the smiles that externalities as transcendent as human capital (or the fruits of R&D) ought to provoke from severe neoclassical economists, including members of the Austrian school. If extra learning generates more output, Austrians will argue along lines sketched in

Chapter 2 that sooner or later somebody should start making money from that fact (say, by providing education more effectively than the state). Were such internalization of the benefits of a higher H^* to occur, Lucas's rationale for the importance of human capital accumulation ceases to make sense.

At least one ambitious piece of data analysis points to an absence of externalities. In a multi-decade project, Jorgenson (1990) has tried to grade components of the United States labor and capital stocks in detail by their "quality" in a sources-of-growth accounting framework; the owners of these inputs have full claim to their returns. For the United States, at least, his results consistently show a minor contribution of the residual (or "technical progress") to growth. In other words, the mathematical contortions required to fit the externality in (6) into an optimal growth framework may not be worth the effort—on strictly neoclassical empirical grounds.

On a more commonsense level, it is also clear that models based on accumulated learning, human capital accumulation, or technological externalities *over*-predict observed productivity growth, at least for high-income countries. Quite clearly, levels of schooling and accumulated research have increased dramatically in the West and Japan over the decades, yet growth rates of per capita income have at best remained the same. It may be that externalities are necessary conditions for sustaining growth but they are not sufficient to accelerate it.

A final comment on the Lucas model is that it bases its growth dynamics on human capital as a produced means of production. The rate of growth is ultimately determined by how much human capital is reinvested to produce more human capital. This causal scheme is the same as that of two important families of development planning models—Feldman-Mahalanobis-Domar (or FMD) two-sector specifications focusing on the allocation of scarce capital goods between production of consumer and more capital goods ("machines to make machines") and "gap" models concentrating on internal, external, and fiscal balance restrictions on capital formation ("foreign exchange to make foreign exchange"). Whether human capital, physical capital goods, or foreign exchange is best treated as "the" binding restriction on growth in a developing economy is a question taken up later.

As noted above, an alternative approach to explaining productivity growth is to drop perfect competition to bring in decreasing average production costs. For example, Romer (1987) "spreads" costs of intermediate inputs across a greater production volume of final goods as in the model set out in section 5 of Chapter 2. Subject to strong behavioral assumptions, he shows that if the intermediates are produced with constant marginal costs, then there will be an aggregate production function for final goods in which the capital tied up in intermediates shows up as an externality like H^* in (6).

It is no doubt true that scale economies as emphasized by authors such as Sraffa (1926), Young (1928), and Kaldor (1972) can underlie "cumulative processes" which upset the balanced, mutual, and self-adjusting growth equilibria characteristic of Walrasian theory. Firms which initially exploit decreasing costs can gain a commanding position, or else unstable price and investment cycles can arise (as noted below, Japanese and Korean planners, in their push for scale economies in production, avoided such problems by hands-on market interventions to preclude what they called "excessive competition"). Under such circumstances, there is no reason for exit and entry of firms to drive "pure" profits to zero.

Indeed, as development economists such as Hirschman (1958) emphasized and Chenery (1959) formalized, relative product prices can shift over wide ranges depending on which production processes with increasing returns are present or absent in the economy (think of the decision whether to import, produce for the domestic market, or produce for export some tradable good, or the impact of decreasing costs on the price of a usually nontraded good such as electricity). Cost-based prices arising from one configuration involving the presence or absence of members of a set of possible decreasing-cost production processes are not an adequate guide for investment project decisions to create another configuration with a markedly different price vector.

The problem is that the new growth models leave out the dynamic, cumulative effects of decreasing costs coupled with backward and forward production linkages which underlie these changes, which were fully recognized by Hirschman, Chenery, and a host of other early development economists. Hirschman's *Strategy of Economic Development* is a far better guide to these connections than exercises in optimal growth with the behavioral unrealism that they impose—just to smooth out the imbalances that Hirschman thought were at the heart of the development matter.

Two more mainstream models can be mentioned before we leave Row A of Figure 11.1. One is set out by Parente and Prescott (2000). They are concerned with the observation (made here in Chapter 5) that in terms of standard growth accounting an enormous differential in capital stock per capita would be needed to generate observed per capita income differentials between rich and poor countries, basically because the nonwage share of output is low. Their solution is to raise both the nonwage share and the stock of capital by counting part of wage payments as investment in "intangible capital" in the form of maintenance and repair, R&D effort, skill training, advertising, and so on. Rigging the numbers to get the "capital share" up to around two-thirds nicely circumvents the problems mentioned in connection with equation (14) in Chapter 5. Whether the exercise makes us any wiser is left for the reader to decide.

Lucas (2000) is more dynamic in generalizing the Japanese productivity catch-up illustrated in Figure 2.1 to all the world. Successive waves of poor countries are supposed to enter into ever more rapid growth as the twenty-first century unfolds, so that everybody is more or less at the same income level by the year 2100. The mechanisms behind the implied succession of increasingly miraculous development spurts are not made clear.

2. Distribution and Growth

Other growth theories can be situated in opposition to the mainstream—not because they are less relevant to serious questions, but because orthodoxy provides a well-known standard of reference. Quite a bit of effort has been devoted in previous chapters to spelling out alternatives appearing in sections B through D of Figure 11.1.

In section B, for example, we already know a lot about the post-Wicksellians (Chapter 3), Schumpeter and Pasinetti (Chapter 2), and Kaldor (Chapter 5). In the development literature, the Schumpeter-Kaldor causal scheme has been extended to several sectors, such as by Latin American structuralists like Furtado (1972). If industrialization beyond production of simple goods like food and textiles is to occur, they said, then under present social conditions greater income concentration is necessary to sustain demand for more sophisticated commodities, since their production is likely to be subject to minimum cost-effective size requirements due to economies of scale. The Taylor-Bacha (1976) knife-edge mentioned above comes from increasing income concentration through a variant of forced saving. It provides macroeconomic adjustment in response to (and feeds back into) rising investment in a luxury goods sector catering to rich people's demands.

Section C of the figure refers to a line of growth theories which take income distribution as determined by institutional factors prior to the economic system. This idea of course traces back to the Classics, and found vibrant form at the hands of Marx.

To summarize Marx's views on growth (or anything else, for that matter) in a way acceptable to all readers is impossible. All we can do here is set out a number of points that he raised, which can be inserted into simple, formal models (Chapters 2 and 5) that fall well short of capturing the complexity and internal contradictions of his perceptions of growth under capitalism and other modes of production.

Indeed, the first thing to note is that Marx emphasized that economies change in irreversible historical time in an overall institutional framework such as "capitalism," "feudalism," or "oriental despotism." Any such mode of production can be characterized by specific social devices for appropriation of surplus product over necessary consumption. This classical insistence on the primacy of processes determining the income distribution is adopted by many nonmainstream authors.

For the most part, Marx concentrated on the capitalist mode, in which growth results from both accumulation and endogenous technical change. Producers adopt new methods to edge out competitors or because rising labor power can wipe out surplus value, thereby wiping out laggard capitalists as well. Schumpeter gave a specific form to such processes when he wrote about innovation-induced "creative destruction" of obsolete technologies and firms.

Competition among capitalists tends to equalize profit rates across sectors. However, sectoral demand and supply levels may not mesh, giving rise to a "disproportionality crisis." Similarly, aggregate demand may not equal supply. Money provides a vehicle for hoarding purchasing power, which can lead to a "realization crisis," or slump.

Both kinds of crises interact in a cyclical theory of growth, well described by Sylos-Labini (1984). At the bottom of a cycle, the real wage is held down by a large "reserve army" of unemployed workers, and capitalists can accumulate freely. As output expands, however, the reserve army is depleted and the real wage may rise. Capitalists search for new labor-saving technologies and also invest to build up the stock of capital and reduce employment via input substitution. Excessive funds tied up in machinery, sectoral imbalances, and lack of purchasing power on the part of capitalists to sustain investment (or of workers to absorb the output that new investment produces) can all underlie a cyclical collapse. The cycle models in Chapter 9 draw upon but do not fully capture this drama.

Although he cited Ricardo and ignored Marx, Lewis (1954) translated this story of cyclical upswing into a long-run theory of economic growth, with "surplus labor" replacing the reserve army. This view from section C of the figure provoked a strong reaction from the neoclassical line A, as discussed later. More recent, explicitly Marxist authors stress the fall in investment that may occur in response to a profit squeeze as labor gains in bargaining power over a sequence of cycles. This view shows up in the demand-driven aggregate growth models located in section D and developed at length in previous chapters. They provide an alternative to mainstream stories as well as to Marx and Lewis, who largely stick with saving-determined capital formation.

Related models in section D have been developed on a multisectoral basis, with steady states defined by stable income distributions and all sectors expanding at the same rate. Such a framework for redistribution lies behind reform proposals that have appeared over the years. The French-Swiss reformer Sismondi (1815) recommended progressive redistribution in the wake of the Napoleonic Wars to stimulate French industrialization—more prosperous workers would demand clothing and textiles and propel investment in those sectors. Similar themes appeared in the writings of last century's Narodniki, or Populists, in Russia and are debated in India today.

As with Furtado's work mentioned above, the key idea here is that demand and distributional changes can stimulate cumulative processes à la Myrdal (1957) and Kaldor (1972) to alter the nature of supply. Many authors have pointed out that redistribution and/or public investment projects may raise demand enough to make profitable production processes with fixed overheads that have constant marginal but decreasing average costs. Activating economies of scale in this fashion can have profound economy-wide effects of the sort invoked by Young (1928) and his student Rosenstein-Rodan (1961) with his "Big Push."

New growth theorists such as Murphy, Shleifer, and Vishny (1989) came late in picking up such possibilities, which were commonly accepted by the post–World War II generation of development economists. Unhindered by Say's Law, they shared a set of ideas which fit well with the growth theories of sections B through E, and included the following.

Schumpeter's views about the disequilibrium nature of the development process are valid, and provide an underlying framework which can be applied widely.

One can postulate conditions under which development will be increasingly rapid, capital-intensive, and reliant upon a greater role of the state. In nineteenth-century Europe, for example, greater relative "backwardness" called forth more dramatic transitions (Gerschenkron 1962).

Economies of scale are important. As already noted, coordinated investment across many sectors in a Big Push may be required to give balanced output and demand expansion to take advantage of decreasing average costs economy-wide. Building upon Schumpeter's metaphor, the idea was to get the economy from a "vicious" to a "virtuous" circle of growth.

The investment must be planned, since pervasive market failures such as decreasing costs and imperfect tradeability mean that price-driven, decentralized investment decisions will not be socially optimal.

Analytical tools such as input-output models and social cost-benefit analysis can make public investment planning possible (Chenery 1959).

On the other hand, planning tools are at best approximations, so that one should be on the lookout for inflationary, balance of payments, and other bottlenecks, and figure out how to break them in a process of perpetually unbalanced expansion (Hirschman 1958).

The distinction between Hirschman's dialectical worldview and Rosenstein-Rodan's "balanced growth" ideas was sharp. But to anticipate later discussion, neither Hirschman nor Rodan disappeared from the mainstream's view because his work was insufficiently formalized, contrary to what Krugman (1993) asserts. Indeed, the mathematics of Chenery's (1959) and contemporaries' planning models with economies of scale was more sophisticated than the apparatus Krugman habitually works with. The difference is that Chenery and friends used integer or dynamic programming methods to solve centralized or firm-level planning problems while Krugman (with the new growth theorists) uses devices such as the Dixit-Stiglitz (1977) formulation of consumer demand to convexify a putative general equilibrium in which firms have fixed costs. Once again, the interesting questions of multiple equilibrium posed by nonconvexities are simply ignored.

Contrary to Krugman's arguments, the old development literature lost impact because it had two ideological drawbacks. One was that while it was rich with diagnoses of development problems, it provided little concrete policy advice. Circular flow, cumulative processes, relative backwardness, balanced and unbalanced growth, and so on were intriguing metaphors but didn't help much with practical decisions. Planning models and cost-benefit analysis proved to be more of academic interest than managerial worth. Later neoclassical approaches claimed (falsely) to be more practical. The second problem is that the early development economists placed limitless faith in the capacity of the state to intervene in the economic system. Its inability to carry out its assigned development role(s) became apparent, almost equally fast. This defect had already been emphasized by first von Mises (1935) and then von Hayek (1935) in the "calculation debate" about socialist planning discussed in Chapter 6. Their teachings were reanimated by Bauer (1972) in the developing country context; the neoliberal resurgence of the 1980s brought them to worldwide prominence.

Realistically or not, neoclassical economics at most requires that the state should be a "night watchman." The early development economists needed the state to be proactive and effective, but provided no reasons why it could or should fulfill its tasks. This omission was soon seized upon by neoclassical economists, who forged a new "market-friendly" consensus about how to further development and growth, a topic to be addressed below.

3. Models with Binding Resource or Sectoral Supply Constraints

In models which don't postulate Say's Law, specific supply limits can still provoke distributional changes like those underlying forced saving. Examples include shortages of crucial inputs like capital goods or foreign exchange, or else interactions between sectors adjusting to excess demand respectively via changes in output and a flexible price. Growth models along these lines have been elaborated by economists in Figure 11.1's section E. Those emphasizing limiting factors such as foreign exchange or capital goods make an interesting contrast with new growth theory models such as Lucas's (1988) described in section 1.

The ever-present danger of "external strangulation" in developing economies is an old theme in structuralist thought, dating to the work of the Economic Commission for Latin America in Santiago in the 1950s at least. The notion was formalized by Chenery and Bruno (1962) in their two-gap model incorporating separate foreign exchange and saving restrictions on growth.

The saving constraint follows naturally from Harrod-Domar or "AK" algebra: investment has to be financed by either national saving or capital inflows from abroad. But the inflows also cover the trade deficit. Industrialization via import substitution (the only way to build up local production capacity that has been discovered so far) means that the economy becomes dependent on imports of intermediate goods—without them, local factories cannot work. At the same time, import substitution rarely extends to capital goods, so that up to half of investment spending takes the form of purchases from abroad. There is a sharp trade-off between current production and capital formation, which only additional foreign exchange can relieve. If domestic output is limited by scarcity of convertible dollars or yen, inflationary forced saving macroeconomic adjustment often occurs. As a consequence, during the 1980s real wages fell on the order of 50 percent in many economies externally strangled by the debt crisis.

The saving and foreign gaps have been extended in recent work (reviewed by Taylor 1994) to take into account two important fiscal effects. First, after the debt crisis, many governments nationalized foreign obligations—the state was liable for external payments on debt. Second, econometric work in the 1980s typically showed that there is a strong "crowding-in" effect of public on private capital formation (contrary to the crowding-out of private by public spending through rising interest rates in financial markets that is frequently presumed). The consequence is a "fiscal gap" limiting growth because public (and therefore total) capital formation is cut back. Attempts to relieve fiscal burdens by relying on forced saving or the inflation tax became ever more frequent in the 1980s. The multiple, interacting problems posed by saving, foreign exchange, fiscal, and inflation gaps are a source of much current policy concern. They are not adequately addressed by growth models in the mainstream tradition, which typically assume that sufficient relative price flexibility will make such woes go away.

Besides foreign exchange, a shortage of physical capital can be an impediment to growth. This point was raised forcefully by the economist G. A. Feldman during the intense—and for many of its participants fatal—debate about industrialization in the Soviet Union in the 1920s. His contribution was brought to Western attention by Domar (1957), at about the same time as Mahalanobis (1953) applied a similar diagnosis to India.

The FMD model assumes that capital is essential to support production of both new capital goods and consumer goods. Diverting machines to make more machines means that present-day consumers will suffer; on the other hand, the long-run growth rate will be faster, the greater is the reinvestment rate. Blessed with a long (infinite?) horizon, an optimizing planner would therefore concentrate efforts on machine building at the start of his or her tenure, to build up a base for consumption in the future. In the USSR of the 1930s it is possible that the *vozhd* (one possible translation is "owner") thought along such lines.

By similar logic, a planner in an economy constrained by foreign exchange would concentrate initial efforts on building up export capacity. If human capital is the key to economic success, then everybody should be educated as intensively as possible (subject to the teacher constraint) during the initial phases of growth. Country histories can be analyzed in terms of all three models—thanks to external assistance and early export success, South Korea never faced a tight external constraint, but its planners did consciously build up both human and physical capital early on—suggesting that single-factor explanations of growth are not likely to bear much fruit.

Like most new growth theorists, Lucas (1988) focuses on steady states, thus ignoring planning issues of the sort just discussed. Moreover, much new theory falls into the single factor trap. Human capital is frequently asserted to be the fundamental growth factor, and it is certainly true that there is a cross-country correlation between education levels and the level (but not the rate of growth) of per capita income. Country histories, however, belie any tight causal link. The Philippines has a well-educated population, but is the laggard in East Asian growth. Well-educated Sri Lanka grew slowly before external assistance eased the foreign exchange constraint in the late 1970s; poorly educated Brazil grew very fast until the debt crisis struck.

If we turn to section E models with two broad commodities domestically supplied, we find that a frequently used specification is based upon one sector where supply is limited by available capacity and the price adjusts to clear the market, plus a second sector in which production meets demand.[4] This two-sector setup blends forced saving, Engel demand effects, and output adjustment in an illuminating fashion. It can be applied in various contexts, for example, to analyze the agricultural terms of trade, to discuss "Dutch disease" problems when a traded goods sector has its price fixed from the world market and a nontraded sector has an adjusting price, and to do global macroeconomics between a "North" exporting industrial goods and a "South" selling primary products. The nature of the model can be illustrated with the food price interpretation here.

Models focusing on the relative price of food (or agriculture's terms of trade) date at least from the controversy between Ricardo and Malthus about whether England's Corn Laws limiting grain imports should or should not be repealed. To address this question, we assume that "industry" has prices fixed by a markup over prime costs and its output is determined by demand, while "agriculture" has fixed supply and a market-clearing price in the short run.

To see how the model works, we can ask how the two markets interact. Suppose that the terms of trade shift toward agriculture, say due to a reduction of food imports. Industrial output can either rise or fall. It will be pushed up by increased demand from higher agricultural income, but also held down by reduced real nonagricultural spending power (real wages drop because of forced saving from dearer food). The latter effect will be stronger insofar as Engel's Law makes food demand income-inelastic, so that the loss in workers' spending power primarily forces down their demand for industrial goods. Under such circumstances, letting more imports into the economy will doubly benefit the industrial sector—food prices fall and output expands. Although Ricardo used a different model to argue his case, this outcome is consistent with his advocacy of repeal of the Corn Laws.

The alternative view was espoused by Malthus in his *Principles of Political Economy,* where the argument can be interpreted in terms of distributional effects on aggregate demand. Agriculture is responsible for a big proportion of income and consumer spending. Farmers (or landlords for Malthus) hit by adverse terms of trade will cut their purchases, reducing economic activity overall. Whether a Ricardian or Malthusian distributional configuration applies in developing countries today is highly relevant for policy—the answer according to applied computable general equilibrium models seems to go either way.

Besides import policy, other state interventions can affect the terms of trade. Fiscal expansion or increased investment, for example, will bid up the flexible price to generate forced saving to help meet the increased injection of demand. Ellman (1975) argues that food price–induced forced saving supported the Soviet industrialization push of the 1930s, in contrast to Preobrazhensky's (1965) suggestion that the terms of trade be shifted *against* agriculture by a monopsonistic state to extract an investable surplus.

Fix-price/flex-price models (a terminology due to Hicks (1965), one of the many co-inventers of such specifications) can also be used to describe growth. Determination of the growth rate depends crucially on how causality in the macroeconomic system runs. If saving-investment balance in the North, for example, regulates expansion of the world economy, then the primary export terms of trade and capital formation in the South will tag along as adjusting variables. Contrariwise, slow growth in a dominant fixed-supply sector can determine behavior of the whole system. How the agrarian question may (or may not) be resolved is an obvious application not taken up by recent mainstream theories.

A final observation about section E is that ideas like Myrdal's cumulative processes and Hirschman's succession of bottlenecks fit well into a category of models based upon binding sectoral performances and constraints. Whether they can be formalized tractably is another question. The fact that the answer is often in the negative does not detract from the usefulness of disequilibrium or dialectical approaches to thinking about the world.

4. Accounting for Growth

Section F appears in Figure 11.1 to emphasize that accounting schemes and contemplation of how the entries within them change over time can provide insight into the development process. The discovery that it makes sense to peruse the numbers was made centuries before running endless regressions of GDP growth rates on a host of right-hand side variables (re)appeared as a recent fad. As observed in previous chapters, it dates back three hundred years to the "political arithmetick" of

William Petty and contemporaries, who for example recognized that the GDP share of agriculture declines as per capita income goes up—a consequence of now predictable technological trends and Engel's Law. Kuznets and Chenery were able discoverers of similar regularities, whose findings are well summarized by Syrquin (1988).

The other theme that should be mentioned in connection with section F is that manipulation of accounting schemes themselves can provide useful insights. As sketched in Chapter 2, Pasinetti (1981) closes the macro accounts (with a lot of emphasis on the input-output system in his own presentations) by assuming that operating surpluses of firms at the sectoral level just finance their investment demands. Under full employment, he shows that if one aggregates gross outputs over sectors using direct-and-indirect labor inputs taking into account investment requirements as weights, a material balance of the form $\sum h_i c_i = 1$ emerges, where the h_i are "hyper-integrated" labor inputs (in Pasinetti's usage) and the c_i stand for public and private sectoral consumption levels per worker. The question is whether full employment can in fact be assured?

Pasinetti first observes that the h_i coefficients decrease when there is labor productivity growth. Second, although per capita demand for a given commodity or service may rise for a time, ultimately it tends to slow or even decline. For example, in the United States in the 1920s and Europe after World War II, surging consumption of automobiles and associated products supported employment growth, even though productivity was going up. But by now, cars are no longer income-elastic items and their c_i coefficient is stable or going down while their h_i also continues to fall.

Both trends can stifle employment expansion—the material balance condition can fail to be satisfied because of either a realization or a disproportionality problem. Even if enough work is available in principle, disproportional demand and productivity trends across sectors may require substantial labor force reallocations if full employment is to be maintained. Such movements are never socially simple; most countries rely on public action to make them as painless as possible.

Similarly, if the employment realization—or stagnation—problem is severe, it can be offset in several ways, but each entails its own complications. One familiar mechanism is capitalism's continual introduction of new goods which people feel impelled to buy. Whether or not entrepreneurs can continue to deluge us with novel temptations with rapidly growing c_i coefficients is always an open question. Second, real wages can rise to offset lower h_i coefficients. But as shown in Chapter 5, Luddite barriers when the economy is wage-led can impede this process. Finally, policymakers can attempt demand stimulation; in a profit-led economy such an effort can easily break down. Contrary to the facile optimism underlying the models of Figure 11.1's section A, there is no automatic mechanism which makes the $h_i c_i$ terms for currently functioning sectors add up to one.

Set up in slightly different form without the input-output complications, Pasinetti-style accounting can also be applied to developing countries (Taylor 2000). In light of the widespread external liberalization that took place in the 1980s and 1990s, looking at a two-sector breakdown between traded and nontraded goods gives useful findings. A fairly consistent pattern has been an acceleration of productivity growth in traded goods following liberalization, but low or negative employment growth in the sector which can be traced to real appreciation and a shift in demand toward nontraded goods. Employment in nontradeds went up or down according to the relative strengths of higher demand and (typically) slow or negative productivity growth.

To see the details, we can begin with a productivity decomposition. Suppose that one has data on employment and output for several sectors over time. Let $\chi_i = X_i/X$ be the share of sector i in real output, with $\sum_i X_i = X$. Similarly for employment: $\lambda_i = L_i/L$ with $\sum_i L_i = L$. The level of labor productivity in sector i is X_i/L_i with a growth rate $\epsilon_i = \hat{X}_i - \hat{L}_i$.

After a bit of manipulation, an expression for the growth rate ϵ_L of economy-wide labor productivity emerges as

$$\epsilon_L = \sum_i [\chi_i \epsilon_i + (\chi_i - \lambda_i)\hat{L}_i]. \tag{7}$$

Overall productivity growth decomposes into two parts. One is a weighted average $\sum_i \chi_i \epsilon_i$ of sectoral rates of productivity growth. The weights are the output shares χ_i. The other term, $\sum_i (\chi_i - \lambda_i)\hat{L}_i$, captures "reallocation effects" (Syrquin 1986). A sector with relatively high labor productivity will have a higher share of output than of the labor force, $\chi_i > \lambda_i$, so that if its employment growth is positive, $\hat{L}_i > 0$, reallocation of labor toward the sector generates a positive contribution to productivity growth economy-wide.

Decomposition (7) has been applied in a number of transition and developing economies for the period after 1980. Without going into the details, two generalizations emerge.

First, if one disaggregates into traded and nontraded goods, the productivity growth rate in the former is higher, and tended to speed up after many countries liberalized in the 1990s. Insofar as nontraded sectors acted as labor sinks, their productivity growth rates declined.

Second, with some exceptions, reallocation effects on productivity tended to be small, upsetting at least some traditional development economics dogmas.

Given these findings on productivity, it is tempting to look at growth rates of employment, which after all are driven by changes in productivity and demand. Very broadly following Pasinetti, one can put together a two-step employment decomposition over time in terms of these two driving forces.

Let P stand for the population, E the economically active population, L the total of people employed, and U the total unemployed or $U = E - L$. The participation rate is $\eta = E/P$ and the unemployment rate is $v = U/E$. The overall employment rate is $L/E = 1 - v = \phi/\eta$, with $\phi = L/P$ as the employed share of the population. Evidently we have $E = L + U$. Dividing by P lets this expression be rewritten as $\eta = \phi + \eta v$. Taking growth rates and a bit of algebra show that

$$0 = (1 - v)(\hat{\phi} - \hat{\eta}) + v\hat{v} = -(1 - v)\hat{\eta} + v\hat{v} + (1 - v)\hat{\phi}. \tag{8}$$

The terms after the first equals sign state that changes in the rates of employment and unemployment must sum to zero. The formula furthest to the right decomposes this condition in terms of the participation rate η, the unemployment rate v, and the employed share of the population ϕ.

In a second step, ϕ provides a useful tool to analyze job growth across sectors. Along with the ratios defined above, let $x_i = X_i/P$ or sectoral output per capita. The labor/output ratio in sector i can be written as $b_i = L_i/X_i$, and let $\phi_i = L_i/P$. Then we have

$$\phi = \sum (L_i/X_i)(X_i/P) = \sum b_i x_i.$$

Transforming to growth rates gives

$$\hat{\phi} = \sum \phi_i(\hat{x}_i + \hat{b}_i) = \sum \phi_i(\hat{x}_i - \epsilon_i), \tag{9}$$

so that the growth rate of the overall employment ratio is determined as a weighted sum across sectors of differences between growth rates of output levels per capita and labor productivity (the weights ϕ_i don't add up to one because they are ratios of each sector's employment to total population).

Combined with (8), equation (9) provides a framework in which sources of job creation can usefully be explored. In expanding sectors (relative to population growth), productivity increases do not necessarily translate into reduced employment; in slow-growing or shrinking sectors, higher productivity means that employment declines. Under liberalization in many developing countries, the interaction of nontraded and traded sectors can be traced in this fashion, along with the behavior of sectors acting as "sources" or "sinks" for labor (agriculture has played both roles recently, in different countries). The most common outcome is that productivity growth has exceeded output growth in traded goods sectors, to the detriment of the creation of high-end jobs.

5. Other Perspectives

The authors cited in section G of Table 11.1 address the forces supporting East Asia's economic success as well as the scale economy and technical innovation mechanisms already discussed. These feed indirectly into endogenous growth theory, and with more salience appear in Arthur's (1989) observations about the likely irreversibility of sensibly modeled processes of technological advance (especially when there are production nonconvexities). Harking back to the balanced/unbalanced growth debate, his results suggest that the unbalanced team was closer to getting the story right.

A related and distinctly nonmainstream view about the importance of "productive forces" traces back to Hamilton and List, who recommended protectionism as a basis for industrial development.[5] Along parallel lines, Polanyi (1944) argued that the state played an essential role in building up the institutions that supported nineteenth-century growth.

From the orthodox point of view, such notions sound heretical, but they certainly encouraged people like Prebisch (1959) in their advocacy of import-substituting industrialization, or ISI. List's *National System of Political Economy* was more widely read than Anglo-Saxon economists in Japan in the 1930s, and his ideas underpin the East Asian "model" which emerged at that time. Studies of South Korea and Taiwan by Amsden (1989) and Wade (1990) respectively describe the model's features. Amsden (2001) extends the story to other industrializing economies around the world. Because East Asia raises issues which any realistic growth or development theory should address, it is worthwhile to summarize the basic points.

A theme continually developed in South Korea's official documents was that "the market mechanism cannot be entirely trusted to increase competitive advantage by industries," so that branches likely to enjoy high productivity growth and/or income-elastic demand were to be promoted as "promising strategic industries" (Chang 1993). They were given custom-designed financial, technical, and administrative support. Picking winners turned out to be an operational concept in an economy like South Korea's (and, earlier, Japan's) which was not operating on world technological frontiers. In "catching-up" situations, it is fairly easy to choose which sectors to favor and what kinds of support they need for success.

Corrective feedback to the selection process was provided by ongoing, broad reporting of activities of "priority" firms to the government. The economic bureaucracy thus had access to detailed business information, which proved essential for effective industrial policy. "Creative destruction" was ensured by the government's use of its business information to weed out inefficient production operations in successive waves of rationalizations, mergers, and liquidations. Individual *chaebols* were clearly subject to discipline, even though as a group they had privileged access to state resources. Noise and static in dealings between the state and producers were reduced by the fact that apex organizations were engaged on both sides of the dialogue.

In line with this strategy, intense effort was devoted to acquiring technology (the huge public investment in education was economically mobilized exactly in this fashion). For this reason, direct foreign investment was strictly regulated while foreign technologies were banned in sectors in which domestic counterparts were available. Firms were encouraged to practice reverse engineering, along with licensing and purchase of technologies not available at home—all under bureaucratic guidance.

There was a consistent emphasis on attaining economies of scale. This goal was reflected in many mergers of small firms initiated or subsidized by the government, for example, in the chemical, automobile, fertilizer, and other sectors. There was an ongoing campaign to restrict entry and control capacity expansion in various sectors to curtail "excessive competition" in the form of big swings and destabilizing cumulative processes in investment and price wars in industries with decreasing costs.

Within the generally expansionary macroeconomic environment, credit allocation was aggressively practiced. The banking system was nationalized early in the Korean industrial drive, giving the state effective control over all important financial flows (aided by tight foreign exchange restrictions). "Policy loans" with subsidized interest rates and/or priority rationing accounted for over half of bank credits in the 1960s and 1970s.

These features of East Asian industrial planning suggest several conclusions relevant to other developing economies. One is that there can be a bargaining solution among peak organizations to restrain "rent seeking" as damned by Krueger (1974), with rapid output growth and the state's power to punish recalcitrants in the background. Rents (or, better, Marshallian quasi-rents or Marxian/Schumpeterian profits) were certainly created for the *chaebols* by their privileged position, yet they became production powerhouses and not leeches thriving on public largesse. Moreover, they were effectively guided by the bureaucracy, since channels were created for it to gain access to business information.

The economic bureaucracy itself was an essential player. In the terminology of economic sociology of the sort pioneered by Polanyi (Evans 1995), it was "embedded" in the society in the sense that it could act autonomously for the public good as it saw fit, without completely being taken over by patronage and rent seeking.

Dialogue between the bureaucracy and enterprises permitted the East Asian nations to practice economic planning effectively in a capitalist environment. Short-term allocative efficiency ("getting prices right") was often sacrificed to long-term productive efficiency or rapid productivity growth. Conscious rent creation on the part of the state was the key to constant industrial upgrading and realization of economies of scale. In the long run, huge steel mills and shipyards made sense.

Finally, following Japan, the institutional basis for other East Asian miracles was put into place over a relatively short time. *Chaebols*, trading companies, planning bureaucracies, and the macroeconomic policy mix all emerged in the early 1960s in a creative burst. Obviously such institutions cannot be transferred without modification to other national contexts, but partial functional equivalents may well prove relevant elsewhere in the world. Exploring such possibilities would be a proper domain for realistic theories of economic growth.

6. The Mainstream Policy Response

The theories of sections B–F of Figure 11.1 might conceivably be up to such an exploration, but the same cannot be said for the orthodox citations toward the right end of section A. They emerged as part of a strong reaction against public guidance of the economy, which got under way in its most recent form in the 1960s. Of course Mises, Hayek, and predecessor liberals had raised the same ideas long before, while the Polanyis of their times fired back.

The first wave of recent critics concentrated on the "inefficiency" of state intervention as it had evolved, particularly in the emphasis that development economists of the Rosenstein-Rodan vintage placed on ISI. Trade theorists, who are imbued with the evils of protectionism at an early age, took the lead. Using then novel analytical tools such as effective rates of protection and domestic resource costs, authors such as Little, Scitovsky, and Scott (1970) and many others showed that the incentive structures created by import substitution were highly unequal for different economic actors. They further sought to correlate "distorted" policy regimes with poor economic performance. Their modest success in this endeavor is a continual embarrassment for the school.

One of the empirical problems is worth flagging explicitly. The "welfare losses" due to distortions emerging from solutions of computable general equilibrium models—the highest tech analytical tools—are usually meager: 100 percent price wedges might reduce GDP by one-half percent. Implicitly, then, the initial neoclassical critique is reduced to an assertion that eliminating distortions will lead the economy to jump to a noticeably more rapidly growing configuration of circular flow. But just how is such a transition supposed to occur? The dynamics of miracles designed by the invisible hand are not easy to describe, because none have happened.

Regardless of this difficulty, when the critics showed that many industries in developing countries had "negative value-added" at world prices, they took the profession by storm. But they also transmitted a more powerful message. Read between the lines, these economists advocated laissez-faire as the only viable alternative to an incentive mare's nest. The rapid growth rates of Taiwan and South Korea—at the time unrealistically postulated to have noninterventionist governments—were cited in support of the free market. Although they are not easy to substantiate, the notions that observed distortions inhibit growth and that rapid growers are noninterventionist now permeate the rhetoric and advice of mainstream development scholars and lending institutions; they are built solidly into the policy recommendations offered by the World Bank and International Monetary Fund.

Similar developments took place on the agricultural front, where Lewis- and Preobrazhensky-style concerns about the dual economy were swept aside by authors emerging from an anti-interventionist American midwestern agricultural economics tradition such as Schultz (1964). Their diagnosis was that farmgate prices had been held down in developing countries, in comparison with world market prices (however distorted by rich-country interventions) as a point of reference. Accumulation and distributive processes within the sector and politico-economic difficulties in altering the way it works were alien to the new price mechanists' ways of thought. Although food production in some countries was aided by subsidies to big farmers to utilize the new technologies offered by the Green Revolution, price reform alone has not been capable of stimulating agriculture over much of the developing world. Africa is only the saddest case.

In the 1980s, the debate on economic policy took another turn.

Echoing Bauer (1972), who had questioned the efficacy of state intervention early on, recent authors postulate that "bureaucratic failure" is
worse than "market failure."

The "public choice" school follows Krueger (1974) in elevating "rent
seeking" induced by government interventions—lobbying for state fa-
vors, paying a bribe to get an import quota or Pentagon contract, fixing a ticket for a traffic violation—to a deadly social ill. If real resources
are devoted to pursuing rents or "directly unproductive profit-seeking"
(DUP) activities in the jargon, the outcome can be a form of suboptimal-
ity for the society as a whole.

Inventing DUP was a technical advance, since deep wells of postulated
corruption allowed numerical models to give satisfyingly large estimates
of welfare losses from distortion. The saving social grace became a thoroughly night-watchmanly state supervising a competitive market—the
latter condition to be guaranteed by international free trade. Under these
conditions, DUP activity supposedly becomes unrewarding, and the invisible hand will guide society toward optimal resource allocation.

A second form of bliss takes a more authoritarian cast. For believers in
DUP, the ideal state mimics the Cheshire Cat by vanishing to avoid being
taken over by the interests. Alternatively, the state can force the interests
to vanish, or in Lal's (1983) words, "A courageous, ruthless, and perhaps undemocratic government is required to ride roughshod over these
newly-created special interest groups." It is not clear why Lal's ruthless,
etc. generals and bureaucrats will abstain from taking over the market
also. The record of Third World authoritarian states in avoiding corruption and distortions is not encouraging in this regard.

Indeed a market distorted by the state for its own ends is a final extreme possibility, which can be associated with North's (1981) theories
of economic history. In a typical North example, a state may choose to
raise revenue by creating monopolies and then marshal political arguments in their support. The fate of Leninist centrally planned systems
suggests that economic damnation may well lie at the end of such a path.

The conclusion is that the state and market in principle can arrive at
extreme configurations which are easy to characterize. Chang (2002),
however, convincingly argues that the combination of a purely night
watchman state and a completely undistorted market has never been observed in practice. If it were ever created, a Lal equilibrium would probably not be stable; recent events suggest that the same is true of statist ex-
tremism along North's lines.

Existing societies combine mixtures of state activism with market distortions. If it were possible to assign numerical scores to nations on the
two accounts, statistical analysis would almost certainly detect scant as-

sociation between degrees or movements of state presence and market imperfections with indicators of economic performance such as GDP growth rates, except for the likelihood of poor growth in countries with extremely distorted markets.

Beyond this hypothetical regression, a much more fundamental point is that the new neoclassical theory of the state is ahistorical and timeless—although it may shed light on tendencies, it elides the messy dynamics of transitions. As with the new growth theory, a typical model would please Dr. Pangloss: all of its "agents" successfully optimize over all possible choices so that the system inevitably arrives at the best (and only, presuming uniqueness) possible world. Not much hope for "development" in Schumpeter's sense of jumping from one pattern of circular flow to another, in such specifications.

7. Where Theory Might Sensibly Go

We are left to ponder how formal growth theory might incorporate some of the foregoing ideas, to become practically useful for policy formation. No instant answers are at hand, but a few thoughts are worth noting.

Mechanisms supporting growth and factors restraining it clearly vary from place to place and time to time. Questions about the different ways in which the broadly similar accounting schemes which underlie all growth models can be closed by behavioral assumptions come immediately to the fore.

Formalizations of the ideas in all the sections of Figure 11.1 can be fit to any single economy's data and will give different answers about its likely evolution and sensitivity to policy moves. Statistical techniques like Granger causality (or lead-lag) tests are of little use in sorting out the closure question, because of absent data and multiple causal patterns. When the techniques are applied, however, they rarely support the macroeconomic vision underlying Figure 11.1's section A. Serious political economy or institutional discussion provides a better means to consider the causal patterns at hand.

Even so, the ideas of Mises and Hayek as propagandized by Thatcher and Reagan continue to dominate the current policy scene, long after these proponents left office. In growth and development theory, the corollaries are an emphasis on price-induced supply responses and the wonders of the invisible hand. The big role played by human capital accumulation in new growth models is a case in point.

The idea that more education can have productive payoffs was raised by Smith and Mill and popularized by Schultz (1963) and Becker (1964) quite some time ago. Dissidents like Amsden (1989) likewise stress the role that a skilled labor force played in East Asia's economic success. The question is whether education is more a necessary or concomitant condition for economic development, than sufficient for it to occur. Examples already mentioned suggest that like any single factor, human capital cannot support sustained growth. It is a multi-factoral process. All available inputs will not automatically be used. However impressive their manipulations of nineteenth-century mathematics, models ignoring these mundane observations fail the credibility test.

As many authors noted in Figure 11.1 pointed out, growth can be strongly influenced by distributive processes unfolding within the social, political, and economic structures that exist. Old Ricardo and Marx were not wrong in setting up models based on socioeconomic classes; the not-so-old *General Theory* was built upon an institutional vision of capitalism which is still valid to a great extent. Structuralist modelers are inspired by these examples, which strike them as far richer than the world of Walras. It makes sense to heed the *justes limites* to Walras's program raised by Poincaré himself: "you regard men as infinitely selfish and infinitely farsighted. The first hypothesis may perhaps be admitted in a first approximation, the second may call for some reservations" (letter of October 1, 1901, cited by Ingrao and Israel (1990)).

In the "really existing" world, even the first approximation is not very good—the planet is evidently populated by impurely "economic" men and women, who certainly have neither unlimited computational capabilities nor perfect foresight. In such a place, development is a transformation which deep minds besides Mises's and Hayek's have tried to understand, without clear-cut success. Nonetheless, one can learn from the theories of capitalism proposed by Marx, Weber, Polanyi, and others. As already observed, Marx stressed the importance of the institutions supporting accumulation and technical advance. Despite Bretton Woods tutelage over the past dozen years, they show no signs of emerging in much of the developing world under allegedly "market friendly" reform programs.

The mature Max Weber (1968) pointed to a complex causal pattern underlying capitalism's origins: "All in all, the specific roots of Occidental culture must be sought in the tension and peculiar balance, on the one hand, between office charisma and monasticism, and on the other between the contractual character of the feudal state and the autonomous bureaucratic hierarchy." All were essential in setting up capitalism as a system of institutionalized strife among shifting but well-defined social groups (quoted in Collins 1980, p. 929). At a more practical level, all successful or semi-successful reform programs in semi-industrialized countries in recent decades—Spain, Chile, Korea, Taiwan—have involved complex causal patterns and contingent historical events.

Polanyi's great insight has also been noted, that the institutions supporting the market system arose historically with state guidance from within society, which also defended itself against their worst excesses—child labor laws were passed early in the nineteenth century and the collapse of real wages in Eastern Europe was arrested at 30–40 percent late in the twentieth. "Double movements" of this sort will continue to occur as other countries develop, peacefully only if the tensions of change do not become unbearable.

As society's superordinate actor, the state will also have to play a central role in forcing both sides of the double movement—markets will be neither created nor regulated without public action. Developing country experience surely shows that states can fail in several dimensions (Evans 1995). They operate under fundamental uncertainty, and may or may not respond to the uneven advances of different sectors, disproportionalities, and balance of payments and inflationary pressures that will inevitably arise (Hirschman 1958). They can try to do too much, thereby achieving little. They can become purely predatory, as in countless petty dictatorships around the world. Nonetheless, as theoreticians of backwardness from Gerschenkron to Amsden have pointed out, when economies do catch up the process is mediated by the state, in particular by an autonomous bureaucracy accepted by (and embedded in) the society overall.

Somehow, new growth theory manages to ignore all these considerations, while many other authors cited in Figure 11.1 have kept them foremost in their minds.

Notes

Introduction

1. Mainstream macroeconometrics, in an interesting contrast, is much more structuralist in its treatment of behavioral relationships. The influential "LSE approach" explicitly theorizes in terms of aggregates. For examples, see the papers collected in Backhouse and Salanti (2001).

2. The label SFC is due to Dos Santos (2002). Stock-flow modeling was pioneered by Wynne Godley from Cambridge and James Tobin from Yale.

3. Attitudes of the people mentioned in the text toward rational actor "microfoundations" for macroeconomics range from outright hostility to cool indifference, in sharp contrast to more mainstream authors such as Phelps (1994) who fly structuralist banners on optimizing flagpoles. Keynes's use of a marginal productivity labor demand model in *The General Theory* is an interesting exception. As his later writings made clear, the model was a sales pitch, a matter of no conviction whatsoever.

1. Social Accounts and Social Relations

1. NIPA and FOF numbers are far from being raw data. They are constructed from various sources (or cooked from diverse ingredients) with a lot of methodological controversy along the way.

2. For practical purposes, Stone and the American economist Simon Kuznets invented the modern form of national income accounting in the 1930s and 1940s (precursor systems go as far back as William Petty's *Political Arithmetick* of the mid-1600s). Godley is an influential exponent of macro models based firmly on complete accounting systems. Stone (1966) gives an early exposition of the SAM approach, Godley and Cripps (1983) discuss modeling for developed economies, and Taylor (1990) presents SAM-based computable general equilibrium models applied in developing countries.

3. In the NIPA system, the first column and row of Table 1.1 are replaced by the rules that value-added economy-wide = the sum of the values of all final demands = gross domestic product or GDP, that is, the value of intermediate input flows (aPX in the cell A1) is not included in GDP to avoid "double

counting." Most macroeconomic theory—unrealistically—does not incorporate intermediate inputs into its analysis of demands and costs. With some exceptions, this unhelpful convention is adopted in this book.

4. *The General Theory of Employment, Interest, and Money* by Keynes (1936) is the *locus classicus*. There is no doubt that Kalecki independently discovered the principle of effective demand in essays published in the early 1930s that are reproduced in Kalecki (1971). Whether he "fully" anticipated Keynes's vision is another question. See Patinkin (1982) for a thoughtful, anti-Kaleckian review of the evidence.

5. We ignore the severe difficulties that arise in constructing a capital aggregate like K from micro foundations. The fact that the English anti-K team won the "Cambridge controversy" over this issue (Harcourt 1972) has dissuaded neither orthodox nor dissident macroeconomists from using aggregates like K or total productive capacity.

6. Household and business sectors were not disaggregated in Figure 1.1 because the former has rather low gross savings rates which generate a spectacularly unstable curve for $I_{household}/S_{household}$ where $I_{household}$ is interpreted as investment in residential construction. In the implied assignments of money flows, there are a few discrepancies between Figure 1.2 and the more detailed data for 1999 in Table 1.4 below, principally with regard to the treatment of estate taxes, government enterprise investment, and transfers of nonproduced assets. Per Gunnar Berglund and Codrina Rada did the real work in putting Figures 1.1 and 1.2 together.

7. SAMs incorporating flows of funds with linked balance sheets along the lines of Tables 1.2 and 1.3 have been in use since the mid-1980s. An early published example appears in Rosensweig and Taylor (1990). Inspired by Godley, Lavoie (2001) uses similar accounts to discuss issues frequently debated by post-Keynesians (discussed here in Chapter 8).

8. All interest flows in the Table 1.2 SAM are treated as transfers from one set of income recipients to another. As will be seen in connection with Table 1.4, national income accounting practice in the United States does not rise to this standard of detail. In the NIPA system, all interest, dividend, etc. payments are treated as being funneled through the financial system. In business practice, it may be more appropriate to treat interest payments (for financing inventories, for example) as a component of cost in column (1). However, such accounting is unconventional and for that reason is not pursued for the moment. See Chapter 3.

9. In many applied accounting schemes, net profits from the banking and financial sectors are transferred to nonfinancial business so that finance's saving and net worth are implicitly set to zero. As will be seen in later chapters, this accounting trick simplifies macro modeling but in the interests of clarity it is not utilized in Table 1.2.

10. If, more realistically, we were to carry the value of public investment PI_g in the accounting, then in almost all economies $S_g - PI_g < 0$.

11. One rationale for accounting for all imports in cell G1 is that in the first in-

stance they come into the control of firms, which then distribute them via sales to other business for intermediate and investment uses and to consumers. In developing countries, imports of capital goods are often slotted into cell G8 in recognition of their essential role in capital formation.

12. In the period 1982–1990, Pollin (1997) shows that internal and borrowed funds respectively amounted to 96 percent and 40 percent of gross capital formation of U.S. nonfinancial corporations—companies seemed to have more financial resources than they needed. "The funds . . . were devoted to asset transfers such as mergers and takeovers as well as current operations. We directly observe this shift in the relative importance of asset transfers in the 1980s through considering the ratio of net new equity issues [to] net increases in liabilities . . . [O]ne-half of the increase in corporate liabilities was devoted only to buying back outstanding equities" (pp. 342–343).

13. If banking system profits and saving are transferred to the business sector, then consolidating row (K) and column (10) gives $\dot{M} = \dot{L}_b + \dot{L}_g + e\dot{R}^*$, in a familiar identity the increase in the money supply results from new loans to business and government and the increase in international reserves.

14. As with most bits of technical economics, q is not new under the sun. In his *Theory of Business Enterprise,* Thorstein Veblen (1904) emphasized the significance of the stock market's valuation of firms. Gunnar Myrdal (1939) based his investment theory on what he called the "valuation ratio," or the value of the existing capital stock divided by the cost of production of new capital ("replacement cost" is not the appropriate concept for the denominator, because of technical progress). If production cost is reflected in asset valuations, the inverse of Myrdal's ratio is tantamount to q.

15. In terms of definitions, general government includes federal government (including social security funds), state, and local government but excludes government-sponsored enterprises, which are put in the business sector. The FOF matrixes do not *consolidate* general government, but show federal and state-and-local separately. All one can do is to *aggregate* the two by adding them up. Consolidation would go beyond aggregation by purging intra-sector flows, assets, and liabilities. General government *net* financial assets will be automatically consolidated; gross financial assets and liabilities will not.

16. A significant (and confusing) difference between NIPA and FOF methodologies in the United States centers on the NIPA convention that the "personal sector" made up of households and institutions does not have direct ownership of any productive assets. They are located in the nonfinancial business sector, supposedly under indirect control by the personal sector. The assets in question are all nonfarm owner-occupied dwellings, about two-thirds of tenant-occupied dwellings, and all assets owned by nonprofit institutions serving households. The FOF accounts do *not* make this asset relocation. Table 1.4 is based on the NIPA, but is adjusted to fit FOF accounting conventions. Four relatively sizable flows were thereby shifted from NIPA non-financial business to households and institutions: wages related to tenant-

occupied housing ($6.7 billion), indirect taxes minus subsidies (−$16.1 billion), mortgage interest payments (a big $340.4 billion), and consumption of fixed capital ($163.2 billion). A few other minor differences give rise to the entries in row QZIT.

17. The interest flow shows up in nonfinancial business in the NIPA numbers, but was transferred to households for the reasons set out in the previous note. A similar observation applies to the subsidy. Also note that rental income of 143.4 includes 86.8 of imputed rentals net of operating costs on owner-occupied dwellings, a "profit-like" imaginary income flow traditionally included (not without controversy) in all national accounts. This convention traces through A. C. Pigou in the 1930s to the "political arithmetick" of Gregory King in 1696.

18. Disconcertingly, general government depreciation appears to be double-counted in the NIPA and thereby the SAM. It is obviously included in general government gross capital formation (= net capital formation + depreciation), but also in the sector's gross value-added, from which it feeds into government consumption expenditure as described below.

19. Malpractice insurance, corporate donations to nonprofits, theft losses, and so on.

20. Agency securities are issued not by fiscal government but by two quasi-federal agencies, Fannie Mae (Federal National Mortgage Association) and the smaller Freddie Mac (Federal Home Loan Mortgage Corporation). Both buy up home mortgage loans from their originators and package or "securitize" them into bonds sold to institutional investors and rich individuals. Wall Street (probably correctly) believes that Fannie and Freddie are implicitly guaranteed against failure by the U.S. government, even though their shares trade on the New York Stock Exchange. This supposition permits them to exert a lot of market clout.

21. The published accounts do not include holding gains and losses as such. In Tables 1.5 and 1.6 they were obtained residually by plugging NIPA and FOF numbers into the equations in the text.

22. There is a standard distinction between "portfolio" and "direct" investment abroad. The FOF rule of thumb is that an equity position in a foreign company exceeding 10 percent counts as FDI; below this threshold, it is portfolio investment. At the beginning of 1999, the outstanding stock of FDI held by U.S. resident sectors was 1,047.8. Net acquisitions during the year were 137.3, and holding gains were −25.3. The corresponding numbers for the rest of the world's FDI in the United States were 928.6, 275.5, and −78.9. (The heavy holding losses for the United States are presumably due to the sharp increase of the dollar exchange rate in 1999, particularly vis-à-vis the then newly introduced euro—see Chapter 10 for more than enough detail on the wealth effects of exchange rate changes.) The United States historically had a strong positive net position in FDI, but consistent with the economy's structural current account deficit it has been shrinking since the 1980s.

23. For the record, note that financial and produced assets are subject to differ-

ent valuation principles in national accounts: Financial assets are valued at current market prices, which implies that any change in current market conditions (stock market booms, interest rate changes, etc.) will be reflected as holding gains (losses) on financial assets (liabilities). Produced assets, however, are valued at (written-down) current *replacement* cost, which means that the prices of second-hand assets are inferred from the supply prices of newly produced assets. In effect the price level of the stock of produced assets is governed by current movements in the price level of gross capital formation. In order to get significant holding gains on produced assets, there must be sharp increases in the cost of investment. Holding gains on produced assets are usually much smaller than on financial assets.

24. Here we have $\hat{P} = (dP/dt)/P = \dot{P}/P$, or the rate of price inflation. The "real" rate of interest j is defined as $i - \hat{P}$ by "Fisher arbitrage" (details in Fisher (1930) and Chapter 3) and the return to holding cash is $-\hat{P}$. As observed in Chapter 2, "hats" are also often used to denote logarithmic differentiation, for example, $\hat{P} = d \log P = dP/P$. Both usages appear in this book, in appropriate contexts.

2. Prices and Distribution

1. For example, rational voters infiltrated political science from their birthplace in Schumpeter's *Capitalism, Socialism, and Democracy* (1947) via Downs (1957). Olson (1965) amplified their impact in determining patterns of collective action. For an entertaining counterattack, see Green and Shapiro (1994). There is a large, recent literature featuring MIRA economists doing "political economy" (Alesina 1988, for example), which we can safely ignore.

2. As with all periods of thought, Schumpeter (1954) gives an excellent review of classical economics. On much of what follows, see also Dutt (1990), Eatwell and Milgate (1983), Garegnani (1984), and Pasinetti (1977).

3. Chapter 1 in Pasinetti (1977) presents a clear sketch of Quesnay's system.

4. Moreover, policies that hold down landlords' spending power could lead to a reduction in effective demand. This was the gist of Malthus's argument against repeal of the Corn Laws—falling agricultural prices induced by import deregulation could provoke a general glut. For a further discussion, see Chapter 11 and Taylor (1991).

5. The convention generally followed in the models of this book is that the profit rate r is realized on fixed capital, while the real interest rate j represents financial returns or costs, for example the borrowing needed to pay for circulating capital in equation (2).

6. If final sales (for consumption, investment, etc.) of sector j are F_j and intermediate sales are Q_j, we have $F_j/Q_j = j^*$, for all j. The product mix across sectors is the same, so that when the standard commodity is used to weight a GDP deflator (the sum of sectoral value-added levels economy-wide) based on the existing set of prices from (2) with the observed wage and interest

rate, then nonlinear terms like those appearing in (4) drop out. Sraffa's formal results are reproduced endlessly in the literature and so are omitted here. The presentation by Pasinetti (1977) is as good as any.

7. Many of the points that follow should be attributed not to Pasinetti himself, but rather to an interpretation of his system set out more fully in Taylor (1995). For more on Pasinetti's accounting, see Chapter 11.

8. If shares $(1 - \delta_i)$ of sectoral profit flows are paid out as dividends, interest, taxes, and so on, the formula in the text is little changed: $\delta_i r_i = \delta_i \pi_i P_i / P_2 \mu_i = g$. Von Neumann (1945–46) got the golden rule result in a very general model presented at seminars thirty years and published fifteen years before Phelps's paper appeared. Chapter 3 contains more on the mainstream interpretation of the golden rule.

9. More formally, the firm wants to minimize $\Gamma = c_1 Z_1 + c_2 Z_2$ subject to the constraint $X - F(Z_1, Z_2) = 0$. Following the traditional recipe, we can define a Lagrangean function $c_1 Z_1 + c_2 Z_2 + \lambda[X - F(Z_1, Z_2)]$ and set its partial derivatives with respect to the Z_i equal to zero to get the optimality conditions $c_i - \lambda F_i = 0$ $(i = 1, 2)$, where $F_i = \partial F / \partial Z_i$. Suppose that one of the c_i changes. At the minimum cost point, we have $dC/dc_i = Z_i + c_1(dZ_1/dc_i) + c_2(dZ_2/dc_i) = Z_i + \lambda[F_1(dZ_1/dc_i) + F_2(dZ_2/dc_i)]$, where the second expression follows from the first after substituting $c_i = \lambda F_i$ from the optimality conditions. But note that the constraint $X - F(Z_1, Z_2) = 0$ must hold at the optimum. From the chain rule, first-order differential changes in Z_1 and Z_2 as one of the c_i shifts must satisfy the equality $F_1(dZ_1/dc_i) + F_2(dZ_2/dc_i) = 0$. Plugging this condition into the equation above for dC/dc_i shows that $dC/dc_i = Z_i$, as Shephard's Lemma asserts.

10. A value of σ approaching infinity signals a flat isoquant in the (K, L) plane; a value of zero shapes the isoquant as two perpendicular lines parallel to the K and L axes and joining at a point in the positive quadrant (a Leontief production function); and a value of unity corresponds to the familiar Cobb-Douglas case $X = \beta L^\psi K^{1-\psi}$, where under the usual assumptions ψ is the labor share wL/PX (constant by construction, regardless of all perturbations) and β is a scale parameter.

11. Jones (1965) gives nice presentations of the Heckscher-Ohlin trade model (drawing on the envelope theorem) and other war horses in hat calculus.

12. He rejected the "second classical postulate" that utility maximization underlies a rising labor supply curve of the sort discussed in connection with equation (16) here. His reasons are discussed in Chapter 4.

13. In the United States, pro-cyclical wage movement shows up fairly consistently but not with great force. Real nonfarm compensation per hour, for example, dropped by less than 1 percent below trend growth on average in postwar recessions (Romer 2001), with declines observed in seven of nine recessions.

14. You can't tell the players without a scorecard. Here are some of their uniforms' details: Keynes used the word "classical" to refer to economic theories ranging from those of Adam Smith to the Marshall/Pigou version of

marginalist economics (since supplanted for the mainstream by more Walrasian constructs). The "new classical" school which emerged in the wake of Friedmanite monetarism in the 1970s and 1980s sees itself as opposing Keynes on MIRA or Walrasian grounds; it has no great interest in resuscitating Ricardo, Marx, or even Marshall. The opposing "new Keynesians," meanwhile, seek to derive Keynes-like policy recommendations from imperfect competition MIRA models in which (ultimately) Say's Law reigns. In turn, their work descends from a "neoclassical synthesis" which supplanted Keynes in mainstream thinking in the 1950s. More complete descriptions follow in subsequent chapters.

15. Ironically in light of his markup theories, Pigou was Keynes's main whipping boy in *The General Theory,* and his "effect" of changing real money stocks on aggregate demand (discussed in following chapters) became the major weapon in the orthodox assault on the principle of effective demand.

16. For simplicity, we write down industry-wide equations, without explicitly considering aggregation conditions across firms. Fancier models such as the one by Blanchard and Kiyotaki (1987) aggregate across identically sized firms sharing the same technology, adding algebra but not much economic content to the presentation in the text. Because enterprises are not identical in practice, applied studies usually measure their "number" by a formula such as the inverse of the Herfindahl index, defined as the sum of squares of firms' market shares.

17. To highlight the effects of decreasing costs, firms are assumed to base their markups on "full cost" Γ as opposed to variable cost wb.

18. The useful new Keynesian textbook by Carlin and Soskice (1990) presents several exercises along such lines, including "insider-outsider" models as championed by Lindbeck (1993).

19. A sketch of a demonstration goes as follows. The firm's first-order condition for minimizing cost $C = \omega b(Z)$ is $b + \omega b' = 0$ and the second-order condition is $\delta = 2b' + \omega b'' > 0$, where $b'' = d^2b/dZ^2$. Applying the envelope theorem while setting $\omega_a = \omega$ shows that $dC/d\epsilon = -\omega b'(\omega - \omega_b) > 0$. Differentiating the first-order condition gives $d\omega/d\epsilon = (\omega - \omega_b)(b' + \omega b'')/\delta > 0$. Because $dC/d\epsilon = \omega(db/d\epsilon) + b(d\omega/d\epsilon)$ we can combine these expressions to show that $db/d\epsilon = -(\omega - \omega_b)(b')^2/\delta < 0$, which for plausible parameters will be small in absolute value. In sum, the higher employment rate increases both the real wage and labor productivity.

20. Menger (1963) provides a useful entry into his thought.

21. Taylor (1988) and Taylor (1993) review the contrary evidence for inflation-prone developing economies. Bruno (1993) is a good presentation of more mainstream views.

22. Taylor's model has been influential in the policy debate, which is why it is presented here. But he is by no means the only new Keynesian to consider questions of labor relations. See, for example, Akerlof and Yellen (1990), who explore the implications for labor productivity of the "fairness" of wages. The crux of Dunlop's theory is that the wage for any given job is

more responsive to changes in wages in jobs "nearer" to it (in terms of remu-
neration, work description, and so on) than further away.

23. To avoid bringing in a lot of notation extraneous to the point of the discussion, we simply assume that the future levels of the wage, output, money
supply, and so on are known with certainty. Although it goes through a
lot of huffing and puffing with "rational" or model-consistent expectations
taken over appropriate information sets, the mainstream basically does the
same thing. A continuous time analog to indexation rules like (26) is introduced in Chapter 3 in the form of "adaptive expectations."

24. In correspondence, Ron Baiman pointed out grievous errors in earlier versions of the model as presented in Taylor (1979) and fairly widely elsewhere.

25. Indeed, the success of Latin American inflation stabilization packages in the
late 1980s (Mexico) and 1990s as opposed to a preceding chain of failures
can be directly attributed to the surge of capital inflows to the region that began around the turn of the decade.

3. Money, Interest, and Inflation

1. Schumpeter (1954) is of course the essential source on all such matters.
Kindleberger (1984) is a nice complement, and Chapter 23 of Keynes's *General Theory,* on mercantilism, usury laws, and related topics, is a good read.

2. Recall from Chapter 1 that this approach is nonstandard. For example, the
SAM in Table 1.2 follows the usual practice of treating interest payments as
transfers among income recipient classes rather than an element of production cost in column (1).

3. The analysis here in continuous time is a bit more straightforward than the
discrete-time version set out by Anyadike-Danes et al.

4. In formal terms, the person behind the diagram wants to maximize utility
$U(x, y)$ subject to $y = f(x)$ with $df/dx < 0$. The optimality condition is
$(dU/dx)(dx/dy) = -df/dx = 1 + j$ where positive time preference guarantees
that $j > 0$.

5. A bit more formally, individuals or firms engage in Ponzi finance when they
borrow to cover current payment (including interest) obligations (Minsky
1986). The eponymous Charles, or Carlo, Ponzi operated in Boston in 1920.
Kindleberger (1996) reports that he promised to pay 50 percent interest on
45-day deposits, to use in arbitrage operations between depreciated foreign
currencies and International Postal Union coupons that could be exchanged
for U.S. stamps. At the time of his arrest, he had taken in $7.9 million and
held $61 worth of stamps. As of this writing, the accounting is still incom-
plete for Ponzi's latter-day successors at Enron, Global Crossing, and so on.

6. As a philosopher and mathematician, Ramsey stood out even in the brilliant
crowd around Cambridge in the 1920s (Keynes, Bertrand Russell and the
rest of Bloomsbury, Ludwig Wittgenstein, and a host of preeminent mathematical, physical, and biological scientists), although the notably critical
Wittgenstein once wrote that he was a "bourgeois thinker" (Monk, 1990).

Ramsey died at age 26. The tone of the writing suggests that he considered his optimal saving paper to be no more than a clever fling of (then) century-old Hamiltonian mechanics at an economic problem of some interest. Had he lived a long life, in the 1980s Ramsey would presumably have been astounded to see his toy machine supplant *The General Theory* as the central model for macroeconomics.

7. It is helpful if $h(0) = 0$, $h'(g) = dh/dg = 0$ when $g = 0$, and $h'' = d^2h/dg^2 > 0$. Because costs of changing the capital stock are written as $gkh(g)$ and are incurred with both decumulation and accumulation, $h(g)$ has the same sign as g.

8. More formally, if an inessential constant is added to the function quoted in the text so that it becomes $u(c) = (c^{1-\eta} - 1)/(1 - \eta)$, then as η approaches the value 1, $u(c)$ goes to the indeterminate ratio 0/0. Application of l'Hôpital's rule shows that the limiting form is log c.

9. In his 1928 paper, Ramsey says that Keynes provided a verbal rationale for a formula like (19) which he derived using the calculus of variations.

10. These "Routh-Hurwitz" conditions are well known. Among many other sources, chap. 4 in McCafferty (1990) gives a useful summary.

11. Recall from Chapter 1 that we are ignoring all results of the "Cambridge controversies" of the 1960s, in particular the fact that because of reswitching, the relationship between a capital aggregate and its "marginal product" need not be negative and monotonic.

12. On a cowboy's saddle, only a ball placed on the "saddlepath" from the base of the horn to the top of the cantle will be able to settle down in the middle of the seat. A ball placed anywhere else will roll off a side.

13. To be fair to Ramsey, in his own model he did not play discounting games like the ones discussed in the text. Rather he assumed that the (undiscounted) felicity function $u(c)$ saturates for some high value of c, leading him to call his steady-state equilibrium "Bliss."

14. Details are available in Romer (2001), for example.

15. This form of instability is emphasized by Marglin (1984), after whom the following argument is patterned.

16. In many economies, typical CES econometrics gives σ in the range between one-third and two-thirds, while π_t might not be far below one-half. Insofar as savings-driven investment and the specific OLG model developed here really apply, unstable or borderline stable growth seems to be in the cards.

17. Romer (2001) goes into the details.

18. The fact that an absurdly high pure rate of time preference ϵ would be required to give a saving rate as low as 0.035 in formula (23) for a Cobb-Douglas felicity function is a complication we ignore.

19. Why the character of the business cycle changed is an intriguing question too historically complicated to be explored here. Nell and Sylos-Labini respectively point toward changes in the nature of technology (replacement of "craft" by mass production activities) and the evolution of social relations (more widespread markup pricing and centralized wage bargaining, for ex-

ample). Using models like those developed in Chapter 5, Block (1997) presents a useful summary of their arguments. Along his lines, distributive dynamics over the cycle are discussed in Chapter 9.

20. Robertson called the inflation tax "induced lacking," and forced saving "automatic lacking," respectively. The notion that the victims of these processes are compelled to "lack" real consumption captures their essence better than the conventional labels.

21. Because $r = \pi u$, the economy of Table 3.2 is on the "wrong" side of the golden rule with $g > r$. A more realistic treatment of transactions among firms, households, and the financial system would remove this "anomaly."

22. The $-(1/V)g$ term in equation (30) says that part of the required saving increase will be attained because households have to build up transactions balances to deal with a growing capital stock.

23. This "effect" is usually traced to Mundell (1963a) and Tobin (1965). It is consistent with the positive relationship between money velocity and the inflation rate discussed later. People and (especially) enterprises cutting back on money balances as $\hat{P}$ accelerates will tend to build up physical assets.

24. Just what an expectation like $E(d\hat{P}/dt)$ really signifies about the future of the economy is discussed at length in later chapters.

25. The derivative of the bracketed term with respect to $\hat{P}$ is $1 - [v\hat{P}/(V_0 + v\hat{P})] - V(\partial Q/\partial \hat{P})$. It will be positive so long as Mundell-Tobin, etc. effects are weak in the effective demand term $\partial Q/\partial \hat{P}$.

26. Wicksell, Robertson, and Co. were not unobservant. They recognized the empirical fact that an economy can stay below its point of full capacity use for an extended period of time. But they did not turn this observation into the keystone of their analyses.

27. The discussion to follow is nonstandard in several ways. For a clear mainstream presentation of many of the same issues, see Agénor and Montiel (1999).

28. For example, if retailers collect sales taxes over one month and only remit the proceeds the first (or maybe the middle or last) day of the month following, the real value of the government's receipts is eroded by ongoing inflation.

29. For practical purposes, a jump in Δ can be approximated by a high value of $d\Delta/dt$ for a short period of time.

30. In most economies the value of the capital stock is several times the GDP, while government liabilities are a fraction (or only slightly above GDP in rich-country outliers like Japan and Italy). Also, the specification in (46) is odd in terms of the data, since in most economies C is around 75–80 percent of GDP and perhaps 15–25 percent of the capital stock. Such a value for γ_h exceeds most real observed interest rates, but to maintain a positive level of real balances we will assume that $j > \gamma_h$.

31. Perhaps households suddenly wake up to the fact that the government is playing a Ponzi game. See Chapter 6 for another *deus ex machina* rescue of a steady state in the blatantly unstable new classical "Ricardian equivalence" model of taxation versus government debt.

4. Effective Demand and Its Real and Financial Implications

1. This point is emphasized by Pasinetti (1974), in a paper containing a slightly different version of scheme (1). Pasinetti compliments Keynes for indulging in Schumpeter's "Ricardian vice," described in Chapter 1.

2. As argued in Chapter 1, it makes sense to attach differential savings rates to income flows, in line with econometric and institutional evidence in both industrialized and developing economies. Formally speaking, we follow Kaldor (1956) in tying saving behavior to type of income rather than to class, as in Pasinetti's (1962) growth model.

3. That is, capacity use is assumed to adjust out of (temporary) equilibrium according to the rule $\dot{u} = \chi(g^i - g^s)$ with $\chi(0) = 0$ and $\chi' > 0$. The stability condition turns out to be $\Delta > 0$.

4. Short-run profit share adjustment follows the rule $\dot{\pi} = \chi[g^i(\pi, \bar{u}) - s(\pi)\bar{u}]$, which will be stable in a wage-led economy.

5. The point is stated clearly in Keynes's introductory Chapter 2 on "The Postulates of the Classical Economics." He says that the "theoretically fundamental" difficulty with the classics' model is that "if money-wages change, one would have expected the classical school to argue that prices would change in almost the same proportion, leaving the real wage and the level of unemployment practically the same as before, any small gain or loss to labour being at the expense or profit of other elements of marginal cost which have been left unaltered" (1936, p. 12). The aggregate demand effects of the "small gains and losses" as well as monetary responses to changing wages and prices are discussed in detail in Chapter 19 of *The General Theory*. The aim is to show that money-wage cuts may raise output by reducing interest rates and stimulating investment (p. 265), but that similar results can be achieved far less painfully by increasing the money supply.

6. They don't show up, for example, in Solow's (1986) lucid presentation of the mainstream model. He says that using the quantity theory to describe aggregate demand is "childishly simple," but goes ahead and does it anyway. With less apology, Modigliani (1944) got the "quantity theory of effective demand" ball rolling in an IS/LM setup four decades before.

7. Once again we follow custom and ignore the fact that an economy-wide inverse relationship between the volume of capital (or its change) and the profit rate cannot generally be shown to exist. For Cambridge ruminations on the macroeconomic implications of this theme, see Eatwell and Milgate (1983). For practical purposes, the results of the reswitching controversy are yet another factor leading to the imprecision of any investment function such as (18).

8. Think of the ozone holes. The CFC chemicals which now open windows for ultraviolet radiation over the Poles were considered environmentally benign in the 1960s—a Ramsey-style optimal plan for resource allocation would have given them an increasingly important industrial role, even under standard dynamic programming procedures for calculating optimal programs subject to Knightian risk. The point is that there was no reason at the time to

anticipate adverse effects of CFCs in the stratosphere. This sort of outcome underlines the view shared by Hayek, Knight, and Keynes that human intelligence can never fathom the socio-techno-economic system. However, in contrast to Keynes, the Austro-Chicago message is that profit-seeking entrepreneurship will force the market to behave as well as it possibly can. If the effects of the ozone holes become truly serious, entrepreneurship will ensure that the holes get (partially) closed.

9. Whether assuming perfect short-term foresight is true to the spirit of Keynes is an interesting question. As discussed in section 8, he certainly thought that informed players are well aware of what other players—that is, "the market"—expect. And as we will see in Chapter 10 he presumed myopic perfect foresight in postulating uncovered interest rate parity for the determination of exchange rates (Keynes 1923). More generally, his views were not uncongenial with the volatility implicit in rational expectations—but only in the short run, of course.

10. In a world subject to repeated inflationary shocks, the system would never quite converge. With di_l/dt usually positive, from (21) the normal yield curve would be observed. Note also that the slope of the saddlepath in Figure 4.5 will be positive—both variables move steadily upward after Γ increases and i_l jumps. To see why, let λ be the *negative*, stable eigenvalue of the Jacobian. The corresponding eigenvector $(v_l, v_{\hat{p}})$ will satisfy the homogenous equations

$$\begin{bmatrix} (1/\phi) - \lambda & -1/\phi \\ -\eta & -(v + \lambda) \end{bmatrix} \begin{bmatrix} v_l \\ v_{\hat{p}} \end{bmatrix} = \begin{bmatrix} 0 \\ 0 \end{bmatrix}$$

The matrix on the left-hand side is singular by construction, so it suffices to consider the equation corresponding to its first row. It can be written as $v_{\hat{p}} = (1 - \phi\lambda)v_l$. In Figure 4.5, the corresponding line SS through C will have a positive slope and may be fairly steep insofar as $\phi \gg 0$.

11. A standard set of restrictions on the partial derivatives of the asset proportion functions (similar to restrictions imposed in complete sets of consumer demand equations) ensures that this "adding-up" constraint will be satisfied. The reader may want to write them out.

12. To go a step beyond counting variables and equations, here is a solution algorithm for (25)–(33). The banking system variables M and L are fixed in (32) and (33). Combining (25) and (26) gives Ω as a function of P_v, while as discussed in the text (29)–(31) solve to give P_v, i_v, and i as functions of Ω, M, V, and the policy-determined T_h. Hence we can solve out for Ω, P_v, and the rates of return just named. We can go back to (26) to get q, and λ comes from (27). Using the profit rate r in (24) finally gives the loan interest rate i_l.

13. The ratio $Z = PK/T$ looks suspiciously like the "velocity" of T-bills with respect to the capital stock. As shown in later chapters, in a structuralist formulation one can write out differential equations in which Z influences inflation dynamics for P, accumulation processes for K, and fiscal deficit dy-

namics for T. The resulting processes usually lead to a self-stabilizing response for Z, that is, $d\dot{Z}/dZ < 0$. Given a stable credit multiplier ζ, much of the renowned empirical stability of money velocity and cognate variables stems from this simple fact.

14. As discussed in section 5, the presence of a liquidity trap due to bond-holders' flight to money if the interest rate falls too far would also produce a horizontal LM schedule. As will be seen in Chapter 9, Minsky's financial instability hypothesis relies on an increasingly shallow slope of the LM curve at high levels of economic activity, as asset-holders forgo liquidity to switch their portfolios toward more speculative assets in a financial boom.

15. Here we take up only economic issues, but the point is more general. Recall Polanyi's (1944) insistence on the socially destabilizing properties of unfettered market forces.

16. The following discussion draws on Eatwell (1996).

17. In fact one can distinguish between "own-rates of own return" (a marginal product divided by an asset price in neoclassical jargon) and "own-rates of money return" (or capital gains). If 100 tons of wheat for spot delivery can buy 102 tons for forward delivery, the "wheat rate of wheat return" is 2 percent. If in addition the wheat price will appreciate in terms of money by 2 percent more (say), then the wheat rate of money return will be 4 percent. The variable ρ defined in the text implicitly includes both physical output and capital gains. The latter can be destabilizing, as discussed in section 9.

18. Kaldor's views are (of course) broadly consistent with the liquidity preference analysis in section 5. Even the perfect foresight jump of the long bond interest rate in Figure 4.5 keeps the slope—though not the level—of the yield curve relatively stable under shifting inflation, an eventuality that Kaldor did not consider.

19. To continue filling out scorecards of economists, the post-Keynesians draw on Cambridge (England) traditions, with the American branch largely concentrating on monetary and financial questions. Besides Minsky, representative players include Davidson (1972), Moore (1988), and Palley (1996). Much of their inspiration comes from two decades' worth of effort by Kaldor, summarized in Kaldor (1982).

20. This observation is not always true, of course. Between 1945 and the mid-1960s, for example, American firms could draw on an asset cushion built up during World War II due to big public spending and official restrictions on investment and dividend payments. This cushion certainly played a role in facilitating the rapid, relatively stable economic growth that took place during the late 1940s to late 1960s "Golden Age."

21. Two more caveats. First, as discussed in Chapter 1, when q is less than one, firms are tempted to "over-borrow" to play merger and acquisition games as in the 1980s. Second, financial systems have evolved differently in the advanced capitalist economies. The institutions discussed in the text are "Anglo-American," whereas banks with close ties to enterprises have played the long-term role in financing capital formation on the Continent and in Japan.

The classic essay on the German banking system is by Gerschenkron (1962). With a twenty-year lag, it set off an active field of comparative studies of financial systems beginning with Zysman (1983). For a review and update, see Pollin (1998a). There is more on financial system structure in Chapter 8.

22. Both "lender's risk" and "borrower's risk" are defined succinctly on p. 144 of *The General Theory,* but these terms are more often associated with Kalecki than with Keynes. New Keynesian reinterpretations of lender's and borrower's risk in terms of the currently chic "informational asymmetries" giving rise to moral hazard and adverse selection are discussed in Chapter 8.

23. Beginning in the 1970s there was a boom in formal neoclassical models exploring "bubble" trajectories off the saddlepath built into unstable dynamic systems like (38)–(40). Working out the mathematics kept theorists amused for a few years, but lack of empirical relevance ultimately put an end to the effort.

24. The colleague was almost certainly Duesenberry.

25. More generally, maximizing a quadratic function subject to linear constraints with additive random errors will produce a linear decision rule with another random term included. If the maximand is not exactly quadratic, the constraints are not exactly linear, or the random term is not additive, however, decision rules can easily be nonlinear in the extreme (Taylor 1970). As will be seen in later chapters, many neat-looking new classical formulations depend on quadratic utility, even though it has peculiar features such as making a risky asset an inferior good (Eichberger and Harper 1997, pp. 30–31).

26. A slump in the expected rate of profit may curtail investment demand, leading asset-holders to flee toward liquidity. In a Keynes/Minsky scenario (see Chapter 9), lower investment is associated with a rising ratio of the interest rate to the profit rate, making recovery unlikely. In another example, consumers may speed purchases at the beginning of an inflation because they are not sure along liquidity preference lines how far prices will rise. This destabilizing response is opposite to that predicted by the real balance effect and the inflation tax.

27. Market transactions are often limited by the short side, but not always. After the 1982 debt crises, for example, the short side would have been *no* additional loans from commercial banks to the developing countries affected. By running up payments arrears, borrowers in effect got new credits but not in the amounts that they desired on the long side. The market "cleared" somewhere between the loan supply and demand schedules.

5. Short-Term Model Closure and Long-Term Growth

1. For the private nonresidential U.S. economy with variables scaled by potential output, rough values for long-run investment and saving parameters are on the order of $\alpha = 0.25, \beta = 0.1, s_\pi = 0.5, s_w = 0.3$ (Gordon 1995), with the savings rates implicitly incorporating taxes and other leakages. Subject to the vagaries of econometrics and data, stability of a forced saving adjust-

ment process (were the economy really at full employment with forced saving as the main adjustment mechanism) would be precarious in the United States. The same conclusion follows from econometric results in Chapter 9 below, which show U.S. demand to be consistently profit-led.

2. The biblical interpretation involving a cruse of oil plus a barrel of flour that were divinely refilled as they emptied was proposed by Keynes (1930). The widow happened to be hosting the prophet Elijah while he was at cudgels with King Ahab (no friend of Yahweh and later reincarnated as the enemy of Moby-Dick). See 1 Kings 17:9–16. With due respect to Maynard, what this fable has to do with a capitalist social order 2,500 years later is moderately obscure.

3. Strictly speaking, the Ramsey-Keynes rule says that the time-derivative of per capita consumption $\dot{c}$ depends negatively on i, so that not the level but the change of per capita saving $\dot{s} = \dot{y} - \dot{c}$ (in obvious notation) will rise with i. As we have seen, this particular dynamic specification forces the economy to leap across saddlepaths, but in the long run the results would not differ greatly if one simply postulated that $s = s(i)$. As discussed in Chapter 3, this sort of relationship is in fact observed in steady states of Ramsey-style models.

4. In terms of Table 4.2, the balance sheets underlying (11) omit equity holdings $P_v V$ but do incorporate loans to firms from households. An LM equation like (11) is used in Chapter 7. See Table 7.2 for the underlying balance sheets.

5. That is, the Olivera-Tanzi effect discussed in Chapter 3. It has long been recognized, at least since the end of the German hyperinflation in the 1920s.

6. Models of cycles as discussed in Chapter 9 expand the range of dynamic options by selectively blending the fast and slow variables that are carefully isolated from one another in most growth models.

7. For example, in Chapter 3's Ramsey model, real consumption and thereby the real wage jump up to absorb the productivity increase in Figure 3.4.

8. Without productivity growth, $g > n$ means that a vibrant capitalism will have to absorb petty modes of production outside its own geopolitical domain to make up for the slow natural rate of growth: imperialism à la Rosa Luxemburg (1951). Massive importation of foreign labor could be such a solution. If $n > g$, capitalism may collapse, or else the ever-expanding reserve army will force the real wage down until additional accumulation increases the warranted rate g to n.

9. It is common in the literature to make $\hat{I}$ depend on g directly as opposed to u. The outcomes are much the same since in (21) u is treated as a function of g.

10. The steady-state capital/output ratio is $\mu = s/n$. For plausible saving and population growth rates μ could easily exceed typically observed capital/GDP levels of three to five, but that is because we are not including depreciation in our growth accounting.

11. As long as the employment rate $e_t = bX_t/H_t$ is "high," the results that follow go through if it is assumed that only employed households make pension contributions which are shared out to all retirees.

6. Chicago Monetarism, New Classical Macroeconomics, and Mainstream Finance

1. One standard justification for an aggregate demand equation of the type $X = MV/P$ is that it emerges as a reduced form from a full IS/LM system. That may be so, but even the simple model of Chapter 7 shows that in such a solution state variables besides money should affect X, for example, other components of wealth and measures of distribution. They never appear in short-run monetarist or rational expectations models.

2. The reference is to a famous passage from *The General Theory:* "It is a great fault of symbolic pseudo-mathematical methods of formalizing a system of economic analysis . . . that they expressly assume strict independence between the factors involved and lose all their cogency and authority if this hypothesis is disallowed; whereas, in ordinary discourse, where we are not blindly manipulating but know all the time what we are doing and what the words mean, we can keep 'at the back of our heads' the necessary reserves and qualifications and the adjustments which we shall have to make later on, in a way in which we cannot keep complicated partial differentials 'at the back' of several pages of algebra which assume that they all vanish" (pp. 297–298).

3. For the record, if a random variable Y is related to another one X by an equation $Y = g(X)$, then its expected value or expectation is $E(Y) = \int g(t)f_x(t)dt$, where f_x is the probability density function of X and the integral covers the domain over which X varies. Since we are dealing with probabilities, it will be true that $\int f_x(t)dt = 1$.

4. Keynes (1921) first set out his views about the vagueness of our knowledge of the future in his *Treatise on Probability.* In apparent reaction, Ramsey (1931) launched the movement toward treating things to come solely as a set of probabilistic "events;" de Finetti (1937) proposed a similar approach. It was given a big impetus by the invention of game theory (featuring an axiomatic treatment of expected utility theory and the later emergence of the idea of "games against nature") by von Neumann and Morgenstern (1944). However, counter-examples by Allais (1953) and Ellsberg (1961) strongly suggested that even the most "rational" decision-maker is likely to behave inconsistently with the axioms of rational choice which have no room for the "ambiguity"—Ellsberg's word—of unavoidable uncertainty. Despite the efforts of Allais and Ellsberg, the expected utility approach carried the day and more so. Completely "objective" probability distributions on the future are the stock in trade of new classical macroeconomics.

5. To quote Friedman (1968), "'The natural rate of unemployment' . . . is the level that would be ground out by the Walrasian system of general equilibrium equations," subject to a few qualifications about market structure and informational barriers which the new classicists were soon to discard.

6. Nor is empirical support for the Friedman-Phelps model strong, as Baker (2000) points out in a critical review (the fact that Baker felt the need to write the piece as late as the year 2000 is itself a testament to the obsession

of mainstream macroeconomists with the NAIRU). Like all bastard Keynesian constructs, the accelerationist story is dogged by its inaccurate prediction of a visibly countercyclical real wage, despite the high employment, rising real wages, and low inflation rates of the late 1990s. Also, job quit rates peak when unemployment falls, and decline sharply in downturns, contrary to the assumptions about the labor supply underlying the model (Okun 1980).

7. This assumption is usually justified on the basis of the demand model due to Spence (1976) and Dixit and Stiglitz (1977), which is widely utilized in the analysis of imperfect competition. When production is subject to decreasing costs, the model's specification smoothes away a number of inconvenient nonlinearities and nonconvexities in diverse contexts.

8. Buchanan (1976) introduced the term "Ricardian equivalence theorem" for Barro's result, while arguing that Ricardo himself toyed with the idea but ultimately rejected it.

9. The adjustments of household consumption and saving to more government spending in the Wicksell and Sargent-Wallace models of Chapter 3 are of the same stripe as the movements described in the text. The inflation tax plays an essential equilibrating role in those models, while Barro relies on dynamic savings optimization.

10. The accounting underlying equation (15) was pioneered by Domar (1944). The significance of the growth rate > real interest rate condition was perhaps first pointed out in print in a book from the World Bank put together by Avramovic (1964). The basic insight was apparently due to the Bank economist Gerald M. Alter in the 1950s.

11. Substituting variables among the accounting balances of the SAM gives other expressions for the steady state. For example, the share β of business in total debt is $\beta = (g - \pi u)/[(1 - \pi)u - \gamma_h - \tau_h)]$. Household consumption γ_h and taxes τ_h together have to exceed wage income $(1 - \pi)u$ (but not necessarily total household income including interest receipts) for the economy to be on the "right" side of the golden rule where $g < \pi u$ with $\beta > 0$. Transfers such as interest payments from firms and government to households again show up as essential components of capitalist financial systems.

12. That is, one lag emerges because saving (= investment, by Say's Law) in period $t - 1$ affects the level of capital stock and output in period t. Substituting out the effects of the assumed one-period autocorrelation of z_t then makes output depend on its values in periods $t - 1$ and $t - 2$. For details, see McCallum (1989), Stadler (1994), or Romer (2001).

13. The need for such violent fluctuations in the level of productivity is reduced if there are "technical" lags of longer than one period in investment projects, or if capital formation is especially stimulated in a cyclical upswing—ideas already present in the writings of Hayek and Wicksell.

14. For those interested in pursuing the topic, Øksendal (2000) is an exemplary text, with several optimization applications. Neftci (2000) is very good on intuition, with an emphasis on financial engineering.

15. In a recent seven-hundred-page text on dynamic methods in macroeconom-

ics, Ljungqvist and Sargent (2000) acknowledge Bellman's curse, but then proceed to get around it by using approximation techniques on toy models and advocating the use of quadratic objective functions and linear constraints. Much more fundamentally, Mirowski (2002) reviews results in computational economics, demonstrating that infinite-horizon dynamic programming models of the sort described in the text make no sense as exact descriptions of economic behavior, because they cannot be solved (or the preference functions underlying them described) with a Universal Turing Machine, the ultimate theoretical computational power.

16. The continuous time analog is equation (18) in Chapter 3, which can be restated as $-d\xi/dt = \xi(f' - \epsilon)$, where ξ is an asset-price costate variable, f' is the marginal product of capital, and ϵ is a pure rate of time preference.

17. CAPM does not fit the data remarkably well, but that does not prevent regressions of the form $r_i - \bar{r} = \beta_i(r_m - \bar{r})$ from being endemic among practitioners. In the equation, r_i is firm i's expected (in practice, average) return, r_m is the cross-firm average "market" return, and $\bar{r}$ is the "riskless" return (to government debt). An asset with a high "beta" will have to pay an extrahigh return (even if its overall returns have low variance) because its positive correlation with the market forces its owners to take additional steps to hedge.

18. The discussion that follows draws on Blanchard and Fischer (1989), chap. 6.

19. As usual in rational expectations models, (36) demonstrates unstable dynamics because typically $\beta U_{C,t+1}/U_{C,t} < 1$ or (ignoring expected values for the moment), $Z_{t+1} > Z_t$. Bubbles or Ponzi games seem ready to appear, but they are ruled out on the assumption that the investor solves (36) forward on an extremal path.

20. Diamond (1967) shows that the stock market can in principle cover all contingencies. One suspects, however, that the number of companies (options, derivatives, hedge funds) needed to span all economically relevant states of nature (assuming that they can be objectively assigned risks) far surpasses the capacity of people to manage, financial gurus to analyze, stock market pages to list, or computers to store in memory.

21. Contrast the Keynes-Minsky vision of Chapters 4 and 8!

22. With caveats to be noted below, their basic arbitrage argument carries over into subsequent general equilibrium treatments of the theorem, such as Stiglitz (1969) and Eichberger and Harper (1997).

7. Effective Demand and the Distributive Curve

1. The basic causal structure of this chapter's model draws heavily on Amadeo's (1994) work on inflation and distribution in Brazil. Chiarella and Flaschel (2000) also set up models with separate wage and price Phillips curves.

2. Insofar as ψ would be the dominant variable in explaining changes in the standard of living and production costs, the model here can be viewed as a first approximation toward a more complete version.

3. For a preview of the cyclical behavior of the wage share, see Figures 9.3 through 9.5.

4. It is easy to show that (7) is equivalent to an adaptive expectations or "error-learning model" $\hat{P}^e = \hat{P} + \rho^p[P - P^e)/P]$ and similarly for the growth rate of the expected wage. As ρ^p approaches zero (the likely case empirically), workers would be responding to the actual as opposed to the expected price inflation rate.

5. As is usual in economics, there is no shortage of potential explanations for a positive association between an increase in labor productivity and the profit share $1 - \psi = ru$ with r as the rate of profit. For example, the level of output may be determined by effective demand, which shifts the position of a neoclassical aggregate production function. "Along" the function, a higher real wage will induce enough capital-labor substitution to reduce the wage share when the elasticity of substitution exceeds one (refer back to Chapter 2). A more Kaldorian story could be based on the idea that higher profits lead to more investment embodying recent, high-productivity technologies. The higher cash flow could also be directed to noninvestment spending that raises productivity. As discussed in Chapter 11, the postulated existence of such "intangible capital" has become a recent neoclassical fad.

6. See Eisner (1996). A curve like the one in Figure 7.1 could emerge from the model discussed in this chapter, if (3) takes the form $\hat{P} = \psi u - au^2$ when $\chi^w = 1$, and the locus along which $\dot{\psi} = 0$ satisfies an equation such as $\psi = b + cu^2$. The reduced form is $\hat{P} = bu - au^2 + cu^3$, which takes the shape of the curve in Figure 7.1.

7. The Luddites were technologically unemployed workers who smashed labor-saving textile machinery in England after 1810, protesting job losses and reduced wages (the possibly mythical Ned Lud took a hammer to his master's machines a decade or two earlier). In response to this issue of his day, Ricardo added a chapter "On Machinery" to the third (1821) edition of his *Principles of Political Economy and Taxation,* in which he allowed that the opinion prevailing in "the labouring class, that the employment of machinery is frequently detrimental to their interests, is not founded on prejudice and error, but is conformable to the correct principles of political economy." Most contemporary and subsequent economists chose to differ.

8. As has been noted in Chapter 4, Fisher's formula also often serves as a monetarist theory of the nominal interest rate i. That is, in the monetarist worldview, $\hat{P}$ is determined by growth of the money supply and r by intertemporal resource allocation of the sort built into Fisher's real interest theory. The nominal rate i follows as a residual, $i = r + \hat{P}$.

9. The monetary side of the economy is restated in Chapter 8 to highlight business debt burdens and their dynamics.

10. Manipulations like those to follow in the text should always be interpreted taking into account *The General Theory*'s famous dismissal of algebraic macroeconomic games, quoted in note 2 of Chapter 6. Many complicated partial differentials underlie equations (5) and (20); just a few are brought "from the back" of the algebra into the discussion that follows.

11. To repeat, "It is the fact that money wages are *too high* relative to the quantity of money that explains why it is unprofitable to expand employment to the 'full-employment' level" (emphasis added). That is, if for a given Velocity curve the Distributive schedule shifts downward, the economy will be in better shape.

12. Blecker (1999c) gives a helpful review of the material covered in this section, plus much more on a Kaleckian approach to open economy macroeconomics in general.

13. In other words, the price of "our" exports in the world market is P/e, and our products are assumed to be in some form of imperfect competition with those of other countries. The "law of one price" does not hold in the sense that the internal price level is determined by an external commodity price P^* according to the relationship $P = eP^*$.

14. In terms of equation (15) of Chapter 4 the tax changes had the effect of driving saving-cum-tax rates like s_π and s_w closer together, making the economy more strongly profit-led.

15. The joint hypotheses that aggregate demand is profit-led and devaluation expansionary seem to be widely accepted for industrialized economies. Recently Phelps and Zoega (2002) have entered a disclaimer: "A weaker real exchange rate hinders overseas competitors and thus invites higher markups, so contracting output and jobs available." Contractionary devaluation looks inevitable, *if* $\partial\pi/\partial\rho > 0$ *and* demand is wage-led. The empirical support appears to involve a regression across OECD countries of employment on local prices of Big Mac burgers as compiled by *The Economist* magazine.

8. Structuralist Finance and Money

1. As Richard Feynman (1985, p. 6) disarmingly put the matter at the beginning of a fascinating set of lectures, "By the way, what I have just outlined is a 'physicist's history of physics,' which is never correct. What I am telling you is a sort of conventionalized myth-story that the physicists tell to their students, . . . and [it] is not necessarily related to the actual historical development, which I do not really know!" Economics is no better than its major disciplinary object of envy in this regard.

2. Recall the discussion in Chapter 4 of how the architecture and function of financial systems can vary substantially, even across advanced capitalist economies. Arguments in sections 1 and 2 herein draw heavily on Caridi (2002), D'Arista (2002), Desai (1989), and comments by Jan Kregel and Yilmaz Akyuz on earlier versions.

3. The major twentieth-century discoverer of endogenous money was probably Dennis Robertson (1922)—others such as Marshall had had the notion previously. Robertson pointed out that the way the London discount market worked, the Bank of England had no choice but to provide the reserves that commercial banks required to hold the amount of debt the government wished to issue, given Bank rate. After his old friendship with Keynes fell

apart over the content of *The General Theory,* Robertson dropped into disfavor among the Cambridge Keynesians. But they had no qualms about appropriating his ideas. Forced saving is another example.

4. This tendency later disappeared. We can briefly recapitulate the reasons why: after the turn of the century, emerging multiplant, multimarket corporate enterprises began to push price formation in the direction of markup rules as opposed to the flexible price variation more commonly observed in markets for raw materials and other commodities. At roughly the same time, unions began to defend the real wage by forcing nominal wage increases. Both processes spilled over into raw material prices, and through markups back into final goods prices.

5. Moral hazard ("hidden action") and adverse selection ("hidden information") are ideas from the literature on insurance which have become popular among new Keynesians. See section 6 below for examples. In the present context, moral hazard means that if a financial agent is protected against downside risk, she or he is more likely to indulge in high risk/high return investment activities. Hidden action and information are treated in detail in all recent texts on microeconomics and game theory.

6. The moral hazard was codified in the Garn-St. Germain Act of 1982, which guaranteed full insurance on an unlimited number of $100,000 deposits in S&Ls held by one individual. When he signed it, President Reagan called the act a "home run." Maybe it was for the silent partners in S&Ls who subsequently got bailed out. For almost everyone else (taxpayers underwriting the bailout included), Garn-St. Germain was more like being on the wrong side of a triple play.

7. Forced saving serves as an example of another channel. Recall how full employment ruled even in Kaldor's own growth models, although he dropped that assumption in later formulations in the late 1960s and 1970s.

8. Dropping the terms for capital gains, equation (8) in Chapter 1 gives $S_b = \dot{\Omega}_b$ in which S_b is business sector saving. Equity prices are reintroduced in the growth model in section 5 of this chapter and in the Minsky business cycle model discussed in Chapter 9. In both cases, short-run changes in wealth levels due to capital gains or losses play important roles.

9. As noted in the text, in practice banks can also meet reserve requirements by borrowing in other securities markets—the more realistic case, in fact, for the United States. Palley (1996) and Franke and Semmler (1999) present models going in the same direction as the one developed here.

10. A household portfolio adjustment like the one described in the text is essential if asset-holders are to absorb an increase in the money supply. Palley (1996) criticizes many post-Keynesians for emphasizing how loans create money without worrying about how it gets absorbed.

11. Post-Keynesians such as Rousseas (1985) put great emphasis on nominal interest rate markups in banks' loan-pricing relationships such as (13) and (14).

12. The basics are from Lavoie and Godley, but the model presented here differs

from theirs in specification details and the use of continuous as opposed to discrete time. An early paper by Shaikh (1989) and several follow-ups deal with similar issues in a disequilibrium framework.

13. As observed in Chapter 1, for the last two or three decades of the twentieth century, in the United States χ was negative.

14. As shown in Chapter 9, a more reactive version of investment behavior transforms the one-dimensional dynamics of Figure 8.4 into two-dimensional cycles.

9. A Genus of Cycles

1. In continuous time, oscillating variables appear in a two-dimensional system when its eigenvalues are conjugate complex (as opposed to real), that is, they can be written in the form $\lambda = \alpha + \beta i$ and $\bar{\lambda} = \alpha - \beta i$ with $\alpha = \text{Tr } J/2$. For the oscillations to converge locally, the real part α of the eigenvalues has to be negative. Steady cycles show up when the real part equals zero, and there are divergent spirals when it is positive. The two standard methods to investigate the properties of such systems are Hopf bifurcations and the Poincaré-Bendixson theorem. The former analyzes the changing nature of cycles as the real part of the eigenvalues shifts through the value zero. The latter sets out global conditions for convergence to a closed orbit. Hirsch and Smale (1974) is a classic text on these matters, and Lorenz (1989) and Medio and Lines (2001) offer helpful intuition.

2. The analysis in sections 2 and 3 draws heavily on work by Nelson Barbosa-Filho. See Barbosa-Filho (2001b) and Barbosa-Filho and Taylor (2003).

3. In the upper diagram, convergence will be oscillatory (the equilibrium point is a "focus") instead of direct (a "node") if the discriminant $(\text{Tr } J)^2 - 4 \text{ Det } J$ of the Jacobian is negative so that the eigenvalues are complex. The (discrete time) econometric results in the following section suggest that this condition is likely to be satisfied.

4. The labor share is from NIPA Table 1.2. Capacity utilization is based on NIPA Table 1.14 and the Congressional Budget Office methodology. Supplemental labor income separated by private and public sources is not available in the tables. Some studies of the labor share incorporate part of proprietors' income into wages. However, there is no obvious way to carry out the needed imputations so we did not pursue this option. Using potential output or capacity instead of the capital stock to define u presupposes no trend in capital productivity. As discussed in Chapter 2, this assumption is probably appropriate for the United States.

5. Recall from Chapter 7 Blecker's (1991) suggestion that the Reagan fiscal package may have pushed the economy in a profit-led direction during the 1980s.

6. Though the details differ, the interpretation of the Tobin model presented here draws on Chiarella and Flaschel (2000).

7. The destabilizing inflationary expectations process just analyzed can gener-

ate cycles in other contexts. It is easy to show that they can arise in the Wicksellian inflation model of Chapter 3, for example.

8. In their Chapter 12, Flaschel, Franke, and Semmler (1997) provide a good discussion of the implications of pursuing the "confidence" approach.

9. The interpretation here differs from that of Taylor and O'Connell (1985), who treated the LM curve as having a negative slope. The importance of nonlinearities in Minsky's model is emphasized by Skott (1995). Minsky's analysis clearly hinges on the existence of something like a liquidity trap, but at high as opposed to low levels of the interest and profit rates as in the traditional story. Although the long-term bond pricing rules discussed in Chapter 4 suggest that the LM curve can flatten more easily at a low interest rate, they certainly do not rule out the same possibility when i is relatively high.

10. To avoid complications not of great priority at the moment, (22) ignores interest payments on government debt. In the following section, a cycle around the debt service burden of firms is presented.

11. The investment function is equation (20) in Chapter 8. Savings rates might also fluctuate with the state of confidence, falling when it is high and rising when it is low. The outcome would be a cycle similar to the one in Figure 9.9 below.

10. Exchange Rate Complications

1. Williamson and Milner (1991) is an institutionally and historically informed mainstream textbook. Krugman and Obstfeld (1997) is a better specimen of the profession's central tendencies.

2. Other specifications, such as treating imports as negative exports or additional components of consumption demand, are possible, but would not change the main results to be presented below.

3. Salter-Swan was the culmination of a long string of models of the trade account based on the assumption that capital flows are exogenous. They included an elasticities approach (featuring "Marshall-Lerner conditions" on trade elasticities of the sort discussed in Chapter 5), an absorption approach, and analysis of internal versus external balance which led to Salter-Swan.

4. Full intertemporal optimization models for open economies unsurprisingly became popular in the 1990s, and represent an alternative to the older formulations discussed in the text. Their dynamic relationships typically include UIP and a Ramsey rule for capital accumulation. Most of the relevant mathematics appears in previous chapters, and can safely be omitted here. Intertemporal models have had no visible impact on the thoughts of practical women and men. As the models' proponents Obstfeld and Rogoff (1995) concede, the Mundell-Fleming approach, "which ignores intertemporal choice and even intertemporal budget constraints, remains overwhelmingly dominant in policy circles." If, as is argued in this chapter, Mundell-Fleming is not a functional model either, it is not obvious where policy circles are supposed to turn.

5. We stick with the standard literature in assuming that the monetary authorities intervene to control their holdings of assets. A post-Keynesian scenario in which interest rates are set exogenously and money supplies adjust would be straightforward to work through. See also section 12.

6. The diagram presupposes that the home country is a net creditor at the ruling exchange rate. To get to the net debtor case, the External assets schedule can be rotated clockwise via exchange appreciation until it crosses the vertical axis above the origin.

7. Another way is to linearize three asset market balance equations around an initial equilibrium and attempt to solve them for small changes in i, i^*, and e, subject to the accounting restrictions mentioned in the text. After great labor, the Jacobian matrix of this system will turn out to be singular. Such an exercise was the genesis of the model presented here.

8. The interest rate changes could induce shifts in the exchange rate over time. On the basis of the comparative static results below, it seems likely that the compensated capital inflow discussed in the text will make i fall and i^* rise. Under UIP and myopic perfect foresight (section 8), the exchange rate would tend to appreciate, $\dot{e} < 0$.

9. To keep the analysis simple, all variables are assumed to be continuously differentiable functions of time. In practice, both stock and flow variables can change discontinuously. But if in so doing they obey all relevant balance sheet and income statements, the transition from portfolio balance to Mundell-Fleming accounting goes through. The extensive theory and notation required to deal with such eventualities as well as changes in prices is best avoided here. Foley (1975) takes up the complications. In theory, accounting consistency between stock and flow variables is a means for linking the future to the present; in practice (in discrete time) it will be observed in sectoral balance sheet and flow-of-funds accounts because they are constructed that way.

10. As observed by Branson and Handerson (1985), there were many papers in the 1970s and early 1980s devoted to dynamic analysis of a portfolio balance model augmented by IS and BP relationships. A typical "finding" was that the dynamic system could be unstable if home country net foreign assets were negative. Unfortunately this literature was flawed, because it assumed the spot rate could be set by portfolio balances and also treated the BP equation as being an independent restriction on the dynamic system.

11. For future reference, a possible instability in (18) due to expectational effects in asset demands is worth noting. With MPF, $\dot{e}$ equals expected depreciation ϵ and (as noted in the text) shows up as a determinant of the interest rates on the right-hand side of (18). Differentiation gives $d\dot{e}/de = (i - i^*) + e[\partial i/\partial e + (\partial i/\partial \dot{e})(d\dot{e}/de)]$, where the $\partial i/\partial \dot{e}$ term comes from the IS/LM system. Minor manipulation shows that $d\dot{e}/de = [1 - e(\partial i/\partial \dot{e})]^{-1}[(i - i^*) + e(\partial i/\partial e)]$. When $0 < e(\partial i/\partial \dot{e}) < 1$ (the traditional inelastic expectations story), the UIP differential equation is locally stable. But strong expectational effects could make $d\dot{e}/de > 0$ even when $\partial i/\partial e$ is negative.

12. That is, a critical point E of the system (18)–(19) in Figure 10.3 can be a stable or unstable focus.

11. Growth and Development Theories

1. Note the contrast with the traditional Ramsey model of Chapter 3, in which the marginal product of capital is equal to the exogenous rate of discount at steady state.

2. Arrow borrowed the basic idea from the "learning curves" used by many World War II aircraft engineers as well as the Cost Analysis section at RAND Corporation, where he was a frequent consultant. For an entertaining discussion of learning and related matters, see Mirowksi (2002), pp. 394–406.

3. In fact, Uzawa (1965) proposed a very similar model in an optimal development planning context twenty years before Lucas, depriving the 1988 paper of most of its originality. It is also fair to add that growth will be endogenous in the Lucas model even if the H^* term in his production function (6) is not present, because the marginal return of labor time devoted to skill acquisition is constant.

4. See Taylor (1991), chap. 9, for formalization of much of the discussion to follow.

5. See Chang (2002) for a fascinating history of the interventionist policies that the now prosperous economies practiced when they were poor and—more important—how they now pressure the rest of the world not to take the road they followed.

References

Abel, Andrew B., and Olivier Jean Blanchard. 1983. "An Intertemporal Model of Saving and Investment." *Econometrica, 51:* 675–692.

Abel, Andrew B., N. Gregory Mankiw, Lawrence H. Summers, and Richard J. Zeckhauser. 1989. "Assessing Dynamic Efficiency: Theory and Evidence." *Review of Economic Studies, 56:* 1–20.

Agénor, Pierre-Richard, and Peter J. Montiel. 1999. *Development Macroeconomics.* 2d ed. Princeton, N.J.: Princeton University Press.

Akerlof, George A., and Janet L. Yellen. 1990. "The Fair Wage-Effort Hypothesis and Unemployment." *Quarterly Journal of Economics, 105:* 255–283.

Alesina, Alberto. 1988. "Macroeconomics and Politics." *NBER Macroeconomics Annual, 3:* 13–52.

Allais, Maurice. 1953. "Le comportement de l'homme devant le risque: Critique des postulats et axioms de l'école américaine." *Econometrica, 21:* 503–546.

Amadeo, Edward. 1989. *Keynes's Principle of Effective Demand.* Upleadon, U.K.: Edward Elgar.

——— 1994. *Institutions, Inflation, and Unemployment.* Brookfield, Vt.: Edward Elgar.

Amsden, Alice H. 1989. *Asia's Next Giant: South Korea and Late Industrialization.* New York: Oxford University Press.

——— 2001. *The Rise of the "Rest": Challenges to the West from Late-Industrializing Economies.* New York: Oxford University Press.

Ando, Albert, and Franco Modigliani. 1963. "The Life Cycle Hypothesis of Saving." *American Economic Review, 53:* 55–84.

Anyadike-Danes, Michael, Ken Coutts, and Wynne Godley. 1988. "IS-LM and Real Stock-Flow Monetary Models: A Prelude to Applied Macroeconomic Modelling." Department of Applied Economics, University of Cambridge.

Arrow, Kenneth J. 1962. "The Economic Implications of Learning by Doing." *Review of Economic Studies, 29:* 155–173.

Arthur, W. Brian. 1989. "Competing Technologies, Increasing Returns, and Lock-in by Historical Events." *Economic Journal, 99:* 116–131.

Avramovic, Dragoslav, ed. 1968. *Economic Growth and External Debt.* Baltimore: Johns Hopkins University Press.

Backhouse, Roger, and Andrea Salanti, eds. 2001. *Macroeconomics and the Real World*. New York: Oxford University Press.

Bagehot, Walter. [1873] 1962. *Lombard Street*. Homewood, Ill.: Irwin.

Baker, Dean. 2000. "NAIRU: Dangerous Dogma at the Fed." Philomont, Va.: Financial Markets Center.

Ball, Laurence. 1990. "Intertemporal Substitution and Constraints on Labor Supply: Evidence from Panel Data." *Economic Inquiry, 28*: 706–724.

Barbosa-Filho, Nelson H. 2000. "A Note on the Theory of Demand-Led Growth." *Contributions to Political Economy, 19*: 19–32.

——— 2001a. "Effective Demand and Growth: An Analysis of Alternative Closures of Keynesian Models." Center for Economic Policy Analysis, New School University, New York.

——— 2001b. "Income Distribution and Demand Fluctuations in the Postwar U.S. Economy: A Structuralist Approach." Center for Economic Policy Analysis, New School University, New York.

Barbosa-Filho, Nelson H., and Lance Taylor. 2003. "Distributive and Demand Cycles in the U.S. Economy—A Structuralist Goodwin Model." Center for Economic Policy Analysis, New School University, New York.

Barro, Robert J. 1974. "Are Government Bonds Net Wealth?" *Journal of Political Economy, 82*: 1095–1117.

——— 1976. "Rational Expectations and the Role of Monetary Policy." *Journal of Monetary Economics, 2*: 1–32.

——— 1989. "The Neoclassical Approach to Fiscal Policy." In Robert J. Barro, ed., *Modern Business Cycle Theory*. Cambridge, Mass.: Harvard University Press.

Barro, Robert J., and Xavier Sala-i-Martin. 1995. *Economic Growth*. New York: McGraw-Hill.

Bauer, P. T. 1972. *Dissent on Development*. London: Weidenfeld and Nicolson.

Becker, Gary S. 1964. *Human Capital*. New York: Columbia University Press.

Bellman, Richard. 1957. *Dynamic Programming*. Princeton, N.J.: Princeton University Press.

Benassy, Jean-Pascal. 1986. *Macroeconomics: An Introduction to the Non-Walrasian Approach*. Orlando, Fla.: Academic Press.

Bernanke, Ben S., and Mark Gertler. 1990. "Financial Fragility and Economic Performance." *Quarterly Journal of Economics, 79*: 14–31.

Bhaduri, Amit, and Stephen A. Marglin. 1990. "Unemployment and the Real Wage: The Economic Basis for Contesting Political Ideologies." *Cambridge Journal of Economics, 14*: 375–393.

Blanchard, Olivier Jean, and Stanley Fischer. 1989. *Lectures on Macroeconomics*. Cambridge: MIT Press.

Blanchard, Olivier Jean, and Nobuhiro Kiyotaki. 1987. "Monopolistic Competition and the Effects of Aggregate Demand." *American Economic Review, 77*: 647–666.

Blanchard, Olivier Jean, and Danny Quah. 1989. "The Dynamic Effects of Aggregate Demand and Aggregate Supply Disturbances." *American Economic Review,* 79: 655–673.

Blanchflower, David G., and Andrew J. Oswald. 1994. *The Wage Curve.* Cambridge: MIT Press.

Blecker, Robert A. 1991. "Profitability and Saving-Spending Behavior in the U.S. Economy: A Test of the Exhilarationist Hypothesis." Department of Economics, American University, Washington, D.C.

—— 1999a. "The Debt Bomb: Is the U.S. International Financial Position Sustainable?" Washington, D.C.: Economic Policy Institute.

—— 1999b. *Taming Global Finance: A Better Architecture for Growth and Equity.* Washington, D.C.: Economic Policy Institute.

—— 1999c. "Kaleckian Growth Models for Open Economies." In Johan Depez and John T. Harvey, eds., *Foundations of International Economics: Post-Keynesian Perspectives.* New York: Routledge.

—— 2002a. "Distribution, Demand, and Growth in Neo-Kaleckian Macro Models." In Mark Setterfield, ed., *The Economics of Demand-Led Growth: Challenging the Supply-Side Vision of the Long Run.* Northhampton, Mass.: Edward Elgar.

—— 2002b. "International Capital Mobility, Macroeconomic Imbalances, and the Risk of Global Contraction." In John Eatwell and Lance Taylor, eds., *International Capital Markets: Systems in Transition.* New York: Oxford University Press.

Block, Thorsten H. 2000. "Essays on Historical Macroeconomics." Ph.D. dissertation, Department of Economics, New School University, New York.

Boddy, Raford, and James R. Crotty. 1975. "Class Conflict and Macro Policy: The Political Business Cycle." *Review of Radical Political Economics,* 7 (1): 1–19.

Bowles, Samuel, and Robert Boyer. 1995. "Wages, Aggregate Demand, and Employment in an Open Economy: An Empirical Investigation." In Gerald A. Epstein and Herbert A. Gintis, eds., *Macroeconomic Policy after the Conservative Era.* Cambridge: Cambridge University Press.

Bowles, Samuel, and Herbert Gintis. 1990. "Contested Exchange: New Microfoundations of the Political Economy of Capitalism." *Politics and Society,* 18: 165–222.

—— 1995. "Escaping the Efficiency-Equity Trade-off: Productivity-Enhancing Asset Redistributions." In Gerald A. Epstein and Herbert A. Gintis, eds., *Macroeconomic Policy after the Conservative Era.* Cambridge: Cambridge University Press.

Bowles, Samuel, David Gordon, and Thomas Weisskopf. 1990. *After the Wasteland: A Democratic Economics for the Year 2000.* Armonk, N.Y.: M. E. Sharpe.

Branson, William H., and Dale W. Henderson. 1985. "The Specification and Influence of Asset Markets." In Ronald W. Jones and Peter B. Kenen, eds.,

Handbook of International Economics, vol. 2. Amsterdam: North-Holland.

Bruno, Michael. 1993. *Crisis, Stabilization, and Economic Reform.* New York: Oxford University Press.

Bruno, Michael, and Stanley Fischer. 1990. "Seigniorage, Operating Rules, and the High Inflation Trap." *Quarterly Journal of Economics, 105:* 353–374.

Bryson, Arthur E., Jr., and Yu-Chi Ho. 1969. *Applied Optimal Control.* Waltham, Mass.: Blaisdell.

Buchanan, James M. 1976. "Barro on the Ricardian Equivalence Theorem." *Journal of Political Economy, 84:* 337–342.

Burns, Arthur, and Wesley C. Mitchell. 1946. *Measuring Business Cycles.* New York: National Bureau of Economic Research.

Cagan, Philip. 1956. "The Monetary Dynamics of Hyperinflation." In Milton Friedman, ed., *Studies in the Quantity Theory of Money.* Chicago: University of Chicago Press.

Caridi, Christy Huebner. 2002. "Keynes's Inactive Balances, the Banking Sector, and Effective Demand." Center for Economic Policy Analysis, New School University, New York.

Carlin, Wendy, and David Soskice. 1990. *Macroeconomics and the Wage Bargain.* Oxford: Oxford University Press.

Carroll, Christopher D., and Lawrence H. Summers. 1991. "Consumption Growth Parallels Income Growth: Some New Evidence." In B. Douglas Bernheim and John B. Shoven, eds., *National Saving and Economic Performance.* Chicago: University of Chicago Press.

Cass, David. 1965. "Optimum Growth in an Equilibrium Model of Capital Accumulation." *Review of Economic Studies, 32:* 233–240.

Cassell, Gustav. 1922. *Money and Foreign Exchange after 1914.* London: Constable.

Cavallo, Domingo. 1977. "Stagflationary Effects of Monetarist Stabilization Policies." Ph.D. dissertation, Department of Economics, Harvard University, Cambridge, Mass.

Chakravarty, Sukhamoy. 1980. *Alternative Approaches to the Theory of Economic Growth.* Delhi: Orient-Longman.

Chang, Ha-Joon. 1993. "The Political Economy of Industrial Policy in Korea." *Cambridge Journal of Economics, 17:* 131–157.

——— 2002. *Kicking away the Ladder: Development Strategy in Historical Perspective.* London: Anthem Press.

Chenery, Hollis B. 1959. "The Interdependence of Investment Decisions." In Moses Abramovitz et al., *The Allocation of Economic Resources.* Stanford, Calif.: Stanford University Press.

Chenery, Hollis B., and Michael Bruno. 1962. "Development Alternatives in an Open Economy: The Case of Israel." *Economic Journal, 72:* 79–103.

Chiarella, Carl, and Peter Flaschel. 2000. *The Dynamics of Keynesian Monetary Growth: Macrofoundations,* Cambridge: Cambridge University Press.

Chick, Victoria. 1986. "The Evolution of the Banking System and the Theory of Saving, Investment, and Interest." *Economies et Sociétés, 20:* 111–126.

Clower, Robert. 1965. "The Keynesian Counter-Revolution: A Theoretical Approach." In F. H. Hahn and F. P. R. Brechling, eds., *The Theory of Interest Rates.* London: Macmillan.

Coase, Ronald H. 1960. "The Problem of Social Cost." *Journal of Law and Economics, 3:* 1–44.

Collins, Randall. 1980. "Weber's Last Theory of Capitalism: A Systematization." *American Sociological Review, 45:* 925–942.

Currie, Lachlin. 1934. *The Supply and Control of Money in the United States.* Cambridge, Mass.: Harvard University Press.

D'Arista, Jane. 2002. "Financial Regulation in a Liberalized Global Environment." In John Eatwell and Lance Taylor, eds., *International Capital Markets: Systems in Transition.* New York: Oxford University Press.

Davidson, Paul. 1972. *Money in the Real World.* New York: John Wiley.

de Finetti, Bruno. 1937. "La prévision: Ses lois logiques, ses sources subjectives." *Annales de l'Institut Henri Poincaré, 7:* 1–68.

Desai, Meghnad. 1973. "Growth Cycles and Inflation in a Model of Class Struggle." *Journal of Economic Theory, 6:* 527–545.

——— 1989. "The Scourge of the Monetarists: Kaldor on Monetarism and on Money." *Cambridge Journal of Economics, 13:* 171–182.

Diamond, Peter A. 1965. "National Debt in a Neoclassical Growth Model." *American Economic Review, 55:* 1126–1150.

——— 1967. "The Role of the Stock Market in a General Equilibrium Model with Technological Uncertainty." *American Economic Review, 57:* 759–776.

Dixit, Avinash, and Joseph E. Stiglitz. 1977. "Monopolistic Competition and Optimal Product Diversity." *American Economic Review, 67:* 297–308.

Domar, Evsey D. 1944. "The 'Burden of Debt' and the National Income." *American Economic Review, 34:* 798–827.

——— 1957. "A Soviet Model of Growth." In E. Domar, *Essays in the Theory of Economic Growth.* New York: Oxford University Press.

Dornbusch, Rudiger. 1976. "Expectations and Exchange Rate Dynamics." *Journal of Political Economy, 84:* 1161–1176.

Dos Santos, Claudio H. 2002. "Cambridge and Yale on Stock-Flow Consistent Macroeconomic Modeling." Department of Economics, New School University, New York.

Downs, Anthony. 1957. *An Economic Theory of Democracy.* New York: Harper and Row.

Duesenberry, James S. 1949. *Income, Saving, and the Theory of Consumer Behavior.* Cambridge, Mass.: Harvard University Press.

Duménil, Gérard, and Dominique Lévy. 1999. "Being Keynesian in the Short Term and Classical in the Long Term: The Traverse to Classical Long-Term Equilibrium." *Manchester School, 67:* 684–716.

Dunlop, John T. 1938. "The Movement of Real and Money Wage Rates." *Economic Journal, 48*: 413–434.

——— 1957. "The Task of Contemporary Wage Theory." In George W. Taylor and Frank C. Pierson, eds., *New Concepts in Wage Determination*. New York: McGraw-Hill.

Dutt, Amitava Krishna. 1984. "Stagnation, Income Distribution, and Monopoly Power." *Cambridge Journal of Economics, 8*: 25–40.

——— 1990. *Growth, Distribution, and Uneven Development*. Cambridge: Cambridge University Press.

——— 1997. "Equilibrium, Path Dependence, and Hysteresis in Post-Keynesian Models." In Philip Arestis, Gabriel Palma, and Malcolm Sawyer, eds., *Essays in Honor of Geoff Harcourt*, vol. 2: *Markets, Unemployment, and Economic Policy*. New York and London: Routledge.

Dymski, Gary, and Robert Pollin. 1992. "Hyman Minsky as Hedgehog: The Power of the Wall Street Paradigm." In Steven Fazzari and Dimitri Papadimitriou, eds., *Financial Conditions and Macroeconomic Performance*. Armonk, N.Y.: M. E. Sharpe.

Easterly, William R., and Carlos A. Rodriguez, eds. 1995. *Public Sector Deficits and Macroeconomic Performance*. New York: Oxford University Press.

Eatwell, John. 1996. *International Financial Liberalization: The Impact on World Development*. New York: Office of Development Studies, United Nations Development Programme.

Eatwell, John, and Murray Milgate, eds. 1983. *Keynes's Economics and the Theory of Value and Distribution*. New York: Oxford University Press.

Eatwell, John, and Lance Taylor. 2000. *Global Finance at Risk: The Case for International Regulation*. New York: The New Press.

Eichberger, Jürgen, and Ian R. Harper. 1997. *Financial Economics*. Oxford: Oxford University Press.

Eichner, Alfred S. 1980. "A General Model of Investment and Pricing." In Edward Nell, ed., *Growth, Profits, and Property*. Cambridge: Cambridge University Press.

Eisner, Robert. 1996. "A New View of the NAIRU." Department of Economics, Northwestern University, Evanston, Ill.

Eisner, Robert, and Robert H. Strotz. 1963. "Determinants of Business Investment." In Commission on Money and Credit, *Impacts of Monetary Policy*. Englewood Cliffs, N.J.: Prentice Hall.

Ellman, Michael. 1975. "Did the Agricultural Surplus Provide the Resources for the Increase in Investment during the First Five Year Plan?" *Economic Journal, 85*: 844–864.

Ellsberg, Daniel. 1961. "Risk, Ambiguity, and the Savage Axioms." *Quarterly Journal of Economics, 75*: 643–669.

Engel, Charles M., and James D. Hamilton. 1990. "Long Swings in the Dollar: Are They in the Data and Do Markets Know It?" *American Economic Review, 80*: 689–713.

Estrella, Arturo, and Frederic S. Mishkin. 1996. "The Yield Curve as a Predictor of U.S. Recessions." *Current Issues in Economics and Finance 2.* New York: Federal Reserve Bank of New York.

Evans, Peter B. 1995. *Embedded Autonomy: States and Industrial Transformation.* Princeton, N.J.: Princeton University Press.

Fair, Ray C. 2000. "Structural Macroeconomic Modeling and the Modern View of Macroeconomics." Department of Economics, Yale University, New Haven, Conn.

Fazzari, Steven M., and Tracy L. Mott. 1986–87. "The Investment Theories of Kalecki and Keynes: An Empirical Study of Firm Data, 1970–82." *Journal of Post Keynesian Economics, 9:* 171–187.

Felipe, Jesus, and J. S. L. McCombie. Forthcoming. "Some Methodological Problems with the Neoclassical Analysis of the East Asian Miracle." *Cambridge Journal of Economics.*

Feynman, Richard P. 1985. *QED: The Strange Theory of Light and Matter.* Princeton, N.J.: Princeton University Press.

Fischer, Stanley. 1972. "Keynes-Wicksell and Neoclassical Models of Money and Growth." *American Economic Review, 62:* 880–890.

—— 1977. "Long-Term Contracts, Rational Expectations, and the Money Supply Rule." *Journal of Political Economy, 85:* 191–205.

Fisher, Irving. [1930] 1967. *The Theory of Interest: As Determined by Impatience to Spend Income and Opportunity to Invest It.* Reprint. New York: Augustus M. Kelly.

—— 1933. "The Debt-Deflation Theory of Great Depressions." *Econometrica, 1:* 337–357.

Flaschel, Peter, Reiner Franke, and Willi Semmler. 1997. *Dynamic Macroeconommics: Instability, Fluctuations, and Growth in Monetary Economies.* Cambridge: MIT Press.

Fleming, J. Marcus. 1962. "Domestic Financial Policies under Fixed and Floating Exchange Rates." *IMF Staff Papers, 9:* 369–379.

Foley, Duncan K. 1975. "On Two Specifications of Asset Equilibrium in Macroeconomic Models." *Journal of Political Economy, 83:* 303–324.

Foley, Duncan K., and Thomas R. Michl. 1999. *Growth and Distribution.* Cambridge, Mass.: Harvard University Press.

Franco, Gustavo. 1986. "Aspects of the Economics of Hyperinflations: Theoretical Issues and Historical Studies of Four European Hyperinflations in the 1920s." Ph.D. dissertation, Department of Economics, Harvard University, Cambridge, Mass.

Franke, Reiner, and Willi Semmler. 1999. "Bond Rate, Loan Rate, and Tobin's *q* in a Temporary Equilibrium Model of the Financial Sector." *Metroeconomica, 50:* 351–385.

Frankel, Jeffrey A., and Andrew K. Rose. 1995. "Empirical Research on Nominal Exchange Rates." In Gene Grossman and Kenneth Rogoff, eds., *Handbook of International Economics,* vol. 3. Amsterdam: North-Holland.

Freeman, Richard B., and James L. Medoff. 1984. *What Do Unions Do?* New York: Basic Books.

Frenkel, Roberto. 1983. "Mercado financiero, expectativas cambiales, y movimientos de capital." *El Trimestre Económico, 50:* 2041–2076.

Friedman, Milton. 1957. *A Theory of the Consumption Function.* Princeton, N.J.: Princeton University Press.

——— 1968. "The Role of Monetary Policy." *American Economic Review, 58:* 1–17.

Furtado, Celso. 1972. *Analise do "modelo" brasileiro.* Rio de Janeiro: Civilização Brasileira.

Galbraith, James K., and William Darity Jr. 1994. *Macroeconomics.* Boston: Houghton Mifflin.

Garegnani, Pierangelo. 1984. "Value and Distribution in the Classical Economists and Marx." *Oxford Economic Papers, 36:* 291–325.

Gerschenkron, Alexander. 1962. *Economic Backwardness in Historical Perspective.* Cambridge, Mass.: Harvard University Press.

Glyn, Andrew, Alan Hughes, Alain Lipietz, and Ajit Singh. 1990. "The Rise and Fall of the Golden Age." In Stephen A. Marglin and Juliet B. Schor, *The Golden Age of Capitalism: Reinterpreting the Post-War Experience.* Oxford: Clarendon Press.

Godley, Wynne. 1996. "A Simple Model of the Whole World with Free Trade, Free Capital Movements, and Floating Exchange Rates." Jerome Levy Economics Institute, Bard College, Annandale-on-Hudson, N.Y.

——— 1999. "Seven Unsustainable Processes: Medium-Term Prospects and Policies for the U.S. and the World." Jerome Levy Economics Institute, Bard College, Annandale-on-Hudson, N.Y.

Godley, Wynne, and T. Francis Cripps. 1983. *Macroeconomics.* London: Fontana.

Goldstein, Jonathan P. 1996. "The Empirical Relevance of the Cyclical Profit Squeeze: A Reassertion." *Review of Radical Political Economics, 28* (4): 55–92.

Goodwin, Richard M. 1951. "The Nonlinear Accelerator and the Persistence of the Business Cycle." *Econometrica, 19:* 1–17.

Goodwin, Richard M. 1967. "A Growth Cycle." In C. H. Feinstein, ed., *Socialism, Capitalism, and Growth.* Cambridge: Cambridge University Press.

Gordon, David M. 1995. "Growth, Distribution, and the Rules of the Game: Social Structuralist Macro Foundations for a Democratic Economic Policy." In Gerald A. Epstein and Herbert A. Gintis, eds., *Macroeconomic Policy after the Conservative Era.* Cambridge: Cambridge University Press.

——— 1997. "Must We Save Our Way out of Stagnation? The Investment-Savings Relationship Revisited." In Robert Pollin, ed., *The Macroeconomics of Saving, Finance, and Investment.* Ann Arbor: University of Michigan Press.

Green, Donald P., and Ian Shapiro. 1994. *Pathologies of Rational Choice Theory.* New Haven, Conn.: Yale University Press.

Greenwald, Bruce C., and Joseph E. Stiglitz. 1993. "Financial Market Imperfections and Business Cycles." *Quarterly Journal of Economics, 108:* 77–114.

Greider, William. 1997. *One World, Ready or Not: The Manic Logic of Global Capitalism.* New York: Simon and Schuster.

Hahn, Frank, and Robert Solow. 1995. *A Critical Essay on Modern Macroeconomic Theory.* Cambridge: MIT Press.

Hall, Robert E. 1978. "Stochastic Implications of the Life Cycle-Permanent Income Hypothesis: Theory and Evidence." *Journal of Political Economy, 86:* 971–987.

Hansen, Alvin. 1938. *Full Recovery or Stagnation?* New York: Norton.

Harcourt, G. C. 1972. *Some Cambridge Controversies in the Theory of Capital.* Cambridge: Cambridge University Press.

Harris, Donald J. 1978. *Capital Accumulation and Income Distribution.* London: Routledge and K. Paul.

Harrod, Roy. 1939. "An Essay in Dynamic Theory." *Economic Journal, 49:* 14–33.

Hazledine, Tim. 1990. "Why Do Free Trade Gain Numbers Differ So Much? The Role of Industrial Organization in General Equilibrium." *Canadian Journal of Economics, 23:* 791–806.

Heilbroner, Robert. 1999. *The Worldly Philosophers.* 7th rev. ed. New York: Simon and Schuster.

Henwood, Doug. 1998. *Wall Street: How It Works and for Whom.* New York: Verso.

Hicks, John R. 1936. "Mr. Keynes' Theory of Employment." *Economic Journal, 46:* 238–253.

——— 1937. "Mr. Keynes and the 'Classics': A Suggested Interpretation." *Econometrica, 5:* 147–159.

——— 1965. *Capital and Growth.* Oxford: Clarendon Press.

——— 1980–81. "IS-LM: An Explanation." *Journal of Post-Keynesian Economics, 3:* 139–154.

Hirsch, Morris W., and Stephen Smale. 1974. *Differential Equations, Dynamical Systems, and Linear Algebra.* New York: Academic Press.

Hirschman, Albert O. 1958. *The Strategy of Economic Development.* New Haven, Conn.: Yale University Press.

Hollander, Samuel. 1979. *The Economics of David Ricardo.* Toronto: University of Toronto Press.

Holmes, Alan. 1969. "Operational Constraints on the Stabilization of Money Supply Growth." In *Controlling Monetary Aggregates.* Boston: Federal Reserve Bank of Boston.

Horgan, John. 1996. *The End of Science.* Reading, Mass.: Addison-Wesley.

Hume, David. 1969. "Of the Balance of Trade." In Richard N. Cooper, ed., *International Finance.* Harmondsworth: Penguin.

Ingrao, Bruna, and Giorgio Israel. 1990. *The Invisible Hand: Economic Equilibrium in the History of Science.* Cambridge: MIT Press.

Isard, Peter. 1995. *Exchange Rate Economics.* Cambridge: Cambridge University Press.

Johansen, Leif. 1960. *A Multi-Sectoral Study of Economic Growth*. Amsterdam: North-Holland.

Jones, Larry E., and Rodolfo Manuelli. 1990. "A Convex Model of Equilibrium Growth: Theory and Policy Implications." *Journal of Political Economy, 98*: 1008–1038.

Jones, Ronald W. 1965. "The Structure of Simple General Equilibrium Models." *Journal of Political Economy, 73*: 557–572.

Jorgenson, Dale. 1990. "Productivity and Economic Growth." In Ernst R. Berndt and Jack E. Triplett, eds., *Fifty Years of Economic Measurement: The Jubilee of the Conference on Income and Wealth*. Chicago: University of Chicago Press.

Kaldor, Nicholas. 1940. "A Model of the Trade Cycle." *Economic Journal, 50*: 78–92.

——— 1956. "Alternative Theories of Distribution." *Review of Economic Studies, 23*: 83–100.

——— 1957. "A Model of Economic Growth." *Economic Journal, 67*: 591–624.

——— 1960a. "Speculation and Economic Stability." In *Collected Economic Essays*, vol. 2: *Essays on Economic Stability and Growth*. London: Duckworth.

——— 1960b. "Keynes' Theory of Own Rates of Interest." In *Collected Economic Essays*, vol. 2: *Essays on Economic Stability and Growth*. London: Duckworth.

——— 1961. "Capital Accumulation and Economic Growth." In F. A. Lutz and D. C. Hague, eds., *The Theory of Capital Accumulation*. London: Macmillan.

——— 1972. "The Irrelevance of Equilibrium Economics." *Economic Journal, 82*: 1237–1255.

——— 1982. *The Scourge of Monetarism*. Oxford: Oxford University Press.

Kalecki, Michal. 1971. *Selected Essays on the Dynamics of the Capitalist Economy: 1933–1970*. Cambridge: Cambridge University Press.

Kendrick, David, and Lance Taylor. 1970. "Numerical Solution of Non-linear Planning Models." *Econometrica, 38*: 453–467.

Keynes, John Maynard. 1921. *A Treatise on Probability*. London: Macmillan.

——— 1923. *A Tract on Monetary Reform*. London: Macmillan.

——— 1930. *A Treatise on Money*. London: Macmillan.

——— 1936. *The General Theory of Employment, Interest, and Money*. London: Macmillan.

——— 1937a. "The General Theory of Employment." *Quarterly Journal of Economics, 51*: 209–223.

——— 1937b. "Alternative Theories of the Rate of Interest." *Economic Journal, 47*: 242–252.

——— 1939. "Relative Movements of Real Wages and Output." *Economic Journal, 49*: 35–51.

Kindleberger, Charles P. 1984. *A Financial History of Western Europe*. London: Allen and Unwin.

—— 1985. *Keynesianism vs. Monetarism and Other Essays in Financial History.* London: Allen and Unwin.

—— 1996. *Manias, Panics, and Crashes: A History of Financial Crises.* 3d ed. New York: John Wiley and Sons.

Knight, Frank H. 1921. *Risk, Uncertainty, and Profit.* Boston: Houghton-Mifflin.

Kocherlakota, Narayana R. 1996. "The Equity Premium: It's Still a Puzzle." *Journal of Economic Literature, 34:* 42–71.

Koopmans, Tjalling C. 1965. "On the Concept of Optimal Economic Growth." In Pontifical Academy of Sciences, *The Economic Approach to Development Planning.* Amsterdam: North-Holland.

Kregel, Jan A. 2000. "Krugman on the Liquidity Trap: Why Inflation Won't Bring Recovery to Japan." Jerome Levy Economics Institute, Bard College, Annandale-on-Hudson, N.Y.

Krueger, Anne O. 1974. "The Political Economy of the Rent-Seeking Society." *American Economic Review, 64:* 291–303.

Krugman, Paul R. 1993. "Towards a Counter-Counter-Revolution in Development Theory." *World Bank Economic Review, 10* (supplement), 15–38.

—— 1998. "It's Baaaack: Japan's Slump and the Return of the Liquidity Trap." Department of Economics, Massachusetts Institute of Technology.

Krugman, Paul R., and Maurice Obstfeld. 1997. *International Economics.* Reading, Mass.: Addison-Wesley.

Kuznets, Simon S. 1946. *National Product since 1869.* New York: National Bureau of Economic Research.

Kydland, Finn E., and Prescott, Edward C. 1982. "Time to Build and Aggregate Fluctuations." *Econometrica, 50:* 1345–1370.

Laing, N. F. 1969. "Two Notes on Pasinetti's Theorem." *Economic Record, 45:* 373–385.

Lal, Deepak. 1983. *The Poverty of "Development Economics."* London: Institute of Economic Affairs.

Lange, Oscar. 1936–37. "On the Economic Theory of Socialism." *Review of Economic Studies, 4* (1–2): 53–71 and 123–142.

Larrain, Felipe, and Jeffrey Sachs. 1986. "Contractionary Devaluation, and Dynamic Adjustment of Exports and Wages." Cambridge, Mass.: National Bureau of Economic Research.

Lavoie, Marc. 1995. "The Kaleckian Model of Growth and Distribution and Its Neo-Ricardian and Neo-Marxian Critiques." *Cambridge Journal of Economics, 19:* 789–818.

—— 2001. "Endogenous Money in a Coherent Stock-Flow Framework." Jerome Levy Economics Institute, Bard College, Annandale-on-Hudson, N.Y.

Lavoie, Marc, and Wynne Godley. 2000. "Kaleckian Models of Growth in a Stock-Flow Monetary Framework: A Neo-Kaldorian Model." Jerome Levy Economics Institute, Bard College, Annandale-on-Hudson, N.Y.

Layard, Richard, Stephen Nickell, and Richard Jackman. 1991. *Unemploy-*

ment: Macroeconomic Performance and the Labour Market. Oxford: Oxford University Press.

Leibenstein, Harvey. 1954. *A Theory of Economic-Demographic Development.* Princeton, N.J.: Princeton University Press.

Leijonhufvud, Axel. 1968. *On Keynesian Economics and the Economics of Keynes.* New York: Oxford University Press.

Lerner, Abba P. 1936. "A Note on Socialist Economics." *Review of Economic Studies, 4:* 72–76.

Lewis, W. Arthur. 1954. "Economic Development with Unlimited Supplies of Labor." *Manchester School of Economics and Social Studies, 22:* 139–191.

Lindbeck, Assar. 1993. *Unemployment and Macroeconomics.* Cambridge: MIT Press.

Lindblom, Charles. 1977. *Politics and Markets: The World's Political-Economic Systems.* New York: Basic Books.

Little, Ian M. D., Tibor Scitovsky, and Maurice Scott. 1970. *Industry and Trade in Some Developing Countries: A Comparative Study.* London: Oxford University Press.

Liviatan, Nissan. 1984. "Tight Money and Inflation." *Journal of Monetary Economics, 13:* 5–15.

——— 1986. "The Tight Money Paradox—An Alternative View." *Journal of Macroeconomics, 8:* 105–112.

Ljungqvist, Lars, and Thomas J. Sargent. 2000. *Recursive Macroeconomic Theory.* Cambridge: MIT Press.

Lorenz, Hans-Walter. 1989. *Nonlinear Dynamical Economics and Chaotic Motion.* Berlin: Springer-Verlag.

Lotka, Alfred Y. 1925. *Elements of Physical Biology.* Baltimore: Williams and Wilkins.

Lucas, Robert E., Jr. 1972. "Expectations and the Neutrality of Money." *Journal of Economic Theory, 4:* 103–124.

——— 1976. "Econometric Policy Evaluation: A Critique." *Carnegie-Rochester Conference Series on Public Policy, 1:* 19–46.

——— 1978. "Asset Prices in an Exchange Economy." *Econometrica, 46:* 1426–1445.

——— 1988. "On the Mechanisms of Economic Development." *Journal of Monetary Economics, 22:* 3–42.

——— 2000. "Some Macroeconomics for the 21st Century." *Journal of Economic Perspectives, 14:* 159–168.

Luxemburg, Rosa. 1951. *The Accumulation of Capital.* London: Routledge and Kegan Paul.

Mahalanobis, P. C. 1953. "Some Observations on the Process of Growth of National Income." *Sankhya, 12:* 307–312.

Malinvaud, Edmond. 1977. *The Theory of Unemployment Reconsidered.* Oxford: Basil Blackwell.

Mankiw, N. Gregory. 1989. "Real Business Cycles: A New Keynesian Perspective." *Journal of Economic Perspectives, 3:* 79–90.

Mankiw, N. Gregory, and David Romer, eds. 1991. *New Keynesian Economics.* Cambridge: MIT Press.

Marglin, Stephen A. 1984. *Growth, Distribution, and Prices.* Cambridge, Mass.: Harvard University Press.

McCafferty, Stephen. 1990. *Macroeconomic Theory.* New York: Harper and Row.

McCallum, Bennett T. 1989. "Real Business Cycle Models." In Robert J. Barro, ed., *Modern Business Cycle Theory.* Cambridge, Mass.: Harvard University Press.

Meade, James E. 1961. *A Neo-classical Theory of Economic Growth,* London: Allen and Unwin.

Medio, Alfredo, and Marji Lines. 2001. *Nonlinear Dynamics: A Primer.* Cambridge: Cambridge University Press.

Mehra, Rajnish, and Edward C. Prescott. 1985. "The Equity Premium: A Puzzle." *Journal of Monetary Economics, 15:* 145–161.

Menger, Carl. 1963. *Problems in Economics and Sociology.* Urbana: University of Illinois Press.

Minsky, Hyman P. 1975. *John Maynard Keynes.* New York: Columbia University Press.

——— 1986. *Stabilizing an Unstable Economy.* New Haven, Conn.: Yale University Press.

Mirowski, Philip. 2002. *Machine Dreams: Economics Becomes a Cyborg Science.* New York: Cambridge University Press.

Mishkin, Frederic S. 1990. "Asymmetric Information and Financial Crises: Historical Evidence." Cambridge, Mass.: National Bureau of Economic Research.

Modigliani, Franco. 1944. "Liquidity Preference and the Theory of Interest and Money." *Econometrica, 12:* 45–88.

Modigliani, Franco, and Richard E. Brumberg. 1954. "Utility Analysis and the Consumption Function: An Interpretation of Cross-Section Data." In Kenneth K. Kurihara, ed., *Post Keynesian Economics.* New Brunswick, N.J.: Rutgers University Press.

Modigliani, Franco, and Merton H. Miller. 1958. "The Cost of Capital, Corporation Finance, and the Theory of Investment." *American Economic Review, 48:* 261–297.

Modigliani, Franco, and Tommaso Padoa-Schioppa. 1978. "The Management of an Open Economy with '100% Plus' Wage Indexation." Princeton Essays in International Finance no. 130. Department of Economics, Princeton University.

Monk, Ray. 1990. *Ludwig Wittgenstein: The Duty of Genius.* New York: Free Press.

Moore, Basil J. 1988. *Horizontalists and Verticalists: The Macroeconomics of Credit Money.* New York: Cambridge University Press.

Mundell, Robert A. 1963a. "Inflation and Real Interest." *Journal of Political Economy, 71:* 280–283.

——— 1963b. "Capital Mobility and Stabilization Policy under Fixed and Flexible Exchange Rates." *Canadian Journal of Economics and Political Science, 29:* 475–485.

Murphy, Kevin M., Andrei Shleifer, and Robert Vishny. 1989. "Industrialization and the Big Push." *Journal of Political Economy, 97:* 1003–1026.

Myrdal, Gunnar. 1939. *Monetary Equilibrium.* New York: Augustus M. Kelley.

Myrdal, Gunnar. 1957. *Economic Theory and Underdeveloped Regions.* London: Duckworth.

Ndikumana, Leonce. 1999. "Debt Service, Financing Constraints, and Fixed Investment: Evidence from Panel Data." *Journal of Post Keynesian Economics, 21:* 455–478.

Neftci, Salih N. 2000. *An Introduction to the Mathematics of Financial Derivatives.* 2d ed. San Diego: Academic Press.

——— 2001. "FX Short Positions, Balance Sheets, and Financial Turbulence: An Interpretation of the Asian Financial Crisis." In John Eatwell and Lance Taylor, eds., *International Capital Markets: Systems in Transition.* New York: Oxford University Press.

Nell, Edward J. 1992. *Transformational Growth and Effective Demand.* New York: New York University Press.

Nelson, Richard R. 1956. "A Theory of the Low-Level Equilibrium Trap in Underdeveloped Economies." *American Economic Review, 46:* 894–908.

North, Douglass C. 1981. *Structure and Change in Economic History.* New York: W. W. Norton.

Obstfeld, Maurice, and Kenneth Rogoff. 1995. "The Intertemporal Approach to the Current Account." In Gene M. Grossman and Kenneth Rogoff, eds., *Handbook of International Economics,* vol. 3. Amsterdam: North-Holland.

Øksendal, Bernt, *Stochastic Differential Equations,* 5th ed. Berlin: Springer.

Okun, Arthur M. [1962] 1983. " 'Potential GNP': Its Measurement and Significance." Reprinted in Joseph Pechman, ed., *Economics for Policy-Making.* Cambridge: MIT Press.

——— 1980. "Rational-Expectations-with-Misperceptions as a Theory of the Business Cycle." *Journal of Money, Credit, and Banking, 11:* 817–825.

Olivera, Julio H. G. 1967. "Money, Prices, and Fiscal Lags: A Note on the Dynamics of Inflation." *Banca Nazionale del Lavoro Quarterly Review, 20:* 258–267.

——— 1970. "On Passive Money." *Journal of Political Economy, 78:* 805–814.

Olson, Mancur. 1965. *The Logic of Collective Action,* Cambridge, Mass.: Harvard University Press.

Ono, Yoshiyasu. 1994. *Money, Interest, and Stagnation: Dynamic Theory and Keynes's Economics.* Oxford and New York: Clarendon Press.

Palley, Thomas I. 1996. *Post Keynesian Economics,* New York: St. Martins's.

Panico, Carlo. 1988. *Interest and Profit in the Theories of Value and Distribution.* London: Macmillan.

Parente, Stephen L., and Edward C. Prescott. 2000. *Barriers to Riches*. Cambridge: MIT Press.

Pasinetti, Luigi L. 1962. "Rate of Profit and Income Distribution in Relation to the Rate of Economic Growth." *Review of Economic Studies, 29*: 267–279.

——— 1974. *Growth and Income Distribution*. Cambridge: Cambridge University Press.

——— 1977. *Lectures on the Theory of Production*. New York: Columbia University Press.

——— 1981. *Structural Change and Economic Growth*. Cambridge: Cambridge University Press.

Patinkin, Don. 1966. *Money, Interest, and Prices*. New York: Harper and Row.

——— 1982. *Anticipations of the General Theory?* Chicago: University of Chicago Press.

Phelps, Edmund S. 1961. "The Golden Rule of Accumulation: A Fable for Growthmen." *American Economic Review, 51*: 638–643.

——— 1968. "Money-Wage Dynamics and Labor Market Equilibrium." *Journal of Political Economy, 76*: 678–711.

——— 1969. "The New Microeconomics in Employment and Inflation Theory." *American Economic Review (Papers and Proceedings), 59*: 147–160.

——— 1994. *Structural Slumps: The Modern Equilibrium Theory of Unemployment, Interest, and Assets*. Cambridge, Mass.: Harvard University Press.

Phelps, Edmund S., and Sidney G. Winter. 1970. "Optimal Price Policy under Atomistic Competition." In Edmund S. Phelps et al., *Microeconomic Foundations of Employment and Inflation Theory*. New York: W. W. Norton.

Phelps, Edmund S., and Gylfi Zoega. 2002. "Portents of a Darkening Outlook: Falling Equities and a Weaker Dollar Herald Economic Slowdown." *Financial Times*. July 31.

Phillips, A. W. 1958. "The Relationship between Unemployment and the Rate of Change of Money Wages in the United Kingdom, 1861–1957." *Economica, 25*: 283–299.

Pieper, Ute, and Lance Taylor. 1998. "The Revival of the Liberal Creed: The IMF, the World Bank, and Inequality in a Globalized Economy." In Dean Baker, Gerald Epstein, and Robert Pollin, eds., *Globalization and Progressive Economic Policy: What Are the Real Constraints and Options?* New York: Cambridge University Press.

Pigou, A. C. 1927. *Industrial Fluctuations*. London: Macmillan.

——— 1943. "The Classical Stationary State." *Economic Journal, 53*: 343–351.

Polanyi, Karl. 1944. *The Great Transformation*. New York: Rinehart.

Pollin, Robert. 1991. "Two Theories of Money Supply Endogeneity: Some Empirical Evidence." *Journal of Post Keynesian Economics, 13*: 366–396.

——— 1997. "Financial Intermediation and the Variability of the Saving Constraint." In Robert Pollin, ed., *The Macroeconomics of Saving, Finance, and Investment*. Ann Arbor: University of Michigan Press.

——— 1998a. "Financial Structures and Egalitarian Economic Policy." In Philip Arestis and Malcom Sawyer, eds., *The Political Economy of Economic Policies*. New York: St. Martin's Press.

——— 1998b. "Can Domestic Expansionary Policies Succeed in a Globally Integrated Environment? An Examination of Alternatives." In Dean Baker, Gerald Epstein, and Robert Pollin, eds., *Globalization and Progressive Economic Policy*. Cambridge: Cambridge University Press.

Prebisch, Raul. 1959. "Commercial Policy in the Underdeveloped Countries." *American Economic Review, 49:* 257–269.

Preobrazhensky, Evgeny. 1965. *The New Economics*. Oxford: Clarendon Press.

Ramsey, Frank P. 1928. "A Mathematical Theory of Saving." *Economic Journal, 38:* 543–559.

——— 1931. "Truth and Probability." In Frank P. Ramsey, *The Foundations of Mathematics and Other Logical Essays*. London: Kegan Paul.

Rebelo, Sergio. 1991. "Long Run Policy Analysis and Long Run Growth." *Journal of Political Economy, 99:* 500–521.

Robertson, Dennis H. 1922. *Money* (Cambridge Economic Handbook). London: Bisbet and Co.

——— 1933. "Saving and Hoarding." *Economic Journal, 43:* 399–413.

Robinson, Joan. 1956. *The Accumulation of Capital*. London: Macmillan.

Romer, Christina D., and David H. Romer. 1989. "Does Monetary Policy Matter? A New Test in the Spirit of Friedman and Schwartz." *NBER Macroeconomics Annual, 4:* 121–170.

Romer, David. 2001. *Advanced Macroeconomics*. 2d ed. New York: McGraw-Hill.

Romer, Paul M. 1986. "Increasing Returns and Long-Run Growth." *Journal of Political Economy, 94:* 1002–1037.

——— 1987. "Growth Based on Increasing Returns Due to Specialization." *American Economic Review (Papers and Proceedings), 77:* 56–62.

Ros, Jaime. 1988. "On Inertia, Social Conflict, and the Structuralist Analysis of Inflation." Helsinki: World Institute for Development Economics Research.

Rosenstein-Rodan, Paul N. 1961. "Notes on the Theory of the Big Push." In H. S. Ellis and H. C. Wallich, eds., *Economic Development for Latin America*. New York: St. Martin's Press.

Rosensweig, Jeffrey A., and Lance Taylor. 1990. "Devaluation, Capital Flows, and Crowding-Out: A CGE Model with Portfolio Choice for Thailand." In Lance Taylor, ed., *Socially Relevant Policy Analysis*. Cambridge: MIT Press.

Rotemberg, Julio, and Garth Saloner. 1986. "A Super Game Theoretic Model of Price Wars during Booms." *American Economic Review, 76:* 390–407.

Rousseas, Stephen. 1985. "A Mark-up Theory of Bank Loan Rates." *Journal of Post Keynesian Economics, 8:* 135–144.

Rowthorn, Robert E. 1982. "Demand, Real Wages, and Economic Growth." *Studi Economici, 18:* 2–53.

Salter, W. E. G. 1959. "Internal and External Balance: The Role of Price and Expenditure Effects." *Economic Record, 35:* 226–238.

Samuelson, Paul A. 1939. "Interaction between the Multiplier Analysis and the Principle of Acceleration." *Review of Economics and Statistics, 21:* 75–78.

Samuelson, Paul A., and Robert M. Solow. 1960. "Analytical Aspects of Anti-Inflation Policy." *American Economic Review (Papers and Proceedings), 50:* 177–194.

Sargent, Thomas J. 1973. "Rational Expectations, the Real Rate of Interest, and the Natural Rate of Unemployment." *Brookings Papers on Economic Activity,* no. 2: 429–472.

Sargent, Thomas J., and Neil Wallace. 1981. "Some Unpleasant Monetarist Arithmetic." *Federal Reserve Bank of Minneapolis Quarterly Review, 5:* 1–17.

Schefold, Bertram. 1997. "The Nature of Capital and Interest." Faculty of Economics, Johann Wolfgang Goethe University, Frankfurt am Main.

Schroeder, Susan K. 2002. "A Minskian Analysis of Financial Crisis in Developing Countries." Center for Economic Policy Analysis, New School University, New York.

Schultz, T. W. 1963. *The Economic Value of Education.* New York: Columbia University Press.

——— 1964. *Transforming Traditional Agriculture.* New Haven, Conn.: Yale University Press.

Schumpeter, Joseph. 1934. *The Theory of Economic Development.* Cambridge, Mass.: Harvard University Press.

——— 1947. *Capitalism, Socialism, and Democracy.* Rev. ed. New York: Harper and Brothers.

——— 1954. *History of Economic Analysis.* New York: Oxford University Press.

Semmler, Willi. 1984. *Competition, Monopoly, and Differential Profit Rates.* New York: Columbia University Press.

Sen, Amartya K. 1963. "Neo-classical and Neo-Keynesian Theories of Distribution." *Economic Record, 39:* 53–64.

——— 1970. "Introduction." In Amartya K. Sen, ed., *Growth Economics.* Harmondsworth: Penguin Books.

Shaikh, Anwar. 1974. "Laws of Production and Laws of Algebra: The Humbug Production Function." *Review of Economics and Statistics, 56:* 115–120.

——— 1989. "Accumulation, Finance, and Effective Demand in Marx, Keynes, and Kalecki." In Willi Semmler, ed., *Financial Dynamics and Business Cycles: New Perspectives.* Armonk, N.Y.: M. E. Sharpe.

Shefrin, Hersh M., and Richard H. Thaler. 1988. "The Behavioral Life-Cycle Hypothesis." *Economic Inquiry, 26:* 609–643.

Shephard, Ronald. 1953. *Cost and Production Functions.* Princeton, N.J.: Princeton University Press.

Sismonde de Sismondi, J. C. L. 1815. "Political Economy." In *Sir J. D. Brewster's Edinburgh Encyclopedia*. Edinburgh.

Skott, Peter. 1995. "Financial Innovation, Deregulation, and Minsky Cycles." In Gerald A. Epstein and Herbert A. Gintis, eds., *Macroeconomic Policy after the Conservative Era*. Cambridge: Cambridge University Press.

Solow, Robert M. 1956. "A Contribution to the Theory of Economic Growth." *Quarterly Journal of Economics, 70*: 65–94.

―――― 1957. "Technical Change and the Aggregate Production Function." *Review of Economics and Statistics, 39*: 312–320.

―――― 1986. "Unemployment: Getting the Questions Right." *Economica, 53* (supplement): s23-s34.

Spence, Michael. 1976. "Product Selection, Fixed Costs, and Monopolistic Competition." *Review of Economic Studies, 43*: 217–235.

Sraffa, Piero. 1926. "The Laws of Returns under Competitive Conditions." *Economic Journal, 36*: 535–550.

―――― 1932a. "Dr Hayek on Money and Capital." *Economic Journal, 42*: 42–53.

―――― 1932b. "Money and Capital: A Rejoinder." *Economic Journal, 42*: 249–251.

―――― 1960. *Production of Commodities by Means of Commodities*. Cambridge: Cambridge University Press.

Stadler, George W. 1994. "Real Business Cycles." *Journal of Economic Literature, 32*: 1750–1783.

Steindl, Josef. 1952. *Maturity and Stagnation in American Capitalism*. Oxford: Basil Blackwell.

Stigler, George J. 1958. "Ricardo and the 93% Labor Theory of Value." *American Economic Review, 48*: 356–367.

Stiglitz, Joseph E. 1969. "A Re-examination of the Modigliani-Miller Theorem." *American Economic Review, 59*: 784–793.

Stone, J. R. N. 1966. "The Social Accounts from a Consumer Point of View." *Review of Income and Wealth, 12*: 1–33.

Summers, Lawrence H. 1981. "Capital Taxation and Accumulation in a Life Cycle Growth Model." *American Economic Review, 71*: 533–544.

―――― 1983. "The Nonadjustment of Nominal Interest Rates: A Study of the Fisher Effect." In James Tobin, ed., *Macroeconomics, Prices, and Quantities: Essays in Memory of Arthur M. Okun*. Washington, D.C.: Brookings Institution.

―――― 1986. "Some Skeptical Observations on Real Business Cycle Theory." *Federal Reserve Bank of Minneapolis Quarterly Review, 10* (Fall): 23–27.

Swan, Trevor. 1960. "Economic Control in a Dependent Economy." *Economic Record, 36*: 51–66.

Sweezy, Paul. 1939. "Demand Conditions under Oligopoly." *Journal of Political Economy, 47*: 568–573.

Sylos-Labini, Paolo. 1984. *The Forces of Economic Growth and Decline*. Cambridge: MIT Press.

—— 1993. *Economic Growth and Business Cycles*. Aldershot, U.K.: Edward Elgar.

Syrquin, Moshe. 1986. "Productivity Growth and Factor Reallocation." In Hollis B. Chenery, Sherman Robinson, and Moshe Syrquin, *Industrialization and Growth*. New York: Oxford University Press.

—— 1988. "Patterns of Structural Change." In H. B. Chenery and T. N. Srinivasan, eds., *Handbook of Development Economics,* vol. 1. Amsterdam: North-Holland.

Tanzi, Vito. 1978. "Inflation, Real Tax Revenue, and the Case for Inflationary Finance: Theory with an Application to Argentina." *International Monetary Fund Staff Papers, 25:* 417–451.

Tarshis, Lorie. 1939. "Changes in Real and Money Wages." *Economic Journal,* 49: 150–154.

Taylor, John B. 1980. "Aggregate Dynamics and Staggered Contracts." *Journal of Political Economy, 88:* 1–23.

Taylor, Lance. 1970. "The Existence of Optimal Distributed Lags." *Review of Economic Studies, 37:* 95–106.

—— 1979. *Macro Models for Developing Countries*. New York: McGraw-Hill.

—— 1988. *Varieties of Stabilization Experience*. Oxford: Clarendon Press.

——, ed. 1990. *Socially Relevant Policy Analysis: Structuralist Computable General Equilibrium Models for the Developing World*. Cambridge: MIT Press.

—— 1991. *Income Distribution, Inflation, and Growth*. Cambridge: MIT Press.

——, ed. 1993. *The Rocky Road to Reform*. Cambridge: MIT Press.

—— 1994. "Gap Models." *Journal of Development Economics, 45:* 17–34.

—— 1995. "Pasinetti's Processes." *Cambridge Journal of Economics, 19:* 697–713.

——, ed. 2000. *External Liberalization, Economic Performance, and Social Policy*. New York: Oxford University Press.

Taylor, Lance, and Edmar L. Bacha. 1976. "The Unequalizing Spiral: A First Growth Model for Belindia." *Quarterly Journal of Economics, 90:* 197–218.

Taylor, Lance, and Frank J. Lysy. 1979. "Vanishing Income Redistributions: Keynesian Clues about Model Surprises in the Short Run." *Journal of Development Economics, 6:* 11–29.

Taylor, Lance, and Stephen A. O'Connell. 1985. "A Minsky Crisis." *Quarterly Journal of Economics, 100:* 871–885.

Tobin, James. 1965. "Money and Economic Growth." *Econometrica, 32:* 671–684.

—— 1969. "A General Equilibrium Approach to Monetary Theory." *Journal of Money, Credit, and Banking, 1:* 15–29.

Uzawa, Hirofumi. 1965. "Optimum Technical Change in an Aggregative Model of Economic Growth." *International Economic Review, 6:* 18–31.

Veblen, Thorstein. 1904. *The Theory of Business Enterprise*. New York: Charles Scribner's Sons.

Verdoorn, P. J. 1949. "Fattori che regolano lo sviluppo della produttivita del lavoro." *L'Industria, 1:* 3–10.

Vernengo, Matias, and Per Gunnar Berglund. 2000. "Empirical Analysis of Okun and Verdoorn Effects in the United States 1961–1998." Center for Economic Policy Analysis, New School University, New York.

Volterra, Vito. 1931. *Leçons sur la théorie mathématique de la lutte pour la vie*. Paris: Gauthier-Villars.

von Hayek, Friedrich. 1931. *Prices and Production*. London: Routledge and Kegan Paul.

——, ed. 1935. *Collectivist Economic Planning*. London: Routledge and Kegan Paul.

—— 1988. *The Fatal Conceit: The Errors of Socialism*, vol. 1 of *Collected Works of F. A. Hayek*. London: Routledge.

von Mises, Ludwig. 1935. "Economic Calculation in the Socialist Commonwealth." In Friedrich von Hayek, ed., *Collectivist Economic Planning*. London: Routledge and Kegan Paul.

von Neumann, John. 1945–46. "A Model of General Economic Equilibrium." *Review of Economic Studies, 13:* 1–9.

von Neumann, John, and Oskar Morgenstern. 1994. *The Theory of Games and Economic Behavior*. Princeton, N.J.: Princeton University Press.

Wade, Robert. 1990. *Governing the Market: Economic Theory and the Role of the Government in East Asian Industrialization*. Princeton, N.J.: Princeton University Press.

Weber, Max. 1968. *Economy and Society,* ed. G. Roth and C. Wittich. New York: Bedminster Press.

Weitzman, Martin. 1982. "Increasing Returns and the Foundations of Unemployment." *Economic Journal, 92:* 787–804.

Wicksell, Knut. 1935. *Lectures on Political Economy*. Vol. 2. London: Routledge and Kegan Paul.

Williamson, John, and Chris Milner. 1991. *The World Economy*. New York: New York University Press.

Wolff, Edward N. 1995. *Top Heavy: The Increasing Inequality of Wealth in America and What Can Be Done about It*. New York: The New Press.

Young, Allyn. 1928. "Increasing Returns and Economic Progress." *Economic Journal, 38:* 527–542.

Zarnowitz, Victor. 1992. *Business Cycles: Theory, History, Indicators, and Forecasting*. Chicago: University of Chicago Press.

Zysman, John. 1983. *Government, Markets, and Growth: Financial Systems and the Politics of Industrial Change*. Ithaca, N.Y.: Cornell University Press.

Index

Abel, Andrew B., 93, 97, 108
Accelerationist theory, 199, 203, 207, 210. *See also* Adaptive expectations; Friedman, Milton; Monetarist theory; Phelps, Edmund S.; Phillips curve; Unemployment
Accelerator, 128, 137, 159, 188, 191, 193, 241, 243, 278, 281, 297. *See also* Investment function
Accommodationist theory of money. *See* Money
Active money. *See* Money
Activity level. *See* Capacity utilization
Adaptive expectations, 72, 120, 136, 205, 235–236, 295–296. *See also* Myopic perfect foresight; Rational expectations
Adiabatic approximation, 296
Adjustment costs, 94–95, 98, 159. *See also* Eisner, Robert; Strotz, Robert H.
Adverse selection, 157n, 263n, 278–279
AK model, 351–354, 363
Amadeo, Edward, 51, 76, 109, 233n
Amsden, Alice H., 294, 350, 370, 375, 377
Ando, Albert, 163–164. *See also* Consumption function
Animal spirits, 25, 138, 245, 303–305; *See also* Keynes, John Maynard; Minsky, Hyman P.
Anyadike-Danes, Michael, 88
Arrow, Kenneth J., 350, 356. *See also* Learning by doing
Arrowhead diagram, 170. *See also* Closure; Disequilibrium theory; Dual decision hypothesis; Malinvaud,

Edmond; Repressed inflation; Unemployment
Arthur, W. Brian, 350, 370
Asset demand function, 149, 267–270, 277, 300, 319–328, 343, 345–346. *See also* Portfolio balance; Tobin, James
Asymmetric information, 200, 278–280
Atomism. *See* Methodological individualism and rational action
Austrian school, 68, 70, 90, 108, 138n, 154, 200, 208, 219, 231, 356. *See also* Menger, Carl; Overinvestment; von Hayek, Friedrich A.; von Mises, Ludwig
Avramovic, Dragoslav, 213n

Bacha, Edmar L., 355, 359
Backward integration, 102, 185, 222, 224, 227. *See also* Dynamic optimization; Terminal conditions; Transversality conditions
Bagehot, Walter, 83. *See also* Lender of last resort
Baker, Dean, 207n
Balance of payments, 22, 77, 81, 312, 314–315, 329–333, 337, 362; as constraint on growth and development, 363–364. *See also* Debt; Deficit
Ball, Laurence, 221
Banana diagram, 193–194, 297. *See also* Robinson, Joan
Banking School, 80, 82, 86, 127, 143, 260, 269. *See also* Currency School; Money; Real bills doctrine
Barbosa-Filho, Nelson H., 190, 197, 284n